Teaching Developmental Reading

Historical, Theoretical, and
Practical Background Readings

Teaching Developmental Reading

Historical, Theoretical, and Practical Background Readings

EDITED BY

Norman A. Stahl

Northern Illinois University

Hunter Boylan

Appalachian State University

Bedford/St. Martin's   Boston ◆ New York

For Bedford/St. Martin's

Developmental Editor: Jeffrey Voccola
Associate Editor, Publishing Services: Maria Teresa Burwell
Senior Production Supervisor: Joe Ford
Production Associate: Christie Gross
Marketing Manager: Brian Wheel
Project Management: Stratford Publishing Services, Inc.
Text Design: Claire Seng-Niemoeller
Cover Design: Donna Dennison
Composition: Stratford Publishing Services, Inc.
Printing and Binding: Haddon Craftsmen, an RR Donnelley & Sons Company

President: Joan E. Feinberg
Editorial Director: Denise B. Wydra
Editor in Chief: Karen S. Henry
Director of Marketing: Karen R. Melton
Director of Editing, Design, and Production: Marcia Cohen
Manager, Publishing Services: Emily Berleth

Manufactured in the United States of America.

8 7 6 5 4 3
f e d c b a

For information, write: Bedford/St. Martin's, 75 Arlington Street, Boston, MA 02116 (617-399-4000)

ISBN: 0–312–24774–5

Acknowledgments

Laura Bauer and Linda Sweeney. "The Use of Literary Letters with Post-Secondary Non-Native Students." From *The Learning Assistance Review,* Volume 4, Number 1, Spring 1999, pp. 33–41. Reprinted by permission of the Midwest College Learning Center Association.

Julia Beyeler. "Reluctant Readers: Case Studies of Reading and Study Strategies in Introduction to Psychology." From *The Learning Assistance Review,* Volume 3, Number 1, Spring 1998, pp. 5–19. Reprinted by permission of the Midwest College Learning Center Association.

Louise Bohr. "College and Precollege Reading Instruction: What Are the Real Differences?" From *The Learning Assistance Review,* Volume 1, Number 1, Spring 1996, pp. 14–28. Reprinted by permission of the Midwest College Learning Center Association.

Acknowledgments and copyrights are continued at the back of the book on pages 455–457, which constitute an extension of the copyright page. It is a violation of the law to reproduce these selections by any means whatsoever without the written permission of the copyright holder.

Preface

Whether an individual is able to read critically with ease the great works of the cannon or is struggling to comprehend *I Know Why the Caged Bird Sings* in a developmental reading class, interacting with text is a personal process. And whether an individual has recently won a Pulitzer Prize for fiction or is a writer struggling to draft his or her first essay of the term, creating text is a personal experience. What's more, most people's experience with text changes as they move through life.

This particular text, *Teaching Developmental Reading,* comes at a transition point in my life, both in the personal and professional realms. On the personal side, I'm comfortable with middle age, although my rekindled fascination with surfing begs the question to a degree. On the professional side, I now have opportunities to work on projects that have a different orientation. In past years, I wrote (either on my own or with valued colleagues such as James King, William Henk, and Michele Simpson) primarily for a body of researchers and theorists. With those pieces, I sought to achieve a form of immortality so important to young Turks in the profession. I don't for a moment mean to imply that young Turks are bad for the profession. On the contrary, we can thank our stars that they strive for new knowledge and alternative answers to the pedagogical questions of the era. But wisdom does come with thirty years in the profession, and with it one's reasons for writing may well shift. I know mine have.

When Aron Keesbury, representing Bedford/St. Martin's, first approached me about this project, he could not have called at a more untimely moment. My first inclination was to suggest that someone else might be better suited to undertake this collection of readings. But then he made a statement that let me know I had to take on the project. He noted that the text you now hold in your hands was designed as a complimentary text to be given to college reading instructors and learning assistance specialists who were new to the field. At that point, participation in this project became very personal. It was my opportunity to pay back a few debts.

You see, I am a developmental studies student. I say that in the present tense with good reason. Once a developmental studies student, always a developmental studies student. When I graduated from Lincoln High School in December of 1967 and then walked up the hill on Phelan Avenue to City College of San Francisco a few short weeks later, I began my long journey in higher education through the portals of developmental education.

Like so many of the students I've worked with over the years, I was none too excited about being placed in "bonehead English" or remedial reading or business math. Still, I was not alone, as virtually all my school buddies — Bill and Bill, Ted and Ray, and also Bob — entered "Harvard on the Hill" in the same manner. But we also all graduated, some years later.

Developmental education and developmental educators provided us with opportunities to revisit content not fully mastered in previous years and to learn new material we hadn't encountered in our secondary school. Yes, we were both underprepared and misprepared. But the bottom line is that something worked for us in the developmental education classroom. In fact, from the steps first taken along our college paths in developmental education to graduation years later, we all found our journeys somewhat less rocky than those of our friends who had gone on to Pac-10 schools right out of high school. For my buddies and me, developmental education got us off on the right foot and provided us with the initial successes in postsecondary learning that assured us a college education was attainable. So now, nearly thirty-five years after my developmental education experience, I have an opportunity to repay the field that helped me and my lifelong friends develop the academic foundation for college success.

As you read through the various chapters that compose this text, you will find a survey of our profession through selected articles from journals that constitute the learned foundation of the field. The first chapter is entitled "Historical Contexts." I'm a firm believer that a field becomes a profession only as it documents and appreciates its history. I'm also a firm believer that you take the first steps in becoming a member of our profession when you begin to read works that trace our history.

The second chapter, "Paradigms and Programs," describes various organizational structures for delivering course work and services to students. Understanding different program designs and their underlying philosophical positions permits members of the field to evaluate programs on their home campuses and to design alternatives for the future.

The third chapter, "Teachers and Praxis," focuses on the role of the developmental reading instructor through a look at specific practices and recommendations for instruction. The chapter that follows, "Strategic Learning," covers the theory and research on this popular approach and describes instructional models for helping students become strategic learners.

College reading and learning programs and learning assistance centers have always served a diverse clientele. With the turn of the century, however, the range of this diversity is greater than ever before. The next two chapters focus on aspects of this diversity. Chapter 5, "New-to-English Learners," includes a description of English language learners in developmental reading programs, followed by articles detailing instructional approaches tailored to this population. The next chapter, "Planning for a Range of Readers," features articles pertaining to students who have Attention Deficit Disorder or are deaf or hard of hearing.

The goal of all college reading classes and learning enhancement services is to prepare students to succeed in courses offered throughout the college experience. Therefore, Chapter 7, "Reading in the Content Areas," focuses on designing a curriculum and offering instruction that specifically prepares students for content field learning.

The next chapter, "The Reading/Writing Connection" provides a theoretical and historical rationale for the integration of reading and writing instruction, along with discussions of various instructional approaches that draw upon the synergy of the reading/writing connection. Next, "Beyond the Reading/Writing Connection" makes a case for expanding the pedagogical boundaries of developmental reading courses to include the spoken and visual arts as well.

The final chapter deals with the brave new world of technology as it impacts college reading instructors and learning assistance professionals, as well as today's college student. "Technology" portrays the fully wired campus and students of the new millennium. It also covers several instructional delivery systems that utilize technology to promote college reading instruction.

While this text provides a range of snapshots of the profession as it exists today, it is not designed to replace initial or advanced professional development in the field of college reading and learning instruction. Reading this book may, however, provide a kind of developmental experience in itself by adding to one's professional foundation. Still, as a member of a profession with a long and quite honorable history, I certainly hope the new college reading instructor or learning assistance specialist will become an active participant in the field through membership in organizations such as the College Reading and Learning Association, the National Association for Developmental Education, or the National College Learning Center Association. In addition, I hope he or she will regularly read the journals from which the articles published here were drawn. And, finally, I hope that, if the opportunity permits, new professionals will seek advanced training through participation in programs for developmental educators such as the Kellogg Institute at Appalachian State University, the National Conference on

Supplemental Instruction sponsored by the University of Missouri – Kansas City, the Annual Institute for Learning Assistance Professionals at the University of Arizona, or through formal degree objectives in developmental education offered at institutions such as National Louis University, Southwest Texas University, or the University of Minnesota.

Finally, let me add that this project would not have come to fruition without the commitment of the staff at Bedford/St. Martin's to the instructors and students involved in the developmental education mission. Next, I want to pay particular thanks to Hunter Boylan of the National Center for Developmental Education, who recommended me for this project. In addition, all due praise and thanks are given to Trudy Palmer for her superb editorial guidance throughout this endeavor. And as always, great appreciation and love is directed to Carolyn and Jennifer, who, as over a hundred times before, found me focused on the computer monitor and keyboard on still one more project. Lastly, thanks are due to all the developmental educators who made a college education a reality for Bill and Bill, Ted and Ray, Bob and Norm. And to you, the reader of this text: You are a member of the finest group of educators in postsecondary education today. Be proud to be a developmental educator.

NORMAN A. STAHL

Contents

Preface   v

Introduction   1

Hunter Boylan
Developmental Education: What's It About?   1

"[W]e really didn't know very much about the students we were trying to bring into the university. We blindly assumed that if we extended the opportunity, they would take advantage of it and succeed. Somehow, they would magically turn out to be just like us. It proved to be much more complicated than that. We could admit countless numbers of [disadvantaged students], but unless we gained an understanding of how they learned, what they needed in order to succeed in college, and how we might provide it, we would never be successful in our efforts to turn them into college graduates."

1   Historical Contexts   11

Monica Wyatt
**The Past, Present, and Future Need for College Reading
Courses in the U.S.**   12

"The need exists today, as it has historically existed, for college reading programs in American higher education. Most importantly, with the changing demographics of the population of the United States, the need for college reading assistance in the twenty-first century will be critical."

Nancy V. Wood
**College Reading Instruction as Reflected by Current
Reading Textbooks** 29

"The changes in reading during the last fifteen to twenty years should also be regarded as a paradigm shift. The changes are significant, they represent real change, and they are pervasive. Change is characterized in this paper as a shift from a traditional, text-based approach to a modern, reader-based approach to teaching reading."

Norman A. Stahl, James R. King, and Ulinda Eilers
Postsecondary Reading Strategies Rediscovered 43

"The passage of time often proves that our professional [romance] with theories and instructional practices is at best fleeting. An academic field demonstrates regularly its fickle behavior, as new favorites are embraced in a cyclical process of initial interest, growing adoration, general acceptance, varied evaluation, and either rejection or relegation to a cult status. In either rejection or cultism, ideas lie dormant and await reincarnation as the cycle repeats itself."

2 Paradigms and Programs 59

Louise Bohr
**College and Precollege Reading Instruction:
What Are the Real Differences?** 60

"[I]t is rare that we delineate for prospective college reading instructors how their practice can be differentiated from the practices of elementary and high school teachers. And there are some crucial questions: Do the same practices work with college students? Are the purposes for instruction the same? Do students have the same needs? If we are to clearly understand the role played by college reading teachers, we should focus on what we can and can't learn from high school and elementary reading teachers."

Mellinee Lesley
**Exploring the Links between Critical Literacy
and Developmental Reading** 72

"The story recorded here is one of students' successful formulation of literacy as measured in test scores, reading interest inventories, and written artifacts. It's also one of success for me as a teacher, taking a huge risk to revamp an entire developmental reading program for my university."

Jim Reynolds and Stuart C. Werner
**An Alternative Paradigm for College Reading
and Study Skills Courses** 86

"A core concept in the learner centered paradigm is that individuals develop personal ways of learning which can be called their learning style characteristics. This pattern of personality and environmental factors related to how one learns is called [learning style.] . . . developmental educators, counselors, and administrators can reconsider their philosophical assumptions about how best to assist college students in developing more effective reading and study skills. We think a new learner centered paradigm in which people develop in their own way and style should be applied."

Nannette Evans Commander and Brenda D. Smith
Developing Adjunct Reading and Learning Courses That Work 95

"As developmental programs expand into learning support programs and colleges seriously begin to address student retention, adjunct courses will become an increasingly important service offered by learning support and assistance programs."

3 Teachers and Praxis 110

Francine C. Falk-Ross
**Toward the New Literacy: Changes in College Students'
Reading Comprehension Strategies following Reading/
Writing Projects** 111

"The educational benefit of following college students' progression through a series of reading and writing assignments lies in discovering relevant and meaningful ways to connect marginalized students with literacy skills and strategies that they have not previously learned or adopted."

Annette F. Gourgey
**Teaching Reading from a Metacognitive Perspective:
Theory and Classroom Experiences** 126

"Students need to be prodded to read actively with each new piece, to overcome their resistance to thinking through their confusion and to changing old habits. Yet, only by struggling with these skills over time did they begin to develop the confidence that they *could* figure out meaning for themselves."

Martha E. Casazza
**Using a Model of Direct Instruction to Teach Summary
Writing in a College Reading Class** 135

"Using a model of direct instruction to teach summarizing provides a natural framework for emphasizing to students that it is their responsibility to bring meaning to the text. Through direct instruction, there is a gradual release of instructor support as students become capable of applying the strategies independently."

Kenneth Wolf and Yvonne Siu-Runyan
Portfolio Purposes and Possibilities 144

"[P]ortfolios are a means, not an end. The goal is not to create wonderful portfolios, but to promote more effective learning. A portfolio can accomplish the goal of advancing student learning only if the experiences documented are worthwhile. That is to say, portfolios are only as good as the curriculum and instructional opportunities afforded to students."

4 Strategic Learning 156

Michele L. Simpson and Sherrie L. Nist
**An Update on Strategic Learning: It's More Than
Textbook Reading Strategies** 157

"Most researchers would agree that strategic learners are those students who have a vast repertoire of strategies that they can selectively apply in order to complete tasks across a variety of content areas. Although the term *strategic learning* involves several complex and interactive factors, at a basic level it suggests that students possess effective strategies for reading textbooks as well as a variety of strategies useful in studying."

Martha E. Casazza
Strengthening Practice with Theory 179

"The field of developmental education is strong in part due to the range of disciplines represented by its practitioners. . . . This multidisciplinary foundation facilitates an integrated approach to educational practice. This integration could be further enhanced by constructing an interdisciplinary theoretical framework."

Claire E. Weinstein, Douglas Dierking, Jenefer Husman,
Linda Roska, and Lorrie Powdrill
The Impact of a Course in Strategic Learning on the
Long-Term Retention of College Students 193

"Developmental education, by definition, includes facilitating students' transition into higher education. The ultimate goal, however, is not only to help students prepare for college-level courses but also to facilitate (a) the transfer of what they are learning to other academic coursework, (b) their retention to graduation, and (c) the successful attainment of their academic goals."

Donna L. Mealey
Understanding the Motivation Problems of
At-Risk College Students 208

"Until at-risk college reading students are motivated to take responsibility for their own learning, until they attribute their success to their own efforts, until they see themselves as learners, they will be unable to take advantage of strategic learning instruction."

5 New-to-English Learners 216

Lía D. Kamhi-Stein
Profiles of Underprepared Second-Language Readers 217

"The placement of L2 students into prebaccalaureate reading courses is usually accomplished through traditional forms of assessment, which [are limited in their descriptive power]. If teachers were to rely solely on information provided by reading comprehension tests, they would not develop an understanding of what strategies their students use or why their students have arrived at a certain decision."

Denise Johnson and Virginia Steele
So Many Words, So Little Time: Helping College ESL Learners
Acquire Vocabulary-Building Strategies 233

"The strong relationship between reading comprehension and vocabulary knowledge presents teachers of ESL learners with the challenge of meeting their unique need for effective vocabulary-building strategies. . . . Teachers must work with students to identify those specific strategies that hold the most promise for helping them become enthusiastic and independent word learners."

Vicki L. Holmes and Margaret R. Moulton
Dialogue Journals as an ESL Learning Strategy 246

"Using a multiple case study design, we collected data to answer the following question: What perspectives do second-language university students have on dialogue journal writing as a strategy for learning English?"

Laura Bauer and Linda Sweeney
The Use of Literary Letters with Post-secondary Non-native Students 255

"According to the transactional theory, reading and writing are reciprocal, part of the same process. . . . With the use of literary letters, a free-form exchange between teacher and student or student and student, based upon the shared reading of novels, we found a wonderful tool that melds the reading/writing process . . . and goes far beyond."

6 Planning for a Range of Readers 265

Shevawn Eaton and Sharon Wyland
College Students with Attention Deficit Disorder (ADD): Implications for Learning Assistance Professionals 266

"More students with Attention Deficit Disorder are coming to college than ever before. Because many of the symptoms of the disorder involve learning, those of us who work within learning assistance, academic support services, and developmental education are increasingly faced with the needs of students with ADD."

Karen S. Kalivoda, Jeanne L. Higbee, and Debra C. Brenner
Teaching Students with Hearing Impairments 277

"There are growing numbers of students with hearing impairments on college campuses today. Due to current admissions and placement testing practices and differences between written English and American Sign Language, many of these students will be admitted into developmental education programs."

7 Reading in the Content Areas 289

Michele L. Simpson
**Conducting Reality Checks to Improve Students'
Strategic Learning** 290

"[I]nstructors involved in academic assistance must become familiar with and immersed in the reading, writing, and thinking demands placed upon their students. Instructors then would use that information to identify relevant strategies that students would practice with actual content area texts."

Julia Beyeler
**Reluctant Readers: Case Studies of Reading
and Study Strategies in Introduction to Psychology** 301

"The implication of this study for professionals planning reading and learning assistance for college students is that if surface level strategies are sufficient to pass a course, those are the strategies the students will utilize. However, when surface level strategies are utilized and the student does not obtain the desired grade, then the student is more willing to apply deep level strategies to improve the grade."

Jodi Patrick Holschuh
**Do as I Say, Not as I Do: High, Average, and Low-Performing
Students' Strategy Use in Biology** 316

"Deep and surface approaches to learning may tie into students' college performance because they are a result of students' perceptions of academic tasks. Students who adopt deep approaches to learning tend to personalize the task and integrate information so that they can see relationships among ideas."

8 The Reading/Writing Connection 330

Karen B. Quinn
**Teaching Reading and Writing as Modes of Learning
in College: A Glance at the Past; a View to the Future** 331

"Those of us who teach academic reading and writing at the college level or, in current parlance, who attempt to help students achieve critical literacy, follow current trends in theory, research, and practice without giving much thought to the historical circumstances which have led up to the changes in the way reading and writing are conceived, researched, taught, and even talked about today."

Amelia E. El-Hindi
**Connecting Reading and Writing: College Learners'
Metacognitive Awareness** 350

"First-year college students are faced with many pressures. . . . Of the many pressures faced by this special population is the demand to integrate information from vast amounts of text. . . . Students who lack the sophistication to rapidly digest text could be set up for failure in reading-intensive courses."

Mary P. Deming and Maria Valeri-Gold
**Making Reading and Writing Connections with
Shay Youngblood's *Big Mama Stories*** 363

"The short story, 'Did Mama Like to Dance', has been very successful with college students. Students were moved by its themes. They were especially intrigued by the emphasis on family and indicated that they longed to learn more about their own families. Since this story spoke to students on such a personal level, it became an accessible arena from which to draw connections between reading and writing."

Cynthia M. Chamblee
**Bringing Life to Reading and Writing for At-Risk
College Students** 369

"The evidence of the importance of the reading and writing relationship has manifested itself in integrated language arts classes and writing in the content areas. Nevertheless, courses designed for basic readers and writers often continue to separate the two processes and, therefore, fail to benefit from the important connections."

Maryann S. Feola
**Using Drama to Develop College Students'
Transaction with Text** 378

"If putting students in touch with what they bring to a text promises reading improvement, what type of literature would best facilitate the process? Dramatic literature, filled with personal conflict, emotion, and moving language, has the potential to transform students in developmental reading courses into more responsive readers."

9 Beyond the Reading/Writing Connection 386

Nannette Evans Commander and Sandra U. Gibson
Ideas in Practice: Debate as an Active Learning Strategy 386

"Developmental reading instructors, therefore, need to use instructional techniques that allow students to transfer reading skills to other kinds of tasks that the students perceive to be real. . . . One active learning technique that involves students in doing things and thinking about what they are doing is formal debate."

Carolyn Beardsley Meigs and Ruth Abernethy McCreary
**Foreign Films: An International Approach
to Enhance College Reading** 397

"Reading foreign films with English subtitles has proved to be an engaging way for our college developmental readers to expand their reading interests. Students gained confidence in their ability to read adult material and developed research skills while completing written assignments related to particular films."

10 Technology 406

Alison V. Kuehner
**The Effects of Computer Instruction on
College Students' Reading Skills** 407

"Most studies suggest that computers can provide motivating and efficient learning and help students improve their reading skills. However, it is not clear whether the computer or the instructing via the computer best accounts for student gains."

Marsha D. Sinagra, Jennifer Battle, and Sheila A. Nicholson
**E-mail "Booktalking": Engaging Developmental Readers
with Authors and Others in the Academic Community** 423

"We have learned that providing developmental students with quality literature, the novelty of E-mail, and authentic audiences can engage them in the type of academic discourse they must develop to be successful in college."

David C. Caverly and Lucy MacDonald

Techtalk: Developing Online Reading Courses   433

"Here we will share how we developed a generation two (G2) online developmental reading course, delivering a class online but adding asynchronous interaction among the students and instructor. Using technology such as e-mail, web-based discussion boards, and interactive web pages, students are able to complete a G2 course at their own time and place."

David C. Caverly

**Back to the Future: Preparing Students to
Use Technology in Higher Education**   438

"Learning centers and developmental education courses are well placed to help develop the students of today grow to meet these demands of tomorrow. . . . Whether we like it or not, the future will come. We need to be prepared to meet it head on and grow with our students."

About the Contributors   **447**

Developmental Education: What's It About?

Hunter Boylan

April 1969 — The Beginning

My first-ever developmental student sat on the other side of my desk. He called himself "Bubbie Tomatoes." That wasn't his real name, of course, but everyone in North Philadelphia street gangs had a nom de guerre.

Bubbie was the Warlord of the Omega Soul Gents, one of a half dozen neighborhood gangs of fifteen- to twenty-year-olds who, in those days, terrorized the North Philadelphia area. Of course, street gangs were different thirty-three years ago. Their members rarely killed each other or anyone else. Instead, they engaged in occasional larceny, assault, and extortion, and they fought to protect whatever they regarded as their territory. When they weren't doing these things, they served as social organizations for the young people of North Philadelphia. They were far from benign, but their actions probably wouldn't make news today.

In street gang hierarchy, the Warlord was second in command, responsible for organizing the defense and expansion of gang territory. Because the Omega Soul Gents seemed to have a larger amount of territory under their control than anyone else in North Philadelphia, I assumed Bubbie was pretty good at what he did.

Bubbie claimed to be nineteen, but there were no records to back up that claim. He had no permanent home, and stayed with various

1

aunts and cousins and friends when the weather was cold, and lived on the street when the weather was warm. He was a wiry five feet eight inches tall, and his face and arms were covered with scars from countless street fights. Since he was still walking around and members of other gangs seemed to be afraid of him, I assumed he'd won most of those fights.

I was a very junior administrator at Temple University. One of my roles was to improve community relations, so through a variety of misadventures, I wound up working with street gangs in the North Philadelphia ghetto surrounding the university. In the process, I was supposed to find talented young kids in the area from disadvantaged backgrounds and recruit them to attend Temple. Bubbie was the first person I'd convinced to attend the university under this new outreach program. And he'd done surprisingly well the previous term as a first semester freshman, earning a 2.70 grade point average as a sociology major.

But on this particular April day, he was explaining to me why he had just dropped out of college. He had two reasons. First, as he told it, every day he spent in the university was a day he didn't spend out on the street. And he was worried that his street skills were atrophying while he was learning how to be a college student. He'd decided that the consequences of not learning how to be a college student were far less critical than the consequences of losing his street skills.

His second reason was that he was experiencing a lot of racism, and he didn't feel like putting up with it. He felt, with some justification, that "everyone treats me like I don't belong here." After all, in order to get to class he had to wear his gang uniform to avoid being attacked. The uniform consisted of a black mesh T-shirt with a bicycle chain for a necktie, which didn't exactly endear him to the faculty of Temple. Speaking of some of his professors, he pointed out with a certain Zen eloquence, "I could kill the dudes, but they wouldn't learn anything from it. Besides . . . what goes around comes around."

So Bubbie said good-bye, thanked me for my efforts, and disappeared back into the wilderness of North Philadelphia's ghetto. He was my first developmental student and my first failure.

I realized as a result of that experience that we really didn't know very much about the students we were trying to bring into the university. We blindly assumed that if we extended the opportunity, they would take advantage of it and succeed. Somehow, they would magically turn out to be just like us. It proved to be much more complicated than that. We could admit countless numbers of "disadvantaged students," but unless we gained an understanding of how they learned, what they needed in order to succeed in college, and how we might provide it, we would never be successful in our efforts to turn them into college graduates.

I've spent most of my career trying to understand those issues. The body of knowledge we now have to help us serve these students has expanded dramatically. And I've been privileged to take part in that expansion of knowledge. Let me share with you a few things I've learned along the way.

The Myth of the Prepared College Student

Many college professors bemoan the passing of the "good old days," when all students going to college arrived fully prepared for the experience. They would probably be chagrined to learn that except for a brief period of time from the late 1950s through the late 1960s, those good old days never existed.

The first students attending Harvard in 1636 had to be tutored because they did not know Greek and Latin well enough to study classical works written in those languages. In the 1700s, colonial colleges limited their admission to "gentlemen," without paying much attention to how well the gentlemen could read or write. Land grant colleges of the late 1800s provided college preparatory departments that taught basic reading and writing to students who were only marginally literate. In the early 1900s, Ivy League admissions officers acknowledged that more than half of their students were not able to pass their college admissions examination (Maxwell, 1997). More recently, the National Center for Education Statistics reported in 1996 that 29 percent of students entering American colleges and universities placed into one or more remedial courses. Like the biblical poor, underprepared college students have always been and will always be with us.

The only exception to this took place roughly between 1956 and 1966. During this period, there were far fewer colleges and universities than there are now, and there was little financial aid available to support college attendance. The people who went to college were, for the most part, white and middle to upper-middle class. Students who made it to college from lower socioeconomic backgrounds either obtained competitive academic scholarships or worked their way through school. In both cases, they were likely to be bright and highly motivated.

The myth of the good old days when everyone in college was prepared to be there was created during this period. Because about 60 percent of those teaching in colleges and universities today were hired between 1965 and 1975, a majority of today's college faculty did their undergraduate work during the 1960s. When they reflect upon their own college experience, they recall being surrounded by bright and motivated students just like they remember themselves to have been. In their recollection, all but the best and the brightest failed. With the exception of weak students with wealthy alumni for parents or poorly schooled athletes playing critical roles on varsity teams, this was probably true.

Most college professors are unfamiliar with the history of American higher education other than their experience with it. Consequently, many of them fail to realize that they did their undergraduate work during the one brief period when colleges and universities actually were filled with a preponderance of bright and motivated students.

As the United States became more concerned with social justice and educational opportunity during the 1960s and 1970s, opportunities to attend college were extended to ever larger numbers of students. Most of these students were from different backgrounds than those students who had immediately preceded them. They were more likely to be ethnic minorities, they were more likely to be single parents, they were more likely to have grown up in poverty, and they were more likely to be older than traditional college students. The very characteristics that made these students nontraditional also meant that many of them suffered from poor schooling and a subsequent lack of academic preparation for college.

In the years since the 1970s, a variety of activities have been undertaken to help these students overcome their underpreparedness. Basic skills courses in reading, study strategies, writing, and mathematics have been added to the curriculum. Colleges and universities have offered tutoring. Learning centers and instructional laboratories have provided programmed learning and individualized instruction. All these services eventually became part of what is now called developmental education.

Who Are the Developmental Students?

Students who participate in developmental education are a very diverse group, particularly at community colleges. The only thing that may consistently be said of them is that they have either a long or a short history of difficulty succeeding in an academic environment. Some of them have been poor students throughout their academic careers while others did well in school and have just discovered that college courses are harder than high school ones.

Across the nation, including universities and community colleges, the average age of developmental students is about twenty-two, though that average is somewhat higher in community colleges. But averages are deceiving. The age distribution of students in developmental education tends to be bimodal. Just under half of those taking developmental courses are eighteen- and nineteen-year-old college freshmen. And just under half are twenty-five to thirty-five years old. The remainder may be as young as sixteen or as old as sixty.

The majority of developmental students are from low-income backgrounds. A 1996 study conducted by the American Council on Education (Knopp, 1996) reported that more than 50 percent of dependent students taking developmental courses came from families with annual incomes of $20,000 or less. On the other hand, about 8 percent came from families with annual incomes of $50,000 or higher.

Minority students tend to be disproportionately represented in developmental education. More specifically, the percentage of minorities in developmental education is about three times higher than the percentage of minorities in American higher education. White students, however, are the majority in developmental courses. The National Study of Developmental Education (Boylan, Saxon, White, & Erwin, 1994) reported that about two thirds of the students enrolled in developmental courses are white.

The vast majority of those taking developmental courses have lower than average SAT scores. According to the American Council on Education (Knopp, 1996), 81 percent of those enrolled in developmental courses have SAT composite scores lower than 1000. However, nearly 20 percent of those enrolled in developmental courses have SAT composite scores over 1000 and 4 percent have scores over 1200. As Hardin (1998) points out, students find themselves in developmental education for a variety of reasons.

Most of today's developmental students avoided college preparatory courses in high school and only decided to attend college either late in their high school careers or after graduation. (Only 45 percent of high school graduates take college preparatory courses, yet more than 60 percent of them eventually go on to some form of postsecondary education [Boylan, 2000].) Other developmental students are adults who graduated from high school five to ten years ago. Those in this group who did take college preparatory courses in high school have forgotten much of what they learned in the intervening years.

Some developmental students have diagnosed or undiagnosed disabilities that made learning difficult for them in elementary and secondary school. Yet they somehow managed to attain high school diplomas and are now participating in postsecondary education. It should be noted, however, that there are far more students who believe themselves to be learning disabled or whose instructors think they are learning disabled than is actually the case.

Others may have gone to elementary or secondary school in a foreign country. They may be quite skilled in some areas but have limited English proficiency. Although they speak English well enough to survive in society, their lack of high-level English speaking and writing skills represents a barrier to success in college.

Still others in developmental education are simply passive students of average ability. In high school, they attended class regularly, didn't cause any trouble, and were often ignored by their teachers. Now, they sit in college classes, continue to be passive, continue to do average work, and find that average high school work is just not good enough in college. Some may also lack maturity and direction. They are not sure what they want to do with their lives and, therefore, have relatively low levels of motivation. Even those who are motivated don't understand what's required to be successful in college.

All of these circumstances contribute to the fact that many college students are not yet prepared, emotionally or intellectually, for college-level academic work. These students need developmental education if they are to have a chance at being successful undergraduates.

What Is Developmental Education?

Today, most courses, services, and activities designed to help underprepared students are organized and delivered under the rubric of "developmental education." At the most basic end, developmental education teaches students to read and write well enough to pass college courses. At the opposite end, developmental education prepares honor students to get higher scores on graduate and professional school entrance examinations such as the GRE, LSAT, or MCAT. Essentially, developmental education helps students develop the skills necessary to achieve their objectives in postsecondary education. This is reflected in the motto of the National Association for Developmental Education: "Helping underprepared students prepare, prepared students advance, and advanced students excel."

Most developmental education is delivered through one of three models. On some campuses, it's provided through a centralized department or program combining reading, writing, and mathematics instruction, along with support services. On other campuses, these courses and services are decentralized and provided within their respective academic departments or units. Sometimes developmental education is delivered through a combination of centralized and decentralized programs. Developmental programs also differ in their level of coordination. Some decentralized programs are highly coordinated, and some centralized programs are loosely coordinated.

Typically, all college campuses provide academic support services to supplement classroom instruction. Sometimes these support services are part of the centralized developmental education, and sometimes they are not. These support services include subject-oriented learning laboratories, which frequently use individualized computer-aided instruction; learning assistance centers, which provide comprehensive learning services; and tutoring programs. Other services may include peer mentoring programs, academic counseling and advising, or diagnosis and testing.

Regardless of the organizational arrangements governing the delivery of developmental education, successful developmental educators utilize a common theory and philosophical base. As Casazza and Silverman point out,

> If we look back at the belief system that many practitioners of developmental education . . . share, we find that one major theme emerges: placing the learner at the center of our practice. Closely aligned with this learner-centered approach is the understanding of the word developmen-

tal. The word denotes an educational process that begins with a determination of where learners are, what they want to achieve, and how to help them realize their greatest potential as they work toward their goals. (1996, p. 260)

One of the most basic principles of developmental education is that students are constantly developing as human beings. Furthermore, the actions, methods, and attitudes of instructors, counselors, and advisors can contribute to this development over time. Because of this, learners' skills measured at one point in time do not represent where learners might be at a later time.

Another principle of developmental education is that students' affective characteristics are just as important to their success in academe as their cognitive characteristics. Affective characteristics are students' beliefs, thoughts, and emotions, such as their attitudes toward education, their motivation, their instructional style preferences, or their level of autonomy. Cognitive characteristics refer to students' knowledge, skills, and information processing styles. As Benjamin Bloom (1976) points out, only about half of how well a student performs academically is determined by cognitive characteristics. The rest of student performance is governed by affective characteristics and the quality of instruction. Recognizing this, developmental educators place great emphasis not only on teaching basic academic skills but also on improving students' attitudes toward learning, autonomy, academic self-confidence, and motivation.

A major purpose of developmental education is to insure that the open door does not become, in the words of Pat Cross (1971), a revolving door. In essence, developmental education helps make educational opportunity meaningful. It helps students develop the skills, values, information, and motivation they need not only to attend college but also to attain their goals while in attendance.

Developmental education is also a field of research, a field of study, and a field of practice. The most effective instructors teaching developmental courses study the research and literature in the field and use this information to inform their teaching. They do not rely on teaching the way they were taught but, instead, are constantly searching for ways of improving the design and delivery of their instruction. They do this because they are fully aware of one of the most basic maxims of developmental education: Developmental students are extraordinarily diverse, and diverse students require diverse instructional methods.

Why Do We Need Developmental Education?

Providing quality developmental instruction and services is, now more than ever, critical to higher education and to our society. As Harold Hodgkinson (1985) pointed out, seventeen people contributed to the benefits of each Social Security recipient in 1950. By the year 2000, only three people were working to support each Social Security recipient. One of those three was a minority, and one of those three had experienced poverty as a child. Since the size of our workforce has declined, it is essential that we improve the amount and quality of education available to the remaining workers. In the words of Robert McCabe (2000), we no longer have anyone to waste.

There are too many slots in our society and in our workforce that require advanced technical, communication, and critical thinking skills to deny anyone the opportunity to attain these skills through postsecondary education. We can no longer afford to deny educational opportunity to those who might not yet be fully prepared to take advantage of it. We must develop the educational potential of all our nation's talent pool if the United States is to survive and prosper in the twenty-first century.

The mission of developing our talent pool, particularly for our least advantaged citizens, will most likely to fall to our community colleges and less selective universities. These are the institutions where the least advantaged members of our society can gain admission. These are the institutions that admit the largest share of students who are poorly prepared for college. These are the institutions that are most likely to admit those students who have grown up in poverty or been exposed to poor elementary or secondary schools. These institutions and their instructors can, therefore, make the greatest difference in enhancing the nation's talent pool through developmental education.

Reading instruction has long been a key component of developmental education. In fact, when the first college preparatory department was established at the University of Wisconsin in 1849 (Brier, 1983), one of its primary purposes was to provide reading instruction. This is no less necessary today.

According to the National Center for Education Statistics (1996), 41 percent of those attending public two-year institutions and 22 percent of those attending public four-year institutions for the first time were enrolled in one or more remedial courses. Among all the nation's college and university freshmen, 13 percent enrolled in remedial reading or study strategies courses. In 2001–2002, about a half million students took these courses, many of whom were from the most disadvantaged social, economic, and educational backgrounds.

These students are not just statistics, however. They are individuals with their own aspirations for a quality life, a meaningful contribution to society, and the ability to provide for themselves and their families. They did not ask to be poor, they did not choose to attend our worst public schools, they did not decide to have poor academic skills, and they did not choose to have low motivation. In fact, people from disadvantaged backgrounds generally have fewer choices than the middle class, and, unfortunately, they often have less information on which to base their choices than the middle class. Consequently, developmental students are frequently the victims of their limited choices and their own poor selection among the available alternatives.

In our society college attendance means many things for many people. To the poverty stricken, to the middle-class-poor choosers, to the displaced workers of our society, college attendance often represents their last chance for a productive and fulfilling life. Many of the students in our developmental classrooms are there because they would not be able to take advantage of this last chance without developmental education. For many of them, developmental education represents a launch pad not only to success in college but to a turnaround in their lives.

Christa McAuliffe, the educator astronaut who died in the space shuttle *Challenger* tragedy, once said, "I touch the future, I teach." In teaching developmental courses, we touch not only the future of our nation but the future of our students' lives. We have the opportunity to make a difference — one student at a time.

A hundred years from now, historians will look back upon the early years of the twenty-first century and ask if our nation was successful in extending the promise of educational opportunity to its most disadvantaged citizens. We do not know if they will answer that we succeeded or failed. We do know, however, that our actions today in serving developmental students will help determine that answer.

Epilogue — 1989

I was at a conference held on the campus of a Pennsylvania university. I had just finished giving the conference's keynote address to a group of developmental educators. An African American man walked up to the podium, shook my hand, and said, "Dr. Boylan, I just wanted to tell you how much I enjoyed your speech. I also wanted to tell you that I appreciated your help."

I didn't recognize the name printed on his name tag, so I said, "I'm sorry but I don't recall what I did to help you." He said, "You probably knew me better in a previous life as Bubbie Tomatoes."

As it turns out, Bubbie eventually went back to school, entering a community college and then transferring to a university. He graduated and went on for a master's degree in sociology. In 1989, he was working at a Pennsylvania university as a recruiter and counselor for minority students.

After he explained all this, Bubbie smiled at me and said, "You know something, Hunter . . . what goes around comes around."

References

Bloom, B. S. (1976). *Human characteristics and school learning.* New York: McGraw-Hill.

Boylan, H., Saxon, D., White, R., & Erwin, A. (1994). "Retaining minority students through developmental education." *Research in Developmental Education,* 11(3), 1–4.

Boylan, H. (2000). "Harvard symposium 2000: Demographics, outcomes, and activities." *Journal of Developmental Education,* 23(3), 2–9.

Brier, E. (1983). "Bridging the academic preparation gap: An historical view." *Journal of Developmental Education,* 8(1), 2–5.

Casazza, M., & Silverman, S. (1996). *Learning assistance and developmental education.* San Francisco: Jossey-Bass.

Cross, K. P. (1971). *Beyond the open door: New students to higher education.* San Francisco: Jossey-Bass.

Hardin, C. (1998). "Who belongs in college: A second look." In J. Higbee & P. Dwinnel (Eds.), *Developmental education: Preparing successful college students* (pp. 15–24). Columbia, SC: National Center for the First-Year Experience and Students in Transition.

Hodgkinson, H. L. (1985). *All one system: Demographics of education, kindergarten through graduate school.* Washington, DC: Institute for Educational Leadership.

Knopp, L. (1996). "Remedial education: An undergraduate student profile." *American Council on Education: Research Briefs,* 6(8), 1–11.

Maxwell, M. (1997). *Improving student learning skills.* Clearwater, FL: H & H Publishing.

McCabe, R. H. (2000). *No one to waste: A report to public decision makers and community college leaders.* Washington, DC: Community College Press.

National Center for Education Statistics (1996). *Remedial education at higher education institutions in fall 1995.* Washington, DC: U.S. Department of Education, Office of Educational Research and Improvement.

1

Historical Contexts

At the time of the dedication of the Franklin D. Roosevelt Library and Museum, President Roosevelt noted that "a nation must believe in three things. It must believe in the past. It must believe in the future. It must, above all, believe in the capacity of its own people so to learn from the past that they can gain in judgement in creating their own future."[1] Such wisdom not only challenges us as citizens, but can also guide our actions as members of a profession with a proud lineage. For these words direct our attention to the relationship between the contributions of college reading teachers and researchers of generations past, on the one hand, and the achievements to be realized in the future, on the other.

To so build the future, we must be fully cognizant of our past. As professionals, we should be knowledgeable of our historical roots, which span well over a century at schools such as Harvard University, Cornell University, and Vassar College among so many others. We should appreciate that many of the greatest scholars and leaders in the field of reading pedagogy — including William S. Gray, Miles Tinker, Nila B. Smith, Ruth Strang, and George Spache — wrote about college readers and college reading and learning programs. We should also revel in the fact that our professional organizations (including the

---

[1]Franklin D. Roosevelt, "Remarks at the dedication of the Franklin D. Roosevelt Library, June 30, 1941." Franklin D. Roosevelt Library and Digital Archives, Marist College/IBM. [cited 5 April 2002], available at <http:www.fdrlibrary.marist.edu/dedicate.html>.

International Reading Association [IRA], the National Reading Conference [NRC], the College Reading Association [CRA], the College Reading and Learning Association [CRLA], the American Reading Forum [ARF], and the Society for the Scientific Study of Reading [SSSR]) began with leadership provided by college reading researchers and instructors.

This is the heritage to which the new college reading professional comes and from which the more established colleague benefits on a regular basis. The articles that follow provide an introduction to the history of our field through three very different types of historical writings. In addition, historical works germane to specific subjects appear throughout the text. Our purpose is both to share an awareness of our past and to promote the pride in accomplishment associated with membership in the field of college reading and learning assistance.

The Past, Present, and Future Need for College Reading Courses in the U.S.

Monica Wyatt

It's likely that during the past decade, more individuals in the field of college reading and learning strategy instruction got to know their historical roots through Monica Wyatt's article "The Past, Present, and Future Need for College Reading Courses in the U.S." than through any other work. Wyatt's careful integration of both primary and secondary sources produced a work that covered two centuries of our history and also looked to the future based on past trends. Even now, a decade after its issuance, this historical work remains a most valuable introduction to the field's heritage, and her predictions are generally accurate as of 2002.

In today's climate of popular despair for education, lamentations about deficiencies in the reading and study habits of American college undergraduates are not unusual. As is demonstrated in the following quotation, they are also not new. In 1929, Charles H. Judd, Director of the School of Education at the University of Chicago, stated his views regarding the limitations of his institution's student body:

> Independent self-directed study is rare among senior-college students, and there is ground for the suspicion that the power of independent, self-directed study is not universal in the graduate school. These facts make it clear that students not only come to junior college intellectually dependent but they leave it in the same immature state. There is every reason to recognize immaturity in methods of self-directed thinking as one of the major deficiencies of college Freshmen (Judd, 1929, p. 5).

As Martha Maxwell has remarked, "It seems that every generation, at some point, discovers that students cannot read as well as they would like or as well as professors expect" (Maxwell, 1979, p. 269).

This article will demonstrate that college students' inadequate reading and study skills have existed from at least the early years of the nineteenth century and have continued unabated to the present, not only in public universities, but also in the nation's most selective and prestigious institutions. The need exists today, as it has historically existed, for college reading programs in American higher education. Most importantly, with the changing demographics of the population of the United States, the need for college reading assistance in the twenty-first century will be critical.

Americans have consistently supported many more institutions of higher learning than have Europeans. There were 9 established colleges in America by 1776 when there were only 2 in England, at that time a much larger and wealthier country. In 1880 England, with a population of 23 million, had 4 universities. At the same time Ohio, with a population of 3 million, had 37 institutions of higher learning. Between the Revolution and the Civil War, perhaps 700 institutions started and failed, competing for scarce resources. Although George Washington's dream of a University of the United States was defeated in Congress, American higher education has moved toward the ideal of education for all, unlike European (Trow, 1989). However, the success of higher education in America has frequently meant assisting the underprepared.

Nineteenth Century: Preparatory Departments

Since formal secondary schools did not exist in the U.S., nineteenth century students either worked with private tutors to prepare for college or simply received no education beyond grammar school. Those who were college bound, prepared or not, often matriculated at a very young age. Typically, prospective students lacked such basic skills as reading, spelling, and writing, and had no idea how to study. Faculty complaints about student ignorance were common throughout American higher education even in selective institutions. Especially on the western frontier, now the Midwest, the influx of underprepared students compelled new universities to adjust their standards to fit the population that was seeking their services.

Admission requirements of many century nineteenth century American colleges were low, often no more than basic grammar school skills in geography, arithmetic, grammar, reading, and spelling (Brubacher & Rudy, 1976). Yet, most students could not meet even those basic standards. Some western institutions, such as the University of Missouri, eliminated entrance requirements entirely, admitting anyone who could pay their fees (Levine, 1978).

Most institutions found methods of raising the abilities of their students so that they could begin training the scholars and professionals they intended to create. Commonly, "preparatory departments" were established to accomplish that task. Underprepared students, sometimes as young as 12, lived and studied in these departments after formal admission to the institution until they had acquired enough basic education to attempt regular courses. In essence, these were university-level high schools. They typically housed young adolescents, a custom not confined to the West. In 1842, Francis Wayland complained about the practice of admitting 14-year-olds to Brown University in Rhode Island (Brubacher & Rudy, 1976).

By the nineteenth century, eastern universities such as Harvard maintained far higher entrance requirements than those of the emerging western institutions. Nevertheless, eastern institutions also experienced difficulty finding students who met their standards, because entrance requirements varied widely from university to university. To accommodate potential students, eastern institutions sometimes established relationships with separate feeder preparatory schools instead of housing their own preparatory departments.

Even so, changes in the curricula of eastern institutions reflected a growing sophistication in their students, implying that those students were unsophisticated at an earlier time. At Yale, for example, geometry was a senior-level course in 1720. By 1743 it was at the sophomore level, in 1825 at freshman level, and by 1855 it had become a requirement for admission (Levine, 1978). The gradual demotion of the course may lead us to infer that matriculating freshmen in the eighteenth century East were no better prepared than their descendants a century later in the West.

Similar Remedies

However, whether the problem of underprepared students arose from a lack of basic skills or from a failure to meet more advanced requirements, educational institutions employed similar remedies. In order to engender enough enrollment to maintain financial viability, colleges and universities found methods of assisting underprepared students. Although departments were established for that purpose at nearly every institution, since recordkeeping was inadequate their existence can sometimes only be detected today through the complaints lodged against them. The existence of underprepared students on American college campuses was decried as early as 1828 at Yale (Brier, 1984). University student bodies often were composed more of preparatory than regular students. Yet their existence on campus was fiercely resented by those who struggled to establish a prestigious image of their schools in the European tradition of high scholarship.

The preparatory department at the University of Wisconsin, established in 1849, was typical. By 1865, out of 331 students registered at that institution, only 41 attended regular classes (Brubacher & Rudy, 1976). The remaining 290 students, 88 percent, attended the preparatory department. The department was finally abolished in 1880, after enduring constant attack for the embarrassment its existence brought to the campus. But complaints were not confined to Wisconsin.

In 1852, the president of the University of Michigan warned against admitting poorly prepared students (Enright & Kerstiens, 1980). Brier (1984), tracing the history of developmental courses in the nineteenth century, uncovered fascinating signs of their existence. In 1869, Cornell University President Andrew Dickson White complained that students' "utter ignorance" in the "common English branches" was "astounding." The *Vassar Miscellany* referred to such students in 1872 as "inferior forms" and "a reproach to be wiped away" and in 1882 as "a vandal horde."

Nevertheless, the presence of preparatory departments on campuses was far more common than their absence; by the 1870s they proliferated on American college campuses. In 1889, it was reported that of nearly 400 universities in the United States, only 65 "have freed themselves from the embarrassment of preparatory departments." The protests against underprepared students have continued unabated until the present, with perhaps less colorful language, but with no less vehemence.

Assistance at Harvard

Despite occupying one of the positions at the apex of American higher education, Harvard University has assisted underprepared students, drawn from the finest educational backgrounds, since at least the late nineteenth century. University President Charles Eliot noted in 1871 that Harvard freshmen displayed "bad spelling, incorrectness as well as inelegance of expression in writing, [and] ignorance of the simplest rules of punctuation."

He called for an entrance examination. In 1879, half of Harvard's applicants failed that examination. Many of these failures nevertheless were admitted "on condition" (Weidner, 1990, p. 4), costing the college time and money to move them into regular college level classes. But the entrance examination results continued to be deficient. W. P. Garrison complained in 1892 that "[u]nhappy instructors were confronted with immature thoughts set down in a crabbed and slovenly hand, miserably expressed and wretchedly spelled" (Weidner, 1990, pp. 4–5).

Harvard educators blamed the poor showing of their college freshmen on a literacy crisis in America. They attempted to show that preparatory schools were deficient. The preparatory schools blamed grammar schools and primary schools. The public blamed "ill prepared teachers, lazy students, neglectful parents, an indifferent society, and the sensationalist press" (Weidner, 1990, p. 6). Thus, today's literacy crisis mirrors that of 100 years ago.

Early Twentieth Century: How to Study Courses

By the turn of the century, the emergence of secondary schools eliminated the need to train adolescent scholars at the college level. Nevertheless, the problem of underprepared students persisted, and American universities continued to respond to their needs. In 1907, over one half of the students enrolled at Harvard, Yale, Princeton, and Columbia failed to meet the entrance requirements (Brubacher & Rudy, 1976; Levine, 1978). Therefore, in that year all four institutions followed the lead established by Wellesley College in 1894 and added formal college-level developmental courses to their curricula. Indeed, by 1915, some 350 colleges still had preparatory departments, as reported to the U.S. Commissioner of Education (Maxwell, 1979).

In 1927, one lone voice began to laud rather than condemn the practice of assisting underprepared students. William F. Book of the University of Indiana responded to an obvious need for such assistance at his institution. In 1926, one half of the Indiana freshmen had not fully met their course requirements with 16 percent failing all of their courses. After determining that a great deal of the students' difficulty lay in the area of reading and study habits, but that intelligence was apparently not a factor in their deficiencies (Book, 1927a), Book invented a How to Study course. His analysis of it revealed its effectiveness in improving time management, reading, and planning among the students who took the course (Book, 1927b).

Book's analysis of college reading (Book, 1927a) was remarkable in its depth of insight. He foreshadowed modern admonitions (Hayes & Diehl, 1982; Nist & Diehl, 1990) on the importance of using actual content material in developmental reading and in focusing on the use to which college readers put information in the real world of the college classroom:

> To measure their ability to master a standard assignment in a text, such as is regularly given by their instructors, a special test was devised by the writer which required the readers not merely to note and comprehend what was read, but to select and evaluate the important points made by the author, to organize and fix these points in mind so well, by relating them to what they already knew, that they would be able to recall and use this information in any way that their instructors might require on the following day (Book, 1927a, p. 243).

Of course. the validity and reliability of Book's test is open to question, but his intentions reflect advanced thinking in the field today. Book did not lament his students' seeming lack of ability; he instead tried to develop their talents to the extent that would allow them to function as productive students.

The problems faced by Book were not unique to the University of Indiana, however. In fact, the first study skills handbook had been published in 1916. Book's concerns were also predated by the University of Buffalo, which required a How to Study course for underachieving applicants in 1926 (Maxwell, 1979). Charles Judd's concerns in 1929 have already been noted. In 1932, the University of Minnesota found it necessary to offer a course entitled How to Study as part of what was considered to be an innovative curriculum for their newly instituted General College, which had been designed to accommodate an open admissions policy mandated by the legislature of that state (Coffman, 1933). In 1936 New York University's Reading Laboratory was established, and in 1938 both Harvard and Dartmouth established remedial reading programs for their students (Maxwell, 1979; Perry, 1959).

Book's enlightened recommendations for college reading held little sway during the next three decades. According to a survey conducted by Charters (1941), college reading courses were widespread, but Charters's description of them implies that they concerned mainly the mechanical aspects of reading. They concentrated their efforts on students' eye movements and eye span in an attempt to improve rate. The reading courses of the midcentury also included study skills. Normally, isolated skills were taught, such as skimming, organizing, and vocabulary (Charters, 1941).

Mid-twentieth Century: Federal Support

The Servicemen's Readjustment Act of 1944, popularly known as the G.I. Bill of Rights, sparked the first fires in a revolution of vast changes that swept across American college campuses following World War II. Prior to the war, higher education had been primarily accessible only to the nation's young male elite who were academically prepared and financially capable. Colleges commonly did not welcome nontraditional students; most of them automatically expelled students who were discovered to be married, for example. The Federal government had provided no significant support either to students or to research. The generosity of the G.I. Bill was based on the assumption that very few veterans would want to go to college (Bonner, 1986).

Nevertheless, the effect of the G.I. Bill brought an enormous expansion in the number of students on colleges and universities. More than a million veterans had matriculated by the fall of 1946. Altogether, about 2,232,000 veterans attended college under the G.I. Bill, including about 60,000 women. Over half of these veterans were married, and

A Chronology of American Developmental Education

1828	*Yale Review* laments the admission of underprepared students
1842	Francis Wayland complains about the practice of admitting 14-year-olds to Brown University
1849	University of Wisconsin establishes its Preparatory Department
1852	President of the University of Michigan warns against admitting poorly prepared students
1865	Of 331 students at the University of Wisconsin, only 41 attend regular classes
1869	Andrew Dickson White, President of Cornell University, complains about the ignorance of students
1870s	Preparatory departments proliferate on American campuses
1871	Harvard President Eliot deplores the writing of Harvard freshmen
1872	The *Vassar Miscellany* calls preparatory students "inferior forms" and "a reproach to be wiped away"
1879	Half of Harvard freshmen fail the entrance examination
1880	The Preparatory Department at the University of Wisconsin is abolished
1882	The *Vassar Miscellany* calls preparatory students "a vandal horde"
1889	Of nearly 400 universities in the United States, only 65 are without preparatory departments
1892	W. P. Garrison complains about the writing of Harvard freshmen
1894	Wellesley College establishes the first formal college developmental course
1898	Remedial Writing at Berkeley
1907	Over one half of students enrolled at Harvard, Princeton, Yale, and Columbia do not meet entrance requirements; developmental courses are established
1915	350 colleges still have preparatory departments
1916	The first How to Study course

half of those had children while still attending college. Most were mature and hardworking, and succeeded beyond the levels of their younger classmates. Many, though, were underprepared, and colleges made resources available to assist them.

In 1948, William S. Gray called for college reading to be taught to all college students, not only to those who were underprepared. He specifically recommended that attention be paid to content and personal reading, and that training for remedial and disabled readers be offered (Bullock, Madden, & Mallery, 1990). The expansion of college reading also gained the attention of other reading researchers. In 1952, Oscar Causey became the first president of the Southwest Reading Conference, later the National Reading Conference, which was specifically devoted to college reading.

A Chronology of American Developmental Education (continued)

1926	Half of freshmen at the University of Indiana do not fully meet their course requirements; 16 percent fail all their courses; the University of Buffalo institutes a required How to Study book
1927	William F. Book publishes results from his How to Study course at the University of Indiana
1929	Charles H. Judd complains about the study habits of freshmen, upperclassmen, and graduate students
1938	Harvard and Dartmouth establish remedial reading courses
1941	Charters publishes his survey indicating that college reading courses were widespread
1948	William S. Gray advises that college reading be taught to all students
1950s	Large influx of underprepared students to colleges after World War II attending on the G.I. Bill. Colleges respond to meet their needs with college reading courses
1952	Oscar Causey becomes the first president of the Southwest Reading Conference (later the National Reading Conference), exclusively devoted to college reading
1959	W. G. Perry's Report to the Faculty on remedial reading at Harvard
1960s	Open admissions policies lead to a second great influx of underprepared students
1963	Maxwell calls for college reading and study strategies to be taught to advanced students
1970s	Peer tutoring programs begin in California community colleges, leading to formal learning centers by the end of the decade
1980s	Developmental courses widespread in 4-year institutions
2000–2020	One third of Americans will be nonAnglo.

Although President Truman in the late 1940s had called for a huge peacetime program to assist college students and had urged extending mass education to the university level, the Eisenhower administration saw no need for Federal assistance. By 1956, the tide of veterans had ebbed on American campuses, and colleges had reverted to admissions standards and homogeneous student bodies similar to those that existed prior to World War II. But on October 4, 1957, the Soviet Union launched Sputnik I, an event that persuaded Congress to pass the National Defense Education Act of 1958. Finally, loans, fellowships for graduate study, and grants for research were provided to nonveteran students. University-level research and mass education were at last perceived to be important to the nation.

By 1960, the faith of Americans in higher education reached its peak; more believed that it should be democratized and broadened. The

Kennedy administration began to provide direct Federal help to the colleges themselves, and in 1965 the Higher Education Act finally provided direct government grants to undergraduate students. Many public institutions instituted open admissions policies, requiring a corresponding increase in academic support services; the experience of those open admissions policies for minority students is discussed below. Students in support programs became the focus of a new emphasis on the "whole person," wherein the personality as well as intellectual factors were addressed as being involved in reading and writing (Enright & Kerstiens, 1980). Counseling became part of the assistance programs; students worked to achieve their own goals rather than a laboratory norm.

Additionally, toward the end of the 1950s the desire to fit the program to the person inspired a move to materials based upon B. F. Skinner's notions of programmed learning. These materials formed the core curriculum of the independent reading programs that were established in 1959 at the University of Florida, in 1962 at the University of Maryland, and in 1965 at the University of Minnesota (Maxwell, 1979).

Even at Harvard

Harvard's difficulties with underprepared students did not end in the nineteenth century. Its college reading course, begun in 1938, was renovated by W. G. Perry, Director of Harvard's Bureau of Study Counsel. Originally titled Remedial Reading, it was devoted to training students' eye movements and about 30 freshmen per year were encouraged to enroll. Most did so reluctantly. Once the course title was changed to The Reading Class, however, it immediately attracted 400 freshmen, 150 upperclassmen, 230 graduate students, and 2 professors from the law school.

In order to limit enrollment to reasonable levels, Perry devised a placement test that was devoted to examining students' abilities to understand lengthy expository texts. His report to the Harvard faculty (1959) describes an entering class of 1,500 freshmen from Harvard and Radcliffe, 99 percent of whom could not write a short sentence concerning the meaning of a history chapter they had read, although all could answer multiple choice questions about details from the chapter. Given answers to a mock essay question on the same chapter, nearly one third of these freshmen chose a chronological reiteration of dates as superior to an essay that directly addressed the intellectual issue of the essay question. These 400 students were allowed to enroll in the renovated reading course, designed to stress study strategies rather than mechanical aspects of reading. Perry concluded that "[t]he possession of excellent reading skills as evidenced on conventional reading tests is no guarantee that a student knows how to read long assignments meaningfully" (Perry, 1959, p. 199).

The writing skills of entering Harvard freshmen have apparently not improved since they so shocked President Eliot in 1871. In 1985, a remedial writing course was required for those who exhibited deficiencies on a placement test. These students made mistakes in their writing similar to those of basic writers at less selective institutions. The basic writing course was at first greatly resented by those required to take it, by the faculty, and by the campus newspaper. However, when the course title was changed from Basic Writing to Introduction to Expository Writing, all questions of its appropriateness to the Harvard curriculum ceased, and some students began to take the course voluntarily (Armstrong, 1988).

We may surmise from the experiences at Harvard that the title of a course makes a crucial difference in its popularity. Students apparently feel a need to improve their reading and writing skills, but will not do so in a course that is labeled " basic" or "remedial."

Late Twentieth Century: Academic Assistance

Today, college reading courses remain widespread in the U.S., having become fixtures in almost all 4-year institutions. A survey completed by the National Center for Education Statistics found that 82 percent of all public and private institutions and 94 percent of public institutions offered at least one developmental course (Abraham, 1987). However, a high burnout rate of developmental studies instructors attests to a continuation of the historic bias against developmental courses in higher education. Universities commonly fail to accept developmental education instructors as full faculty members, and tend to limit their opportunities for advancement and for conducting research (Bullock et al., 1990).

Harvard, of course, is not the only prestigious institution to offer academic assistance. The University of California system accepts only the top 12.5 percent of high school graduates into its 4-year undergraduate programs. Yet, remedial writing was first taught at Berkeley in 1898, and by 1979 more than half of the entering freshmen at the Berkeley campus were still required to take such a course (Callas, 1985; Maxwell, 1979; Roueche, 1985). In 1981, 33 percent of freshmen at the Davis campus entering with a 4.0 high school grade point average and 49 percent of those with a grade point average of 3.5 or higher were held for the same course (Myers, 1984). The Los Angeles campus required half of its entering freshmen to enroll in remedial noncredit math or English courses in 1985 (Astin, 1985).

Stanford University established a learning center in 1972 for the provision of remedial programs to its students. By 1976, over half of its freshmen received assistance; that proportion has persisted in later years (Henry, 1986; Roueche, 1985).

If the most selective institutions in the nation find it necessary to provide assistance to their students, how necessary must such assistance be to the public institutions who accept a more diverse student body? At New Mexico State University, Blake (1985) found that only 37 percent of the entering freshman class of 1976 had graduated by 1985, even though those students had been screened to eliminate the insufficiently skilled and the unmotivated. She concluded that the institution was meeting the needs of only 4 out of 10 students.

Platt (1986) cites statistics that indicate about 28 percent of all college freshmen need help in reading. In 4-year colleges with entrance requirements, 21 percent of freshmen need remedial reading. Most students, especially, have not acquired higher order thinking skills by the time they enter college. Content area curricula are particularly challenging; most science texts used by nonscience majors are written at a reading level above the ability of average college students (Simms & Leonard, 1986).

There appears to be a continuing general need for support courses. In a survey designed to observe the actual study habits of college students, Thomas (1987) found that even students who were succeeding at a highly competitive major university did not use efficient study strategies; in fact, they used strategies that he described as "desultory": nonstrategic, nonselective processing of texts. When average and advanced students entered college from high school, they encountered learning contexts previously unknown to them and for which they had no experience or training.

Maxwell (1963) has argued that the study strategies and skills normally taught in developmental courses might be equally valuable to advanced students. In my own informal conversations with college development reading instructors, most of whom are graduate assistants enrolled in coursework for their doctorates, I discovered that even these advanced students had only recently begun to use the study strategies they had learned to teach to freshmen.

Late Twentieth Century: Exclusion

Many students who are underprepared are not unable (Hardin, 1988). Higher education may be losing a large number of able students because institutions do not know how to deal with their deficient skills. Exclusion rather than development has become a policy often used by universities to cope with the underprepared. Indeed, the pursuit of excellence alone provides an excuse to exclude (Willie, 1982). Platt (1986) argues that the excellence movement, driven by the pursuit of prestige, may eventually create an elitist educational system.

In an analysis of ways through which institutions attempt to enhance their prestige, Conrad and Eagan (1989) warn that exclusion tends to reduce student diversity by drawing students from an increasingly narrow pool. Through their actions, these institutions deny themselves the benefits of a more heterogeneous mix of students and sacrifice their institutional uniqueness. Seeking prestige, then, may not improve quality, but instead may militate against it.

Willie also reproves the exclusion of underprepared students. "Indeed," he writes, "the reputation of many schools is based in part on the proportion of applicants rejected" (Willie, 1982, p. 16). He agrees with Conrad and Eagan that such institutions deny themselves the wisdom and wit unique to groups that diverge from the norm. Myers argues that the ultimate value of well educated college graduates is far greater than the cost — in dollars or in prestige — of remediation. Without remediation as an aid in attracting and retaining diverse populations, the value of the bachelor's degree may be undermined or the underprepared students may have little chance of success (Myers, 1984).

Finally, Newman summarizes the need for assistance of underprepared students:

> We simply must not tolerate having 20 percent of the population unable to understand and unwilling to be concerned with what is going on around them. A nation cannot function as a democracy if a significant part of its population is not involved in and feels no sense of responsibility to the society in which they live (Newman, 1988, p. 10).

Seeking Social Equality

Trow (1989) argues that American higher education now seems ready to provide service to all nontraditional students. As such, higher education has become not only a supplier of advanced skills, but may become a source of greater social equality. Many ethnic minority and nontraditional students who are extremely able and well prepared for college will become students in the twenty-first century and will not need compensatory academic assistance. Many other ethnic minority and nontraditional students will be able but will also be underprepared due to inadequate and unequal schools they attended as children. It is the purview of this article to discuss the predicament of these underprepared students and their need for academic assistance.

In this nation, the right of all students to attend desegregated schools was not established until 1954, and civil rights legislation and adjudication has continued from that time to the present (Bullock et al., 1990). Yet, universal compliance within the nation's schools has never truly been attained; inequity still exists in schools. Orfield and Paul (1987–1988) cite some inequities in disadvantaged innercity schools as opposed to suburban schools, including (1) more crowded classrooms, (2) teachers with fewer advanced degrees, and (3) fewer counseling services. Students attending innercity schools are often tracked into classes that experience less advanced curricula, and are exposed to less vocabulary and to a less rich academic program. Results of such deficiencies in innercity schools include high dropout rates and students who are generally less well prepared for college.

American ethnic minority children, then, especially those who live in poor and disadvantaged areas, often still suffer from inadequate and unequal education. Those who persevere in their education and go on to college encounter increasing college costs, a lack of commitment to equal opportunity, and inadequate academic assistance.

Clearly, ethnic minorities in America still confront sizeable social and economic barriers (Applegate & Henniger, 1989). Minority high school students are likely to attend school in poor districts where their academic preparation is limited (Wilson & Justiz, 1988). These students are far more likely than nonminority Americans to be from poor families with limited education (Collison, 1988).

Twenty-First Century: Disadvantaged Minorities in College

Because of the inequities that unfortunately still exist in the education of ethnic minority and nontraditional students in the U.S., it is reasonable to surmise that some proportion of these students may need assistance in order to achieve their full potentials in college. If the numbers of minority and nontraditional students rise in the future, we may expect the need for compensatory academic assistance to rise as well.

Between the years 2000 and 2020, fully one third of Americans will be "nonAnglo," meaning not from families with a European ethnic heritage (Rainsford, 1990). By 2025, minorities may make up 40 percent of all 18–24 year olds (Applegate & Henniger, 1989). Within the next decade, 42 percent of all public school students will be from ethnic minorities. Already, the 25 largest school districts in the nation have nonAnglo majorities (Rainsford, 1990). In 1985, the University of California at Berkeley for the first time had a freshman class of 52 percent minorities (Trow, 1989).

Reasons for the changing demographics of the population of the United States include a decline in the birthrate of nonminority Americans while ethnic minority birthrates grow, and the immigration of minorities (Estrada, 1988). Two thirds of the world's immigration is to the United States, with one third going to California. By 2010, western nations may have only 9 percent of the world's population. There is a serious question that these nations may not continue to lead the remaining 91 percent (Hodgkinson, 1986).

The above statistics alone may give pause to those in higher education who continue to resist the presence of college reading programs on their campuses. As long as minority students suffer from unequal elementary and secondary education, their opportunity to achieve their full potential will be limited. The effects of demographic changes at the elementary school level have included providing more remediation (Estrada, 1988). It is apparent that during the twenty-first century, colleges and universities will be compelled to follow suit, or may lose a significant and vitally important segment of the population of the United States.

Although there is considerable evidence that the underprepared and disadvantaged can achieve success in college with assistance, there has been a recent decline in minority access and help has been less forthcoming than in the 1970s. Collison (1988) believes that America is moving backward in efforts to achieve full participation of ethnic minorities. Half a million disadvantaged students were dropped from Federal programs during the Reagan administration (Bullock et al., 1990). Minority enrollment in higher education is falling (Rainsford, 1990). Professor Shirley Chisholm believes that part of the reason for the decline is that "colleges and universities have failed to budget a fair and reasonable percentage of money for remedial and tutorial programs" (Keeter, 1987, p. 19).

Nevertheless, even though the enrollment rate for some minorities is falling, their population is growing so strongly that even small changes in rate will have a major impact on colleges (Trow, 1989). Also, although the overall population of high school students is declining, American college enrollment is still growing, partly due to the enrollment of women and ethnic minorities.

Open Admissions

The experience of the open-admissions policies of the 1960s clearly points to the necessity of assistance for underprepared students. Maxwell reports that during the 1960s and 1970s, colleges who treated open-admissions students as they treated any other student found that this approach failed (Maxwell, 1979). During their second year of open admissions, these colleges introduced required developmental courses. Many open-admissions programs experienced a high attrition rate, however; 90 percent of students either failed or withdrew. Often, early developmental programs were either watered-down versions of regular college courses or elementary courses badly redesigned for adults (Roueche, 1985). And all too often, institutions took credit for enrolling minorities but did not commit to seeing that these students graduated. Civil rights objectives focused on enrollment, not graduation (Rainsford, 1990).

However, some efforts were quite successful. Established in 1969, the Higher Education Opportunity Program (HEOP) gained recognition for the disadvantaged on New York campuses. The support services in the form of diagnostic testing, learning centers, and courses in critical thinking and communications were deemed "crucial" to the success of their students in competitive environments (Glazer, 1985).

A more recent program to aid disadvantaged minority students in medical school continues to realize much success. The Preentrance Enrichment Program (PEP) at Boston University School of Medicine began in 1973, and is credited with assisting program participants to outscore their peers who did not participate in the program during their first year of school. Participation in PEP was one of the consistent predictors of overall performance (Ugbolue, Whitley, & Stevens, 1987).

Institutions that have been effective in retaining minorities incorporate academic support services into their programs (Applegate & Henniger, 1989; Collison, 1988; Maxwell, 1979; Walters & Marcus, 1985; Wilson & Justiz, 1988).

In order to maintain enrollments, higher education will have to draw on a broader portion of the overall pool of college-age youth. To do so, it must recruit and serve minorities. The inequities that still exist in America's public school system, whether due to economics or to some other cause, might still be remedied by the colleges and universities of our nation. American children who have been disadvantaged by unequal schools may yet find an avenue toward achieving their potentials in higher education, if they have access to compensatory assistance.

Looking Back and Looking Forward

Although the presence on campus of college reading courses has been viewed as a stigma and has been excoriated by embarrassed American educators for at least 128 years, it has remained with us. While exclusion through selective admissions policies successfully limits the numbers of underprepared students on campuses, it also limits the talent pools from which institutions draw, and the benefits that diversity brings.

Admitting and then assisting underprepared students to meet the standards of excellent universities will better help American higher education to achieve widespread excellence than will exclusion. It is toward that goal that William F. Book looked. The most prestigious institutions in America do not shrink from the task.

Notwithstanding the historic and continuing need for assistance of well prepared, above average, and average students, assistance for the rising population of disadvantaged minorities will be crucial to the nation in the next century. NonAnglos will make up one third of the population. Many, though able, will be underprepared through no fault of their own. Academic assistance will be vital to attract them to college, to retain them, and to their eventual academic success. Without their success, and without the success of underprepared Anglo students, the nation as a whole may be weakened in the twenty-first century. American college reading courses thus may prove to be acutely important in years to come.

References

Abraham, A. A. (1987). *A report on college-level remedial / developmental programs in SREB states.* Southern Regional Education Board. (ERIC Document Reproduction Service No. ED 280 369)

Applegate, J. R., & Henniger, M. L. (1989). Recruiting minority students: A priority for the '90s. *Thought & Action,* 5(1), 53–60.

Armstrong, C. (1988, March). *Basic writers' problems are basic to writing.* Paper presented at the 39th annual meeting of the Conference on College Composition and Communication, St. Louis, MO. (ERIC Document Reproduction Service No. ED 298 152)

Astin, H. S. (1985). Providing incentives for teaching underprepared students. *Educational Record, 66*(1), 26–29.

Blake, M. (1985). *Is higher education an educational process or a screening process?* (ERIC Document Reproduction Service No. ED 271 087)

Bonner, T. N. (1986). The unintended revolution in America's colleges since 1940. *Change, 18*(5), 44–51.

Book, W. F. (1927a, August). How well college students can read. *School and Society, 26*(669), 242–248.

Book, W. F. (1927b, October). Results obtained in a special "How to Study" course given to college students. *School and Society, 26*(669), 529–534.

Brier, E. (1984). Bridging the academic preparation gap: An historical view. *Journal of Developmental Education, 8*(1), 2–5.

Brubacher, J. S., & Rudy, W. (1976). *Higher education in transition: A history of American colleges and universities, 1636–1976.* New York: Harper & Row.

Bullock, T. L., Madden, D. A., & Mallery, A. L. (1990). Developmental education in American universities: Past, present and future. *Research & Teaching in Developmental Education, 6*(2), 5–73.

Callas, D. (1985). Academic placement practices: An analysis and proposed model. *College Teaching, 33*(1), 27–32.

Charters, W. W. (1941). Remedial reading in college. *The Journal of Higher Education, 12*(3), 117–121.

Coffman, L. D. (1933). Fundamental reforms in instruction. In W. S. Gray (Ed.), *Needed readjustments in higher education* (pp. 39–56). Chicago, IL: The University of Chicago Press.

Collison, M. N. K. (1988). Neglect of minorities seen jeopardizing future prosperity: U.S. seen 'moving backward;' colleges are urged to act. *The Chronicle of Higher Education, 34*(37), 1, A20.

Conrad, C. F, & Eagan. D. J. (1989). The prestige game in American higher education. *Thought and Action, 5*(1), 5–16

Enright, G., & Kerstiens, G. (1980). The learning center: Toward an expanded role. In O. T. Lenning & R. L. Nayman (Eds.), *New directions for college learning assistance* (pp. 1–24). San Francisco, CA: Jossey-Bass.

Estrada, L. F. (1988). Anticipating the demographic future. *Change, 20*(3), 14–19.

Glazer, J. S. (1985). *Education for the disadvantaged: The Higher Education Opportunity Program in New York State.* Rockefeller Institute Reprints, n. 18, 1–10. (ERIC Document Reproduction Service No. ED 323 833)

Hardin, C. J. (1988). Access to higher education: Who belongs? *Journal of Developmental Education, 12*(1), 2–6, 19.

Hayes, D. A. & Diehl, W. (1982). What research on prose comprehension suggests for college skills instruction. *Journal of Reading, 25*(7), 656–661.

Henry, T. C. (1986). Needed: Comprehensive evaluation of education program efforts. *Community College Review, 14*(2), 46–52.

Hodgkinson, H. L. (1986). Look who's coming to college. AGB *Reports, 28*(6), 24–27.

Judd, C. H. (1929). Adapting the curriculum to the psychological characteristics of the junior college. In W. S. Gray (Ed.), *The junior college curriculum,* Vol. 1 (pp. 1–13). Chicago, IL: University of Chicago.

Keeter, L. (1987). Minority students at risk: An interview with Professor Shirley Chisholm. *Journal of Developmental Education, 10*(3), 18–21.

Levine, A. (1978). *Handbook on undergraduate curriculum.* San Francisco, CA: Jossey-Bass.

Maxwell, M. J. (1963). College reading has no future. *The Journal of the Reading Specialist, 3*(1), 3–5.

Maxwell, M. (1979). *Improving student learning skills.* San Francisco, CA: Jossey-Bass.

Myers, C. (1984, April). *Promises to keep, indeed, and miles to go before we sleep.* Paper presented at the annual meeting of the American Educational Research Association, New Orleans, LA. (ERIC Document Reproduction Service No. ED 252 167)

Newman, F. (1988). Reconnecting youth: The new wave of reform. In J. E. Lieberman (Ed.), *Collaborating with high schools. New Directions for community colleges, No. 63* (pp. 5–11). San Francisco, CA: Jossey-Bass.

Nist, S. L., & Diehl, W. (1990). *Developing textbook thinking: Strategies for success in college* (2nd ed.). Lexington, MA: D. C. Heath.

Orfield, G., & Paul, F. (1987–1988). Declines in minority access: A tale of five cities. *Educational Record, 68–69*(4 & 1), 57–62.

Perry, W. G., Jr. (1959). Students' use and misuse of reading skills: A report to a faculty. *Harvard Education Review, 29,* 193–200.

Platt, G. M. (1986). Should colleges teach below-college-level courses? *Community College Review, 14*(2), 19–25.

Rainsford, G. N. (1990). The demographic imperative: Changing to serve America's expanding minority population. In D. W. Steeples (Ed.), *Managing change in higher education* (pp. 91–100). San Francisco, CA: Jossey-Bass.

Roueche, S. D. (1985). *Basic skills: Dealing with deficiencies.* (ERIC Document Reproduction Service No. ED 271 087)

Simms, R. B., & Leonard, W. H. (1986). Accommodating underprepared students. *Journal of College Science Teaching, 16*(2), 110–112.

Thomas, J. W. (1987, April). *Proficiency at academic studying.* Paper presented at the annual meeting of the American Educational Research Association, Washington, DC.

Trow, M. (1989). American higher education — Past, present and future. *Studies in Higher Education, 14*(1), 5–22.

Ugbolue, A., Whitley P. N., & Stevens, P. J. (1987). Evaluation of a preentrance enrichment program for minority students admitted to medical school. *Journal of Medical Education, 62*(1), 8–16.

Walters, J., & Marcus, L. R. (1985, March). *Maximizing retention rates in collegiate programs for disadvantaged students.* Paper presented at the annual meeting of the American Educational Research Association, Chicago, IL. (ERIC Document Reproduction Service No. ED 261 122).

Weidner, H. Z. (1990, March). *Back to the future.* Paper presented at the 41st annual meeting of the Conference on College Composition and Communication, Chicago, IL. (ERIC Document Reproduction Service No. ED 319 045)

Willie, C. V. (1982). Educating students who are good enough: Is excellence an excuse to exclude? *Change, 14*(2), 16–20.

Wilson, R., & Justiz, M. J. (1988). Minorities in higher education: Confronting a time bomb. *Educational Record, 68–69*(4 & 1), 9–14.

College Reading Instruction as Reflected by Current Reading Textbooks

Nancy V. Wood

Individuals who have been active, contributing members of the college reading instruction profession have shaped its modern history. For them, the profession's past is both experiential and most personal. In the article "College Reading Instruction as Reflected by Current Reading Textbooks," by Nancy V. Wood, we learn how changes in theory, research, and best practices across the past forty years influenced this individual's teaching and scholarship. In addition, Wood adds to the field's content analysis research by discussing how current texts have responded to changes in theory and research.

No one can describe with certainty what college reading instructors teach on a daily basis in their reading classrooms. Studies and research reviews like those conducted in recent years by O'Hear (1993) and Maxwell (1995/96) suggest considerable change in the teaching of reading, particularly in the past twenty-five years or so. The assumption in this paper is that an examination of a sample of the most current college reading textbooks will also provide information not only about change but also about current practice in modern reading classrooms. Textbook publishers and their sales representatives certainly encourage reading faculty to link available textbooks with actual classroom practice. This link may, understandably, be a qualified one for many faculty who do not always follow in an exact manner the textbooks they select. Still, reading faculty customarily participate in the selection of the textbooks they use, and their decisions reflect preferences and, at least to a degree, actual teaching practice as well.

Many of the available reading textbooks have changed considerably in the past forty years, the time period examined in this paper, and they imply parallel changes in classroom instruction. Changes in reading theory and pedagogy have influenced some of this change. The focus of this paper is change: change in theory, change in textbooks, and change in classroom practice. The paper describes traditional and modern models for teaching college reading, it examines current textbooks to see how they reflect these models, and it speculates about how much change has occurred in reading classrooms since the 1950s.

A Reading Class of Forty Years Ago and the Traditional Model

I want to provide an historical perspective on change in reading classes by describing my first reading class, which I taught in 1958. It was part of the curriculum of Walter Pauk's Reading and Study Skills Program at Cornell University. This class was an elective for Cornell students, and it was representative of college reading classes of its time. Cornell was a major center for teacher training, and Pauk trained many reading teachers in his graduate classes to follow the methods taught in the general Cornell reading classes. My impression from the professional literature and the reading textbooks of that time was that the Cornell reading classes represented the state of the art in college reading instruction. In this paper my 1958 reading class will be designated as a "traditional" reading class to help create, by contrast, a definition of what a "modern" reading class might look like.

Students in this college reading class of 1958 began each semester with a reading test. The purpose was to identify areas of student deficiency and thus to define an instructional starting place for each student. Students read a timed essay, answered multiple choice questions, and put the results of their speed and comprehension on a graph. Even though many of the students who signed up for this reading class were also enrolled in the Cornell Law School or in one of the Cornell engineering or liberal arts colleges, we nevertheless assumed that they would not be signing up for a reading class unless they were somehow deficient.

After the first day of testing, the classes typically included three types of activities: instruction in a reading skill, a check of textbook comprehension, and practice to improve reading speed. We began each class by teaching one discrete reading skill. For example, we taught main ideas and details, followed by organizational patterns, tone and intent, vocabulary building, and formulas for reading college textbooks, such as Robinson's SQ3R and Pauk's OK4R. We also taught critical reading, which was a very underdeveloped concept at that time, and we taught students to recognize the bad reading habits of vocalization and regression. We warned them that these bad habits could slow their reading. Our method for teaching was to give lectures, which we illustrated with short paragraphs that we had marked ahead of time. Thus we were able to point out special features of these paragraphs, like topic sentences or context clues, which we, as the expert readers, could then bring to our students' attention.

After we had presented the skill for the day, we turned to the reading assignment. We used Cornell professor Marvin Glock's reading book, which contained articles about reading, each followed by multiple choice questions. The articles in this book had titles like "The Hygiene of Reading." That particular article dealt with posture, adequate lighting, placement of lighting, and so forth. We checked student comprehension of these daily reading assignments by asking them to call out in unison their answers for each question. We worked through these answers quickly. There was no discussion.

We then turned to speed reading. The 1950s were the days of the speed reading machines. We used the tachistoscope, a machine which we were told had also been used during the second World War to help train fighter pilots to identify quickly which planes to shoot down and which to leave alone. Tachistoscope literally means "viewing fastest." The machine, as it was used in our reading classes, flashed phrases of three to seven words on the screen at rates of 1/25th to 1/100th of a second. We could adjust the speed. When we had flashed a phrase, students would call out what they had seen. "A red apple" was one of the phrases. As long as the phrases were short and familiar, students could see them and call them out. In my experience, however, students were never able to identify the seven-word phrases, and the students who had less familiarity with English phrases because they were learning in a second language would invariably come up after class to complain that they had not seen anything at all when we used the tachistoscope.

We also used the perceptoscope to improve reading speed. A page of print was projected onto the screen, and a flashing light illuminated each line of print in two regular and rhythmic movements. Student eyes were to move with the light, fixating on half a line of print at a time in a regular cadence. Finally, we used speeded reading films which we projected with a special 16-millimeter projector which we were able to set to run a little faster each day. We started these films at 200–300 words per minute at the beginning of the course and advanced their projected speed to 500–700 words per minute by the end of the course. We checked student comprehension of the short essays and stories on these films with multiple choice questions.

In addition, students were assigned to go to the reading lab where they were to read short, easy articles of general interest in the reading books housed there. One of these articles, for example, was about the vitamins found in different foods. The books were just the right size and format to place in the reading machines. These machines were equipped with opaque shutters that could be set to descend the page at preset rates. Students read to keep ahead of these shutters, and when they finished reading the essays, they answered the multiple choice questions that accompanied them. Then they checked their answers and marked their speed and comprehension scores on a graph. Thus we were able to measure gains on a regular basis both in class and in the lab.

Rarely was assigned reading material in class or lab at college level, despite the given talent and ability of the students. Furthermore, if students missed multiple choice questions, we moved them to even easier materials. We did not ask students to practice reading on their own textbooks or any other materials they had been assigned to read in their other classes.

We delivered most of the classroom instruction via lectures and reading machines. We believed that information came from the words on the page, through the eyes, to the brain where it was taken in as knowledge. We believed we could shorten the time for the words to get from the page to the brain by speeding up the eyes. To show them what they were working to improve, we had students watch each other's eye fixations as they read. We cautioned against vocalization because that would involve the ears and slow the whole process down. Finally, we relied on formulas for teaching study reading even though we did not know any students who followed all of the steps in these formulas.

Reading teachers today may be tempted to identify this 1950s model of teaching reading as an "old-fashioned" model. For many modern reading teachers, however, this model contains elements that represent familiar and reliable practices that have worked well in the past and that can keep right on working in the future. This class of forty years ago has evolved into what is now the "traditional" model for teaching college reading. And it is, in fact, a model that is far from obsolete, as evidenced by a number of modern reading textbooks.

Behaviorist Theory and the Traditional Model

My reading class of 1958 was heavily influenced by behaviorism, which assumes that observable and measurable behavior is the only type of behavior worth studying. My 1950s psychology professor told his students on the first day of class that the goal for studying psychology was to learn "to predict and control human behavior." The instructional methods we employed in our reading classes of that time, including the graphs that showed reading gains and the training that improved eye fixations, made the otherwise private process of reading as observable, measurable, and controllable as we could make it. The reading machines, in fact, were called controlled readers. The class began with a test to identify deficiencies, it prescribed material to remediate them, it quantified gains in speed and comprehension, and it made them visible on graphs. It taught discrete skills, it emphasized skill level, it relied on short, easy reading passages for practice, and it relied on multiple choice questions to measure comprehension. It also made reading levels available for just about everything assigned, taught formulas like SQ3R for study reading, did little with critical reading or critical thinking, and taught various ways to speed up reading and to improve vocabulary. Furthermore, all students read the same material in the same way. They were also all expected to come up with the same correct answers about what they had read. The instructors assumed the role of expert readers who could demonstrate to student readers just what was important or significant in a given text. Instructors modelled desired reading behavior. Classes and textbooks that mainly follow this model are identified as "traditional" from now on in this paper.

Psycholinguistic Theory and the Modern Model

Some modern textbooks differ considerably from the traditional model. There has been change in these modern textbooks, and there are identifiable causes for change. Cognitive psychology, with its emphasis on the study of unseen mental processes such as thinking, feeling, learning, remembering, and judging, is partly responsible for the change. So is modern psycholinguistic theory, which has had a strong influence on the way many reading faculty think about and teach reading.

I remember when I first encountered some of the new ideas about reading at a College Reading and Learning Association conference in the early 1980s in California. A graduate student was reporting on her research. She had been reading the new psycholinguistic theorists, and she was talking rather hesitatingly about the notion that reading can be viewed as an interactive process. The idea that the words do not simply travel from the page to the brain, as so many of us had taught for years, but that readers use what they already know to make sense of the words seemed a revolutionary idea at that time. It changed the way I thought about reading entirely and permanently, and I think it did the same for many reading teachers. Psycholinguistic theory moved the focus of attention in reading classes away from the text and the teacher as expert reader, and placed it instead on the student, including what that student either knows or needs to learn in order to read a particular text.

A number of reading researchers were describing the psycholinguistic approach to reading in the late 1970s and early 1980s (Goodman, 1976; Just & Carpenter, 1980; Rosenblatt, 1978; Rumelhart, 1977; Stanovich, 1980). An author whose early works also date from that period of time and who influenced many reading teachers is the Canadian scholar, Frank Smith. The fifth edition of his book, *Understanding Reading: A Psycholinguistic Analysis of Reading and Learning to Read* (1994), presents a clear explanation of the psycholinguistic approach to reading. I have extracted ten pervasive ideas from this book to summarize some of the major tenets of the psycholinguistic theory of reading. These ideas define and describe the "modern" approach to teaching college reading. Note how Smith's ideas suggest applications for classroom instructors and for textbook authors alike.

1. Reading is **thinking.** "Reading," Smith says, "might be defined as thought that is stimulated and directed by written language" (p. 20). When people read, their minds are active. This means that teachers should be able to ask students to describe either orally or in writing what they are thinking as they read. Students who have difficulty identifying and verbalizing their thoughts are not, by definition, reading. Textbooks influenced by psycholinguistic theory define reading as an active, thinking process, they teach special "meta" thinking techniques such as metacognition (thinking about what one knows) and metacomprehension (thinking about what one has understood), and they require written or oral responses to reading.

2. Reading is **interactive.** Readers depend on both "visual" and "nonvisual" material (p. 67) to achieve comprehension. This means that readers combine the information they can visualize on the page

with the nonvisual information already in their minds to create meaning. Furthermore, since no two readers bring exactly the same information to the page, no two readers comprehend a page in exactly the same way. Textbooks that ask students to respond and react to their reading in unique and individual ways, as opposed to looking for one correct answer from all students, are influenced by psycholinguistic theory.

3. **Prior knowledge** is organized in readers' minds as a "theory of the world" (p. 7). Readers constantly add to their "theory of the world," and they use it to learn even more. "Reading is basically a matter of increasing returns" (p. 147). Students can be encouraged to read widely and to increase their prior knowledge in order to become better readers. Textbooks influenced by psycholinguistic theory require large quantities of reading on a variety of subjects, invite holistic approaches to reading, and teach reading strategies that include accessing and using prior knowledge.

4. "Reading depends on **prediction**" (p. 17). Readers bring their prior knowledge or "theory of the world" to the text and use it to predict. In the classroom, students can be taught to discover what they already know and then to use this information to anticipate or predict an author's ideas. Textbooks that teach prereading strategies that include predicting from prior knowledge are influenced by psycholinguistic theory.

5. **Asking questions** is critical to comprehension. "Prediction means asking questions, and comprehension means being able to get some of the questions answered" (p. 19). Learning to ask questions about reading material can help students comprehend it. Textbooks that ask open-ended questions or that have students ask their own questions are influenced by this theory.

6. A knowledge of **writing conventions** is important. Such conventions, Smith says, are the "common currency" of reading and writing (p. 44). As an example, in writing class students are taught to clarify and emphasize important ideas with transitions, and in reading class they are taught to recognize transitions to locate important ideas. Knowing that writers use transitions helps readers predict and locate them. College reading textbooks that link reading and writing through the conventions of writing are influenced by psycholinguistic theory.

7. Students need to **apply** what they read. This helps students make sense of what they have read by moving it into a context that is meaningful to them. Reading textbooks that have students apply what they learn to "real" reading situations and to their own real life experiences are influenced by psycholinguistic theory. In such books longer passages are often favored over short ones as being more "real."

8. "Reading is a **social activity**" (p. 45). Teachers and learners can, in fact, collaborate in a social context to improve reading. Collaborative learning and peer groups are regarded as effective. Modern textbooks that include collaborative reading exercises and peer group activities are influenced by psycholinguistic theory.

9. Standardized **reading tests** are artificial. Furthermore, students do not learn to read better by taking standardized reading tests. Instead, the best reading test is the homemade test, constructed on the spot, that reassures the teacher that the student is understanding. Textbooks that test comprehension with discussion, open-ended questions, and written responses, as opposed to multiple choice questions, reflect this modern theory.

10. Reading is a **purposeful** activity. "A person who has no purpose in reading can bring nothing to the reading, and the activity is bound to be meaningless" (p. 3). Teachers can help students set purposes for reading, and textbooks that encourage students to do this are influenced by this theory.

Psycholinguistic theory provides several descriptive criteria that can be used to define the modern model of teaching reading. To recapitulate, this theory suggests that reading can be taught as an interactive process, that reading is thinking, that prior knowledge is the basis of comprehension and that, as a result, not everyone comprehends in identical ways. Predicting and questioning are critical to comprehension, and understanding writing conventions helps readers find their way through a text. This theory suggests that reading is a social activity, and it values collaborative and peer group reading activities. It also recognizes reading as a purposeful activity, it insists that students apply what they read in contexts meaningful to them, and it tests comprehension with writing and discussion as opposed to multiple choice questions. It employs longer reading selections and a greater variety of reading material than are typically found in traditional textbooks, including selections from a variety of college textbooks, various types of nonfiction, and imaginative fiction. Classes and textbooks that are influenced by these criteria are classified as "modern" in the rest of this paper.

A Reading Class of the 1990s and the Modern Model

I still teach reading, but the classes I teach now differ considerably from those I taught forty years ago. Rather than beginning my classes by testing for reading deficiencies as I did in 1958, I begin by asking students to describe their current reading processes. My purpose is to validate what students already do, since most people like what they do, and then to help them discover ways to improve. I no longer teach a prescribed reading process, like the SQ3R method, assumed to be equally effective for all students, but I do encourage students to consider what they might do differently before they read, while they read, and after they read to improve their ability to comprehend and think. The skills I taught in 1958 are now described as strategies, with the emphasis on what students can do to help themselves to discover ideas and comprehend. I no longer lecture extensively or use reading machines in class. More typically, brief lectures are followed by class discussion of reading assignments or by structured collaborative group work where students read, discuss, make decisions, and report results to the rest of the class. I no longer rely on multiple choice questions to test comprehension. I am much more interested in what students have to say or want to write about the material they have read. In discussion, I allow room for reasonable variations in student response. The possible reasons for these variations are a frequent topic for discussion and this helps students become aware of their prior knowledge and how it influences their comprehension. For writing, I teach students to write reading notes, summaries, summary/responses, critical reactions, and creative responses inspired by their reading. I still teach students to study, learn, and remember, but I also teach them to think, analyze, and evaluate.

I now link reading and writing on a regular basis in my classes by asking students to recall what they have learned about writing conventions and to use this information to help them read. I also ask students to write as they read. They learn to write before they read to discover what they know, to write while they read to focus and concentrate, and to write after they read to summarize and discover what they have learned. I do not read all of their writing, but I do check to see that it gets done. I tend to assign much longer reading selections now than I did forty years ago, and these selections are more like the reading students are assigned in their other classes. I further teach students to make mental links among the readings from all of their classes and to synthesize information from several sources. I still teach students how to vary their reading speeds, but I caution them against reading difficult material so rapidly that they lose comprehension. I teach them that purpose should control their use of speed reading strategies.

If I had to describe briefly how I have changed as a reading teacher in forty years, I would say the biggest change is one of focus. In the 1950s, we focused on the text. We thought meaning resided in the text, that it had been put there by the author, that the reader's job was to discover it, and that the teacher's job was to show how to discover it. In the 1990s, many of us have switched from a focus on the text to a focus on the reader. Those who have made this change now recognize that no meaning is created without the active participation of the reader. We still teach students to read the words on the page, but we now stress that meaning is achieved through an interaction between the reader and those words. The traditional model, as described in this paper, is predominantly a text-based model, and the modern model is a reader-based model.

Which Approach Do Modern Textbooks Follow: The Traditional or the Modern?

Conventional wisdom holds that textbooks are the last to register change in a discipline. Textbook editors typically advise authors to be different, but not too different, or to change, but not to change too much. The motivating fear is that not all instructors change, and that textbooks must, as much as possible, reflect the varieties in actual classroom practice. I have examined a sample of 20 college reading textbooks with copyright dates that range from 1993 to 1997, to determine which of them fall mainly into the traditional category and which into the modern category. I obtained these textbooks from the publishers' exhibits at the 1996 national conventions of the National Association for Developmental Education and the College Reading and Learning Association. These are not the only current reading textbooks available to reading and learning professionals, but they are the books that were displayed in 1996, and several of them are described by publishers' representatives as "best sellers" in the field. They are the books that conference-goers are likely to pick up and consider for their classes. They have a relatively high profile among available reading textbooks.

My method in examining these books was, first, to survey them and then to read significant chunks of each to identify prominent characteristics. Later, when I reread the notes I took during this process, I found that I could work inductively to formulate criteria, drawn from the books themselves, which I could use to place them in either traditional or modern categories. When I had applied these criteria, which I will describe directly, I found that of the twenty books I had examined, eight were predominantly traditional, eight were predominantly modern, and four were a mix of traditional and modern. It would be unfair, by the way, to suggest that any one of these books is a pure example of either the traditional or the modern model. Most of the books I classified as modern retain vestiges of the traditional, and most of the books I classified as traditional include some modern features. I looked for predominant tendencies. The books in each category are identified by author in a note at the end of this paper.

My criteria for identifying the eight traditional textbooks include the following items. Traditional textbooks teach discrete skills, many of them followed by practice drills. Reading passages tend to be short and relatively easy. Reading level is often identified. Many of the traditional books adhere to a workbook format that contains brief explanations and short practice exercises. These are followed by multiple choice, true-false, and fill-in-the-blank questions, and, in some cases, examples of completed summaries and outlines from which students are to select the best. SQ3R is usually taught. Students often record their speed and comprehension scores, and scores are based on how many questions students answer correctly. Some of these books include mastery tests, and some say the instruction they offer will help students perform on standardized tests. Computer programs that accompany these books tend to offer additional skill and drill activities. These programs are not billed as interactive.

Vocabulary improvement is a common feature in the traditional books, and it is a common feature in the modern books as well. In fact, two aspects of much in traditional and modern reading textbooks that resist change are the ways vocabulary and speed reading are taught. Context clues, word parts, vocabulary in context, and dictionary and thesaurus skills appear in both types of books. Skimming, scanning, various types of pacing methods, and word recognition skills are also taught in both.

My criteria for identifying the eight modern textbooks include the following items. Modern reading textbooks contain multicultural reading selections. I had not predicted that, but I should have, since authors include such selections to appeal to the unique prior knowledge of diverse groups of student readers. Some of these books also teach a whole language approach to reading, with the focus on content and building background through lots of "real" reading. A variety of types of reading selections are usually available that include essays, textbook passages, and sometimes imaginative literature. Other features include assignments that ask students to write about what they read at various stages of the reading process and to make various other connections between reading and writing. Collaborative reading activities encourage sociable reading, open-ended questions invite discussion and writing, and authors warn students that there are no correct, only possible, answers to reading questions. Strategies are featured in these books in the place of skills and drills, and predicting exercises are included to introduce reading selections. Reading is described as an active thinking process, and students learn what they might do at various stages and in response to different reading problems. These books also feature writing-to-learn activities and reading across the disciplines, with applications to specific disciplines in some cases. Critical reading and critical thinking are featured more prominently and pervasively than in the traditional books. The computer programs that accompany a few of these books, emphasize process and claim to be interactive. If these modern books have multiple choice questions in them at all, they often appear in an appendix or are presented with the rejoinder that they are included only for those who want to use them.

The four books that fell in the middle, those that have both traditional and modern features, tend to be books that have already gone through several editions, and their authors and editors have, perhaps, been cautious about throwing out the old as they have added the new. These books may, for example, teach both skills and strategies, include open-ended questions and multiple choice questions, and focus mainly on college textbook reading but still try to identify readability levels. The old familiar materials and approaches in these books are set side by side with new ideas that include teaching students to make mental connections among readings on the same topic, to activate existing knowledge, to relate old knowledge to new, to predict, and generally to interact with the text in various ways.

Paradigm Shifts and What Lies Ahead

In the 1970s and early 1980s, as I have shown, some major theoretical changes influenced the way in which many reading instructors thought about reading. The same thing was happening with writing. Reading teachers who regard reading and writing as two sides of the same coin are inevitably influenced by shifts in theory that impact the teaching of both reading and writing. A comparison of the rate of change in both areas provides insight into some of the unique characteristics of the profession of teaching college reading.

In 1982 Maxine Hairston wrote a well-known article called "The Winds of Change: Thomas Kuhn and the Revolution in the Teaching of Writing," first delivered as a keynote address at the Conference on College Communication and Composition and later published in *College Composition and Communication*. Hairston described the change from the traditional product approach to teaching writing to the modern process approach. She called this change a paradigm shift, borrowing that concept from Thomas Kuhn (Hairston, 1982). Paradigm shifts are major changes that represent a whole new way of looking at things, and they occur when old ways are no longer working or no longer serving. The shift from teaching writing as a product to teaching writing as a process happened fairly quickly in writing classrooms. The transition occurred during a period of about ten years. In the late 1970s, the writing process was not a dominant concept in writing textbooks. It became more and more dominant during the 1980s. Now, in the 1990s, it is difficult to find a writing textbook that does not profess to teach a process approach to writing. Some modern writing textbooks still teach the modes, long associated with the current-traditional approach, and contain long sections on grammar, but most advertise themselves as predominantly modern, with a commitment to process writing.

The changes in reading during the past fifteen to twenty years should also be regarded as a paradigm shift. The changes are significant, they represent real change, and they are pervasive. Change is characterized in this paper as a shift from a traditional, text-based approach to a modern, reader-based approach to teaching reading. When we compare the shifts in reading and writing that have occurred during roughly the same period of time, evidence suggests that the shift to the modern in the teaching of writing has been made faster than the shift to the modern in the teaching of reading. The shift in writing is virtually complete. The shift in reading is making its strongest presence now, during the middle and late 1990s, but it by no means dominates current reading textbooks and, by implication, reading classrooms. Instead, there seems to be roughly a 50-50 split between traditional and modern approaches to teaching reading, at least as evidenced by the sample of recent textbooks examined for this paper.

I believe that reading teachers have been slower than writing teachers to respond to new theories of reading in their classes and textbooks for several reasons. One reason is standardized reading tests. These tests encourage an adherence to the traditional model. Reading teachers who are obligated to demonstrate gains in student reading via these tests will have a difficult time abandoning the traditional model. Another reason some reading instructors are slow to change is that the traditional model is easier and more predictable for teachers to follow. Also, teachers do not need to relinquish so much of their authority in traditional classes. Teachers in these classes know the correct answers to the reading questions, and that provides a privileged and comfortable position. In modern classes, by contrast, what the student knows becomes privileged. The teacher gives up some authority but, at the same time, is often obliged to work harder to keep student learning on track. Other possible reasons for slow change include the fact that graduate training, which usually includes a grounding in theory, is not so readily available for college reading teachers as it is for college writing teachers. Finally, many college reading teachers have such large teaching loads that they have little time or opportunity to learn new methods or to make significant changes in the way they teach.

Reading teachers who are cautious about embracing radical change may be most comfortable with a mix of traditional and modern practices. A *New York Times* editorial of January 25, 1997, entitled "Teaching Johnny to Read" reports on a long-term study of children's reading problems conducted by the National Institutes of Health. This report shows that one in five American children has "substantial difficulty" (p. 16) in learning to read, but that 96 percent can improve after intensive help. What constitutes effective help becomes an issue, however. Individuals disagree about "the relative merits of the 'whole-language' approach, which often immerses children in literature at the expense of phonetic drill and practice, and the phonics approach, which provides drill and practice in phonetics and grammar" (p. 16). The National Institutes of Health report resolves this controversy by concluding that "both literature and phonics practice are necessary for impaired and unimpaired children alike" (p. 16). It may be that at the college level a mix of the traditional and the modern will be the most effective model of instruction as well.

For myself, however, having been a traditional teacher in the 1950s and having made the transition to the modern model during the 1980s, I now favor the modern model. I have several reasons for my preference. The modern model is more interesting to teach. Classrooms become more lively for teachers and students alike when students are given the power to explore texts and construct meaning on their own. By drawing on their own experiences and knowledge instead of relying mainly on the teacher's, students often generate insights into texts that teachers might never otherwise see. For example, a student whose entrance into college has been impaired by affirmative action policy and who reads an article on that subject will often describe its meanings and implications in a different way from teachers and students who have not been affected. When students are allowed to contribute their meanings, teachers learn along with their students.

Another reason I favor the modern model is that teaching critical reading and critical thinking, required by law in some states and considered an important responsibility of higher education in many others, becomes easier. The modern model emphasizes reading as thinking, and it recognizes the importance of prior knowledge, including opinion. The modern model encourages students to use such knowledge to form considered judgments and to develop original insights as they read. Many of the open-ended questions in modern textbooks invite such critical and original perspectives. The multiple choice questions of traditional texts and standardized tests do not invite original thinking, and instead require students to read a text and to answer questions about it in exactly the same way that the testmaker did.

I also like the modern model because it emphasizes reading as a social activity. I can more easily engage reluctant readers in reading improvement by assigning them to collaborative reading groups. For example, various prereading activities can be assigned to different groups of students in a given class period. One group can make predictions, one can write questions, another can identify difficult vocabulary, another can survey and discover the organization, and still another can identify the background information that most students will need for adequate comprehension. Students then share the results of these activities, and all students benefit. As a second example, groups of students can map the organization of an essay or a chapter, and then display their maps on the wall. Students can be encouraged to compare maps, discuss, and defend them. Reading, an activity that in the past has been lonely and frustrating for many students, now becomes both a sociable and a successful experience as a result of group activities. Reading students who have had trouble in the past often report that at last they are learning.

Finally, I favor the modern model because it is more transportable. It permits students to apply what they have learned in reading class to their other classes. For instance, students may learn to write summaries of reading textbook selections and then be asked to write summaries of chapters in other textbooks. Or students may learn to survey their reading textbook and then to survey all of their other textbooks. The transfer of learning from one class to another, a difficult accomplishment at any educational level, becomes easier when reading assignments are open-ended and encourage application. There are other advantages of the modern model, and, like those I have just cited, most of them benefit students in direct ways. The modern model now has a strong presence in current reading textbooks. Because of the advantages of the modern model, I predict that it will gain more and more momentum until it finally dominates the reading textbooks and the reading classes of the twenty-first century.

Notes

1. The traditional textbooks referred to in this paper include Adams; Broderick; Hancock; Jacobus; Langan; Langan and Broderick; Miller and de Orozco, Books I and II. The mixed traditional/modern textbooks include Leo, Smith (two titles), and Wasserman and Rinsky. The modern textbooks include Cortina, Elder, and Gonnet; Fjeldstad; Hennings, McGrath; McWhorter (two titles); Wood; and Zinn and Poole. Full bibliographical information for each of these books appears in References.

References

Adams, W. R. (1996). *The reading light.* Fort Worth, TX: Harcourt Brace.

Broderick, B. (1994). *Ten steps to building college reading skills. Form B* (2nd ed.). Marlton, NJ: Townsend Press.

Cortina, J., Elder, J., & Gonnet, K. (1995). *Opening doors: Understanding college textbooks.* New York: McGraw Hill.

Fjeldstad, M. C. (1994). *The thoughtful reader: A whole language approach to college reading.* Fort Worth, TX: Harcourt Brace.

Goodman, K. S. (1976). Behind the eye: What happens in reading. In H. Singer and R. Ruddell (Eds.), *Theoretical models and processes in reading* (2nd ed.). Newark, DE: International Reading Association.

Hairston, M. (1982). The winds of change: Thomas Kuhn and the revolution in the teaching of writing. *College Composition and Communication, 33* (1), 76–88.

Hancock, O. H. (1995). *Reading skills for college students* (3rd ed.). Upper Saddle River, NJ: Prentice Hall.

Hennings, G. H. (1996). *Reading with meaning: Strategies for college reading* (3rd ed.). Upper Saddle River, NJ: Prentice Hall.

Jacobus, L. A. (1995). *Developing college reading* (5th ed.). Fort Worth, TX: Harcourt Brace.

Just, M., & Carpenter, P. (1980). A theory of reading: From eye fixations to comprehension. *Psychological Review,* 87, 329–54.

Langan, J. (1993). *Ten steps to advancing college reading skills* (2nd ed.). Marlton, NJ: Townsend Press.

Langan, J., & Broderick, B. (1993). *Ten steps to building college reading skills* (2nd ed.). Marlton, NJ: Townsend Press.

Leo, E. S. (1994). *Powerful reading, efficient learning.* Needham Heights, MA: Allyn and Bacon.

Maxwell, M. (1995–96). New insights about teaching college reading: A review of recent research. *Journal of College Reading and Learning, 27* (1), 34–42.

McGrath, J. L. (1995). *Building strategies for college reading: A text and thematic reader.* Upper Saddle River, NJ: Prentice Hall.

McWhorter, K. T. (1994). *Academic reading* (2nd ed.). New York: Harper-Collins.

McWhorter, K. T. (1996). *Efficient and flexible reading* (4th ed.). New York: Harper Collins.

Miller, W. M., & de Orozco, S. S. (1996). *Reading faster and understanding more, Book 1* (4th ed.). New York: Harper Collins.

Miller, W. M., & de Orozco, S. S. (1996). *Reading faster and understanding more, Book 2* (4th ed.). New York: Harper Collins.

O'Hear, M. (1993). College reading programs: The past 25 years. *Journal of College Reading and Learning, 25* (2), 17–24.

Rosenblatt, Louise M. (1978). *The reader, the text, the poem: The transactional theory of the literary work.* Carbondale, IL: Southern Illinois University Press.

Rumelhart, D. (1977). Toward an interactive model of reading. In S. Dornic (Ed.), *Attention and performance.* Hillsdale, NJ: Erlbaum.

Smith, B. D. (1995). *Breaking through: College reading* (4th ed.). New York: Harper Collins.

Smith, B. D. (1993). *Bridging the gap: College reading* (4th ed.). New York: Harper Collins.

Smith, F. (1994). *Understand reading: A psycholinguistic analysis of reading and learning to read* (5th ed.). Hillsdale, NJ: Erlbaum.

Stanovich K. (1980). Toward an interactive-compensatory model of individual differences in the development of reading fluency. *Reading Research Quarterly, 16* (1), 32–71.

Teaching Johnny to read. (1997, January 25). *New York Times,* 16.

Wasserman, R., & Rinsky, L. A. (1997). *Effective reading in a changing world* (2nd ed.). Upper Saddle River, NJ: Prentice Hall.

Wood, N. V. (1996). *College reading and study skills* (5th ed.). Fort Worth, TX: Harcourt Brace.

Zinn, A., & Poole, C. (1996). *Strategies for interactive reading.* Fort Worth, TX: Harcourt Brace.

Postsecondary Reading Strategies Rediscovered

Norman A. Stahl, James R. King, and Ulinda Eilers

As professionals in the field of college reading and learning pedagogy, we are so often involved in a race to the future through the generation of new knowledge and best practices that we all too quickly forget Anthony Manzo's admonition that the field is also the repository of considerable wisdom. The article "Postsecondary Reading Strategies Rediscovered" shows how valid college reading and study strategies have become lost, altered, or borrowed as resea·*ch and instruction have changed over the past century. The authors also demonstrate how past practices are useful as we define and evaluate future approaches.*

To one who chronicles the ebb and flow of trends in a professional field, the passage of time often proves that our professional "romance" with theories and instructional practices is at best fleeting. An academic field demonstrates regularly its fickle behavior, as new favorites are embraced in a cyclical process of initial interest, growing adoration, general acceptance, varied evaluation, and either rejection or relegation to a cult status. In either rejection or cultism, ideas lie dormant and await reincarnation as the cycle repeats itself.

An unfortunate implication in our wanton cycling is that many ideas that are abandoned are presumably of lesser value than newer ideas. Certainly this premise should not be taken as a statement against the generation of new ideas, theories, or pedagogical practices. Still, the danger is real that valid practices may be lost to the times for a number of reasons. This article examines how pedagogical practices that influenced the field of postsecondary reading instruction have filtered in and out of our instructional practices and our research agendas.

We propose that fully viable learning strategies have been "lost to the times" in varying degrees since the first decades of the century. In fact, lost learning strategies from the postsecondary reading/study literature (and by logical association the content area reading literature) can be classified into four working categories: (a) fully lost to the times, (b) partially lost to the times, (c) reincarnated or transmuted in form after being lost in time, and (d) existing in parallel forms with one or more variations being lost.

Furthermore, we propose that the longevity of instructional methods is not necessarily based upon research findings (Stahl, Simpson, & Brozo, 1988) but equally based on a combination of factors. Some of these factors include political status, market factors, timeliness of visibility, and even tenacity of purpose demonstrated by both individuals and institutions associated with the instructional strategies

This article undertakes one of Lewis's (1975) three modes of historiography by *recovering* specific learning strategies (also known successively across the years as work methods, work study methods, study methods, and study skills) that have been forgotten at some stage or rejected for some reason by the communal memory. Bird's (1931) Inductive Outline Procedure with the Self-Recitation Study Method will be used to represent Category (a): Fully Lost to the Times. We use the original recitation stage of Robinson's (1946) Survey Q3R as an example for Category (b): Partially Lost to the Times. We have selected Frederick's (1938) Block Method as an example of Category (c): Reincarnated or Transmuted in Form. And finally, we use the Bartusch Active Method and the Unified Notetaking Procedure as described by Palmatier (1971) to represent Category (d): Parallel Forms.

Through this patterned discussion of the ebb and flow of strategies, we also intend that readers will learn much about the historical roots for many of today's popular strategies (e.g., the Cornell System for notetaking, textbook-study systems, mapping) and also learn about a number of learning strategies and tactics that may warrant research attention in the 1990s.

Fully Lost to the Times

It might be said that the strength of a method of instruction lies in its ability to stand the test of time. Hence, we could judge the Socratic Method to be a robust method from the perspective of pedagogy based on longevity. The same mode of evaluation might work equally as well for methods of study. If so, one would consider strategies such as outlining, underlining, and notetaking to be equally timeless. But what do we say about strategies that did not stand the test of time? Were these inferior in nature? Perhaps some *were* inferior. But, it might just as well be said these were simply valid ideas that have been lost to the times for a range of reasons.

Bird's (1931) Inductive Outline Procedure is an example of a strategy that has simply been lost to succeeding generations. The inductive outline was put forth as a method that would prove quite useful in taking notes from text in which discussions of specific facts lead to general conclusions. In addition, it would appear to be an extremely useful technique for learners who have difficulty sorting out the superordinate ideas from the subordinate ideas.

In Bird's scheme the learner was told to record the various facts encountered in brief statements at an initial stage of study. Bird felt that the main divisions of a subject are usually indicated by boldfaced type, and so it was beneficial for the learner first to determine the basic ideas and facts within each section and then only later search for the greater meanings.

Figure 1 presents a student-developed inductive outline of this section of our article. The design looks somewhat like a modern textbook map in linear format, except that it is presented in a reverse order. In building the study guide, the student first writes the title of the chapter to be studied across the top of a page. Then the page is separated into three vertical columns with the following headings: (a) What are the facts? (b) What is their immediate significance? and (c) What is the overall significance?

Then, the actual reading/study procedure begins as the learner reads the first subsection of the chapter on a paragraph-by-paragraph basis. Each of the specific facts encountered in the subsection is jotted down and numbered in the first column. Text features such as italicized words, dates, figures, and proper nouns often signal the reader that an important fact is at hand.

After readers have completed all the paragraphs in a subsection, they glance over the notes in column one (the facts), and then skim over the entire subsection in the text. Based on this second reading, the

Figure 1. Inductive Outline

What are the facts?	What is their immediate significance?	What is the overall significance?
1. Useful in taking notes where discussion of specific facts leads to general conclusions.	There are two main advantages of an inductive outline.	The inductive outline is a useful strategy that was fully lost to the times.
2. Useful technique for sorting superordinate facts from subordinate ones.		
3. Record, in brief statements, the facts from the initial stage of study.		
4. Divide outline into three columns: (a) What are the facts? (b) What is their immediate significance? (c) What is the overall significance?		
5. Read text paragraph by paragraph and record the facts in the first column.	There are five steps to be used in creating an inductive outline.	The inductive outline is a step-by-step reading strategy.
6. Skim the text to find the importance of these facts and record them in the second column.		
7. Review statements in column two along with subheadings in text to find significance of statements in column two and record them in column three.		
8. Reason one for being lost: perceived as being overly complicated to use.	There are two primary reasons why this strategy may have been lost to the times.	We should be careful not to lose valuable learning strategies to the times.
9. Reason two for being lost: rapid reading more valued in the 1950s.		

learner records statements in the middle column that stress the importance of the observed facts. Accuracy is checked through rereading any topic sentences or summaries provided by the writer.

Each subsection of text is read in a like manner until the entire section has been charted out in columns one and two of the inductive outline. Now the student is ready to undertake the final step of the method. This begins with a review of the statements in column two as well as the subheadings throughout the section. The reader then writes a general statement in column three concerning the significance of the statements in column two. The accuracy of the general statement is evaluated by skimming over the introductory statements, topic statements, summary statements, and concluding remarks found throughout the section.

Bird (1931), in his own writings and later with his wife (Bird & Bird, 1945), recommended that the inductive outline also could be used in helping students to write themes. Perhaps this aspect of the inductive outline has not been totally lost in substance. The procedure, as Bird instantiated it for writing, follows the format stated previously. The writer first lists personal insights and facts from associated readings in a column on the far left-hand side of a page. Having enough ideas in place is one thing, but providing a sense of order or organization is quite another. Here, the learner uses the middle column to rearrange the details so that the ideas are both interdependent and meaningful. Trivial information may be discarded at this point, and it is not included in column two. The remaining facts serve as the core of the paragraphs for the paper. Still, paragraphs must have topic sentences, and the development of these topic sentences is undertaken in the third column. As they are formed, such generalizations can be numbered so as to indicate the sequence of the paragraphs in the final draft of the composition.

Bird concluded that once the inductive outline was complete, writing could proceed with the outline as the map to guide the basic drafting process. Nevertheless, Bird warned that being a "slave" to the outline would hamper the creative factors involved within the tasks of composing.

Why was the strategy lost to the times? We may offer what we see as informed conjecture. Perhaps the procedure was simply viewed as being overly complicated to use regardless of whether it was of benefit. While Bird provided support for the technique based on pre-World War II descriptive data from the University of Minnesota, the postwar students in college reading programs were more apt to spend their study energy and a major part of their time in curricular activities designed to make them more efficient readers — translated as more rapid readers. The inductive outline procedure was a rather laborious, time-consuming procedure that would appear to hinder rapid reading. Indeed, the 1950s and 1960s were the height of modernity, and with modernity, education prized efficiency, replicability, and accuracy. An elaborate, if not baroque, approach would not have been desirable or valued. During this period the traditional outline was the time-honored and most favored technique taught regularly to college students in general writing courses.

Furthermore, the more deductive methods such as SQ3R (1946), which were based on the scientific management theories of Gilbreth (1914), Taylor (1911), and Gantt (1913, 1916) and the pedagogical version of work methods theories of Seashore (1939), focused upon the more modern typographical aids (i.e., headings, subheadings, questions) and top-down text structures used in the textbooks of the 1950s that did not exist to the same degree in Depression-era texts.

Instructors stressed rapid reading with survey-type activities, along with other efficient steps promoting "work methods" in the systems approach (now called a sequential strategy approach) to learning. Even Bird and Bird (1945) fell sway to the deductive approach for textbook learning as they provided a step-by-step system as found in a number of texts from the pre-SQ3R era (e.g., Cole & Ferguson, 1935; Robinson, 1941).

The inductive outline may have simply outlived its usefulness or acceptability for the class of 1950. Then, across the next 25 years, it was lost to the times. Yet it was in the 1970s that Bird's Inductive Outline Procedure might have had some of its greatest success. As the doors of U.S. higher education — particularly through the community college — opened to individuals who sought "the dream," but possessed limited reading and writing capabilities, inductive outlining may have proved productive. With knowledge bases not fully valued by the academic community, these nontraditional or "new" students of the era might best have used the inductive outline approach as a way to connect prior knowledge with formidable text, foreign topics, and controlled writing assignments. Inductive approaches to knowledge, however, were not in favor during an efficiency-based, course-centered time in education.

Partially Lost to the Times

We now shift our focus to look at a strategy that has been partially lost to the times. Here, we examine the changes that have reshaped the original Survey Q3R proposed by Robinson in 1946. In SQ3R, students undertake five steps as they move through a section of text. First, the student *surveys* the entire section to obtain a bird's-eye view of the piece. This step is followed by the student's development of a *guiding question* for the first section of text to be studied. Then the learner would *read actively* the first section passage to answer the question. The next step involves the tactic of *recitation* in which the student would respond specifically to the question. Finally, the student is expected to *review* in a systematic manner. Few of us practice this strategy, but many of us were told we should be using it every time we read content material.

We see SQ3R as only partially lost to the times because of the extreme popularity of the system with the authors of study strategy texts and even basal reading systems through the years. It is a study strategy that has been cloned to such an extreme that there are over 100 variations in the study strategy and reading literature base (Stahl, 1983). Yet, with all the copying and all of the revising of SQ3R, many authors and many learning specialists have never read Robinson's (1946) primary writings, in which he spelled out the nature of the method and the theoretical rationale that underlies it. What we discover then is that across the nearly 50 years since the system was introduced, the recitation stage has changed in nearly all the clones from a step that evoked the power of writing to a step that focuses almost solely on oral recitation.

What then is the written component of this textbook study system? Simply put, the students are told to develop working notes on the materials that have been read. This form of summarization does not happen during the initial reading as it does with most traditional note-taking or annotation systems. Rather, as students respond to the self-developed question after reading the text section, their task is to draft working notes in the form of a "jot list," a précis, or an informal outline. As they produce written texts for sections of the text, the cycle of survey, question, read, recite continues for each section within the chapter under study — not unlike the tactics in Bird's (1931) Self-Recitation Study Method.

The readers' written texts are then used as part of the ongoing review function. Students are told to look over all the points within their texts to get a global as well as an integrated perspective of the chapter's content. The students perform the review step by reciting the major points and recalling the respective subpoints found in their written study guides.

In his original writing on SQ3R, Robinson (1946) shared his belief in the superiority of the written approach to recitation. He noted that self-recitation could take the form of either mentally reviewing the answer or writing it. He believed that the latter was far more effective because it forced students to articulate an answer more fully. Furthermore, simple mental review could, in fact, mislead readers into believing that a vague feeling of comprehension was actually content mastery. Robinson also felt that writing notes provided the student with greater independent learning power, because visual and kinesthetic cues, as well as verbal imagery, were employed in thinking about the content.

Why has the writing stage, for the most part, been lost? Actually, this is not particularly hard to understand. All one has to do is look at Robinson's own initial description of the step. The writing component is staged low in the set of the paragraphs detailing the recitation activity.

Hence, at first glance one is likely to see the oral response aspect but fail to see the written component. Further, as the system gained such broad popularity with the writers of study strategy texts and content area reading methods texts, it is likely that authors from the 1980s onward never read Robinson's admonitions. Rather, these authors simply may have taken the steps for SQ3R from preceding summaries of the strategy as found ubiquitously in the workbooks and the methods texts of the 1970s. There is some support for this contention, as current writers quite regularly and erroneously credit Robinson's 1941 text as the source of SQ3R when in fact it did not appear as a unified system in text until 1946.

This writing component has not been fully lost. One of the few reading methods books that continues to present the early form of the recitation step is the one by Readence, Bean, and Baldwin (1992). These authors advocate the use of a split-page question and answer response form where the student writes down the guiding question on the right-hand side of the page, and then after reading the respective section, the student follows up with the answer in the left-hand section. Of course, the question can be raised as to whether this technique is based on Robinson's ideas or has been reborn because of the influence of Pauk's integrating various notetaking tactics into the Cornell System.

It is interesting to conjecture as to whether the research base for SQ3R would be more positive if all of the researchers had fully trained the participants to use the working notes aspect of the system. In PORPE (Predict, Organize, Rehearse, Practice, Evaluate), the test preparation strategy by Simpson (1986), writing is an intricate tactic, and the research with the overall strategy has been most positive with college developmental readers (Hayes, Simpson, & Stahl, 1994; Simpson, Hayes, Stahl, Connor, & Weaver, 1988). Perhaps research will be undertaken with writing as a formal part of SQ3R in the future.

Reincarnated or Transmuted in Form

In this third case, we will examine the Block Method for studying a complete book, a chapter in a textbook, or an article in a journal. The technique was first mentioned in the widely distributed *How to Study Handbook* (Frederick, 1938), and then apparently lost during the World War II years. At that time, the field's infatuation with systems like SQ3R, as well as the reading efficiency emphasis of the postwar years, may have pushed other approaches off the stage. Later, a variant of the Block Method appears to have been reincarnated as the textbook mapping system put forth by Hanf (1971), which provided the foundation for the multitude of graphic organizers we find in the study strategy texts and in the reading methods texts of the current era.

Like so many of the approaches from the "work method" era of the 1930s, the recommendations for the Block Method were presented in the form of ordered steps. The learner was instructed to first, and foremost, consider the title most carefully. This step entailed the simple act of pondering the nature of the content that was likely to be encountered in the chapter. This was done first by the reader developing and then pondering a number of rather broad questions that focused on the title.

Step 2 of the Block Method was presented as the most important activity, as it required the learner to block out the section to be read. In blocking out a chapter, the reader sets up the framework on which selected information is hung. Hence, the main divisions, topics, or subordinate ideas of each chapter were referred to as blocks. By understanding the chapter's framework, readers could more quickly and easily fill in the details during reading.

Frederick called this second step skimming, but it is much more akin to the survey/preview activities found in many texts today. The student was encouraged to skim through each section of the chapter, and by using each section heading, the student would begin to verbalize expectations of what content might be found in the section. These thoughts could be written down in the form of an outline or a diagram. The two examples of diagrams advocated by Frederick, provided as Figure 2 and Figure 3, are similar to what we now call a "pyramid" or "linear" map (Baldridge, 1976; Kump, 1979; Solon, 1980) and to what we now call a "radial" map (Adams, 1980).

The third step of the Block Method required the learner to read something about each block. Frederick informed the learner that following the chapter's section-by-section order was not necessary; each block could also be approached in a different manner. On the basis of prior knowledge, the reader could select to read over a block of text composed of relatively familiar information, or, on the other hand, read a section with content that was relatively unknown. In either case, blocks were processed as discrete sets of ideas.

Figure 2. Block Method

Learning strategies		
Fully lost to the times—Inductive Outline Procedure	Partially lost to the times—Recitation stage of Survey Q3R	Reincarnated or transmuted in form—Block Method
	Existing in parallel forms—Unified Notetaking Procedure	Three concluding themes emerge to explain lost strategies	

Figure 3. Variation of the Block Method

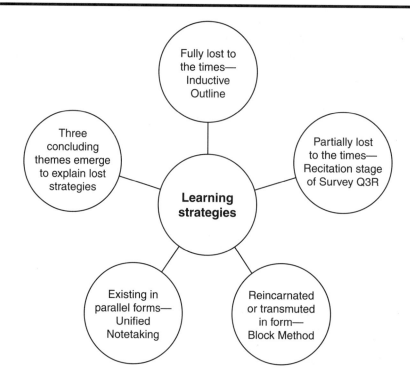

In the last step, the student would review the chapter's content through the use of the block design. The titles of each of the blocks were committed to memory. Furthermore, the students were to think of the ideas that were subordinate to the key idea in each block. The student was told that it might be profitable to put down from memory the ideas in each block on note paper and fill in missing information from the text. As the activity was completed, the student would have a map in hand that would compare to any found in current classrooms of 1995.

Why was this system lost to the times — or at least misplaced for 25 years? Earlier, we proposed that the Block Method was lost because of the very success of SQ3R and other acronym-based study approaches of the 1950s. These were rather lock-step, sequential systems that fit in well with the times. The Block Method's author was not as well known as the leaders of the college reading field in the prewar era such as Robinson, Crawford, Pressey, and Triggs, or the cadre of mostly young and all multitalented college reading and study skills authors (such as Spache, Berg, Pauk, etc.) who emerged on the scene during the Cold War period.

Furthermore, the Block Method was a graphic organizer in a period in which the American student (as part of the pretelevision generation) was not yet accustomed fully to graphic forms of presentation in instructional contexts. The populace and, even more important, the teaching profession, was not yet using flow charts and other forms of graphic presentation of text. The concept of the written advance organizer (Ausubel, 1960), which later led to the development of the structured overview (Barron, 1969), was still in the formative stages. By the 1970s when the Hanf (1971) mapping system slowly began to have an impact, the college reading programs were ready for new approaches to handle the great influx of new students flooding the newly designed developmental studies programs of that decade.

With the mid-1980s, the graphic organizer, or student-designed chapter map, was a staple in the field's texts and was taught widely in the classroom. Furthermore, the popularity of trade books (e.g., Buzan, 1976; Rial, 1977) linking popular press conceptions of the cognitive research on left brain/right brain functions to techniques such as "mind-mapping" further supported the use of graphic organizers in the college reading and study skills course. Yet to this day, few professionals who train students to develop maps as study materials know of the debt owed to Frederick.

Existing in Parallel Forms

A number of strategies quite similar in nature may have been born across the years, yet only one of these techniques will have received the greatest interest and support from the profession. The group of note-taking strategies is an example. The best known approach to notetaking is the Cornell System, which has been advocated by Pauk, one of the pioneers of the modern college reading and learning movement. Pauk (1989) noted in the fourth edition of his classic text, *How to Study in College,* that he developed the technique 40 years before at Cornell University. The system is well known, but the specifics bear repeating.

The student uses 8-1/2-by-11-inch paper to create the notetaking sheet, which has a vertical line drawn 2-1/2 inches down the entire left side of the sheet. During the lecture, the learner takes notes in the 6-inch wide section. Then to facilitate the study (i.e., recitation) of the notes, the individual writes questions or cue words in the narrower 2-1/2-inch recall column. A summary is written in the section generally created in the 2 inches at the bottom of the page.

Pauk provides two versions of the Cornell System: the Six R Version and the One Q/Five R Version. Both stress systematic, multiple passes at the material recorded during the class lecture. The primary difference between Pauk's two versions is whether or not students write cues or questions in the recall column. In either way, the Cornell System is probably the best known notetaking procedure of the century.

Still, it is interesting to note that several other methods evolved at essentially the same time. As far back as 1926, Headley offered an early version of a split-page method, where supplementary information, such as details or examples, was placed in a separate column drawn down the right side of the notebook page. Later, Aiken (1953) proposed a notetaking procedure that used the same split page as the Cornell design. Another example, the Bartusch Active Method, or BAM (Palmatier, 1971), was developed over several student generations at the University of Michigan and at Syracuse University. Later, an adapted form was to appear in the *Journal of Reading* as the Notetaking System for Learning or NSL (Palmatier, 1973). There were few differences among the BAM, the NSL, and the Cornell System. Other texts, such as Morgan and Deese (1969) and even Pauk's (1962) *How to Study in College,* presented numerical acronyms (e.g., 2-5-1 format, 2-6-2 format) that provided cues for the layout of the notetaking paper and consequently the progression of notetaking tactics that made up the respective strategies.

How is it, then, that we have come to associate notetaking systems with Pauk? More directly, how has the Cornell System become the dominant system in the minds of so many of our colleagues? The reason may be much like that presented for the popularity of SQ3R. Certainly, the actual construct was not particularly novel for the times. Yet the name or acronym coined for a technique can be right for the times. Somehow it strikes a chord with the professionals who are writing methods texts and worktexts, as well as individuals implementing curriculum in the college reading programs. With SQ3R, the New Deal-militaristic acronym (Survey Q3R as shortened to SQ3R) was quite appropriate to use in college reading texts and college reading classes whose ranks were swelled with former U.S. World War II and Korean War service personnel receiving G.I. Bill benefits (Stahl, 1983).

The same type of argument might be used with the Cornell System/Method. While the overall system as advocated by Pauk and others was clearly the method of choice by worktext writers, and we will assume that for college reading instructors by the 1960s, the term Cornell Method did not truly come into its own until the publication of the second edition (1974) of *How to Study in College.*

To understand the complete domination of the technique, one must understand the era and the contributions of Pauk. These were the boom years for college reading programs, as a community college was opening virtually every week across the U.S. Remedial education, and later developmental education, were well-accepted missions of the community/junior college. Yet the vast majority of instructors were self-trained and came from a wide variety of academic fields. The initial method of self-training came through the reading of texts designed to be used in the study skills classes. *How to Study in College* (1974) with the Cornell Method as one of its cornerstones was a classic for the times.

Furthermore, in a field facing a marginalized existence, the teaching of a study strategy with an apparent lineage tracing back to a highly selective university provided a degree of respectability with faculty peers and perhaps an equal amount of comfort to the college reading instructor. The association of the system with Cornell University carried with it a most positive connotation for students enrolled, usually not by choice, in remedial or developmental reading classes. A greater degree of acceptability and self-worth was generated when developmental studies students thought that they were learning the same methods being presented to students at an Ivy League university.

Finally, the system was advocated by one of the few scholars of national caliber who had not abandoned college reading for the more prestigious and lucrative fields of elementary reading or remedial reading. Through his many writings, presentations, and service activities, Pauk was a giant in the field of college reading in an era when only a handful of other national leaders (e.g., Martha Maxwell, Alton Raygor) offered new ideas and scholarship for a field striving to be recognized as a profession.

While techniques similar to the Cornell System/Method continued to appear in the literature, individuals saw them simply as renditions of the Cornell System. The pedagogical version of Kleenex tissues or Xerox copiers was born. The other notetaking approaches, while continuing to exist, were so overshadowed by the Cornell System that they also became lost to the times.

Timing, Politics, and Efficiency

Across our analysis of instructional strategies that have been lost to the times, and in some ways recovered in this article, three themes have emerged. These themes are important, as one of the benefits of historical study is to help us predict the future through understanding the past.

First, several of the strategies that were lost did not fit with the tenor of the times, as college reading programs went through two succeeding boom periods during the G.I. Bill era and later the Open Door era of higher education. These times demanded systematic, sequential strategies that reflected society's complete adoption of, if not adoration for, "Taylorism" (i.e., scientific management theory) during the height of the military-industrial complex in the 1950s, 1960s, 1970s, and into the 1980s.

With the advent of the postmodern era, we have entered a period where there is an acceptance of more recursive forms of knowing that build cumulatively upon introspective actions. In some ways, these newer approaches are similar to ways of learning accepted at the turn of the century (when the college reading and study movement was in its infancy). In the years ahead we may find greater acceptance of cumulative strategies in which a range of activities based upon individual needs and desires is viewed as more acceptable than "one best" sequential strategy.

Second, we have observed what seems to be the politics of adoption and promotion of ideas. Indeed, we have seen examples where the persona of the proponent (individual or institutional) of a particular technique leads to its being accepted while similar techniques are lost to the times. While in the positive sense, as with our examples, this persona may be based upon academic respectability and service to the field, we must be aware that acceptance of particular teaching techniques may also be based on political clout of institutions or research centers, on personal charisma, or on proponents' connections to others with like ambitions. Also ideas put forth by one individual can ultimately be claimed by another individual or group, leading the former to be forgotten.

Finally, there is the issue of efficiency of innovation. We raise the regularly asked question: Does the technique work with controlled research samples in the lab *or* with actual students in the classroom? Even more important, does the strategy work given the communal, the philosophical, and the practical mind-sets of the academic community (i.e., the college learners and the instructors) during the era it was first proposed? And, finally, is the question raised again for each successive era and unique cohort of students then forming the undergraduate population? Even the most effective technique will not stand the test of the times if students in the current era are not willing to embrace the construct in the same way as earlier generations. In a sense, we see the need for recurring research to be carried out on each generation — a job that was once the partial domain of the all-but-extinct master's thesis.

We end this article with a point so well articulated by Manzo (1983). College reading is both a generator of new ideas and a repository of considerable wisdom. This is a powerful observation that should provide sage guidance to the profession. Yet with the field's compulsive desire to always be on the cutting edge, we often sacrifice both our heritage and the useful knowledge from the past. Hence, we echo a warning (Stahl, Hynd, & Henk, 1986) from the past decade. We must always be aware that the varied parts of the past will add up to the sum that is our future. To stress the future without a memory and an understanding of the past does a disservice to the field and to individuals who have served with distinction — indeed, we then condemn them to be lost to the times.

References

Adams, W. R. (1980). *Reading beyond words.* New York: Holt, Rinehart & Winston.

Aiken, D. J. (1953). *You can learn how to study.* New York: Rinehart.

Ausubel, D. P. (1960). The use of advance organizers in the learning and retention of meaningful verbal material. *Journal of Educational Psychology* 51, 58–88.

Baldridge, K. P. (1976). *Study techniques for academic subjects.* Greenwich, CT: Baldridge Reading Instruction Materials.

Barron, R. F. (1969). The use of vocabulary as an advance organizer. In H. L. Herber & P. L. Sanders (Eds.), *Research in reading in the content areas: First year report* (pp. 29–39). Syracuse, NY: Syracuse University, Reading and Language Arts Center.

Bird, C. (1931). *Effective study habits.* New York: Century.

Bird, C., & Bird, D. M. (1945). *Learning more by effective study.* New York: Appleton-Century.

Buzan, T. (1976). *Use both sides of your brain.* New York: Dutton.

Cole, L., & Ferguson, J. M. (1935). *Student's guide to effective study* (rev. ed.). New York: Farrar & Rinehart.

Frederick, R. W. (1938). *How to study handbook.* New York: Appleton-Century.

Gantt, H. L. (1913). *Work, wages and profit.* New York: Engineering Magazine.

Gantt, H. L. (1916). *Industrial leadership.* New Haven, CT: Yale University Press.

Gilbreth, F. (1914). *Primer of scientific management.* New York: D. Van Nostrand.

Hanf, M. B. (1971). Mapping: A technique for translating reading into thinking. *Journal of Reading, 14,* 225–230.

Hayes, C. G., Simpson, M. L., & Stahl, N. A. (1994). The effects of extended writing on students' understanding of content-area concepts. *Research & Teaching in Developmental Education, 10,* 13–34.

Headley, L. A. (1926). *How to study in college.* New York: Henry Holt.

Kump, P. (1979). *Breakthrough rapid reading.* West Nyack, NY: Parker.

Lewis, B. (1975). *History remembered, recovered, invented.* Princeton, NJ: Princeton University Press.

Manzo, A. V. (1983). College reading: Past and presenting. *Forum for Reading, 14,* 5–16.

Morgan, C. T., & Deese, J. (1969). *How to study* (2nd ed.). New York: McGraw-Hill.

Palmatier, R. A. (1971). Comparison of four note-taking procedures. *Journal of Reading, 14,* 235–240, 258.

Palmatier, R. A. (1973). A notetaking system for learning. *Journal of Reading, 17,* 36–39.

Pauk, W. (1962). *How to study in college* (1st ed.). Boston: Houghton Mifflin.

Pauk, W. (1974). *How to study in college* (2nd ed.). Boston: Houghton Mifflin.

Pauk, W. (1989). *How to study in college* (4th ed.). Boston: Houghton Mifflin.

Readence, J. E., Bean, T. W., & Baldwin, R. S. (1992). *Content area reading: An integrated approach* (4th ed.). Dubuque, IA: Kendall Hunt.

Rial, A. F. (1977). *Speed reading made easy.* New York: Doubleday.

Robinson, F. P. (1941). *Diagnostic and remedial techniques for effective study.* New York: Harper.

Robinson, F. P. (1946). *Effective study.* New York: Harper.

Seashore, R. (1939). Work methods: An often neglected factor underlying individual differences. *Psychological Review, 46,* 123–141.

Simpson, M. L (1986). PORPE: A writing strategy for studying and, learning in the content areas, *Journal of Reading,* 29, 407–414.

Simpson, M. L., Hayes, C. G., Stahl, N. A., Connor, R. T., & Weaver, D. (1988). An initial validation of a study strategy system. *Journal of Reading Behavior,* 20, 149–180.

Solon, C. (1980). The pyramid diagram: A college study skills tool. *Journal of Reading,* 23, 594–597.

Stahl, N. A. (1983). *A historical analysis of textbook-study systems* (Doctoral dissertation, University of Pittsburgh). University Microfilms No. 8411839.

Stahl, N. A., Hynd, C. R., & Henk, W. A. (1986). Avenues for chronicling and researching the history of college reading and study skills instruction. *Journal of Reading,* 29, 334–341.

Stahl, N. A., Simpson, M. L., & Brozo, W. G. (1988). The materials of college reading instruction. A critical and historical perspective from 50 years of content analysis research. *Reading Research and Instruction,* 27(3), 16–34.

Taylor, F. W. (1911). *The principles of scientific management.* New York: Harper Brothers.

Additional Readings

Boylan, H. R., & White, W. G. (1987). "Educating all the nation's people: The historical roots of developmental education." *Research in Developmental Education,* 4 (4), 1–4.

Bullock, T. L., Madden, D. A., & Mallery, A. L. (1990). "Developmental education in American universities: Past, present, and future." *Research & Teaching in Developmental Education,* 6 (2), 5–74.

Cross, K. P. (1976). *Accent on learning.* San Francisco: Jossey-Bass.

Leedy, P. D. (1958). *A history of the origin and development of instruction in reading improvement at the college level.* Unpublished doctoral dissertation, New York University, New York. (University Microfilms #59-01016)

Lundell, D. B., & Higbee, J. L. (2002). *Histories of developmental education.* Minneapolis: The Center for Research on Developmental Education and Urban Literacy, University of Minnesota.

Kersteins, G. (1998). "Studying in college, then & now: An interview with Walter Pauk." *Journal of Developmental Education,* 21 (3), 20–24.

O'Hear, M. (1993). "College reading programs: The last 25 years." *Journal of College Reading and Learning,* 25 (2), 17–24.

Pauk, W. (1999). "How SQ3R came to be." In J. R. Dugan, P. E. Linder, W. M. Linek, & E. G. Sturtevant (Eds.), *Advancing the world of literacy: Moving into the 21st century, The 21st yearbook of the College Reading Association* (pp. 27–35). Commerce, TX: College Reading Association.

Piper, J. (1998). "An interview with Martha Maxwell." *The Learning Assistance Review,* 3 (1), 32–39.

Stahl, N. A., & King, J. R. (2000). "A history of college reading." In R. F. Flippo & D. C. Caverly (Eds.), *The handbook of college reading and study strategy research* (pp. 1–23). Mahwah, NJ: Erlbaum.

2

Paradigms and Programs

Most institutions of higher education in the United States offer students some form of academic enhancement services. The academic home for these support services varies from institution to institution, depending upon the unique convergence of institutional history, faculty politics, funding priorities, pedagogical "turfism," and even influential personalities at any given school. In addition, these institutional factors are usually influenced by similar variables determining postsecondary policy in the state legislature and the state higher education authority. Yet, even with all these variables that come to bear on the college reading program and the learning assistance center (as well as other developmental education units or academic assistance services), their fundamental organizational schemes are quite similar from program to program across the country.

This chapter focuses on program design and philosophy. In the first article, Louise Bohr provides a context for our examination of paradigms and programs through a discussion of the differences between college and precollege reading instruction. Then, Mellinee Lesley discusses how a critical literacy philosophy led her to redesign a developmental reading course that had previously been driven by a traditional remedial model. An article by Jim Reynolds and Stuart C. Werner next covers the three stages of a learner-centered paradigm that helps students identify their learning styles. And, finally, in a widely cited article, Nannette Evans Commander and Brenda D. Smith describe the adjunct course model they developed at Georgia State University.

College and Precollege Reading Instruction: What Are the Real Differences?

Louise Bohr

Instructors enter the field of college reading from a range of professional backgrounds. Many come to it after having taught in elementary schools, middle schools, or secondary schools. Louise Bohr raises five questions often voiced by newcomers to the field: "What do college and precollege instruction have in common?" "Why is college reading instruction so different?" "What are the differences between college and precollege reading classrooms?" "Is there overlap between college and precollege instruction?" "What are the implications for college reading instructors?" While showing the common bonds between precollege reading instruction and postsecondary reading instruction, Bohr explains the significance of the fact that college developmental reading and learning programs employ curricular designs and instructional models for individuals at a unique juncture in their educational experience.

Since we have so much more to draw upon in primary and secondary reading instruction, it's tempting to assume that what is right for elementary and high school classrooms is right for college classrooms. However, it is prudent to ask whether college reading instructors are actually in the same practice as elementary and high school teachers. Eighty-two percent of American public postsecondary institutions *offer reading courses,* and further, 13 percent of all American college students take *at least one reading course* (National Center for Educational Statistics, 1991). As the number of college students taking reading courses increases, more and more college reading instructors join the profession. With few exceptions, however, there is little difference in the way they and other reading teachers are prepared.

College instructors are generally included among the array of reading professionals (Barclay & Thistlewaite, 1992), and there is a small body of literature on the training of college reading professionals (Austin & Gilford, 1993; Garcia, 1981; Matthews, 1981; Maxwell, 1981). However, it is rare that we delineate for prospective college reading instructors how their practice can be differentiated from the practices of elementary and high school teachers. And there are some crucial questions: Do the same practices work with college students? Are the purposes for instruction the same? Do students have the same needs? If we are to clearly understand the role played by college reading teachers, we should focus on what we can and can't learn from high school and elementary reading teachers.

Much has been borrowed by precollege reading educators in literacy pedagogy; notions of teaching composition with process rather than product emphasis was generated in college, not precollege, research

(Hillocks, 1986). But more has been borrowed by college reading educators from the far larger field of precollege reading; however, specific cautions should be exercised in the process. In this discussion, the phrase "precollege reading" is used to describe the teaching of reading to elementary and high school students.

The following will address the shared, exclusive, and modified components of college and precollege reading instruction. Presented first is a summary of shared components: those which precollege and college reading have in common. After a discussion of the reasons for real differences between college and precollege reading instruction, the exclusive components are presented. Exclusive components are those which the fields do not share. Finally, there are some components of precollege reading which could be applied in a college setting if appropriately altered. These areas of modification and reconsideration are presented. The implications of distinctions are then discussed.

What Do College and Precollege Instruction Have in Common?

Central notions regarding where comprehension takes place have evolved and impacted practice in both college and precollege reading. In early reading theory, the author just threw the ball, and the reader just caught it. But the author wasn't standing anywhere in particular, and the reader was floating in space, could only catch in one manner, and couldn't throw back. The "grand prize" in reading comprehension theory in the past decades once belonged to the author, then moved to the text itself, and now has flown off the page, where the reader and the reader's culture do battle for it.

Our current understanding of the varied contexts, goals, and world views which students bring to their reading has led us to a view behind and beyond the text (Rogers-Zegarra & Singer, 1985; Steffensen, et. al., 1979) and has revealed the economic (Ogbu, 1987; Willis, 1977) and social (Cazden, 1986) imperatives guiding the process. In addition, linguistic particularities of the reader and the structures of the text influence comprehension (Halliday & Hasan, 1976; Fasold & Shuy, 1970; Rosenthal, et. al., 1983). Further, the reader has a personal wealth of prior knowledge and schemata (Anderson & Pearson, 1984) which he brings to the process, as well as certain effective or ineffective strategies (Raphael, 1982) and metacognitive processes (Paris & Winograd, 1991) which he or she uses to interact with text (Rumelhart, 1985) and to monitor the dialogue which ensues. The reading process appears to be quite situation specific (Brown, 1989) and depends upon the goals of the reader and the purposes of the reading material itself (Shanahan, 1988). Furthermore, we now understand that learning to write is an integral part of the reading process (Shanahan, 1984; 1988; 1990). What an individual reader does during and after the comprehension process to construct personal meaning and to change himself and change his world (Freire & Donaldo, 1986; Rosenblatt, 1978) can also be considered part of comprehension itself. These findings have shaped both college and precollege reading instruction.

College and precollege reading pedagogy share the most in recognizing the impact that *culture, socio-economic condition, and schema* have on students' comprehension. It is crucial that the cultural context of the reader be taken into account in college and precollege reading instruction. Children who are privy to certain cultural contexts (either inside or outside the mainstream) will excel if pedagogy is based on knowledge from that culture (Labov, 1972; Hunt, 1975; Au, 1980; Heath, 1983). For college readers living outside the boundaries of academic culture, the acknowledgment of the students' special background abets literacy development (Rose, 1989; Shaughnessy, 1977).

Interwoven with issues of culture, socio-economic conditions arrange the posture of reader, text, and instructor. On a universal scale, readers with lower economic status don't meet standards on the comprehension assessments created, primarily, by those who have higher economic status (Thorndike, 1973; Coleman, 1966). Developmental (Chall, et al., 1990; Covington & Beery, 1976; Deutsch, 1960; Warren-Leubecker & Carter, 1988), deliberate (Ogbu, 1988; Weis, 1985; Willis, 1977), and instructor (Rist, 1970; Haller & Davis, 1981) behaviors are blamed for this discrepancy.

Related to the cultural and socio-economic influences on both college and precollege reading is a reader's immediate psychological predisposition, background knowledge, or schema. The schema model (Pichert & Anderson, 1977) allows deeper understanding of a reader's use of metacognition and strategy. In both precollege and college reading, a student is directed toward strategies, for attention, memory, summary, questioning, and regulation of his or her own reading. These strategies have long been recommended for elementary school (Palincsar & Brown, 1984) and for the development of college literacy (Hillocks, 1986; Nist & Kirby, 1991; Stahl, et. al., 1992; Simpson, 1994; 1995).

Four further dimensions of the comprehension process shared by college and precollege readers deserve attention. The first concerns the situation in which the reader comprehends, the second concerns the genre of the text, the third concerns the reader's purpose, and the fourth concerns the use of technology in literacy development.

First, it appears that comprehension processes accomplished in one situation are not always easily transferred to another. This means that if students practice a particular strategy on a particular text in a classroom in September, the experience does not necessarily enable them to do it at home with text homework for another class in December, or even later that day in the library. Some unknown ambience is lost the second time around, which has led researchers to believe learning is "situated" (Brown, 1989). Second, as comprehension is different from one situation to the next, it is different when a text is from another genre. Comprehension instruction in lower and higher education must show the reader different processes for comprehension in the many genres which elementary, secondary, and postsecondary readers share. Third, the purpose for reading, or the reason a student sets out to read what he or she has in hand, should make students use different strategies (Janiuk & Shanahan, 1988). A heightened awareness of purpose enhances comprehension for readers of all ages. Finally, as computer competency in reading and writing become necessary for those who will and will not attend college, students and teachers at all levels must work to integrate technological processes with literacy development (Kiefer, 1991).

Why Is College Reading Instruction so Different?

A number of reasons account for the very real differences between college and precollege reading instruction: 1) Students in elementary and high schools attend by law; students in college attend by choice. 2) There is a wide range of ages in each setting, but for the most part the age ranges do not overlap. 3) There are differing ability ranges for each of the settings, though here the overlap is pretty large. 4) Grade school pedagogy prepares readers for all reading; college reading pedagogy prepares students for academic reading. College reading instruction is limited to that which helps students to succeed in college; it is not intended to help students with literacy styles outside of academe. Some may disagree, but most practice does, in fact, address primarily college tasks (Fairbanks, 1974). In some very special cases developmental educators and the administrators of a college or university agree to literacy goals outside academic success, but generally a developmental reading program at a college *earns its keep* by trying to help college students succeed in classes.

What Are the Differences between College and Precollege Reading Classrooms?

Following are six basic differences between college and precollege reading which separate the tasks of educators in those two areas. The ages, abilities, motivations, and goals of "clientele" account for most of these differences. For the purpose of this discussion, college success is assumed to be the primary goal of college reading programs.

   1. *Only precollege reading is concerned with reading readiness and emergent reading.* A very rich collection of works helps early

childhood educators to prepare children for the new phenomenon of reading (Mason & Au, 1990). This type of activity, of course, appears prior to kindergarten, and has registered successes which may endure even through college age, but few conceivable circumstances would ever involve the college reading educator in this literature.

2. *Only precollege reading is concerned with early, first language development.* Not only is reading new at some age for every child, but so is a sort of integration with one's own language. First language acquisition in children has been characterized by many types of grammars and their resultant "stages," and these concerns may or may not have interplay with the reading a very young child accomplishes (Brown, 1973; Clark, 1973). However, these issues do not concern college reading educators, with the exception of lexical acquisition.

3. *The ability range of college readers excludes some of the range of precollege readers.* While we hope that the top of the achievement range for college students is higher for college readers than for precollege students, we know that the bottom of the range is not generally equal to the bottom of the precollege range. According to recent studies, the number of students with no knowledge of sound-letter relationships is only about 6 percent of the adolescent population (Davidson & Koppenhaver, 1993). For this reason, college reading is usually not concerned with orthography, phonics, and word recognition. Some open admissions postsecondary institutions do report reading instruction of this sort. Yet it is unclear that even those college students in the extremely low ability ranges would benefit from instruction of this nature. Curricula designed for reading disabled college applicants might be one exception. However, for the most part college reading instruction does not include instruction in sound-letter association or sight word recognition. For this reason, assessment issues for college readers should also not address word recognition, and should instead address the difficulty, purposes, lengths, and genres of college texts (Quinn, 1992).

4. *Only precollege reading uses early reading materials (e.g., basals, big books).* There is widespread disagreement regarding what materials best facilitate reading at all levels (Heinrichs & La Branche, 1986), but even with extremely low achieving college applicants materials designed for the primary grades are not used. Because basals and early reading materials are engineered to perform functions mentioned in 1–3 above (Mason & Au, 1990), they appeal to the taste of children, and they are psychologically distracting to adults for a number of reasons.

5. *College reading is usually not concerned with functional, survival, vocational, or other extra-academic "utility" reading.* We

teach grade schoolers to read in many more ways than we do college students. We prepare them to be citizens, to labor, to pay taxes, to be consumers, to stay healthy, and to understand personal communications. Some pedagogy broaches the question, "What are the natural uses of literacy in the world?" In a sense, language experience approaches in the classroom and whole language approaches in pedagogy give rise to conceptions of literacy's unlimited, personal, and natural uses (Mason & Au, 1990). Some of the whole language and language experience techniques should certainly be applied by college educators, but only if the focus returns to the academic uses of literacy. In short, precollege readers face a different group of literacy experiences.

6. *Instruction for college readers is androgogy, not pedagogy.* Androgogy is instruction for adults, not for children. The teacher of college reading pursues a classroom discourse more suited to adults. Classroom management is a very different proposition for children. Good precollege reading instruction requires a teacher to guide and conduct groups of children toward comprehension. Conducting this type of "orchestra" requires attention to the management of a group which may still be developing social control and may not know how to keep the learning task a priority (Doyle, 1986). It should be acknowledged that some excellent recent work points to the possibility that developmental college classes are comprised of students who do not share all the characteristics of adult learners (Davis, 1995). In a good *college* class, however, much of the responsibility for the management of productivity is shared with the students (McClusky, 1958; Newton, 1976). The essence of the adult is independence and self-direction (Kidd, 1966; Knowles, 1973).

Is There Overlap between College and Precollege Instruction?

While many of the features that follow have been mentioned in the last section, the emphasis here is to show how some considerations are *modified* for the college reader. In these six areas, college reading instructors must be careful to adapt pedagogical styles in order to work with postsecondary students.

1. *Developmental college reading, though it addresses a more advanced, sophisticated audience, might not apply some of the more sophisticated advancements in reading theory.* As reading theory shifted focus away from the text and author, it became possible for readers to follow suit. The activities of the reader in reader response, constructivist, post-structural, and in a discourse synthesis approach (Rosenblatt, 1978; Foucault, 1981; Spivey, 1990) are generally not the

initial focus of college reading. An immediate focus for a low achieving college reader on personal response and action may confuse this reader who has never entered an academic dialogue in the first place. Delpit goes so far as to indicate that process approaches can confuse or frustrate readers "on the boundary," who want to know common rules for academic interpretation (Delpit, 1988). Applications of newer theories should be made, but constraints of the college's goals (which must usually be addressed in one short academic term) are limiting factors.

2. *Purposes are different for precollege and college readers.* As we have mentioned, college readers face a different group of literacy experiences. These experiences go beyond "catching the ball," from writers of droll introductory texts, and beyond the text itself to include synthesis of academic texts, understanding underlying grammars of discourse in the disciplines, interpretation, criticism, syntopical synthesis, and the construction of argument (Bartholomae & Petrosky, 1986). Literature dialogue in higher education may also address the outer limits of knowledge and how this knowledge has been created, and the creation of further knowledge.

3. *Genres and expectations are different for precollege and college readers.* College reading programs may exclude "workplace," or "functional" reading strategies and materials. The precollege reader in high school, for example, may learn to distinguish between argument and comparison, or between scientific and non-scientific prose, but probably does not learn to distinguish among historical types of argument, or among varied methods for research in sociology, for example. The high school student may have to read a small amount of text as homework, but probably is not expected to read and integrate extended text with little or no instructional support as are college students (Carson, et. al., 1992). Emphasizing discipline-specific strategies for reading academic genres of considerable expectation separates precollege and college reading instruction.

4. *Motivation is different for precollege and college readers.* We don't sell a new concept of literacy to college readers. They've bought it. We may sell certain types of text, for example, philosophical text or texts explaining quantitative analysis, but few college-aged students are without understanding of the importance and uses of literacy in society. The college student's readiness for learning is inherent in his role as a college student, and he or she has already experienced demands for literacy (Kidd, 1966).

5. *Prior lexical, psychological, and cultural knowledge are different for precollege and college readers.* The mature individual is a storehouse of language and experiences which can help him to

comprehend text. Instructional strategies should attempt to tap this knowledge base, which may be richer than that of a precollege reader (Knowles, 1993).

6. *Family ties are different for precollege and college readers.* Much important recognition and research on family influence for young readers points to the potency of family effects for young readers (Maehr & Stallings, 1975; Marjoribanks, 1979). Family influence is different for the college reader, and by the time a student is 18, much of what a family has done for a student is indelible. In fact, where precollege reading focuses on the positive contributions of a family for the young reader, the college impact literature which concerns family ties reflects primarily negative family influence — the constraints of living with parents or children, or the great benefits of leaving the family behind to be immersed in college at a dormitory (Pascarella & Terenzini, 1991). In short, college reading practitioners do not usually look to family learning models to understand reading gains.

What Are the Implications for College Reading Instructors?

How does this delineation of the shared, exclusive, and adapted help inform new and prospective college reading teachers? Those preparing to teach reading at a postsecondary level do not need to concentrate at all on many areas which are important only for precollege instruction. College reading teachers don't need to study the features of preliteracy, literacy emergence, or initial language learning. They may comfortably expect to go beyond the teaching of sound-letter relationships. Rarely will college readers benefit from instruction of this nature. In particular, postsecondary reading instructors must avoid using basals and other reading materials designed for precollege readers. Neither the genre nor the focus will help the college reader.

College reading teachers also need not focus on functional and "utility" reading. Where a high school teacher could appropriately show students how to read a checkbook, a job application, a tax form, a bus schedule, or a newspaper advertisement, the parameters of academic genre dictate a classroom focus which is separate from these tasks. "Utility" in college reading is the direct academic use of literacy.

The teacher of college reading must pursue a classroom discourse to which adults respond. Since college students attend by choice and not by law, the postsecondary instructor can count on a more motivated group, yet a group which may demand quality and challenge. A college instructor may indeed be teaching students about the discipline and rules of college classes, but unlike the precollege teacher, generally works with students who are eager to participate if the game is clearly described and the content is substantive. Again, few college-aged students are without understanding of the importance and uses of literacy in society.

The college instructor has an obligation to make clear exactly which types of interpretations of text and which written assertions are acceptable in the academy. The college reading instructor clearly teaches for a distinct purpose: to foster comprehension of texts that fulfills academic expectations. College texts themselves are unlike those taught in precollege classrooms (i.e., social science texts, texts about scientific method, literacy criticism, written in formats particular to each of the fields in a liberal arts core curriculum). College reading requires more indepth processing and analysis.

These differences in the nature of the student, the context, and the genres of college literacy should guide college reading instruction as a field distinct from precollege fields in knowledge and style. While it is clear that precollege and college reading practice share similar features, the distinctions must be addressed.

References

Anderson, R. C., & Pearson, P. D. (1984). A schema-theoretic view of basic processes in reading comprehension. In P. D. Pearson (Ed.), *Handbook of reading research* (pp. 255–291). New York: Longman.

Au, K. (1980). Participation structures in a reading lesson with Hawaiian children. *Anthropology and Education Quarterly, 11,* 91–115.

Austin, R., & Gilford, M. (1993). Implementing a teaching excellence program for developmental educators. *Journal of College Reading and Learning, 26*(1), 11–15.

Barclay, K. D., & Thistlewaite, L. (1992). Reading specialists of the 90's: Who are they and what do they want? *Reading Research and Instruction, 31*(4), 87–96.

Bartholomae, D., & Petrosky, A. (1986). *Facts, artifacts and counterfacts.* New Jersey: Boynton/Cook Publishers.

Brown, J. (1989). Situated cognition and the culture of learning. *Educational Researcher, 18,* 32–42.

Brown, R. (1973). *A first language: The early stages.* Cambridge, MA: Harvard University Press.

Carson, J., Chase, N., Gibson, S., & Hargrove, M. (1992). Literacy demands of the undergraduate curriculum. *Reading Research and Instruction, 31*(4), 25–50.

Cazden, C. (1986). Classroom discourse. In M. Wittrock (Ed.), *Handbook of research on teaching.* New York: MacMillan Publishing Company.

Chall, J. S., Jacobs, D. A., & Baldwin, L. E. (1990). *The reading crisis: Why poor children fall behind.* Cambridge, MA: Harvard University Press.

Clark, E. (1973). How children describe time and order. In C. A. Ferguson & D. I. Slobin (Eds.), *Studies of child language development.* New York: Holt, Rinehart and Winston.

Coleman, J. S. (1966). Equality of educational opportunity survey. Washington, D.C.: National Center of Educational Statistics, United States Office of Education.

Covington, M., & Beery, R. (1976). *Self-worth and school learning.* New York: Holt, Rinehart and Winston.

Davidson, J., & Koppenhaver, D. (1993). *Adolescent literacy: What works and why.* New York: Garland Publishing.

Davis, D. (1995). Self-direction and adults in college reading and learning programs: An exploratory study of personal autonomy. Unpublished doctoral dissertation, Northern Illinois University.

Delpit, L. (1988). The silenced dialogue: Power and pedagogy in educating other people's children. *Harvard Educational Review, 58*(3), 280–298.

Deutsch, M. (1960). Minority group and class status as related to social and personality factors in scholastic achievement (Applied Anthropology, Monograph #2).

Doyle, W. (1986). Classroom organization and management. In M. Wittrock (Ed.), *Handbook of research on teaching* (pp. 392–431). New York: MacMillan Publishing Company.

Fairbanks, M. (1974). The effect of college reading improvement programs on academic achievement. In P. L. Nacke (Ed.), *Twenty-third yearbook of the national reading conference* (pp. 105–114). Washington, D.C.: The National Reading Conference.

Fasold, R., & Shuy, R. (1970). *Teaching standard English in the inner city.* Washington, D.C.: Center for Applied Linguistics.

Foucault, M. (1981). The order of discourse. In R. Young (Ed.), *Untying the text.* London, England: Routledge and Kegan Paul.

Freire, P., & Donaldo, M. (1986). *Literacy: Reading the word and the world.* South Hadley, MA: Bergin and Garvey.

Garcia, S. (1981). The training of learning assistance practitioners. In F. Christ & M. Coda-Messerle (Eds.), *Staff development for learning support systems: New directions for college learning assistance,* (Volume 4). Washington, D.C.: Jossey-Bass Inc., Publishers.

Haller, E., & Davis, S. (1981). Teacher perceptions, parental social status, and grouping for reading instruction. *Sociology of Education, 54,* 162–174.

Halliday, M. A. K., & Hasan, R. (1976). *Cohesion in English.* London: Longman.

Heath, S. (1983). *Ways with words.* Cambridge, MA: Cambridge University Press.

Heinrichs, A. S., & La Branche, S. P. (1986). Content analysis of 47 college learning skills textbooks. *Reading Research and Instruction, 25*(4), 277–287.

Hillocks, G. (1986). *Research on written composition* (NCRE/ERIC). Urbana, IL.

Hunt, B. C. (1975). Black dialect and third and fourth graders' performance on the Gray Oral Reading Test. *Reading Research Quarterly, 10,* 103–123.

Janiuk, D., & Shanahan, T. (1988). Applying adult literacy practices in primary grade instruction. *The Reading Teacher,* 880–886.

Kidd, J. (1966). *Implications of continuous learning.* Toronto, Canada: W. J. Gage.

Kiefer, K. (1991). Computers and teacher education in the 1990's and beyond. In G. Hawisher & C. Self (Eds.), *Evolving perspectives on computer and composition studies.* Urbana, IL: National Council of Teachers of English.

Knowles, M. (1973). *The adult learner: A neglected species* (2nd ed.). Houston, TX: Gulf Publishing Company.

Labov, W. (1972). Academic ignorance and black intelligence. In M. L. Maehr & W. M. Stallings (Eds.), *Culture, child, and school* (pp. 63–81). Monterey: Brooks/Cole Publishing.

Maehr, M. L., & Stallings, W. M. (1975). *Culture, child, and school.* Monterey: Brooks/Cole Publishing.

Marjoribanks, K. (1979). *Families and their learning environments.* London, England: Routledge and Kegan Paul.

Mason, J., & Au, K. (1990). *Reading instruction for today.* Glenview, IL: Scott, Foresman and Company.

Matthews, J. (1981). Becoming professional in college level learning assistance. In F. Christ & M. Coda-Messerle, (Eds.), *Staff development for learning support systems: New directions for college learning assistance, 4* (pp. 1–18). Washington, D.C.: Jossey-Bass Inc., Publishers.

Maxwell, M. (1981). An annual institute for directors and staff of college learning centers. In F. Christ & M. Coda-Messerle (Eds.), *Staff development for learning support systems. New directions for learning assistance, 4* (pp. 39–45). Washington, D.C.: Jossey-Bass Inc., Publishers.

McClusky, H. (1958). Central hypotheses about adult learning. Report of the Commission of the Professors of Adult Education. Washington, D.C.: Adult Education Association of the United States of America.

National Center for Educational Statistics. (1991, May). College-level remedial education in the fall of 1989. Macknight Black, O.E.R.I., Washington, D.C.

Newton, E. (1976). Andragogy: Understanding the adult as a learner. *The Reading Teacher, 30*(3), 361–363.

Nist, S., & Kirby, K. (1986). Teaching comprehension and study strategies through modeling and thinking aloud. *Reading Research and Instruction, 25,* 254–264.

Ogbu, J. (1987). Variability in minority school performance: A problem in search of an explanation. *Anthropology and Education Quarterly 18*(4), 312–334.

Ogbu, J. (1988). Literacy and schooling in subordinate cultures. In E. R. Kintgen, B. Kroil, & M. Rose (Eds.), *Perspectives on literacy* (pp. 227–242). Carbondale, IL: Southern Illinois University Press.

Palincsar, A., & Brown, A. (1984). Reciprocal teaching of comprehension-fostering and comprehension monitoring activities. *Cognition and instruction, 1,* 117–175.

Paris, S., & Winograd, P. (1991). How metacognition can promote academic learning and motivation. In B. F. Jones & L. Idol (Eds.), *Dimensions of thinking and cognitive instruction, 1.* Hillsdale, NJ: Earlbaum.

Pascarella, E., & Terenzini, P. T. (1991). *The impact of college on students.* San Francisco: Jossey-Bass Inc., Publishers.

Pichert, J. W., & Anderson, R. C. (1977). Taking different perspective on a story. *Journal of Educational Psychology, 69,* 309–315.

Quinn, K. (1992). Developing a college level reading/writing placement test. IAPLP Newsletter. Chicago, IL: IAPLP.

Raphael, T. (1982). Question-answering strategies for children. *The Reading Teacher, 36,* 186–190.

Rist, R. (1970). Student social class and teacher expectations: The self-fulfilling prophecy in ghetto education. *Harvard Educational Review, 40*(3), 411–451.

Rogers-Zegarra, N., & Singer, H. (1985). Anglo and Chicano comprehension of ethnic stories. In H. Singer & A. B. Ruddell (Eds.), *Theoretical Models and Processes of Reading* (pp. 611–617). Newark, NJ: IRA.

Rose, M. (1989). *Lives on the boundary.* New York: Penguin.

Rosenblatt, L. (1978). *The reader, the text, the poem: Transactional theory of the written word.* Carbondale, IL: Southern Illinois University Press.

Rosenthal, A. S., Baker, K., & Ginsburg, A. (1983). The effect of language background on achievement level and learning among elementary school students. *Sociology of Education, 56,* 157–169.

Rumelhart, D. (1985). Toward an interactive model of reading. In H. Singer & A. B. Ruddell (Eds.), *Theoretical models and processes of reading* (pp. 722–750). Newark, NJ: IRA.

Shanahan, T. (1984). The nature of the reading-writing relationship: An exploratory multivariate analysis. *The Journal of Educational Psychology.*

Shanahan, T. (1988, March). The reading-writing relationship: Seven instructional principles. *The Reading Teacher, 41*(7), 637–647.

Shanahan, T. (1990). *Reading and writing together: New perspectives for the classroom.* Norwood, MA: Christopher-Gordon Publishers, Inc.

Shaughnessy, M. (1977). *Errors and expectations: A guide for the teacher of basic writing.* New York: Oxford University Press.

Simpson, M. (1995). Talk throughs: A strategy for encouraging active learning across the content areas. *Journal of Reading, 38*(4), 296–304.

Simpson, M., & Nist, S. (1990). Textbook annotation: An effective and efficient student strategy for college students. *Journal of Reading, 34*(2), 122–131.

Spivey, N. (1990). Transforming texts: Constructive processes in reading and writing. *Written Communication, 7*(2), 256–287.

Stahl, N. A., Simpson, M. L., & Hayes, C. G. (1992). Ten recommendations from research for teaching high-risk college students. *Journal of Developmental Education, 16*(1), 2–10.

Steffensen, M. S., Joag-Dev, C., & Anderson, R. C. (1979). A cross-cultural perspective on reading comprehension. *Reading Research Quarterly, 15,* 10–29.

Stein, N. L., & Glenn, C. (1979). An analysis of story comprehension in elementary school children. In Freedle (Ed.), *New directions in discourse processing.* Norwood, Ablex.

Thorndike, R. L. (1973). *Reading comprehension education in fifteen countries.* New York: Wiley and Sons.

Warren-Leubecker, A., & Carter, B. W. (1988). Reading and growth in metalinguistic awareness: Relations to socioeconomic status and reading readiness skills. *Child Development, 59,* 728–742.

Weis, L. (1985). *Between two worlds: Black students in an urban community college.* Boston: Routledge and Kegan Paul.

Willis, P. (1977). *Learning to labor.* Westmead, England: Saxon House.

Exploring the Links between Critical Literacy and Developmental Reading

Mellinee Lesley

Through this article, we accompany Mellinee Lesley on the journey she undertook as she revamped a developmental reading program at her open-enrollment state university. The end result was a course driven by a critical literacy philosophy rather than a remedial model.

With critical literacy as her curricular goal, four basic tenets supported the author's instruction: Writing would be the primary tool to promote reading, thinking, and learning; Lives on the Boundary *and other selected readings would serve as class texts; basic skills in reading would be taught as minilessons through reading and responding to natural text; and themes for the course would emphasize translation into academic discourse, territories for reading, and literacy narratives. Specific goals for the students included reconstructing individuals' identities as readers and writers, developing writing as a tool for thinking, building critical and analytical reading competencies, and promoting metacognitive awareness. Both qualitative and quantitative evaluation of the course are provided.*

> Through all my experiences with people struggling to learn, the one thing that strikes me most is the ease with which we misperceive failed performance and the degree to which this misperception both reflects and reinforces the social order. Class and culture erect boundaries that hinder our vision . . . and encourage the designation of otherness, difference, deficiency. . . . [S]ome of our basic orientations toward the teaching and testing of literacy contribute to our inability to see. To truly educate in America, then, to reach the full sweep of our citizenry, we need to question received perception, shift continually from the standard lens. (Rose, 1989, p. 205)

Mike Rose speaks to my experiences both as a student and as a teacher. I think first of the ways I have failed students in my hurried evaluations of their literacy, but I realize that even my failures have taught me an immense amount as a teacher. To keep learning, I must keep assessing myself. I must have "failures" to be able to recognize and know success. I must misperceive in order to perceive. I like this passage because it reminds me to think differently about literacy, how I teach it, and how to recognize it in its most nascent forms.

The story recorded here is one of students' successful formulation of literacy as measured in test scores, reading interest inventories, and written artifacts. It's also one of success for me as a teacher, taking a huge risk to revamp an entire developmental reading program for my university. It took a great deal of risk to try to sell a pedagogy of critical literacy to instructors and graduate assistants with minimal amounts of training in literacy in general and absolutely no comprehension of constructivist approaches to literacy (Atwell, 1998; Johnston, 1992;

Noguchi, 1991) let alone any understanding of the domain of critical literacy (Bee, 1993; Brady, 1995; Ellsworth, 1992; Freire, 1995; Giroux, 1993; Lankshear & McLaren, 1993; Shor, 1996).

The other risk occurred in the classroom with my own students. Attempting to evoke a pedagogy of questions (Freire, 1995), bring students out of "intellectual Siberia" (Shor, 1996), and deal with resistance (Bigelow, 1990; Ellsworth, 1992; Lather, 1992) was not easy. In some ways these actions paralleled the professional development work I undertook with the other instructors and graduate assistants. Unlike some of the other instructors, my students were able to navigate the process of critical literacy and come to a measured level of "conscientization" (Freire, 1995), working through false consciousness (Lather, 1992) and resistance (Ellsworth, 1992; Lather, 1992) to obtain a new degree of control over their literacy development, histories, and futures. To say the least, learning more about the possibilities in enacting critical literacy with a "remediated" population of students was an important experience for me as a teacher.

Local and National Trends in Developmental Studies

The current status of basic skills, "remediated" courses in English, reading, and mathematics has reached a critical juncture in the history of developmental studies programs in higher education across the U.S. Every year enrollment in such noncredit courses increases along with student attrition and academic failure rates (The Institute for Higher Education Policy, 1998). This increase in remedial student population is concomitant with an overall increase in the number of students attending college, thanks to open enrollment admission standards (The Institute for Higher Education Policy, 1998).

While attention to developmental studies programs tends to be nonexistent in institutions of higher education, remediation constitutes a core function of these programs (Brittain, 1982; The Institute for Higher Education Policy, 1998). A 1995 survey conducted by the National Center for Education Statistics (NCES) found that 78 percent of higher education institutions offered at least one remedial reading, writing, or mathematics course. All too often, pedagogy in developmental studies courses is "hit or miss" with little, if any, oversight of the curriculum and staff responsible for teaching these courses. In such courses, our most academically at-risk students are subjected to part-time adjunct instructors and teaching assistants with very little institutional efficacy or permanency. Another concern with developmental studies courses lies with the fact that there are no national criteria to determine placement in such courses. In other words, there are no standards for what constitutes "college-level" work and consequently what constitutes remedial college work. This phenomenon peculiar to developmental studies further alienates these courses from the intellectual rigor that is heralded in the academy proper.

At my university, we offer developmental courses in mathematics, English, and reading to provide students with prerequisite skills for entry into college-level coursework. From the fall 1994 semester to the fall 1998 semester, the average percentage of first-year students enrolled in English 100 was 49.3 percent. In the same period, the average percentage of first-year students in Reading 100 was 27.5 percent. Despite the numbers of students enrolling in developmental studies courses, the status of these courses has remained low. The developmental reading course, for instance, had been moved from the Reading Education program to administration by Student Academic Services in the early 1980s. Locating Reading 100 in a service program heightened the nonacademic reputation of the course. With this shift in administrative placement, Reading 100 suffered from little administrative oversight and no curricular attention. As a result of my preliminary research on the developmental reading program a year prior to conducting this study, Reading 100 was returned to the oversight of the Reading Education Program in the Department of Curriculum and Instruction. This simple yet important shift signaled the transition of this course from marginalized to a status of more import, recognizing the relationship of this course to subsequent credit courses offered in the institution.

In an effort to ameliorate the current status of developmental studies courses, I was appointed to chair a committee to study the problems afflicting these courses. While the committee addressed many issues related to the problems troubling our developmental studies courses, the greatest concern was over the pedagogy of these courses. I was appointed as the Coordinator for Reading 100 and permitted to teach one section of the class during the fall 1999 semester.

Prior to my appointment as the coordinator, Reading 100 consisted of weekly vocabulary drills, basic comprehension of brief texts (paragraphs), and eye exercises to increase students' reading rates (speed reading). The course concluded with a full-blown research paper. The course did not ask students to do any reading of the sort that would be required of them in a university-level academic setting. Furthermore, Reading 100 was predicated on a restrictive philosophy of remediation that taught basic skills with repetitive drills. Another glaring problem with the design of this course was the fact that the curriculum followed an illogical practice of teaching lower level drill activities and then expecting students to write a research paper. Little emphasis was placed on reading "real" texts or the interconnectedness of reading and writing, and certainly no attempt was made at reflexive practice or evoking a pedagogy of critical literacy. These identified weaknesses in the pedagogy of Reading 100 led to my research and restructuring of the course to reflect constructivist notions of literacy as well as a pedagogy of critical literacy.

Collecting the Data

Broadly stated, the objective for this research was to design an alternative pedagogy for a developmental studies reading course offered at an open enrollment state university. In an attempt to foster the successful literacy acquisition required to survive in a university setting, I examined the effects of enacting a critical literacy pedagogy within the course. The curriculum developed in this study emphasizes the interrelatedness of processes of reading and writing as well as critical reading and writing within an academic discourse community. Consequently, the pedagogy presented in the new course incorporated research from the domains of critical literacy, adult literacy, emergent literacy, and developmental studies in order to shed light on developmental reading programs in higher education.

The following research questions guided my study:

1. What happens when students enrolled in a basic skills reading course experience critical literacy (reading and writing conscientization) as an entrance into academic modes of discourse?

2. To what extent do the students enrolled in this course construct or begin to construct themselves as readers and writers through the means of critical reflection and critical literacy pedagogy?

To answer these questions I first had to design a literacy program where critical literacy was a curricular goal. Consequently, I began by restructuring the course around the following tenets that I would require of all Reading 100 instructors:

- Writing will be used primarily as a tool for strengthening processes of reading/thinking/learning.

- Texts will consist of Mike Rose's (1989) book *Lives on the Boundary,* readings chosen from the Freshman Seminar Reader, and selections chosen by the instructor.

- "Basic skills" in reading (e.g., summarizing, synthesizing, developing inference, developing vocabulary) will be embedded in the processes of reading "real" texts and explicitly taught as minilessons that are to be applied to immediate experiences with reading and responding to reading.

- Themes for the course will emphasize translation into academic modes of discourse (especially critical and analytical reading), "territories" for reading (Atwell, 1998) (how people read or learn to read in authentic venues), and literacy narratives.

Goals for the students included the following:

- Reconstruct their identities as readers and writers,

- Develop fluency in using writing as a tool for thinking,

- Develop skills to foster critical and analytical reading ability, and

- Develop metacognitive awareness about their reading processes.

With these tenets and goals, I grounded the course in a constructivist philosophy (Vygotsky, 1978). Through the texts chosen for the course, the reflective assignments, and the first student goal, I also set the stage for establishing a pedagogy of critical literacy in the course.

I collected data through qualitative interpretive (Erickson, 1986) methods. However, I also collected quantitative data from norm-referenced test scores and surveys. My stance was primarily that of a teacher-researcher (Cochran-Smith & Lytle, 1993, 1999). There were 22 students enrolled in my course. As recent graduates from high school, all of the students in the course could be categorized as "traditional" students. Fourteen of the students were female, and eight were male. Eight of the students were Hispanic, two were African American, and one was Native American.

Data sources for the study consisted of pre- and poststudy Nelson-Denny Test scores, interest inventories, and responses to literature; writing samples; transcripts from focus group interviews and class discussions; archives of student writing; and a reflective journal of my experiences as a teacher. I analyzed each source of qualitative data through linguistic coding according to Fairclough's (1995) work on critical discourse analysis and Vine and Faust's (1993) work on situated reading. With these tools for analysis, I looked specifically for trends in students' reflection and self-ascribed literacy labels. I also coded the data for personal connections students were making in reading, intertextual connections in their reading and writing, and instances of critical observations about developmental studies. Through all of this analysis, I was looking for trends in students' abilities to read the texts analytically as well as position themselves as readers in the broader contexts for literacy the institution entails (e.g., developmental studies). As revealing as the qualitative data was, the most compelling data were the increases made in students' reading scores on the Nelson-Denny Test. (See Table 1.)

Developmental Reading

Focusing as it does on a lack of vocabulary and comprehension skills, research on developmental reading methods is almost exclusively predicated on a deficit model of learning. Developmental reading courses are similarly constructed as "college success" courses with a

Table 1. Nelson-Denny Reading Test Results

Year	Section number	Beginning*	Ending*
Fall 1998	104	11.5	10.5
Fall 1998	101	9.0	8.4
Fall 1998	102	8.6	9.1
Fall 1998	103	10.9	9.9
Fall 1999	101	9.1	9.8
Fall 1999	102	9.9	12.0
Fall 1999	103	10.0	10.9
Fall 1999	104	8.8	9.1
Fall 1999	105	9.1	10.2

*Average grade equivalency as scored on the Nelson-Denny Reading Test

great deal of emphasis placed on study skills and content area reading strategies (Barksdale-Ladd & Rose, 1997). Nearly two decades ago, Brittain (1982) found that college reading instruction invariably fell into one of the following two categories: (a) courses where reading was constructed as a series of study skills, and (b) courses where reading was constructed in relation to a combined content area course. While Laine, Laine, and Bullock (1999) found that successful developmental reading instruction is contingent upon innovative teaching and learning strategies, little research to date has been conducted on evoking critical literacy pedagogy in either of Brittain's two categories within the framework of a developmental reading course (see McFarland, Dowdey, & Davis, 1999 for an exception). This study fills a gap in the research on developmental reading programs, where basic skills in reading are reconceptualized through the lens of critical literacy.

In my study, basic skills of reading (e.g., comprehension, vocabulary development, inference, synthesis) were subsumed into a larger framework of critical literacy. Critical literacy is defined by researchers such as Lankshear and McLaren (1993), Giroux (1993), Bee (1993), Brady (1994), and others as literacy that begins with a rising consciousness of not merely the functionality of print but also the power of language to both silence and give voice to instances of oppression in issues of socially determined disparities. In this vein of consciousness, Paulo Freire (1995) wrote that students first had to read the world before they could read the word. Emergent literacy research (Avery, 1993; Calkins, 1994; Cooper, 1993; Morrow, 1997) espouses a similar philosophy, that children read their environment long before they begin to decode print. In other words, literacy at all levels always begins with the impetus of the context for reading, writing, and speaking. The impetus of the context for students in developmental reading courses exists within a system of social stratification. The construction of developmental studies courses by the larger academic community as subacademic courses teaching subacademic skills creates a relevant context for developmental studies students to delve into issues of power and language from a personal, experiential vantage point.

Students in basic skills courses need to read the world of the academy before they can read and write for an academic community. Critical pedagogues (e.g., Shor, 1996) would argue that we cannot successfully invite students into the world of academic reading by drilling them in a series of disconnected subskills in literacy. Rather, we must give them complete, contextualized reading and writing experiences first and then work on skills through student-driven assessment and instruction. Similarly, we must redefine the concept of "basic skills" in reading through the stance of critical literacy. While this is a seemingly compelling argument in favor of critical literacy in a developmental reading course, fully realizing critical literacy in such a context is problematic. The definition and experience of critical literacy is so utterly dependent upon the students' relationships with the texts of their lives that the story of critical literacy within the population of "remedial" students is always, necessarily, delicately contingent upon these relationships.

In the section of Reading 100 that I taught, critical literacy began with a pedagogy of questions (Freire, 1995) pertaining to discussions surrounding the nature of a developmental studies course in reading. These initial dialogues were pivotal in establishing a culture conducive to critical literacy. The dialogues were difficult for me as a teacher because some students expressed open hostility to being placed in the course based on an arbitrary score on the ACT test, receiving no credit toward graduation, and being required to pay for it.

Rose's (1989) account of remediation, tracking, and the academy in *Lives on the Boundary* served as the core text for the course. The text further fueled class discussions about the perceived unfair placement of students into the course. From this text, students read, wrote, and talked about the larger system of developmental studies across the U.S. as well as their own experiences. The assignments I gave students to keep a dialogue journal, write in-class reflective essays, compile a reader's resource notebook, and write a literacy narrative facilitated their learning and growth from skill development to critical reflection and questioning.

Bound by university guidelines and expectations for developmental studies coursework, I wasn't able to negotiate course assignments to the extent that Shor (1996) did. I did, however, seek to provide assignments that were student-driven. The assignments for the class began with an in-class dialogue journal. This journal consisted of students first responding to class readings and discussions and then responding to their classmates' responses. I also participated in this weekly activity. I included this assignment as a mechanism to give each student a chance to voice ideas and receive feedback on these ideas. The journals also gave students less structured opportunities for writing practice. Over time, students began to generate more in-depth responses and questions with their audience in mind. The following exchange from a dialogue journal exemplifies the beginning of student reflection on their educational experiences.

Student 1: If I was designing a reading developmental class I would do pretty much the same things that we are doing in here but I would have prepared students for things like this in earlier grades so they wouldn't have to take these courses in college. I think reading should be taught by understanding what you are reading along with how to read a certain word.

Student 2: I agree they should prepare students in earlier grades and maybe they wouldn't fall behind in college. Understanding what you read might make the reading more interesting.

Mellinee: What happened in your earlier school experiences that led to your having to take a developmental studies course in reading? What were you not taught?

Student 1: I don't think that there really is anything that I haven't learned, that maybe I should've learned. Maybe I don't comprehend all the time but I don't think that it is to the point where I should have to take a basic reading class in college, but that's what the test proved. (Dialogue journal, September, 1999)

In addition to modeling writing and responding for my students, I was also participating in learning through joining this activity.

Students also kept a reader's resource notebook. The purpose of this assignment was for students to create an archive to assist them in their reading and literacy skills. The notebook provided students with an opportunity to personalize skill aspects of their learning in a contextualized and systematic fashion. The reader's resource notebook was a compilation of vocabulary encountered in course readings, notes from class discussions on the readings, and reading strategies that worked for the student. I presented this assignment largely as an investigative tool for students to explore the mechanics of their literacy development. As such, it served the purposes of both skill exploration and metacognitive awareness development.

Every class period, we concluded with a summary of what we did on one side of an index card and what we learned on the other side. These cards not only helped students distill key ideas and recall class events, but also served as data for me. With the cards, my students were able to give me continual and instant feedback on each class. I was also able to monitor my students' literacy development (e.g., questioning, reflection, analysis, rising consciousness) through their observations of the class. The following are examples of responses to one class:

What did we do?

- Today we read pp. 111–114 and got into groups and discussed what went on and how Mike Rose is dealing with what is going on. We responded in our journals about our literacy lessons.
- We read out of *Lives on the Boundary* and David gave his presentation on a soccer player.
- Article presentation; went over Monday dialogue journals; read 111–114 in *Lives on the Boundary,* discussion in small groups about what we read; Nov. 1 class feedback.
- Discussed our journal topic, heard David's presentation. Read pgs. 111–114, got in small groups.
- We did dialogue journals and students volunteered to read from pg. 111–114 in *Lives on the Boundary.* We read 11/1/99 What did we do/ What did we learn and I explained the info I got from it.

What did we learn?

- I learned how Mike Rose feels about students. I learned what other students are learning about Mike Rose.
- I learned what *tracking, resistance,* and *remediation* meant.
- Mike Rose really cares about the kids.
- What I learned was that the children Mike Rose taught live in very harsh environments.
- How others felt about *Lives on the Boundary,* the literacy words *tracking, resistance,* and *remediation.*
- Everybody will have trouble in some subject, but you can't let it take you down. Never give up.
- We learned different people's ideas in their journal and what Mike Rose's students' lives are like.
- I learned what Dr. Lesley does with these cards. I realized that remediation will help in the long run.

(Class archive, November 3, 1999)

From these statements, I could tell how many of my students were developing reading skills such as inference (e.g., how Mike Rose *really* felt about his students), empathy (e.g., how my students felt about the students in the book), and critical analysis (e.g., how concepts of tracking, remediation, and resistance figured into the book).

Another assignment in the course consisted of in-class reader response essays written about excerpts from *Lives on the Boundary*. On one occasion toward the end of the semester, I asked students to revise essays written in the previous class to include five vocabulary words from their reader's resource notebooks. I used this revision request to demonstrate for the students Noguchi's (1991) notion of the ways writing signifies class distinctions. By incorporating and applying the academic vocabulary students were encountering in their writing, they were able to begin to emulate the discourse patterns of the academy. This assignment demonstrated the students' growing control of academic discourse. By couching the assignment in terms of social class markers in discourse, I was attempting to move students toward a critical literacy insight on the ways language intertwines with societal power.

The final assignment was to write a literacy narrative (Soliday, 1994) of the story of how students acquired literacy. Through this assignment students noted social and emotional "disconnects" in their education and their lives at times when they were supposed to be developing literacy. For instance, one student wrote the following:

> Reading out loud in front of the class was always a challenge for me. My problem was that I would get nervous because I wouldn't want to mess up in front of my friends. But, of course I would get really nervous and mess up or I couldn't pronounce a word correctly. Sometimes the other students would giggle when I would read or make fun of me. So, therefore, I didn't have a strong self-confidence and I wouldn't push myself to do better because I thought I couldn't be as smart as them. (December, 1999)

Another student wrote about similar disconnects in his literacy narrative:

> From first grade to the fifth grade it got harder and easier at the same time if that makes sense. Reading was the easy part; it was the whole English part that through me off. I understood what a noun and a verb was but I didn't know how to use them. So I was screwed so to speak. Teachers at my elementary school had other things to worry about or they just didn't care. A teacher later on in the sixth grade stumbled across my disability and I was placed in a chapter one class where I was basically taught everything over again. To my disbelief it help. I was teased and picked on for being in the class. The teasing took a toll on my self-esteem. I felt really small and stupid and that caused me to drop the whole idea of reading except in school. My reading skill dropped once again and I didn't care. (December, 1999)

One of the most powerful literacy narratives was written by a student who through our discussions of expanding literacy beyond written texts, realized her literacy was disconnected at home long before she learned to decode print. This student wrote:

As I was growing up I learn many ways of reading. I learn how to read my father's attitude, I learn to read books from school and on my own, I learn to take care of my younger brothers and sister by reading my mother, I also read feeling and objects to write my poetry.

Since I can remember my father has had a drinking problem. I always knew what to do and how to act after reading him for a few years. Some days my dad would come home smelling weird and had blood shot eyes. I never understood what that was all about, I just knew he was going to be a different person from hours before. At first I would see that my dad's walk was weak and he wore a wicked smile. I would walk by him to see if he had that strong bitter smell on him. Once I smelled that ugly odor I had to think fast, I had to think of ways to tell my mom without him knowing. By reading his actions I learn to act fast and think quickly. As I watched him speak to my mother his words were mixed, his voice was very sharp and deep. Each time he would start talking, he would talk about all the happy and good times they had. Then he moves on to all the bad things that happen between them, after that he gets very angry and he would take his anger out on my mother. As I was reading him I knew that I had to do something once he started to raise his voice. (December, 1999)

These examples of students' writing and reflection about their literacy development mark the beginning of a journey of self-awareness within a larger social and academic structure facilitated by critical literacy. My approach to critical literacy was to bring critical reflection on constructions of literacy into the course content. The themes of the course initiated from this point as we explored concepts of being present, place, silence, play, teachers, community, justice, and transformation. We found that what's transformative for one student within a critical literacy context may not be for the next. Also, simply approaching literacy in relationship to critical reflection about the status of language and placement of courses within a university leads to critical literacy.

Critical Literacy Fosters Academic Success

I want to conclude with some of the compelling statistics collected on the pre- and poststudy inventories. In each of these measures, students made significant gains, and students' attitudes toward reading and practices with reading improved. (Please see Figures 1–4 for a breakdown of these results.) Perhaps even more impressive was the increase in average reading level of students in all sections of Reading 100. In previous years, students' reading scores had actually decreased upon completion of the course. The section I taught, with an explicit focus on critical literacy (section 102), made the most dramatic gains — moving from an average ninth-grade reading level equivalency to a twelfth-grade equivalency. (Please see Table 1.)

Figure 1. How many books do you own?

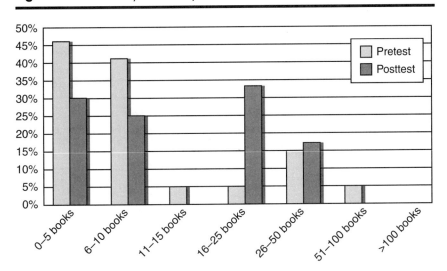

Figure 2. How many books have you read in the last four months?

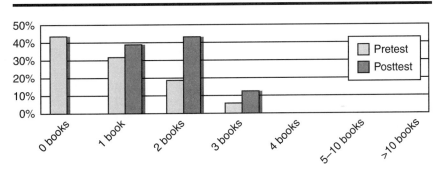

Figure 3. How often do you read for pleasure?

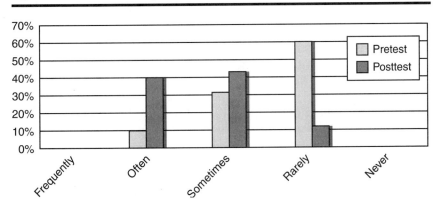

Figure 4. How often do you read for school purposes?

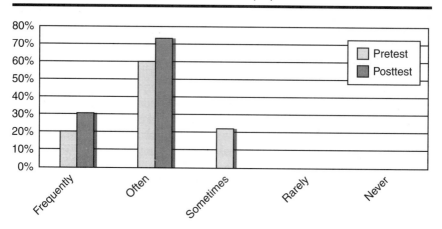

The instructors for the other sections followed some of the assignments for the course and did not complete Rose's *Lives on the Boundary* with their classes. These instructors similarly did not attempt a pedagogy of critical literacy in their sections. The results support the previously cited research in favor of critical literacy. If we can learn anything from this study it's the fact that it's critical for students enrolled in developmental reading courses to experience the level of reading — reflection and analysis — that critical literacy fosters.

Critical literacy is a problematic philosophy to translate into practice (Ellsworth, 1992; Lesley, 1997). Yet the ideals of equity that shape critical literacy make the philosophy particularly compelling for developmental course work. This research suggests that teaching reading as a complex analysis even to "remediated" populations of students yields positive gains in students' literacy skills. The study also highlights the fact that critical literacy occurs in practice as a process. In effect, critical literacy is its own content area for students to master before they can enact a pedagogy of action. Introducing critical literacy to "developmental" readers begins students' successful introduction to academia where complex questions and analysis of answers drive inquiry in every discipline. If "remedial" students are to survive in the world of the academy, they cannot do so through lower level drill practice. They must learn to read analytically, beginning with their own circumstances of tracking, social stratification, and marginalization.

From this experience, I have come to believe that critical literacy fosters critical questioning and thinking and thus enhances students' comprehension skills in reading. Certainly, this study warrants further longitudinal investigation into the potential of academic success that critical literacy pedagogy fosters for developmental students. Finally, my attempt in this study to enact critical literacy hinged on my ability to create an environment where students could develop their own understanding of the concepts of critical reading and writing in the academy. Eminent purposes for literacy compel us all to engage more deeply.

References

Atwell, N. (1998). *In the middle. New understandings about writing, reading, and learning.* Portsmouth, NH: Heinemann.

Avery, C. (1993). *And with a light touch: Learning about reading, writing, and teaching with first graders.* Portsmouth, NH: Heinemann.

Barksdale-Ladd, M., & Rose, M. (1997). Qualitative assessments in developmental reading. *Journal of College Reading and Learning, 28*(1), 34–55.

Bee, B. (1993). Critical literacy and the politics of gender. In C. Lankshear & P. McLaren (Eds.), *Critical literacy: Politics, praxis, and the postmodern.* Albany, NY: State University of New York Press.

Bigelow, W. (1990). Inside the classroom: Social vision and critical pedagogy, *Teachers College Record, 91,* 437–448.

Brady, J. (1995). *Schooling young children: A feminist pedagogy for liberatory learning.* Albany, NY: State University of New York Press.

Brittain, M. (1982). *Developmental and remedial reading instruction for college students.* Paper presented at the 9th World Congress on Reading, Dublin, Ireland.

Calkins, L. (1994). *The art of teaching writing.* Portsmouth, NH: Heinemann.

Cochran-Smith, M., & Lytle, S. (1993). *Inside/outside: Teacher research and knowledge.* New York: Teachers College Press.

Cochran-Smith, M., & Lytle, S. (1999). The teacher research movement: A decade later. *Educational Researcher, 28,* 15–25.

Cooper, P. (1993). *When stories come to school.* New York: Teachers and Writers Collaborative.

Ellsworth, E. (1992). Why doesn't this feel empowering? Working through the repressive myths of critical pedagogy. In C. Luke & J. Gore (Eds.), *Feminisms and critical pedagogy* (pp. 90–119). New York: Routledge.

Erickson, F. (1986). Qualitative methods in research on teaching. In M. C. Wittrock (Ed.), *Handbook of research on teaching* (3rd ed., pp. 119–161). New York: Macmillan.

Fairclough, N. (1995). *Critical discourse analysis: The critical study of language.* New York: Longman.

Freire, P. (1995). *Pedagogy of hope: Reliving Pedagogy of the Oppressed.* New York: Continuum.

Giroux, H. (1993). Literacy and the politics of difference. In C. Lankshear & P. McLaren (Eds.), *Critical literacy: Politics, praxis, and the postmodern* (pp. 367–377). Albany, NY: State University of New York Press.

The Institute for Higher Education Policy. (1998, December). *College remediation: What it is, what it costs, what's at stake.* Washington, DC: Author.

Johnston, P. (1992). *Constructive evaluation of literate activity.* New York: Longman.

Laine, M., Laine, C., & Bullock, T. (1999). Developmental reading in the United States: One decade later. *Research and Teaching in Developmental Education, 15*(2), 5–17.

Lankshear, C., & McLaren, P. (1993). *Critical literacy: Politics, praxis, and the postmodern.* Albany, NY: State University of New York Press.

Lather, P. (1992). Critical frames in educational research: Feminist and poststructural perspectives. *Theory Into Practice, 35*(2), 70–71.

Lesley, M. (1997). The difficult dance of critical literacy. *Journal of Adolescent & Adult Literacy, 40,* 420–424.

McFarland, K. P., Dowdey, D., & Davis, K. (1999). *A search for nontraditional pedagogies in teaching developmental reading and writing.* (ERIC Document Reproduction Service No. ED 432 784)

Morrow, L. M. (1997). *Literacy development in the early years: Helping children read and write.* Boston: Allyn & Bacon.

Noguchi, R. (1991). *Grammar and the teaching of writing: Limits and possibilities.* Urbana, IL: National Council of Teachers of English.

Rose, M. (1989). *Lives on the boundary.* New York: The Free Press.

Shor, I. (1996). *When students have power: Negotiating authority in a critical pedagogy.* Chicago: University of Chicago Press.

Soliday, M. (1994). Translating self and difference through literacy narratives. *College English, 56,* 511–526.

Vine, H., & Faust, M. (1993). *Situating readers: Students making meaning of literature.* Urbana, IL: National Council of Teachers of English.

Vygotsky, L. S. (1978). *Mind in society.* Cambridge, MA: MIT Press.

An Alternative Paradigm for College Reading and Study Skills Courses

Jim Reynolds and Stuart C. Werner

In this article, Jim Reynolds and Stuart Werner posit that two very different paradigms or philosophical approaches underpin college reading and learning skills programs. They describe the first paradigm as a "one size fits all" approach. The other — favored by the authors — provides a more individualized orientation that is learner centered and focuses on personal learning styles.

The authors go on to present a developmental model for the learner-centered paradigm. This design that is presented leads college students to (1) discover their personal learning style; (2) evaluate the pros and cons of their approaches to reading, writing, and learning; and (3) try out, evaluate, and choose alternate strategies for particular learning tasks. In the course of their presentation, Reynolds and Werner make a strong case for empowering students to take charge of their learning.

The improvement of college students' reading and study skills is a widespread concern for developmental educators, counselors, and college administrators in the U.S. There is a long, well documented history of trying to help new college students who are poorly prepared in academic content areas or who have weak reading skills and learning strategies (Brier, 1984; Mickler & Chapel, 1989; Wyatt, 1992).

The development of effective reading skills and study strategies has often been viewed as a remedial process that should focus only on at-risk or underprepared students. Our view is that most college students would benefit from programs designed to develop stronger learning skills and strategies.

The main objective of this article is to review two very different paradigms or philosophical approaches used to support college reading and study skill programs. One paradigm might be described simply as "one size fits all." We do not favor it because it assumes there are tried and true ways to study and that all learners should conform to them.

We support an alternative paradigm that is more learner centered, where individuals are allowed to develop skills and strategies in their own way and style. A core concept in the learner centered paradigm is that individuals develop personal ways of learning which can be called their learning style characteristics. This pattern of personality and environmental factors related to how one learns is called "learning style."

Another objective of this article is to outline a developmental model that supports the learner centered paradigm. The model is designed for learners to (a) recognize their unique pattern of learning style characteristics, (b) examine strengths and weaknesses in their current reading/writing skills and learning strategies, and (c) explore, evaluate, and select alternate learning skills and strategies where needed.

Learning Skills and Strategies

The literature on learning and studying uses terms which, at times, are defined differently. Terms such as skills, habits, tactics, techniques, activities, and methods are frequently used synonymously with other terms such as strategies, plans, behaviors, or sequences. Since we believe the terminology associated with the concept of learning and studying can be confusing, we want to define how we are using the terms "learning skills and strategies."

We use the terms learning skills and strategies to describe a wide range of ways in which people approach the learning process. Learning skills are defined here as components of a learning strategy. For example, several learning skills, including reading, writing, and finding and organizing information, compose the learning strategy for producing a research paper.

We use the term learning strategy to describe a process of selecting and organizing one's skills. A learning strategy may be ineffective either because the skills needed are weak or their organization is not appropriate. For example, a learner's strategy for producing a research paper can be impaired by weak reading comprehension, ineffective writing skills, poor research skills, or lack of organizational skills.

One-Size-Fits-All View

Cross (1976) questioned the assumption that one method or methods could be found that would assist *all* learners. When Anderson and Armbruster (1984) reviewed research on "studying" covering more than 50 years, they found inconsistent results about what works well. They concluded that almost any learning skill or strategy can be effective when used in the right way and under the right conditions, Dworkin and Dworkin (1988) later agreed that the search for a universal learning strategy has not been successful and probably will not be in the future. These findings bring into question the usefulness of the one-size-fits-all view.

In higher educational environments, the development of reading skills and study strategies has been associated with study skill books, workshops, and courses that focus on teaching reading skills and study strategies. These study skills books or workshops tend to focus on just one method for learners to use. A good example would be a book or workshop presenting the SQ3R reading strategy for textbooks (S=Survey, Q=Question, R=Read, R=Recite, and R=Review). This stepwise reading strategy has become very popular since it was originally outlined by Francis P. Robinson 50 years ago. Robinson's study skills book *Effective Study* was last published in 1970, but SQ3R's five steps live on (in teaching if not in student use).

Deese and Deese (1979) have suggested all learners can improve with the SQ3R reading strategy. Other authors recommend that SQ3R be made shorter by just doing the 3Rs (Orlando, 1980) or made more complex by adding a step to make it SQ4R (Walter & Siebert, 1990). We are not suggesting the SQ3R reading model or its variations are ineffective. Rather, our concern is that any one strategy might be viewed as best for all learners.

Caverly and Orlando (in Flippo & Caverly, 1991) reviewed the empirical literature that analyzed the SQ3R reading strategy. Of the 25 studies reviewed, less than half reported improvement while using SQ3R. Their general conclusion was "that most study strategies are effective, but no one study strategy is appropriate for all students in all study situations" (p. 155), echoing Anderson and Armbruster's (1984) conclusion.

The assumption that one study strategy will work for all learners overlooks learner differences. For example, SQ3R may not be effective for a visual learner who needs or prefers activities that involve displaying the material being learned, such as drawing pictures or maps of textbook material (Jones, Pierce, & Hunter, 1989). Although this technique may not be appropriate for all learners, the technique of "concept" or "mind" mapping may be useful for visual learners.

How-to-study books often advocate a one-size-fits-all approach. Hettich (1992) and Pauk (1989) encourage reading in a quiet environment, while in reality some learners need and prefer background music or sound when they read or study (Dunn & Dunn, 1993). Similarly, cooperative learning may be effective for many learners but may not be the answer for everyone. The new U.S. federal educational reform initiative called Tech Prep also seems to be blinded by the one-size-fits-all philosophy. In an article on Tech Prep and applied academics, Atkinson, Lunsford, and Hollingsworth (1993) write that "research on learning styles identifies the applied approach as appropriate for *all* students" (p. 10). Yet the research literature just does not support the one-size-fits-all view.

Learner Centered Paradigm

The learner centered approach to developing learning skills and strategies recognizes each individual's ability to grow in one's own way and style. In particular, Rogers (1969) emphasized that trust enabled individual learners to develop their learning potential and he encouraged learners to choose both the way and direction for their own learning. The focus on the needs of individual learners is important today because of the diverse student population in American colleges (McKeachie, 1988). Diverse students are enrolled in community colleges, where the literature has supported the need for instructional approaches to be more student centered (Cross, 1981; Deegan, 1985).

Smith (1983) described a sequence that might be viewed as a learner centered model for developing learning skills and strategies. First, learners need to identify areas in need of improvement, for example, improving one's strategy in reading textbooks. Next, the learner should examine his or her current way of reading a text, such as underlining, highlighting, or writing notes in the book. Subsequently, the learner investigates alternate ways of reading text. In this case, the learner may discover SQ3R or one of its many variations.

Although this sequence encourages learners to identify and select new or different strategies, a missing element is the need for each learner to better understand the pattern of her or his learning style characteristics and subsequently exert more control over the learning process. Insights into learning style characteristics can be used to develop more effective skills and strategies for all learners (Griggs, 1990).

The concept of learning style is associated with sensory preferences individuals have in their learning. For example, a learner's preference for the visual (seeing) mode over the auditory (hearing) mode is an example of a preferred learning style. The preference for visual stimulation suggests that the learner may need to study and learn by techniques that require seeing the material. Visual learners may prefer information presented by way of graphs, charts, and drawings, as well as print. The area of perceptual preferences (visual, auditory, tactile, etc.) is only one of several categories of learning style characteristics.

Although differing definitions have been advanced, the importance of the concept of individual learning styles with variable characteristics is recognized by many writers and researchers (Claxton & Murrell,

1987; James & Galbraith, 1985; Keefe, 1987; Kolb, 1984; McCarthy, 1990; Smith, 1982). Most experts would agree that the concept of learning style should be viewed as multidimensional. A multidimensional conceptual model of one's unique pattern of learning style characteristics encompasses, but is not limited to, the six categories of perceptual preference, physical environment, social environment, cognitive style, time of day, and motivation. Similar categories and characteristics can be found in the Dunn model (Productivity Environmental Preference Survey: PEPS Manual, 1982) and also in the Hill (1976) model of "cognitive mapping."

We do not suggest that the six categories listed are the only categories of learning style characteristics, nor do each of the six categories contain the same number of elements. For example, the category of "cognitive style" has a number of different models (e.g., Hill, 1976; Kolb, 1984; Witkin & Goodenough, 1981), and Keefe (1987) summarized 12 different cognitive styles.

The six categories presented here were selected because they are prominent in the research literature and cover areas that we have identified as major in learning styles. In our view, a learner centered philosophy is what is needed. This increased awareness of individual learning style preferences may be useful for all learners, regardless of their academic achievement or lack thereof.

A Three Stage Developmental Model

The second objective of this article is to present a three stage model to support the new learner centered paradigm. This three stage model asks learners to investigate their unique learning style characteristics, identify ineffective methods, and pursue alternate learning skills or strategies. This model is grounded in the humanistic learning theories of Rogers (1969, 1980) and Maslow (1991) and thereby "trusts" each learner (Rogers, 1980) to identify personal learning style characteristics and to take responsibility to select alternate ways to learn.

In Maslow (1991), a horticultural metaphor is used to describe a learner centered model for counseling and education. Maslow writes "that we try to make a rose into a good rose, rather than seek to change roses into lilies" (p. 104). This metaphor emphasizes our concern that people should be given the chance to develop in their own way.

Our three stage model also has a cognitive orientation that stresses the "learning to learn" concept expressed in the work of Smith and Associates (1990) and in such books as *Learning and Study Strategies* (Weinstein, Goetz, & Alexander, 1988). This cognitive orientation supports the popular slogan of trying to learn how to study "smarter" not "harder." This is the underlying value of combining a humanistic approach with a cognitive orientation.

Developing Learner Centered Learning Skills and Strategies

Stage	Developmental concern	Developmental activities
I	Knowing one's unique pattern of learning style characteristics	Workshops, courses, or counseling for assessment of learning style characteristics
II	Identifying learning skills or strategies that may be ineffective	Analysis of learning skills and strategies now being used
III	Knowing ways to improve the ineffective learning skills and strategies identified in Stage II	Use and practice of alternate strategies that are congruent with the learning style revealed in Stage I

Stage I

The Figure suggests a three stage model for developing learner centered reading skills and study strategies. In the first developmental stage, the major concern is the identification of individual learning style characteristics.

At this stage, the activities require learners to acquire insights about learning style characteristics through a variety of formats which may include workshops, study skill courses, or counseling intervention at both secondary and postsecondary school levels.

To assist in the identification of learning style characteristics, assessment instruments might be used. A number of learning style inventories now exist and may be available from college academic advisors or counselors. In a recent article, DeBello (1990) reviews and compares 11 major learning style models and their corresponding assessment instruments.

As with any type of assessment, individuals will have their preferences. Two learning style instruments we prefer are the Productivity Environmental Preference Survey (PEPS) (1982) and Kolb's Learning Style Inventory (1985). These have been useful to us because of their focus on adult learners.

For a selected bibliography of learning style assessment, see Cornett (1983).

Stage II

In the second stage of the developmental model, the concern is to identify skills and strategies that are not working well for the learner. For example, a learner might decide that notetaking or textbook reading is an area that needs improvement. The activity for this stage is for the learner to consider methods and activities being used and to analyze which ones are not working. For example, is the learner taking notes in an outline or doing concept mapping? When reading textbooks, is the learner just reading, reading and underlining, reading and taking notes, or reading and drawing concept maps? Assessment instruments also may be used to assist in the identification of ineffective skills or strategies.

One of the instruments for assessing learners' weaknesses is the Learning and Study Strategies Inventory (LASSI) (1987). The LASSI uses a self-report format and yields 10 scores for 10 different scales, which include such areas as time management, study aids, selecting main ideas, test strategies, etc. The LASSI or a similar inventory can be used in Stage II as a diagnostic instrument to help learners identify strengths and weaknesses.

Stage III

The last stage of the developmental model requires that the student acquire insight into alternatives to ineffective skills and strategies. Alternate methods need to use processes that incorporate the strengths of the learner's unique pattern of learning style characteristics. For example, a visual learner might decide to try concept or mind mapping for notetaking. Consequently, the activity for this stage is for the learner to practice the alternate method or process.

Effective alternatives may be pursued in a number of ways, such as using how-to-study books or participating in reading or study skill courses, workshops, and seminars. Several how-to-study books are available, including *Becoming a Master Student* (Ellis, 1991) or Pauk's (1989) *How to Study in College* and reading books like Adams and Brody's (1991) *Reading Beyond Words*. One of our major concerns with most of the how-to books is their prescriptive nature, a view that tends to support the one-size-fits-all philosophy. To provide a wider range of alternatives, a learner may find it advantageous to reference several how-to books.

To operationalize this approach, a learning-to-learn course using the three stage model was started at our community college. Students who enroll in this course reflect the general student population of the community college. The course is open to all students and is not a developmental course for at-risk students. The current course has evolved over the last 3 years from part of a one-credit orientation class to a separate 2-semester-hour student development course. The three stage model is presented in the course by using an earlier draft of this article as the first reading assignment.

The course introduces Stage I by encouraging students to investigate their learning style characteristics through in-class inventories, small group exercises, selective reading, writing a learning journal, and class presentations/discussions. Stage II makes use of a learning strategy inventory, small group work, and the learning journal. Stage III relies on the use of how-to-study books, videotapes, and class discussions.

Lynch (1990) described a number of college learning-to-learn programs supporting students in their search for more effective reading and study strategies. Flippo and Caverly and their colleagues (1991) have identified a number of reading and study strategies for college teachers and students. One popular and effective reading/study skills course is offered at the University of Texas (Weinstein, 1988). The importance of such courses for underprepared but able college students has been documented by Wyatt (1992).

Knowledge Is Power

This article has provided an overview of two different philosophical viewpoints for developing reading skills and study strategies for college students. Empirical research on learning strategies suggests that no one learning strategy fits all learners. We suggest that the one-size-fits-all paradigm should be replaced with an alternative learner centered approach that stresses individual learning style characteristics and learner control.

Individuals enhance their ability to develop effective learning skills and strategies when they understand their own unique patterns of learning style characteristics. After identifying ineffective skills or strategies, each learner can analyze and explore alternate ways of learning. Evaluating the application of individual learning patterns should produce more effective learning skills and strategies. We believe that a three stage learner centered model produces more effective learning and study skills.

In our view, developmental educators, counselors, and administrators can reconsider their philosophical assumptions about how best to assist college students in developing more effective reading and study skills. We think a new learner centered paradigm in which people develop in their own way and style should be applied. Learning is a lifelong process during which individuals gain insight about their unique learning style. They are empowered to direct and to take charge of their own learning.

References

Adams, W. R., & Brody, J. (1991). *Reading beyond words* (4th ed.). Fort Worth, TX: Holt, Rinehart & Winston.

Anderson, T. H., & Armbruster, B. B. (1984). Studying. In P. D. Pearson (Ed.), *Handbook of reading research* (pp. 657–679). New York: Longman.

Atkinson, J. S. C., Lunsford, J. W., & Hollingsworth, D. (1993). Applied academics: Reestablishing relevance. *The Balance Sheet, 74*(2), 9–11.

Brier, E. (1984). Bridging the academic preparation gap: An historical view. *Journal of Developmental Education, 8*(1), 2–5.

Claxton, C. S., & Murrell, P. H. (1987). *Learning styles: Implications for improving educational practices.* ASHE-ERIC Higher Education Report No. 4. Washington, DC: Association for the Study of Higher Education.

Cornett, C. E. (1983). *What you should know about teaching and learning styles* (Fastback 191). Bloomington, IN: Phi Delta Kappa Educational Foundation.

Cross, K. P. (1976). *Accent on learning: Improving instruction and reshaping the curriculum.* San Francisco: Jossey-Bass.

Cross, K. P. (1981). *Accent on learning: Increasing participation and facilitating learning.* San Francisco: Jossey-Bass.

DeBello, T. C. (1990). Comparison of eleven major learning styles models: Variables, appropriate populations, validity of instrumentation, and the research behind them. *Journal of Reading, Writing, and Learning Disabilities, 6,* 203–222.

Deegan, W. L. (1985). *Renewing the American community college: Priorities and strategies for effective leadership.* San Francisco: Jossey-Bass.

Deese, J., & Deese, E. K. (1979). *How to study* (3rd ed.). New York: McGraw-Hill.

Dunn, R., & Dunn, K. (1993). *Teaching secondary students through their individual learning styles.* Boston, MA: Allyn & Bacon.

Dworkin, A., & Dworkin, N. (1988). *Problem solving assessment.* Novato, CA: Academic Therapy.

Ellis, D. B. (1991). *Becoming a master student* (6th ed.). Rapid City, SD: College Survival, Inc.

Flippo, R., & Caverly, D. C. (Eds.). (1991). *Teaching reading & study strategies at the college level.* Newark, DE: International Reading Association.

Griggs, S. A. (1990). Counseling students toward effective study skills using their learning style strengths. *Journal of Reading, Writing, and Learning Disabilities, 6,* 281–296.

Hettich, P. I. (1992). *Learning skills for college and career.* Pacific Grove, CA: Brooks/Cole.

Hill, J. E. (1976). *The educational science.* Bloomfield Hills, MI: Oakland Community College.

James, W. B., & Galbraith, M. W. (1985). Perceptual learning styles: Implications and techniques for the practitioner. *Lifelong Learning, 8*(4), 20–23.

Jones, B. F., Pierce, J., & Hunter, B. (1989). Teaching students to construct graphic representations. *Educational Leadership, 46*(4), 20–25.

Keefe, J. W. (1987). *Learning style theory and practice.* Reston, VA: National Association of Secondary School Principals.

Kolb, D. A. (1984). *Experiential learning: Experience as the source of learning and development.* Englewood Cliffs, NJ: Prentice-Hall.

Lynch, A. Q. (1990). Helping college students take charge of their education. In R. M. Smith (Ed.), *Learning to learn across the life span* (pp. 219–246). San Francisco: Jossey-Bass.

Maslow, A. H. (1991). Critique of self-actualization theory. *The Journal of Humanistic Education and Development, 29,* 103–108.

McCarthy, B. (1990). Using the 4MAT system to bring learning styles to schools. *Educational Leadership, 48*(2), 31–37.

McKeachie, W. J. (1988). The need for study strategy training. In C. E. Weinstein, E. T. Goetz, & P. A. Alexander (Eds.), *Learning and study strategies: Issues in assessment, instruction, and evaluation* (pp. 3–9). San Diego, CA: Academic Press.

Mickler, M. L., & Chapel, A. C. (1989). Basic skills in college: Academic dilution or solution? *Journal of Developmental Education 13*(1), 2–4, 16.

Orlando, V. P. (1980). Training students to use a modified version of SQ3R: An instructional strategy. *Reading World, 20*(1), 65–70.

Pauk, W. (1989). *How to study in college* (4th ed.). Boston: Houghton Mifflin.

Robinson, F. P. (1970). *Effective study* (4th ed.). New York: Harper & Row.

Rogers, C. R. (1969). *Freedom to learn.* Columbus, OH: C. E. Merrill.

Rogers, C. R. (1980). *A way of being.* Boston: Houghton Mifflin.

Smith, R. M. (1982). *Learning how to learn: Applied theory for adults.* Chicago: Follett.

Smith, R. M. (1983). The learning-how-to-learn concept: Implications and issues. In R. M. Smith (Ed.), *Helping adults learn how to learn* (pp. 97–103). New Directions for Continuing Education, No. 19. San Francisco: Jossey Bass.

Smith, R. M., & Associates. (1990). *Learning to learn across the life span.* San Francisco: Jossey-Bass.

Walter, T., & Siebert, A. (1990). *Student success* (5th ed.). Fort Worth, TX: Holt, Rinehart & Winston.

Weinstein, C. E. (1988). Assessment and training of student learning strategies. In R. R. Schmeck (Ed.), *Learning strategies and learning styles* (pp. 291–316). New York: Plenum Press.

Weinstein, C. E., Goetz, E. T., & Alexander, P. A. (Eds.). (1988). *Learning and study strategies: Issues in assessment, instruction, and evaluation.* San Diego, CA: Academic Press.

Witkin, H. A., & Goodenough, D. R. (1981). *Cognitive styles: Essence and origins.* New York: International Universities Press.

Wyatt, M. (1992). The past, present, and future need for college reading courses in the U.S. *Journal of Reading, 36*(1), 10–20.

Developing Adjunct Reading and Learning Courses That Work

Nannette Evans Commander and Brenda D. Smith

Adjunct courses are taught in conjunction with content field courses, which generally cover lower division, general education subjects. Students enrolled in the content area course are simultaneously registered in an adjunct course, where they learn reading and learning strategies appropriate to both the subject matter of and the assignments in the content area course. Transfer of learning strategies is promoted, and opportunities for small group interaction are provided. Numerous versions of adjunct courses exist, but most trace their roots to the supplemental instruction model designed at University of Missouri–Kansas City.

Nannette Commander and Brenda Smith describe the adjunct model they established at Georgia State University. They also reflect upon the effectiveness of two slightly different versions of the model, and based on their experiences, they make recommendations for designing adjunct courses.

American institutions of higher learning have offered college reading and study courses since the early twentieth century. In fact, the historic and present need for developmental education in America is well documented (Wyatt, 1992). Currently, though, as the numbers of first-generation and economically disadvantaged students increase on college campuses, so do the various populations of able but underprepared students. As a result, many different learning support programs are emerging to meet the demand for academic assistance. This article will show how one successful model, the adjunct learning course, was adapted to the campus situation at Georgia State University. Its results were encouraging and led to some clear recommendations for effective ways to structure this sort of learning support program.

Origins

One rapidly growing area of academic support is in Supplemental Instruction (SI), a model originally developed to help medical students at the University of Missouri–Kansas City (Martin, 1980). SI programs are taught by trained graduate students who attend designated content area classes and act as learning leaders for students who voluntarily attend the organized learning sessions.

With the financial support of the National Diffusion Network, a team of professors in the Kansas City program have spread the message of SI to over 400 colleges and universities around the world. Because of its effectiveness, the SI program has become one of the few postsecondary programs to be designated by the U.S. Department of Education as an Exemplary Educational Program. The proponents, however, acknowledge that institutions may need to create variations of the original SI model in order to meet the needs of local populations. One such variation of SI is the adjunct course model.

Adjunct courses are taught generally in conjunction with college content courses such as history, political science, psychology, or biology. Adjunct courses offer reading and learning strategies to students who are simultaneously registered in the credit-bearing content course. Thus, students are able to apply their learning strategy instruction in the adjunct course to the actual paired content course immediately. In addition, adjuncts provide a support system and opportunities for small group interaction.

Many different versions of adjunct courses have begun to evolve. Some are voluntary, and others are mandatory extensions of developmental studies courses. Some instructors assign course grades based on tests related to the content course, while other programs are strictly tutorial. Some award college credit, while others carry "institutional credit" (not counting toward a degree but included in the calculation of tuition), extra credit from the content professor, or no credit at all.

This article will describe the adjunct model as we established it on our campus and will evaluate the academic outcomes of two slightly different versions. On the basis of the strengths and weaknesses of each variation and on our experiences, we make recommendations for designing adjunct courses.

The Adjunct Pilots

In preparation for designing the first adjunct course at our university and as instructors who would be team teaching the course, we met with a consultant from the University of Missouri–Kansas City SI Program. Our goals were to understand the SI model and adapt it to the needs of our university. Many successful features of SI were incorporated later into two adjunct courses. Each course, however, varied from the SI adjunct model in two areas: method of course pairing and population served.

Course Pairing

How the learning course is paired with a content course is a critical aspect of the adjunct course program. One key element of SI is that, rather than identify high-risk students, SI identifies high-risk course sections — those having a rate of 30 percent or higher D or F final course grades and withdrawals. At our university — Georgia State University, an urban institution with 25,000 students — most sections of History 113, a survey of American history, were identified as high risk since 34 percent of the students enrolled failed to complete the course with a C or better. We therefore decided to pair our pilot adjunct course with History 113.

The History Department welcomed the adjunct pilot and fully cooperated with us. We were not, however, able to reserve all needed spaces in a single section of History 113 for our adjunct students. To maximize options for student scheduling, students in the first pilot were allowed to register for any of 15 different sections of History 113. Thus, we paired our adjunct course not with a particular high-risk section, as defined by SI, but with a high-risk course. SI proponents would insist that supplemental instruction be specific to only one course section. We, however, had no choice about the scheduling.

A first version of our adjunct learning course was taught during the fall quarter, and after modifications a second version was piloted during the following winter quarter. Both adjuncts were 5-hour courses that met on Tuesdays and Thursdays from 10:50 a.m. to 1:05 p.m. for 10 weeks. The two adjunct courses were entitled Learning Strategies for History (LSH).

Preparation

Another key element of the SI model is that the instructors attend all content course sessions, take notes, read all assigned materials, and take all tests. This was not feasible in our case since our learning strategy course was not paired with one specific section of American History. Since we knew of this problem beforehand, each instructor visited a section of History 113 for one academic quarter prior to the beginning of the adjunct course. We attended all classes, took lecture notes, and recorded observations of student behaviors. We did not, however, take the tests.

To us, our experiences in the history class were an important part of our preparation. We were able to experience the lecture firsthand and to view the course from the student's perspective. A research study on the academic literacy demands of American History courses at our university also provided us with background information about the course requirements, as well as instructors' and students' expectations (Carson, Chase, Gibson, & Hargrove, 1992).

Recruitment

Student recruitment into the LSH adjunct courses proved challenging. The fall enrollment of 16 students was not as high as expected. In addition, these 16 students were enrolled in eight different sections of American history with eight different professors. As predicted, registration in multiple sections was a handicap.

In the second adjunct version, the history section options were to be limited to two professors. Because of registration complications, however, the 21 students enrolled in LSH for winter quarter were registered in three different sections of History 113 with three different professors.

Population

Another way our adjunct course differed from the traditional SI model was that the students served were developmental studies students designated by the university as high risk, conditionally admitted, and required to take a course in reading. Prior to this course, students in developmental studies with a reading requirement had to successfully complete a reading course before registering for any content area course. The adjunct course called LSH permitted students to coregister for reading and history.

To be eligible to enroll, students within the developmental studies program were required to have at least a 340 on the verbal section of the Scholastic Aptitude Test (SAT) as well as be placed in the exit level of a two-course developmental studies reading program sequence. The students enrolled in LSH were not identified to the history professors.

Course Content

The curriculum for both adjunct courses included the following instructional components: learning strategies, metacognitive awareness, and historiography — the key ideas that give structure to the study of history.

Learning Strategies

One workable definition of learning strategies is a variety of behaviors that learners consciously invoke to increase the comprehension and retention of information (Gillis & Olson, 1989) and that have been proven to enhance overall student achievement (Long & Long, 1987). Chiseri-Strater (1991) calls the result "academic literacy," and Nist (1993) says that academic literacy "covers reading, writing, listening, studying, and critical thinking processes" (p. 11).

Traditional study and learning strategies as outlined by Nist were taught in LSH with application to students' materials in American history. The following activities were among those included in instruction:

1. Students practiced time management techniques with specific guidance in dividing and planning their history assignments. The emphasis was on making an immediate start and striving to fulfill a daily and weekly plan.

2. Students practiced annotating texts, outlining, and notetaking. They prepared notes for quizzes and practiced essay responses for exams.

3. Lecture note review occurred primarily in small groups according to the class sections. Chase, Gibson, & Carson (1993) found that high school history students were required "to do very little, if any, notetaking" (p. 8). Thus attention was given to organizing class notes and planning for later study.

4. Collaboration in studying was strongly emphasized and enhanced with the exchange of phone numbers and the assignment of a variety of small group activities. Assignments were frequently given to groups rather than individuals.

5. Typical reading comprehension concepts such as main idea, detail, patterns of textbook organization, summarizing, and critical reading were discussed and practiced using the students' materials from their history class.

6. Metamemory, or information on how memory works, was discussed. Specific memory techniques were practiced using history materials.

7. Testwiseness was reviewed, and multiple choice questions from a history textbook bank were practiced on the computer. Students worked in pairs and enjoyed this activity, although their history tests were not multiple choice. Most of their history exams were divided between identifying historical terms and essay questions. Strategies for identification of terms and answering essay questions were modeled by instructors. Students practiced answering such items using history materials.

Metacognitive Awareness

Research studies have demonstrated the positive results of efforts to enhance metacognitive skills of learners (Weinstein, Goetz, & Alexander, 1988). Instructional efforts in the LSH course were designed to increase awareness of the students' successful and nonsuccessful learning behaviors and strategies.

1. A weekly two-page learning log was required, in which students were asked to reflect on their own progress as learners, usually regarding the use of a strategy taught during the previous week. Sometimes specific assignments were made to prompt introspection. For example, students seemed to enjoy an assignment of writing a script for a scenario showing themselves in the midst of a typical behavior that did not lead to academic success.

2. As an extension of the learning log, students were asked to record weekly observations of student behavior in history as well as other college classes. Through describing the successful and nonsuccessful behaviors of fellow students, many students recognized some of their own weaknesses.

3. Early in the quarter, students were alerted that they would be asked to develop a list of "Tips for History 113" for incoming students in future learning strategies courses. Another such list they developed was "Ways that College and High School Are Different." (See Tables 1 and 2.)

4. The Myers-Briggs Type Indicator was administered. Feedback from this instrument provides students with information on their personality type. Specific emphasis was placed on how one's personality type may affect one's learning style.

5. In order for students to become cognitively aware of their background knowledge in history, or historical schema, a 50-item true-false inventory on American history, developed by the LSH instructors, was administered at the beginning of the quarter. Students received feedback on their performance along with information on the influence of schema on learning.

6. To provide visual opportunities for learning and to expand students' schemata, excerpts from Alistair Cooke's *America* television series and other films on several historical figures were shown.

Historiography

Hennings (1993) asserted that each discipline has essential ideas — or ways of reading, writing, and thinking that give structure to the study

Table 1. Tips for Developmental Students Enrolled in History 113

1. Ask for help on papers.
2. Don't wait until the last minute to prepare for an exam. Use a full week.
3. Often your attitude will make a major difference on how well you do in class.
4. Ask questions in class to discover what the professor wants (s/he usually doesn't volunteer info).
5. Ask for a recommended professor.
6. Attend all classes — unless you're really sick.
7. Make it a point to call or let the professor know if you will not be in class.
8. Don't miss any quizzes!!!
9. Keep an open mind in learning.

Table 2. Students' Summary of Differences between High School and College

1. You have fewer classes, but a lot of work.
2. You need to adapt more quickly to the pace of your classes, because if you don't, you will fall behind a great deal (especially with the quarter system).
3. You don't get punished (a detention) for not completing an assignment. Your punishment's the grade you get in the end.
4. If you fail the class, you are out hundreds of dollars, plus you have to take the course over and spend more money.
5. You need to use various resources other than your textbooks, including classmates and other books.
6. You are treated like an adult. You are expected to take care of digging out what your status is in the class and what is to be covered on tests.

of that discipline. Our curriculum stressed the following essential ideas as ways of knowing history:

1. Time as a major organizing idea of history was discussed. Timelines assisted students with developing a meaningful time frame for organizing events and people. Instructors modeled ways of interpreting and relating significant dates.

2. Space as a major organizing idea of geography was discussed. In order to interpret events, readers of history must be able to locate where events occurred. Maps were used to assist students with developing a meaningful geographic space for organizing events and people. Again, instructors modeled ways of interpreting and relating to a sense of the geographical space in which significant historical events occurred.

3. Generalizing about the meaning of events was encouraged. Readers were asked to consider the ultimate significance of historical events. For example, students were asked not only to describe the New Deal but to discuss its impact on people living in the U.S. today.

4. The significance and application of specific historical terms was emphasized. For example, students were required not only to learn the meaning of particular terms, such as *reconstruction,* but also to provide examples of reconstruction in modern times. Hence, the reconstruction of the South that occurred after the U.S. Civil War was compared to the reconstruction of Japan after World War II, and to the reconstruction of Viet Nam, etc.

Results

To measure the success of the adjunct courses, we looked both at how many of the adjunct students passed the course with a grade of C or better and at the final history grade average for our adjunct students, comparing the latter with the average grade for all 15 History 113 sections.

Three fourths of the adjunct students passed the history course with a grade of C or better. However, the class average when compared to the general population was lower than we anticipated. Table 3 shows individual grades and the averages. For fall quarter, our adjunct students' average grade on a 4.0 scale was 1.5 in history, while the overall average for history 113 was 2.3.

Such a direct comparison, however, is not an entirely acceptable measure. Our adjunct students were designated as high risk by the university while the other History 113 students were admitted with no risk designation. Under usual circumstances, our adjunct students would not have been allowed to enter any History 113 class.

Our experiences and the fall quarter results prompted us to make some changes for the next pilot. As described previously, we limited the next adjunct registration to only three sections of History 113. We also increased the requirements in the LSH course by adding more opportunities for students to practice and apply learning strategies to history. For the second pilot the average grade for students taking the adjunct course rose to 2.3, which compared more favorably with the average of 2.5 for all winter quarter history sections.

Because of the 10 weeks during which we attended the history classes prior to offering the adjunct course, we knew that many of the history students with whom we were comparing our high risk adjunct students were not freshmen. We had talked to sophomores, juniors, and even graduating seniors. Thus, we decided to compare our newly enter-

Table 3. Success of Regular vs. Developmental Studies
Students in History 113

Final course grade	Fall quarter (1993)		Winter quarter (1994)	
	Number of history students	Number of learning strategies students	Number of history students	Number of learning strategies students
A	114	1	127	0
B	194	3	272	8
C	179	5	202	8
D	81	1	77	1
F	58	1	36	1
WF	10	1	10	
W	114		102	
I	15		15	2
Total number of students	765	12	841	20
Average grade	2.3	1.5	2.5	2.3

ing adjunct students with only the newly entering regularly admitted freshmen who took history during the same period.

Of those students who entered the university for the fall quarter as regularly enrolled freshmen and took history in either the fall or winter quarter, 80 percent passed History 113. Our adjunct students, also newly admitted in fall quarter, passed history at a rate of 89 percent. These findings encouraged our view of the benefit of the adjunct courses.

Since we were interested in the connection between prior course experience and success in history, we also looked at the History 113 success of fall quarter students who had been admitted to the university at least a year earlier. We found that they were more likely to pass the course than were first-year students (see Table 4). Of the regularly enrolled freshmen who took History 113 during their first fall quarter, 45 percent earned a C or better. Of those with prior course experience, 55 percent earned a C or better.

Since many developmental studies students are fulfilling only a math or English requirement (no reading course) and would be allowed by the university to take a history course, we compared the history grades of the newly admitted and previously admitted developmental studies students. Of those in the developmental studies program who took History 113 their first quarter, only 15 percent earned a C or

Table 4. Effect of Previous College Experience on Success in History 113

Type of students	Percentage earning a grade of C or better
Regularly admitted students	
Freshmen taking course in their first quarter	45%
Students with previous college course experience	55%
Developmental studies students	
Freshmen taking course in their first quarter	15%
Students with previous college course experience	85%

better, but of those with more college experience, 85 percent earned a C or better.

Thus, prior course experience seems to influence academic achievement in history with all students but more dramatically for developmental students. Developmental studies students, even those without a reading requirement, seem to benefit enormously from taking other courses before taking History 113.

Recommendations

As developmental programs expand into learning support programs and colleges seriously begin to address student retention, adjunct courses will become an increasingly important service offered by learning support and assistance programs. After piloting adjunct courses for 6 years at California State University at San Bernardino, Dimon (1988) summarized her six reasons why adjunct courses work by saying "they have a definable purpose, function as a support group, challenge students, promote participation, are flexible, and do what they say they do" (p. 33).

In our pilot courses at Georgia State University, we found the same advantages. The definable purpose was motivational. Students began to accept the responsibility for small group interactions, monitor their progress, and actively request instruction in areas of need. The immediate rather than simulated application created a desire for action.

In the design of adjunct courses, several questions germane to ultimate success must be addressed. Our positive and negative experiences in the two pilot versions of LSH suggested answers and led us to make the following recommendations:

1. How should adjunct courses be paired?

Students are best registered in only one content course section. Enrollment in multiple versions of the same History 113 was a severe handicap in both our first and second pilot. Our LSH students had different history textbooks, different assignments, and different dates for tests. In the first pilot, 7 of the 8 history professors were teaching chronologically, starting with the Paleo Indians or colonization. One professor, however, started with World War II and moved backwards. In demonstrating and applying learning strategies, we had to use simulated materials for many of our class activities rather than student textbooks or assigned materials, thereby negating one of the strengths of the adjunct model.

We concluded that regardless of skill, experience, and charisma of the adjunct course instructor, allowing registration in more than one content section severely limits teaching options. Although we did not experimentally control for this variable, our resulting history grade averages were better with fewer course pairings. We strongly recommend pairing an adjunct course with only one content course section.

2. What should adjunct courses teach?

Adjunct courses should teach learning strategies, develop metacognitive awareness, and focus on the structure of the discipline. A crucial element of our curriculum may have been the degree to which we required the application of the learning strategies to the history content.

In the first pilot we did test students, but we relied heavily on students to tell us how they were doing in history and what they needed from us. We assigned little beyond what was already assigned by the history professor. The problem was that student perception of progress and the reality according to the history professor were not always a match. Unfortunately, we did not discover this mismatch until after students had received low grades on the first test and the situation was critical.

In the second LSH we increased the demands. We required significantly more practice in application of the learning strategies to students' history materials. In addition to a midterm and final exam designed to provide practice in answering test questions similar to those required in the content course, we frequently quizzed students on dates, maps, and historical terms.

In essence, the second LSH course had a complementary content curriculum. We came to believe that our tests and quizzes probably provided a preliminary review for students' history tests. By giving our own tests, we gained a quicker insight into their studying behaviors. Thus, we monitored student progress through our own grade feedback, rather than relying on their perception of the history course. Again, although we cannot isolate this variable, history grades were much higher for the second pilot.

3. How should students be graded in adjunct courses?

Daily grades should be used to motivate learners. Pairing the adjunct course with only one history course section would offer many opportunities for constructively using daily grades for motivation. All the students in the class would have the same textbook, tests, and assignments. Other than tests on maps, dates, and essay responses, an obvious grading opportunity would be to give a short true-false quiz on the assigned reading for each week. Daily grades need not be heavily weighted, but they can be used as small steps of success to encourage students and foster self-confidence.

Frequently, students who need learning support also need structure. Dividing the demands of the course into daily goals encourages attendance and gives structure to a large body of material beyond the content professor's structure of a midterm and final exam.

4. Who should be taking which adjunct course?

Underprepared students should probably not be immediately paired with the college's most difficult course. We chose History 113 for our pilot because it filled the criteria for a high-risk course. What we did not consider is that few students take History 113 as their first "reading" course in the university, and prior course experience may influence academic achievement. For most developmental studies students, a psychology or a sociology course would be less threatening than history as the first regular college course and still would provide valuable academic experience in the core curriculum.

Although the argument could be made that offering the adjunct in the hardest course helps the students get through it, perhaps a sequential plan of academic growth would be better than asking students to work at frustration levels. A solution would be to offer adjunct courses in many academic disciplines and to encourage students to take the more difficult courses later.

5. What methods are effective in teaching adjunct courses?

Modeling is the essential teaching technique for adjunct courses. You must model for students how to fulfill the various requirements of the content course. Show students exactly what constitutes a good essay response, a good term paper, and a good set of lecture notes. For many students, each discipline and each professor seems to have a different definition of excellence. Have you seen a student look at a C paper and say "I answered the question. Why didn't I get an A?" Obtain examples of excellence from content professors and then provide students with many opportunities for practice and application of the learning strategies in order to achieve success.

6. How can students find out about adjunct courses?

Simplify registration so that students can understand the opportunity. In both pilots we wanted more students than actually were registered. To promote the course, we attended orientation, counselors advised students of the pairings, and we distributed handouts to eligible students. The message, however, was not clear. Pairing the course with only one content section would certainly simplify the instructions but would not solve the promotional issues. Even after 6 years of piloting adjuncts, Dimon (1988) concluded that student recruitment was still a major problem.

Benefits of Adjunct Courses

An increased emphasis on student retention, particularly for first-generation and economically-disadvantaged students, is a priority for higher education. A study by the American College Testing Program (1992) indicates that the freshman to sophomore dropout rate is 43 percent for postsecondary institutions with open admissions policies. Tinto (1987) predicted that of the 2.8 million students who in 1986 entered U.S. higher education for the first time, over 1.8 million would leave their first institution without receiving a degree. Noel, Levitz, Saluri, & Associates (1985) examined academic records and discovered that attrition is highest in the first 6 weeks of the first year of a student's academic term and that entry profiles did not necessarily predict high-risk students.

Recruitment on college campuses has become increasingly more competitive. Successful retention effects, such as adjunct courses, would alleviate some of the pressure in recruitment. At Georgia State University, for example, an increase in retention of only 1 percent would be the equivalent of recruitment of 17 percent of the incoming freshman class.

Given the retention concerns of higher education, the potential university populations for adjunct courses goes far beyond developmental studies students. Supplemental Instruction is one avenue of support and adjunct courses are another. With computerized placement tests offering additional data on incoming freshman and transfer students, marginally prepared students who could be identified might benefit from an adjunct course in a special area. Colleges that are serious about retention might consider making adjunct courses a prescription for students who do not need developmental studies yet are not predicted to excel. Although our pilots met for 5 hours a week, we feel that the curriculum could be shaped into a 3-hours-per-week schedule for regularly admitted students. The adjunct courses could be viewed as learning labs for the paired course.

Variations of adjunct courses will continue to evolve. They are important to the students and to the institutions in the retention of students. Adjunct courses are proactive in that they begin to deliver assistance before students experience academic difficulty. The purpose of learning strategy instruction is clearly defined for the students. Thus, whether serving developmental studies students, students enrolled in core curriculum classes, or transfer students, adjunct courses are a highly effective method of delivering academic support.

References

American College Testing Program. (1992). *ACT institutional data file,* 1992. Iowa City, IA: Author.

Carson, J. G., Chase, N. D., Gibson, S. U., & Hargrove, M. F. (1992). Literacy demands of the undergraduate curriculum. *Reading, Research, and Instruction,* 31, 25–30.

Chase, N. D., Gibson, S. U., & Carson, J. G. (1993). Preparing students for college: Making the transition. *Georgia Journal of Reading,* 19, 4–10.

Chiseri-Strater, E. (1991). *Academic literacies: The public and private discourse of university students.* Portsmouth, NH: Heinemann.

Dimon, M. (1988). Why adjunct courses work. *Journal of College Reading and Learning,* 21, 33–40

Gillis, M. K., & Olson, M. W. (1989). *Effects of teaching learning strategies with course content.* (ERIC Document Reproduction Service No. ED 339 259)

Hennings, D. G. (1993). On knowing and reading history. *Journal of Reading,* 36, 362–370.

Long, J. D., & Long, E. W. (1987). Enhancing student achievement through meta-comprehension training. *Journal of Developmental Education,* 11, 2–5.

Martin, D. C. (1980). Learning centers in professional schools. In K. V. Lauridsen (Ed.), *New directions for college learning assistance: Examining the scope of learning centers.* San Francisco: Jossey-Bass.

Nist, S. L. (1993). What the literature says about academic literacy. *Georgia Journal of Reading,* 19, 11–18.

Noel, L., Levitz, R., Saluri, D., & Associates. (1985). *Increasing student retention: Effective programs and practices for reducing the dropout rate.* San Francisco: Jossey-Bass.

Tinto, V. (1987). *Leaving college: Rethinkng the causes and cures of student attrition.* Chicago: The University of Chicago Press.

Weinstein, C. E., Goetz, E. T., & Alexander, P. A. (Eds.). (1988). *Learning and study strategies.* San Diego: Academic Press.

Wyatt, M. (1992). The past, present, and future need for college reading courses in the U.S. *Journal of Reading,* 36, 10–20.

Additional Readings

Casazza, M. E., & Silverman, S. L. (1996). *Learning assistance and developmental education: A guide for effective practice.* San Francisco: Jossey-Bass.

Caverly, D. C., & Peterson, C. L. (1996). "Foundation for a constructivist, whole language approach to developmental college reading." In J. L. Higbee & P. L. Dwinell (Eds.), *Defining developmental education: Theory, research, & pedagogy* (pp. 39–48). Cold Stream, IL: National Association of Developmental Education.

Heerman, C. E., & Maleki, R. B. (1994). "Helping probationary university students succeed." *Journal of Reading,* 37 (8), 654–61.

Henry, J. (1995). *If not now: Developmental readers in the college classroom.* Portsmouth, NH: Boyton/Cook.

Higbee, J. L. (1999). "New directions for developmental reading programs: Meeting diverse student needs." In J. R. Dugan, P. E. Linder, W. M. Linek, & E. G. Sturtevant (Eds.), *Advancing the world of literacy: Moving into the 21st Century, The 21st yearbook of the College Reading Association* (pp. 172–81). Commerce, TX: College Reading Association.

Johnson, L. L., & Carpenter, K. (2000). "College reading programs." In R. F. Flippo & D. C. Caverly (Eds.), *Handbook of college reading and study strategy research* (pp. 321–63). Mahwah, NJ: Erlbaum.

Maxwell, M. (1997). *Improving student learning skills: A new edition.* Clearwater, FL: H & H Publishing.

Maxwell, M. (1994). *From access to success.* Clearwater, FL: H & H Publishing.

Pugh, S. L., Pawan, F., & Antommarchi, C. (2000). "Academic literacy and the new college learner." In R. F. Flippo & D. C. Caverly (Eds.), *Handbook of college reading and study strategy research* (pp. 25–42). Mahwah, NJ: Erlbaum.

Roueche, J. E., & Roueche, S. (1999). *High stakes, high performance: Making remedial education work.* Washington, DC: Community College Press.

3

Teachers and Praxis

Martha Maxwell (2000) has pointed out that only four institutions of higher education in the United States offer a graduate major in developmental reading and study strategies. It comes as no surprise, then, that she goes on to describe the problematic tradition of individuals entering the field who are generally inexperienced in and only minimally trained for teaching postsecondary level students. (In all likelihood, these individuals' training focused on literacy at the primary level.) Unfortunately, the International Reading Association, the largest literacy organization in the world, does little to help this situation. In fact, its national standards for literacy professionals only exacerbate the problem, for the association doesn't even acknowledge postsecondary reading and learning instruction as a unique field in need of standards drawn from its own body of theory, research, and best practice.

Given this situation, it is imperative that college reading instructors and learning assistance professionals strive to learn as much as possible about the teaching practices that best serve a diverse postsecondary developmental reading population. This chapter can't possibly cover the full scope of best practice for college reading and learning programs, but it does provide several examples of instructional practice that serve as frames of reference for both the seasoned and the neophyte college reading and learning specialist.

The first article, Francine C. Falk-Ross's "Toward the New Literacy," follows the growth of four students as they undertake inquiry-based research, participate in independent and shared reading activities, and receive direct instruction in reading comprehension strategies.

Annette F. Gourgey describes another student-centered strategy: a metacognitive approach to college reading. She also shows how she applied this approach in her classroom. Then Martha E. Casazza discusses the direct instruction model and describes her use of this model in helping students improve their reading through the writing of summaries. Finally, Kenneth Wolf and Yvonne Siu-Runyan offer a framework for distinguishing between styles of portfolios (ownership, feedback, and accountability), along with guidance in determining which type of portfolio is most appropriate for a particular pedagogical purpose.

Toward the New Literacy: Changes in College Students' Reading Comprehension Strategies following Reading/Writing Projects

Francine C. Falk-Ross

Two questions directed Francine C. Falk-Ross's development of a new syllabus for a college developmental reading course offered at an urban, inner-city university that primarily prepares students for careers in the fine arts. The first question asked, "How can we approach these students' problems with effective instruction and academic support that allows for meaningful and appropriate comprehension strategy development?" The second asked, "How do we, as professors and facilitators, motivate self-direction and personal literacy strategy development?"

Throughout the article, Falk-Ross follows four students as they engage in inquiry-based research (the I-Search project), independent and shared reading activities, and direct instruction reading comprehension strategies. Case studies describe how the students' competencies changed in discussion and critical thinking, reading and writing, language and vocabulary, purposeful reading, and standardized testing. Implications of the study are provided, as are recommendations for both college reading specialists and content area teachers.

A small but significant number of U.S. first-year college students commence their studies with less than adequate reading comprehension strategies and enter developmental reading classes or attend assistance labs. This number may be as high as 20 percent of the student body at a public 2-year college, 8 percent at a public 4-year college, and from 5–10 percent at private colleges (U.S. Department of Education, 1995). These students come unprepared for the academic literacy requirements that typically characterize college coursework (Pugh,

Pawan, & Antommarchi, 2000) and that may very well be a part of their upcoming job responsibilities. Assuming that there are multiple factors responsible for these difficulties, such as linguistic or cultural differences and inadequate or inappropriate educational preparation, educators are pressed to determine answers to the following questions: How can we approach these students' problems with effective instruction and academic support that allows for meaningful and appropriate comprehension strategy development? How do we, as professors and facilitators, motivate self-direction and personal literacy strategy development? These questions directed the development of a new syllabus for two college reading classes that I taught at a private 4-year institution.

The educational benefit of following college students' progression through a series of reading and writing assignments lies in discovering relevant and meaningful ways to connect marginalized students with literacy skills and strategies that they have not previously learned or adopted. Assignments that activate and promote students' thoughtful interaction with textual material for various purposes, such as for story, procedural knowledge, or resource information, gain importance as educators encounter students who challenge traditional literacy instruction. Identifying teaching methods that support students' interests, prior understandings, and choice in directing applications for new knowledge is key to developing a new literacy (Willinsky, 1990). In this study, three areas of students' progress are considered: reading and writing connections, language and vocabulary, and purposes for reading.

Theoretical Perspective

The theoretical perspective that supported the development of strategies for four students in this course was a social-constructivist view of learning, which posits that cognitive development follows immersion in language and experiences in which members can construct knowledge together (Wells & Chang-Wells, 1992). More specifically, this perspective of reading focuses on the social intention between reader and text, and on reflection among teacher and students as they help one another construct meaning about the process and product (Kucan & Beck, 1997). Educators are seen as facilitators for students as they construct lessons and modify instruction to suit the needs of individual class members. Problem-based learning using strategies such as inquiry, reflection, and discussion can support and heighten learning (Blumenfeld et al., 1991).

This perspective underlies the movement toward a more "connected" literacy, referred to as the New Literacy (Willinsky, 1990). The New Literacy encourages development of an authentic reason to read text, that is, to answer a question or solve a problem, and imposes a need for effective ways to read. In essence, the New Literacy is a school of thought in which students are seen as authors and meaning makers. That is, reading and writing become a realization and connection of self (Willinsky, 1990). Willinsky defined the New Literacy as consisting of "those strategies in the teaching of reading and writing which attempt to shift the control of literacy from the teacher to the students; literacy is promoted in such programs as a social process with language that can from the very beginning extend the students' range of meaning and connection" (1990, p. 8). Willinsky's New Literacy is supported by the models presented by other theorists who share his premise that reading must be meaningful and useful to students Freire and Macedo (1987) explained that students' literacy competencies — that is, their ability to read the word — are built on their ability to read the world around them. Rosenblatt (1994) characterized the reading process as a transaction between the reader and the text, strengthening the importance of the reader's prior knowledge and goals.

As previous studies have indicated the need for strong reading-writing connections (Shanahan, 1997) and reading-writing-research connections (Many, Fyfe, Lewis, & Mitchell, 1996), it follows that the nature of reading comprehension strategy instruction in college classes must be relevant and applicable as the students immerse themselves in a highly literate environment (Applebee, 1984). And yet, according to Allen, Swearingen, and Kostelnik (1993), many college-level developmental reading courses and tutoring clinics are still primarily skills-based. These studies support the need for development of reading comprehension strategies using the I-Search paper (Macrorie, 1988). It consists of free writing on a topic that is uniquely important to the student. Macrorie explained the differentiating quality of what he and other researchers call

> *I-Searches* — not Researches, in which the job is to search again what someone has already searched — but original searches in which persons scratch an itch they feel, one so marvelously itchy that they begin rubbing a finger tip against it and the rubbing feels so good that they dig in with a finger nail. A search is to fulfill a need, not that the teacher has imagined for them, but one they feel themselves. (Macrorie, 1988, p. 14)

The Focus Students

Participants were four students at an urban, inner-city university, primarily focused on pursuing careers in the fine arts. All students were voluntarily enrolled in a class entitled College Reading, although the four in this case study had been alerted to the need for inclusion in such a class following their performances on a reading test (Test of Adult Basic Education, or TABE) required for entrance into the university. Eight students were enrolled in the class, but only the four focal students described here attended 80 percent of the classes and completed the final assignment. These students were reading below an eighth-grade level with additional difficulties in reading comprehension. The four focal students differed in their educational and ethnic backgrounds, gender, and age, but all expressed a need to become better readers and to understand course material as their motivation to enroll in the class. All were first-generation college attendees. Their ages ranged from 18 to 22. All students have been given pseudonyms. Each student initially completed an informal survey of personal reading strategies compiled from several formal sources (e.g., Schumm & Post, 1997).

Robert was 19 years old and of Polish ancestry. He was a first-year student at the college and was attending full time. He was bilingual, fluent in both English and Polish. He commented that he didn't pay much attention to classwork in high school, mostly due to disinterest in the lectures but also due to a lack of confidence in his abilities. He lived with his family, who supported his decision to attend college but were unable to help him with content material. He stated that he was aware that he needed to read and write more proficiently in order to reach his goal of becoming a playwright.

Rose was 18 and also a first-year student. She was Mongolian in ethnicity, and was able to converse fluently in Mongolian, English, Russian, and French. Her family lived in the city where the college was located but she shared an apartment with a friend. Rose admitted to having problems with the reading comprehension questions on the entrance reading test, but felt that this hadn't been a problem for her in completing assignments in her high school classes. Rose had chosen to major in filmmaking, although she knew very little about the topic and had no past experience in this area.

Susan was 22 and was a returning first-year student. She had completed a few courses during the previous school year, but left so she could work full time. She was African American, had medical problems that interfered with her full-time status at school, and lived in an apartment with her mother. She was qualified for special education supportive services, which she received in addition to attending classes. Her only fluent language was English. Susan felt confident about her reading and writing abilities, and was interested in broadcasting and media presentation careers.

Raymond was 21 years old, African American, and a junior. He was a full-time student, and had a full-time job as well. As a result, he was slightly disorganized and often distracted during our conversations. Raymond felt that the reading comprehension test was difficult, and that he struggled to find the appropriate answers among the choices. He spoke using the dialect referred to as African American Vernacular English (AAVE), which was strongly reflected in his writing samples.

He had not decided upon a major focus in his college studies and chose coursework that interested him each semester.

Course Content

Three main teaching and learning assignments helped develop reading comprehension for these students. These were not presented in chronological order; instead there was overlap in the introduction of parts of each component. The syllabus was constructed to include teaching and learning activities to improve reading comprehension in a classroom context in which the reading-writing-research connections were clear. The assignments included inquiry-based research (the I-Search project), independent and shared reading events, and direct instruction of reading comprehension strategies. The I-Search project applied reading and writing strategies and new insights gained from the other two activities.

I-Search Paper

The inquiry paper was introduced as the central, critical project and culminating assignment for the class. During the third week of classes, each student chose a topic of inquiry relevant to his or her interest, in most cases directly related to his or her college major. These topics were discussed among the class members in order to help the writer further shape, narrow, and focus the questions that would drive the inquiry. Consistent with the scope of Macrorie's (1988) self-developed information search, the students were provided with opportunities to gather data through varied experiences. Students were directed toward resources that would inform their inquiry from a list provided in class and from classroom members' suggestions. These resources included, but were not limited to, interviews with college professors using guided questions concerning reading and writing advice, Internet searches using university computer systems, online discussions among students and experts, journal references taken from library sources, and expository and narrative text chosen from varied sources. Instructions for using these sources and comprehending the content were provided through introduction and hands-on experience with the genre, guiding questions for first contacts, ongoing reference, and monitoring of independent completion. Weekly conferences between students and professor monitored the papers' progress toward completion, through development of the topic and three successive drafts.

Independent and Shared Reading

Ella Price's Journal (Bryant, 1972), a fictional narrative, was read as a group activity to situate and practice new reading comprehension strategies and initiate discussion. The book is about a young woman returning to college, immersing herself in classes within a social environment that is confusing and unsettling. Her need to acclimate to new study patterns and the college environment was similar to the needs of the students in the class. In the text, significant events are shared with the reader through Ella's personal journal entries for her English class. There were several themes that the students identified throughout the text, such as racial and cultural discrimination, feminist concerns of "double standards" and sexual relationships, moral issues of honesty and truth, and educational relevance and independent thought.

Weekly group discussions for reading response used text examples for support and independent experiences for further connections. Representative text selections were read in pairs or individually, followed by completion of book reviews. In most cases, these texts were the same ones used in the I-Search project.

Direct Instruction of Reading Comprehension Strategies

In order to enhance the content and guide the completion of the I-Search paper, review and instruction in reading preparation and comprehension strategies accompanied the classroom discussions. First, students were instructed to identify purposes and foci for college reading, that is, whether they were reading for factual information, for basic ideas and connections, or as resource material for an application or project. Second, students learned to identify and compare various genres of text in terms of organization and content, using this information as a preassessment strategy for reading in the college classes for which they were enrolled. Third, the prereading strategy of skimming for essential chapter material was explained, modeled, and practiced using excerpts from texts they were using in our class and others. Fourth, we discussed the specifics of morphemic analysis, that is, looking for meaningful or recognizable parts or roots of difficult vocabulary words in order to better understand the statements in reading passages. Fifth, we experimented with various forms of notetaking strategies (Pressley & Woloshyn, 1995; Schumm & Post, 1997) in order to support each student's preferential form of (re)collecting information from text. Last, formats for summary statements were reviewed as midreading and postreading strategies to aid comprehension and self-monitoring. In all cases, college texts were used for application of comprehension activities in class. These were all monitored through writing activities such as journal entries, application exercises, and drafts of students' I-Search papers.

Procedures

Approximately half of each class, about 1 hour, was devoted to an in-depth investigation of the genres of the resource materials. This was a core element in our reading class because even though they were aware of the nature of these resources from previous exposure, students were unfamiliar with how to independently use or comprehend the content. For example, in order to introduce students to e-mail and Internet use, we visited the computer laboratory to register each student for Internet access. To learn the necessary technical vocabulary and strategies for e-mail use, we discussed and practiced exchanging e-mail as a class. Students were assisted in their use of online discussions among peers, Internet browsing for content information from experts, and e-mail communication. At the library, these students acquired a library card, reviewed information access, and discussed journals as a genre. Names of cooperative college professors were provided for interviews, and a set of guided questions concerning reading and writing advice was compiled with student input. Expository and narrative text were chosen from varied sources, including the students' own content-area textbooks.

Each week, at least 1 or 2 hours of class time were devoted to the development of progressive aspects of the I-Search paper through small-group discussions and paper comparisons. We methodically discussed strategies for improving reading comprehension through prior knowledge, fluency, rate, accuracy, word identification, vocabulary analysis, notetaking, and test taking. We discussed the importance of understanding the author's perspective and tone and of becoming critical readers. Each week, we used text passages to complete exercises in specific areas of reading comprehension, discussing and sharing experiences along with introductions to new strategies for reading comprehension. The ongoing writing process, a series of continually modified drafts, was explained. For the vocabulary sections, we reviewed root words and their meanings. To increase comprehension we reviewed before, during, and after strategies for reading. To increase rate, we discussed the importance of highlighted information and the beginning of most paragraphs, skimming other parts for information, and rereading parts that may have been confusing. For test taking, we decided to look at the questions first to identify foci and develop a purpose for reading. We applied each of these strategies to reading for the I-Search paper, as well.

The progression of the I-Search paper's component parts was cumulative, building on each week's lessons. Individual writing and conferences followed class discussions, similar to a reading or writing workshop approach (Atwell, 1987, Reutzel & Cooter, 1991). As a culmination of the semester's studies of the many components of reading comprehension, we used part of the last four class sessions to talk through the completion of reading comprehension exercises. When necessary, the anticipated progression of classroom events was changed to respond to students' questions and help with the papers. (See Table 1.)

Table 1. Overview of Course Assignments

	Activity description	Content materials	Theoretical rationale
I-Search (self-selected inquiry)	A purposeful approach to reading through development of a free-writing assignment.	Research inquiry deriving from a student's life and needs.	Macrorie, 1988; Many, Fyfe, Lewis & Mitchell, 1996
Independent and shared reading	Portions of a narrative, fictional text were assigned for home readings and for in-class read-alouds.	*Ella Price's Journal*	Bryant, 1972
Direct instruction activities	Several strategies were explicitly introduced to assist students with reading comprehension of narrative and expository text, in preparation for university content area reading and research assignments.	• Prereading assessment of text's organization. • Skimming of essential chapter material. • Forms of notetaking. • Formats for summary statements using representative reading materials.	Fry, 1977; Schumm & Magrum, 1991 Schumm & Post, 1997 Palmatier, 1973 Applegate, Quinn, & Applegate, 1994

Data Collection and Analysis

The data sources for this study consisted of field notes of class events, participant observations, audiotapes of class members' discussions (concerning reading comprehension strategy use and paper comparisons), and literacy artifacts consisting of students' journal entries with reflective comments and photocopies of students' work. Field notes were added following each class. Artifacts were photocopied before and after grading and conferences. The sources were varied in order to compare information and to provide for triangulation in results.

Consistent with the methodology of action research through teacher inquiry, cycles or spirals of observation, reflection, and action (Pappas, Kiefer, & Levstik, 1999) characterized the analysis of data collected during class activities. Ongoing formative analyses of discourse samples and descriptive field notes using a constant comparative method (Strauss & Corbin, 1990) provided a determination of major patterns in changes in the students' reading comprehension. Evaluative judgments were made at several levels of intervention and analysis in order to identify, support, and monitor changes in students' literacy competence. During the study, those problems that seemed to initially limit or interfere with progress in a particular curricular activity became the target for observation or instruction in my subsequent classroom visits. An analysis was then made of new attempts at reading effectively, and new instruction would follow over the course of the semester.

Direct participant observation during classroom activities allowed for "on-the-spot" decision making about the appropriateness of responses to text, allowing for immediate (re)introduction of literacy skills when necessary. Indications for intervention included increased signs of frustration as students struggled to express an idea or interpret a sample of text. Feedback relating to the effectiveness of the strategy was both immediate, in that the change allowed or interfered with students' competent participation, and delayed, as we also discussed the changes at a later date.

The second level of analysis was through consideration and coding of transcribed discourse samples and the situational notes that accompanied them. Review of students' reading strategies and of the teacher's and students' antecedent and consequent comments provided further insight on the areas where students required support or clarification. Interpretations and goal setting that followed this analysis were done with occasional input of another reading comprehension professor. This collegial collaboration allowed for extended discussion and strategy recommendations.

A third level of analysis derived from informal conversations with students in locations other than the classroom, such as in hallways or in my office. These important interactions were initiated by members of the study. These meetings were unscheduled and not audiotaped, but were alluded to in the field notes.

These patterns, grounded in field experiences within a one-semester course, evolved through discussion and reflection. This set of forms of analysis was well matched to the study because it provided a way for me to reflect upon the nature of students' progress with reading comprehension strategies. Explanations of the nature and occurrence of specific patterns are offered throughout the text. Examples of narratives from classroom discourse are included for illustration and explanation.

Comparative data were also available from the pre- and posttest forms of the TABE reading comprehension test results and the reading survey form developed for this class.

Improvements to Students' Comprehension

Changes in several areas of development occurred in the four students' reading comprehension strategies and their application of newly learned information. Their reading became more focused, more critical, and more productive. These changes were noticeable in their individual contributions through classroom discourse participation, in small-group meetings, and in paper and assignment completions.

Discussions and Critical Thinking

Throughout the semester, the students' comfort in sharing ideas and frustrations with one another increased. Students revealed that they had not commented on peers' assignments, progress, or problems in previous classes, and that this process was instructive for (re)constructing their own understandings. These conversations helped each of them to consider prior knowledge of their topics and to integrate new information with their own previous constructions.

The students did not choose to read one another's early drafts of inquiry papers because they were struggling to compose their own constructions and preferred to learn from specific suggestions and problem-solving models. Issues of process and organization were resolved for individual students. Eventually, however, students began to share questions about their own papers. For example, Robert wanted suggestions for finding core ideas and usable information in the resources he chose so he could formulate a plan for devising a play of his own. Rose needed language and vocabulary support as she read expository information and developed her paper. Susan requested help with organization of information as she struggled to transfer the new information she learned into her own words. Raymond required guidance with finding the main ideas in expository text, as was obvious from his early writing samples.

Critical thinking and interpretive response were used more frequently. Students collaboratively used higher level forms of information analysis, such as critiquing text for deeper meaning and usefulness. For example, Rose observed that Robert had integrated a lot of new information concerning other people's experiences with filmmaking, but needed to apply the information to his own efforts. She suggested that he refer to a computer disk that might provide him with explicit information for his paper. Susan questioned the formal nature of the information she was reading and how she could clearly articulate her own "voice" in her interpretation. Raymond argued that the use of his own dialectical grammar made his arguments more powerful as he discussed text and his own opinions. These practices helped them to trust one another and to mitigate the competitive nature of discussing text.

Reading and Writing Connections

Although the emphasis of the class was on reading strategies for comprehension, we discussed and used writing activities as well. Initially, students were not comfortable with the number of journal entries that accompanied the readings. Some students were able to reflect orally but were at a disadvantage when they first tried to keep journals. They were not used to formalizing their reactions to reading or to responding in a critical and personalized manner. In addition to difficulties with reading comprehension, several students in the class had problems with writing organization, quality, and quantity. As a result, they were still having trouble writing their thoughts about how they approached reading assignments as the semester ended. I did, however, notice progress in their thinking about reading and in their critical stances.

For their I-Search projects, the students chose topics in which they had vested interests. Raymond chose to write about the use of nonstandard English in educational settings. Susan researched the educational resources available on our campus and others for assistance with students' chronic medical problems. Robert investigated the process of scriptwriting and offered his own first draft of a play. Rose chose to study the opportunities and experiences of women as filmmakers.

Two examples provide illustrations of the reading and writing connections made by the students in the assigned reading, which stretched their writing abilities during the final I-Search drafts. Rose wrote brief summaries of the chapters with a short added comment such as "This made me feel sad," in her journal entries focused on assigned reading. In her final book report she wrote,

> At the beginning I felt the same way like Ella, how she thought that she might not be able to write journal everyday. Then at the end she said that she has filled a whole notebook, and she admits that it's getting easier. I'm thinking to myself if I really try hard I can do it, I mean, I can write journals in all of my classes.

Raymond, whose summaries of initial reading assignments varied greatly from those of the other members of the class, was able to more accurately pinpoint his difficulties and solutions by the end of the class when he wrote, "Be more focus when I read and start looking up words that I don't understand. Also, try not to hide my potential. And the most important, stop taking my time and [instead] ask question." In all cases, journal entries focused on responses to text and on analysis of the students' reading progress.

In addition, information in early drafts of the I-Search paper was reworded and regrouped into meaningful and individual thought organizations, not merely borrowed from the text. For example, Rose rewrote the component parts of the paper with a different focus than in the previous submissions. The original draft of her explanation of the two interviews that she conducted as she collected information consisted of two organizations. The first interview was in a question-answer format; the second was a two-paragraph narrative with the quoted material included in the text of the paragraph. She organized the final draft around three focal points gained from the interviews, explained in her own words.

Raymond's paper was originally simple reviews of the two texts he chose to read as resources. Both reviews originally included 4–5 short paragraphs, each containing a fact or event and a limited response to it. In the final paper, following class discussion of text organization and comprehension, he discussed three main points that he extracted from each text, and provided examples for support. These changes were clear indications of an expansion in his approach to reading and reflection with regard to text.

Language and Vocabulary

Rose and Raymond, among other students in the class, experienced difficulties with standard English. Positive changes in their understanding and use of Standard English occurred with the amount of reading they did each week. They were not originally aware of the differences between their language and Standard English. Following feedback from classroom members concerning Raymond's consistent use of the African American vernacular, he chose the subject for his I-Search paper. He questioned and reasoned in his paper, "If Standard English is considered the official language, why are some people who were born in America still having a hard time communicating with the English Language? Part of the reason is that we never talk Standard English. . . . The answer is to adapt to what [people] are saying in order to communicate with each other."

Rose was unfamiliar with the vocabulary of language and textual analysis, such as *resources, metaphors,* and *connotation.* She didn't remember being exposed to these terms in her high school writing classes. For her, textbook vocabulary had slowly become uncomfortably varied and sophisticated, creating frustration. Rose admitted in discussion and in writing that she wanted to have a larger vocabulary. She had difficulty as a second-language learner attempting to write in an acceptable way. Rose found our discussions of root words and morphemic analysis helpful in developing vocabulary.

Susan had problems with word retrieval, which interfered with her reading and writing fluency. Vocabulary suggestions from other class members were beneficial to all, initiating discussions of word connotation and use. Both she and Robert struggled with finding vocabulary that appropriately articulated their ideas.

Purposeful Reading

Robert and Susan were pleased to have developed clearer foci for their inquiry topics and explained that they had chosen topics in other classes more carefully, instead of detaching from assignments as was their usual approach. Robert commented, "This is really a great idea. This is really what I needed to do. We will *use* this information now. I should be doing this all the time." Susan wrote that she had begun to "surf the Internet for information on subjects, gather as much information from books as I can, and speak to other instructors" as sources of purposeful learning. These students, who admitted to rarely taking notes or forming summary statements during lectures or reading assignments, had developed notetaking strategies to recall information in text for classroom questions and discussion. With the added effort and knowledge, their use of critical thinking and response were more obvious. These students were making connections with the information rather than simply recalling facts.

Results of Standardized Tests (TABE)

The changes in reading comprehension were not only apparent in qualitative evaluation of the students' writing; results from formal testing revealed mild differences in reading comprehension measures between the pretest (Form 7) and posttest (Form 8) scores; that is, each of the four focal students gained the equivalent of at least three grade levels in reading achievement (see Figure 1). Although reading material was provided in the students' other classes, reading instruction was not emphasized in lieu of hands-on activities for procedural knowledge in the fine arts. Comparable pre- and posttest TABE scores for the other students in the class were not available, however, it is believed that the coursework promoted change over and above the college classes in which these four focal students were enrolled.

Helping Students Construct Useful Literacy Strategies

The college-level developmental reading program I have discussed and my case studies provide further insight into the development of meaningful reading comprehension strategies that connect with the purposes and needs of struggling college readers. Although the study involved a small number of students in one program, it provides a depth of knowledge about complex phenomena (Hammersley, 1992) and responds to the need for an increased number of investigations of integrated approaches

Figure 1. Pretest and Posttest TABE Results for Focal Students

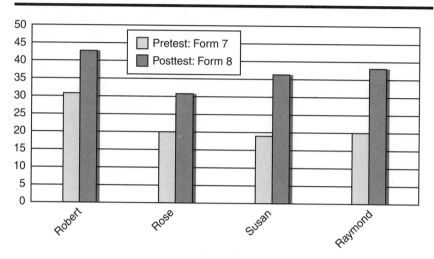

to literacy teaching and learning (Shanahan, 1997). The implications of this study relate to more effective instructional approaches for students' own construction of useful literacy strategies for success in college classes and application in their chosen careers. The study also answers questions about the process and context of college developmental reading programs.

An important consideration is the integrated nature of the reading and writing assignments that seemed to be central to this developmental reading program. The focus was on the importance of integrating the specific elements that have been used at earlier educational levels and are still necessary for all reading activities. These include "before" reading strategies, such as identifying a purpose for reading and analyzing text structure and organization through language and writing activities; "during" reading activities, such as reviewing and clarifying ideas through questioning in oral and written forms; and "after" reading skills, such as summarizing and applying information in papers and journals (Valeri-Gold & Deming, 2000). Other studies have proposed similar integration of reading and writing activities for more critical reading and comprehension through workshop organization (Bartholomae & Petrosky, 1986), theme development (Segall, 1995), diverse literary selections (Valeri-Gold & Deming, 1994), and strategy planning (Stahl, Simpson, & Hayes, 1991). Students in college developmental reading classes need to be introduced to all of these strategies, and to have them explicitly modeled, practiced, and discussed in order to construct (and reconstruct) conceptual understandings. In addition to becoming familiar with these processes, they need to learn to use those that work for them in successive college classes.

Researchers have advocated the importance of content-area reading and writing using interdisciplinary approaches in middle and secondary school (Alvermann & Phelps, 1998; Lapp, Flood, & Farnan, 1996; Vacca & Vacca, 2002). Teacher education programs must include and stress the importance of introduction and mastery of these new literacy goals and critical thinking tasks prior to students' entrance into postsecondary programs (McKenna, 1998). New foci on the application of reading strategies for vocational and professional purposes must begin in earlier grades, especially for students from nonmainstream populations, to equally provide all students with choices for successful careers.

References

Allen, D. D., Swearingen, R. A., & Kostelnik, J. L. (1993). University reading clinics: Changing focus for changing needs. In T. V. Rasinski & N. D. Padak (Eds.), *Inquiries in literacy learning and instruction* (15th yearbook, pp. 73–79). Kent, OH: College Reading Association.

Alvermann, D. E., & Phelps, S. F. (1998). *Content area reading and literacy: Succeeding in today's diverse classrooms.* Needham Heights, MA: Allyn & Bacon.

Applebee, A. (1984). *Contexts for learning to write: Studies of secondary school instruction.* Norwood, NJ: Ablex.

Applegate, M. D., Quinn, K. B., & Applegate, A. J. (1994). Using metacognitive strategies to enhance achievement for at-risk liberal arts college students. *Journal of Reading, 38,* 32–40.

Atwell, N. (1987). *In the middle: Writing, reading, and learning with adolescents.* Portsmouth, NH: Heinemann.

Bartholomae, D., & Petrosky, A. (1986). *Facts, artifacts, and counterfacts: Theory and method for a reading and writing course.* Upper Montclair, NJ: Boynton.

Blumenfeld, P. C., Soloway, E., Marx, R. W., Krajcik, J. S., Guzdial, M., & Palincsar, A. (1991). Motivation project-based learning: Sustaining the doing, supporting the learning. *Educational Psychologist, 26,* 369–398.

Bryant, D. (1972). *Ella Price's journal.* New York: The Feminist Press.

Freire, P., & Macedo, D. (1987). *Literacy: Reading the word and the world.* Granby, MA: Bergin & Garvey.

Fry, E. B. (1977). Fry's readability graph: Clarifications, validity, and extension to level 17. *Journal of Reading, 21,* 242–252.

Hammersley, M. (1992). *What's wrong with ethnography? Methodological explorations.* London: Routledge.

Kucan, L., & Beck, I. L. (1997). Thinking aloud and reading comprehension research: Inquiry, instruction, and social interaction. *Review of Educational Research, 67,* 271–299.

Lapp, D., Flood, J., & Farnan, N. (1996). *Content area reading and learning: Instructional strategies.* Needham Heights, MA: Allyn & Bacon.

Macrorie, K. (1988). *The I-Search paper.* Portsmouth, NH: Heinemann.

Many, J. E., Fyfe, R., Lewis, G., & Mitchell, E. (1996). Traversing the topical landscape: Exploring students' self-directed reading-writing-research processes. *Reading Research Quarterly, 31,* 12–35.

McKenna, M. C. (1998). Afterword to 20th century literacy: Prospects at the millennium. *Peabody Journal of Education, 73,* 376–386.

Palmatier, V. A. (1973). A notetaking system for learning. *Journal of Reading, 17,* 36–39.

Pappas, C. C., Kiefer, B. Z., & Levstik, L. S. (1999). *An integrated language perspective in the elementary school: An action approach.* New York: Longman.

Pressley, M., & Woloshyn, V. (1995). *Cognitive strategy instruction* (2nd ed.). Cambridge, MA: Brookline.

Pugh, S. L., Pawan, F., & Antommarchi, C. (2000). Academic literacy and the new college learner. In R. F. Flippo & D. C. Caverly (Eds.), *Handbook of college reading and study research* (pp. 25–42). Mahwah, NJ: Erlbaum.

Reutzel, D. R., & Cooter, R. B., Jr. (1991). Organizing for effective instruction: The reading workshop. *The Reading Teacher, 44,* 548–555.

Rosenblatt, L. M. (1994). The transactional theory of reading and writing. In R. B. Ruddell, M. R. Ruddell, & H. Singer (Eds.), *Theoretical models and processes of reading* (4th ed., pp. 1057–1092). Newark, DE: International Reading Association.

Schumm, J. S., & Magrum, C. T. (1991). FLIP: A framework for fostering textbook thinking. *Journal of Reading, 35,* 120–125.

Schumm, J. S., & Post, S. A. (1997). *Executive learning.* Upper Saddle River, NJ: Prentice Hall.

Segall, M. T. (1995). Embracing porcupine: Redesigning a writing program. *Journal of Basic Writing, 14*(2), 38–47.

Shanahan, T. (1997). Reading-writing relationships, thematic units, inquiry learning . . . In pursuit of effective integrated literacy instruction. *The Reading Teacher, 51,* 12–19.

Stahl, N. A., Simpson, M., & Hayes, C. (1991). *How college learning specialists can help college students* (ERIC Digest). Washington, DC: Office of Educational Research and Improvement.

Strauss, A., & Corbin, J. (1990) *Basics of qualitative research. Grounded theory procedures and techniques.* Newbury Park, CA: Sage.

U.S. Department of Education. (1995). *Digest of educational statistics.* Washington, DC: Author.

Vacca, R. T., & Vacca, J. L. (2002). *Content area reading: Literacy and learning across the curriculum* (5th ed.). Boston: Allyn & Bacon.

Valeri-Gold, M., & Deming, M. P. (1994). *Making connections through reading and writing.* Belmont, CA: Wadsworth.

Valeri-Gold, M., & Deming, M. P. (2000). Reading, writing, and the college developmental student. In R. F. Flippo & D. C. Caverly (Eds.), *Handbook of college reading and study research* (pp. 149–174). Mahwah, NJ: Erlbaum.

Wells, G., & Chang-Wells, G. L. (1992). *Constructing knowlege together: Classrooms as centers of inquiry and literacy.* Portsmouth, NH: Heinemann.

Willinksy, J. (1990). *The new literacy: Redefining reading and writing in the schools.* New York: Routledge.

Teaching Reading from a Metacognitive Perspective: Theory and Classroom Experiences

Annette F. Gourgey

Developmental reading and learning specialists have long understood the importance of assisting in developing a more comprehensive or metacognitive approach to learning. Here, Annette F. Gourgey asks, "What are the specific metacognitive skills that developmental college readers need, and how can they be taught?"

In answering these two questions Gourgey examines research and theory from the past two decades. From this review, she describes a metacognitive approach to teaching as one that trains a student to identify his or her learning goals and select appropriate methods for achieving them, to monitor understanding of and progress toward those goals, and to clarify misunderstandings leading to the loss of comprehension. Finally, two exercises that promote the development of metacognitive skills are detailed: vocabulary in context and metacognitive reading strategies.

Educators are increasingly recognizing the value of instruction that focuses on the development of comprehensive strategies for thinking and independent learning (Stahl, Simpson; & Hayes, 1992). Included in this formulation are *metacognitive* skills, or skills for fostering awareness and control of one's learning (Baker & Brown, 1984). A metacognitive approach to education involves teaching students to identify learning goals, to choose the most appropriate strategies for reaching those goals, to monitor their understanding and their progress toward their goals, and to clarify misunderstanding when they have lost comprehension (Flavell, 1979; Palincsar & Brown, 1984, 1989; Sternberg, 1986). Students who have developed these skills are more able to understand, retain, and transfer knowledge to new situations than students who have been taught discrete skills without a broader context of strategic learning (Hartman & Sternberg, 1993).

What are the specific metacognitive skills that developmental college readers need, and how can they be taught? This article describes research on metacognitive skills important to reading comprehension, followed by two sample classroom exercises used by the author to teach these skills in a developmental reading course.

Metacognition in Reading

Research on metacognition in reading has focused on strategies for monitoring and improving comprehension. Palincsar and Brown (1984, 1989) have described six strategies found to enhance comprehension: (1) clarifying the purpose of reading; (2) activating relevant background knowledge; (3) allocating attention to the important ideas; (4) evaluating content for internal consistency and compatibility with prior knowledge; (5) self-monitoring to verify comprehension; and (6) drawing and testing inferences. Metacognitively skilled readers seek to establish "meaningfulness" in their reading and value careful selection of appropriate strategies and careful monitoring of their comprehension.

Developmental educators have documented the metacognitive strategies used by proficient, in contrast to less competent, college readers (Long & Long, 1987). Proficient readers see knowledge as an organization of concepts rather than as isolated facts; work to understand meanings and relationships rather than simply to recall details;

anticipate test questions about their reading; engage in self-questioning for understanding and test preparation; paraphrase in their own words; and make inferences. Less competent readers tend to be passive, to underline rather than to reformulate, to follow directions rather than to invent their own strategies.

Other research has verified that independent learning is enhanced when students generate and use their own strategies and self-questions rather than respond solely to teachers' questions and directions (Hartman, 1994; Palincsar & Brown, 1984; Paris, Wixson, & Palincsar, 1986). When developmental college readers were encouraged to create their own questions to identify and integrate the important concepts in a college psychology text, and were trained to differentiate between "knowledge" questions and "analytic" questions, they learned for the first time the difference between cramming facts and understanding meaning (Aldridge, 1989).

Self-questioning helps students both to identify important concepts and to monitor and clarify comprehension difficulties. The reciprocal teaching model (Hartman, 1994; Palincsar & Brown, 1984) emphasizes self-questioning to predict important ideas in the reading, to review important concepts, and to identify parts of text that students do not fully understand. Generating questions forces students to focus on what is important; answering them forces students to rework their understanding until it is satisfactory. Students may use a variety of strategies to rework understanding; some common ones are reading ahead, rereading, relating the text to prior knowledge, and relating ideas that appear in different parts of the passage to draw inferences that are not explicitly stated.

Observation of my own developmental reading students confirmed those of Long and Long (1987) that developmental readers tend to be passive readers: they underline, sometimes highlighting most of the text because they cannot tell which ideas are important; they rely on others for clarification rather than trying to figure out connections for themselves; and they overlook important ideas without even realizing it because they have not engaged in self-questioning or self-testing. Moreover, when they encounter an unfamiliar word, they often skip over it; or they may look it up in the dictionary but still be unclear about its meaning in the broader context of the passage. Without metacognitive skills, students all too often experience frustration and failure and give up prematurely. Therefore, in order to help students develop skills for figuring out vocabulary in context and for predicting ideas, generating and answering self-questions, monitoring comprehension, and clarifying confusion, I developed two collaborative learning exercises. These exercises, their rationale, and their outcomes are described below. Students were freshmen enrolled at a four-year urban public college, placed in an "upper developmental" reading course based on their performance on a vocabulary and reading test.

Exercise I: Vocabulary in Context

All metacognitive exercises have the common purpose of encouraging students to discover and rely on their own reasoning abilities rather than to depend only on external sources. I began with a vocabulary in context exercise both as a prelude to passage comprehension and to help students realize that their own reasoning, in addition to dictionaries, could be an important resource of knowledge: even when they do not know a particular word, they have many cues that they can pull together to figure out meaning.

In order to create a situation in which students would be forced to rely on their own reasoning because outside sources were unusable, I chose Lewis Carroll's poem *Jabberwocky* (Carroll, 1960, p. 136). *Jabberwocky* is composed largely of nonsense words, yet the poem tells an understandable story. Students were divided into collaborative learning groups of four and instructed to read the poem and to help each other find the meanings of as many unfamiliar words as they could. My role was to pose questions to help draw out students' thoughts if they got confused, but not to suggest definitions for them.

Despite the fact that I had told students that the words were made up, the impulse to look them up was so strong that a few students actually took out their pocket dictionaries. When they realized that they would have to reason out the meanings for themselves, they began to list words and their supposed meanings, and correctly defined most of them. At the end of the class period, the groups came together to explain their definitions and how they had derived them.

The following cues were most commonly used to figure out meanings: the sound of the word (e.g. "slithy" sounds like slithery or slimy); the form of the word ("ing" at the end of a word means a verb); the immediate context (e.g. "'Twas" implies a description of a time or setting, so "'Twas brillig" must describe that setting); and the broader context in the story.

Some sample definitions illustrate how students reasoned out meanings. Since "brillig" describes the setting, they reasoned that it must refer to the weather, or to the land and the creatures or plants in it, which are also alluded to by the other words in that verse. The Jabberwock must be some kind of beast: it has claws, teeth, and fiery eyes; one must beware of it, so it is dangerous; it "came whiffling," so it moves fast; it was "burbling," so it makes a characteristic noise; and there was joy when it was killed. The phrase "and with its head/He went galumphing back" describes a victory in battle; "galumphing" is a verb describing how the hero went — either galloping or strutting triumphantly because he had killed the beast and was carrying its head home. And "my beamish boy" must mean good and heroic, because the boy's father is happy and proud of him.

What began as an arduous exercise ended up as a fun and exciting project as students got into the spirit of the poem and discovered previously unappreciated capabilities for figuring out the meanings of words. It is my belief that if students become dependent on others, whether people or dictionaries, to do their thinking for them, they lose confidence in their own intelligence; if so, then metacognitive exercises may have the dual purpose of expanding students' skills and their self-confidence as thinkers.

Exercise II: Metacognitive Reading Strategies

In this exercise, I adapted the reciprocal teaching model (Palincsar & Brown, 1984, 1989) to help students learn the metacognitive skills of prediction, question generation, comprehension monitoring, clarification of confusing statements, and summarizing important ideas. The context for these skills was a real newspaper article that was chosen because it contained a built-in ambiguity that would force students to examine their strategies for monitoring and clarifying a comprehension failure. The article, "Defiant Bicyclists to Snub S.F. Mayor" (Matier & Ross, 1997, p. A1) described plans for a grass-roots bicyclists' rights movement to stage a demonstration called Critical Mass in San Francisco's business district during the Friday evening rush hour. The ambiguity in the article was that, having been written for informed San Francisco residents, it never explained what Critical Mass was, only focusing on the contentious negotiations between the bicyclists and the mayor.

This exercise took four class sessions to complete. On the first day, students were asked to look over the article quickly and to generate questions on things they wanted to know and predictions of what they thought the article would be about. I made no suggestions and only listed students' ideas on the board, prompting them with "What else?" when there was a lull. The goal was to have students become aware of the many ways they could activate their thinking before and while they read.

Students used the title, subtitle, inset caption, headings and phrases that quickly caught their eye to generate the following lists, which actually captured many of the significant points in the article:

Questions

1. What is Critical Mass?

2. What does the mayor have to do with bicyclists?

3. Where is "everyone invited"?

4. Is there a demonstration?

5. Will there be a new rule about "hats and bats"? Will it apply to the police or to the cyclists?

6. Will there be a new law for cyclists?

Predictions

1. This is about bicyclists defending their right to ride.
2. There will be a boycott of talks with the mayor.
3. The bicyclists are going against the mayor.
4. It is political because the mayor is involved.
5. The cyclists will ride Friday.
6. They are affecting traffic control.
7. There may be violence.
8. The article will probably describe the traffic problems between the cars and the cyclists, maybe describe an accident.
9. The article will probably describe the political issue: The mayor will emphasize the traffic problems and the cyclists will emphasize their rights.
10. The article will discuss security measures.

On the second day I had students form groups of four. They were to read the article, search for the answers to their questions, verify the accuracy of their predictions, write down any new questions and try to answer them, and note any places where they got confused and what they did to clarify their confusion. These directions were listed on the blackboard. I asked each group to select one facilitator to see that everyone in the group contributed to the discussion and one secretary to write down and report the group's findings.

Whereas the first day generated enthusiasm, the second day generated frustration. Students quickly realized that the article never explained what "Critical Mass" was. Typical reactions were: "Is this the whole article? Is there something missing?" "What does 'hats and bats' refer to?" "We can't figure it out, we need a clue." "Why can't you just tell us the answer?" "How is this going to be useful to me?" Students were focused on getting the right answers to the questions, but had great difficulty identifying and describing the processes they used to find the answers. I had to repeat the instructions and give examples of what I meant by the instruction to describe not just the answers but *how* they got them. I also had to reassure them that the thinking process they used was more important than the answers, that they could do it, and that going through this would be beneficial to them because it would enable them to figure out the meaning of difficult reading passages when a teacher was no longer present to tell them. With encouragement and prompting, students began to work together to describe their answers and the steps they took to find them.

On the third day, each group reported their experiences. All agreed that "Critical Mass" was never explicitly defined and that they had to figure out its meaning. Here are some strategies they used:

1. *Think about what the words mean.* "Critical" means important; "mass" means amount; therefore, "critical mass" means to reach an important amount, i.e. enough cyclists to have an impact. (No one had heard the term "critical mass" in reference to atomic reactions.)

2. *Put together all the facts or phrases mentioned throughout the article and then see what they add up to.* For example, "demonstration," "lots of cyclists," "will block traffic," "will assert their right to ride" taken together paint a picture of a confrontational demonstration for cyclists' rights.

3. *Guess; then reread the confusing part of the passage and see if it makes sense.* For example, one student said he read the section headed "Hats and Bats," found the statement containing this phrase ("It's going to be hats and bats . . . with arrests") and concluded that it must refer to the police making arrests. In response to my prompt, "What will that be like?" they answered, there will be physical violence, like nightsticks against bicycle helmets.

At this point I commented that reading is not a sequential process, but a back-and-forth process. Pre-reading activates and focuses your thinking; then you jump around the article and relate different parts to each other as you look for the answers to your questions.

On the fourth day, we reviewed some guidelines for summarizing (write in paragraph form, include all the main points but not all the details, examples, or dialogue in the original article). How did they decide what to include? They answered:

1. Use the questions that you created before reading to help you read.

2. Use the section divisions of the article and work with the main ideas in each section.

3. Use the quotes in the article, but not word for word — just to identify what the people want.

4. See what the article is mainly speaking about.

5. Use the title, headings, subheadings, and insets for clues.

6. Find the outcome of the main idea — what happened.

A few of the summaries were excellent, a few too detailed, most too terse. The most common outcome was to state what the conflict was without telling the *events* described in the article: what the parties did and what those parties predicted would happen next. Summarizing is hard, and the hardest aspect for students was to go beyond obedience of the rule that a summary should be short to a thoughtful consideration of what ideas are important. Development of good summarization skills requires a great deal of practice, possibly more than any of the other skills.

Finally, I asked students for their reactions to this holistic approach vs. the textbook exercises they had done previously to identify the topic, main idea, and supporting details of an isolated paragraph. Two to one, the majority preferred the holistic method, for two reasons: (1) You can get the big picture of what the article is about and that can help you to understand each paragraph. (2) You can get clues about the meaning of a paragraph by reading ahead or by looking back to other parts of the article. This, in a nutshell, captures the process of actively thinking to construct meaning from a written text.

Conclusions

These exercises demonstrate a holistic approach to reading, that is, reading with the whole context in mind. It is likely that good readers take this approach; they do not focus narrowly on the meaning of a word or the main idea of a paragraph in isolation, without paying attention to the meaning and direction of the whole piece. If we want to prepare students for real reading, we should teach reading skills in context, not in isolation, so that students can employ the full range of their thinking skills. Many of the skills attributed to proficient readers, such as constructing knowledge as an organization of concepts rather than as isolated facts, understanding meanings and relationships rather than recalling details, predicting the development of ideas, drawing inferences, and clarifying confusion (Long & Long, 1987; Palincsar & Brown, 1984, 1989) can best be built when students work with complete passages that have a fully developed conceptual structure. Attempting to develop students' comprehension using isolated paragraphs may seem simpler, but for my students who wanted to put clues together from the larger context of the article, it was actually more difficult.

Moreover, developing metacognitive reading skills is not a single-stage process. These skills require much repeated practice, and have to be learned many times over with different reading passages in order to become more comfortable and habitual. When I repeated this procedure using progressively lengthier and more technical passages, students still struggled to master the metacognitive skills, and needed to review them again and again. Students need to be prodded to read actively with each new piece, to overcome their resistance to thinking through their confusion and to changing old habits. Yet, only by struggling with these skills over time did they begin to develop the confidence that they *could* figure out meaning for themselves.

Students initially found the metacognitive process arduous and frustrating because it forced them to think in ways they were not used to. However, as they worked together, they became more excited and enjoyed what they did, and afterward they were proud of what they had accomplished. They smiled as they reported what they had figured out. And the experience stayed with them: while reviewing these skills later with subsequent passages, they would frequently exclaim, "Oh, it's like Critical Mass!" The article that was initially frustrating became their symbol of struggle and success.

References

Aldridge, M. (1989). Student questioning: A case for freshman academic empowerment. *Research and Teaching in Developmental Education, 5*(2), 17–24.

Baker, L., & Brown, A. L. (1984). Metacognitive skills and reading. In P. D. Pearson, R. Barr, J. L. Kamil, & P. Rosenthal (Eds.), *Handbook of reading research.* New York: Longman Press.

Carroll, L. (1960). *Alice's adventures in wonderland and Through the looking glass.* New York: Signet.

Flavell, J. H. (1979). Metacognition and cognitive monitoring: A new area of cognitive-developmental inquiry. *American Psychologist, 34*(10), 906–911.

Hartman, H. J. (1994). From reciprocal teaching to reciprocal education. *Journal of Developmental Education, 18*(1), 2–8, 32.

Hartman, H., & Sternberg, R. J. (1993). A broad BACEIS for improving thinking. *Instructional Science, 21,* 401–425.

Long, J. D., & Long, E. W. (1987). Enhancing student achievement through metacomprehension training. *Journal of Developmental Education, 11*(1), 2–5.

Matier, P., & Ross, A. (1997). Defiant bicyclists to snub S.F. mayor. *San Francisco Chronicle,* July 21, p. A1.

Palincsar, A. S., & Brown, A. L. (1989). Instruction for self-regulated reading. In L. B. Resnick & L. E. Klopfer (Eds.), *Toward the thinking curriculum: Current cognitive research.* Alexandria, VA: Association for Supervision and Curriculum Development Yearbook.

Palincsar, A. S., & Brown, A. L. (1984). Reciprocal teaching of comprehension-fostering and comprehension-monitoring activities. *Cognition and Instruction, 1*(2), 117–175.

Paris, S. G., Wixson, K. K., & Palincsar, A. S. (1986). Instructional approaches to reading comprehension. *Review of Research in Education, 13,* 91–128.

Stahl, N. A., Simpson, M. L., & Hayes, C. G. (1992). Ten recommendations from research for teaching high-risk college students. *Journal of Developmental Education, 16*(1), 2–10.

Sternberg, R. J. (1986). *Intelligence applied: Understanding and increasing your intellectual skills.* New York: Harcourt Brace Jovanovich.

Using a Model of Direct Instruction to Teach Summary Writing in a College Reading Class

Martha E. Casazza

In this article, Martha E. Casazza presents the theory-based direct instruction model EMQA, along with a description of how to use its component steps: explanation, modeling, questioning, and application. Casazza also illustrates the use of this model with a version of Brown and Day's well-researched summarization strategy for developing comprehension skills. In conclusion, the advantages of teaching summarization with the EMQA direct instruction model are provided.

One of the primary goals of a reading program offered at the postsecondary level is to assist students in becoming successful learners. The program needs to produce active, thoughtful readers who can monitor their own comprehension and who have a set of strategies for interacting with text and organizing the information into a meaningful context. These strategies increase both comprehension and later retrieval.

One strategy that reinforces this interaction and manipulation of text is writing summaries. Through it, students can almost see the cognitive process that underlies successful comprehension. In addition, they are practicing critical thinking skills, often for the first time. As Rose (1989) asserts, "I couldn't imagine a more crucial skill than summarizing: we can't manage information, make crisp connections or rebut arguments without it" (p. 138).

While Rose speaks from direct experience with adult learners, Kintsch and van Dijk (1978) and Irwin (1986) provide a theoretical foundation. Irwin has described macroprocessing, the procedure one uses to construct meaning, as "the process of synthesizing and organizing individual idea units into a summary or organized series of related general ideas" (p. 5). Good readers distinguish the most important ideas in a passage and summarize them according to an appropriate organizational pattern. Irwin suggests that the major purpose of this activity is to enhance recall of the material by organizing it and by decreasing the number of ideas that need to be remembered.

Using a model of direct instruction to teach summarizing provides a natural framework for emphasizing to students that it is their responsibility to bring meaning to the text. Through direct instruction, there is a gradual release of instructor support as students become capable of applying the strategies independently. Vygotsky (1984) laid the foundation for this concept of release through his "zone of proximal development" where the learner, with external assistance, progresses from her present state of knowledge to a more advanced one where she can function independently.

Using direct instruction to teach summarizing has been investigated in a number of studies. Most often direct instruction has been linked with teaching students how to use a set of rules for summarizing (Hare, 1992). The rules that are most often used are derived from the work of Brown and Day (1980), who modeled them after Kintsch and van Dijk's explanation of the reading process. Hare (1992) advocates introducing students to the rules of summarizing so as to avoid their inferring a low level strategy of "delete, then copy."

One model of direct instruction that provides a framework for teaching the rules of summary writing is provided by Irwin (1986). This model, EMQA, includes the following components: explanation, modeling, questioning, and application. When used in a college classroom, this method has successfully taught students how to summarize.

Explanation

Most learners, especially college students who have been placed into a developmental reading course, need to know *what* they are learning and *why* it is important. In this first component of the EMQA model, summarizing is introduced and described explicitly. Students learn that to summarize text they must reduce the material to the key concepts, put these in their own words, and omit personal opinion. Through discussion, they discover that summarizing will help them to monitor their comprehension and thus learn more efficiently.

The instructor emphasizes that summarizing is a skill that will facilitate learning across the curriculum. To reinforce this idea, the primary materials used for instruction should come from content textbooks or periodicals; they should never be short exercises written to teach summarizing. As a result, from the beginning, students will see the relevancy of the task and have a purpose for learning it.

The second part of the explanation component is an explicit description of four rules for writing a summary. The rules have been adopted from the work of Brown and Day (1980), and include the following:

- *Delete* minor and redundant details,
- *Combine* similar details into categories and provide a label, then
- *Select* main idea sentences when the author provides them or
- *Invent* main idea sentences when the author is not explicit.

Students are told that all the rules must be integrated to construct a good summary. Practice and direct instruction, however, are provided for each rule individually. Since Brown and Day (1980) have found that the students apply the rule of deletion most successfully, instruction can begin here and then move into the more difficult areas of combining ideas and selecting or inventing the main ideas.

The latter three rules demand higher order processing from the students and need to be explained in concrete terms as they are applied to college text. To combine ideas, students must synthesize across the text and selectively delete information. To do this, they must construct relationships among ideas; one type of relationship is that of general to specific. The following example demonstrates how an instructor can lead a class to identify such relationships.

> *Instructor to class:* [referring to text previously read] The author discusses how the school corridors are in disrepair, the clocks in the classrooms don't work, and the speaker system rarely carries announcements to all classrooms. She also relates that the rate of student absenteeism is high, the number of dropouts increases each year, and few graduates go on to college. There seem to be two general problems with this high school; can you identify them? What specific details led you to this conclusion?

When the students identify the two general concepts within this text, building disrepair and student motivation, the instructor has them list the specific details that support each one. S/he then explains how only the two general labels would need to be included in a summary of this text. The specific supporting details would be deleted.

Providing direct instruction in main idea selection and invention is important because students often have misconceptions that they have not articulated before. They often expect the main idea to be explicit in the first or last sentence of each paragraph. Due to this expectation, they tend to use one of these sentences uncritically to guide their comprehension. It often surprises them to hear that if a main idea has been stated, it may be located elsewhere. In addition, they need to know that the main idea may be implicit; the author may not have provided one directly.

At this point, students need to be guided through paragraphs that exemplify both styles of writing and shown what it means to construct meaning. It is often a new concept that there is not always one sentence that serves as the main idea and that often the reader must actually invent one to make sense of the material. The student must begin to read critically and fill in the gaps where the author may not have been explicit.

Modeling

The next step in the instructional process is perhaps the most important and the one that must be repeated regularly in classroom activities. This is the modeling component of EMQA. For the four rules of summarizing to really make sense to the students, they must be modeled both verbally and in writing. The modeling should include examples of both the process and the product that results.

There are several ways in which modeling can occur. One way is for the instructor to articulate the thought process that s/he applies as s/he reads a text. Davey (1983) has described this activity as "think-alouds." The students can be instructed to read silently as the instructor reads aloud from a given text. The following examples demonstrate how the instructor reflects aloud after reading selected portions of text.

1. "The author doesn't seem to have one sentence that provides the main idea for this section; I guess I'll have to invent one. I'd better reread to see what really connects these ideas."

2. "The author includes so many details here that aren't important; if I try to remember them all, I'll only get confused. I think I'll cross out some of these names and numbers that aren't that significant."

3. "I didn't really understand this section; I'd better reread it and see what connects these ideas."

This instructor-led modeling gradually leads into a paired reading activity. Initially, a student is paired with the instructor to alternate in a read-aloud. As the class follows along silently, the instructor again articulates his/her thought process for short sections. At the end of each section, the instructor summarizes what s/he thinks the main idea is and why. The student who is paired with the instructor must agree with this summary, stating her/his reasons, or challenge it by asking for a specific rationale. This can lead to an active dialogue in which ideas are reconsidered and reconnected.

Once consensus has been reached on the main idea for a section, the roles are reversed, and the student reads aloud as the instructor listens.

Following several demonstrations of this process, the class is given a text and the students are placed in pairs with the instructor acting only as facilitator. The students are urged to become actively involved as they replicate the read-aloud with each other.

Following this activity, a spokesperson for each pair of students shares with the class the set of main ideas that they have constructed from the text. Discussion is encouraged, and groups often engage in lively sessions as they defend their choices. Following the class discussion, students return to their pairs where they collaborate on writing a summary based on the main ideas they have determined.

In addition to the think-alouds, the instructor needs to provide written models of summaries. These can come directly from the work submitted by the students or can be constructed by the instructor. When using students' summaries, the instructor should search for examples of how each of the four rules has been used.

If appropriate examples cannot be found in the students' work, the instructor can develop a summary that highlights the areas in which the students are experiencing trouble. For instance, by preparing a summary based on a text the students have been assigned, the instructor can highlight how implied main ideas can be stated and how certain details should be deleted.

One effective means of sharing these written models is through the use of an overhead transparency. The entire class can then discuss what appear as strengths and weaknesses. Following discussion, small groups can write revisions.

Questioning

The questioning portion of the direct instruction model should occur naturally within each of the other components, but the instructor can structure activities to ensure that it becomes a part of the direct learning experience. Too often students in postsecondary developmental reading classes are passive learners. Consequently, the instructor needs to provide strategies for active learning in addition to specific reading strategies. This often includes leading the students to ask appropriate questions. With this in mind, the instructor needs to provide opportunities for both process and product questions (Irwin, 1986) to direct the learning.

Students regularly ask product questions, those that relate to the finished product. They want to know if their paper is correct or incorrect. Does it have the correct number of pages? Should it be typed or handwritten? When is it due? All instructors are familiar with this type of question, and it does need to be addressed, but the students' focus needs to be shifted. Often product questions can be helpful if they are framed correctly.

One method for reframing product questions is for the instructor to ask students to compare their final summaries to a written model that is based on the same text. As the comparisons are made, the students' attention can be directed to the application of particular rules. For example, if students are experiencing difficulty with deleting details, they can be asked to look at a summary where the minor details were deleted successfully. The instructor can then model questions for them to ask, such as: What details does my summary include that were deleted from the model? What point do these details serve in my summary? If I delete these details, will I improve my summary? Why?

Process questions, those that occur as the summary is being written, should be encouraged and reinforced regularly. In part, this can be accomplished by requiring drafts of summaries that are evaluated and revised until they are acceptable. For each revision, the instructor can confer with the student and focus on the following types of process questions: How did you select this main idea statement? How did you decide to use this label to connect these ideas?

After several conferences, and in keeping with the concept of gradually releasing responsibility to the student, the instructor could assign students to raise their own process-related questions. Credit could be given to students for asking appropriate questions about their own work as well as that of their peers.

Application

The final component in the EMQA model is application, providing a range of opportunities for students to construct summaries. The students work both individually and in groups.

Every week, as an outside assignment, each student is responsible for finding an article to summarize from a journal that is related to her/his major field of study. (Within this field, s/he must choose one focused topic for the semester.) These articles represent a variety of organizational patterns and are usually the first ones the students have read in an academic journal format. Understandably, they are confused but always motivated since the content relates to their area of interest.

One class session is scheduled with the university librarian, who provides an overview on how to conduct a library search. In addition, instruction is provided in class regarding the general organization of these materials.

To reinforce the relevancy of the written summaries they have produced outside of class, students report orally on their latest article at the beginning of each class. They must provide the significant points for the other students and then be prepared to answer any questions. A major purpose is to make them take responsibility for becoming "experts" in one area so that during the last class session everyone shares an overall summary of what they have learned through their set of outside articles. We hold a symposium to hear everyone's new knowledge and to hear how individual summaries can lead to an overall understanding of a topic.

In addition to the symposium, the students each complete a synthesis paper in which they summarize all their summaries, thus applying the rule of summarizing at a macro level: Each summary must be reduced to only the most significant points. A section must be included in this final paper that reflects on all the individual summaries and describes how they relate to the student's topic.

While the students are discovering the relevancy of summary writing through the natural text that they find in academic journals, the class sessions are spent summarizing, most often in groups, and using text that is well organized with a variety of reader cues such as subtitles, abstracts, conclusions, and boldface highlights. Gradually throughout the quarter, text is introduced in class that is less formally structured.

Specific Ways to Get Students to Ask Their Own Process Questions

Students develop their ability to ask process-related questions during a peer editing activity that is modeled initially through student-instructor conferences. During these conferences, which are built into class sessions, the instructor asks the student questions about how the summary was constructed. Using the evaluation guidelines for student summaries as a basis for the questions, the instructor guides the student through a discussion of the process that occurred as the summary was originally being written.

Following several such conference sessions, the class as a whole constructs a series of questions that the students agree have been the most helpful when revising their own summaries. Students are then assigned to pairs where they edit each other's work using the questions agreed upon by the class to guide the process. The following questions are usually included in the peer editing activity:

- Why did/didn't you delete this detail?
- Which ideas from the text does this phrase represent?
- How did you decide that these ideas should be combined by using this phrase?
- What ideas led you to think this was the author's purpose?
- How did you identify the topic of this article?
- How does the main idea help you to narrow the focus of this topic?
- Does the author follow one organizational pattern? How many different patterns are used? Why do you think the author chose this pattern/s? How did the organization help you to understand the material?

The text is taken from periodical articles that represent a range of student interests, but care is taken by the instructor to initially use articles with obvious cues.

Working collaboratively in groups of three or four, the students must reach consensus on what material from an article to include, delete, or combine for a summary. Often they write their suggestions on a transparency in the form of lists (one each for deletions, main points, and labels for combining ideas) and then share their ideas through an overhead projector with the other groups in the class. As each group presents, the students must defend their ideas to the other groups who may have conflicting ones. After the groups have shared their suggestions with the whole class, the students return to their small groups and produce one cooperative summary.

Once the cooperative summaries have been completed, they are exchanged among the groups and edited according to guidelines provided by the instructor for evaluating summaries. Following the editing

Evaluation Guidelines for Student Summaries

The student:		Points earned		
Deletes minor details	0	1	2	3
Combines/chunks similar ideas	0	1	2	3
Paraphrases accurately	0	1	2	3
Reflects author's emphasis	0	1	2	3
Recognizes author's purpose	0	1	2	3
Identifies topic	0	1	2	3
Identifies main idea	0	1	2	3
Recognizes author's organization	0	1	2	3
Stays within appropriate length	0	1	2	3
Excludes personal opinions	0	1	2	3

Total points earned: _____ out of 30 possible

Additional comments:

Evaluation code: 0=never; 1=sometimes; 2=frequently; 3=always

activity, the summaries are returned to the groups that produced them. Each group individually discusses how the suggested revisions could be incorporated, and then the instructor leads a whole group session in which the students discover patterns of errors across the class.

The same guidelines that the students used to evaluate the cooperative summaries are used by the instructor to evaluate individual summaries (see Figure).

Multiple Advantages of EMQA

Teaching summary writing through a model of direct instruction provides developmental students with a learning strategy that increases their comprehension and that can be applied across the curriculum. The direct instruction model satisfies their need to know why they are taking the class and also provides the gradual release of responsibility for learning that is necessary if they are to succeed in their other coursework.

By using text that stimulates the students' initiative and by conferring "expert" status on them based on their independent reading, the reading course takes on a relevancy for students. The following comments were written by students who were asked to describe how they had changed as a result of the reading course.

> The advanced reading class that I have taken has been very beneficial in helping me do better in my other classes. (Note the descriptor "advanced" for a basic skills course.)

Presenting the Deletion Rule

The following text illustrates how the deletion rule can be demonstrated for students:

> The upstart E-men, with their law-and-order approach, made few friends at the EPA. Not all the agency's leaders were convinced they should be in the law-enforcement business. The squad grew slowly, from an initial 23 investigators to 48 by 1986. Fifteen more slots are expected under the 1990 federal budget, which still would mean just a handful of agents in each of the EPA's 10 regions. To bridge the gap, the E-men have offered training to state law-enforcement and environmental officers as well as to Drug Enforcement Administration and FBI agents. Bush's EPA administrator, William Reilly, has promised that the agency "will get tougher on enforcement, which is the cornerstone of EPA's environmental program. We expect to see even more activity in the future." (excerpted from *U.S. News and World Report*, Oct. 9, 1989)

This passage contains a variety of details that students often include in their summaries, e.g., numbers, quotations, and names. Following a direct explanation of the types of information that should be deleted for a summary and the rationale for the deletion, the instructor can use a text such as this one to model the process.

By reading aloud the sentences with details, the instructor can comment to the class on the author's purpose for including them. The instructor can also model how, when related to the whole passage, the details assist in determining the main idea but are individually insignificant.

A sample explanation from this passage might include the following:

Instructor: "The squad grew slowly, from an initial 23 investigators to 48 by 1986. Fifteen more slots are expected under the 1990 federal budget, which still would mean just a handful of agents in each of the EPA's 10 regions." [reflecting aloud] I think the author wanted to make the point that the squad of E-men is small and, while it will continue to grow, the plan is not to greatly increase the number of agents. The numbers in both sentences helped me to understand this. Twenty-three and 48 didn't seem too small until I read the last sentence and found out that they were spread out over 10 regions. That means only four or five men per region and the 15 additional slots doesn't even add two men to each one. I guess it wouldn't make much sense to try to remember the numbers, but the important point to remember is that the squad is small and will continue to have few men.

Now that I have taken this class my readings for other classes do not seem as tough. My reading time for other classes has been cut down now that I have been taught the correct way to read. It has helped my transition into college life.

References

Brown, A. L., & Day, J. D. (1980). *The development of rules for summarizing text.* Unpublished manuscript, University of Illinois, Urbana-Champaign.

Davey, B. (1983). Think-aloud-modeling the cognitive processes of reading comprehension. *Journal of Reading, 27,* 36–45.

Hare, V. C. (1992). Summarizing text. In J. Irwin & M. A. Doyle (Eds.), *Reading / writing connections: Learning from research.* Newark, DE: International Reading Association.

Irwin, J. (1986). *Teaching reading comprehension processes.* Englewood Cliffs, NJ: Prentice-Hall.

Kintsch, W., & van Dijk, T. A. (1978). Toward a model of text comprehension and production. *Psychological Review, 85,* 363–394.

Rose, M. (1989). *Lives on the boundary.* New York: Penguin Books.

Vygotsky, L. (1984). *Thought and language.* (E. Hanfmann & G. Vakar, Trans.). Cambridge, MA: The MIT Press.

Portfolio Purposes and Possibilities

Kenneth Wolf and Yvonne Siu-Runyan

As Kenneth Wolf and Yvonne Siu-Runyan point out, the underlying purposes for using the portfolio in developmental reading instruction define the form the portfolio will take. Here, the authors offer a definition and a framework that help instructors not only distinguish between various types of portfolios but also decide which type is appropriate for a particular pedagogical purpose. They accomplish this in part by identifying and describing three portfolio models: ownership, feedback, and accountability. For each model the article covers the author, audience, and purposes of the portfolio; the structure, contents, and process of portfolio use; and the strengths and limitations of portfolios. The authors also offer sage advice about the goals that should underlie the use of portfolios in effective developmental reading classrooms.

Portfolios in the United States have moved from innovation to convention in a remarkably short time. Ten years ago, they were largely an idea unfolding in conversations around the country. Today, portfolios are in place at the national level with the New Standards Project (Flanagan, 1994), in statewide assessments in Vermont and elsewhere (Brewer, 1990), and in many school districts, (Valencia & Place, 1994;

Wolf, 1989), schools (Hansen, 1992), and classrooms (Graves & Sunstein, 1992; Tierney, Carter, & Desai, 1990). In these many different settings, portfolios, not unexpectedly, have taken a variety of forms.

What is called a "portfolio" can range from a collection of personalized student products to a comprehensive array of student work and teacher records to standardized student assessments. While all of these versions fall under the label of portfolio, these collections of information vary considerably in what they contain, in how they are constructed, and in the way they are organized. However, even though they differ on many important dimensions, the various manifestations of portfolios are all shaped by the same consideration — the portfolio's purpose.

The purposes for keeping a portfolio ultimately determine the form that the portfolio will take. A portfolio system that promotes self-assessment and self-confidence in students as readers and writers, for example, will look very different from a portfolio that provides a valid and reliable basis for a statewide evaluation of student performance in literacy.

Given that portfolios can take a variety of forms, how do educators decide which models are the most appropriate for their purposes? Should portfolios be structured or open ended? Should they contain only students' self-selected work or a variety of information contributed by students, teachers, and parents? Should they reflect process as well as product?

With these considerations in mind, we offer a definition and a framework that we believe can help educators distinguish between different kinds of portfolios and make informed decisions about the types of portfolios that best suit their purposes. We begin with a brief overview of the theoretical and empirical underpinnings of portfolios. We follow with a definition of a portfolio, then present three different portfolio models that capture the essential differences between the many versions of portfolios that have unfolded in practice.

In describing each of these models, we discuss how the purpose for the portfolio shapes crucial decisions about the portfolio structure, content, and process. We then consider the strengths and limitations of each of the models. We conclude by discussing the relationship between productive portfolios and effective classrooms.

Theoretical Connections and Empirical Findings

The movement to student portfolios has been driven by new conceptions of teaching and learning, and by dissatisfaction with the dominance of standardized tests (Wolf, Bixby, Glenn, & Gardner, 1991). In particular, the cognitive revolution, along with an increasing recognition of the social and contextual nature of learning, has led to the view that learning is a dynamic and complex process that is strongly shaped by the social context and setting in which it occurs (Resnick & Resnick, 1992; Vygotsky, 1978).

At the same time, criticisms of current testing practices are on the rise. Educators have criticized multiple choice standardized tests, the dominant mode of testing in the U.S., for narrowing the curriculum (McNeil, 1988), distorting teaching (Haertel, 1990), undermining student motivation (Paris, Lawton, Turner, & Roth, 1991), deprofessionalizing teaching (Smith, 1991), and misrepresenting student achievement (Cannell, 1987). As a result, educators have begun to explore alternative forms of assessment.

Portfolios fit well with these new views of learning and assessment. Portfolios are malleable enough to capture individual styles and varied contexts, and are robust enough to reflect broad and significant features of learning. Moreover, if carefully conceptualized, portfolios not only present a window on learning but also promote growth by providing a textured picture of learning as it unfolds over time, enabling students and teachers to examine, discuss, and reflect on student performance and perspectives.

As for the value of portfolio-based collaborations and conversations, a number of theoretical and empirical research lines converge. Vygotsky (1978) has convincingly argued that learning is first and foremost a social process, while Slavin (1988) has highlighted the contribution that cooperative learning can make in advancing individual learning. Furthermore, the value of exploratory talk in deepening our understanding of concepts and in examining our work from a variety of perspectives has been documented by a number of educational researchers (Barnes, 1976; Dyson, 1993).

Although the theoretical support for portfolios is compelling, the professional literature on student portfolios is rich in rhetoric but slender in empirical evidence (Herman & Winters, 1994). Proponents argue that portfolios promote ownership of the learning process, foster reflection, enhance teaching, and open up assessment, to mention a few of the many claims (e.g., Wolf, 1989).

As for actual evidence of the effects of student portfolios, however, Herman and Winters (1994) found that most of the published articles on the topic were anecdotal or conceptual and few reported research-based results. We must recognize, however, that despite their widespread emergence, portfolios are in the early stage of development, and it may be too soon to draw strong conclusions about their effectiveness as learning strategies or assessment tools.

A Definition

This definition describes features that we believe are essential to all portfolios:

A portfolio is a selective collection of student work and records of progress gathered across diverse contexts over time, framed by reflection and enriched through collaboration, that has as its aim the advancement of student learning.

A PORTFOLIO IS SELECTIVE. A portfolio is not a random assortment of odds and ends, but a selective collection of information gathered for specific purposes. These purposes vary depending upon the person creating the portfolio and the context in which it is constructed, but all portfolios are assembled for specific (if sometimes implicit) purposes. The purpose may be to promote student self-assessment, to document student learning, to guide teaching, to communicate with parents about their child's progress, or to provide administrators and policy makers with information about the impact of the school's or district's instructional program. These purposes shape the portfolio products and processes and give a portfolio its focus.

A PORTFOLIO IS A COLLECTION OF STUDENT WORK AND RECORDS OF PROGRESS. The heart of a portfolio is student work, such as writing samples, reading journals, collaborative projects, and artistic creations. It is through the examination of collections of student work, which represent contextualized and complex performances, that students and teachers can gain insights into ways to support student learning. In addition to student work, records of student progress such as student-made reading logs and self-assessments, or teacher-constructed checklists of writing skills or observational notes, are invaluable as well. Records of progress not only complement the student work in the portfolio, but also provide information about important features of student learning, such as attitudes and motivation, that may not be visible in the student work itself.

A PORTFOLIO CONTAINS DIVERSE INFORMATION. Portfolios should contain a diverse set of information gathered across a variety of learning contexts, content areas, and forms of communication; otherwise, the full range of an individual's talents and interests may not be revealed. Qualitative researchers describe this process as triangulation (Erickson, 1986), an attempt to build a more complete and accurate picture by drawing on multiple sources of information.

A PORTFOLIO SHOWS DEVELOPMENT OVER TIME. One of the chief values of a portfolio is its ability to show the growth of a piece of work or of a learner over time. Standardized tests provide the equivalent of black-and-white snapshots, while a portfolio, by comparison, is more like a movie that shows not only events over time, but shows them with sound and color as well. Viewing learning over time also allows the documentation of process as well as product and enables students and teachers to see patterns in their performances.

A PORTFOLIO IS REFLECTIVE.   More than anything else, the portfolio process should inspire reflection. Collecting and examining one's work provides a powerful opportunity for studying the "biographies of a work" (Wolf, 1993, p. 227) as well as one's development as a learner. Reflection is what allows us to learn from our experiences; it is an assessment of where we have been and where we want to go next. Reflection in portfolios often takes the form of written comments by students on topics such as the quality of their work or the role of revision in their writing. Reflection may also take alternate forms, such as students drawing story graphs that capture their development as literate thinkers or designing book covers that represent them as readers.

Each portfolio might also include reflections from others about the learner and her/his work as well. With reflection, the portfolio can become "an episode of learning" (Wolf, 1993, p. 213); without reflection, the portfolio may be little more than a scrapbook.

A PORTFOLIO IS COLLABORATIVE.   Learning is not a solitary process, and constructing a portfolio should not be either. Interactions with others — peers, teachers, parents — should permeate the portfolio process as students set goals, carry out their work, and reflect on their accomplishments. Collaboration is a form of social reflection that provides learners with responses to and critiques of their work (Wolf, 1993). By discussing our ideas with others, we deepen our ability to reflect on our own work from a variety of perspectives. Moreover, through portfolio-based interactions we can create a portfolio culture within a community of learners.

THE AIM OF A PORTFOLIO IS TO ADVANCE STUDENT LEARNING.   While portfolios are constructed for a number of purposes, all of these purposes must serve one ultimate goal — to promote student learning. Helping students to assess themselves as readers and writers in order to develop their own learning goals, informing parents of their children's progress, guiding teachers in making effective instructional decisions, or providing administrators and policy makers with information about the overall quality of the instructional program are all legitimate purposes for keeping portfolios. However, no matter what the purposes are for using portfolios, the advancement of student learning must be central, otherwise the endeavor is misguided.

True portfolios, we believe, share the characteristics we have described. Thus, no matter the particulars of any portfolio system, all portfolios are constructed for clear and sound purposes, contain diverse collections of student work and records of progress assembled over time, are framed by reflections and enriched through collaboration, and have as their ultimate aim the advancement of student learning.

Even when honoring these criteria, however, the specific form that a portfolio takes can vary greatly depending upon its purposes. In the following section, we describe three different portfolio models, each reflecting a different primary purpose.

Three Models

We have identified three distinct portfolio models: *ownership, feedback,* and *accountability* portfolios. While *all* portfolios should (a) promote student ownership over the learning process; (b) present students, teachers, and parents with ongoing feedback to guide teaching and learning; and (c) provide information about student performance for accountability, what distinguishes these three types is that the primary purpose of each portfolio differs.

In practice, most portfolios cannot be neatly categorized into one of these three models but often are combinations of two or more. We have, however, drawn sharp contrasts between the various models to illustrate the key features of each and to help practitioners and policy makers understand the trade-offs in the portfolio models they are considering or have implemented

OWNERSHIP PORTFOLIOS. Ownership portfolios are personalized collections of student work that emphasize student choice and self-assessment. Typically, students collect a variety of information that illustrates their progress in reading and writing, they reflect on the development of their work and their learning, and they set goals for themselves as learners. The main purpose of the ownership portfolio is to provide students with an opportunity to explore, extend, display, and reflect on their own learning.

FEEDBACK PORTFOLIOS. Feedback portfolios are comprehensive collections of student work and teacher records, co-constructed by student and teacher, that provide ongoing documentation of student learning. These portfolios typically contain student work and reflections and teachers' records on student learning — such as running records (Clay, 1985) or observational records (Goodman, 1991) — as well as information from parents and peers.

Teachers, students, and parents use these portfolios to obtain a broad picture of student strengths and needs. The primary purpose of the feedback portfolio is to guide teachers and students in identifying effective learning and instructional strategies, as well as to communicate this information to parents.

ACCOUNTABILITY PORTFOLIOS. Accountability portfolios are selective collections of student work, teacher records, and standardized assessments that are submitted by students and teachers according to structured guidelines. Accountability portfolios typically contain student responses to standardized performance assessments, a selection of student work created according to specific criteria, and structured records from teachers. The primary purpose of this type of portfolio is to evaluate student achievement for accountability and program evaluation.

As illustrated by the three definitions, each of these portfolio models — ownership, feedback, and accountability — is driven by a different primary purpose and, as a consequence, has a different emphasis in terms of its authorship, audience, structure, content, and process. In the following section, we elaborate on how these three types of portfolios differ from one another on each of these dimensions, and we then comment on the respective strengths and limitations of each model.

Author, Audience, and Purpose

Portfolios vary according to their purposes, and these different purposes determine the portfolios' authors and audiences (see Figure 1).

The ownership portfolio is owned and authored by the student, and the main audience for the portfolio is that student. The purpose of ownership portfolios is to promote student ownership over the learning process. To achieve this purpose, students must be given the authority for making decisions about what they want to learn and the responsibility for evaluating their own learning.

The feedback portfolio is developed cooperatively by students, teachers, and in some instances parents, and may contain submissions from each. Because its purpose is to guide teaching and learning by providing a comprehensive view of student learning, its primary audiences are the student, teacher, and parents.

The accountability portfolio is authored by the student, teacher, and individuals and institutions outside of the classroom, such as assessment developers or state departments of education. While the accountability portfolio can provide valuable insights for those inside the classroom, its primary audience is external. Its purpose is to present a summary evaluation of student achievement for accountability.

Structure, Content, and Process

Besides determining author and audience, the portfolio purpose is instrumental in shaping the form, content, and process of the portfolio as well. Depending upon the purpose, portfolio structures can range from open-ended to highly organized, portfolio contents can range from idiosyncratic collections to standardized sets of performances, and the portfolio processes can range from ongoing self-assessments to formal evaluations of student achievement (see Figure 2).

The ownership portfolio is loosely structured and contains a variety of work selected by the student to illustrate his or her reflection and progress towards self-chosen goals. An ownership portfolio contains student work and student-generated records of progress, along with the student's periodic reflections on his or her learning.

Figure 1. Portfolio Purposes

	Ownership	**Feedback**	**Accountability**
Author	Student	Student/teacher	Student/teacher/ assessment developer
Audience primary	Student	Student/teacher/ parent	Policy maker/public
secondary	Teacher/parent	Administration/ policy maker/public	Student/teacher/ parent/administration
Purpose primary	Promote independent learning	Guide teaching and learning	Inform accountability
secondary	Guide teaching and learning	Promote independent learning	Guide teaching and learning
	Inform accountability	Inform accountability	Promote independent learning

Figure 2. Portfolio Possibilities

	Ownership	**Feedback**	**Accountability**
Structure	Open-ended, student determined	Semistructured; student, teacher, and parent choices	Highly structured, standardized
Content	Student work and records such as reading logs, writing samples, videotapes of performances	Student work and records, teacher records, information from parents	Selected student work, structured responses, standardized
Process	Students reflect on and assess their own goals.	Teacher, student, and parents together assemble and review portfolio.	Students respond to standardized prompts and collect work according to specified criteria. Evaluation is often done by those outside classroom.

The feedback portfolio is semistructured with both student and teacher, and in some instances parents, submitting information for it. The teacher, students, and parents then work together to assemble a profile of each student's strengths, needs, and progress in order to plan effective teaching and learning activities.

A feedback portfolio contains student work samples such as writing samples and content area projects, student progress records such as reading logs or self-assessments, and teacher progress records such as running records and classroom observations. Parents may offer information about the student's literate activities outside of school. A contrast between students' school and home literate activities can provide useful insights for guiding instruction (Heath, 1983).

The accountability portfolio is highly structured, and a portion of the contents are usually externally mandated. This type of portfolio is tightly constrained so that student performance can be more fairly, efficiently, and reliably evaluated on a large scale. Contents typically include student responses to performance assessments, and student work created and collected under carefully specified conditions.

Strengths and Limitations

The same features that make a portfolio attractive for one purpose often render it less helpful for others. For example, the personalization of the portfolio is a virtue when the purpose is to allow students to explore an area of their own choosing, but it can be a severe liability when the purpose is to evaluate student learning reliably and efficiently. No portfolio approach can address all purposes equally well; there are always tradeoffs to consider (see Figure 3).

The ownership portfolio's strengths are its flexibility and its role in promoting independent student learning. Its weaknesses are that it may not provide a broad view of student learning and is limited in use for accountability purposes. The ownership portfolio is the best choice when the goal is to stimulate and deepen student interests, motivation, and self-assessment.

The feedback portfolio's primary strengths are its comprehensiveness and its role in providing teachers, students, and parents with ongoing feedback to help identify the most effective teaching and learning activities. Its weaknesses are that student ownership is reduced, and it can be time-consuming and cumbersome for teachers and students to manage. The feedback portfolio is a good choice when the goal is to obtain an ongoing and broad view of student learning.

The accountability portfolio's main strength is its focus on clear learning outcomes that can be measured in a reliable and efficient fashion. Its weaknesses are that it allows less flexibility for student choice and it can be artificial in nature. The accountability portfolio is most appropriate when the goal is a large-scale assessment of student achievement for accountability and program evaluation.

Goals

In this article, we have emphasized that portfolios can serve a variety of purposes, and, as a result, they can take many different forms. While no single portfolio approach can meet all needs, a careful consideration

Figure 3. Portfolio Tradeoffs

	Ownership	Feedback	Accountability
Strengths	Is student driven and has great flexibility	Offers a comprehensive view of teaching and learning	Provides a summary measure of performance against clear standards and benchmarks
	Promotes student independence and self-reflection	Guides teaching and learning by providing immediate and ongoing feedback	Shows individual and group performance
	Provides insights into student interests and into how students see themselves	Gives teachers, students, and parents a departure point for substantive discussions about student learning	Allows comparisons
Limitations	Can be idiosyncratic	Reduces student ownership	Limits student ownership
	May not provide broad view of student learning	Can be time consuming and cumbersome to to maintain	May be artificial
			May not tap into student interests and strengths

of the purpose for the portfolio can guide students, teachers, parents, administrators, and policy makers in making informed decisions about the design and use of portfolios.

It is important to keep in mind, however, that portfolios are a means, not an end. The goal is not to create wonderful portfolios, but to promote more effective learning. A portfolio can accomplish the goal of advancing student learning only if the experiences documented are worthwhile. That is to say, portfolios are only as good as the curriculum and instructional opportunities afforded to students. As L. S. Shulman (personal communication, April 1991) has commented, it is difficult to fashion a silk purse portfolio out of a sow's ear curriculum.

Thus, the portfolio definition that we propose not only describes what we believe are essential features of an effective *portfolio,* but also critical features of an effective *classroom.* We have argued that portfolios should present a picture of student learning across diverse and engaging activities, be infused with reflection and collaboration, and promote student development. This definition implies that classrooms should provide students with diverse and engaging experiences, along with frequent opportunities for reflection and collaboration, with the ultimate aim of advancing student learning. Fortunately, carefully designed portfolios can make such classrooms more possible.

References

Barnes, D. (1976). *From communication to curriculum.* Harmondsworth, England: Penguin.

Brewer, R. (1990). *The development of portfolios in writing and mathematics for state-wide assessment in Vermont.* Paper presented at the Institute on New Modes of Assessment, Cambridge, MA.

Cannell, J. J. (1987). *National norm-referenced elementary achievement testing in America's public schools: How all fifty states are above the national average.* Charleston WV: Friends of Education.

Clay, M. M. (1985). *The early detection of reading difficulties.* Auckland, New Zealand: Heinemann.

Dyson, A. H. (1993). *Social worlds of children learning to write in an urban primary school.* New York: Teachers College Press.

Erickson, F. (1986). Qualitative methods in research on teaching. In M. Wittrock (Ed.), *Handbook of research on teaching* (3rd ed., pp. 119–161). New York: Macmillan.

Flanagan, A. (1994, September). ELA teachers engaged in massive portfolio project. *The Council Chronicle: The National Council of Teachers of English,* pp. 1, 4–5.

Goodman, Y. (1991). Informal methods of evaluation. In J. Flood, J. Jensen, D. Lapp, & J. Squire (Eds.), *Handbook of research on teaching the English language arts* (pp. 502–509). New York: Macmillan.

Graves, D. H., & Sunstein, B. S. (Eds.). (1992). *Portfolio portraits.* Portsmouth, NH: Heinemann.

Haertel, E. (1990). Student achievement tests as tools of educational policy: Practices and consequences. In B. R. Gifford (Ed.), *Test policy and test performance: Education, language, and culture* (pp. 13–14). Boston: Kluwer Academic.

Hansen, J. (1992). Literacy portfolios: Helping students know themselves. *Educational Leadership,* 49, 66–68.

Heath, S. B. (1983). *Ways with words: Language, life, and work in communities and classrooms.* New York: Cambridge University Press.

Herman, J., & Winters, L. (1994). Portfolio research: A slim collection. *Educational Leadership,* 52, 48–55.

McNeil, L. (1988). Contradictions of control, Part 2: Teachers, students, and curriculum. *Phi Delta Kappan,* 69, 433–438.

Paris, S. G., Lawton, T. A., Turner, J. C., & Roth, J. L. (1991). A developmental perspective on standardized achievement testing. *Educational Researcher,* 20, 12–20.

Resnick, L., & Resnick, D. (1992). Assessing the thinking curriculum: New tools for educational reform. In B. R. Gifford & M. C. O'Conner (Eds.), *Changing assessments: Alternative view of aptitude, achievement, and instruction,* (pp. 37–75). Boston: Kluwer Academic.

Slavin, R. (1988). Cooperative learning and student achievement. *Educational Leadership,* 45, 31–33.

Smith, M. L. (1991). Put to the test: The effects of external testing on teachers. *Educational Researcher,* 20, 8–11.

Tierney, R. J., Carter, M. A., & Desai, L. E. (1990). *Portfolio assessment in the reading-writing classroom.* Norwood, MA: Christopher-Gordon.

Valencia, S., & Place, N. (1994). Literacy portfolios for teaching, learning, and accountability. The Bellevue Literacy Assessment Project. In S. Valencia, E.

Hiebert, & P. Afflerbach (Eds.), *Authentic reading assessment: Practices and possibilities* (pp. 134–156). Newark, DE: International Reading Association.

Vygotsky, L. (1978). *Mind in society.* Cambridge, MA: Harvard University Press.

Wolf, D. P. (1989). Portfolio assessment: Sampling student work. *Educational Leadership, 46,* 35–39.

Wolf, D. P. (1993). Assessment as an episode of learning. In R. Bennett and W. Ward (Eds.), *Construction versus choice in cognitive measurement: Issues in constructed response, performance testing, and portfolio assessment* (pp. 213–240). Hillsdale, NJ: Erlbaum.

Wolf, D. P., Bixby, J., Glenn, J., & Gardner, H. (1991). To use their minds well: Investigating new forms of student assessment. In G. Grant (Ed.), *Review of Research in Education* (pp. 31–74). Washington, DC: American Educational Research Association.

Additional Readings

Gallik, J. D. (1999). "Do they read for pleasure? Recreational reading habits of college students." *Journal of Adolescent & Adult Literacy, 42*(6), 480–88.

Hayes, C. A., Stahl, N. A., & Simpson, M. L. (1991). "Language meaning and knowledge: Empowering developmental students to participate in the academy." *Reading Research and Instruction, 30*(3), 89–100.

Iannuzzi, P., Strichart, S. S., & Mangrum, C. T. (1998). *Teaching study skills and strategies in college.* Boston: Allyn and Bacon.

Martino, N. L., Norris, J. A., & Hoffman, P. R. (2001). "Reading comprehension instruction: Effects of two types." *Journal of Developmental Education, 25*(1), 2–12.

McKeachie, W. J. (2000). *Teaching tips: Strategies, research, and theory for college and university teachers,* 11th ed. Boston: Houghton Mifflin.

Nist, S. L., & Holschun, J. L. (2000). "Comprehension strategies at the college level." In R. F. Flippo & D. C. Caverly (Eds.), *Handbook of college reading and study strategy research* (pp. 75–104). Mahwah, NJ: Erlbaum.

Nist, S. L., & Simpson, M. L. (2000). "College studying." In M. L. Kamil, P. B. Mosenthal, P. D. Pearson, & R. Barr (Eds.), *Handbook of reading research: Volume III* (pp. 645–66). Mahwah, NJ: Erlbaum.

Simpson, M. L., & Randall, S. L. (2000). "Vocabulary development at the college level." In R. F. Flippo & D. C. Caverly (Eds.), *Handbook of college reading and study strategy research* (pp. 43–73). Mahwah, NJ: Erlbaum.

Stahl, N. A., Simpson, M. L., & Hayes, C. G. (1992). "Ten recommendations from research for teaching high-risk college students." *Journal of Developmental Education, 16*(1), 2–11.

4

Strategic Learning

With the coming of the elective system to higher education in the first half of the twentieth century, practitioners and researchers alike became more interested in helping students become effective and efficient learners of content area subject matter. In the early years of the century, authors of study methods textbooks often based their recommendations upon the introspective reports of reading/study activities undertaken by successful students. Then, with educators' adoption of the principles of scientific management theory, the work method students used to approach a learning task gained importance in college reading research and teaching. As theory was translated into practice, the view emerged that a single best — most effective and efficient — way to approach a learning task existed. From this belief came one-size-fits-all learning methods known over the years as work-type methods, work-study skills, and later simply study skills.

With the cognitive revolution in the second half of the twentieth century, however, the concept of strategic and tactical theory sparked interest in the field of postsecondary reading and learning. And during the last twenty years, this concept has been welcomed into classrooms and assistance centers across the country. Unfortunately, however, the term *strategy* has been so regularly misused that in too many cases the power of the strategic approach has been lost on the student. We hope this chapter will help solve that problem through its coverage of current theory, research, and practice about strategic learning.

This chapter begins with an article in which Michele L. Simpson and Sherrie L. Nist point out five theory and research driven generalizations about strategic learning, along with the practical implications of these points for the classroom. The article by Martha E. Casazza that follows employs theories from cognitive science, linguistics, adult education, reading, and psychology to show how students in developmental education programs learn. Next, Claire E. Weinstein and her colleagues from the University of Texas at Austin present their Model of Strategic Learning, along with their design of a learning-to-learn course based on that model. They also share results from a five-year longitudinal study of participants in this course. Finally, Donna L. Mealey demonstrates the correlation between students' low academic performance in developmental reading courses, on the one hand, and their poor motivation and negative self-concepts on the other. In addition, she proposes specific interventions based on strategic learning and metacognition that help students become more highly motivated, independent learners.

An Update on Strategic Learning: It's More Than Textbook Reading Strategies

Michele L. Simpson and Sherrie L. Nist

Here, the authors share the five theory and research driven generalizations about strategic learning that emerged from their extensive literature review. They are: (1) Task understanding is critical to strategic learning; (2) Beliefs about learning influence how students read and study; (3) Quality instruction is essential; (4) It is important to teach a variety of research-based strategies; and (5) Cognitive and metacognitive processing should be the instructional focus. In addition, the authors offer six practical suggestions for program and course development. Finally, an extensive reference list updates past literature reviews.

Most researchers would agree that strategic learners are those students who have a vast repertoire of strategies that they can selectively apply in order to complete tasks across a variety of content areas (Pressley, 1995; Weinstein, 1994). Although the term *strategic learning* involves several complex and interactive factors, at a basic level it suggests that students possess effective strategies for reading textbooks as well as a variety of strategies useful in studying. As Rohwer (1984) so aptly pointed out, studying is an integral part of our literacy curriculum because the strategies we teach provide students with the "principal means of self-education throughout their life" (p. 1).

Some educators have assumed that students have internalized these critical strategies and have mastered the complexities of strategic learning because they have been assigned homework, projects, and tests throughout their high school career (Zimmerman, 1998). However, the reality may set in when high school graduates enter college and soon realize that they lack the mature strategies necessary to succeed academically. Many of these students are passive learners who possess rote-level strategies for reading and studying (Pressley, Yokoi, van Meter, Van Etten, & Freeburn, 1997). In order to address these problems that college freshmen face, many universities offer some vehicle of academic assistance to help students become more strategic learners (Maxwell, 1997; Simpson, Hynd, Nist, & Burrell, 1997). Some institutions have entire programs to provide students with a variety of academic assistance options; others offer Learning to Learn courses that focus on teaching students specific reading and studying strategies.

To be successful, practitioners in academic assistance need to incorporate what is known from the extant theory and research. Fortunately, during the past 10 years many important research studies have investigated strategies for reading and studying. Moreover, there is a burgeoning body of literature that has examined other factors that have an impact on students' academic success and contribute to strategic learning. These more recent studies, however, have not been summarized and synthesized since Anderson and Armbruster (1984). Hence, we decided to review this literature in a format useful for practitioners who are looking for guidance as they develop and refine their curriculum.

We begin by examining five generalizations that emerged from our review of the literature. Then we offer some practical suggestions for academic assistance programs and courses. The studies and articles we selected for this review came from several sources: recent scholarly books, peer-reviewed reading and educational psychology journals from the past 10 years, and yearbooks from respected conferences such as the National Reading Conference. These search procedures assured us that we had included the most current and scholarly information in our review of the literature.

Five Generalizations about Strategic Learning

Although strategies for reading and studying have been part of an assumed or hidden curriculum, researchers have acknowledged their importance and have churned out numerous studies investigating their efficacy. Most of the studies during the 1960s, 1970s, and early 1980s were experimental or correlational and attempted to identify a superior study strategy system or to determine which strategy was more effective in a particular situation.

The earlier studies offered an equivocal array of findings for practitioners and researchers. For example, the conclusions drawn from the numerous studies on notetaking and outlining indicated that these strategies were no more effective than passive techniques such as rereading and memorizing (Brown, 1982). Accordingly, the reviews of the extant literature on strategy instruction and strategy programs have been cautious, at best. In fact, Anderson and Armbruster (1984) concluded that "empirical research fails to confirm the purported benefits of the popular strategies" and "the effort to find the one superior method has not been successful" (p. 665). Anderson and Armbruster also suggested that most strategies were being taught because of tradition or instructors' personal beliefs about their effectiveness, rather than because the empirical research confirmed their advantages and benefits.

The strategy research studies conducted during the mid-1980s and 1990s changed focus in several significant ways. Rather than attempting to identify a superior strategy, most of these studies investigated whether the performance of college students could be altered with instructional intervention. These later studies were particularly noteworthy in that the interventions were often quite intensive and explanatory, employing what Brown, Campione, and Day (1981) characterized as informed training. Unlike the earlier blind training studies where students were only told to use a strategy, informed training encouraged students to use a strategy and provided them specific information on how the strategy worked and why it was important.

During this same period the most significant change in the research on reading and studying strategies occurred with the emergence of the "cognitive constructivist vision of learning" (Mayer, 1996, p. 364). Such studies typically occurred in more authentic situations, such as in actual classroom settings, and viewed the learner as an active participant and "sense maker." Researchers, although diverse in their approaches, agreed that strategies embodied the essential cognitive and metacognitive processes necessary for college students to make meaning or sense of the world of academia (e.g., Mayer, 1996; Weinstein, 1994). In our analysis of these cognitive constructivist studies conducted during the past decade, we have found five generalizations that seem particularly relevant to academic assistance programs where the overall goal is to develop strategic learning.

Generalization 1: Task Understanding Is Critical to Strategic Learning

Academic tasks are the products students are asked to formulate, (e.g., tests or papers) and the operations or thinking processes (e.g., organizing, elaborating) they should use to create these products (Doyle, 1983). For example, a task in a biology course may be a 50-item multiple-choice test that requires students to understand the relationships between hormones and glands in the endocrine system. The task in history may be to read, analyze, and synthesize several different texts for an essay and short-answer exam. In order to be successful in their reading and studying, college students must understand the characteristics and nuances of academic tasks and then adjust their strategies accordingly. That is, for that biology course students might need to create a map or chart in order to understand the relationships, whereas for that history course students might need to predict possible questions and organize their answers into outlines or study sheets.

Tasks have been studied in a variety of ways. Some of the earlier researchers used laboratory settings to investigate the impact of students having complete, partial, or no task knowledge on their recall or recognition test performance (e.g., Rickards & Friedman, 1978). Although these studies have contributed to our understanding of the importance of specific and accurate task knowledge, the more recent research studies have moved to actual classroom settings where academic tasks are no longer defined and manipulated by the researcher. Rather, researchers have used classroom observations, interviews, and surveys to describe tasks across a variety of content areas (Chase, Gibson, & Carson, 1994; Chiseri-Strater, 1991; Donald, 1994; Hofer, 1998). Moreover, these more recent studies have focused on whether professors and their students hold similar perceptions about the tasks required in a particular course (Burrell, Tao, Simpson, & Mendez-Berrueta, 1996; Chase et al., 1994; Donald, 1994; Schellings, Van Hout-Wolters, & Vermunt, 1996a, 1996b; Simpson & Nist, 1997).

In general, the findings from these studies suggest that academic tasks are not only specific to a content area, but also specific to an instructor and a setting. That is, two history professors might very well expect students to read and think in totally different ways. Moreover, the findings indicate that students and instructors frequently have different perceptions of what is considered the essential reading and thinking processes in a particular course. When examining the differences in the sciences, Donald (1994), for example, found that the match in task perceptions between instructors and students was the closest in engineering courses and the furthest away from congruency in physics courses.

Another group of studies has investigated academic tasks using case study methodology in order to describe in depth the patterns that seem to exist between students' interpretation of academic tasks, their choice of strategies, and their subsequent academic performance. Simpson and Nist (1997), for example, studied one history course in depth to determine if the behaviors of students who performed successfully were different from those who performed unsuccessfully. In addition, they investigated how tasks were communicated to the students and whether the professor and students' perceptions of the tasks were congruent. Simpson and Nist concluded that students who earned high grades in the history course either initially understood the professor's academic tasks, or were flexible enough to modify their task perceptions and strategies over a period time. In contrast, those students who performed poorly did not understand the tasks and were inflexible in their beliefs and behaviors.

It appears that students' understanding of task is an important determinant of whether students select and employ appropriate strategies. The extant literature suggests that task identification must precede strategy selection or students are doomed to spend vast amounts of wasted time using inappropriate strategies and, in the end, not performing well in their courses.

Generalization 2: Beliefs about Learning Influence
How Students Read and Study

What students believe about learning and studying has an influence on how they interpret the task, how they interact with text, and, ultimately, the strategies they select. Because student beliefs are so important, Thomas and Rohwer (1987) suggested that beliefs serve as the "filter" through which students decipher and interpret the tasks and the materials they read. Students' beliefs about knowledge construction and how those beliefs influence learning are currently receiving considerable attention from researchers.

Perry (1968, 1970) was the first to discuss beliefs in an academic setting, and much of the subsequent work is rooted in his findings. The most current line of research examines beliefs that may influence students' performance on academic tasks. For example, Schommer and her colleagues have investigated students' beliefs about the nature of knowledge and learning by isolating their views about the certainty of knowledge, the organization of knowledge, and the control of knowledge acquisition (Schommer, 1994; Schommer, Calvert, Gariglietti, & Bajaj, 1997; Schommer & Hutter, 1995).

A slightly different approach, the reflective judgment model (King & Kitchener, 1994; Kitchener, King, Wood, & Davidson, 1989), posits that beliefs are developmental and, therefore, age related. It also assumes that individuals progress through seven stages, without skipping any. Although these approaches to thinking about beliefs differ in some respects, all models assume that individuals move from naïve to mature beliefs with experience.

Some of the most recent research in this area focuses on how students' beliefs influence factors such as motivation, strategy use, and academic performance. In a series of correlational studies, Schommer (1990, 1993) found significant relationships between certain scales on her beliefs questionnaire and student performance. For example, belief in "quick learning" led to poor performance on mastery tests and overconfidence in test performance (Schommer, 1990). In later studies, Schommer concluded that beliefs about knowledge may also influence students' self-report of strategy use (1993). Using more qualitative data collection methods, Simpson and Nist (1997) and Simpson, Nist, and Sharman (1997) found that students' beliefs about knowledge in general, and more specifically their beliefs about what history is, strongly influenced the strategies they selected and their interpretation of the task in a college history class.

One final area currently of interest related to beliefs and task definition is the controversy over whether beliefs are content specific or whether college students have the same underlying beliefs across all content areas (Hofer & Pintrich, 1997). Although this issue has not been investigated intensively, most of the research indicates that at a particular point in time students' beliefs about learning and knowledge would be at the same stage across all content areas (e.g., Schommer & Walker, 1995).

These and other studies (e.g., Hofer, 1998) suggest that students' beliefs play an important role in both task interpretation and strategy selection. It stands to reason that if students are not aware of their own beliefs, and of how those beliefs are in concert with those of their professors, they will have difficulty in both analyzing academic tasks and selecting appropriate strategies.

Generalization 3: Quality Instruction Is Essential

As noted by Paris, Wasik, and Turner (1991), it is imperative that students receive quality strategy instruction if the goal is to ensure that they can apply the strategies to their tasks and texts. One important legacy from the research studies of the 1980s and early 1990s is that we have a clearer sense of the characteristics of quality strategy instruction or training.

First, we know that in order to develop strategic learners who have a repertoire of approaches, a substantial amount of time must be committed to instruction (Garner, 1990; Pressley, 1995). The strategy instruction that students receive should be intensive and of significant duration. For example, in a study that validated the importance of sustained time, Nist and Simpson (1990) taught students the metacognitive processes of planning and evaluating. They found that students' metacognition gradually improved over time, but distinct and significant improvement did not emerge until 4 weeks after the initial instruction. Had the instruction and data collection ended with the first test, after only 1 week of intensive instruction, improvement would not have been detected and very different conclusions might have been drawn.

Second, strategy instruction should include not only the definition or "what" of a strategy, but also the procedural and conditional knowledge (Garner, 1990; Pressley, 1995). When students have procedural knowledge they understand the steps or processes involved in using a strategy. Conditional knowledge requires students to know the *why, where,* and *when* to select and apply a strategy as well as *how* to evaluate its effectiveness. For students to gain conditional knowledge, it is critical that they practice strategies with authentic texts and tasks and that they learn how to analyze the texts and tasks in order to determine which strategies are the most appropriate (Butler & Winne, 1995; Simpson, Hynd, et al., 1997). Moreover, the texts and tasks should be challenging and complex enough so that students will not opt for more simplistic routines (e.g., rereading) that are familiar to them and deemed more cost effective (Garner, 1990; Paris & Byrnes, 1989; Pressley, 1995).

Third, and perhaps most important, strategy instruction for college students should occur within a specific content area and situation (Alexander, 1996; Garner, 1990; Mayer, 1996; Pressley, 1995). As Garner (1990) pointed out, "One thing that we already know about strategy use is that it is embedded. It does not occur in a vacuum. When context varies, the nature of strategic activity often varies as well" (p. 523). The advantages of teaching strategies within a context are numerous. Students can learn how to define and interpret academic tasks, establish goals, select the appropriate strategies, and then evaluate the utility of those strategies in relationship to the specific context.

Finally, effective strategy instruction should be explicit and direct (Garner, 1990; Pressley, 1995). Explicit and direct instruction includes (a) strategy descriptions; (b) discussions of why the strategy should be learned and its importance; (c) think-alouds, models, and examples of how the strategy is used, including the processes involved and the relationship between the processes; (d) explanations as to when and where it is appropriate to apply the strategy; and (e) suggestions for monitoring and evaluating whether the strategy is working and what to do if it is not. Moreover, explicit instruction should include guided practice situations where students can apply the targeted strategies to authentic tasks. Students should receive specific instructor feedback on those practice attempts because such process checks are critical to the development of active learners (Butler & Winne, 1995). We have observed that very few researchers have actually collected and analyzed students' strategies to determine whether they have been correctly interpreted and applied, and few researchers, if any, have provided them with feedback on their strategy attempts (Simpson et al., 1997).

Strategy instruction, then, involves more than mere exposure to a specific strategy. The research indicates that in order to be effective, instruction should be direct, intensive, and occur over a sustained period of time. In addition, college students must be taught the procedural and conditional knowledge of a strategy. Finally, it is critical that strategy instruction be embedded in a realistic context because strategies taught in isolation have little transfer value.

Generalization 4: It Is Important to Teach a Variety of Research-Based Strategies

Our review of the literature found that there are a limited number of research-based strategies useful for students. The four reading and studying strategies we will examine have been tested in several research studies and have been conducted, in most situations, by a variety of researchers rather than just one. In addition, these studies have included explicit instruction and had high school or college students as participants. Although these strategies are discussed because they have demonstrated a consistent impact on or relationship to students' performance, one caveat should be noted: Their selection in no way implies that they are useful for all students, textbooks, or tasks. Research that has investigated these variables in a consistent manner simply does not exist.

QUESTION GENERATION AND ANSWER EXPLANATION   When students generate questions about what they have read and answer those questions, they are actively processing text information and monitoring their understanding of that information (Graesser & McMahen, 1993; King, 1990; King, 1995; Spires & Donley, 1998). In addition, students' comprehension of text improves, as revealed in Rosenshine, Meister, and Chapman's (1994) meta-analysis of 26 question-generation studies.

In order to train students to create task-appropriate questions that elicit higher levels of reading and thinking, several methods have been used. For example, in King's research studies (1989, 1992) she used generic question stems that asked students to analyze, predict, compare and contrast, apply, and evaluate (e.g., "What is an example of . . . ?"). Other research studies have capitalized on the power of reciprocal teaching in which students worked cooperatively in pairs, or small groups, asking each other questions and answering them in a reciprocal manner (e.g., King, 1990; King & Rosenshine, 1993). The findings from these studies and others have suggested that the question answering is of equal importance to the question asking because students are encouraged to clarify concepts, create alternative examples, or relate ideas to their partners' prior knowledge in order to answer the questions from their partners (King, 1995).

TEXT SUMMARIZATION   Writer-based summaries are external products that students create for themselves in order to reduce and organize information for subsequent study and review. According to Wittrock's (1990) model of generative comprehension, for a summary to be effective students must use their own words to form connections across the concepts and relate the concepts to their own prior knowledge and experiences. Such a definition of summarization implies that it is not a strategy quickly mastered. In fact, summarization is complex, causing many students difficulty (Brown & Day, 1983; Pressley et al., 1997). Because of the inherent difficulties in producing generative summaries, many of the earlier research studies, which did not provide explicit instruction of some duration, found that summaries had no impact on students' reading comprehension and performance (e.g., Howe & Singer, 1975). However, the majority of the more recent studies have found that writer-based summaries not only improve students' comprehension, but also help them monitor their understanding (King, 1992; O'Donnell & Dansereau, 1992; Wittrock, 1990).

Summarization as a strategy has taken a variety of forms. Many of the studies in the mid-1980s involved teaching students summarization rules and hoping to make explicit the steps that expert readers use when they read and study text (Day, 1980; Hare & Borchardt, 1984). Other investigations (e.g., O'Donnell & Dansereau, 1992) have examined the combined impact of dyad learning and summarization on students' performance. For example, O'Donnell and Dansereau reported that students who worked in dyads to summarize outperformed those who worked alone, recallers learned more than listeners, and dyads that were heterogeneous in ability and cognitive style tended to be more effective than dyads that were homogenous.

Nist and Simpson (1988) incorporated many of Wittrock's principles of summarization into a text-marking strategy called annotation, training students to write brief summaries in the margins of their texts and to note other key ideas. These researchers and others have found that students' test performance and summary writing abilities improved when they were taught to summarize and annotate (Harris, 1991; Hynd, Simpson, & Chase, 1990; Strode, 1991).

STUDENT-GENERATED ELABORATIONS   When students generate elaborations, they create examples or analogies, draw inferences, and explain the relationships between two or more concepts (Gagne, Weidemann, Bell, & Anders, 1984). Anderson and Armbruster's (1984) review of studying indicated that there were few studies investigating the effect of elaboration on students' learning from text. Since that time, however, several studies have investigated this impact (Pressley, McDaniel, Turnure, Wood, & Ahmad, 1987; Simpson, Olejnik, Tam, & Supattathum, 1994; Woloshyn, Willoughby, Wood, & Pressley, 1990). These studies confirmed earlier findings (e.g., Diekhoff, Brown, & Dansereau, 1982) that students can be trained to create elaborations. More important, however, the recent studies have demonstrated rather consistently that self-generated elaborations can have a significant impact on students' performance on both recall and recognition measures.

Pressley and his colleagues have conducted numerous studies on elaborative interrogation (e.g., Kaspar & Wood, 1993; Pressley, McDaniel, et al., 1987; Pressley, Symons, McDaniel, Snyder, & Turnure, 1988; Woloshyn et al., 1990). Elaborative interrogation involves students in making connections between ideas they have read and their prior knowledge by generating "why" questions and then answering those questions. Because the elaborative interrogation studies have examined a variety of issues having an impact on students' strategy use (e.g., role of prior knowledge, developmental trends), several important findings have emerged. First, older students, such as college learners, generally are more able to use the elaborative interrogation strategy than younger students. Second, the quality of the generated elaborations does not have an impact on students' understanding when the targeted topic is one for which they have some prior knowledge. Finally, average-achieving students generally provide higher quality elaborations than lower-achieving students.

In a different type of elaboration study, Simpson et al. (1994) trained students to select key ideas from their reading, to create elaborations, and then to recite them orally. Findings were similar to those from the elaboration interrogation studies; the students who produced oral elaborations performed significantly better than their counterparts on immediate recall and recognition measures. Simpson et al. also investigated the long-term impact of the strategy, discovering that oral elaborations had a significant impact on students' delayed recall that occurred 2 weeks later in an unannounced situation.

ORGANIZING STRATEGIES   Perhaps the most researched of the strategies are those that help students organize information from what they have read or studied. Several researchers have sought to validate the effectiveness of strategies that help students visually organize and represent important relationships among ideas present in written or oral text (Bernard & Naidu, 1992; Briscoe & LeMaster, 1991; Kiewra, 1994; Lambiotte, Peale, & Dansereau, 1992; McCagg & Dansereau, 1991). Most of these organizing strategies involve students in identifying main ideas and subordinate ideas, making connections among those ideas, and then choosing a way to visually represent those relationships in an abbreviated spatial format. Although there appear to be many variations, the two basic types are concept maps and network representations.

Concept maps generally depict hierarchical or linear relationships, and can be created in such a way to represent complex interrelationships among ideas. When students have been trained to map and then have studied the maps they constructed, they have performed better on comprehension measures than their counterparts (Bernard & Naidu, 1992; Lipson, 1995). Mapping appears to be especially effective in situations where students must read and study complex expository text and then demonstrate their understanding on measures requiring higher levels of thinking, such as synthesis and application (Bernard & Naidu, 1992; Briscoe & LaMaster, 1991). As such, much of the research on mapping has been conducted in the sciences. In addition, the studies seem to suggest that mapping best benefits students who are persistent in using the strategy and who have high content knowledge (Hadwin & Winne, 1996).

Another type of organizing strategy is network representations. They differ from concept maps in that students link key ideas with a generic set of labels or links (Lambiotte, Dansereau, Cross, & Reynolds, 1989). These links are either dynamic (e.g., results, influences), static (e.g., part, function, characteristics), or elaborative (e.g., analogy, example). Perhaps the earliest study on network representation was done by Diekhoff et al. (1982) who found that college students using the Node Acquisition and Integration Technique or NAIT strategy performed significantly better on recall measures than their counterparts who selected their own strategies.

NAIT gradually evolved into a strategy that was renamed as the knowledge map or k-map. The effectiveness of the k-map has been investigated with both oral and written text (Lambiotte et al., 1992; McCagg & Dansereau, 1991). In both studies, the researchers have found that students using k-maps perform better than their counterparts using alternative methods. It should be noted, however, that the type of thinking demanded on the researchers' tests and the content area (e.g., physiology versus statistics) used as the study material have influenced the success of k-maps.

Our review of the strategy literature suggests that very few reading and studying strategies have been thoroughly researched. In fact, most of the strategies touted in study skills books rely on conventional wisdom and tradition. The evidence that does exist provides strong support for the strategies of self-questioning, summarizing, and elaborating and less compelling support for the strategies that involve students in organizing. Perhaps this is why researchers who have attempted to synthesize the literature in order to calculate an overall "effect" have concluded that strategies have only a meager research base and minimal impact on students' comprehension and performance (e.g., Hadwin & Winne, 1996).

Generalization 5: Cognitive and Metacognitive Processing
Should Be the Instructional Focus

In a quest to determine a superior strategy or to train students to use a specific strategy, previous researchers targeted their efforts on the strategy itself, more often than not overlooking processes underlying it. Recent researchers (e.g., Mayer, 1996; Pintrich, Smith, Garcia, & McKeachie, 1993) however, have focused their investigations more on processes, believing that what makes a difference in students' understanding are the cognitive and metacognitive processes that students enact as they read and study. Although there are some slight differences in the terminology, the processes typically include selecting and transforming ideas, organizing, elaborating, monitoring, planning, and evaluating (Hadwin & Winne, 1996; Mayer, 1996; Pintrich et al., 1993; Weinstein, 1994).

These cognitive and metacognitive processes have been studied in a variety of ways. Mayer (1996), for example, theorized that the Selection-Organization-Integration model represents the cognitive processes involved in students' meaningful learning from expository text and has identified several reading strategies for enhancing each process. Other researchers have trained students to employ certain processes such as elaborating, planning, monitoring, and evaluating (Pressley, Snyder, Levin, Murray, & Ghatala, 1987; Nist & Simpson, 1990).

A majority of these studies have used quantitative methodologies and, in particular, correlational designs, which have attempted to determine what relationships exist between students' self-reported cognitive and metacognitive processes and their performance in a particular course or their overall grade point averages. For example, Pintrich and his colleagues collected self-report data from 2,000 college students over 5 years in order to investigate the role that rehearsal, organization, elaboration, and self-regulation played in the students' course grades (Pintrich & Garcia, 1991). In general, they concluded that students who were engaged in deeper levels of processing, such as elaboration and organization, were more likely to do better in terms of grades on assignments or exams, as well as overall course grades.

The renewed emphasis upon process rather than strategies has significant implications for program evaluation efforts and for studies on strategy transfer. That is, students could be employing certain cognitive or metacognitive processes as they read and study, but not using the specific strategy that embodies these processes. When practitioners and researchers ask students in interviews or in questionnaires to list or check the strategies they are presently using, they may be overlooking the most important data. The irony of this oversight is that we want students to focus on the thinking processes they are using when they read and study, not just the strategies. If students can learn to think about the cognitive and metacognitive processes essential to understanding a text or task, they then can define their goals and proceed appropriately (Hadwin & Winne, 1996; Pressley, 1995).

The more recent focus on the cognitive and metacognitive processes underlying strategies seems to have considerable potential for unlocking key information about strategic learning. Most important, the research findings have reminded us that the processes underlying a strategy, not the strategy itself, are what make the difference in students' understanding, learning, and performance.

Practical Implications for Program and Course Development

In this section we examine the implications of the extant literature for those college instructors involved in academic assistance efforts. These implications are described in terms of six characteristics of effective programs and courses.

1. *Academic assistance programs and courses should focus on helping students succeed in their core courses.*

Effective academic assistance programs and courses should reflect the academic tasks and texts that students encounter during their first 2 years of college. However, our 20 years of experience in the field have taught us that many programs still rely upon a generic model that uses either standardized tests or commercial materials to dictate what students will be taught. Because most commercial materials provide atypical practice opportunities in the form of paragraphs and multiple choice questions, many students have difficulty modifying and transferring the reading and studying strategies to their own textbooks and tasks. More troublesome is that many of these commercial materials teach students only one study system (e.g., SQ3R) or a limited number of strategies, as if there were one best way for all students to read and study across all content areas.

According to our literature review, a more powerful approach is for instructors to begin curriculum development with an explicit understanding of the tasks expected of the students on their own campuses during the first 2 years of college. For example, are students in history courses asked to read a variety of primary and secondary sources and take essay exams over these texts? If so, then the objectives and materials of academic assistance programs should reflect these tasks. That is, students should be taught how to read historical nonfiction or a diary for a history course, how to synthesize and analyze multiple perspectives on an issue such as slavery, and how to write effective essay answers for history professors.

There are several ways in which academic assistance instructors can conduct reality checks in order to understand what students are asked to do in their core courses (Simpson, 1996). A few years ago we developed a faculty questionnaire that we distributed to all the professors teaching core curriculum courses (Burrell et al., 1996). In that questionnaire we asked professors to describe the thinking, reading, writing, and mathematics demands of their courses. Using the information from the completed questionnaires, we have made several modifications in the objectives of our courses. For example, one modification was to spend more time teaching students how to predict and write short-answer questions because 48 percent of our core curriculum professors told us they used this testing format regularly. We also have shared the information gleaned from the faculty questionnaire with our students so that they know, for example, that some professors grade their essays and papers on grammar and organization as well as content.

Another way to conduct a reality check would be for academic assistance instructors in the program to interact with core curriculum faculty members in a variety of ways. Having been involved in academic assistance for many years, we know how easy it is to become isolated from the rest of the institution. However, we have recently conducted some qualitative and action research studies that have introduced us to a variety of biology, botany, and history professors. In addition, we have invited ourselves to take tours of chemistry and biology labs so that we can meet the professors and teaching assistants who have developed the software programs and activities. We have learned a tremendous amount from these informal interactions, information that has redefined our program objectives. For example, we have realized that we must teach our students how to download class notes from the Internet and how to use these professor-provided notes effectively if they are to succeed in their biology courses.

2. *Academic assistance programs should use a variety of delivery models.*

Although there are a variety of delivery models that will help students become strategic learners, the two most prevalent are Learning to Learn courses and paired or adjunct courses. Effective academic assistance programs generally use both models because they teach strategies in embedded or content-specific situations. Learning to Learn courses are designed to teach students a variety of reading and study strategies using simulated experiences. With the simulation model, academic assistance instructors immerse students in content-specific situations such as history or biology. Students read typical material from the content area (i.e., lab manuals, essays, textbook chapters) and listen to professors' lectures, both of which focus on a specific topic such as the Vietnam conflict or the endocrine system. During the simulation instructors introduce students to the task-appropriate strategies for reading, listening, and studying the targeted material. At the end of the unit the students take an exam over the material and then evaluate their performance as to the strategies that worked best for them. In a semester we usually introduce three or four of these simulations so that students have an opportunity to practice and modify strategies across the content areas. Learning to Learn courses have been implemented by a variety of larger U.S. universities such as the University of Michigan, the University of Texas, and the University of Georgia.

In paired or adjunct courses, also known as supplemental instruction (Martin & Arendale, 1994), an instructor "pairs" strategy instruction with a particular high-risk core curriculum course. The instructor attends the targeted course, reads the assigned material, takes lecture notes, and then organizes sessions outside the class period on how to read and study, making sure that the strategies pertain to the professor's tasks and texts. Although these adjunct sessions vary across the content areas in terms of their specific goals, they generally focus on the following topics: (a) reading strategies, (b) methods for taking effective lecture or discussion notes, (c) organizational and rehearsal strategies for test preparation, and (d) monitoring and fixing-up strategies. At our university we have created adjunct courses, taught by trained doctoral students, for the core curriculum courses of biology, botany, anthropology, political science, and history. Because our model allows students to volunteer for the 1-hour pass/fail adjunct course, we serve a variety of freshmen and sophomores. Other models, however, require certain at-risk students to take the adjunct course while they are enrolled in the core curriculum course. Both models have their advantages.

3. *Academic assistance programs and courses should teach students how to interpret academic tasks.*

Some students are "cue seekers" and others are "cue blind" (Gibbs, 1990). Cue-blind students use the same strategies and approaches for whatever tasks they encounter. They are also the same students who have significant difficulties in college (Simpson & Nist, 1997). What we want to do is to teach students how to become cue seekers so they have enough information to select and modify their reading and studying strategies to fit their academic tasks. Obviously, the question is how to teach students to decipher their academic tasks.

We have used a variety of activities to help students become aware of how tasks vary across content areas and professors. One way we help students interpret academic tasks is to involve them in interviewing their professors. This assignment has many advantages for students. The most obvious is that students interact one on one with their professors during their office hours to learn more about their tests, quizzes, papers, and projects. The second advantage of the interview assignment is that professors and students begin a dialogue, which usually continues throughout the semester.

Some students have asked their professors for sample test questions to guide their reading and studying. In order to prepare our students to analyze their test questions, we discuss the levels of thinking (e.g., memory, comprehension, application) that professors can tap on exam questions and share specific examples with them. Students are usually quite shocked to realize that multiple choice questions can require them to do more than just memorize definitions. Other students have taken a sample of their lecture notes or textbook annotations to their professors in order to receive their feedback on their reading and studying efforts.

Once students conduct their interviews, we discuss their findings in class. The discussions are quite productive in that students learn how different professors approach sociology or psychology, and they often gain more task information about their own professors. Given that most students do not seek out their professors for assistance or feedback, this assignment has proven particularly powerful in helping students understand the world of academia, especially at large institutions where students are often little more than identification numbers.

Another way in which we try to build students' task awareness is through the use of case studies and scenarios. Gibbs (1990) and Nist and Diehl (1998) have developed several case studies and scenarios that can be used to help students analyze situations and to think about task-appropriate processes and approaches. For example, we use this brief situation at the beginning of the semester:

> Imagine that you are in a biology course where the professor displays many overheads during her lecture. Because she speaks so rapidly, you are not able to get down what she says in class or what she shows on the overhead. What should you do to make sure your notes are of high quality? List several options.

Students read, respond, and discuss these scenarios in a way that enables them to analyze the tasks they are asked to perform and to think about themselves as learners. More important, during the discussions of the scenarios students are gaining their classmates' perspectives about strategic learning.

4. Academic assistance courses and programs should help students become aware of their beliefs about knowledge and learning.

As previously mentioned, most college freshmen believe learning is simple, can be accomplished quickly, and that knowledge and learning occur when someone else "does something to you" such as when a professor delivers a lecture or organizes a lab activity. Hence, we need to teach students that learning demands their active participation and construction and that their professors probably are also working from that assumption. In fact, we have found from our teaching experiences that students are reluctant to employ the active strategies we teach them until they relinquish these passive and naïve conceptions about learning and knowledge construction.

One way to nudge students into thinking about their personal beliefs is to have them complete assessment instruments such as the Epistemological Beliefs scale (Schommer, 1990) and then ask them to reflect on the information they learned from such instruments in classroom discussions and written assignments. Rather than use a published instrument, we ask our students in our Learning to Learn and adjunct courses to write their definitions of reading, studying, and learning at the beginning of the semester. As we introduce students to a variety of reading and studying strategies, we return to those definitions they wrote earlier in order for them to see the connection between their actions and their beliefs. Then, at the end of the semester, we assign the students to reflect on those definitions and to modify them if they believe it appropriate.

5. *Academic assistance programs and courses should teach students a variety of research-based strategies and processes.*

Because the extant literature suggests that there is no superior strategy or study system, it seems reasonable that students should be taught a repertoire of strategies. Some of these should be general cognitive and metacognitive strategies (e.g., how to read textbooks) and others should be content-specific or professor-specific (e.g., problem-solving steps for mathematics). In our Learning to Learn and adjunct courses we want our students to know how to select, organize, elaborate, monitor, and rehearse. Hence, we teach them research-based strategies such as the talk through, textbook annotation, self-questioning and question prediction, summarizing, mapping, and charting. Moreover, after students become comfortable with a reading strategy such as annotation, we then teach them how to modify it for a biology course where they must understand important functions, processes, and relationships or for a history course where it's important to note cause and effect and historical trends.

In order to address content-specific tasks, we also teach students a variety of strategies pertinent to the core courses they will encounter. For example, we teach them how to adapt their reading style and purposes when they read primary sources such as novels or diaries used in their history courses. We also teach students how to interpret and summarize the dense diagrams that they encounter in their chemistry or biology courses. In addition, we have found it necessary to teach students how to use the professor supports provided in their science courses. That is, many professors are now providing their class lecture notes or practice exams on their Web sites. In order to make sure that students use these notes and exams productively and not use them to replace their own notetaking or class attendance, we now teach them how to compare and contrast their lecture notes with the textbook and notes on the Internet.

6. *Academic assistance programs and courses should provide instruction that emphasizes strategy transfer and modification.*

Because the extant literature suggests that students do not automatically or immediately transfer strategies in a flexible manner, it is also important that students learn how to modify and apply strategies to their own textbooks and tasks (Pressley, 1995). For transfer to occur, students must understand strategies and be able to discuss "knowingly" the courses and tasks for which they are appropriate (Butler &

Winne, 1995; Campione, Shapiro, & Brown, 1995). In addition, students must understand the advantages of a particular strategy, especially if they are expected to abandon their usual approaches, which may be more comfortable and accessible (Pressley, 1995; Winne, 1995).

To encourage strategy transfer and modification, we provide students with explicit instruction and practice opportunities across a variety of textbooks and tasks. As students try out the strategies, we offer them specific feedback on their attempts. Although it is a time-intensive endeavor to read all our students' annotations or charts, we have found checklists to be extremely useful in reducing our time commitment. More important, these strategy checklists give students specific and timely feedback about their attempt to annotate a text or create a chart. Gradually, students then learn how to use the checklists to evaluate the quality and appropriateness of their own strategies.

Finally, in order to promote flexible strategy use, it is important for students to reflect on and evaluate their performance and the strategies they choose to employ (Campione et al., 1995). Students in our courses and adjuncts are required to evaluate their performance on each simulation unit or exam, noting which strategies worked for them and which ones did not. We have found that written activities such as these help students take control of their reading and learning. In addition, these reflection and evaluation activities help students attribute their successes or failures to their effort and the strategies they employed rather than to luck or an unfair professor.

In sum, we believe that the last decade of research has helped clarify the components necessary to make a program or course effective in helping students learn from text, and hence become more strategic learners. Most important, the literature suggests that academic assistance efforts should reflect the interactive and multidimensional nature of learning from text. Rather than concentrate on a few traditional strategies, practitioners involved in academic assistance should help students become more sensitive to their beliefs and to the contexts in which they must read and study.

References

Alexander, P. A. (1996). The past, present, and future of knowledge research: A reexamination of the role of knowledge in learning and instruction. *Educational Psychologist, 31,* 89–92.

Anderson, T. H. & Armbruster, B. B. (1984). Studying. In P. D. Pearson, R. Barr, M. Kamil, & P. Mosenthal (Eds.), *Handbook of reading research* (Vol. I, pp. 657–679). New York: Longman.

Bernard, R. M., & Naidu, S. (1992). Post-questioning, concept mapping, and feedback: A distance education field experiment. *British Journal of Educational Technology, 23,* 48–60.

Briscoe, C., & La Master, S. U. (1991). Meaningful learning in college biology through concept mapping. *The American Biology Teacher, 53,* 214–219.

Brown, A. L. (1982). Learning to learn from reading. In J. A. Langer & M. T. Smith-Burke (Eds.), *Reader meets author / Bridging the gap* (pp. 26–54). Newark, DE: International Reading Association.

Brown, A. L., Campione, J. C., & Day, J. D. (1981). Learning to learn: On training students to learn from text. *Educational Researcher, 10,* 14–21.

Brown, A. L., & Day, J. D. (1983). Macrorules for summarizing texts: The development of expertise. *Journal of Verbal Learning and Verbal Behavior, 22,* 1–14.

Burrell, K. I., Tao, L., Simpson, M. L., & Mendez-Burreuta, H. (1996). How do we know what we are preparing students for? A reality check of one university's academic literacy demands. *Research and Teaching in Developmental Education, 13,* 55–70.

Butler, D. L., & Winne, P. H. (1995). Feedback and self-regulated learning: A theoretical synthesis. *Review of Educational Research, 65,* 245–281.

Campione, J. C., Shapiro, A. M., & Brown, A. L., (1995). Forms of transfer in a community of learners: Flexible learning and understanding. In A. McKeough, J. Lupart, & A. Marini (Eds.), *Teaching for transfer: Fostering generalization in learning* (pp. 35–68), Mahwah, NJ: Erlbaum.

Chase, N. D., Gibson, S. U., & Carson, J. G. (1994). An examination of reading demands across four college courses. *Journal of Developmental Education, 18,* 10–16.

Chiseri-Strater, E. (1991). *Academic literacies: The public and private discourse of university students.* Portsmouth, NH: Boynton/Cook.

Day, J. D. (1980). *Training summarization skills: A comparison of teaching methods.* Unpublished doctoral dissertation, University of Illinois, Champaign-Urbana.

Diekhoff, G. M., Brown, P. J., & Dansereau, D. F. (1982). A prose learning strategy training program based on network and depth-of-processing models. *Journal of Experimental Education, 50,* 180–184.

Donald, J. G. (1994). Science students' learning: Ethnographic studies in three disciplines. In P. R. Pintrich, D. R. Brown, & C. E. Weinstein (Eds.), *Student motivation, cognition, and learning* (pp. 79–112). Hillsdale, NJ: Erlbaum.

Doyle, W. (1983). Academic work. *Review of Educational Research, 53,* 159–199.

Gagne, E. D., Weidemann, C., Bell, M. S., & Anders, T. D. (1984). Training thirteen-year-olds to elaborate while studying. *Human Learning, 3,* 281–294.

Garner, R. (1990). When children and students do not use learning strategies: Toward a theory of settings. *Review of Educational Research, 60,* 517–529.

Gibbs, G, (1990). *Improving student learning project briefing paper.* Oxford, England: Oxford Centre for Staff Development, Oxford Polytechnic.

Graesser, A. C., & McMahen, C. L. (1993). Anomalous information triggers questions when adults solve quantitative problems and comprehend stories. *Journal of Educational Psychology, 85,* 136–141.

Hadwin, A. F., & Winne, P. H. (1996). Study strategies have meager support. *Journal of Higher Education, 67,* 692–715.

Hare, V., & Borchardt, K. M. (1984). Direct instruction of summarization skills. *Reading Research Quarterly, 21,* 62–78.

Harris, J. (1991, November). *Text annotation and underlining as metacognitive strategies to improve comprehension and retention of expository text.* Paper presented at the meeting of the National Reading Conference, Miami, FL.

Hofer, B. K. (1998, April). *Personal epistemology in context: Student interpretations of instructional practice.* Paper presented at the annual meeting of the American Educational Research Association, San Diego, CA.

Hofer, B. K., & Pintrich, P. (1997). The development of epistemological theories: Beliefs about knowledge and knowing and their relation to learning. *Review of Educational Research, 67,* 88–140.

Howe, M. J. A., & Singer, L. (1975). Presentation variables and students' activities in meaningful learning. *British Journal of Educational Psychology, 45,* 52–61.

Hynd, C. R., Simpson, M. L., & Chase, N. D. (1990). Studying narrative text: The effects of annotation vs. journal writing on test performance. *Reading Research and Instruction, 29,* 44–54.

Kaspar, V., & Wood, E. (1993, April). *Academic achievement as a predictor of adolescent success in elaboration strategies.* Paper presented at the annual meeting of the American Educational Research Association, Atlanta, GA.

Kiewra, K. A. (1994). The matrix representation system: Orientation, research, theory, and application. In J. Smart (Ed.), *Higher education: Handbook of theory and research* (pp. 331–373). New York: Agathon.

King, A. (1989), Effects of self-questioning training on college students' comprehension of lectures. *Contemporary Educational Psychology, 14,* 1–16.

King, A. (1990). Enhancing peer interaction and learning in the classroom through reciprocal questioning. *American Educational Research Journal, 27,* 664–687.

King, A. (1992), Comparison of self-questioning, summarizing, and note taking review as strategies for learning from lectures. *American Educational Research Journal, 29,* 303–323.

King, A. (1995). Cognitive strategies for learning from direct teaching. In E. Wood, V. Woloshyn, & T. Willoughby (Eds.), *Cognitive strategy instruction for middle and high schools* (pp. 18–65). Cambridge, MA: Brookline.

King, A., & Rosenshine, B. (1993). Effects of guided cooperative questioning on children's knowledge construction. *Journal of Experimental Education, 61,* 127–148.

King, K. S., & Kitchener, P. M. (1994). *Developing reflective judgement.* San Francisco: Jossey-Bass.

Kitchener, P. M., King, K. S., Wood, P. K, & Davidson, M. L. (1989). Sequentiality and consistency in the development of reflective judgement: A six-year longitudinal study. *Journal of Applied Psychology, 10,* 73–95.

Lambiotte, J. G., Dansereau, D. F., Cross, D. R., & Reynolds, S. B. (1989). Multirelational maps. *Educational Psychology Review, 1,* 331–367.

Lambiotte, J. G., Peale, J., & Dansereau, D. F. (1992, April). *Knowledge maps as review devices: Like 'em or not.* Paper presented at the annual meeting of the American Educational Research Association, San Francisco, CA.

Lipson, M. (1995). The effect of semantic mapping instruction on prose comprehension of below-level college readers. *Reading Research and Instruction, 34,* 367–378.

Martin, D. C., & Arendale, D. (1994). *Review of research concerning the effectiveness of SI from the University of Missouri-Kansas City and other institutions across the United States.* Paper presented at the annual conference of the Freshmen Year Experience, Kansas City, MO. (ERIC Document Reproduction Service No. ED 370 502)

Maxwell, M. (1997). *Improving student learning skills.* Clearwater, FL: H & H Publishing.

Mayer, R. E. (1996). Learning strategies for making sense out of expository text: The SOI model for guiding three cognitive processes in knowledge construction. *Educational Psychology Review, 8,* 357–371.

McCagg, E. C., & Dansereau, D. F. (1991). A convergent paradigm for examining knowledge mapping as a learning strategy. *Journal of Educational Research, 84,* 317–324.

Nist, S. L., & Diehl, W. (1998). *Developing textbook thinking* (4th ed.). Boston: Houghton Mifflin.

Nist, S. L., & Simpson, M. L. (1988). The effectiveness and efficiency of training college students to annotate and underline texts. In J. E. Readence & R. S. Baldwin (Eds.), *Dialogues in literacy research, 37th yearbook of the National Reading Conference* (pp. 251–257). Chicago: National Reading Conference.

Nist, S. L., & Simpson, M. L. (1990). The effect of PLAE upon students' test performance and metacognitive awareness. In J. Zutell & S. McCormick (Eds.), *Literacy theory and research: Analyses from multiple paradigms, 39th yearbook of the National Reading Conference* (pp. 321–328). Chicago: National Reading Conference.

O'Donnell, A. M., & Dansereau, D. F. (1992). Scripted cooperation in student dyads: A method for analyzing and enhancing academic learning and performance. In R. Hertz-Lazarowitz & N. Miller (Eds.), *Interaction in cooperative groups: The theoretical anatomy of group learning* (pp. 120–141). New York: Cambridge University Press.

Paris, S. G., & Byrnes, J. P. (1989). The constructivist approach to self-regulation and learning in the classroom. In B. J. Zimmerman & D. H. Schunk (Eds.), *Self-regulated learning and academic achievement: Theory, research, and practice* (pp. 169–200). NY: Springer-Verlag.

Paris, S. G., Wasik, B. A., & Turner, J. C. (1991). The development of strategic readers. In R. Barr, M. L. Kamil, P. B. Mosenthal, & P. D. Pearson (Eds.), *Handbook of reading research* (Vol. II, pp. 609–640). New York: Longman.

Perry, W. G. (1968). *Patterns of development in thought and values of students in a liberal arts college. A validation of a scheme.* Cambridge, MA: Harvard University. (ERIC Document Reproduction Service No. ED 024 315)

Perry, W. G. (1970). *Forms of intellectual and ethical development in the college years: A scheme.* New York: Holt, Rinehart & Winston.

Pintrich, P. R., & Garcia, T. (1991). Student goal orientation and self-regulation in the college classroom. In M. L. Maehr & P. R. Pintrich (Eds.), *Advances in motivation and achievement: Goals and self-regulatory processes* (Vol. 7, pp. 371–402). Greenwich, CT: JAI Press.

Pintrich, P. R., Smith, D. A., Garcia, T., & McKeachie, W. J. (1993). Reliability and predictive validity of the Motivation Strategies for Learning Questionnaire (MSLQ). *Educational and Psychological Measurement, 53,* 801–813.

Pressley, M. (1995). More about the development of self-regulation: Complex, long-term, and thoroughly social. *Educational Psychologist, 30,* 207–212.

Pressley, M., McDaniel, M. A., Turnure, J. E., Wood, E., & Ahmad, M. (1987). Generation and precision of elaboration: Effects on intentional and incidental learning. *Journal of Experimental Psychology: Learning, Memory, and Cognition, 13,* 291–300.

Pressley, M., Snyder, B. L., Levin, J. R., Murray, H. G., Ghatala, F. S. (1987). Perceived readiness for examination performance (PREP) produced by initial reading of text and text containing adjunct questions. *Reading Research Quarterly, 22,* 219–236.

Pressley, M., Symons, S., McDaniel, M. A., Snyder, B. L., & Turnure, J. E. (1988). Elaborative interrogation facilitates acquisition of confusing facts. *Journal of Educational Psychology, 80,* 264–278.

Pressley, M., Yokoi, L., van Meter, P., Van Etten, S., & Freebern, G. (1997). Some of the reasons preparing for exams is so hard: What can be done to make it easier? *Educational Psychology Review, 9,* 1–38.

Rickards, J. P., & Friedman, F. (1978). The encoding versus external storage hypothesis in notetaking. *Contemporary Educational Psychology, 3,* 136–143.

Rohwer, W. D. (1984). An invitation to an educational psychology of studying. *Educational Psychologist, 9,* 1–14.

Rosenshine, B., Meister, C., & Chapman, S. (1994). Reciprocal teaching: A review of the research. *Review of Educational Research, 64,* 479–530.

Schellings, G. L. M., Van Hout-Wolters, B. H. A. M., & Vermunt, J. D. (1996a). Individual differences in adapting to three different tasks of selecting information from texts. *Contemporary Educational Psychology, 21,* 423–446.

Schellings, G. L. M., Van Hout-Wolters, B. H. A. M., & Vermunt, J. D. (1996b). Selection of main points in instructional texts: Influences of task demands. *Journal of Literacy Research, 28,* 355–378.

Schommer, M. (1990). Effects of beliefs about the nature of knowledge on comprehension. *Journal of Educational Psychology, 85,* 498–504.

Schommer, M. (1993). Comparisons of beliefs about the nature of knowledge and learning among post-secondary students. *Research in Higher Education, 43,* 355–370.

Schommer, M. (1994). An emerging conceptualization of epistemological beliefs and their role in learning. In R. Garner & P. A. Alexander (Eds.), *Beliefs about text and instruction with text* (pp. 25–40). Hillsdale, NJ: Erlbaum.

Schommer, M., Calvert, C., Gariglietti, G., & Bajaj, A. (1997). The development of epistemological beliefs among secondary students: A longitudinal study. *Journal of Educational Psychology, 89,* 37–40.

Schommer, M., & Hutter, R. (1995, April). *Epistemological beliefs and thinking about everyday controversial issues.* Paper presented at the annual meeting of the American Educational Research Association, San Francisco, CA.

Schommer, M., & Walker, K. (1995). Are epistemological beliefs similar across domains? *Journal of Educational Psychology, 87,* 424–432.

Simpson, M. L. (1996). Conducting reality checks in order to improve students' strategic learning. *Journal of Adolescent &Adult Literacy, 40,* 102–109.

Simpson, M. L., & Nist, S. L. (1997). Perspectives on learning history: A case study. *Journal of Literacy Research, 29,* 363–395.

Simpson, M. L., Nist, S. L., & Sharman, S. J. (1997, December). *"I think the big trick of history is . . . ": A case study of self-regulated learning.* Paper presented at the annual meeting of the National Reading Conference, Scottsdale, AZ.

Simpson, M. L., Hynd, C. R., Nist, S. L., & Burrell, K. I. (1997). College academic assistance programs and practices. *Educational Psychology Review, 9,* 39–87.

Simpson, M. L., Olejnik, S., Tam, A. Y., & Supattathum, S. (1994). Elaborative verbal rehearsals and college students' cognitive performance. *Journal of Educational Psychology, 86,* 267–278.

Spires, H. A., & Donley, J. (1998). Prior knowledge activation: Inducing text engagement with informational texts. *Journal of Educational Psychology, 90,* 249–260.

Strode, S. L. (1991). Teaching annotation writing to college students. *Forum for Reading, 23,* 33–44.

Thomas, J. W., & Rohwer, W. D. (1987). Grade-level and course-specific differences in academic studying: Summary. *Contemporary Educational Psychology, 12,* 381–385.

Weinstein, C. E. (1994). Strategic learning/strategic teaching: Flip sides of a coin. In P. R. Pintrich, D. R. Brown, & C. E. Weinstein (Eds.), *Student motivation, cognition, and learning* (pp. 257–273). Hillsdale, NJ: Erlbaum.

Winne, P. H. (1995). Inherent details in self-regulated learning. *Educational Psychologist, 30,* 173–187.

Wittrock, M. C. (1990). Generative processes of comprehension. *Educational Psychologist, 24,* 345–376.

Woloshyn, V. E., Willoughby, T., Wood, E., & Pressley, M. (1990). Elaborative interrogation facilitates adult learning of factual paragraphs. *Journal of Educational Psychology, 82,* 513–524.

Zimmerman, B. J. (1998). Academic studying and the development of personal skill: A self-regulatory perspective. *Educational Psychologist, 33,* 73–86.

Strengthening Practice with Theory

Martha E. Casazza

Martha Casazza employs theories from fields such as cognitive science, linguistics, adult education, reading, and psychology to discuss how students in developmental education programs learn. In "Strengthening Practice with Theory," case studies of three students are interspersed throughout discussions of the construct of intelligence, varied ways of knowing, constructivism, and strategic learning to show how theory informs practice. The ideas of leading theorists and researchers — such as William Perry, Paulo Freire, Howard Gardner, and Lev Vygotsky — who have influenced postsecondary learning across the twentieth century are discussed.

The field of developmental education is strong in part due to the range of disciplines represented by its practitioners. Developmental educators come from a multitude of backgrounds including psychology, student development, reading, and adult education to name a few. This multidisciplinary foundation facilitates an integrated approach to educational practice. This integration could be further enhanced by constructing an interdisciplinary theoretical framework. Such a framework would serve as a standard point of reference for training new practitioners and for facilitating decision making in the field. It would also help to ensure that practices are not randomly implemented and, as a result, could increase communication and collaboration.

This article begins to construct a framework for practice by exploring theory related to ways of knowing. This includes taking a new look at how intelligence is defined as well as levels of thinking and reasoning. It also considers how learners think about what knowledge really is and how it is acquired.

Looking at Some of Today's Learners

In order to more easily integrate theory with practice in the article, three students are introduced and utilized as a living context. They characterize many of the learners enrolled in postsecondary educational systems today. Through descriptive narratives, students' general circumstances, goals, and backgrounds are detailed; they each embody many features of the students we work with daily. As you read their brief histories, you will probably find that they share much in common with the students you encounter regularly.

These three students will serve as case studies throughout the article to clarify connections between theoretical foundations and the teaching and learning process. Readers are encouraged to reflect on their students to try and make similar connections and to find relevance and clarity that may come with concrete applications.

Descriptive Narratives of Students

Eva: Case Study #1

Eva is a former ESL (English as a Second Language) student who has recently completed her English language course work. She had been living in the U.S. for 1 year when she first enrolled at Urban Commuter University (UCU) 3 years ago. Before that, she had immigrated from Poland with her family to join extended family members who lived in a large metropolitan area of the Midwest. Eva spoke little English, and her parents spoke none at all. Since they lived in a Polish-American community where it was easy enough to find jobs for which English was not required, learning English was not a priority.

After 1 year, Eva began to feel the restrictions associated with her job in the neighborhood and the missed opportunities due to her lack of English. She discovered through friends that UCU had a good ESL program, but she was a little apprehensive. Her family did not see the need for her to leave the community; after all, she had a good job and a secure environment. After much encouragement from her friends, however, she went to UCU and was assessed by the ESL faculty. They placed Eva into level one of the five-level English language program, and she diligently worked her way through all five levels.

It took her almost 2 years to complete the course work by attending classes in the evenings. She worked full time during the day and joined her growing group of young classmates in the evenings. More and more, she looked forward to meeting them for dinner to practice her English before going to class. Eva was finding less time for her family, and when she was home she spent most of her time studying. As much as she wanted to help, she became increasingly resentful of the additional family responsibilities she had to assume due to her increasing proficiency in English. She also wanted to speak English while at home, and she offered to help her parents learn. She found, however, that speaking Polish provided a comfort zone and a tie to their heritage that her family did not want to give up.

Shortly before completing the fifth level of English study, Eva moved into an apartment downtown with some of her friends. She found a new job near school where she had to speak English, and she chose a program of study at UCU that would lead to a career in Medical Technology. Although she was excited and extremely proud of her accomplishments, her family did not want to talk about them and spoke very little when she came home to visit.

Mike: Case Study #2

Mike went to work full time at his uncle's auto body shop after his graduation from high school. High school had seemed pretty easy to Mike; after all, based on standardized test scores he had been advised at the beginning of his freshman year to focus on vocational/technical courses, and as he grew up he had spent a great deal of time in his uncle's shop. He felt very comfortable in the shop atmosphere of vocational classes and often felt that he knew more than the teachers. Mike and his friends, in fact, developed a reputation for being confrontational and difficult both in and outside the classroom. Their attitude was that they were already doing "real" work in their part-time jobs as mechanics, and there was nothing relevant going on at school. Mike rarely did homework and often skipped class or was asked to leave when he became too disruptive. Teacher expectations were low, however, so, in spite of this, he passed all his classes and graduated in 4 years.

This experience in high school left Mike with the feeling that formal education was for others; he would rather learn on the job where the work was exciting and fulfilling. He worked long hours for his uncle, and, because of his dedication and growing expertise, the customers often personally asked for his service. At the end of 2 years he was working "on the side" for so many customers that his work week had stretched to an average of 65 hours. He began paying his friends to help him out with the extra work and eventually rented space in an empty garage down the street from his uncle's where he worked evenings.

Facing pressure from his friends to cut down on his hours, Mike decided to leave his uncle's shop and direct his efforts toward developing his own business. He figured that he already had plenty of customers and good, dependable help from his friends. What he didn't have, and didn't know he needed, was formal training in the various components of running a small business. He knew his trade, but he needed a framework for budgeting, marketing, accounting, and training. The first year was tough because he had to depend on others for this expertise which frustrated Mike when he couldn't adequately communicate. In addition, many of his friends left because he wasn't able to pay them on a regular basis.

Mike asked his uncle for advice and, after listening to him, decided to go back to school in the evenings and take a few classes. He registered for an accounting class in the continuing education program at his former high school where he immediately began to experience the assignments as irrelevant. He struggled with the math examples from the text and wondered what they had to do with his goal of running a business. All of this led to a return of the feelings of frustration and inadequacy he had previously experienced in high school.

Anna: Case Study #3

Anna graduated from college with a 3.5 GPA in English literature and went to work for a small company that specialized in corporate training. Her job was to write up the training proposals that were sent out to potential clients; she primarily worked alone and at her own pace. She was quite successful, and her interest in writing continued to grow. After 10 years Anna grew tired of this position and also felt that she needed to spend more time at home raising her two children.

She decided that returning to graduate school might be the answer; it might provide her with the opportunity to refocus her career and at the same time allow her to meet the increasing time demands of her young family. She found a graduate program that seemed to be a good fit; it had a writing specialization and also offered the option of delivering the instruction through an interactive video delivery system. That meant Anna would not have to spend time driving the 30 miles to class; rather, she could simply go to the interactive video classroom at the local community college and be connected to her classmates and teacher through a video camera. All instruction originated from the primary site, where the other students attended; Anna was the only one actually present in the local community college classroom during the time of instruction.

Even though Anna had no prior experience with technology, and the monitors and cameras scared her a little, she welcomed the opportunity to be a part of this new distance learning process. She quickly learned how to work the controls and participate in discussions. She had always been resourceful and independent, so she was accustomed to figuring things out on her own. Soon, however, she began to notice the informal conversations going on among her classmates before the teacher arrived. And even though she was always included in group projects and activities, she felt a little like an outsider as she watched the others handling and distributing the materials for a presentation that she had helped to create.

One evening, the teacher invited a guest speaker to class who had never experienced an interactive delivery system. Anna was present via the video link, but the speaker kept forgetting about her and rarely looked in her direction as she spoke to the group. Anna was able to ask questions at the end, but still it was unsettling to feel so removed. It was then that she decided to make the 30-mile trip and attend the next class at the primary site. She had never met her teacher or classmates face-to-face, and she felt that she needed that connection.

Connecting the Theory

If we "take these students along with us" as we look at some theoretical constructs, the theory may seem more relevant and directly connected to the teaching and learning process. By continuously asking questions raised by the various theories and then critically reflecting on how they could directly enhance the learning and development of these students, the reader can begin to experience the value of integrating theory with practice.

Chances are that when we prepare to teach a class or lead a workshop, we design instructional materials that fit our own ways of knowing. We may even reflect on what has been most effective in our personal learning experiences and, feeling comfortable with it, adapt it to the subject at hand. For instance, if we have always found visual reinforcement helpful, we probably enter the classroom armed with a folder of carefully constructed overhead transparencies. If we go beyond this, our preparation may include what we have heard at the latest professional conference where research from a presentation has confirmed that the lecture is dead and collaborative learning is the way to go. With this information, we systematically design small-group activities and let the students work on their own. After all, we believe that knowledge isn't simply transferred from us to our students through lecture and note taking; knowledge is built by connecting new ideas to experience and integrating others' thoughts with our own. Or maybe our colleagues have suggested that there is one particular method that works best for our discipline. In a workshop on time management or in a chemistry lab, for example, there may be a "tried and true" set of materials developed around a formula that is believed to work for everyone.

What these assumptions are missing is a theoretical framework that can inform educators about the learners' different understandings of what knowledge is and also how they approach the task of learning. Once we have a better idea of the variables affecting the many ways of knowing, we can construct a more effective range of instructional approaches to meet the needs of the increasing variety of learners pursuing their further education.

Different Intelligences

Let's first take a look at Mike and what has been effective for him as he developed into a sought-after mechanic. He seems to be most successful when he is involved in an environment that is relevant to his interests. Brown, Collins, and Duguid (1989) suggest that learning is highly effective when the learner is engaged in realistic, "messy" problems rather than those that are more linear and predictable as is the case so often in formal educational settings. From their research with "Just Plain Folks," they conclude that cognitive apprenticeships in which the learner is engaged in authentic activities in a relevant context help to foster learning. For Mike this suggests that he might learn best through an internship or independent study situation with a plan of study that includes at least several hours a week at a work site under the guidance of an expert in the field. If this is not possible, perhaps a simulated work environment where in-class teams design a business plan and then are expected to find solutions to realistic problems associated with their "own" businesses would better fit Mike's learning needs.

If Mike were engaged in such a learning environment, his practical intelligence would be highlighted and perhaps serve as positive reinforcement that would further motivate him to come to grips with more abstract concepts and ideas associated with his vocational interest. In other words, he may not do well in the analytic tasks required of him in school, but he excels in an environment in which practical performance is valued. Tennant and Pogson's notion of tacit knowledge (1995) supports this concept. They contend that adults develop expertise in domains indirectly through experience. Often they are unable to articulate their knowledge base, but rather they depend on an implicit memory that does not diminish with age. They refer to the importance of procedural rather than declarative knowledge. Gardner's (1983) ideas may also help our understanding of how to help Mike. His theory of multiple intelligences describes an intelligence as a set of tacit knowledge related to performance in a particular domain. Gardner outlines seven intelligences; Mike may be strong in several of them including bodily-kinesthetic and interpersonal abilities.

Another factor related to Mike's lack of success in a formal learning setting seems to be the stress that it elicits. McLeod (1996) theorizes that when fear and stress are present, hormones may be released that actually interfere with meaningful learning. He refers to the presence of a "Deep Learning State" that occurs only when the brain's neurotransmitters are open and there is a more efficient flow of information. The learning environment can act as a stimulus that determines which mode the brain enters.

In the case of Mike, he may be so fearful that he actually is not able to take in the information during class that he needs in order to further process it for learning. If this is the case, it could interfere with his ability to input and store material for later use. Such an information processing model in which learners take in information from the external world through their senses has been described by Bruer (1993). After initial intake, information is subsequently processed in working memory where decisions are made regarding its usefulness. From here, information is either sent on to long-term memory or used for immediate output to answer a question in class or make a response to an instructor's comment, for example. It is in the working memory that Bruer describes a possible "bottleneck in our cognitive system" that may occur if it becomes overloaded. If this overload is not managed efficiently, the learner probably will not progress from lower level to higher level skills (p. 15). Due to his high level of stress, Mike may be unable to make the necessary decisions that determine where information is directed. Consequently, he may not forward information to his long-term memory systems or, if he does, he may be too anxious to manage an organized storage system from which he can retrieve it when needed.

Emotions such as those related to the anxiety of Mike can also contribute to one's cognitive processing in a positive way. Mayer and Salovey (1997) have described this concept as emotional intelligence. They define it as a developmental process that starts with learners perceiving and accurately expressing needs related to their emotional state and moves to a level with individuals consciously regulating emotions and reflecting on them regularly. In the case of Anna, she seems to be able to understand and to express her needs related to distance learning. She understands that her feelings of isolation and lack of involvement stem from her physical separation from the larger group of learners. She does not attach these feelings to resentment toward the instructor or to any inability to understand the content. It is likely that Anna has moved through level two of Mayer and Salovey's emotional intelligence development as she has allowed an analysis of her feelings to help her direct attention to the significant variables in the situation; she appears to be a learner who enjoys collaborative processing, and she realizes that she must change her environment in order for that to be satisfied. If she were at the highest level of emotional development, Anna would be able to consciously detach herself from the negative feelings she attaches to the off-site approach to instruction by reflecting and concentrating on the positive, utilitarian aspects of it which led her to enroll in the first place.

Anna is in the process of adapting to her environment based on a personal understanding of her emotional state. This experience leads us to Sternberg's (1988) triarchic theory. He contends that intelligence consists of three components: analytical, synthetic, and contextual. The analytical piece is perhaps best reflected in traditional approaches to learning in more formal settings. There the learner frequently processes information by analyzing how to solve a given problem and then monitoring and evaluating the effectiveness of the solution. Following this, the solution is implemented, and subsequently knowledge is acquired by sorting out the most relevant information for storage and connecting it to prior knowledge. The process here follows a linear format and is characterized by an internal, mental methodology.

Anna has always been successful using this type of process, as measured by her standardized test scores and consistently high grades in college. For Mike, however, this area causes the most trouble. He is not particularly interested in learning through an internal, mental analysis of information that is presented to him. This could account for his low grades and for low performance on standardized tests. Mike's performance in the second area of the triarchic theory, synthetic, is probably higher. Here is where many traditionally high achievers in school experience difficulty; they cannot go beyond what is given them in order to create solutions for novel situations. The internal world of mental processing often collides with the external world of messy, complicated situations where neatly learned solutions don't work. Mike's ability to deal effectively with the daily problems of his business indicates his strength not only in this second component but in the third piece of Sternberg's (1988) theory, the contextual.

This contextual piece is where one is able not only to adapt successfully to the everyday world but also to go beyond adapting to actually selecting and shaping the environment. Mike, as we know, has been quite successful in the real world of work and relating to people as clients. He also has experienced taking an active role in selecting and shaping his environment by breaking away from his uncle's business and starting his own. He has understood that, if some of his needs are not being met, he can take the actions necessary to make a change.

Collaboration and Constructivism

The work of Vygotsky (1965) helps the understanding of the significant role played not only by the overall environment but by the facilitators in that environment as well. Vygotsky describes an individual's zone of proximal development as being the area between one's latent ability and realized potential. He has theorized that guided instruction which leads one across that zone is a necessary ingredient for learning and that intelligence is most related to performance following the mediation of guided instruction. In Mike's high school environment, no one provided the scaffolding necessary for him to cross this zone. He was never challenged and chose to remain in his comfort zone. Eva, on the other hand, received the guided instruction from teachers as well as more English proficient friends as she gradually became more independent and realized her potential. Vygotsky's framework outlining the effectiveness of an external mediator who gradually releases the responsibility of learning to the learner relates to the concepts of collaboration and constructivism.

Although there is no one constructivist approach to learning, most emphasize social interaction and adaptability. To view learning through this lens, it is necessary to rethink the traditional idea of what knowledge is. In the traditional view, knowledge is considered foundational and most often the expert, or instructor, utilizes Freire's (1970) "banking concept" by making deposits into a willing, passive recipient, the learner. The constructivist viewpoint, on the other hand, suggests that knowledge is nonfoundational and is "a socially constructed sociolinguistic entity and that learning is inherently an interdependent, sociolinguistic process" (Bruffee, 1993, p. 3). Bruffee discusses this approach as it relates to collaborative learning. He makes the assumption that learning occurs as people talk and work toward a consensus about the knowledge they need for the task at hand. He suggests that when heterogeneous groups of learners work together, the zone of proximal development expands due to the varied experiences of all members in the group and consequently increases the potential learning power of each individual (p. 39).

When Eva first enrolled at UCU, she assumed that she would learn English by taking extensive notes and having her teachers correct the grammatical mistakes she made in her papers. She was not prepared for the collaborative peer discussions that took place each evening in her classes. At first she was angry because she did not see how she could possibly learn from other students who also were learning English. She resented her teachers for not simply providing the rules and letting her memorize them. Gradually, as she became more comfortable, she realized how helpful it was to practice the language and listen to others as they practiced also. Through their "sociolinguistic processing," they could actually learn from each others' mistakes and become more independent at the same time.

Related to Bruffee's (1993) emphasis on individuals learning from each other is the work of Brookfield (1986). He has researched adult learners using Witkin's (1949, 1950) concepts of field dependence and field independence. Within the field of adult learning, there is often the assumption that self-directed learning is a sign of maturity and that being characterized as a field-independent learner is more likely to lead to success. Field-independent learners are considered to be more analytical, inner-directed, and individualistic and also to have a stronger sense of self-identity; field-dependent learners are extrinsically oriented, in need of external reinforcement, and also in need of more structure from a mediator (Brookfield, p. 41). What Brookfield's research has shown is that successful self-directed learners exhibit characteristics of field dependency rather than indepedency. "Their learning activities are explicitly placed within a social context, and they cite people as the most important learning resource. Peers and fellow learners provide information, serve as skill models, and act as reinforcers of learning and as counselors in times of crisis" (p. 44).

Looking back at Anna's plight, we see that she is expected to be self-directed as she sits at the far end of a camera, but she does not feel the connectedness that she needs from her peers. She needs their reinforcement and more direct opportunities to collaborate in order for her to effectively process information. The distance from the primary site acts as a barrier to her learning.

Constructivism has much to do with how the learner understands what knowledge is. This has been reflected in reading comprehension theory. Schraw and Bruning (1996) discuss readers' implicit models of reading and explain how the different perspectives regarding knowledge that one brings to the task of reading determine how one attempts to understand. The transmission model involves the reader acting passively with the purpose of simply extracting information from the text. This sounds like the perspective that many developmental learners bring to studying, probably as a consequence of the positive reinforcement they may have received in high school for memorizing facts and then restating them on tests. More than likely, they may also rely on the translation model which involves readers finding meaning only from within the text: They decode the message without connecting it to previous knowledge or experience. If instructors do not encourage students to interpret information, the students simply may not consider it their right to evaluate it critically or to raise questions about the material as it relates to their own experiences, The students' understanding of knowledge is often that someone else "has it" and they need to collect it. This may explain, in part, why Mike has so much trouble relating text-based information to his actual work.

However, if Mike's instructor showed him how to ask questions before reading, it could encourage him to relate the text to what he already knows and to what he needs to know. From there he might move into an active transaction with the author of the text. The third model of reading comprehension discussed in Schraw and Bruning (1996) connects directly to a constructivist point of view and is called the transactional model. The constructivist perspective assumes that comprehension results from a reader who actively engages in the process of building meaning by setting goals and purposes and relating new information to prior knowledge. They contend that most readers are not conscious of the perspective they bring to the reading task and that this often leads to their comprehension being author or text centered. This implies that instructors need to provide some direct instruction on how to read a text before making assignments to encourage active reading. They could direct students to set a purpose for reading by outlining critical questions beforehand and articulating expectations for connecting new material to prior knowledge.

Meaning Systems and Schemata

Mezirow (1991) has introduced the concept of "meaning systems" which act as filters through which learners take in information and try to make sense of it. These systems are constructed by individuals based on their own personal experiences. Learners use their experiences to develop sets of beliefs, theories, and assumptions. These, in turn, become the filter through which incoming information is processed. If they are distorted and organized without careful thought, or critical reflection as Mezirow describes it, then new experiences will be processed through the same "distorted" filters. Eva and Mike embrace two very different meaning systems when it comes to formal schooling. For Eva, school was the obvious place for her to go when she decided to learn English. It never occurred to her to learn on her own or through social interaction in more informal settings. Mike, on the other hand, has experienced his most relevant learning on the job, outside the formal setting of school. He had to experience a crisis to return to school.

The two very distinctive meaning systems provide the filter for students' attitudes toward school. In order for Mike to have a meaningful experience at school, his instructors will need to understand this and address it. Mike will need to engage in a process of critical reflection regarding his goals and how best to connect his work to school rather than seeing them as two separate environments.

Cross and Steadman (1996) also talk about this and refer to it as schemata. Without schemata, learners would have to rely on memorization for learning. The authors provide a good image for this by the description, "Our existing knowledge base is the Velcro of the mind to which new information sticks. However, in the same way that lint can keep Velcro from sticking, misconceptions in a schema can interfere with connecting new information to existing knowledge" (p. 41).

Ways of Knowing

Some of these ways of knowing and various understandings of what knowledge is have been related to the developmental stages through which a learner moves. This notion began with the work of Perry (1970) when he established his nine classic stages of cognitive development. According to him, learners progressed through four major categories of knowing: *absolutist or dualist* (where they view the world in terms of right or wrong with experts holding the "right" answer), *multiplicity or problematic* (where uncertainty creeps in), *relativism* (where knowledge becomes contextual and learners make their own judgments), and *commitment* (which leads to a personalized set of values, lifestyle, and identity). Mike probably functions at an absolutist level when he is in a formal learning situation; he most likely is intimidated by his instructors in part because he sees them as authorities who hold the answers. He becomes frustrated when he cannot seem to find "their" answers, and that is when he returns to the "real" world. In the context of his world of mechanics, his level of knowing may be at the level of relativism as he makes judgments regarding work to be done based on varying sets of conditions. He has sufficient experience and knowledge to know that repairs frequently are personal judgments and not set in stone. Perry's levels are most useful to us if we apply them, not developmentally but within a context, as a way of understanding different thinking patterns.

Whereas Perry's (1970) work was limited to males, Belenky, Clinchy, Goldberger, and Tarule (1986) extended the notion of various ways of knowing to females and found five levels. Even though the researchers did not suggest that these ways were developmental, they have been widely interpreted as such. These positions include *silence* (where one feels voiceless), *received knowing* (where knowledge comes from an external source), *subjective knowing* (where knowing is intuitive rather than based on evidence), *procedural knowledge* (where procedures for processing information are developed), and *constructed knowledge* (where knowledge is considered to be contextual and the knower is part of the context).

More recently, Baxter-Magolda (1992) has looked at college students' ways of knowing and reasoning. She discovered patterns of thinking that were related to, but not dictated by, gender. She argues that attributing characteristics to gender is primarily a social construct and that differences between the sexes result from interactions within particular contexts and also vary within gender. She has identified four stages of ways of knowing that evolve from simple to more complex; within the stages, she has found *patterns* of gender differences. These stages are very similar to those of Perry (1970) and Belenky et al. (1986), but the patterns within them make them significantly different.

At the *absolute level* the learner sees knowledge as held by an external authority. Females at this level tend to function as receivers, taking notes and studying to do well, whereas the males function here in a mastering pattern, exhibiting more verbal interaction with the instructor. At the *transitional level* of reasoning the females tend to exhibit an interpersonal pattern, relying on the opinions of others through dialogue and the collection of others' ideas to help construct their own knowledge, whereas the males more often engage in an impersonal pattern, using the opinions of others as material for debate or challenge. At the *independent stage* of knowing females are often engaged in an interindividual pattern; males at this stage tend to use a pattern of independent processing. Within the interindividual pattern, learners have their own interpretations but value an exchange of ideas; on the other hand, the individual pattern focuses more on the learners' own independent thinking. The *contextual level* of knowing, according to Baxter-Magolda (1992), rarely appears during the undergraduate years. Consequently she does not suggest any patterns within this level. It is generally characterized by thinking that one is able to make informed judgments and evaluate distinctions among perspectives.

As Eva began her studies, she viewed knowledge of the English language as something her instructors had and that she needed to "get." She was clearly behaving at an absolute level of thinking as she studiously took notes on grammatical constructions and was very reticent to experiment with the language. She did not understand it when instructors would require collaboration and have students work orally in small groups. She felt this was a waste of time because the others didn't know any more than she did, and she believed she was there only to take the knowledge from the instructor. Gradually, she came to understand that the rules she struggled so hard to memorize from her notes came much more easily if she tried to construct language by actually engaging in it through the small groups. This more developed level of reasoning carried over into her other classes. There she began to experience how her interpretation of the material often helped others to rethink their own positions and vice versa.

Mike will eventually move from the absolutist level of reasoning once he begins to discover the connection between what he does at work and the knowledge being discussed in the formal classroom. When he does begin to integrate his own experiences and prior knowledge with that of the text and the instructors, he will enter the transitional level and most likely challenge both in active debate in order to figure out what he really thinks.

Conclusion

This study has outlined a brief look at theories related to cognitive development and different ways of understanding what knowledge is. In the classic work of Perry (1970), he outlined a hierarchical stage theory with the learner progressing through three major categories of thinking. Belenky et al. (1986) used this framework and discovered through interviewing women that their stages of cognitive development were somewhat different and not necessarily hierarchical. Baxter-Magolda (1992) studied undergraduates and found that there were gender patterns within broader categories of thinking and that the patterns did tend to build on one another.

Bruffee's (1993) notion of knowledge as "constructed collaboration" led us to think about students as active participants in the learning process. Freire (1970) gave us the dualistic concept of banking versus problem solving to describe the difference between passive receivers of knowledge and those who actively seek answers. Bruer (1993) offered an information processing model for how this happens, whereas Mezirow (1991) and Cross and Steadman (1996) described systems that affect the organization and storage of information for use later on.

The notion of different kinds of intelligence has also been examined in the article. Gardner (1983) provides seven talents that individuals possess to varying degrees, and Sternberg (1988) theorized a triarchic model that he contends can be taught. Another way of looking at intelligence came from Mayer and Salovey's (1997) ideas regarding emotional intelligence and the developmental nature of four stages.

Looking back at this framework, some common denominators emerge: Cognitive development occurs in stages, not necessarily hierarchical ones, which may be related to gender; intelligence is not one generalized factor underlying all learning; learning is an active process in which collaboration plays a significant role; and knowledge is, at the very least, partially constructed by the learner.

These theories raise as many questions as they provide answers. The next step is to engage in a process of critical reflection regarding practices in developmental education to see if they lead to a reconstruction of the principles currently used as a framework.

References

Baxter-Magolda, M. B. (1992). *Knowing and reasoning in college: Gender-related patterns in students' intellectual development.* San Francisco: Jossey-Bass.

Belenky, M. F., Clinchy, B. M., Goldberger, N. R., & Tarule J. M. (1986). *Women's ways of knowing: The development of self, voice, and mind.* New York: Basic Books.

Brookfield, S. D. (1986). *Understanding and facilitating adult learning.* San Francisco: Jossey-Bass.

Brown, J. S., Collins, A., & Duguid, P. (1989, January–February). Situated cognition and the culture of learning. *Educational Researcher, 18*(1), 32–42.

Bruer, J. T. (1993). *Schools for thought: The science of learning in the classroom.* Cambridge: The MIT Press.

Bruffee, K. A. (1993). *Collaborative learning: Higher education, interdependence, and the authority of knowledge.* Baltimore, MD: The Johns Hopkins University Press.

Cross, K. P., & Steadman, M. H. (1996). *Classroom research: Implementing the scholarship of teaching.* San Francisco: Jossey-Bass.

Freire, P. (1970). *Pedagogy of the oppressed.* New York: Herder and Herder.

Gardner, H. (1983). *Frames of mind: The theory of multiple intelligences.* New York: Basic Books.

Mayer, J. D., & Salovey, P. (1997). What is emotional intelligence? In P. Salovey & D. Sluyter (Eds.), *Emotional development and emotional intelligence: Implications for educators* (pp. 3–31). New York: Basic Books.

McLeod, A. (1996). Discovering and facilitating deep learning states. *The National Teaching & Learning Forum, 5*(6), 1–7.

Mezirow, J. (1991). *Transformative dimensions of adult learning.* San Francisco: Jossey-Bass.

Perry, W. G. (1970). *Forms of intellectual and ethical development in the college years.* New York: Holt, Rinehart & Winston.

Schraw, G., & Bruning, R. (1996). Readers' implicit models of reading. *Reading Research Quarterly, 31*(3), 290–305.

Sternberg, R. J. (1988). *The triarchic mind: A new theory of human intelligence.* New York: Penguin Books.

Tennant, M., & Pogson, P. (1995). *Learning and change in the adult years: A developmental perspective.* San Francisco: Jossey-Bass.

Vygotsky, L. S. (1965). *Thought and language.* New York: Wiley.

Witkin, H. A. (1949). The nature and importance of individual differences in perception. *Journal of Personality, 18,* 145–170.

Witkin, H. A. (1950). Individual differences in ease of perception of embedded figures. *Journal of Personality, 19,* 1–15.

The Impact of a Course in Strategic Learning on the Long-Term Retention of College Students

Claire E. Weinstein, Douglas Dierking, Jenefer Husman, Linda Roska, and Lorrie Powdrill

In "The Impact of a Course in Strategic Learning on the Long-Term Retention of College Students," Claire Weinstein and her colleagues describe a specific conceptual model of strategic learning and a research-evaluated, one-semester learning-to-learn course derived from this model. The model itself is based on four primary components. The skill component includes five elements focusing on the knowledge that a student must possess in order to become an expert learner. The will includes six elements that focus on the motivational factors required to become a successful learner. The self-regulation component includes both macro- and micro-level elements that support the management of the skill and will components. The model also includes an academic environment component, which addresses factors in the learning environment that are external to the student.

The history and content of the long-running course built on this model is fully described here. The authors also cover the importance of facilitating transfer of competencies developed through this model to other courses the students will take during their academic careers. Finally, the success of the course is demonstrated through data from a five-year longitudinal study that looked at both the GPA and graduation rates of University of Texas freshmen who successfully completed the course.

Developmental education, by definition, includes facilitating students' transition into higher education. The ultimate goal, however, is not only to help students prepare for college-level courses but also to facilitate (a) the transfer of what they are learning to other academic coursework, (b) their retention to graduation, and (c) the successful attainment of their academic goals. This chapter will describe a conceptual model of strategic learning, a one-semester course derived from this model, and some of the results of a five-year longitudinal study of freshman students who participated in this course in either the fall semester of 1990 or the spring semester of 1991. The tremendous long-term success of this course in strategic learning has strong implications for teaching strategies which help students learn how to learn. One of the major reasons for the success of this course is the consistent use of a model based on theories of strategic and self-regulated learning, in-class design, and instruction.

Model of Strategic Learning

The Model of Strategic Learning (Weinstein, 1994; Weinstein, Husman, Dierking, & Powdrill, in press; Weinstein & McCombs, in press) that is used in the strategic learning course includes the following four components with elements (in parentheses) under each component: skill (e.g., cognitive learning strategies and study skills, reasoning skills); will (e.g., motivation, positive affect toward learning, self-efficacy for learning); self-regulation (e.g., time management, comprehension monitoring, strategic planning); and the academic environment (e.g., teachers' expectations and beliefs, plus available resources). The model, as depicted in Figure 1, emphasizes the direct effects and interactions among the elements across these components in specific academic environments and learning contexts.

An underlying concept of the Model of Strategic Learning is that learners need to be aware of the elements from the four major components of the model: skill, will, self-regulation, and the academic environment. The interactions among these elements are crucial to strategic learning, transfer of learning, and ultimately, students' academic success, retention, and graduation.

Figure 1. Weinstein's Model of Strategic Learning.

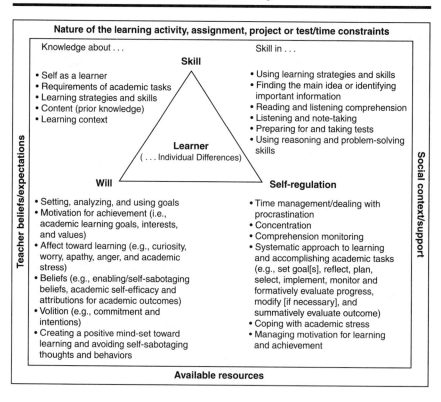

Skill Component

There are a number of different elements within the skill component. All of these elements are important in and of themselves, but for students to be able to reach their academic goals they must also be aware of how these elements interact. For purposes of description, a number of these elements will be described individually.

Within the skill component five of the elements identify types of knowledge that students need to possess in order to become expert learners: 1. knowledge of self as a learner; 2. knowledge of different kinds of academic tasks; 3. knowledge about strategies and skills; 4. knowledge about content often called prior knowledge; and 5. knowledge about the learning context. Each of these five essential types of knowledge are discussed below.

1. *Knowledge of self as a learner* is a key step toward metacognitive awareness (a critical feature of strategic learning) and the ability to think strategically about learning. This includes knowing one's strengths and weaknesses as a learner and one's attitude, motivation, and anxiety level towards learning. Knowledge of self as a learner provides crucial information to learners about areas where they may anticipate difficulties in a given learning context so that they may plan to avoid or minimize potential problems. For example, knowing that you do not like science courses and that you have had difficulty taking science exams can alert you to the potential benefits of participating in a study group or finding out about the availability of science tutors at the learning center. Students need to reflect and think about their answers to a number of possible questions, such as: What are your preferences? What are your strengths? What are your weaknesses? What is the best time of day for you? The worst time? What are your interests and talents? What do you know about study habits and what are your current study habits and practices? Knowing about themselves as learners can help students orchestrate the resources they need to accomplish the studying and learning activities necessary for academic success. Management of resources includes both external resources (i.e., number of visits to the tutor) and internal resources (i.e., use of appropriate cognitive strategies, feelings, and study habits).

2. *Knowledge of the requirements of different academic tasks.* The student needs to understand what is required to complete successfully various academic tasks, such as writing a term paper, taking an essay test, taking notes, or giving an oral presentation. This knowledge includes the steps to be taken and the amount of time required for each step. This type of knowledge helps clarify the procedure that the learner needs to think about, plan for, and accomplish in order to reach a desired outcome.

3. *Knowledge about learning strategies and skills* is the third type of knowledge in the skill component of this model (Weinstein, 1994) and includes the acquisition, integration, reflection, and application of new learning. Learning and thinking strategies and skills are the tools students need to generate meaning, monitor learning progress, and store new information in ways that facilitate future recall or application.

Learning strategies can take a variety of forms ranging from simple paraphrasing to complex content analysis. The common factor underlying each of these forms is the active involvement of the student. Active cognitive involvement is crucial for meaningful learning. Students cannot be passive and expect to reach their learning goals; they must build meaning and memories by actively engaging the material and by using learning strategies to help guide this active engagement. Strategic learners need a variety of strategies available in order to generate appropriate strategies for different learning goals and for different learning problems.

The simplest forms of learning strategies involve repetition or review, such as reading over a difficult section of text or repeating an equation or rule. A bit more complexity is added when students try to paraphrase or summarize in their own words the material they are studying. Other strategies focus on organizing the information by creating some type of scheme for the material. For example, creating an outline of the main events and characters in a story, making a time line for historical occurrences, classifying scientific phenomena, or separating foreign vocabulary into parts of speech are all organizational strategies. Some learning strategies involve elaborating on or analyzing new material to make it more meaningful and memorable. For example, using analogies to access relevant prior knowledge, comparing and contrasting the explanations offered by two competing scientific theories, and thinking about the implications of a policy proposal are examples of elaboration strategies.

There are two major reasons why students need a repertoire of learning strategies that they can use and adapt to a variety of academic as well as everyday learning situations. First, learners need to know about a variety of strategies and methods for learning before they can make mindful decisions about their preferences or the methods that seem to be most effective for them. Second, when students encounter different academic difficulties, they need a set of tools that they can use to resolve the various problems.

4. *Knowledge about content,* often referred to as prior knowledge, is the fourth type of essential knowledge. It is easier for individuals to learn something new about a subject when they all already know something about it. Part of the reason for this is that they already

have an existing knowledge base that they can use to help organize, understand, and integrate the new information.

5. *Knowledge about the learning context* is the last type of knowledge under the skill component. Students need to know about present or future contexts in which they will need the new information they are currently trying to learn. In order to set realistic and challenging learning goals for themselves, students need to identify the importance or utility of the new information in meeting their personal, social, academic, or occupational goals (Lens & Rand, 1997). Students must value the outcomes of learning enough to translate their motivation into action (McCombs & Marzano, 1990).

The model is presented as a series of four components, each with its own sets of elements. The concept of strategic learning comes out of systems theory and Gestalt psychology. Strategic learners know that it is the interaction among the components and the elements within those components that is important. There are emergent properties of the system that only appear when it is operating as an interactive system; the whole is greater than the sum of the components or elements. For example, students' knowledge about themselves as learners helps them identify task characteristics that may be particularly problematic. Identifying these potential problems helps them think about which learning strategies and study skills will help address these particular problems. When students can think about information they have already acquired in an area, they can create more meaning for the new material in order to complete the task successfully.

Will Component

The second major component in the model is the will component. It is not enough for students to know how to study and learn new material, they must also want to do it. Motivation is a result of things we do or think, as well as things we do not do or think. Motivation has many elements, and interacts with and results from many factors (McCombs & Marzano, 1990; Pintrich & DeGroot, 1990; Pintrich, Marx, & Boyle, 1993; Pintrich & Schunk, 1996; Schunk, 1989). Goal-setting, analyzing, and using new information are central elements of motivation. The desire to reach learning goals becomes a driving force that can be used to help generate and maintain motivation, as well as the thoughts and behaviors necessary to accomplish the goals. Strategic learners set realistic, yet challenging, goals for their study and learning activities (Locke & Latham, 1990). Learning goals are both a standard to be met and a way to relate immediate task completion to long-term life and occupational goals. It is the usefulness or utility value of the learning goals for accomplishing present and future educational, personal, social, and occupational goals that helps to keep students on track (Raynor, 1981). Unrealistically high goals (often a symptom of students experiencing academic difficulty) can lead to frustration, feelings of helplessness, avoidance, and failure.

Motivation is also related to self-efficacy beliefs. Self-efficacy is defined as the degree to which students believe they can accomplish a task (Bandura, 1977, 1986). Self-efficacy beliefs affect both effort and persistence applied to a task: If students do not believe they can accomplish the task, then why should they try? Attributions (causal inferences) about learning also determine students' perceptions of whether or not their efforts will improve their grades (Weiner, 1986). To what do students attribute their successes? To what do they attribute their failures? If students do not attribute what happens to them in academic situations to their own efforts and abilities rather than to the system, the instructor, or the difficulty of the test, why would they ever try again? Students must have a sense of empowerment to believe that their efforts will make a difference.

Positive or negative emotions associated with learning goals and actions also will impact the behaviors students exhibit toward a task. Motivation is also related to a number of other variables such as interest, valuing, instrumentality, and a positive mind-set. Similar to the skill component elements, it is the interactive effects of these and other elements that ultimately results in what is called motivation.

Self-Regulation Component

The self-regulation of thoughts, beliefs, and actions in the model focuses on the self-management aspects of learning. Strategic learners manage both their skill and will factors through self-regulation. Essentially, self-regulation involves awareness and control of relevant factors in order to achieve a desired outcome. Strategic learners regulate on a macro level (such as using time management and a systematic approach to studying) and on a micro level (such as focusing concentration, monitoring comprehension, and using coping strategies to manage academic stress).

Time management is one of the major macro elements of self-regulation and refers to the learner's use of time resources in the pursuit of learning tasks and goals. Self-regulation includes monitoring and controlling time management to help attain a desired learning outcome (Zimmerman, Greenberg, & Weinstein, 1994). Students need to balance the many demands on their time to help them meet their goals.

Another macro-level element of the self-regulation component is the use of a systematic approach to learning and accomplishing academic tasks. This systematic approach involves eight steps that are essential for self-regulated learning (Weinstein, 1988, 1994). These eight steps are discussed in some detail below and are shown in Figure 1 as elements in systematically approaching a learning task under the self-regulation component.

1. *Setting a goal.* This first step requires setting a goal for the desired outcome (for example, a specific grade in a course, a certain level of performance on an assessment instrument, or a level of proficiency in performing an academic task). To be most effective the goal needs to be specific, measurable, challenging, and realistic; in addition, an effective goal must have a specific completion date.

2. *Reflecting on the task.* In order to identify the requirements of a task, strategic learners must spend some time thinking about the task. During this reflection, they will consider task requirements in terms of their own levels of skill and will, and then determine how the task relates to their goals. Furthermore, strategic learners will reflect on relevant external contextual factors, such as the resources available to help them achieve the desired outcomes, the expectations of the instructor, and the social support upon which they can draw.

3. *Planning for achievement.* Having reflected on all the requirements involved in the task, the strategic learner moves to the third step, developing a plan. This planning step is best accomplished by brainstorming in order to identify several potential strategies. Mulling over these potential strategies leads to the next step.

4. *Selecting a plan.* From among the several plans considered, the strategic learner selects the most effective and efficient plan for achieving the desired outcome.

5. *Implementing the plan.* After selecting the best and most appropriate plan, a strategic learner then implements the plan.

6. *Monitoring and formatively evaluating progress.* At various stages during the implementation of the plan, the learner monitors and formatively evaluates the effectiveness of each strategy as it is being implemented. If the results are disappointing, the strategic learner will proceed to the next step.

7. *Modifying the plan.* If necessary, the self-regulated learner modifies the plan by replacing ineffective strategies with alternative strategies. These alternatives are then monitored and evaluated. If necessary, the learner may even decide to modify the learning goal itself.

8. *Evaluting outcome.* When the learning task has been completed successfully or unsuccessfully, the self-regulated learner performs the eighth and last step, which is summative evaluation, to measure the effectiveness and efficiency of the learning strategies applied and the outcome achieved. The summative evaluation becomes a future reference when similar learning tasks arise. This final step contributes

both to avoiding unsuccessful approaches in the future and also to increasing cognitive efficiency by helping the learner build up a set of useful approaches for similar future learning tasks.

On the micro level, strategic learners know ways to monitor and manage their level of stress, motivation, concentration, and personal comprehension. To monitor and manage their comprehension students need to know how to use self-assessment or self-testing to determine whether they are meeting their goals. There are many forms of self-assessment, which can be as simple as paraphrasing while reading or as complex as trying to teach new information or skills to someone else. Other forms of monitoring include trying to apply new knowledge, transforming it into any other form (such as a diagram or outline), and summarizing it. Each of these activities is designed to help students determine how well they understand the new material. Often students believe that they understand, but they do not test themselves to confirm or refute this belief. When they are wrong, that is, when they have only the "illusion of knowing," students think that they have reached their achievement goals and do not realize that they have not.

Expert learners can also generate fix-up strategies when problems in their comprehension arise. Fix-up strategies are the approaches and methods that students use to help remedy a learning problem. These methods can range from very simple activities (such as rereading a confusing text section) to more complex activities (such as trying to reason through a problem-solving method, going to a tutor for help, or teaming up with someone else who is taking the same course in order to study difficult sections together). Each of these activities is designed to help solve a learning problem. Students need a repertoire of fix-up strategies so they can deal with a variety of academic problems that might occur.

Academic Environment Component

The Model of Strategic Learning also includes elements in the learning environment that are external to the learner. These are represented in the outside boundaries of the model (see Figure 1) and include: resources available to the learner; instructor expectations; nature of the learning activity, assignment, project, or test; time constraints; and social support. Each of these elements is discussed below.

Available resources refers to any materials or learning aids that the learner can use in acquiring knowledge, such as workbooks, reading materials, computers, reference materials, diagrams, examples, and case studies. Available resources also include campus resources such as labs, tutors, learning skills centers, teaching assistants, and advisors.

Teacher expectations refer to the expectations held by the instructor or course developer. These expectations could include the skill level of students, specific tasks the students should be able to perform, and appropriate teaching methods for the students. The extent to which the teacher's expectations match or do not match the learner's abilities and needs can have a major impact on the acquisition, retention, and transference of information. If the teacher's expectations exceed the learner's ability, the learner may not be able to acquire the information and may be less motivated to put forth the effort to learn or utilize the subject matter. If the teacher's expectations are below the learner's ability, the learner may become bored or place less value on the subject matter and subsequently experience less motivation to learn or utilize the subject matter.

The nature of the learning activity, assignment, project, or test refers to the specific task requirements the learner must complete in order to acquire the new information. This might include listening to a lecture, taking notes, role playing, demonstrating proficiency, writing a paper, or taking a timed test. The nature of a specific task assigned in a class interacts with the learner's level of skill and helps determine the degree of learning success. If the task calls for an activity for which a learner lacks skill or motivation, he or she may have difficulty in performing that activity or may seek to avoid it altogether.

Time constraints within which the course material is delivered, or other time constraints that may be impacting the learner (e.g., outside deadlines not related to the course), affect the learning outcomes. If the class time is limited, students may not be able to practice using the knowledge acquired in the program. Learners might also be overwhelmed if a large amount of information is presented in a short period of time, especially if their learning strategies and skills are limited.

Social support refers to the support learners receive from peers, fellow students, and family. Such support might include roommates and other students with whom the learner can study and share class experiences, and advice from siblings or parents. Beliefs of peers and family members, supportive or antagonistic, can also affect a student's motivation to learn course content and to participate in class discussions.

All of these external factors interact with the internal factors associated with the skill, will, and self-regulation components of the model. In this sense, the model is a dynamic system (i.e., change in one factor can produce changes in other factors). As in all systems, it is important to consider all factors. Strategic learners try to be aware of and control as many of these factors as possible so that new knowledge can be acquired, retained, integrated with existing knowledge, and ultimately transferred to new situations. This model seeks to emphasize the impact of changes in one factor on other strategic learning factors.

Strategic Learning Course

In 1977, Weinstein developed a semester-long course to determine the effects of teaching learning strategies to undergraduates at risk for low academic achievement or failure. The success of this experimental course resulted in its inclusion as a three-credit elective in the general educational psychology (EDP) undergraduate courses offered at the University of Texas at Austin. This course (EDP 310) has remained highly popular among student advisors and undergraduates with 16 sections filled to capacity each major semester. Two to three sections of the course are offered during each of the two summer sessions. Enrollment is limited to 28 students in each section. The course is taught by graduate students in the Educational Psychology doctoral program, primarily from the Learning, Cognition, and Instruction concentration. The course is highly structured; the course content, pacing, policies, testing, and assignments are the same across all 16 sections. The instructors receive extensive training in the Model of Strategic Learning, the specific topics covered during the course, and varied teaching and instructional methods.

The students enrolling in EDP 310 vary greatly in terms of academic standing, skill, motivation, and reason for taking the class. The majority of these students are freshmen or sophomores, frequently on scholastic probation (i.e., cumulative grade point averages less than 2.0 using a four-point system), or otherwise predicted to be at risk of leaving the university.

On other college campuses, many learning skills courses do not teach students how to select and evaluate appropriate study strategies for different learning tasks. As a result, these students have only a group of study techniques at their disposal with a limited understanding of the conditions under which these techniques will be most effective and what to do when the techniques do not work. Often students have learned a specific learning strategy in a highly contextualized manner. This is likely to limit their application of this strategy in other relevant situations that differ from the situation in which it was learned.

The EDP 310 course attempts to provide students with an awareness of the systems nature of strategic learning, the range of factors that influence learning, and the impact and interaction among factors. Students in this course receive instruction in both the theoretical underpinnings of the Model of Strategic Learning as well as practical applications of specific strategies, methods, and self-management techniques. With this awareness and knowledge, students should be better able to (a) strategically match their selection of learning strategies to task demands and their own learning goals, (b) identify problems and potential problems in the application of their strategies, and (c) generate alternative learning strategies when current strategies fail. By increasing awareness and knowledge about study skills, students will learn how to transfer these skills across tasks and courses.

Transfer

The ultimate goal of any learning strategies or study skills class is to facilitate transfer to other coursework and future learning. Salomon and Perkins' (1989) concept of high-road transfer — particularly forward-reaching high-road transfer — and their concept of "mindful abstraction" seem to fit quite well within the tenets of Weinstein's Model of Strategic Learning as well as other conceptions of self-regulated learning. In each of these conceptions the learner is metacognitively aware that the new information has potential current and future applications outside of the original learning context. The strategic learner goes forward from the learning-to-learn course in search of new contexts in which to apply what has been learned. Salomon and Perkins (1989) state that "the main distinction of the high-road to transfer is the mindful generation of an abstraction during learning and its later application to a new problem or situation from which basic elements are similarly abstracted" (p. 113).

The learning skills course, EDP 310, is based on Weinstein's Model of Strategic Learning as shown in Figure 1; but EDP 310 is also compatible with Sternberg and Frensch's (1993) model which posits four mechanisms that determine the successful transfer of knowledge. These four mechanisms are: encoding specificity, organization, discrimination, and set. Each of these mechanisms is discussed in more detail below.

The first mechanism is *encoding specificity,* in which the retrieval of information from memory is dependent upon the manner in which the information was encoded. Information that is encoded as context-specific is likely to be accessed only within that context. Students in the learning-to-learn course, EDP 310, complete assignments that require them to apply new information in a variety of contexts. Having students practice learning strategies on real coursework from other classes results in more natural strategy transfer (Stahl, Simpson, & Hayes, 1992). EDP 310 uses examples from a wide variety of academic settings to provide a "bottom-up" teaching approach as suggested by Bassock and Holyoak (1993). This should serve to generalize the encoding and enhance recall and subsequent transfer. Students who become strategic learners use many knowledge-acquisition strategies; for example, they are more likely to learn new information by applying it to themselves or their situation, making it meaningful within new settings. Therefore, the new information is embedded in several contexts and, hence, is more likely to be recalled in a wider range of situations.

The second mechanism is *organization* (Sternberg & Frensch, 1993), which refers to how the information is organized in memory. Organizing information within a clear framework and connecting it to prior knowledge improves the retrieval of the new information. The use of knowledge acquisition strategies and the ability to identify important information are also parts of Weinstein's Model. Learning strategies involve actively organizing information into a format that is meaningful to the learner and linking new information to the learner's prior knowledge. With a framework in mind, learners can identify which information is of primary importance (i.e., worthy of their focused attention) versus which information is of secondary importance (i.e., supporting details).

Sternberg and Frensch's (1993) third mechanism is *discrimination,* the ability to tag information as relevant or irrelevant to a novel situation. If students perceive new information to be useful in their coursework or occupation, they are likely to tag that information as relevant and plan ways to apply it. The ability to identify important information is also a critical factor in learning. The learner's perceived usefulness of new information determines what information will be tagged as important or relevant, and subsequently what information will be accessible in a transfer situation. Through the use of diagnostics, such as the Learning and Study Strategies Inventory (LASSI) (Weinstein, Schulte, & Palmer, 1987), class lectures, and exercises, students in the learning-to-learn course receive diagnostic and prescriptive feedback in order to enhance their ability to identify important information. In addition, exercises throughout the course encourage students to identify the relevant features of successful strategic learning situations, thus addressing Bassock and Holyoak's (1993) recommendations for a "top-down" approach to teaching for transfer.

The fourth mechanism in the model by Sternberg and Frensch (1993) is *set,* which indicates how the learner mentally approaches a problem or learning task (i.e., whether or not the learner is planning to transfer or use new material). This mechanism is also addressed in the Model of Strategic Learning by Weinstein. From the will component, motivation and attitude towards learning apply to *set.* If learners do not value the course or are not interested in actively participating, then they are not likely to have a *set* towards learning that is conducive to transfer of the study strategies to subsequent coursework. Within the self-regulation component, *set* is implied in the monitoring strategy in which the student checks to see if the material is being understood and can be applied at the desired level of performance. Knowledge of the learning context from the skill component of the model is also related to *set* (i.e., the more learners perceive the new information to be relevant to current or future coursework, the more likely they are to have a positive *set* towards the learning task). In other words, with a positive *set* towards the learning task, the student is more likely to demonstrate transfer.

In many cases transfer of learning strategies cannot be directly observed, but must be inferred from other measures. In an academic setting there are two sources of information that are commonly used to indicate transfer of learning from academic assistance programs to future academic situations: grade-point average and retention/graduation rates (Simpson, Hynd, Nist, & Burrell, 1997).

The learning-to-learn course, EDP 310, addresses many of the issues that impact academic achievement, retention, and graduation rates. Weinstein's Model of Strategic Learning (as shown in Figure 1) is the foundation for this course; the model emphasizes the importance of being aware of and knowing how and when to use specific learning strategies as well as managing motivation, goals, and other self-regulatory factors. The model also addresses the environmental factors of social support (such as family and friends), available resources (such as money and computers), nature of the academic task (such as the size of classes and level of difficulty), and teacher beliefs and expectations (such as the amount of support provided by the teacher). These have all been identified as important factors that impact academic achievement, retention, and graduation rates.

Through learning about and using the Model of Strategic Learning, students in the learning-to-learn course develop three kinds of knowledge: (a) declarative knowledge which defines many different learning strategies, (b) procedural knowledge which explains ways to apply these strategies, and (c) conditional knowledge which examines appropriate conditions for application of specific strategies. The course provides direct instruction and practice in all three knowledge areas. Declarative, procedural, and conditional knowledge are all crucial in providing students with a systematic way of learning new material in any academic context. Not only are strategic learners fluent and flexible in that they possess a toolbox full of many different learning strategies, they are also able to choose which strategy to apply within a given situation to reach a desired outcome.

Simpson et al. (1997) indicate that learning-to-learn courses, such as the one which is being investigated in this study, should be one of the most effective types of academic assistance programs in producing a positive impact on follow-up measures such as grade point average, retention, and graduation rates. Learning-to-learn courses are based on theories of learning and cognition; such courses create strategic learners who possess a wide range of learning strategies and the ability to adapt those strategies to a variety of academic contexts and demands. Strategic learners, therefore, should demonstrate transfer of learning from the learning-to-learn course to other coursework through increased grade point average, retention, and graduation rates.

Results of a Five-Year Longitudinal Study of Freshmen

From semester evaluations of the pre- and post-data on the Nelson-Denny and LASSI scores, students showed highly significant gain on these measures. The research question for this study was: Did the course improve students' subsequent GPAs and retention at the university. A summary of the data for students who entered the university in the 1990 fall semester is presented in Table 1.

The most dramatic data appear in the fifth-year follow-up statistics. Approximately 55 percent of the students who entered in 1990 and did not take the strategic learning course (EDP 310) graduated after five years; this statistic has remained the same for a number of years. However, despite significantly lower standardized test scores, approximately 71 percent of the students who successfully completed EDP 310 (i.e., did not drop out or fail due to excessive absences) graduated after

Table 1. Students Enrolled in EDP 310: Fall 1990 and Spring 1991

	First-Year Retention		Fifth-Year Retention	
	Freshmen Successful in EDP 310	All Other Freshmen	Freshmen Successful in EDP 310	All Other Freshmen
Dropped out — academic dismissal	1.9% 3	6.9% 373	0.6% 1	12.7% 687
Enrolled/Retained (continuing students)	92.3% 143	84.9% 4576	7.1% 11	10.7% 577
Graduated			71.4% 110	55.3% 2981
SAT — Verbal	458.3 140	512.5 5180	458.3 140	512.5 5181
SAT — Quantitative	523.1 140	586.3 5180	523.1 140	586.3 5181
Cumulative GPA	2.75 155	2.68 5392	2.72 154	2.58 5392
Course hours failed	.79 155	1.74 5392	2.55 154	4.91 5392
Course hours passed	29.23 155	31.00 5392	103.5 154	94.79 5392
Course hours undertaken	30.19 155	32.87 5392	106.5 154	100.2 5392

Note: Italicized numbers represent cell sizes.

five years. This 16-point difference is a dramatic finding that supports the long-term retention effects of an intervention in learning strategies. In addition, the cumulative GPAs for these students were higher than for the general population. These data offer strong support for the importance of developmental education for at-risk students.

Conclusion

At a time when developmental education is being attacked by policy makers, it is imperative to conduct research to demonstrate the achievements of our field. Developmental educators must remain open and susceptible to new learning theories being explored in other disciplines (i.e., instructional psychology, adult development, and cognitive and educational psychology). Ideas from these fields should be continually incorporated into theories from developmental educators to build more powerful models to describe how people learn. Also, additional research of this course and other developmental programs can provide a supportive database to strengthen further the field of developmental education. Such a database can be used by developmental educators, faculty, administrators, policy makers, and the voting public to make informed decisions about providing entry to and success in higher education for a broader range of our citizens. The research reported in this chapter documents an important fact: Developmental education makes a critical difference in the lives of many students.

References

Bandura, A. (1977). Self-efficacy: Toward a unifying theory of behavioral change. *Psychology Review, 84*(2), 191–215.

Bandura, A. (1986). *Social foundations of thought and action: A social cognitive theory.* Englewood Cliffs, NJ: Prentice-Hall.

Bassock, M., & Holyoak, K. J. (1993). Pragmatic knowledge and conceptual structure: Determinants of transfer between quantitative domains. In D. K. Detterman & R. J. Sternberg (Eds.), *Transfer on trial: Intelligence, cognition and instruction.* Norwood, NJ: Ablex.

Lens, W., & Rand, P. (1997). *Combining intrinsic goal orientations with professional instrumentality/utility in student motivation.* Unpublished manuscript.

Locke, E. A., & Latham, G. P. (1990). *A theory of goal setting and task performance.* Englewood Cliffs, NJ: Prentice-Hall.

McCombs, B. L., & Marzano, R. J. (1990). Putting the self in self-regulated learning: The self as agent in integrating will and skill. *Educational Psychologist, 25*(1), 51–69.

Pintrich, P. R., & DeGroot, E. V. (1990). Motivational and self-regulated learning components of classroom academic performance. *Journal of Educational Psychology, 82*(1), 33–40.

Pintrich, P. R., Marx, R. W., & Boyle, R. (1993). Beyond "cold" conceptual change: The role of motivational beliefs and classroom contextual factors in the process of conceptual change. *Review of Educational Research, 63,* 167–199.

Pintrich, P. R., & Schunk, D. H. (1996). *Motivation in education.* Columbus, OH: Prentice Hall.

Raynor, J. O. (1981). Future orientation and achievement motivation: Toward a theory of personality functioning and change. In G. D'Ydewalle & W. Lens (Eds.), *Cognition in human motivation and learning* (pp. 199–231). Hillsdale, NJ: Lawrence Erlbaum.

Salomon, G., & Perkins, D. N. (1989). Rocky roads to transfer: Rethinking mechanisms of a neglected phenomenon. *Educational Psychologist, 24*(2), 113–142.

Schunk, D. H. (1989). Social cognitive theory and self-regulated learning. In B. J. Zimmerman & D. H. Schunk (Eds.), *Self-regulated learning and academic achievement* (pp. 83–110). New York: Springer-Verlag.

Simpson, M. L., Hynd, D. R., Nist, S. L., & Burrell, K. I. (1997). College academic assistance programs and practices. *Educational Psychology Review, 9*(1), 39–87.

Stahl, N. A., Simpson, M. L., & Hayes, C. G. (1992). Ten recommendations from research for teaching high risk college students. *Journal of Developmental Education, 16*(1), 2–8.

Sternberg, R. J., & Frensch, P. A. (1993). Mechanisms of transfer. In D. K. Detterman & R. J. Sternberg (Eds.), *Transfer on trial: Intelligence, cognition and instruction.* Norwood, NJ: Ablex.

Weiner, B. (1986). *An attributional theory of motivation and emotion.* New York: Springer-Verlag.

Weinstein, C. E. (1988). Executive control processes in learning: Why knowing about how to learn is not enough. *Journal of College Reading and Learning, 21,* 48–56.

Weinstein, C. E. (1994). Strategic learning/strategic teaching: Flip sides of a coin. In P. R. Pintrich, D. R. Brown, & C. E. Weinstein (Eds.), *Student motivation, cognition, and learning: Essays in honor of Wilbert J. McKeachie* (pp. 257–273). Hillsdale, NJ: Lawrence Erlbaum.

Weinstein, C. E., Husman, J., Dierking, D., & Powdrill, L. (in press). Strategic learning. In C. E. Weinstein & B. L. McCombs (Eds.), *Strategic learning: The merging of skill, will and self-regulation.* Hillsdale, NJ: Lawrence Erlbaum.

Weinstein C. E., & McCombs, B. L. (Eds.). (in press). *Strategic learning: The merging of skill, will and self-regulation.* Hillsdale, NJ: Lawrence Erlbaum.

Weinstein, C. E., Schulte, A. C., & Palmer, D. R. (1987). *The learning and study strategies inventory (LASSI).* Clearwater, FL: H & H.

Zimmerman, B. J., Greenberg, D., & Weinstein, C. E. (1994). *Self-regulating academic study time: A strategy approach.* In D. H. Schunk & B. J. Zimmerman (Eds.), *Self-regulation of learning and performance* (pp. 181–199). Hillsdale, NJ: Lawrence Erlbaum.

Understanding the Motivation Problems of At-Risk College Students

Donna L. Mealey

For too many students enrolled in developmental reading courses, low motivation and a negative self-concept lead to poor academic performance. Mealey argues that such students will be unable to take advantage of strategic learning instruction until they are motivated to take responsibility for their learning, attribute success and failure to their own efforts, and view themselves as college learners.

In "Understanding the Motivation Problems of At-Risk College Students," the author describes how achievement motivation pertains to autonomous, self-regulated learning. She also examines the relationship of motivation to strategic learning, with specific instructional recommendations for college reading courses. Mealey then goes on to demonstrate how motivation is tied to a student's metacognitive abilities. Finally, she reviews the tenets of attribution theory as related to developmental learners. This article offers developmental reading instructors valuable insight into the affective issues that promote academic literacy.

Many developmental college reading students are at risk for academic failure. Some believe, correctly or not, that their failures are caused by a lack of ability; others simply do not persevere in the face of difficulty. While many of these students do work hard in order to exit from developmental studies programs, a large number are not successful because their academic motivation and self-concept are low, contributing to their poor academic performance.

These students lack both the learning and metacognitive strategies that they need to compensate for deficits. Until at-risk college reading students are motivated to take responsibility for their own learning, until they attribute their success to their own efforts, until they see themselves as learners, they will be unable to take advantage of strategic learning instruction.

According to Paris, Lipson, and Wixson (1983), there are three key areas of strategic learning: (a) whether studying and performing well on tests is meaningful to the students, (b) how students perceive the usefulness and efficiency of strategic learning, and (c) how well students can manage their time, study behavior, etc. The authors indicate that strategy use "represents the fusion of cognitive skills and motivational will" (p. 310). Indeed, each of the three behaviors has a strong motivational component.

In order to understand how achievement motivation is related to autonomous, self-regulated learning, the nature of motivation will be examined here briefly. Then, its role in strategic learning will be discussed, with applications made to the developmental college reading population, incorporating the three strategic learning behaviors noted by Paris et al.

Nature of Motivation

Refuting animal psychologists' ideas that motivation was an instinct or drive, White (1959) introduced the notion that human motivation was a drive toward competence that was reinforced by feelings of efficacy following success. Motivation is fueled by each successful experience, thereby increasing self-efficacy (Bandura, 1977), the belief in our effectiveness to cope with given situations. In an academic situation, therefore, motivation can be increased when students (a) strive for competence by exerting a certain amount or quality of effort and persistence, (b) achieve success, and (c) believe in their ability to cope with academic tasks.

There is an added component to these ideas of motivation, however. Deci (1975) stated that the individual must be self-determining, making deliberate choices about actions. Relating these ideas to developmental college learners, it appears that students must not only know and use learning strategies to be academically successful, but they must also use metacognitive strategies. Development of metacognitive capabilities enables students to decide when and how to use various tactics in a given academic situation.

Described below is a developmental college reading program that emphasizes both learning and metacognitive strategies with the aim of increasing academic success, motivation, and self-concept.

Motivation and Strategic Learning

Because motivation is the key predictor of academic performance (Harter, 1982, 1985), at-risk college students must become aware of (a) their negative attitudes toward learning in general and (b) themselves as learners specifically before they can change. Only when this realization occurs is it possible for students to become motivated to learn and use cognitive and metacognitive strategies in their coursework.

This growth on the students' part, however, may be heavily dependent upon the philosophical approach of the developmental reading program in which they are enrolled. Many reading programs at the college level are skills based; that is, they focus on teaching skills, such as finding the main idea and distinguishing between fact and opinion. These skills are presented in isolation and are not shown to be directly related to college course demands. As a consequence, students are less likely to perceive skills instruction as relevant and practical and to find studying and performing well on tests to be meaningful.

In contrast, college reading programs are likely to be more practical and relevant if they employ a content-based, strategic learning approach. Rather than emphasizing skills mastery, developmental reading instructors can focus on teaching a variety of reading, study, recitation, and test preparation strategies, such as text annotation, mapping and charting, questioning, and use of test preparation strategies such as PLAE (Simpson & Nist, 1984) and PORPE (Simpson, 1986). The strategies are taught using chapter-length, naturally occurring, intact texts taken from content areas such as psychology, biology, computer science, or history.

Applying the notions of Paris et al. (1983) to at-risk college students, a content-based, strategic learning emphasis will seem personally significant, relevant, and practical for students when they take content courses concurrently or upon successful completion of a developmental reading course. Perceived utility and relevance will be more likely to occur with a content-based program and may be more likely to result in students' transfer of strategy use.

Motivation and Metacognition

A strategic learning program, however, will probably not be successful unless a strong metacognitive component is included. Students can be taught how to use study strategies, but without the knowledge of when and why to use them, students are likely to experience continued academic failure.

Control is an integral part of both academic motivation and metacognition. McCombs (1986) stated that the self must preserve itself and the illusion of control, especially in the face of a possible threat, such as failure. Without that preservation, motivation and achievement, regardless of ability, will decrease to the point that strategic and autonomous learning cannot occur (Wittrock, 1986).

Metacognitive strategies can be taught in order to show students that they can control their learning and performance. Metacognitive development can take many forms, but two are suggested here.

(1) Weekly journals can be assigned that focus on increasing metacognitive awareness. For example, at the beginning of a semester, students are asked to write a journal in which they discuss how they perceive themselves as learners. They examine a variety of areas, such as motivation, attitude, time management, anxiety level, concentration, ability to apply old information to new, selection of important information in text, and use of study and test preparation techniques. After a strategy such as text annotation is introduced and students have had guided and independent practice in it, they can discuss in a journal assignment their experiences (successes and difficulties) in learning how to annotate. They are encouraged to cite sentences or paragraphs from their content chapters where they experienced difficulty comprehending and annotating.

As the test over the material approaches, students can write a journal about how they have prepared for the test, what strategies they did and did not use, how much time they studied, what grade they expect, what topics they feel (un)prepared for, etc. After the test, they would be encouraged to write about their experience during test taking and their subsequent thoughts, such as the difficulty of the test, grade received, how much or how little they prepared, what they plan to do differently in the future, where they need help, and where most of their errors fell (objective or subjective parts of the test).

Initially, students' metacognitive awareness is not well developed, and writing about their comprehension presents difficulties for them. As the semester progresses, however, and they are given ample opportunities and encouragement to examine their comprehension, they improve considerably. Students begin to perceive that they have control over their learning.

(2) On-line monitoring of comprehension can be included in testing. For example, students can participate in on-line monitoring of their test item responses. As they answer multiple choice or true-false questions over chapter content in biology or psychology, for example, they can be asked to indicate for each question how confident they are in the accuracy of their answer. Similarly, after finishing an essay, they can write a few sentences evaluating their response and how well they expressed themselves in writing. They can also be asked what grade they think they will get.

After the test is graded and returned, they can examine their metacognitive evaluations of objective and subjective item responses and see where they went wrong, or what it was about a particular question that led them to choose an incorrect answer. As they learn to monitor their responses during testtaking over the course of a semester, students become better at preparing for and taking tests (Nist & Simpson, 1989).

Metacognitive development is important because students need to monitor their comprehension and become aware of when they are experiencing difficulties with academic material and when to use appropriate fix-up strategies. Motivation is predicted to improve because of the self-control implicit in their awareness and subsequent actions and the self-management of their resources. If students are shown that strategy use will improve their achievement, they can become convinced that their efforts will make a difference and that their learning is under their control.

This concept relates to White's (1959) notions of competence, where feelings of efficacy result in motivation following fruitful interaction with the environment. McCombs (1984) cited evidence that if perceptions of personal control are developed, students will transfer the use of strategies they have been taught. In any developmental program, after all, transfer and independent learning are the most important goals.

Motivation and Attributions

Students with full knowledge of their negative attitudes toward learning and the opportunity to learn strategies still may not change, however. Eccles (1983, 1984) claimed that one's interpretation of a situation, its requirements, and one's abilities determine one's actions more than actual events. This perception problem may be explained by the tenets of attribution theory.

Briefly, attributionists believe that motivation results from an individual's beliefs in the causes of success and failure. Weiner (1979) separated perceived causes into four factors: ability, effort, luck, and task

How Students See the Causes of Success and Failure

Perceived causes	Stability of causes	Controllable by student?	Locus of control
Ability	Stable	Uncontrollable	Student
Effort	Unstable	**Controllable**	**Student**
Luck	Unstable	Uncontrollable	External
Task difficulty	Stable	Uncontrollable	External

Based on Weiner (1979)

difficulty. He then classified these factors according to whether each is stable or unstable, controllable or uncontrollable, and has an internal or external locus of control. Thus, ability is stable, uncontrollable, and internal; effort is unstable, controllable, and internal; luck is unstable, uncontrollable, and external; and task difficulty is stable, uncontrollable, and external (see Chart).

The main hypothesis held by attributionists is that students will be motivated when they attribute their successes and failures to the amount of effort they invest in a task, rather than to their ability. With an effort attribution, they retain a sense of control. If they attribute failure to ability or luck (factors outside their control), however, self-esteem and perception of personal control decrease. Anxiety will result, and students will be motivated to evade the task and the requisite studying demands. In addition, at-risk students may develop learned helplessness, the feeling that failure cannot be overcome. If students are taught to attribute failure to effort rather than ability, their anxiety levels may not be as debilitating, and they will be more likely to face the fact that because academic demands will not change, learners must.

It is important to recognize that self-esteem and self-identity are functions of development and experience (McCombs, 1986). We may be expecting a lot of college reading students when we attempt to teach them metacognitive strategies for use in learning academic material. Students' problems with low self-esteem start long before they reach college. Often, they have "not developed the cognitive complexity necessary to organize information in such a way that it enhances or preserves self-esteem" (McCombs, 1986, p. 323). Nevertheless, a strategic learning/reading program, relevant to students' needs, appears to be an appropriate place for students to begin developing that necessary cognitive complexity.

Students with negative learning experiences, therefore, require much support as they become autonomous and regulate their own learning. Teaching them a variety of study and test preparation strategies using lengthy text will help them gain a sense of control over what they may perceive as daunting academic tasks. In addition, sparking and nurturing the development of metacognitive awareness is an over-riding component to a learning strategies program. Without the metacognitive awareness of why and when to use learning strategies, transfer to independent learning may not occur.

References

Bandura, A. (1977). Self-efficacy: Toward a unifying theory of behavioral change. *Psychological Review, 84,* 191–215.

Deci, E. L. (1975). *Intrinsic motivation.* New York: Plenum.

Eccles, J. (1983). Expectancies, values, and academic behaviors. In J. T. Spence (Ed.), *Achievement and achievement motives: Psychological and sociological approaches.* San Francisco: Freeman.

Eccles, J. (1984). Self-perceptions, task perceptions, socializing influences and the decision to enroll in mathematics. In M. W. Steinkamp (Ed.), *Advances in motivation and achievement: Women in science,* vol. 2. Greenwich, CT: JAI Press.

Harter, S. (1982). A developmental perspective on some parameters of self-regulation in children. In P. Karoly & F. H. Kanfer (Eds.), *Self-management and behavior change: From theory to practice.* New York: Pergamon.

Harter, S. (1985). Processes underlying self-concept formation in children. In J. Suls & A. Greenwald (Eds.), *Psychological perspective on the self.* Hillsdale, NJ: Erlbaum.

McCombs, B. L. (1984). Processes and skills underlying continuing intrinsic motivation to learn: Toward a definition of motivational skills training. *Educational Psychologist, 19,* 199–218.

McCombs, B. L. (1986). The role of the self-system in self-regulated learning. *Contemporary Educational Psychology 11,* 314–332.

Nist, S. L., & Simpson, M. L. (1989). PLAE: A validated study strategy. *Journal of Reading, 33,* 182–186.

Paris, S. G., Lipson, M. Y., & Wixson, K. K. (1983). Becoming a strategic reader. *Contemporary Educational Psychology, 8,* 293–316.

Simpson, M. L. (1986). PORPE: A writing strategy for studying and learning in the content areas. *Journal of Reading, 29,* 407–414.

Simpson, M. L., & Nist, S. L. (1984). PLAE: A model for independent learning. *Journal of Reading, 28,* 218–223.

Weiner, B. (1979). A theory of motivation for some classroom experiences. *Journal of Educational Psychology, 71,* 3–25.

White, R. W. (1959). Motivation reconsidered: The concept of competence. *Psychological Review, 66,* 297–333.

Wittrock, M. C. (1986). Students' thought processes. In M. C. Wittrock (Ed.), *Handbook of research on teaching.* New York: Macmillan.

Additional Readings

Caverly, D. C., Mandeville, T. F., & Nicholson, S. A. (1995). "PLAN: A study-reading strategy for informational text." *Journal of Reading,* 39 (3), 190–99.

Caverly, D. C., Orlando, V. P., & Mullen, J. L. (2000). "Textbook study reading." In R. F. Flippo & D. C. Caverly (Eds.), *The handbook of college reading and study strategy research* (pp. 1–23). Mahwah, NJ: Erlbaum.

Commander, N. E., & Smith, B. D. (1996). "Learning logs: A tool for cognitive monitoring." *Journal of Adolescent & Adult Literacy,* 39 (6), 446–53.

Commander, N. E., & Valeri-Gold, M. (2001). "The learning portfolio: A valuable tool for increasing metacognitive awareness." *The Learning Assistance Review,* 6 (2), 5–18.

Grant, R. (1993). "Strategic training for using text headings to improve students' processing of content." *Journal of Reading,* 36 (6), 482–88.

Harri-Augstein, S., Smith, M., & Thomas, L. (1982). *Reading to learn.* London: Methuen.

McWhorter, Y. (1994). "Processes and learning strategies: What works for postsecondary students." In E. G. Sturtevant, & W. M. Linek (Eds.), *Pathways for literacy: Learners teach and teachers learn, The 16th yearbook of the College Reading Association* (pp. 127–38). Commerce, TX: College Reading Association.

Nist, S. L., & Simpson, M. L. (1989). "PLAE, A Validated Study Strategy." *Journal of Reading,* 33 (3), 182–86.

Simpson, M. L. (1986). "PORPE: A writing strategy for studying and learning in the content areas." *Journal of Reading,* 29 (8), 407–14.

Smith, R. M. (1990). *Learning to learn across the lifespan.* San Francisco: Jossey-Bass.

Spires, H. A. (1989). "The directed notetaking activity: A self-questioning approach." *Journal of Reading,* 33 (1), 36–39.

Stahl, N. A., King, J. R., & Henk, W. A. (1991). "Enhancing students' notetaking through training and evaluation." *Journal of Reading,* 34 (8), 614–22.

5

New-to-English Learners

The United States is in what could be said to be the greatest period of immigration in our history. Because of a range of cultural, economic, pedagogical, and political factors and policies during previous periods of immigration, it was unlikely that English language learners would be enrolled in postsecondary education to the same degree we see in our schools today. Whether an institution labels such individuals as Limited English Proficient students, English as a Second Language learners, New-to-English learners, or English Language Learners (the field continues to hunt for the best term), a key factor for success in college courses is the ability to use college-level communication skills in the learning process.

Two groups of English language learners can be found on the college campus today. The first group is made up of international students who have come to the United States to undertake postsecondary or graduate-level education. Many of these students will be served by English language centers often associated with English departments. Once the international students have successfully undertaken the training provided by such programs, they, like any other student on the campus, have access to the services of learning assistance centers, tutorial programs, supplemental instruction programs, and so forth.

The second group of students would be identified as immigrants to the United States. Such students may or may not have gone through the public school system in this country. Whether basic English training is initially undertaken in an adult education program or in a K-12 ESL or bilingual education program, should the individual not demonstrate the reading competency level required for college admission, he or she will likely receive services from that college or university's developmental reading program.

The articles in this chapter cover ways that new-to-English learners might be served by college reading programs. Lía D. Kamhi-Stein explains how she used a think-aloud text, a prior knowledge measure, a demographic questionnaire, and a summarization task to develop profiles of students' facility with the English language. Denise Johnson and Virginia Steele discuss learning principles and strategies recommended for building the vocabulary levels of new-to-English learners. Vicki L. Holmes and Margaret R. Moulton show how dialogue journals promote academic literacy with English language learners. Finally, Laura Bauer and Linda Sweeney explain the use of literary letters in the development of comprehension skills.

Profiles of Underprepared Second-Language Readers

Lía D. Kamhi-Stein

Lía D. Kamhi-Stein argues that when instructors rely solely on the data provided by standardized reading measures, they cannot develop an understanding of the strategies used by students or of the reasons those students approach reading in a particular manner. The study reported in this article developed in-depth profiles of underprepared university-level Spanish speakers who had attended varying degrees of K-12 schooling in the United States. Kamhi-Stein used these profiles to distinguish more successful readers from less fluent, underprepared English-dominant readers with a Spanish-speaking background. Students were assessed with a think-aloud text, a prior knowledge measure, a demographic questionnaire, and a summarization task. The profiles of three readers detail their respective approaches to reading as well as the strategies they employed while undertaking the assessment tasks. Implications for practice and research are provided as well.

Increasing numbers of underprepared students from non–English-speaking home backgrounds are entering U.S. colleges and universities. For example, in the fall of 1993, of the nearly 24,000 first-year students entering California State University (CSU), between 5,000 and 6,000 reported that English was their second language (L2). Of these, only 1,000 evidenced college-level English proficiency. Comparable numbers of L2 students are enrolling in other urban university systems. The City University of New York (CUNY) statistics for the fall of 1992 indicate that 44.3 percent of the entering students were L2 speakers. In addition, CUNY statistics for 1990 show that 15 percent of the entering first-year students were placed in English as a second language (ESL) classes (Benesch & Block, 1995).

Moreover, a vast majority of the underprepared L2 students entering U.S. colleges and universities are from immigrant families. Specifically, as shown in a report by the U.S. Department of Education (1997), in 1995 approximately 546,420 recent immigrants were taking ESL classes as part of their college courses, and approximately 41,000 first-time, first-year students came to the U.S. to pursue a college degree (in a public university) and return to their country of origin (U.S. Department of Education, 1995).

The placement of L2 students into prebaccalaureate reading courses is usually accomplished through traditional forms of assessment, which "are limited in their descriptive power" (Cohen, 1987, p. 131). If teachers were to rely solely on information provided by reading comprehension tests, they would not develop an understanding of what strategies their students use or why their students have arrived at a certain decision.

This study was designed using a premise advanced by Block (1986). In her view, an understanding of the readers' internal reading process is needed for the development of reading programs tailored to meet the actual needs of L2 readers. To develop such an understanding, this study relied on the think-aloud method, which involves readers verbalizing their thought processes while they are reading a text (Wade, 1990).

While the think-aloud technique has been widely used by first-language (L1) reading researchers (see Pressley & Afflerbach, 1995, for a description of think-aloud research), its use in the L2 reading field has been more limited (e.g., Block, 1986, 1992; Calcavanti, 1987; Davies & Bistodeau, 1993). Possible reasons for this may be the researchers' concerns with the added cognitive demands placed on L2 readers (Cohen, 1996) and the incomplete reports that may result from the readers' limited L2 proficiency (Block, 1992).

Think-aloud research in the L2 reading field has shown that the comprehension-monitoring processes of L1 and L2 readers are similar (Block, 1992) and differences in monitoring and reading strategy result more from reading proficiency than from language background (Block, 1986, 1992). In addition, when compared to less proficient bilingual readers, more proficient bilingual readers exhibit a multistrategic approach to reading and view their bilingualism as a resource (Jiménez, García, & Pearson, 1995, 1996). Finally, L2 readers have been found to be affected by their lack of L2 vocabulary (e.g., Davies & Bistodeau, 1993), which leads readers to employ an approach to reading that is word-centered — or what Jiménez, García, and Pearson (1995) call "logocentric" (p. 76).

This study was designed to provide in-depth information about underprepared university-level native Spanish speakers from an immigrant background — a population that is not yet achieving at the same level as their native English-speaking peers. Specifically, the purpose of this investigation was to create profiles that would help to distinguish more successful from less successful underprepared English-dominant readers from a Spanish-speaking background reading in English.

Participants

Three bilingual, English-dominant, Latino/a first-year college students enrolled in an introductory Health Science course participated in this study. The students were considered to be underprepared, as indicated by their scores on the reading skills section of the California State University (CSU) English Placement Test (EPT) (150 or below) and the Gates-MacGinitie Reading Test (56 or below). Therefore, they were required to enroll in the introductory reading course for L2 readers and a minimum of two remedial writing courses prior to taking the required English Composition class.

Three criteria were used to select the study participants. First, the three students reflected the first-year student population at CSU, Los Angeles, where 75 percent of the entering first-year students are language-minority students, and 82 percent of these are required to enroll in remedial reading and writing courses on the basis of their EPT scores. Second, the students were able to speak and write in Spanish, though each participant differed in writing skill level. Finally, the students were selected on the basis of their willingness to participate in the think-aloud task. Table 1 presents background information on the study participants and information related to the participants' patterns of L1 and L2 use.

Materials

Think-Aloud Text

The article selected for the think-aloud task was related to the introductory Health Science course in which the students were enrolled. The article, entitled "The Safer Sex" (Fackelmann, 1991), was from *Science News*; its word count was 2,144, and the ratio of sentence length to word length indicated that the article was aimed at students at the college level (Fry, 1977). The total number of main ideas in the article was 19, as determined by 10 independent readers. The text, which had features characteristic of descriptive and comparative texts (Meyer, 1981), was selected because it presented information about gender differences in heart attack, a topic that was addressed in the introductory Health Science course in which the students were enrolled.

Table 1. Participant Background Information

Name	Country of birth	Length of U.S. residence	U.S. schooling	Reading scores	Language used at home	outside the home	Self-reported ability to read/write in Spanish	Language used in reading		
								news-papers	magazines	books
Estela	Nicaragua	9 years	Since Grade 5	132 (EPT)	Spanish	English	Good	English	English	English
Julio	Mexico	5 years	Since Grade 10	50 (Gates-MacGinitie Reading Test)	Spanish	English	Very good	Spanish/English	Spanish/English	Spanish
Juan	U.S.	Since birth	Since Kindergarten	43 (Gates-MacGinitie Test)	Spanish	English	Very good	English	English	English

Prior Knowledge Assessment

Prior to the completion of the think-aloud task, the three participants' prior knowledge of the topic of the article was assessed by asking the students to write, in 5 minutes, what they knew about the topic about which they would be reading (Kamhi-Stein, 1995). Although the students were instructed to use either English or Spanish, the three readers chose to write in English.

Questionnaire

The participants completed a questionnaire designed to provide demographic information and information regarding their patterns of L1 and L2 use.

Summarization Task

After completing the think-aloud task, the three participants completed a timed summary. This task was selected because the ability to summarize information is common to most, if not all, academic literacy tasks in the general education curriculum (Kamhi-Stein, 1995).

Data Collection Procedures

The three participants completed the questionnaire in their introductory Health Science class at the beginning of the term. To ensure that the reading strategies observed through the think-aloud task were not random, the same think-aloud task was completed twice — the first time at the beginning and the second time at the end of the term.

Prior to engaging in the think-aloud task, thinking aloud was modeled on a videotape — a technique also used by Jiménez, García, and Pearson (1995) — and students practiced thinking aloud with a passage different from the one used for data collection purposes. Only when the students indicated that they felt comfortable using the technique did the think-aloud task start. Once students completed the think-aloud task, they wrote the timed summary.

Instructions for the think-aloud task included asking students to read silently or out loud, as they usually did, and to say everything that they were thinking when they read. Additionally, students were told to complete the think-aloud task in Spanish or English, as they would naturally do when they read at home. To ensure that students would remember to stop and think aloud, a red dot was placed after each sentence (Block, 1986).

Drawing on prior research by Jiménez, García, and Pearson (1995), individual student profiles were created by combining the number of main ideas included in the summary protocols with data from the think-aloud task and the questionnaire. The following two procedures were followed to create the readers' profiles.

First, the number of main ideas recalled by each of the three readers in the summarization task was counted. To identify the number of main ideas reproduced in each of the summary protocols, three raters read one summary protocol at a time and determined which of the main ideas from the source text were reflected in the protocol (Kamhi-Stein, 1995).

Second, data from the think-aloud task were first transcribed; then, categories of individual reading strategies adapted from Block (1986) were identified through a process of recursive reading. The reading strategies were then grouped into three major categories (Jiménez, García, & Pearson, 1996): (a) reader-initiated strategies (strategies prompted by the reader), (b) text-initiated strategies (strategies prompted by the reading passage), and (c) interactive strategies (strategies prompted by the interaction of the reader with the text). Table 2 presents the individual reading strategies included under each of the three major categories followed by their definitions.

Analyses of the think-aloud data were combined with and supported by the results of the summarization task and the students' scores on reading examinations. Two profiles were created, one for more successful and the other for less successful underprepared L2 readers. These two profiles assumed that more successful and less successful L2 readers would differ in a combination of qualitative and quantitative features. The qualitative features observed included whether or not the readers exhibited characteristics typical of good readers, including having a multistrategic and flexible approach to reading and engaging in a process of meaning construction. The quantitative features observed included the number of main ideas and the readers' scores on reading tests or college entrance examinations.

Estela, a More Successful L2 Reader

Estela can be considered a more successful underprepared reader. Though Estela's approach to reading is linear, as she reads she engages in an active process of meaning construction and makes use of multiple reading strategies — typical of good readers. Estela's characterization as successful is made further evident by the fact that, when compared with the other two readers, she identified the highest number of main ideas in the source text (8 of 19).

Estela's approach to reading is characterized as being linear, word-centered as a means to construct meaning, and multistrategic.

Reading as a Linear Process

Although she uses many other reading strategies, Estela does not act as a strategic reader initially in that she does not construct a goal for

Table 2. Classification of Reading Strategies Used

Reading Strategies

Reader-initiated (strategies prompted by the reader)	Text-initiated (strategies prompted by the reading passage)	Interactive (strategies prompted by the reader's interaction with the text)
Detecting comprehension problems: The reader expresses his/her lack of understanding	Paraphrasing: The reader rephrases the idea using different wording	Integrating information: The reader finds connections between new information and ideas previously stated in the text
Attempting to solve comprehension problems: The reader takes action to correct comprehension problems	Using the dictionary: The reader looks up words in the dictionary	Interpreting the text: The reader hypothesizes or makes an inference about the text
	Rereading: The reader rereads a portion of the text	
	Recognizing important information: The reader identifies important information	

reading the text. Instead, she dives into the text and reads it in a linear, nonselective manner, from front to back (Pressley & Afflerbach, 1995). Absent from Estela's protocol are strategies that characterize good readers, like reading the article title ("The Safer Sex") or subtitle ("Probing a Cardiac Gender Gap") and generating a hypothesis about the text. In fact, Estela's first encounter with the text consists of reading and paraphrasing the first sentence in the article.

His mother died quite, quite, um, early from heart disease.

Estela's linear approach to reading is further made evident by the fact that absent from her protocol is the strategy of jumping ahead to understand an important point that may be fully explained in a subsequent paragraph (Pressley & Afflerbach, 1995).

Word-Centeredness as a Means to Construct Meaning

Estela acts as a less successful L2 reader in that — to use Grabe's (1991) term — she is "word-bound" (p. 391). Whenever Estela encounters an unknown word, she stops reading and looks the word up in the dictionary. Not once does Estela attempt to guess the meaning of a word she does not understand. Following is an example of what Estela says when she encounters unknown vocabulary words.

> I have to read it [the word] again. I'm looking for the word, um, *poignant,* poignant. Poignant means to prick, sharp, repugnant to smell; or formerly, formerly to taste, to taste, keenly affecting the other senses, other senses. Okay.

Although Estela's approach to reading is driven by her focus on unknown vocabulary words, this does not prevent her from constructing meaning. In fact, as will be shown in the example below, Estela uses her word-centeredness as a means to comprehend text.

> I'm looking for the word *innate,* i-n-n-a-t-e. Innate means to be born in, originate in, originate in. The question's asking that. Let me read it again. The question's asking if the mortality gap, I assume, for men and a woman, um, show or reflects a built-in or born-in difference in biological, um, senses between men and women. That's what the question is asking.

Estela's concern about unknown vocabulary has been found to exist among bilingual readers (Jiménez, García, & Pearson, 1995, 1996). These readers may be affected by their limited vocabulary and this, in turn, may affect the students' ability to read fluently. What is unique to Estela is that, in contrast to bilingual readers in prior studies (Jiménez, García, & Pearson, 1996), looking up words in the dictionary is the sole strategy to which she resorts when trying to understand the meaning of unknown words.

Multistrategic Approach

Although Estela's approach to reading is driven by her concern about unknown vocabulary words, she employs a variety of reader-initiated strategies, interactive strategies, and text-initiated strategies as a means to construct meaning. The reader-initiated strategies that Estela employs include detecting comprehension problems at the sentence level and attempting to solve them. An example from the protocol follows:

> I have to read it again. It's a long sentence [she proceeds to read the sentence one more time].

The interactive strategies that Estela uses are interpreting the text and integrating new information with previously stated content. Interpreting the text appears consistently in Estela's protocol and is introduced by words like "I guess," "I think," "Maybe," and "So it could be." Following is an example of how Estela interprets text:

> I guess the reason why it effects [sic] more women is because the hormone estrogen decreases so then, it stops, uh, protecting the women's body.

The second interactive strategy, integrating new information with previously stated content, can be observed in no more than two occasions. What follows is an example from Estela's think-aloud protocol:

> Okay, this is, I think this is kind of important. It's connected with the other paragraph.

The third type of reading strategy that Estela uses is text initiated. As already explained, Estela pays attention to unknown words. She also paraphrases. When she reads the following sentence, she says:

> Um, the sentence is saying that when a woman has the first heart attack, um, they have a higher risk in getting one a few weeks after.

The final text-initiated strategy Estela uses is recognizing important information in the text, as she does in the following protocol:

> This is kind of important.

Estela's multistrategic approach to reading, which has been found to be characteristic of better L2 readers (e.g., Carrell, 1989; Devine, 1987; Jiménez, García, & Pearson, 1996), results in high engagement with the article. When reading, Estela resorts to the use of multiple local (as opposed to global) reading strategies (e.g., understanding the meaning of unknown words, paraphrasing, monitoring and repairing comprehension at the sentence level) as a means to comprehend ideas and construct meaning.

Julio, Another More Successful Reader

Although Julio's approach to reading is also linear, he exhibits a multistrategic approach, which characterizes good readers. In addition, Julio has recognized 6 of the 19 main ideas in the source text.

Reading as a Linear Process

Much like Estela, Julio, while strategic in several other ways, does not construct a purpose for reading the text or use other initial reading strategies characteristic of good readers (e.g., reading the article title or subtitle and predicting information that might be presented in the article; paying attention to the structure of the text). Julio's reading process is linear; like Estela, he dives into the reading task and completes it in a nonselective manner (Pressley & Afflerbach, 1995).

Julio's first encounter with the article consists of paraphrasing the first sentence.

> Someone's mom died, um, of heart disease some time ago.

Multistrategic Approach

Julio employs reader-initiated strategies, interactive strategies, and text-initiated strategies. As will be shown in the example that follows, Julio's reader-initiated strategies include detecting comprehension problems and attempting to solve them.

> What's this saying? Okay, I'm gonna read the sentence again.

Julio uses interactive reading strategies. First, as shown in the following example, he interprets the text.

> It might be the fact that, em, as they get older they, they tend to, to suffer from other conditions or other diseases that might make it harder, em, for their treatment.

An interactive reading strategy that appears consistently in Julio's think-aloud protocol is integrating previously read information with new information presented in the text. An example from the think-aloud protocol follows:

> Again, more women died within the next, within the next year, after suffering the heart attack.

The only text-initiated strategy that Julio uses is paraphrasing:

> In other words, when performing surgery of the heart, eh, careful attention is being paid to, em, to the subject of gender.

In contrast to Estela, Julio never focuses his attention on individual words, nor does he resort to the dictionary. Julio is interested in identifying important ideas, which he mentally underlines by saying "again." What follows is an example from Julio's protocol:

> Again, um, uh, physicians, physicians might not pay much attention to the, to the, to the condition of women . . .

Julio's multistrategic approach to reading results in an active process of meaning construction, characteristic of better L2 readers (Block, 1986). As shown in this section, critical to Julio's process of meaning construction is the fact that he is interested in understanding important information. To reach such an understanding, Julio consistently resorts to mentally underlining important information and to integrating previously read information with new information presented in the same text.

Juan, a Less Successful L2 Reader

A combination of factors, including Juan's lack of engagement with the text, the limited variety of reading strategies in his protocol, and the low number of main ideas he recognizes on the summarization task (3 of 19), resulted in Juan's characterization as a less successful underprepared L2 reader. As will be explained, Juan's approach to reading is linear and monostrategic.

Reading as a Linear Process

Juan's approach to reading is similar to that of Estela's and Julio's in that it is linear. He dives into the reading task and completes it from front to back, in a nonselective manner. Juan, much like Estela and Julio, never attempts to overview the text in order to develop an understanding of the whole text, a strategy that is characteristic of strategic readers (Pressley & Afflerbach, 1995). Juan's first encounter with the text occurs when he reads and paraphrases the first paragraph:

> Okay, um, what it says is that, um, that 15 years ago, um, this person's mom died and yes, he's looking, um, didn't do the first paragraph. And now he's, um, he, now, um, secretary at the Department of Health and Human Services. Next paragraph.

Monostrategic Approach to Reading

Juan's reading strategies include only one text-initiated strategy, paraphrasing, and one reader-initiated strategy, identifying comprehension problems. The following examples reflect how he paraphrases and identifies comprehension problems, respectively:

> It says that, uh, the Yale report, it's saying that, um, male and female are unequal, related to stay in the hospital from a heart attack.
> Uh, I don't understand this sentence [continues reading].

Although Juan can identify his comprehension problems, he never attempts to solve them. This behavior has been found to be typical of poor L2 readers in previous studies (e.g., Block, 1986; Jiménez, García, & Pearson, 1996). Juan, much like other less proficient L2 readers, may lack the resources necessary to repair his comprehension problems (Block, 1986).

In addition, Juan's approach to reading is characterized by his limited engagement with the text. The same pattern of behavior has been found to exist among poor L2 readers in prior research (e.g., Bean & Hedgcock, 1996; Jiménez, García, & Pearson, 1996). In contrast to good L2 readers, who view the reading process as one that allows them to construct meaning, poor L2 readers view the reading process as one that allows them to "get through" the reading task, whether they comprehend or not.

Summary of Findings and Discussion

The results of this study show that while there are similarities among the three readers, there are also considerable variations in the reading behaviors exhibited by the three underprepared readers. Table 3 presents a summary of the reading strategies observed in the three readers' think-aloud protocols.

As can be observed in Table 3, Estela's approach to reading is linear, word-centered, and multistrategic, Julio's approach to reading is linear and multistrategic, and Juan's approach to reading is linear and monostrategic. Estela and Julio, the two more successful readers, differ from Juan, the less successful reader, in that they exhibit a wide repertoire of reading strategies and are more flexible strategy users. These findings are consistent with prior research (e.g., Block, 1986; Carrell, 1989; Devine, 1987) which indicates that better readers have a wide repertoire of reading strategies to which they can resort.

Critical to Estela's and Julio's approaches to reading is the fact that they are involved in a process of meaning construction that is characterized by their high engagement with the text. This finding supports the notion that better readers exhibit an active approach to meaning construction (Block, 1986; Jiménez, García, & Pearson, 1996). However, Estela and Julio differ in the process in which they engage in order to construct meaning. Specifically, Estela pays attention to individual words as a means to understand the ideas in the text. In contrast, Julio never focuses on unknown words; instead, when he identifies important information, he seems to mentally underline it by saying "again." The word *again,* for Julio, seems to operate as a mnemonic device assisting him to construct the global meaning of the text.

When compared to the reading behavior exhibited by Estela and Julio, the more successful readers, Juan's reading behavior is characterized by his low engagement with the reading passage. Juan's focus is on completing the reading task and not on negotiating the meaning of text. This finding supports prior research conducted with at-risk English-dominant bilingual readers from a Spanish background (Bean & Hedgcock, 1996). Also consistent with prior studies on poor L2 readers (e.g., Block, 1992; Jiménez, García, & Pearson, 1995, 1996) is the fact that Juan does not take action when he becomes aware of a reading difficulty.

Table 3. Reading Strategies Observed in the Think-Aloud Protocols

Reader's name	Approach to reading	Reader initiated	Strategies used		
			Text-initiated	Interactive	
Estela	Linear Word-centered Multistrategic	Detecting comprehension problems Attempting to solve comprehension problems Rereading	Paying attention to unknown words Paraphrasing Recognizing important information	Interpreting text Integrating new information with previously stated content	
Julio	Linear Multistrategic	Detecting comprehension problems Attempting to solve comprehension problems Rereading	Paraphrasing Recognizing important information	Interpreting text Integrating new information with previously stated content	
Juan	Linear Monostrategic	Detecting comprehension problems	Paraphrasing		

Second-language reading research has shown that L2 readers are affected by their lack of vocabulary knowledge (e.g., Davies & Bistodeau, 1993; Jiménez, García, & Pearson, 1995, 1996; Scarcella, 1996). This seems to be the case for Estela, whose lack of reading fluency seems to result, at least in part, from her limited knowledge of vocabulary.

The results of this investigation suggest a positive correlation among reading strategy use, number of main ideas recognized, and degree to which the readers can use Spanish and English. Although the students' ability to use Spanish was not formally measured, results of an informal written assessment and an oral interview in Spanish point to the fact that a higher degree of Spanish proficiency was observed for Estela and Julio. These two students received primary language instruction in Nicaragua and Mexico prior to entering the U.S. educational system in Grades 5 and 10, respectively.

Common to Juan, Estela, and Julio is that in attempting to understand written text, they never resort to their first language or to the use of cognates. In Juan and Estela's case, it could be assumed their length of participation in the U.S. educational system may have resulted in stronger academic language skills in English than in Spanish, leading Juan and Estela to resort to their L2 skills in academic situations. In the case of Julio, who reports reading books in Spanish and reading magazines and papers in Spanish and English, it is not clear whether or not he views his L1 as a resource. Questions like these and others regarding the relationship between L1 and L2 literacy could be investigated in future studies focusing on bilingual, English-dominant university-level readers. This work would build upon prior research on bilingual children from a Spanish-speaking background and their views about their L1 (Jiménez, García, & Pearson, 1995, 1996).

Another characteristic common to Estela, Julio, and Juan is their linear approach to reading. None of the three readers consider a goal in reading. As noted by Pressley and Afflerbach (1995), this lack of planning of how to approach the reading task, which has been found typical of poor readers, "often affects subsequent reading" (p. 32). In the case of the three readers in this study, it is not clear the extent to which planning how to approach the reading task would have affected the readers' processing of the source text.

Research has shown that main idea construction is facilitated by the readers' prior knowledge of the topic (Afflerbach, 1990). In the current study, none of the three readers exhibited familiarity with the topic of gender differences and heart attack. This lack of prior knowledge of the topic may have affected the readers in their process of main idea construction and may have prevented them from constructing an initial hypothesis, which — as explained by Afflerbach (1990) — could have contributed to lowering the readers' cognitive load.

Implications for Practice and Research

The findings arising from the think-aloud protocols support the idea that underprepared L2 readers have, to varying degrees, a repertoire of reading strategies. Therefore, reading teachers could draw upon the strategies that L2 readers have — a suggestion also made by Block (1986) — and could help students to build upon them. For example, students like Estela, whose reading process is driven by her word-centeredness, need to understand that, in order to comprehend written text, they do not need to know the meaning of every word they read. These students would also benefit from learning how to guess the meaning of vocabulary in context (Jiménez & Gámez, 1996) and how to allocate resources to understand written text. Students like Juan, who may be aware of but do not resolve their reading problems, could be taught the importance of rereading when failing to understand the meaning of the text.

In addition, L2 readers like Estela, Julio, and Juan would benefit from instruction that consistently integrates reading strategy instruction into the language or subject-matter curriculum. Positive changes have been observed in L2 classrooms where instructors combine subject matter teaching with reading strategy instruction by providing students with models, training with awareness, and support for learning (Grabe & Stoller, 1997; Jansen, 1996; Kamhi-Stein, 1997). Teachers could model reading strategy use through the think-aloud technique. In this way, underprepared L2 readers would be explicitly exposed to models of expert behavior, and the reading process (often obscure to underprepared L2 readers) would be demystified.

A further use of the think-aloud technique in the L2 classroom could involve students verbalizing reading strategy use in whole-class and small-group activities. This would allow underprepared L2 readers to become aware of what strategies they are using to understand written text. As noted by Kucan and Beck (1997), the strength of the think-aloud technique as an instructional method lies in its potential to reveal what readers do.

Future research on underprepared university-level L2 readers should focus on the relationship between biliteracy skills and reading strategy use. Think-aloud research in the students' L1 and L2, combined with formal assessments of the readers' L1 literacy skills, oral retellings and summaries (as opposed to written summaries), and interviews about the readers' views of their L1 would contribute to the growing number of studies focusing on underprepared L2 readers. This line of research would help researchers and practitioners develop an in-depth understanding of the strengths possessed as well as the challenges faced by underprepared L2 readers. Only by drawing upon this understanding will it be possible to develop reading programs designed to meet the needs of underprepared L2 students.

References

Afflerbach, P. P. (1990). The influence of prior knowledge on expert readers' main idea construction strategies. *Reading Research Quarterly* 25, 31–46.

Bean, M. S., & Hedgcock, J. S. (1996, October). *¿Para qué? Latino readers reflect on ESL literacy tasks and motives.* Paper presented at the meeting of the Second Language Research Forum, Tucson, AZ.

Benesch, S., & Block, E. (1995). Issues in ESL: The cost of public education, *College ESL*, 5, 47–51.

Block, E. (1986). The comprehension strategies of second language learners. TESOL *Quarterly*, 20, 463–494.

Block, E. (1992). See how they read: Comprehension monitoring of L1 and L2 readers. TESOL *Quarterly*, 26, 319–343.

Calcavanti, M. C. (1987). Investigating FL reading performance through pause protocols. In C. Faerch & G. Kasper (Eds.), *Introspection in second language research* (pp. 230–250). Clevedon, England: Multilingual Matters.

Carrell, P. L. (1989). Metacognitive awareness and second language reading. *Modern Language Journal*, 73, 121–134.

Cohen, A. D. (1987). Mentalistic measures in reading strategy research: Some recent findings. *English for Specific Purposes*, 5, 131–145.

Cohen, A. D. (1996). Verbal protocols as a source of insights into second language learner strategies. *Applied Language Learning*, 7(1 & 2), 5–24.

Davies, J. N., & Bistodeau, L. (1993). How do L1 and L2 reading differ? Evidence from think aloud protocols. *Modern Language Journal*, 77, 459–472.

Devine, J. (1987). General language competence and adult second language reading. In J. Devine, P. Carrell, & D. Eskey (Eds.), *Research in reading in English as a second language* (pp. 73–86). Washington, DC: TESOL.

Fackelmann, K. A. (1991). The safer sex: Probing a cardiac gender gap. *Science News*, 139, 139–140.

Fry, E. (1977). Fry's readability graph: Clarifications, validity, and extension to level 17. *Journal of Reading*, 21, 242–253.

Grabe, W. (1991). Current developments in second language reading research. TESOL *Quarterly*, 25, 375–406.

Grabe, W., & Stoller, F. L. (1997). Content-based instruction: Research foundations. In M. A. Snow & D. M. Brinton (Eds.), *The content-based classroom: Perspectives on integrating language and content* (pp. 5–21). White Plains, NY: Addison Wesley Longman.

Jansen, J. (1996). Teaching strategic reading. TESOL *Journal*, 6, 6–9.

Jiménez, R.T., & Gámez, A. (1996). Literature-based cognitive strategy instruction for middle school Latina/o students. *Journal of Adolescent &Adult Literacy*, 40, 84–91.

Jiménez, R. T., García, G. E., & Pearson, P. D. (1995). Three children, two languages, and strategic reading: Case studies in bilingual/monolingual reading. *American Educational Research Journal*, 32, 67–97.

Jiménez, R. T., García, G. E., & Pearson, P. D. (1996). The reading strategies of bilingual Latina/o students who are successful English readers: Opportunities and obstacles. *Reading Research Quarterly*, 31, 90–112.

Kamhi-Stein, L. D. (1995). *The effect of explicit instruction on the summarization strategies of "underprepared" native Spanish-speaking freshmen in university-level adjunct courses.* Unpublished doctoral dissertation, University of Southern California, Los Angeles.

Kamhi-Stein, L. D. (1997). Enhancing student performance through discipline-based summarization-strategy instruction. In M. A. Snow & D. M. Brinton (Eds.), *The content-based classroom: Perspectives on integrating language and content* (pp. 248–262). White Plains, NY: Addison Wesley Longman.

Kucan, L., & Beck, I. L. (1997). Thinking aloud and reading comprehension research: Inquiry, instruction, and social interaction. *Review of Educational Research, 67,* 271–299.

Meyer, B. J. F. (1981). *Prose analysis: Procedures, purposes, and problems* (Prose Learning Series, Research Report No. 11). Tempe, AZ: Arizona State University. (ERIC Document Reproduction Service No. ED 201 972)

Pressley, M., & Afflerbach, P. (1995). *Verbal protocols of reading: The nature of constructively responsive reading.* Hillsdale, NJ: Erlbaum.

Scarcella, R. C. (1996). Secondary education in California and second language research: Instructing ESL students in the 1990s. *The* CATESOL *Journal, 9,* 129–151.

U.S. Department of Education, National Center for Education Statistics. (1995). *Integrated postsecondary education data system: Fall enrollment survey.* Washington, DC: U.S. Government Printing Office.

U.S. Department of Education, National Center for Education Statistics. (1997, June). *Statistics in brief.* Washington, DC: U.S. Government Printing Office.

Wade, S. E. (1990). Using think alouds to assess comprehension. *The Reading Teacher, 43,* 442–453.

So Many Words, So Little Time: Helping College ESL Learners Acquire Vocabulary-Building Strategies

Denise Johnson and Virginia Steele

New-to-English students in the developmental reading courses delivered by Denise Johnson and Virginia Steele readily acknowledge the need to expand their vocabularies in academic content areas. In attempting to address this need, the authors discovered that very little has been done to examine how ESL students approach academic literacy requirements, and more precisely, how limited English-proficient students expand their vocabularies for college reading. This is not surprising since vocabulary acquisition by college developmental readers is an under-researched area.

Here, the authors share a number of strategies that build on one or more of the following theoretical points: (1) vocabulary learning should be integrated with content instruction; (2) students should be introduced to vocabulary-building activities in nonthreatening, cooperative contexts; and (3) learning activities should be scaffolded in order to increase students' background knowledge. Strategies covered in the article focus on peer teaching, personal word lists, semantic mapping, and imagery, among others. The article concludes with the students' evaluation of the strategies, and the authors' call for instructors to use a mixed approach to teaching vocabulary.

The fact that vocabulary is an important component of reading comprehension for all readers has been well established (Anderson & Freebody, 1981; Bensoussan & Laufer, 1984; Davis, 1944; Farr & Carey, 1986; Hague, 1987; Nation, 1990; Thorndike, 1917). First language reading researchers have estimated recognition vocabularies of fluent readers to range from 10,000 words to 100,000 words (Nagy & Herman, 1987). Recognition vocabularies of second language readers are far lower, ranging from 5,000 to 7,000 words (Singer, 1981). This limited vocabulary does not meet the needs of second language learners who must deal with highly technical, infrequently used terms encountered in academic subject matter at the college level.

In our developmental reading classes, ESL students identify the ability to quickly expand their vocabularies in the context of academic subjects as one of their most critical needs. Recognizing that this need could be a major obstacle to success in college courses, we searched for effective vocabulary-building strategies supported by research in second language acquisition. We quickly found that although researchers have proposed several strategies for acquiring the vocabulary of a second language, little research has been conducted as to the effectiveness of specific learning strategies (Brown & Perry, 1991). Especially in the subject areas, little research has been done to explore how language minority students cope with literacy requirements (Reyes & Molner, 1991). Consequently, little is actually known about how competent ESL students expand their vocabularies to meet the demands of college reading.

We were enthusiastic, however, about experimenting with some of the strategies that have been proven to help ESL learners gain greater control over their own vocabulary-building processes. In this article, we describe several specific strategies and the research that supports them. We also give examples of students' applications of some of these strategies to materials presented in our developmental reading course.

Identifying Generative Strategies

In our classes, we teach generative reading strategies in the context of entire chapters from college-level textbooks. Generative strategies are those that are student-initiated and monitored and can be employed in a variety of situations. Although there are a number of effective instructional strategies described in the literature, our interest was in identifying effective generative strategies that would enable students to become independent learners of the conceptual meanings of new words (Nist & Diehl, 1994).

Each of the following strategies has been proven to help ESL learners develop their vocabularies as they learn from content materials. Most of the strategies can be used with mixed groups of English-speaking and non-English-speaking students. Each strategy incorporates one or more of the principles of effective vocabulary instruction offered by Stahl (1986). Both definitional and contextual information is included, students are involved in active processing, and students are given multiple exposures to the words.

Each strategy also includes at least one of the three characteristics believed to be important in teaching language-minority students — first, that vocabulary learning is integrated with content instruction; second, that students are given access to vocabulary-building activities in a nonthreatening, cooperative context; and third, that learning activities are "scaffolded" so as to build background and promote learning (Reyes & Molner, 1991).

Vocabulary Selection Strategies

Research has shown that effective readers can tolerate a high degree of ambiguity, up to 15 percent of words in a passage (Irvin, 1990). Many ESL learners, on the other hand, have developed the habit of word-by-word reading, feeling the need to stop and look up, or even translate into their native language, most unknown words they encounter.

Research by Parry (1991) with ESL students indicates that teachers "should encourage the students in our classes to do rapid reading without spending too much time on each word. Less frequent and more specialized words, however, may need more careful treatment to be remembered" (p. 650). She suggests that teachers lead students in a process of identifying "crucial terms," those words whose meaning they must know accurately in order to understand a particular text.

This view is supported by Irvin (1990). "Wide reading should be the primary vehicle for vocabulary learning, yet some selected words can be the focus of direct instruction or study" (p. 12). "Words that are introduced in a leading sentence and then thematized by repetition or by the use of reference items are obvious candidates for dictionary work, so also are those that are printed in bold or italic type. Most other words, however, need not be looked up, and they should not be because it takes so much time and interrupts the flow of reading" (Parry, 1991, p. 650). Other criteria offered by Diekhoff, Brown, and Dansereau (1982) are "italicized terms, terms used in headings, terms defined by the author, terms listed in glossaries, etc." (p. 181).

Peer Teaching

This is a strategy adapted from Haggard's (1986) Vocabulary Self-Collection Strategy and Parker's (1990) Desktop Teaching model. First, the student is asked to select *one* word from a section of the chapter the class is studying. The student must develop a justification for investing time in studying that particular word. The student then chooses a strategy such as a word map or an image that s/he can use to teach the word's meaning to another student. The next day students share their words and the criteria they used to select them. Students are then paired according to Parker's model and alternately teach their word and learn the word of their partner. This leads to a good discussion of

Figure 1. A Student's Use of Vocabulary Selection Strategies

And Connie would say nervously, "Oh, her. That dope." She always drew thick clear lines between herself and such girls, and her mother was simple and kindly enough to believe her. Her mother was so simple, Connie thought, that it was maybe cruel to fool her so much. Her mother went scuffling around the house in old bedroom slippers and complained over the telephone to one sister about the other, then the other called up and the two of them complained about the third one. If June's name was mentioned her mother's tone was approving, and if Connie's name was mentioned it was disapproving. This did not really mean she disliked Connie and actually Connie thought that her mother preferred her to June because she was prettier, but the two of them kept up a pretense of exasperation, a sense that they were tugging and struggling over something of little value to either of them. Sometimes, over coffee, they were almost friends, but something would come up—some vexation that was like a fly buzzing suddenly around their heads—and their faces went hard with contempt.

From the short story, "Where Are You Going, Where Have You Been?" Copyright ©1970 by Joyce Carol Oates. Reprinted by permission of John Hawkins and Associates, Inc.

the criteria for crucial terms, and it also gives students the opportunity to compare the effectiveness of the different strategies used by their classmates.

Crucial Term Identification

In this strategy the teacher selects an excerpt from the reading being studied by the class. The students are then instructed to read the excerpt and underline only those unfamiliar words that they feel they must know to comprehend the text. The next day, students compare their responses and discuss the criteria they used to select the words (see Figure 1). This strategy is especially useful for illustrating the differences between the selection criteria for different types of reading assignments. For example, in a short story it is important that words relating to the plot be understood, while details about the appearance of a character may or may not be equally important. In a chapter from a textbook, words that appear in the introduction or summary may be targets for more intensive study, as are any words in bold type. Students are then asked to use one of the other strategies — context, imagery, or key word — to learn the meanings of the terms they have identified as crucial.

Personal Word Lists

Researchers have come to view vocabulary development as a gradual process, "the result of many encounters with a word towards a more precise grasp of the concept the word represents" (Parry, 1993, p. 127). If repeated encounters with a word in a meaningful context is the way most vocabulary is learned, a logical inference is that ESL readers should develop their ability to use context clues.

Although the effectiveness of context as a strategy for vocabulary growth in a first language has been debated, research has shown that a great deal of word meaning for an ESL student can be inferred from context (Parry, 1991). Nation (1990) also points out that the analysis of words into affixes and roots is an effective learning strategy.

Too often, ESL students ignore context and structure and instead quickly turn to their dictionaries. Their reading is peppered with frequent "stopper words" that break their concentration and comprehension (Anders & Bos, 1986). This is especially problematic if the student relies on bilingual dictionaries, which is frequently the case.

Recognizing the importance of using context to infer word meaning, we have begun to teach explicit strategies for using both local (sentence level) and global (whole passage or background knowledge) context clues. We then structure assignments so that students will have many opportunities to apply these strategies as they read.

In our classes, we study full-length chapters from college textbooks representative of a variety of disciplines. The Personal Word List or Personal Dictionary (Nist & Simpson, 1993) requires the student first to select an unfamiliar word from the current chapter. The student, rather than the teacher, does the selecting. Obviously, not all unfamiliar words have equal utility. We often spend time in class discussing the criteria for selecting a word for careful study.

The student is then directed to use either context or the structure of the word to infer a reasonable meaning. If the student is not satisfied that s/he has determined a close approximation of the meaning, or if there are no context or structure clues, s/he may go to the dictionary to find a definition (see Figure 2). In this way, the Personal Word List is a combination of definitional and contextual approaches, but the emphasis is on determining meaning from context or structure when possible. Because the strategy is used within the context of studying an entire chapter, it is likely that the word will reappear, thus naturally reinforcing its meaning.

Figure 2. Students' Personal Word List Entries

Word	What I think it means	Clues (either context or structure)	Dictionary definition (only if you need it)
1. sacred	religious	they were entering a sacred building that loomed out of the night to give them what <u>haven</u> and what <u>blessing</u> they yearned for	
2. vexation	displeasure	but something would come up—some vexation that was like a <u>fly buzzing</u> around their heads.	
3. lurch	movement	she took a step toward the porch lurching	a sudden movement forward or sideways

1. encounter	meet or face	When students <u>encounter</u> stress, very often it is psychological and <u>involves the pressure</u> to achieve in school	
2. unrelieved	not move. the stress still there because too much stress	un - not re - again lieved - leave, move <u>A little</u> practice helps keep the hormonal system in good shape, but too much <u>stress unrelieved</u> is <u>exhausting</u>	
3. incubate		in - not cubate?	to place under conditions favorable for growth

    This strategy is supported by Nation's (1990) finding that the primary strategy for dealing with low-frequency vocabulary should be to teach students how to guess words in context or how to use word-part analysis. Only when these strategies fail should students look up the word in a dictionary and gloss it in the text or their notes.

    The Personal Word List is a means of "scaffolding" what should become a natural, automatic process of learning vocabulary while reading. The goal is to encourage good vocabulary-building habits. Keeping a word list has also been shown to increase sensitivity to new words and enjoyment in word learning for American students (Haggard, 1986).

In the beginning, Personal Word List assignments are very structured to ensure that students understand the process. Later the students are asked to gloss the meaning in their texts or simply list words and definitions to approximate a more realistic vocabulary learning experience.

Semantic Mapping

There is general agreement among educators that vocabulary development involves the complex process of relating words to ideas that exist in the schema of the reader (Irvin, 1990). One explanation for vocabulary acquisition is the Knowledge and Access Hypothesis outlined by Hague (1987). According to this hypothesis, "new words are best learned in semantically related groups that are somehow related to words and knowledge that the reader already knows" (p. 219). Hague suggests that the vocabulary of second language learners should be taught "in semantic networks to the point of automatic access" (p. 220). Further research by Meara (1980) supports the view that words in a second language are meaningfully integrated with words in a first language to form a complex whole lexicon. These meaningful associations are often referred to in the ESL literature as "collocations" or "paradigmatic relationships."

The use of semantic maps to facilitate the learning of new words is strongly supported by this "knowledge position" of vocabulary acquisition. Coady (1993) contends that "many current techniques for teaching vocabulary are artificial and frequently ineffective because they do not induce the readers to associate the new word-forms and concepts in their minds together with the schemata they already know" (p. 12). Research also supports the effectiveness of semantic maps over more traditional techniques (Johnson & Pearson, 1984).

We do a variety of mapping activities in our classes. One generative vocabulary strategy is making a "word map." The student first selects a word s/he feels is worthy of special study, then tries to write down as many words as possible that relate to that word. S/he then organizes the words and relates them to one another in a meaningful way in the form of a map (see Figure 3). Word maps enable students to relate new words to those they know well. Because semantic mapping helps students see relationships between ideas and connect known information with new information, it is a valuable tool for developing their vocabulary.

The challenge is to give ESL learners sufficient practice in creating word maps to the point that they will appreciate their usefulness and continue to use them independently as a means of building their vocabularies. We must find new ways to get students actively involved in assimilating new vocabulary in a meaningful fashion. The learners must take responsibility for relating new ideas to those already

Figure 3. Students' Word Maps

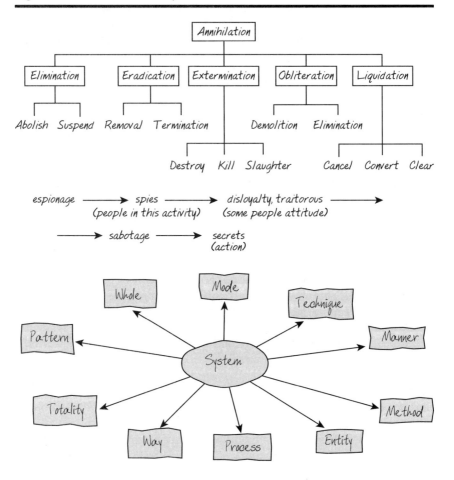

possessed. "Ownership of vocabulary occurs when students can relate the word in an appropriate schema. Instead of asking, 'What is the definition of this word?' students should be asking themselves, 'Where does this word fit?' " (Thelen, 1986, p. 606).

Imagery

Relating a distinct visual image to a new word is a widely accepted learning tool. Likewise, associating a word with its visual or acoustic properties seems to improve recall for ESL learners (Brown & Perry, 1991). We encourage our students to create images whenever possible as a means of increasing understanding and retrieval.

An approach to using imagery to develop vocabulary, which is often referred to in the ESL literature, is the "key word" method originally designed by Raugh and Atkinson (1975) for learning a foreign language. An associative link is created between a new word and a known word, phrase, or image that is acoustically and/or visually similar. "For example, the Spanish word for duck is *pato*. Employing the English word 'pot' as the key word, one could imagine a duck hiding under an overturned flower pot with its webbed feet and tufted tail sticking out below" (p. 1). The new word is associated with a more familiar word in the student's first language, thereby enhancing comprehension and memory. There is some evidence that when learners create their own images they recall even more than when they are provided with the images (Simpson & Dwyer, 1991).

Because we have a wide range of first languages in a typical class, we have used a modified key word technique by showing the students how to choose an English key word and then write a sentence with the new word and the key word that creates a distinct visual image (see Figure 4).

An example we have used is learning the verb *caress* by placing the key word *cares* in the sentence, "Because he *cares* for her, he *caresses* her face gently." The sentence is presented along with a simple drawing of hands caressing a woman's face.

According to Stoller and Grabe (1993) "the mnemonic key word approach has no rivals with respect to vocabulary recall. The skill is generalizable, permitting students to use the strategy on their own to build their vocabularies" (p. 36). Although the key word technique has been found to be superior to other methods (Nation, 1990), we have found that our adaptation of the technique is somewhat complex to teach and very time consuming for the students to construct.

Although extremely effective for a small number of new words, the key word method seems to have limited usefulness in helping ESL students with the large number of abstract terms they must learn to deal with. In fact, Parry (1991) reports that more than 40 percent of words identified as "difficult" by the ESL learners she studied came from "bridging vocabulary, general terms that characterize formal prose and often express relationships and other abstractions" (p. 637), words like *stipulating, augmented,* and *unsubstantiated.* "In sum, memory techniques have a demonstrated power, but teachers and researchers need to understand that such techniques gloss over the complexity of what it means to know a word" (Coady, 1993, p. 13).

Computer-Assisted Instruction

Although not a truly generative strategy, we provide computer-assisted instruction (CAI) to supplement the strategies we teach in our classes and to provide our students with additional exposure to new vocabulary in a variety of contexts. Some of the advantages of using CAI are increased student involvement and motivation and the capacity to

Figure 4. Students' Use of Imagery

provide ample practice outside of class time (Wheatley, Muller, & Miller, 1993). In addition, the computer can offer individualized instruction with immediate reinforcement, all with unending patience. CAI has also been found to have a strong positive effect on the amount of student learning, the time spent in student learning, and student attitudes toward learning.

The program we use is *Word Attack, Plus!* (Davidson, 1988). We chose it because of the "editor" function whereby instructors can enter selected vocabulary and sample sentences. We use words and sentences from the chapters we teach in our reading course, including chapters from health, history, literature, and economics. Instructors survey the chapters and choose vocabulary based on three criteria. Words that are judged to be difficult for most students, critical for comprehension of the text, and likely to be repeated in other courses are selected.

Through CAI, we provide at least five exposures to the selected words, one in the original context of the chapter, and four in *Word Attack, Plus!* — the definition in the Word Display activity, the sample sentence in Word Display, definition matching in the Multiple Choice activity, and fill-in-the-blank in the Sentence Completion activity. (The inability to delete the definition that appears in the Sentence Completion activity is one frustration we have experienced with the program. The presence of the definition above the sentence enables the student to use the definition rather than the context of the sentence to supply the missing word, thus reducing the possibility that the activity will help students develop their use of context clues.) Each time the words are used in class or appear on a quiz additional exposures to the words in meaningful contexts are provided.

The students are given a new list of 25 words each week, taken from the chapter we are studying in class. Because structural analysis is widely recognized as a useful aid for students, we also encourage them to complete additional lists of common prefixes and roots available on *Word Attack, Plus!* for extra credit. Completion of the lab assignments is compulsory and makes up 10 percent of the final grade for the course. We find that the percentage of students using the lab is very high and the response from students is generally very positive. The following is an example of a *Word Attack, Plus!* entry:

Word: metabolism
Definition: chemical changes that produce energy in living cells
Sample sentence: Hormones secreted during the stress response alter the metabolism of every cell in your body.
Sentence completion: _____ in living organisms produces the energy that makes growth possible.

Students' Evaluations of Strategies

In order for a strategy to become generative (one that students will independently choose to use in the future), the strategy must be carefully modeled. Students must also be given ample practice in deciding how and when to apply the strategy effectively. Like any new skill, a new strategy requires extra effort in the beginning, and like all other learners, ESL students often resist doing something in a new way. It is a challenge for us as teachers to provide ample practice while maintaining motivation so that our students will "own" the strategies we teach.

As ESL students enter our classes they identify using a dictionary as their primary strategy for finding a word's meaning as they read and study. At the end of the course, students more often mention using context and keeping a word list. Other strategies mentioned are using word cards, imagery, and key words. In future semesters we hope to identify the generative strategies ESL learners find most useful.

A Mixed Approach Works

Certainly reading is one of the most important skills for second language learners in academic settings. The strong relationship between reading comprehension and vocabulary knowledge presents teachers of ESL learners with the challenge of meeting their unique need for effective vocabulary-building strategies.

Although specific strategies for effective vocabulary learning have not been the subject of extensive research, both theory and research in second language acquisition seem to support a mixed approach to vocabulary acquisition in ESL. This includes encouraging extensive reading as well as teaching decontextualization and semantic mapping skills and strengthening students' abilities to select vocabulary worthy of careful study. Teachers must work with students to identify those specific strategies that hold the most promise for helping them become enthusiastic and independent word learners.

References

Anders, P. L., & Bos, C. S. (1986). Semantic feature analysis: An interactive strategy for vocabulary development and text comprehension. *Journal of Reading, 29,* 610–616.

Anderson, R. C., & Freebody, P. (1981). Vocabulary knowledge. In J. T. Guthrie (Ed.), *Comprehension and teaching: Research reviews* (pp. 77–117). Newark, DE: International Reading Association.

Bensoussan, M., & Laufer, B. (1984). Lexical guessing in context in EFL comprehension. *Journal of Research in Reading, 7,* 15–32.

Brown, T. S., & Perry, F. L. (1991). A comparison of three learning strategies for ESL vocabulary acquisition. TESOL *Quarterly, 25,* 655–670.

Coady, J. (1993). Research on ESL/EFL vocabulary acquisition: Putting it in context. In T. Huckin, M. Haynes, & J. Coady (Eds.), *Second language reading and vocabulary learning* (pp. 3–23). Norwood, NJ: Ablex.

Davidson, J. (1988). *Word attack, plus!* [computer software] Torrance, CA: Davidson and Associates.

Davis, F. (1944). Fundamental factors of comprehension in reading. *Psychometrika, 9,* 185–197.

Diekhoff, G. M., Brown, P. J., & Dansereau, D. F. (1982). A prose learning strategy training program based on network and depth-of-processing models. *Journal of Experimental Education, 50,* 180–184.

Farr, R., & Carey, R. (1986). *Reading: What can be measured?* Newark, DE: International Reading Association. (ERIC Document Reproduction Service No. 266 438)

Haggard, M. R. (1986). The vocabulary self-collection strategy: Using student interest and word knowledge to enhance vocabulary growth. *Journal of Reading, 29,* 634–642.

Hague, S. (1987). Vocabulary instruction: What L2 can learn from L1. *Foreign Language Annals,* 20, 217–225.

Irvin, J. L. (1990). *Vocabulary knowledge: Guidelines for instruction. What research says to the teacher.* Washington, DC: National Education Association. (ERIC Document Reproduction Service No. ED 319 001)

Johnson, D. D., & Pearson, P. D. (1984). *Teaching reading vocabulary.* New York: Holt, Rinehart & Winston.

Meara, P. (1980). Vocabulary acquisition: A neglected aspect of language learning. *Language Teaching and Linguistics: Abstracts,* 13(4), 221–246.

Nagy, W., & Herman, P. (1987). Breadth and depth of vocabulary knowledge: Implications for acquisition and instruction. In M. McKeown & M. Curtis (Eds.), *The nature of vocabulary acquisition* (pp. 19–35). Hillsdale, NJ: Erlbaum.

Nation, I. S. P. (1990). *Teaching and learning vocabulary.* New York: Newbury House.

Nist, S. L., & Diehl, W. (1994). *Developing textbook thinking* (3rd ed.). Lexington, MA: D. C. Heath.

Nist, S. L., & Simpson, M. L. (1993). *Developing vocabulary concepts for college thinking.* Lexington, MA: D. C. Heath.

Parker, J. F. (1990). *Workshops for active learning.* Delta, BC: JFP Productions.

Parry, K. (1991). Building a vocabulary through academic reading. TESOL *Quarterly,* 25, 629–65 1.

Parry, K. (1993). Too many words: Learning the vocabulary of an academic subject. In T. Huckin, M. Haynes, & J. Coady (Eds.), *Second language reading and vocabulary learning* (pp. 109–129). Norwood, NJ: Ablex.

Raugh, M. R., & Atkinson, R. C. (1975). A mnemonic method for learning a second-language vocabulary. *Journal of Educational Psychology,* 67, 1–16.

Reyes, M. L., & Molner, L. (1991). Instructional strategies for second-language learners in the content areas. *Journal of Reading,* 35, 96–102.

Simpson, M. L., & Dwyer, E. J. (1991). Vocabulary acquisition and the college student. In R. F. Flippo & D. C. Caverly (Eds.), *Teaching reading and study strategies at the college level* (pp. 1–41). Newark, DE: International Reading Association.

Singer, H. (1981). Instruction in reading acquisition. In O. Tzeng & H. Singer (Eds.), *Perception of print* (pp. 291–311). Hillsdale, NJ: Erlbaum.

Stahl, S. A. (1986). Three principles of effective vocabulary instruction. *Journal of Reading,* 29, 662–671.

Stoller, F. L., & Grabe, W. (1993). Implications for L2 vocabulary acquisition and instruction from L1 vocabulary research. In T. Huckin, M. Haynes, & J. Coady (Eds.), *Second language reading and vocabulary learning* (pp. 24–45). Norwood, NJ: Ablex.

Thelen, J. N. (1986). Vocabulary instruction and meaningful learning. *Journal of Reading,* 29, 603–609.

Thorndike, E. (1917). Reading as reasoning. *Journal of Educational Psychology,* 8, 512–518.

Wheatley, E. A., Muller, D. H., & Miller, R. B. (1993). Computer-assisted vocabulary instruction. *Journal of Reading,* 37, 92–102.

Dialogue Journals as an ESL Learning Strategy

Vicki L. Holmes and Margaret R. Moulton

Dialogue journals have become an important educational technique in helping college students become more competent readers and writers. They have also been useful in working with second-language learners. In this article, Vicki L. Holmes and Margaret R. Moulton use case study methodology, along with the review of dialogue journals and in-depth interviews, to discover what their postsecondary, second-language learners feel about the use of this method for mastering English. The authors found that writing fluency and the motivation to write were particularly rich subthemes among the students' responses.

In the last decade, dialogue journal writing has emerged as a learning strategy to support the writing process (Peyton, 1990; Peyton & Reed, 1990; Peyton, Staton, Richardson, & Wolfram, 1990; Staton, Shuy, Peyton, & Reed, 1988). This support evolves from the authenticity of partners engaging in a two-way written interaction (Edelsky, 1986; Silva, 1990; Urzua, 1987). Unlike personal journals, which involve private written communication (Lucas, 1990), dialogue journals involve participants, typically the teacher and a student, exchanging information in writing. These unedited, uncorrected dialogues usually extend over an entire semester or year of instruction and are generally collected in notebooks, although other formats such as computer networking are becoming more popular (Sayers, 1986).

Research in the use of dialogue journals with second-language students is a relatively recent phenomenon (Isserlis, 1991). One of the first studies conducted with students learning English as their second language (Kreeft, Shuy, Staton, Reed, & Morroy, 1984) outlined the features that make dialogue journals a productive strategy for language acquisition. Using a case study design, the researchers concluded that dialogue journals provide the following conditions for learning: interaction about topics relevant to learning, focus on interaction rather than form, enhancement of reading skills, modeling of correct grammatical forms, natural evolution of grammatical structures, and interaction in a private, nonthreatening way.

The general contexts for learning alluded to by Kreeft et al. (1984) formed the foundation for a handful of other studies that addressed several important issues in the use of dialogue journals with L2 populations: speaking and writing connections (Peyton, 1986), appropriate teacher response (Peyton & Seyoum, 1989), improvement in writing product (Peyton, 1990), and effects on student motivation (Lucas, 1990; Peyton et al., 1990). Yet none of these studies explored dialogue journal writing from the student perspective.

This perspective is often overlooked in the learning process, suggested Krapels (1990). She argued that more information is needed about what occurs in the "real space of writing" from the "collective consciousness of the people making and then sharing that meaning" (p. 51). Krapels called on researchers to include participants' points of view in the research process, claiming that ethnography is perhaps the best research design for questioning assumptions about writing processes. We responded to that call by using ethnographic tools to investigate dialogue journals as an ESL learning strategy from the students' perspectives.

Methodology

Using a multiple case study design (Stake, 1994; Yin, 1989), we collected data to answer the following question: What perspectives do second-language university students have on dialogue journal writing as a strategy for learning English? The study was conducted in a 15-week intermediate composition class within the English language program of an urban southwestern U.S. university. The course included the writing of both formal rhetorical patterns and weekly dialogue journals (which the teacher introduced as "letters"). All 21 students enrolled in the intermediate composition class volunteered for this study. Six were selected to participate on the basis of their responses to a questionnaire regarding their perceptions of themselves as writers (Holmes, 1994). These 6 represented a "maximum variation sample" (Schumacher & McMillan, 1993, p. 381) that included the full range of a priori perceptions held by the class as a whole.

Data collected and analyzed for this study included the students' weekly journals and transcripts of four in-depth guided interviews (Seidman, 1991) with each participant. Using the constant comparative method (Glaser & Strauss, 1967), we searched for patterns in the students' journal entries and interview transcripts. Three broad patterns about dialogue journals emerged: interpersonal perspectives, intrapersonal perspectives, and developmental perspectives. The last pattern yielded the most promising data for understanding the students' views. Within this pattern two subcategories emerged, writing fluency and motivation to write, which demonstrated that these ESL students regarded dialogue journal writing as an effective strategy for learning English.

The students' reflections on their writing throughout the semester showed a gradual growth of writing fluency and motivation. The students attributed this growth to the dialogue journal process and often pointed out what they believed were the reasons for it.

Writing Fluency

In describing the increase in their writing fluency, students used words such as "easier," "comfortable," "better," "directly," "quickly," and "improve." A further examination of the context of the participants' comments revealed that specific attributes of journal writing that are similar to conversation might account for their perceived improvements: topic choice, spontaneity, and frequency.

Topic Choice

Students perceived that writing about topics of their own choosing, a characteristic more often associated with speaking, was an important factor in their growing fluency. For example, 6 weeks into the semester, Yanik, a 20-year-old Belgian male, indicated that writing had become easier: "You write more . . . you write differently . . . the sentence are more easy . . . because you write what you want." Ceci, a 25-year-old Korean woman, also noticed the changes in her writing fluency in the journal, especially in comparison with the traditional paragraph-writing assignments, because she could write about her own topics: "I like the letters. It's more Americanized my writing. More comfortable. More easier. Journal is I can explain about myself and what I want to talking." Mikhail, a 32-year-old Bulgarian man, said choosing his own topic to write about in the journal contributed to his ease and fluency in writing: "To pick up some choices, it is more easy. Because you don't must to follow only one topic. You form your opinion in your mind. It's more easy to write."

Spontaneity

The students noted that, as in conversation, they experienced a freedom of expression in the journal unfettered by the act of translation and the focus on structure. They stopped using dictionaries and focused on the interactive, communicative aspects of their writing, which led to their increased fluency. Yanik indicated that writing, for him, had become as easy as conversation: "It shows your sentence. Letters, I think, it is more like talking." Early in the semester, Yanik had relied on translation, writing his entries first in French and then using a dictionary for the English version. Now he noted a change, which he attributed to dialogue journal writing:

> It changed because I go more quickly now when I write. I remember
> before when I begin was long time in the library . . . to write in English.
> Because before I was thinking more to make my sentence, now it go faster
> and I don't looking in my dictionary. Before . . . I make first my sentence
> in French, then in English. Now, yesterday, I make it directly in English.
> Now, [whistles] I go quickly. I am cool to write.

Like Yanik, Ceci noticed a decreasing dependence on the dictionary as her fluency increased in the journal. "At first I always have to find dictionary," she claimed, "but after one month, a little bit I don't need dictionary." However, it was the change in her ability to think spontaneously in English that Ceci credited most to the journal writing. In her final journal entry she wrote:

> I'm going to tell about what was good for me through this journal. First, I could arrange my thought from Korean language to American grammatical sentence. I can arrange my thinking better than before. At first I was confused because of Korean language. Korean language in head and was coming out confusing. Second, I feel writing more comfortable. My English sentence much better than before.

Demi, a 33-year-old Korean woman, also claimed the dialogue journal process improved her fluency because it caused her to think spontaneously in English. "Improve my English, the expression of myself. When I wrote I have to think English, not Korean," she declared. As a result, she was able to write more easily and quickly as the semester progressed. "For me, time saving writing. Faster than before. Compared to before when I had to think a long time. . . . That is nice way to write," she explained. Dang, an 18-year-old Taiwanese male, also noted improvement in his ability to think in English: "I think it is better my letter. I can write down what I think more easily in English. I think it is getting help me a lot."

Frequency

Although most students engage in conversation daily, few students write as frequently. The participants, who wrote daily, acknowledged the connection between writing frequently and developing fluency. Wanita, a 29-year-old Indonesian woman, suggested that her increasing fluency occurred as a result of writing regularly in a form more like conversation:

> It become a habit for me. I like to write every day. I can improve myself because I just do more — write, write, write. I think it like a conversation, you know dialogue. Talking, just like that. I think that is very nice. It make it just like a habit writer. I feel more responsible to write more.

Wanita also noticed changes in the quality of her journal writing as the semester unfolded. "It really is good exercise for me. My husband see my change. Lately, I don't do much mistake. It is getting better," she offered.

Daily writing was one of the elements of dialogue journals that Mikhail, too, claimed contributed to his improved fluency: "Practice, practice, practice. When you practice everyday it helps. It give me homework for write the letter. I think this help." In his final journal entry, Mikhail wrote about an additional change he noticed as a result of the journal: I think writing these letters have been graet [*sic*] help to me. First, this has helped to build my vocabulary. Second, it has increased my proper knowledge of English."

In the view of the participants, dialogue journal writing contributed to their growing fluency in writing English by mirroring the act of conversation. Mikhail, Ceci, and Yanik noted that writing about their own topics encouraged their English language development. Writing in the journal helped Yanik, Ceci, and Demi learn to compose with ease and speed, without relying on dictionaries and translation. Demi and Ceci also emphasized the journal's contribution to their ability to convert their thinking directly into written English, while Wanita and Mikhail claimed that the repetitive practice provided by the journal writing, the "habit writer" as Wanita called it, improved their writing fluency.

Motivation to Write

In describing the motivational aspects of dialogue journal writing, the participants used words and phrases such as "no scare," "feel good," "like to write more," "feel free," and "excited." The attribute of dialogue journals that seems to account most for the students' enhanced motivation for writing was the uncorrected, ungraded format. This format allowed students to test their ideas in written English without the fear of judgment.

After only 6 weeks, Ceci noted: "Maybe it give to me more comfortable writing. . . . At first, I was scared about writing, but is now it is funny. I get like writing because of journal." In the final interview, Ceci reiterated the value of the motivational aspects of dialogue journal writing. When asked what was best about the dialogue journal experience, she responded: "I am not afraid about writing anymore. That is best for me."

Yanik also articulated feelings of comfort, freedom, and reduced apprehension after only 3 weeks of the semester. He focused specifically on the lack of corrections as a motivating factor:

> I feel free. Yes, you feel good and you think you can scribe good because you know when she give back [the journal] you see nothing you feel happy. You say, OK. [laugh] But with the composition, you feel a little bit sick. You understand? It's real. It's like this. She said, "I don't want to agress [sic] you so I don't correct." Yeah, it's good psychologically because every time we see mistake, you know, it is not good for the students. They are too much demotivated.

The reduced apprehension he experienced, Yanik declared, helped him take greater risks with his writing because "you don't scare for the structure." In the final interview, Yanik elaborated on the motivational aspects of uncorrected dialogue journal writing:

> If you are too constipated, you write nothing, you know? First, you have to make your mistake. Than you can write. But first you have to put

something on the paper. That is what you say in French. It [dialogue journal] helps you because your idea on the paper. You put something. If you are scared to scribe and you say this is not good, not good, you have only three line to write. But if you do not scare to make fault, you write, write, write. Then later you can rectify, you know?

Demi also concluded that the journal reduced her fear of writing and motivated her to write more. "So now I felt I didn't afraid to writing. I feel comfortable. Even spelling is wrong, I don't care. Just writing more," she stated. Demi suggested that this uncorrected kind of communication showed the teacher's acceptance and respect for the student, an aspect that Demi valued highly:

> She didn't correct the journal. Maybe she accept as person, the feelings and things and the way they expression. Maybe she doesn't understand some words, but she accept for us. She respect the person. If she correct every time, but sometimes afraid to write. If she correct every time is nice way, but the other hand is criticize. So maybe she give us the expression of whatever we can tell her. The respect as person. I feel very happy with that.

Demi claimed that dialogue journal writing motivated her to write comfortably and easily, focusing less on errors. "That is nice way to write. I write easily. Makes really comfortable. Even though the spelling will be wrong it doesn't bother me much because now I can writing more comfortably."

Mikhail also discussed being motivated by the process of exploring his ideas in a written format that was uncorrected and ungraded. He concluded:

> I think so letter is more enjoyable to me. I hate to have rules about mine to manage. It's just ideas where you have in your head. You explain your ideas. This is more easy for me. I know it's not for grade this letter. This just more enjoyable when it's not for grade.

Throughout the semester, students viewed the dialogue journal process as motivational, claiming that it spurred them to write more often with greater comfort and less apprehension. Most students accredited these benefits directly to the ungraded, uncorrected attributes of the dialogue journal.

Learning Through Modeling

The 6 students in this study observed changes during the semester in their English fluency. The students' perceived improvement validated Vygotsky's (1978) assumptions about the connections between learning and modeling through social interaction. According to Vygotsky, learners mimic the teacher's language guide until they internalize the structures that allow them to guide themselves. The acquisition of the forms and syntax of written language — fluency — is controlled by learners who, consciously or unconsciously, gradually pattern their writing, just as they do their speaking, after the teacher's model and learn to communicate the way the teacher does. In this study, the students' journals provided a highly visible and credible demonstration of modeling and of students' ability to write fluently and communicatively, though not necessarily without error.

Students reported increased fluency not only in writing but also in thinking in English. What began as a difficult process for most of the students — thinking up ideas to write about, thinking through those ideas, and communicating about them in written English — became noticeably easier for all the students during the semester. This finding corroborates what both L1 and L2 writing researchers suggest about the act of composing; that is, writing is a tool of thought and communication. Writing is not the manipulation of prefabricated ideas or pieces of sentences. On the contrary, writing is a highly demanding cognitive task, which involves higher order thinking skills that can be enhanced through dialogue journal writing.

Adult ESL writers typically bring to the task of writing a plethora of fears about grammar and form (Gungle & Taylor, 1989). The nonthreatening, uncorrected, unedited communicative format was particularly empowering for these students, who reported "feeling more comfortable" about their writing. As Lucas (1990) suggested, the students' attitudes about writing changed as a result of the open, nonjudgmental nature of dialogue journal writing.

Unlike traditional writing assignments in which the teacher acts as evaluator, the teacher's role as communicator in the dialogue journal is important in building students' motivation to write. Through responding to the content of students' writing and not correcting their errors, teachers can, as Leki (1992) suggested, "minimize fear, nervousness, and self-consciousness" by controlling affective variables that affect the writer's motivation (p. 17).

The students' freedom to write about what was important in their own lives was another motivating factor, as Freire (1973; Freire & Macedo, 1987) and Knowles (1984) have emphasized. Without struggling to discover a topic that was pleasing to the teacher, students were free to explore issues of personal significance, playing with language along the way. As one student noted, "You can scribe what you want. You can learn this way."

Implications and Need for Further Study

The students' positive reactions to dialogue journal writing as a learning strategy suggest the need for adult ESL writing teachers to expand the contexts for writing. Zamel (1983) argued that teachers must overcome the strong temptation to overcontrol the writing of students who are not competent in the target language. By dictating the form and content of their writing, Zamel (1983) suggested, teachers limit the students' cognitive and linguistic growth. Teachers must remind themselves that adult ESL students bring with them complex histories and individual perspectives spun from the existential fabric of their lives. By allowing students to write about the "stuff" of their lives in a non-threatening format, teachers encourage cognitive and linguistic growth while motivating students to write.

This study suggests the need for additional research regarding ways in which dialogue journal writing affects second-language acquisition. Most students in the study reported increased fluency and motivation to write in English, but a critical question remains: Does dialogue journal writing promote writing skills that transfer to other writing tasks across age groups? The answer to this question is of utmost importance to writing teachers who work with both L1 and L2 populations.

Dialogue journal writing is an enormously time-consuming task for teachers. To commit to such a task, teachers need to believe that their efforts will make a lasting difference in the writing abilities of their students, for changes in students' motivation alone may not warrant the effort involved in sustaining the dialogue over time. While this study suggests that fluency was, according to the participants, enhanced in the process of dialogue journal writing, no objective measure was used to validate the students' views. Nor was any speculation advanced about the transfer of that fluency to other writing contexts.

Future studies might answer the transfer-of-skills question and increase the knowledge base about dialogue journal writing with adult ESL populations. Furthermore, is it necessary that the dialogue partner be the teacher? Would adult university ESL students benefit equally from dialogue communication with another, more fluent, student as their dialogue partner? Can native speaker volunteers from the community be effective dialogue journal partners for adult ESL students? These questions suggest the need to explore, from both students' and teachers' perspectives, the range of roles and role models that are appropriate and beneficial to dialogue journal communication as a learning strategy for language acquisition.

References

Edelsky, C. (1986). *Writing in a bilingual program: Habia una vez.* Norwood, NJ: Ablex.

Freire, P. (1973). *Education for critical consciousness.* New York: Seabury Press.

Freire, P., & Macedo, D. P. (1987). *Literacy: Reading the word and the world.* South Hadley, MA: Bergin & Garvey.

Glaser, B. G., & Strauss, A. L. (1967). *The discovery of grounded theory: Strategies for qualitative research.* Chicago: Aldine.

Gungle, B. W., & Taylor, V. (1989). Writing apprehension and second language writers. In D. M. Johnson & D. H. Roen (Eds.), *Richness in writing: Empowering ESL students* (pp. 235–248). White Plains, NY: Longman.

Holmes, V. L. (1994). *Six adult university ESL students' perspectives of dialogue journal writing: A multiple case study.* Unpublished doctoral dissertation, University of Nevada, Las Vegas.

Isserlis, J. (1991). Dialogue journal writing as part of a learner-centered curriculum. In J. P. Peyton & J. Staton (Eds.), *Writing our lives: Reflections on dialogue journal writing with adults learning English* (pp. 45–51). Englewood Cliffs, NJ: Prentice Hall Regents.

Knowles, M. S. (1984). *Andragogy in action: Applying modern principles of adult learning.* San Francisco: Jossey-Bass.

Krapels, A. (1990). An overview of second language writing process research. In B. Kroll (Ed.), *Second language writing: Research insights for the classroom* (pp. 37–56). New York: Cambridge University Press.

Kreeft, J., Shuy, R., Staton, J., Reed, L., & Morroy, R. (1984). *Dialogue writing: Analysis of student-teacher interactive writing in the learning of English as a second language* (Final Report to the National Institute of Education, NIE-G-83-0030). Washington, DC: Center for Applied Linguistics.

Leki, L. (1992). *Understanding ESL writers: A guide for teachers.* Portsmouth, NH: Heinemann.

Lucas, T. (1990). Personal journal writing as a classroom genre. In J. K. Peyton (Ed.), *Students and teachers writing together: Perspectives on journal writing* (pp. 99–123). Alexandria, VA: Teachers of English to Speakers of Other Languages.

Peyton, J. K. (1986). *Literacy through written interaction* (Report No. FL-015-912). (ERIC Document Reproduction Service No. ED 273 097)

Peyton, J. K. (1990). Dialogue journal writing and the acquisition of English grammatical morphology. In J. K. Peyton (Ed.), *Students and teachers writing together: Perspectives on journal writing* (pp. 67–97). Alexandria, VA: Teachers of English to Speakers of Other Languages.

Peyton, J. K., & Reed, L. (1990). *Dialogue journal writing with nonnative English speakers: A handbook for teachers.* Washington, DC: Teachers of English to Speakers of Other Languages.

Peyton, J. K., & Seyoum, M. (1989). The effect of teacher strategies on students' interactive writing: The case of dialogue journals. *Research in the Teaching of English, 23,* 310–334.

Peyton, J. K., Staton, J., Richardson, G., & Wolfram, W. (1990). The influence of writing task on ESL students' written production. *Research in the Teaching of English, 24,* 142–171.

Sayers, D. (1986). Interactive writing with computers: One solution to the time problem. *Dialogue, 3*(4), 9–10.

Schumacher, S., & McMillan, J. H. (1993). *Research in education: A conceptual introduction.* New York: HarperCollins.

Seidman, I. E. (1991). *Interviewing as qualitative research.* New York: Teachers College Press.

Silva, T. (1990). Second language composition instruction: Developments, issues, and directions in ESL. In B. Kroll (Ed.), *Second language writing: Research insights for the classroom* (pp. 11–23). New York: Cambridge University Press.

Stake, R. E. (1994). Case studies. In N. K. Denzin & Y. S. Lincoln (Eds.), *Handbook of qualitative research* (pp. 236–247). Thousand Oaks, CA: Sage.

Staton, J., Shuy, R. W., Peyton, J. K., & Reed, L. (Eds.). (1988). *Dialogue journal communication: Classroom, linguistic, social and cognitive views.* Norwood, NJ: Ablex.

Urzua, C. (1987). "You stopped too soon": Second language children composing and revising. TESOL *Quarterly, 21,* 279–297.

Vygotsky, L. S. (1978). *Mind in society: The development of high psychological processes* (M. Cole, V. John-Steiner, S. Scribner, & E. Souberman, Eds. and Trans.). Cambridge, MA: Harvard University Press.

Yin, R. K. (1989). *Case study research: Design and methods.* Newbury Park, CA: Sage.

Zamel, V. (1983). The composing processes of advanced ESL students: Six case studies. TESOL *Quarterly, 17,* 165–187.

The Use of Literary Letters with Post-secondary Non-native Students

Laura Bauer and Linda Sweeney

Here, the authors describe an instructional model appropriate for use with new-to-English readers (but equally valid for any developmental reading student) that draws upon transactional theory. Students read novels, write letters about their reading to both the teacher and a peer, participate in literary circles, and reflect upon instructors' comments about the content of each of the letters. Examples of letters from the ESL students to the instructors are provided and analyzed.

Accessording to transactional theory, reading and writing are reciprocal, part of the same process (Rosenblatt, 1994). Research further indicates that intensive reading and writing are natural ways to gain command of a language — prolific writing, in particular, produces fluency (Deen, 1992).

Of course, such research is primarily based on instruction with native speakers of English. As instructors of second-language students, we have always believed that a similar approach — intensive reading and writing — would also give such students a greater command of the English language. With the use of literary letters, a free-form exchange between teacher and student or student and student, based upon the shared reading of novels, we found a wonderful tool that melds the reading/writing process . . . and goes far beyond.

Communication Development — Pre-101 English with Second Language Freshmen

The non-native students at National-Louis University have usually completed the acclaimed ESOL program of the University's Department of Applied Language. These students, mainly Polish, with a mix of Latin American, Asian, and students from other countries, were already high school graduates or had received their GEDs before entering the ESOL program. They may have taken as many as five to six quarters of English already and have a solid background in grammar, basic vocabulary development, and sentence composition. If they decide to continue their studies in one of the University degree programs, they must take a placement exam which may require them to complete Communication Development I and II, two ten week quarters of six hours-per-week intensive developmental English classes meant to hone their reading, writing, and speaking skills. An important goal of Communication Development has simply been to get students to relax with their new language, to make it their own while they're acquiring further skills for an American institution of higher learning.

Through the years, reading articles, stories, and short novels has been included in the syllabi of both Communication Development I and II. In addition, vocabulary acquisition and study skills have been emphasized, as well as the writing of essays and a variety of creative, "fun" approaches to composition, such as writing answers to newspaper advice columns or composing class-collaborative stories. Acculturization has also been a goal, though not an overt one set down to help students "fit into" American society, but rather, the presentation and explanation of attitudes or approaches that lead to success in this country's universities and workplaces.

Attempting to make writing fun while sharing attitudes about culture is not easy. Essays are good practice but do not always engage a student at the level at which he or she will willingly wrestle with new vocabulary and enthusiastically embrace higher thinking skills with which to express him or herself.

When we encountered Jeanne Henry's book, *If Not Now, Developmental Readers in the College Classroom* (1995), which explores the technique and process of reading novels and exchanging letters about them, we adopted it with delight. In turn, Henry had read *In the Middle — Writing, Reading, and Learning with Adolescents* by Nancie Atwell (1987) and adapted the fiction reading/dialogue journal technique that Atwell details in her book. Though Atwell's students were junior high students and Henry's native born, we thought a similar approach would work with second-language freshmen. Like Atwell and Henry, we preferred *inspired* practice to skills tactics. For though nonfiction expresses the mind of a culture, we believe fiction is its heart . . . and what is more powerful than the heart?

Our Initial Approach and Expectations

Laura and Linda required that a novel be read each quarter and allotted time in classes for silent sustained reading. We also required the students to write letters about the novels, though we varied in our methods. Laura began with a single novel assignment but moved to a free choice of novel for two quarters. Her students were expected to submit one letter per week based on their reading — a letter to the instructor, as well as one to a student peer (which was not read by the instructor). Linda, on the other hand, to reduce the complexity of the task and the time involved for the instructor, assigned one novel for Communication Development I classes and gave a choice of two or three novels for Communication Development II classes. Linda required at least three letters between student and instructor and two between peers during the ten week quarter. Neither instructor specified, even at repeated requests from students, how many pages a letter "should" be.

Whether or not there was more than one book being read by different groups within the class, both Laura and Linda divided the students into separate discussion teams or "literary circles" (Daniels, 1994). Discussion was an important part of the process in all classes, along with reading and writing, since speaking English could be worked on that way and questions about the text interpreted or explained. Laura found it particularly effective to return a complete set of each student's letters along with instructor replies by the second to last week of class. Students reread these sets, then wrote a final letter on how they felt about the process and how they had changed as readers and writers.

Initially, we expected the students to use English in a free, safe way — we did not correct the letters, though we asked questions in our own replies to prod the students to elaborate or revisit the text when we couldn't understand what the student was trying to say. This particular approach has also been used by other educators with ESL students via dialogue journals (Holmes & Moulton, 1997). As in the use of journals, we wanted to "focus on interaction rather than form" (p. 616). We wanted to provide a safe environment for interaction between the text, students, and instructor. If we felt a student needed to learn correct usage, we wanted them to do so by reading our more fluent letters to them. We modeled English, rather than taught it directly.

More importantly, we hoped to engage students at a deeper level than the most literal, to encourage them to interact with the text, to compare events in it to their own lives and experience. We hoped the students would be highly motivated by interest in this unique way of communicating, from the authenticity of partners engaging in a two-way written interaction (Edelsky, 1986).

We offered reading options from a wide variety of texts from which discussion and writing were based, other than length — Communication Development I needed a shorter book — and complexity of vocabulary. Novel choices ranged from classics such as Salinger's *Catcher in the Rye* (1945) to modern literature such as Barbara Kingsolver's *Animal Dreams* (1990) or Marilynne Robinson's *Housekeeping* (1980), to plain old popular fiction such as Michael Crichton thrillers or Nevada Barr environmental mysteries.

Though the choice of novels could not help but depend on our own knowledge of available novels, on what we ourselves had read, we tried to avoid imposing our ideas of what was interesting, as long as most of the class liked or were engaged by what they were reading. We hoped against hope we had found a way for them to lose themselves in the language.

Results from a Year's Worth of Experience

No assignment is perfect. Just as in any other situation, there were some students who said they didn't like the tasks expected of them, who claimed they were bored by their books, and who insisted that writing so much was far too difficult. Each quarter, a student or two might want to abandon the novel. However, through our letters and discussions, we persuaded the student to "hang tough," and sometimes allowed that student to choose a topic in which articles might be found to share with the class. Luckily, such students were in the minority.

The first class of each quarter started with students eyeing American novels suspiciously and counting the pages with alarm. Yet, they seemed interested by the initial letters they received which invited their individual responses. As the weeks wore on, we spotted Communication Development students in the lounge area of the school and in the cafeteria . . . actually reading the novels on their own time. Some finished their novels before the end of the quarter and asked for additional novels by the same author or recommendations for similar novels.

Furthermore, throughout the quarter, the students actively participated in discussions about the books and most wrote longer and longer letters as the exchange went on, often "testing" new vocabulary words. Some told us how much they liked the experience: *Dear Laura — I enjoy reading letters, especially which are from friends. Do you mind being my friend? I like to read them as soon as I receive them. I always read them again after a short time.* (Min, Chinese, CD2, based on *Animal Dreams*)

Many other students expressed in their letters their profound surprise that their teacher would write letters to *them,* that they had our undivided attention. They were also sensitive to the amount of time instructors spent responding to each student and expressed their appreciation.

Touched by Min's letter quoted above, Laura answered with encouragement: *I'm so happy you're enjoying your letters. I'd love to be your friend. Thank you for asking.*

It was no use trying to get into a lecture or other project when we handed our response letters back to Communication Development students. As soon as they received them, they became engrossed in reading. As instructors, we also had to admit we loved getting letters from the students, which varied from the expected summary of events in the text, to surprisingly personal disclosures about students' lives, to more simple topics we hadn't even thought of when we began the letter exchange process, such as the type of greeting one "should" use in an

American style letter: *I am sorry this letter is late. I hope you don't mind. I hope Dear Ms. Sweeney is the right way to start. Actually I didn't feel very good these days. I felt annoyed because there was an unhappy arguement between my friend and I. When I am in a bad mood, I don't want to do anything except to work out . . . Is it a little far from the book? OK, I am coming back.* (Xan, Chinese, CD1, based on *A River Runs Through It*)

Linda answered: *Yes, either Dear Linda or Dear Ms. Sweeney would be considered the correct way to start an American letter . . . I can understand your being in a really down mood after fighting with a friend. I'm surprised to learn you were in a bad mood at all, though, since you always look and act so happy. I guess it only goes to prove that no one can tell what is going on in another person's head. All of us can be good at hiding our emotions.* Then Linda went on to ask Xan what kind of exercise he practiced, another unobtrusive way to "connect" before continuing on with comments and questions about the book and Xan's interpretation/reaction.

Most students had no trouble relating to the events in the novel or understanding the basic action and emotion, even when they didn't know every single word they read: *The story is so sad that it makes me full of sadness. Cosima led an unhappy life in Grace. Her mother death is a blight on her. She says she is a stranger in her hometown, which makes me think about my feelings to my village.* (Min, CD2, based on *Animal Dreams*)

Laura replied: *I'm sorry that* Animal Dreams *makes you sad. Please believe me when I tell you there are some happy parts of the novel, too.* Furthermore, Laura reinforced Min's identification with the situation by admitting, *For me, when I go back home, I feel as if I no longer belong, that life there has gone on without me and I've missed important events with my family.*

Almost all students made predictions about where the novels' plots were heading, some with no prompting from instructors' letters, others because of the questions posed to them. In her initial letter to one class, the instructor asked: *This book is full of emotion and has some interesting characters who suffer a lot. Can you identify with any of them? What do you think might happen next?*

A student answered: *First, I thought this is a women book — borring and telling a love story, but later I found out that it's going to be something more . . . I knew something interesting and bad will happened.* (Rafal, Polish, CD2, based on *The Horse Whisperer,* 1995).

Many students backed up their opinions by revisiting the text and quoting it in their letters: *The more I read, the more I'm convinced how little I know. Many books give us knowledge and teach us in many ways. Camps for Japanese? In the United States? . . . Hatsue's soul was "made impure," living among white people "has tainted" her (Chapter 14, p. 202).* (Bianca, Polish, CD2, based on *Snow Falling on Cedars,* 1995.)

The instructor admitted: *I'm ashamed to say that I didn't know about Japanese concentration camps either until some years back. Prejudice causes such terrible things!* To get the student to think critically, however, the instructor asked Bianca if the Japanese were also being prejudiced when they thought that Hatsue's soul had been tainted by Caucasians.

The ability to not only predict the action a novel's storyline will be taking but also reviewing those predictions shows a high level of reading comprehension. As Rosenblatt (1994) states, "From a to-and-fro interplay between reader, text, and context emerges a synthesis or organization, more or less coherent and complete" (p. 1064) and, again, "The reader may return to the original text to recapture how it entered into the transaction, but must 'find words' for explaining the evocation and the interpretation" (p. 1074).

Based on most of the letters we received, we were elated that CD students understood so much about what they were reading. Prolific readers ourselves, with many literature courses in our backgrounds, we found that some students made literary interpretations that could be considered products of very high level thinking (Holmes & Moulton, 1997), helping to explain events to other students, as well as the instructor: *But in my opinion, Tom Booker made a suicidal after Annie told him that she's going to let her husband know about them and live him. He didn't want to crash their marriage so he killed himself. And I also think the kind of death he choose, Tom did on purpose. He wanted to be killed by a horse as a symbol. The horse connected Tom and Annie and because of the horse he could be close to her.* (Rafal, CD2, based on *The Horse Whisperer,* 1995.)

Students did not have to possess high level writing skills to understand the basics of what they were reading or why the author wrote the way he or she did, but were encouraged to work with the language before they had complete control of it. For example, a young Chinese woman who had trouble articulating words aloud and wrote short letters because the process was so difficult for her, nevertheless, composed an insightful statement about *A River Runs Through It* (1976) that could be considered literary criticism as to how the structure and style of the novel reflected one of its main themes: *I had ever been fishing, but this was many years ago. I think the book moves slow because the story told how to fish. Fishing is very slow action . . .* (Su, CD1).

Some students identified deeply with characters. Van Horn (1997) speculates that readers pretending to be a character or trying to help a character figure out a problem will not only make reading a more meaningful experience, but will come to see themselves as readers/writers who have a duty to think and create. Min, the Chinese student mentioned earlier, wrote these poignant comments about two major characters in *Animal Dreams,* an estranged father and daughter: *I'm a person who hides love deep in my heart, just like Dr. Homer. I sometimes hate Cosima. No matter how he seems to be a bad father, he is her only real father. I don't want her to regret not treating him nicely when he's still in her sight. Whenever I think the person I love is gone without knowing my love, my heart crashes like glass.*

In reply, the instructor wrote: *The relationship between Doc Homer and Codi is pretty strange to me, too. I feel the same way you do about relationships with parents. Even if they make us crazy, we have to be there for them when they need us.*

A young Polish man in CD1 identified so much with the doomed brother in *A River Runs Through It* that he changed his name in his letters from Pawel (which is Paul in Polish) to Poul, to, finally, Paul. His remarks about the character showed his growing attachment: *I hope we will talk about Paul in class because his person is very interesting and hard to describe* (first letter). *It is almost not possible to find the cause of his* (Paul's) *death because Norman is a person who tells us this story, and we know that Paul didn't like to talk with him about his problems, so the Paul's inside is unknown for us, and we can just speculate about the reasons of his death* (second letter). *You wrote in your letter that another student came up with opinion that Paul felt inferior to Norman. My opinion is different. I think that Paul felt better than Norman and more independent. He was better at fly-fishing which both brothers knew and I think that Paul had more freedom* (third letter). *My final opinion about this book — I think that Norman wrote this book like document which should tell us that he wasn't guilty Paul's death* (fourth letter).

Of course, the student actually did think Norman guilty of neglecting to save his brother, somehow, and expressed this in class. In response to both letters and discussion, the instructor wrote: *Perhaps you are right about Norman not being brave enough to approach his brother regarding his problems . . . However, as adults, we have to allow each other to make our own decisions. Think about the alcoholics you've known — were their families able to change them? Still, I admire your deep feelings on this matter. If a person were in trouble, he or she should appreciate having a friend or brother like you. I think you would fight to the death for the people you love.*

The instructor also added: *I'm so happy you found a character to care about in* A River Runs Through It. *I think caring about Paul is the whole point of this book. If he were alive, Norman Maclean would be thrilled to know that his work touched you, that you made Paul, his beloved brother, come back to life, if only in your mind and words.*

We believe the support for his opinions may have helped Pawel/Paul be willing to learn so much from his own process of reading and writing, as is shown in the introduction to his final essay, a compare/contrast summary of *A River Runs Through It* and the film that was based on the book: *I would like to send a few words to my teacher which was the best I've ever had. I would like to thank you for your all work which you had to do to teach me and my friends. I feel that I've learned a lot and I'm really appreciate. When I learned my own language in Poland, my teacher didn't like when I wrote a composition about the book which included my deep feelings. She always said to me that I was flew so high in my imagination and I could fail my final exam because somebody could dislike my interpretation. I thought about it a lot and know that it didn't make sence, but sometimes when I read my previous compositions I couldn't understand myself because I wrote on paper my feelings which I had in my head right after reading the book.*

I liked the idea about writing the letters because I could write about everything which I wanted. Sometimes my opinions were misleading, but everybody can interpretate the book in a different way. These letters were like sheets of paper which were a copies of our picture which book made in our minds.

Rosenblatt (1994) would certainly agree that everyone can interpret a book in a different way:

> There is no such thing as a generic reader or a generic literary work; there are in reality only the potential millions of individual readers of individual literary works. . . . The reading of any work of literature is, of necessity, an individual and unique occurrence involving the mind and emotions of some particular reader (p. 1057).

From the transactional standpoint, we had met our goals of helping our students increase their reading comprehension. We had helped pave the way for them to express themselves as sophisticated readers in English, readers who could consciously articulate information about a character's emotional state (Barton, 1990) and remark on their own processes. Furthermore, and of great importance, the quotes from students above show an increased level of trust and connection by the student for the instructor, minds reaching across cultural boundaries and communicating, if only for the transient and fragile interlude of three letter exchanges.

The process of acculturization can only be enhanced by such an approach. In two students' own words: *I am so happy you liked this process too. From your letter, I know you more and want to continue our communication* (Su, CD1). *I know I will never be an American but my Polish roots aren't as pure as they were. The question where I belong to, will always come to my mind. Dilemmas are the price we have to pay for freedom* (Bianca, CD2).

We believe that interaction with a novel and with letter exchanges between instructors and students regarding that novel are complicated transactions, reciprocal relationships within the classroom environment which broadens to include the whole institutional, social, and cultural context of the situation (Rosenblatt, 1994). We became far more enlightened about what was going on with our students, particularly the silent, reluctant population that attended class but never had much to say. We believe many students got to know us better as well, along with the complex American culture that shaped us. We found ourselves explaining (and sometimes looking up) anything from who General Custer was to why the United States became embroiled in military problems with El Salvador.

Implications and a Few Final Words

Literary letters are a powerful tool for enhancing literacy. Though we have no official count, since the inception of this classroom tool in 1997, the number of students who are admitted to English 101 from Communication Development II, rather than continuing in yet another developmental writing class, has increased from 20–30 percent to 50 percent or more.

We do not offer this information with graphs and official statistics. Rather, we present it as practical inquiry (Richardson, 1994). Like most teachers, we like to begin with a general idea, focus on content and activities, then connect our experiences with formal research as we examine the results of what we have done.

Are there drawbacks to the letter and novel reading method? Absolutely. Like dialogue journal writing, the process is labor intensive (Holmes & Moulton, 1997). It helps if instructors have computers and know how to use a keyboard. They also need to believe their efforts will make a lasting difference in the abilities of their students (Holmes & Moulton, 1997).

We do.

We constantly encounter students from past classes in the hallways who say, "I still have all your letters and I read them again once in awhile." We respond the same way, "So do I."

References

Atwell, N. (1987). *In the middle: Writing, reading, and learning with adolescents.* Portsmouth, New Hampshire: Boyton/Cook Publishers.

Barton, J. (1996). Interpreting character emotions for literature comprehension. *Journal of Adolescent & Adult Literacy, 40*(1), 22–28.

Daniels, H. (1994). *Literature circles — voice and choice in the student-centered classroom.* York, Maine: Stenhouse Publishers.

Deen, R. (1994). Notes to Stella. In Tate, Corbett, & Myers (Eds.), *The writing teacher's sourcebook* (3rd ed., pp. 55–64). New York: Oxford University Press.

Edlesky, C. (1986). *Writing in a bilingual program: Habia una vez.* Norwood, NJ: Ablex.

Evans, N. (1995). *The horse whisperer.* New York: Dell.

Guterson, D. (1995). *Snow falling on cedars.* New York: Vintage Books.

Henry, J. (1995). *If not now: Develomental readers in the college classroom.* Portsmouth, New Hampshire: Boynton/Cook Publishers.

Holmes, V. L., & Moulton, M. R. (1997). Dialogue journals as an ESL learning strategy. *Journal of Adolescent & Adult Literacy, 40*(8), 616–621.

Kingsolver, B. (1990). *Animal dreams*. New York: HarperCollins Publishers.

Maclean, N. (1976). *A river runs through it*. New York: Pocket Books.

Ollmann, H. E. (1996). Creating higher level thinking with reading response. *Journal of Adolescent & Adult Literacy, 39*(7), 576–581.

Richardson, V. (1994). Conducting research on practice. *Educational Researcher.* June-July, 5–10.

Robinson, M. (1980). *Housekeeping*. New York: The Noonday Press.

Rosenblatt, L. (1994). The transitional theory of reading and writing. In R. Ruddell, M. R. Ruddell, & H. Singer (Eds.), *Theoretical models and processes of reading* (4th ed., pp. 1057–1092). Newark, DE: International Reading Association.

Salinger, J. D. (1945). *Catcher in the rye*. New York: Little, Brown.

Van Horn, L. (1997). The characters within us: Readers connect with characters to create meaning and understanding. *Journal of Adolescent & Adult Literacy, 40*(5), 342–347.

Additional Readings

Burrell, K. I., & Kim, D. J. (1998). "International students and academic assistance: Meeting the needs of another college population." In P. L. Dwinell & J. L. Higbee (Eds.), *Developmental education: Meeting diverse student needs* (pp. 81–96). Carol Stream, IL: National Association of Developmental Education.

De la Pena, A. M. M., & Soler, L. R. (2001). "Cognitive strategies for academic reading and listening in EFL." *Journal of College Reading and Learning,* 31 (2), 217–32.

Dupuy, B. (1996). "Bringing books into the classroom: First steps in turning college ESL students into readers." *TESOL Journal,* 5 (4), 10–15.

Gonzalez, O. (1999). "Building vocabulary: Dictionary consultation and the ESL student." *The Journal of Adolescent & Adult Literacy,* 43 (3), 264–70.

Harklau, L. (2001). "From high school to college: Student perspectives on literacy practices." *Journal of Literacy Research,* 33 (1), 32–70.

Kasper, L. F. (1995). "Using discipline-based texts to boost college ESL reading instruction." *Journal of Adolescent & Adult Literacy,* 39 (4), 298–306.

Mokharti, K., & Sheorey, R. (2002). "Measuring ESL students' awareness of reading strategies." *Journal of Developmental Education,* 25 (3), 2–10.

Pintozzi, F. J., & Valeri-Gold, M. (2000). "Teaching English as a second language (ESL) students." In R. F. Flippo & D. C. Caverly (Eds.), *The handbook of college reading and study strategy research* (pp. 261–89). Mahwah, NJ: Erlbaum.

Reynolds, P. F. (1993). "Evaluating ESL and college composition texts for teaching the argumentative rhetorical form." *Journal of Reading,* 36 (6), 474–80.

Wilson, K. (1999). "Notetaking in the academic writing process of non-native speaker students: Is it important as a process or product." *Journal of College Reading and Learning,* 29 (2), 166–79.

6

Planning for a Range of Readers

The breadth of the cultural, economic, social, national, and disability backgrounds of students enrolled in postsecondary education is greater than ever before. Indeed, the nontraditional student of the previous generation has become part of the mosaic that is today's traditional student body. The cross section of this "traditional" college population can readily be found in college reading and learning assistance programs and in writing centers. Hence, the instructors and staff specialists in these programs need to be knowledgeable about the unique learning issues the various subgroups on campus are facing. In addition, college reading and learning specialists need to be aware of the campus support programs — such as accessibility centers, international student offices, educational opportunity programs, and student services programs — available to students.

The two articles that follow look at two unique populations on campus — those with Attention Deficit Disorder and the deaf and hard of hearing. Both articles discuss the unique issues facing these populations and offer recommendations for better serving them. The articles listed in the "Additional Readings" section cover other special populations on campus.

College Students with Attention Deficit Disorder (ADD): Implications for Learning Assistance Professionals

Shevawn Eaton and Sharon Wyland

The number of students entering higher education with diagnosed Attention Deficit Disorder (ADD) is growing. Many of these individuals will enroll in reading and learning strategy courses and workshops through learning assistance centers, academic support services, or developmental studies programs. Shevawn Eaton and Sharon Wyland cover the theory and research related to ADD students in postsecondary education, and provide information on how instructors and learning assistance professionals can effectively serve students with ADD.

Recently, in a conversation with a colleague, a faculty member voiced his concern about Shelly, a student in his class. "She's always late," he said, "and often shows up completely unprepared for class, even though we worked together the day before." His frustration, however, was not so much about these characteristics, as it was about Shelly's erratic performance. "On some days, she comes up with the most incredible thoughts about the topic we are discussing. Her work can be excellent. But on other days, she spends the entire class doodling. She seems to be paying attention, but something doesn't seem right, like she somehow is not really there. When I call on her, she can paraphrase what we are discussing, but her understanding seems "wobbly" somehow, as though she is just not getting it."

He went on to talk about her exams. "She says she studies, and I believe her, but her exams have been very poor. I have tried to break down concepts into small parts, but she gets caught up in just memorizing lists and just can't grasp the larger issues. She told me that she panics during the exams as soon as she sees a question she can't answer. She is just sure she is going to fail." And sadly, Shelly usually does. His frustration was not that Shelly wasn't trying, but that she wasn't making progress in the course despite her efforts, and his, to succeed.

Is this a case of an average student having problems in a class, or is it something more? Students with Attention Deficit Disorder may look a lot like other students, but the problems can be much more deeply rooted, and the frustration to the students and those who work with them can be great. Sensitivity to how a student with ADD may appear in the college environment can help a learning assistance professional work more effectively in enhancing student success.

Currently, the incidence of Attention Deficit Disorder (ADD) in college students has been estimated from anywhere between 1 percent and 9 percent (Faigel, 1995; Barkley, 1993). As awareness of the disorder increases, so too are numbers of school age children being diagnosed (Westby & Cutler, 1994). Along with better definitions and increases in diagnosis has come successful treatment of many of the symptoms that are associated with ADD. The result is that more students with the disorder are and will be attending college. Consequently, more than ever before, those of us who work with learning assistance programs, academic support services, and developmental education will be faced with the needs of students with ADD.

As more is learned about the disorder, the stereotype of students with ADD continues to change. Because ADD is a disorder that has a direct effect on educational activities and demands, a college learning center is one resource these students are likely to turn to for assistance. While many students come to college knowing that they have ADD, pressures of the academic environment may encourage them to seek new coping strategies. The college experience may motivate others to seek assistance with academics for the first time. The more that learning assistance professionals know about ADD, its symptoms and its treatment, the better this growing population of students can be served. In this article, we will address several issues that will touch learning assistance providers as the number of students with ADD on campus continues to increase.

Specifically, four questions will be addressed here, based on the research and theory that have emerged in the last several years. These include:

1. What is Attention Deficit Disorder?

2. What are the characteristics of college students with ADD?

3. What are some reasons why learning assistance professionals should increase their knowledge of ADD?

4. How can learning assistance professionals help meet the needs of college students with ADD?

What Is Attention Deficit Disorder?

According to the Diagnostic and Statistical Manual of Mental Disorders, fourth edition (DSM-IV), Attention Deficit Hyperactivity Disorder (referred to as ADD in this article) is a complex mental disorder with three primary types of symptoms. The categories of symptoms include inattention, hyperactivity, and impulsivity (American Psychiatric Association, 1994). Individual cases may demonstrate any combination of these characteristics.

Observable symptoms of the disorder include "difficulty directing attention appropriately, impulsive behavior, hyperactivity, mood swings, low stress tolerance, and difficulty in following rules. It is an invisible disability that often affects an individual's performance in early school years, postsecondary education, and throughout life" (Latham, 1995, p. 53). Individuals frequently report being unable to concentrate in social and educational situations, often drifting off or appearing "spacey." They may also be distracted or experience concentration difficulties when faced with certain elements of the surrounding environment, including noise, light, or movement. Individuals with ADD also seem to be prone to accidents. Further, the disorder is often accompanied by other disorders, including mood disorders, depression, and most frequently, learning disabilities (Cantwell & Baker, 1992; Barkley, 1990). In sum, ADD may interfere with academic, social, and emotional components of an individual's life (Faigel, 1995).

Historically, ADD was diagnosed as a disorder that affected children. It was thought that most outgrew the disorder by puberty. More recent research, however, determined that while in many cases the symptom of hyperactivity may decrease or disappear at puberty, other symptoms of the disorder such as poor concentration and difficulty with organization may be with the individual through life (Denckla, 1993; Wender, 1987). In follow-up studies of adults that were diagnosed in childhood, 50 percent to 80 percent were found to exhibit some symptoms of ADD into adulthood (Leimkuhler, 1994; Hallowell & Ratey, 1994; Hechtman, 1989; Gittleman, Manuzza, Shenker, & Bonguara, 1985; Weiss, Hechtman, Milroy, & Perlman, 1985).

Perhaps one of the most perplexing characteristics of ADD is the variation in specific symptoms from one case to another. Different individuals with the disorder can exhibit polar opposite symptoms. For example, one individual can be hyperactive and impulsive (usually labeled as ADHD), while another may be quiet and withdrawn (ADD without hyperactivity). Some individuals may be severely distracted by external environmental factors, while others can easily adapt (Leimkuhler, 1994). In short, no single stereotype fits the profile of all individuals with ADD, making diagnosis tricky at best.

Those individuals that exhibit hyperactivity as a child are more likely candidates for correct diagnosis. Those that do not conform to this stereotype, however, may never be identified, or may be identified much later in life. This is especially the case for bright students who develop successful coping strategies for educational settings prior to their college experience (Lahey & Carlson, 1992).

Along with the clarification of a definition for ADD from a medical and psychological perspective, in recent years, the disorder has also received clarity from a legal perspective. Under the protection of the Americans with Disabilities Act of 1990 and Section 504 of the Rehabilitation Act of 1973, ADD has become accepted as a disability that requires accommodation. This recognition requires that postsecondary institutions like other educational institutions have an obligation to provide services and assistance for this population (Latham, 1995). The legal rights of students with ADD are comparable to those of students with other disabilities, that of "reasonable accommodation." The result is not only the increase of such students on college campuses, but also the expected reaction of institutions to meet the needs of these students.

What Are the Characteristics of College Students with ADD?

As mentioned earlier, a student with ADD who enters a learning center probably will look like many other students in need of academic support services. It is beneficial, however, for those who work with such students to be aware of cues in behavior that may suggest a more complicated problem. Willis, Hoben, and Myette (1995) provide a theoretical framework that helps to characterize college students with ADD. The framework includes five key components which will be summarized here: self-esteem, family and peer support, stress, organizational skills, and personal resistance/acceptance of the disorder as a part of life.

Self-Esteem

Individuals with ADD, like many other students with disabilities that affect learning, experience negative academic self-esteem that is brought on by a number of factors. Many students with ADD have a history of inconsistent performance in academic work, often ranging from A's to F's (Javorsky & Gussin, 1994). Teachers often characterize this phenomenon as a lack of effort or laziness (Leimkuhler, 1994). Accordingly, while these students often recognize their own potential, they also witness their own underachievement (Ratey, Greenberg, Bemporad, & Linden, 1992). Consequently, they have a poor academic self-concept that can cause an increase in stress in future academic settings. Such students may develop self-defeating attitudes, which, when compounded by concentration deficits from the disorder, may create a downward spiral of failure.

The combination of failure and frustration in academic settings can result in depression. The incidence of depression in students with ADD is so common that it is difficult to determine if the depression is a coexisting condition with ADD or one brought on because of it.

Apart from the academic context, self-esteem in social situations is also affected by the disorder. As children, many students with the disorder felt stigmatized by their peers (Willis, Hoben, & Myette, 1995). Labeling in school and being singled out for special programs and services or disciplinary problems were a constant reminder that they were different.

In social situations as well as academic ones, concentration and focus problems contribute to esteem problems for students with ADD. Some may "space out" during conversations, or they may not respond when addressed. They may also frustrate peers with their hyperactive or impulsive behaviors. These social failings frustrate students with ADD, making them more sensitive and subject to bursts of anger or social withdrawal, both symptoms of weak self-esteem.

Family and Peer Support

ADD creates an isolation for many students with the disorder. It is therefore very important that an individual with ADD is made to feel supported by family and friends. Such relationships can be crucial to a student's academic success (Willis, et al., 1995). "When any part of the family or friends' support system is primarily negative, a student with ADD may expend additional energy repairing his/her psychological wounds" (p. 39).

Friendships and long-term personal relationships can be difficult and complex for individuals with ADD. For many, the distractibility and impulsiveness of the disability interfere with the ability to build a foundation for personal and social relationships (Ratey, et al., 1992). Many experience multiple failures in relationships. Some may protect themselves by avoiding relationships while others establish complex, co-dependent relationships because of their own insecurities (Ratey, et al., 1992). Studies have also shown that children with ADD were found to be less popular in school than their peers, some being actively disliked, and others choosing to be socially inactive (Lahey & Carlson, 1992).

Stress

The continuing battle that students with ADD face over symptoms of the disorder is extremely frustrating. Because the college environment often intensifies many of these symptoms, students may tend to overreact to stressful situations (Aust, 1994). The individuals may exhibit emotional difficulties, such as mood swings or bursts of anger. They may try to self-medicate by turning to illegal drugs and alcohol to deal with their symptoms and their stress. "The level of stress for these students seems to be greater than that of their college peers because of the typical attributes of ADD and learning disabilities" (Willis, et al., 1995, p. 39). In particular, the stressors that college can present to these individuals include responding to deadlines, time limits on exams, exams which are poorly written or difficult to comprehend, multiple choice tests, and lack of structure in academic tasks (Willis, et al., 1995).

Organizational Skills

Organizational problems resulting from the disorder can manifest themselves in a number of ways. For some students, problems may occur when attempting to create structure within course work where little or none exists. Other problems may be in the areas of time management, test preparation, or organizing work necessary to write a paper. A larger problem may be an inability to gain a "big picture" perspective from lectures and/or readings by making connections between details and major themes and constructs (Nadeau, 1995; Willis, et al., 1995; Leimkuhler, 1994).

Daily tasks requiring organizational skills may also demonstrate symptoms of the disorder. Students may have problems being on time for classes and meetings. Their finances may always be in turmoil, and they may have difficulty in managing money. They may also have problems in getting and keeping a job (Javorsky & Gussin, 1994).

Personal Resistance / Acceptance of the Disorder

In college, when many students are facing issues of independence, students with ADD may choose this point to disregard the disorder and ignore the support services, medication and other help that has guided them in the past (Willis, et al., 1995). The reaction to the disorder of ADD can be varied among individuals, ranging from extreme relief at an initial diagnosis to complete denial. The reactions and choices in coping with the disorder may also change within an individual over time. The result of such reactions can feed into the inconsistent array of successes and failures that many such students experience. In short, growing to accept the disorder can be difficult, but acceptance will increase a student's capacity for academic, personal, and social success.

What Are Some Reasons That Learning Assistance Professionals Should Increase Their Knowledge of ADD?

The number of students with ADD who are attending college is on the increase. This is due to a number of factors. The use of Ritalin and other medications has been shown to be successful in assisting children in increasing concentration and attention in educational settings. Before the advent of successful diagnosis and treatment, hyperactivity and inability to concentrate made many individuals with the disorder turn away from education (Javorsky & Gussin, 1994). Now, more students are able to have successful and positive experiences in school, thus encouraging more of them to attend college.

In addition, individuals with moderate ADD or ADD without hyperactivity may be more difficult to diagnose early in their educational experience. Particularly, if students come from high school environments where classes were small, academics were well structured, and in which they received large amounts of support from family and friends, they may have been able to accommodate for problems effectively (Nadeau, 1995). In college, however, the environments are often quite different, and these differences can affect performance.

The increased intensity of course work, challenging reading, difficult assignments and examinations, a less structured academic environment, and a change in support structure may all tax a student who has coped successfully in the past. Students with ADD can be particularly sensitive to distractions, such as variations in noise and light (Latham, 1995). College life is filled with a variety of challenges to someone with such sensitivities. The combined elements of the college experience may intensify symptoms, bringing many students to counselors, physicians, and learning centers for assistance for the first time.

A learning center has at its disposal some key interventions that can assist such students to become successful. Research has shown that basic learning and study skills, time management, and test taking strategies provide a good foundation to assist these students. But other interventions, either medical or psychological, may also be necessary. To be most effective, learning assistance professionals should collaborate with other offices on campus when beginning to work with a student with ADD.

Students may come to a learning center self-reporting the disorder, or a learning assistance professional may suspect a certain student has ADD. In either case, diagnosing the disorder should fall to a psychiatrist or physician using the DSM-IV. Documentation of the diagnosis should be available on campus, usually in the office for disabled student services. That office can also provide insights into how to approach an undiagnosed student in making an effective referral.

A good diagnostic report is one that includes a clinical diagnosis as well as other evaluative information. Most important for the learning center is a list of recommendations and accommodations, supported by evaluative data on the student, including academic support services that can be provided by the center.

Learning assistance professionals who are able to make educated referrals and connections with other campus and medical services offer students with ADD the best opportunity to acquire a comprehensive intervention program that can help overcome what could be a lifetime of academic and social problems. For many students, diagnosis of the disorder, and some direction in terms of supports, can bring great relief and an understanding of performance problems in college.

How Can Learning Assistance Professionals Help Meet the Needs of College Students with ADD?

Students with ADD have a number of specific academic needs. However, because ADD frequently is found to be associated with other learning, cognition, and emotional disorders, the needs of students with ADD cover medical and psychological areas as well (Shaywitz, Fletcher & Shaywitz, 1994). As stated earlier, it is advisable for learning assistance personnel to develop a collaborative approach with other professionals, especially those in disabled student services, in working with students to achieve the best possible support system. However, there are some consistent academic needs within the group of college students who have the disorder that can be addressed by learning assistance.

In a learning center, a variety of strategies and supports can be offered for students with ADD. These include developmental course work, academic counseling, tutoring services, special services for exam situations, enhancement of organizational skills, advocacy, and education of professors and staff (Weiss & Hechtman, 1993).

Developmental course work is a good beginning service for a number of students with ADD. These courses inherently are designed to address many of the typical problems experienced by students with the disorder. Since students who have ADD are often characterized as having spotty skill development (due to concentration problems) and study skill weaknesses (due to poor organization), such course work would be of great benefit to fill in the gaps that the disorder may have created in previous educational experiences (Javorsky & Gussin, 1994; Nadeau, 1995).

Students with ADD require support from learning centers in getting and staying organized but perhaps with more attention to the unique characteristics of the individual student's particular form of disorganization. Assessment and diagnosis of organizational problems is imperative for the student with ADD, as is gaining strategies that are effective in moving towards better organization. Perhaps the most important tool that students with ADD can gain from those of us that work with learning assistance is the ability to build structure where none exists.

As with all students who need academic support services, students with ADD can gain self-esteem when given opportunities to feel successful in academic and social situations. Learning assistance staff who are supportive and positive in their interactions with such students can provide them with opportunities for esteem building and personal growth. They can also assist in helping students structure academic activities in ways in which they can achieve small successes that can build a foundation for more consistent, future accomplishments.

In addition to academic successes, those who work with students who have ADD can also, through peer and professional relationships, provide opportunities for these students to begin building positive and supportive relationships that can enhance academic and social integration into the institution.

Educators have the capacity to build trust with students in significant ways. Being in a trusting relationship with a learning assistance professional, the student may be more receptive to a recommendation to seek out assistance in dealing with personal and psychological problems through counseling or psychological services. As with most other students who require academic assistance, often it is the recognition that someone genuinely cares for the individual that motivates the student to change in positive directions and become successful in many areas of life.

Another service that learning assistance personnel can provide which can contribute to a student's academic achievement in college is attention to planning, organization, and goal setting. Depending on the needs of the student, planning can encompass a range of considerations from day-to-day activities to short and long term educational, career, and personal goals. In terms of long range goals, students may need assistance in choosing a career that best matches their skills and abilities. In the short term, they also may require advice in registering for a course load which offers a balanced combination of courses, particular teaching styles, and a good match between skills and course requirements (McKinney, Montague & Hocutt, 1993).

Leimkuhler (1994) provides some specific recommendations for assisting students with ADD with short term organizational problems. These include using a calendar, breaking tasks into smaller pieces, and working on them in priority order, establishing personal deadlines for smaller pieces of an entire project and creating an environment that minimizes distractions, interruptions, and stressors.

Coping with all types of stressors is another important part of adjustment to college for students with ADD. Learning assistance can offer students with ADD many ways of dealing with stress caused by academic tasks such as taking exams or meeting deadlines. Stress management and coping strategies, time management, and test taking skills can assist students in taking control. Academic stress caused by poor test performance, comprehension, or writing problems may be best addressed through academic services, especially tutoring.

Students with ADD are found to perform better in one-on-one or small group learning situations than in large groups (Javorsky & Gussin, 1994). Tutors who understand the special problems of students with ADD will gain a better understanding of how the disorder affects the tutoring relationship. Tutors also play an important role in helping students learn to stay organized, overcome procrastinations, and stay motivated. They can coach them on specific skills such as memory enhancement, test preparation, and academic problem solving (Leimkuhler, 1994; Weinstein, 1994).

Individual contact with other positive role models is a good way to help a student with ADD become more successful. "Coaching" and "anchoring" are two treatment models for assisting students with ADD.

"Coaching," as a specific type of assistance for students with ADD, has been shown to be a highly effective way to enhance success with adults (Hallowell & Ratey, 1994). The coach can be a therapist, friend, or colleague who is willing to invest time and regular conversation with an individual with ADD. An ADD coach works to help keep the individual with ADD focused on the task at hand and offer encouragement along the way. She takes time to help the student clarify goals, and maintain the day-to-day activities needed for success.

An important success factor for adults with ADD is the presence of a positive role-model or mentor. College students with ADD can benefit by "anchoring" themselves to a counselor, faculty member, learning assistance professional, or a successful older student with ADD. Having an "anchor" or a coach available can greatly assist students in more rapid recovery from setbacks and in avoiding prolonged downward spirals in academic performance or emotional adjustment (Richard, 1995).

In addition to individual assistance, outreach and advocacy are important roles that learning assistance professional must play to educate faculty, staff, and administrators about students with ADD. Faculty education, for example, can be an important part of a student's success. The quality and style of teaching can have a large impact on the performance of the student with ADD. Students with ADD benefit from instruction that is multisensory. Faculty who are able to shift their teaching to accommodate can provide significant benefits.

Faculty need to be aware that ADD is not an excuse for special treatment, but a disability that requires special accommodation and understanding. Small changes in traditional presentation of material such as preferential seating, providing lecture outlines and copies of overhead transparencies in advance, a quiet non-distracting environment, and extra time for exams can help a student dramatically (Faigel, 1995).

Javorsky and Gussin (1994) provide a series of recommendations for faculty that can help students with ADD in their courses, as adapted from Vogel (1993). They suggest a number of practices that can assist faculty in streamlining course experiences in ways that can help all students, but most specifically can improve the organization, comprehension, and academic success of students with ADD. Sensitized faculty, staff, and administrators may be more willing to open the door to negotiations for the special services a student with ADD may need to be successful. An adaptation of specific recommendations for faculty and exam situations is included in Appendix A. Appendix B provides a list of twelve suggested readings for faculty, learning assistance professionals and students.

Perhaps the most important consideration when working with students with ADD, is offered by Weiss and Hechtman (1993): "When adult subjects assessed the treatment they had received as children and what factors had helped them the most, they chose individual persons (a parent, teacher, a counselor, or a friend) who had been particularly significant for them" (p. 218). As it is with other populations of students who require academic support services, for students with ADD, it is the perception of care, mentorship, and belonging that can make a student become successful.

Appendix A

Strategies for Faculty / Learning Center Professionals in Accommodating Students with ADD

Author's Note: Strategies which faculty can employ to assist students with ADD are effective strategies that will enhance success for *ALL* students. The strategies and suggestions listed here do not require extra time and/or effort, but rather are simply good teaching practices that would be appreciated by any student.

- Making the syllabus available four to six weeks before the beginning of class, and when possible, discussing it in advance with students considering the course.

- Beginning lectures with a review of the previous lecture and an overview of topics to be covered that day.

- Emphasizing important points, main ideas, and key concepts orally and/or highlighting them.

- Speaking distinctly and at a relaxed pace, pausing to respond to questions or for students to catch up in their note-taking.

- Noticing and responding to nonverbal signals of confusion or frustration with explanations and assistance.

- Trying to eliminate or at least reduce auditory and visual classroom distractions such as outside noise.

- Leaving time for a question-answer period and/or discussion periodically and at the end of each lecture and providing periodic summaries and highlights.

- Giving assignments in writing as well as orally.

- Being available during office hours for clarification of lecture material, assignments, and readings.

- Offering question and answer sessions, and/or review sessions.

- Providing study questions for exams that show test format and content.

- Encouraging students to schedule difficult classes in accordance with their individual "body clocks."

- Encouraging students to enroll in classes that are small (under 30 students) and scheduled for short durations of time (under one hour and fifteen minutes).

- Encouraging students to schedule classes to allow for breaks in between them, especially classes that require intense concentration for lectures and note-taking.

- Allowing students to enroll in a reduced course load and extending the time for completion of degree requirements.

- Working cooperatively with the Disabled Student Services office as resources for each other to verify the appropriateness of a particular accommodation with a particular student.

Suggestions for Specific Testing and / or Evaluation Accommodations

- Allowing extended time for exams.

- Providing the exam in an alternate format (e.g., essay versus objective).

- Permitting students to take exams in a room that is distraction-free, allowing students the privacy needed to subvocalize to maintain attention and recall of information.

- Allowing students to answer exam questions using methods other than handwriting (such as, orally or typing).

- Allowing students to verify an exam question by rephrasing.

- Providing alternatives to exams to show mastery of course objective (e.g., a research project, class presentation).

- Allowing students to use computational aids, such as a calculator, and word processing assistance for exams.

- Avoiding complex sentence structure, such as double negatives and embedding questions within questions on exams.

- Providing ample blank space or additional exam booklets for students with overly large handwriting.

Adapted from Javorsky, J., & Gussin, B. (1994, May). College students with attention deficit hyperactivity disorder: An overview and description of services. *Journal of College Student Development, 35*(3),170–177.

Teaching Students with Hearing Impairments

Karen S. Kalivoda, Jeanne L. Higbee, and Debra C. Brenner

With the increasing numbers of deaf and hearing impaired students at postsecondary institutions across the nation, specialized services are being offered on a regular basis. Yet as this article explains, these students are often enrolled in developmental reading and basic writing classes because of the differences between written English and American Sign Language, coupled with current admissions practices and placement testing. The authors review existing services available to deaf and hearing impaired students and discuss how literacy instructors in developmental programs can better serve this population.

The 1990 passage of the Americans with Disabilities Act (ADA) brought the issue of disability access to the forefront at institutions of higher education. A first-page article of the *Chronicle of Higher Education* (Jaschik, 1993) reported that colleges are struggling to determine how to implement this new federal regulation. The ADA defines disability as a physical or mental impairment that substantially limits one or more major life activities, such as walking, seeing, breathing, working, and learning. Examples of disabilities covered by the ADA include orthopedic, visual, speech and hearing impairments, cerebral palsy, epilepsy, muscular dystrophy, multiple sclerosis, cancer, heart disease, diabetes, emotional illness, specific learning disabilities, and HIV disease (Office of the Attorney General, 1991). This legislation has contributed to the rapid growth of educational opportunity for students with disabilities at institutions of higher education. As their participation increases, it is anticipated that faculty will encounter more students with disabilities in their classrooms. As a result, faculty will be responsible for the provision of reasonable accommodations in the classroom as outlined in the ADA.

There are growing numbers of students with hearing impairments on college campuses today (Karchmer & Rawlings, 1991; Rawlings, Karchmer, DeCaro, & Allen, 1995). The greatest increase occurred as a result of maternal rubella. This was reflected in an increase in the number of students with hearing impairments attending postsecondary institutions in the first half of the 1980s. Though the numbers may not reach such epidemic proportions as we approach the twenty-first century, students with hearing impairments continue to aspire to higher education in growing numbers. The services are available, the information is accessible, and the deaf consumer increasingly seeks equality in education.

With the growing number of students with hearing impairments also has come an increase of programs providing services to this population (Rawlings, Karchmer, DeCaro, & Allen, 1995). There are several institutions, such as Gallaudet and the National Technical Institute for the Deaf, that have specific charters to serve deaf students. Although these are excellent programs specifically designed for this population of students, deaf students should not be limited in their choice of institution. Students with hearing impairments are applying to colleges and universities that may have never previously enrolled a deaf student. Like other students, deaf students may be influenced to attend a specific institution because of its academic reputation, excellence in a specific field of study, or geographic location. All institutions of higher education, whether or not they are "specialized" colleges for the deaf, are required to provide accommodations that will meet the communication needs of deaf and hearing impaired students. Due to admissions and placement testing practices and differences between written English and American Sign Language (ASL), many students with hearing impairments will be admitted or placed into developmental education programs. Mounty (1990) states, "standardized tests are problematic for deaf individuals, primarily due to difficulties with English" (p. 13). Even testing with accommodations such as extended time and an interpreter to sign the instructions has not shown considerable gains in scores. "As a group, deaf students have been found to earn lower SAT-Verbal and SAT-Math scores than the general population" (Mounty, 1990, p. 13). Studies that explore differences between written English and ASL studies have found the language of deaf students to be similar in English usage to that of nonnative speakers. The test scores that most students who are deaf receive on standardized admissions tests and institutional placement tests are lower than their hearing peers (Mounty, 1990; Ragosta, 1987; Willingham, Ragosta, Bennett, Braun, Rock, & Powers, 1988). As a result, many students with hearing impairments are placed in developmental education programs.

Although the fairness of standard admissions procedures deserves further discussion, the purpose of this article is to address equal access measures that are essential for deaf and hearing impaired students to be successful in developmental education programs. The intent is to provide an introduction to common concerns and needs of students with hearing impairments. It is hoped that this article will enhance understanding of how developmental education faculty can meet the instructional needs of these students in the classroom.

ADA Guidelines

To assure equal opportunity to all programs and activities, institutions are required to provide what the ADA refers to as auxiliary aids. The Federal Register (Office of the Attorney General, 1991), which provides guidelines for addressing the communication needs of people with hearing impairments, defines auxiliary aids as follows:

> Auxiliary aids and services include qualified interpreters, notetakers, transcription services, written materials, telephone handset amplifiers, assistive listening devices, assistive listening systems, telephones compatible with hearing aids, closed caption decoders, open and closed captioning, telecommunication devices for the deaf (TDDs), videotext displays or other effective means of making aurally delivered materials available to individuals with hearing impairments. (p. 35717)

The listed items above are examples of accommodations that may assist in providing equal access to classes and campus activities. The Federal Register (Office of the Attorney General, 1991) specifies that this is not an exhaustive list of auxiliary aids and services; new devices continue to become available through emerging technology. Federal legislation further dictates that it is not only the institution's responsibility to provide equal access through appropriate auxiliary aids and services but also to demonstrate a good faith effort to provide the student's preferred accommodation (Office of the Attorney General, 1991). The regulations accentuate the importance of responding to each person with a disability on an individual basis rather than assuming that the same auxiliary aid or service will accommodate an entire group of deaf people. For instance, it may be presumed that the provision of a sign language interpreter meets the communication needs of students with hearing impairments; in actuality many people who are hearing impaired do not utilize sign language as their preferred mode of communication.

Oral Communication

The most challenging obstacle for students with hearing impairments is in the area of oral communication. Communication is of utmost importance in classroom instruction. Students who are totally deaf may request the use of a sign language interpreter. Others who have some residual hearing may rely on speech reading or use an assistive listening device in the classroom. In order for the student to communicate with the faculty member by telephone, an amplified receiver or a telecommunication device may be necessary. Together, the instructor and student must determine the best mode of communication to provide access to the spoken lecture, question and answer periods, group discussions, audio and video presentations, review sessions, and individual meetings between the student and the instructor.

Speech Reading

Some students rely on speech reading, also referred to as lip reading. Speech reading is a skill that is dependent on previous training, practice, proximity to the speaker, lighting, and clarity of the speaker's oral presentation. It is affected by differences in facial features (e.g., a mustache) and the limited mouth movement of some speakers. Group discussion precludes the ability to speech read except in very controlled situations in which the speech reader is given sufficient time to locate and focus upon each new speaker.

Speech reading is extremely difficult because only 30 percent of spoken English is visible on the lips (Newby, 1964; Zemlin, 1968). For example, sounds may look alike because they are produced at the same point of articulation, such as mat, pat, and bat. The beginning sounds of these words are bilabial sounds articulated by the lips. Sounds that are articulated at the juncture of the tongue and the hard palate, such as dog, tog, and log, are only partially visible. The remaining 70 percent of English speech is formed in less visible locations. For instance, the beginning sounds in the words cot, hot, and got are formed in the back of the mouth. Skilled speech readers look for contextual cues to assist them in determining the message. This is extremely difficult when the subject matter is new to the student and when the conversation is not rooted in a known context. Other barriers to speech reading are an inadequate view of the speaker, facial hair, foreign or regional accents, poor lighting, or instructors turning their backs to the class in order to write on the board.

Assistive Listening Devices

Depending on the classroom environment, students with hearing impairments may choose to use an assistive listening device (ALD). These systems are beneficial to students who have sufficient residual hearing to enable them to benefit from the increased amplification and decreased environmental noise. The ALD amplifies and transmits the instructor's voice to students anywhere in the lecture hall as if the students were situated in close proximity to the instructor. The ALD reduces interference from environmental noises such as air conditioners, conversation between other students, shuffling of papers, and other distracting noises in a typical classroom setting. The most common types of ALDs are frequency modulated (FM) systems, which operate on radio frequencies, and infrared systems, which operate on infrared light waves. Depending on the institutional needs (e.g., size of classroom, number of users, acoustics), a determination can be made regarding which type of system would be most beneficial to the student as well as practical for the academic setting.

The FM system, which is comprised of a pocket size transmitter and receiver, is a convenient and transportable system for college students. The instructor wears a lapel microphone attached to the amplifier. The amplifier unit can be placed in a pocket or clipped on a belt or waistband. If the instructor intends to remain in one place, the microphone can be clipped onto a podium or connected directly to the sound system. Amplification occurs for the speaker only; therefore, questions and comments from the other participants must be repeated by the instructor. The student wears the receiving unit, which functions similarly to a powerful hearing aid. These and other helpful devices are available through a number of different companies, such as Comtek and Phonic Ear. It is our recommendation that the institution invite regional representatives to demonstrate available technology and discuss the compatibility of equipment with the institution's specific needs (i.e., large lecture halls, compatibility with existing sound systems, technical support from the manufacturer). When involved in renovations or new construction, it is important to refer to the Federal Register (Office of the Attorney General, 1991), which states:

> such assembly areas, if (1) they accommodate at least 50 persons, or if they have audio-amplification systems, and (2) they have fixed seating, shall have a permanently installed assistive listening system. . . . The minimum number of receivers to be provided shall be equal to 4 percent of the total number of seats, but in no case less than two. (p. 35616)

Included in this stipulation are concert and lecture halls, playhouses, movie theaters, and meeting rooms.

Interpreters

Students with severe hearing impairments may not benefit from hearing aids or assistive listening devices. If the student's preferred mode of communication is sign language, a sign language interpreter should be used to facilitate communication between the student, the instructor, and the class. The interpreter's role is to convey all verbal communication to the deaf student and to voice all signed responses, enabling the student to actively participate during class sessions. A student who does not know sign language may request an oral interpreter. The oral interpreter is situated in close proximity to the student and is responsible for presenting information via mouth movement, facial expression, and appropriate rephrasing to assure clarity of reception of spoken material. The interpreting process occurs simultaneously while the class is being taught.

As information is being presented to the class, a natural 5- to 10-second delay occurs as information is received and transmitted by the interpreter. It is helpful to allow for this brief delay when calling upon students to answer a question in order to allow sufficient time to receive and process the information. It is important to talk directly to the student and use natural speech patterns. A common pitfall for those new at working with interpreters is to refer to the student in the third person, such as "tell her that the test is postponed." It is more appropriate and efficient to direct communication to the student.

Based on the student's preference, the interpreter may sit directly in front of the student, stand on a platform with the instructor, or even follow the instructor if he or she moves around or frequently uses the chalk board. At first the presence of the interpreter may be a distraction for students and a new experience for the instructor, but after a few days the novelty of the experience wears off and all parties adjust. It has been our experience that the majority of faculty members are quite willing to accommodate an interpreter in their classrooms. One way to enlist cooperation and support is by conducting teaching orientation sessions prior to the first day of class. This time can be utilized to explain the role of the interpreter, demonstrate the communication mode, discuss learning and teaching styles, request additional copies of handouts, and observe the actual classroom location to determine the appropriate interpreter placement and lighting.

Sign language interpreters who are state or nationally certified are professionals, work under a strict code of ethics, and are not permitted to share information about the student. The Registry of Interpreters for the Deaf Code of Ethics states that interpreters should not "counsel, advise, or interject personal opinions" (Caccamise et al., 1980, p. 12). If instructors have questions or concerns pertaining to the student's performance, attendance, or understanding of the lecture, they are encouraged to first approach the student directly, and if necessary to consult with a representative from the institution's disability resource office. The Code of Ethics also emphasizes the importance of accurately conveying the message of the instructor. It states that it is the interpreter's responsibility to "render the message faithfully, always conveying the content and spirit of the speaker" (Caccamise et al., 1980, p. 12). The interpreter does not rearrange the lecture of a disorganized professor or convey a boring rendition of an animated and enthusiastic instructor. Faculty should be assured that the interpreter's presence is solely for the purpose of facilitating accurate communication in the classroom.

The responsibility for hiring qualified interpreters belongs with the college or university. According to both the ADA (1990) and Section 504 of the Rehabilitation Act of 1973, auxiliary aids may include taped texts, interpreters, or other effective methods of making orally delivered materials available to students with hearing impairments. In the United States v. Board of Trustees for the University of Alabama (1990), both the district and appeals courts held that a university must provide auxiliary aids to students with documented disabilities for whom aids are necessary to enable learning.

Telecommunication Devices for the Deaf

Students with communication disorders may also wish to converse with faculty over the telephone. To place telephone calls, students with a speech or hearing disability commonly use a Telecommunication Device for the Deaf (TDD). The TDD has a keyboard and visual display to assist in the communication. Both parties must have a TDD unless the Telecommunication Relay Service (TRS) is utilized. Further information about this service is available in the local telephone book. The TRS allows a student using a TDD to communicate with faculty who only have access to a standard voice telephone. The student uses the TDD to call the TRS; then the TRS provider communicates the student's message orally to the faculty member and vice versa. However, direct contact with the student via a TDD is preferred. TDDs range in cost from $300 to $700. It would be helpful to install a portable TDD in each major building on campus and develop an interdepartmental policy for sharing this resource. If this is not possible, the availability of a TDD in the institution's student center as well as in the primary administration building is imperative.

Suggestions for Oral Communication

There are several suggestions that can assist faculty in teaching students who are deaf or hearing impaired. It is important to enunciate clearly and speak at a moderate pace. It is not necessary to overexaggerate.

Remaining in front of the classroom and facing forward to present a clear view of the face while lecturing enhances the student's ability to read the faculty member's lips. When the instructor turns toward the board, students with hearing impairments lose a main source of information. When writing on the board is necessary, the teacher must pause long enough to give students an opportunity to read the board before continuing to speak. It is critical that instructors do not smoke, chew gum, or otherwise block the area around the mouth with hands or other objects while lecturing. During question and answer sessions, questions from students in the class should be repeated. Before small group discussions, students should be reminded that only one student may speak at a time. This is common courtesy, and need not be addressed in a manner that singles out or embarrasses students with hearing impairments.

The use of visual aids in class enhances learning for students with diverse learning styles, not just those with hearing impairments. By using an overhead projector, faculty can continue to face the class while writing information that might otherwise be written on the chalkboard. The use of captioned videotapes is also recommended. Most current educational films as well as theatrical releases are encoded with closed or open captions. A symbol on the jacket of the video indicates whether captions are present. Televisions with closed captioned decoders are an essential equipment purchase for any institution serving students with hearing impairments. All new televisions are now equipped with decoders.

As much structure as possible should be provided. The course syllabus should be precise, providing attendance policies, grading criteria, test dates, and due dates for any assignments or papers. When possible, the faculty member can provide considerable assistance by giving the student (and interpreter, if appropriate) an outline of each lecture in advance. The use of handouts is also encouraged. Handouts assist all students in the class, not just those with hearing impairments. The instructor should be available immediately before and after the lecture to provide clarification and respond to questions. Office hours should be listed on the syllabus. If appointments outside of class are necessary, arrangements for an interpreter must be made in advance.

Written Communication

Many people believe that hearing loss implies merely the inability to hear sounds, but that is certainly not the only impact that deafness has upon an individual. Depending on the age of onset and the severity of the hearing loss, an individual's spoken language development may be radically affected. Normally, language development begins with an infant's babbling and relies heavily on repetition of sounds that are heard in the child's environment. As hearing children develop their language, they modify it and model the language of people around them, incorporating vocabulary development, syntax, and grammatical structures (Meier, 1991). "Prelingual deafness refers to the condition of persons whose deafness was present at birth or occurred at an age prior to the development of speech and language" (Moores, 1982, p. 7). Individuals with prelingual hearing loss cannot rely on auditory means of learning English as a spoken language; they have had no opportunity to do so. An individual who has a postlingual hearing loss, "the condition of persons whose deafness occurred at an age following the spontaneous acquisition of speech and language" (Moores, 1982, p. 7), may initially develop similarly to that of a hearing child. At the onset of the hearing loss, however, the monitoring system and the modeling that continues to occur for a hearing child no longer exists. Spoken language development, therefore, is an integral part of hearing loss that also affects an individual's ability to utilize the English language in written form.

A prelingually deaf student will generally demonstrate a more restricted vocabulary, grammatical errors in verb and tense agreement, and errors in word usage. For example, a freshman student wrote, "a boy from the other team came charging through my nose with his elbow." A hearing student would select different word usage. Hearing people often check their written language by playing an imaginary audio tape in their heads and correcting their word usage or verb tense agreement by saying "that doesn't sound right." A deaf student does not have the luxury of relying on the sound or familiarity of which words go together in spoken speech.

In opposition to learning through auditory modeling, deaf students learn English in a printed form or visual form. Many college students who utilize sign language may not be exposed to sign language prior to the age of four or five. Some deaf students experience a delay in their development of English because they are not exposed to an effective communicative method until they enter a formal educational setting. This late introduction may present a delay in language development and could be avoided if the parents took the initiative to learn sign language immediately after the child is born (Meier, 1991). Children that are born to deaf parents have an advantage in language development because they are exposed to signing from their infancy. However, 90 percent of deaf children are born to hearing parents and will not be exposed to sign language until either their parents learn or they enter an educational institution that utilizes manual communication (Meier, 1991).

American Sign Language and Written English

A deaf child that is born into a deaf family and utilizes ASL has the distinct advantage of early language development. ASL is considered a language as is English, French, or any other language (Meier, 1991). It has a grammatical structure, a syntactical structure, and many other components that linguists have documented to determine that it does indeed exist as a formal language. It differs greatly from English in its word order and its grammar and how concepts and subtleties are expressed. For example, an English greeting such as "Thank you for coming this morning. I'm pleased to see so many people interested in this topic" would be expressed in ASL via the following glosses: "Thank you (plural) come here today. Many you (plural) interested topic. Happy me." This example of ASL "gloss" in written form appears to contain many errors in English usage and grammar. However, it contains no English at all. It is an example of ASL and follows the rules set forth by ASL. Thus, the student who has developed ASL skills will also have difficulty with standard English in the written form. The writing of students whose native language is not English will exhibit some of the same characteristics as international students for whom English is a second language.

Suggestions for Written Communication

When faculty members encounter a deaf student, they should meet with the deaf student's counselor in order to gain a better understanding of how the disability affects written language and to discuss appropriate accommodations (Kelly, 1995). In an English class, it is crucial to explain writing errors to the student and how to improve them. Weekly appointments with the instructor would assist both the deaf student and the instructor in getting to know each other and recognizing recurring errors that are directly related to the deafness. Students need to utilize a dictionary, thesaurus, and a grammar check software program if available. These are excellent tools for improving written English. A proofreader can be very helpful in eliminating glaring errors in English usage. The proofreader can circle errors so that the deaf student can improve writing skills by making corrections. If a student is enrolled in a class with an emphasis on content, such as a history class, instructors should be encouraged to focus on content rather than English proficiency when grading a deaf student's paper.

Written tests may also demonstrate the implications of the disability (Mounty, 1990). A deaf graduate student recently tested using a multiple choice and essay format test answered all the multiple choice items correctly. However, the student's responses on the essays did not reflect an understanding of the content at all. The instructor felt strongly that the deaf student demonstrated knowledge both in class and in the multiple choice section of the test and proposed clarifying both the essay questions and the student's answers to them. In order to reconcile the apparent miscommunication, the instructor suggested that the student have an opportunity to clarify the answers without relying on the written word. This is an excellent example of an accommodation that should be considered in similar situations. Essay exams can be administered orally with an interpreter present.

Faculty Responsibility

In order to provide appropriate accommodations, faculty will need support from other resources on campus. However, it is imperative that faculty members understand that they bear the responsibility for insuring that students with hearing impairments have equal access to the information presented in their classrooms. Many campuses do not have specific offices to serve students with disabilities. Even on campuses that do have centralized services, it may be the responsibility of the teacher to arrange for a notetaker in the class or to make the necessary arrangements for audiovisual services.

Developmental educators are likely to be among the first to need to rise to this challenge. Fortunately, most developmental classes are kept small to provide individualized instruction. Developmental educators are aware of the importance of maintaining a high level of structure in the developmental classroom (Higbee, 1991, 1988). Many of the suggestions for serving students with hearing impairments will improve the learning environment for all students. Although the placement of students with hearing impairments in developmental education programs may, to some extent, be based upon criteria that discriminate against students with disabilities, developmental educators may be among those best equipped to assure that these students' initial college experiences are positive ones.

References

Americans with Disabilities Act of 1990, 42 U.S.C. § 12101 (1990).

Caccamise, F., Dirst, R., DeVries, R. D., Heil, J., Kirchner, C., Kirchner, S., Rinaldi A. M., & Stangarone, J. (1980). Registry of Interpreters for the Deaf (RID). Code of ethics. In Caccamise et al. (Eds.). *Introduction to interpreting for interpreters/transliterators, hearing-impaired consumers, hearing consumers* (pp. 10–14). Silver Spring, MD: Registry of Interpreters for the Deaf.

Higbee, J. L. (1988). Student development theory: A foundation for the individualized instruction of high risk freshmen. *Journal of Educational Opportunity, 3*(1), 42–47.

Higbee, J. L. (1991). The role of developmental education in promoting pluralism. In Cheatham, H. E. (Ed.), *Cultural pluralism on campus* (pp. 73–87). Alexandria, VA: American College Personnel Association.

Jaschik, S. (1993). Backed by 1990 law, people with disabilities press demands on colleges. *The Chronicle of Higher Education, 39*(22), A 26.

Karchmer, M. A., & Rawlings, B. W. (1991). Changes in postsecondary education opportunities for deaf students during the 1980s. In E. G. Wolf-Schein, & J. D. Schein (Eds.), *Postsecondary Education for Deaf Students* (pp. 27–37). Alberta, Canada: University of Alberta.

Kelly, L. P. (1995). Processing of bottom-up and top-down information by skilled and average deaf readers and implications for whole language instruction. *Exceptional Children, 61*(4), 318–334.

Meier, R. P. (1991). Language acquisition by deaf children. *American Scientist, 79*(1), 60–70.

Moores, D. F. (1982). *Educating the deaf: Psychology, principles, and practices.* Dallas, TX: Houghton Mifflin Company.

Mounty, J. L. (1990). Testing deaf individuals: Equity in test conditions and test format. *Selected Proceedings of the 1990 AHSSPPE Conference,* 13–18.

Newby, H. A. (1964). *Audiology.* New York: Meredith Corporation.

Office of the Attorney General, Department of Justice. (1991, July). Nondiscrimination on the basis of disability in state and local government services: Final rule. *Federal Register,* 28 CFR Part 35.

Ragosta, M. (1987). *Students with disabilities: Four years of data from special administrations of the SAT: 1980–1983.* New York: College Entrance Examination Board.

Rawlings, B., Karchmer, M., DeCaro, J., & Allen, T. (1995). *College and career programs for deaf students* (9th ed.). Washington, DC: Gallaudet University.

Section 504, Rehabilitation Act of 1973, 29 U.S.C. § 794 as amended (1973).

United States v. Board of Trustees for the University of Alabama, 908 F.2d 740 (1990).

Willingham, W. W., Ragosta, M., Bennett, R. E., Braun, H., Rock, D. A., & Powers, D. E. (1988). *Testing handicapped people.* Boston: Allyn and Bacon.

Zemlin, W. R. (1968). *Speech and hearing science.* Englewood Cliffs, NJ: Prentice-Hall.

Additional Readings

Fink, R. J. (1998). "The educational challenge of multiple disabilities in the postsecondary setting." *Journal of College Reading and Learning,* 28 (2), 148–55. (To be read after Leone & Hylton [1998] below.)

Leone, P., & Hylton, J. (1998). "It's all your fault!" *Journal of College Reading and Learning,* 28 (2), 141–47. (To be read before Fink [1998] above.)

Nelson, R. R. (1998). "Achievement difficulties for the academically gifted." *Journal of College Reading and Learning,* 28 (2), 117–23. (To be read before Weinsheimer [1998] below.)

Peltzman, B. (1990). "Techniques to help learning disabled students meet the challenges of college life." *Research and Teaching in Developmental Education,* 6 (2), 97–101.

Rose, M. (1989). *Lives on the boundary.* New York: Penguin Books.

Smith, C. M., & Wiener, J. (1999). "Development and validation of the Smith Learning Disabilities Screen." *Journal of College Reading and Learning,* 30 (1), 62–84.

Sweener, K., Kundert, D., May, D., & Quinn, K. (2002). "Comfort with accommodations at the community college level." *Journal of Developmental Education,* 25 (3), 12–18, 42.

Valeri-Gold, M., Callahan, C. A., Deming, M. P., & Mangram, M. T. (1997). "Reflections: Experience commentaries by urban developmental studies students." In P. L. Dwinell & J. L. Higbee (Eds.), *Developmental education: Enhancing student retention* (pp. 3–18). Carol Stream, IL: National Association of Developmental Education.

Vogel, S. A., & Adelman, P. B. (1992). *Success for college students with learning disabilities.* New York: Springer-Verlag.

Weinsheimer, J. E. (1998). "Helping students get off probation and on with their education." *Journal of College Reading and Learning,* 28 (2), 124–31. (To be read after Nelson [1998] above.)

7

Reading in the Content Areas

This century has brought a growing recognition that learners must master particular strategies in order to read and study in specific content fields. Literacy theorists and instructors have come to understand not only that students need to develop "reading to learn" strategies so that they can locate, comprehend, recall, and retrieve information, but also that they must master "reading to do" strategies in order to conduct lab experiments, complete case reports, construct mechanical/technological devices, and so on.

As early as 1937 William S. Gray championed the idea that every teacher should include reading instruction in his or her content area courses, but the reality is that content area instructors at both the secondary and postsecondary level are primarily concerned with the delivery of their subject matter. Indeed, it is unlikely that professors offering general education courses have even had general training in pedagogy much less in academic literacy skills. So, college reading instructors and learning assistance specialists are often asked to fill the void through classes and workshops. Consequently, helping students transfer skills from developmental reading and study strategy classes to content area courses has been of paramount interest to both researchers and instructors.

The articles in this chapter focus on students' learning in the content areas. Through Michele Simpson's work we learn of a number of methods by which college reading instructors and learning assistance personnel can become acquainted with the academic demands of content area classes. The articles by Julia Beyeler and Jodi Patrick

Holschuh tell how college students approach content field reading and learning demands in a psychology course and a biology course, respectively.

Conducting Reality Checks to Improve Students' Strategic Learning

Michele L. Simpson

A fundamental mission of learning strategies instruction is to promote students' willingness and ability to transfer strategies from a developmental reading and learning course to content courses. Michele Simpson points out that to promote such a transfer of strategies, instructors must know of the actual reading, writing, and learning demands of the professors in each of the core content area courses. Given the sheer number of courses at any school, this is not an easy task.

Here, Simpson reviews the "reality checks" she has used to determine the tasks and texts her students encounter beyond her classroom. We learn of procedures such as observing course sessions, interviewing instructors, reviewing sample syllabi, surveying faculty about course literacy demands, and having students interview faculty. Finally, the author demonstrates the value of both one-time telephone interviews and longitudinal case studies of former students to learn about their use of various learning strategies they were taught.

Most academic assistance program models at the college level in the U.S. share a common goal — the development of strategic learners (Nist, 1993). Students who are strategic have a repertoire of effective and efficient strategies for reading their texts, taking notes from lectures, and preparing for exams and papers. More importantly, strategic learners know how and when to modify and transfer those strategies to their own tasks in their content area courses (Stahl, Simpson, & Hayes, 1992).

Strategy transfer, however, is difficult to promote (Pressley, 1995). One reason it becomes difficult for students to transfer spontaneously the strategies they have learned in academic assistance programs is that the instruction they have received has often been "isolated from the rest of the instructional system" and practiced in "contrived texts" (Schallert, Alexander, & Goetz, 1988, p. 213). As a result, when students confront a difficult history or chemistry lab exam that seemingly does not fit the generic study skills they have learned, they become overwhelmed and generally resort to ineffectual approaches such as memorizing facts and details (Simpson & Nist, 1992).

Pintrich and Garcia (1994) and others (e.g., Carson, Chase, Gibson, & Hargrove, 1992; Nist, 1993) have suggested that college students can learn to become strategic learners when academic assistance efforts reflect the actual learning tasks required by professors in the core content area courses. The obvious implication is that instructors involved in academic assistance must become familiar with and immersed in the reading, writing, and thinking demands placed upon their students. Instructors then would use that information to identify relevant strategies that students would practice with actual content area texts.

Given that most instructors in academic assistance programs teach countless students and classes, this immersion in the academic milieu of their institution seems a formidable task. However, there are several ways in which instructors can discover more about the tasks and texts their students encounter daily. I have used these ways or "reality checks" as a means of gathering information that has enabled me to help students become more strategic.

This article will explain these reality checks as well as what information should be gathered from a reality check. Although the ideas shared in this article are from the perspective of a professor who teaches required and elective reading/learning strategy courses for underprepared and regularly admitted students, I think instructors in other settings would benefit.

What Should Be Learned from a Reality Check?

Many questions need to be examined if learning strategy instructors are to understand the reading, writing, and thinking demands placed upon students in their content area courses. The following questions are examples:

1. What types of reading materials are students being assigned? Are any of the assigned readings primary sources such as diaries or letters?

2. What is the relationship between the assigned readings and the activities in class?

3. Are students assigned to read merely one text or are they expected to synthesize ideas across multiple texts?

4. Do professors expect students to read the assignments before class?

5. Do professors provide an overview of their lectures in the form of an outline or a map?

6. Do professors organize their lectures inductively or deductively?

7. Are students required to write papers outside of class? What type of paper (research, reaction, or critique)?

8. What type of tests will students be given (essay, objective, or some other variation)?

9. What level of thinking is required to answer those exam questions?

10. What criteria are used to evaluate the students' essay answers or written work?

These are some of the questions that need to be answered so that students' transfer of strategies can occur. In the next section some general methods for conducting reality checks will be shared.

General Methods for Conducting Reality Checks

There are many ways in which learning strategy instructors can obtain more information about the academic demands facing their students. The most obvious way is to observe some of the core content area courses that baffle students. Because this type of reality check necessitates a large commitment of time, I have tried limiting my participation and observation in a course to one unit of instruction and the first exam.

A second way of conducting a reality check is to interview the professors teaching a particular core course. Because it is impossible to interview all professors, especially on a large campus, I have found it useful to select the high-risk courses that first- and second-year students typically fail. The questions previously discussed in this article are usually a good starting point for the interview. In addition, I have found it useful to try to define how the professor perceives learning and the academic discipline, whether it be history, geography, or sociology. For example, does the instructor have a social-political or military perspective of history?

The major disadvantage of these visits and one-on-one interviews is that they require a lot of time. Given my teaching load, I could never hope to interview all the history professors at my institution, nor could I visit all the biology labs. Hence, in order to really understand what happens in a biology or history course, I have learned to rely on some more efficient ways of conducting reality checks. Some of these are from the perspective of the professors and some are from the perspective of the students. Four of these methods will be discussed in the next section.

Time Efficient Methods for Conducting Reality Checks

The following methods, when combined with actual classroom observations or professor interviews or with one another, are efficient ways of conducting reality checks.

Requesting Sample Syllabi from Professors

About 4 years ago a colleague of mine decided to write to the professors teaching core content area courses at our institution and request copies of their syllabi. I initially laughed at her naiveté because I thought that this letter would become filed under a mountain of bulletins and other requests seemingly distributed hourly at our institution. Remarkably, about 50 percent of the professors replied by sending their syllabi, and some others sent additional materials such as sample study questions or problems.

I used the information from those syllabi to help me revise my lessons and units in my courses. For example, I learned that many professors in history and sociology were requiring students to read novels. Therefore, I decided to include a unit in the required reading course on how to read and study literature when it is used to explain or reinforce content area concepts.

In addition, those syllabi helped me educate first-quarter students about the demands of the core content area courses they would soon be taking. To help students become familiar with these courses and their reading demands, I distributed copies of these sample syllabi and required the students to analyze them using questions much like the following:

1. Does the professor list the required texts? If so, how many are there? Any novels, magazines, or newspapers required? Any materials from the professor? Does the professor recommend optional readings in the library?

2. Does the professor explain the goals of the course or how he/she wants you to think about the content of the course?

3. Does the professor explain the types of tests given? If so, what kind are given? Is the final comprehensive? How many tests will be given during the quarter?

4. Does the professor provide a schedule of reading assignments? How many chapters are assigned each week? Given that most college chapters are about 30 pages long, how many pages per week are you expected to read and study?

This assignment was an impressive reality check for the students. Most of them were shocked to discover the number of chapters or pages covered in 1 week, especially in the history and political science courses.

Requesting sample syllabi from core content area professors is a quick and informative way of conducting a reality check. The information obtained from the syllabi can also supplement a learning strategy instructor's classroom observations and validate the many comments from students about a particular course or professor.

Sending Out Faculty Questionnaires

Questionnaires are a time efficient way to define the academic literacy demands of any institution. These questionnaires can be written to investigate the academic literacy demands of a certain curriculum from the perspective of the professors or the students. Some researchers have sent questionnaires to faculty members in order to define one type of academic literacy such as the use of language and writing tasks across the academic disciplines (e.g., Anderson, Best, Black, Hurst, Miller, & Miller, 1990). Other researchers have examined the demands placed upon special populations such as nonnative speakers (e.g., Christison & Krahnke, 1986).

At my institution several faculty members who were involved in the Academic Literacy Committee decided to create a questionnaire that would describe the reading, writing, listening, speaking, and problem-solving processes essential for student success in the core content area courses. The faculty members involved in the committee were from the Division of Academic Assistance, the College of Arts and Sciences, and the College of Education.

The committee began by describing the purposes for the instrument that eventually became the Academic Literacy Questionnaire (ALQ). Specifically, we wanted to answer three questions: (a) What are the academic literacy demands that beginning college students should meet in order to succeed in their core courses? (b) What are the differences in academic literacy demands among professors and across academic disciplines? and (c) What are faculty concerns about these academic literacy processes?

We then spent 6 months writing sample questions and piloting the items with five different professors who taught core courses and with a committee of professors from the Office of Instructional Development. The final version of the ALQ contained 35 open-ended and close-ended items so that we could collect both quantitative and qualitative data. The open-ended questions asked the professors to explain the most serious cognitive and affective problems that students have in their courses and to offer suggestions on how students could be better prepared for their courses. The close-ended questions were created so that the professors could check the appropriate answers or fill in the blanks with one or two words. The first set of close-ended questions asked professors about their predominant class format, types of required texts and tests/quizzes, and the level of thinking required in their courses. The rest of the close-ended questions focused on issues relevant to reading, studying, writing, problem solving, and numeracy. Some of those questions are illustrated in Figure 1.

The committee sent the questionnaire to 440 professors and received 223 back, a return rate of 51 percent. Obviously, the professors' answers to our questions produced voluminous amounts of data. In fact, it took us almost 3 months just to analyze and organize the data. When the data were coded and analyzed, we learned a lot about the core courses and the academic demands expected of first- and second-year students at our institution.

Figure 1. Sample Questions from the Academic Literacy Questionnaire

1. When I give an essay test, I emphasize (check all that are appropriate):
    ____ Synthesis/summarization of material in the course
    ____ Analysis or critique of concepts
    ____ Definition and examples of concepts
    ____ Application of concepts
    ____ Comparison/contrast of concepts
    ____ Problem solving
    ____ Argumentation of a thesis or point of view
    ____ Other (explain)

2. The writing demands in my class consist of (check the appropriate answers):
    ____ Filling in the blanks on exams
    ____ Short answers on exams
    ____ Essay exams
    ____ Lab reports
    ____ Library research projects
    ____ Other (explain)

3. I use the following criteria for evaluating students' written assignments:_____
   _____

4. On the average, I expect my students to read _____ number of pages per week from the textbook and other materials.

5. I expect students to be able to understand on their own the concepts from the assigned textbook:
    ____ Most of the time   ____ Occasionally   ____ Rarely

I discovered from the ALQ that many of the strategies I was teaching students in our required courses and elective learning strategy courses were appropriate and relevant. What was needed, however, was more practice across the content areas so that students would have the opportunity to modify the strategies.

For example, I learned from the ALQ that short-answer tests were more prevalent than I had imagined. In fact, 46 percent of the professors reported that they gave short-answer questions on their exams. Hence, I decided to place more emphasis on PORPE (Simpson, 1986) because the goal of the five-step strategy (Predict, Organize, Rehearse, Practice, Evaluate) is to help students prepare for recall tests.

In the revisions of the elective learning strategy course, I now include for each content area chapter some activities that help students learn how to predict possible test questions. In addition, the students learn how to answer those questions completely and accurately, because many of the professors indicated in their comments that students were far too general in their responses to essay and short-answer questions.

As a result of the comments on the ALQ from geology, biology, physics, and chemistry professors, I decided to spend more time teaching strategies for reading and studying scientific and process-related material. The students in my class read a chapter on the endocrine system taken from a college-level biology textbook. I added lessons that involved my students in taking notes from a biology professor who lectured on negative feedback loops and the male and female reproductive systems. The students then had to integrate that information from the lecture with the key ideas from their assigned reading. In addition, I spent time discussing how to study charts and diagrams in biology and other process-oriented classes. At the end of the unit the students took an exam similar in format to the ones given in the biology department.

The committee members also learned from the ALQ that library projects were not a common assignment. This finding was surprising to me since I had assumed that library research was an integral part of many of the core courses such as sociology and political science. However, only 19 percent of the professors reported that they assigned students a library project or paper as a course requirement. Many of the professors reported in the questionnaire that they had at one time or another required library research, but gave up on this assignment because students did so poorly on it. From the professors' comments it appeared that students had difficulty not only using the library, but also synthesizing the research and then writing it into a cogent paper.

The only students coerced into learning how to use the library and its databases are the ones required to take the reading course from the Division of Academic Assistance. The committee decided that it would be important for all students to learn how to conduct research and write a research paper; thus, the Division of Academic Assistance now offers an elective course called Writing a Research Paper, which is open to any undergraduate student at the university.

A faculty questionnaire such as the ALQ can inform and confirm hunches about what students need to know to survive and thrive as strategic learners. However, to successfully obtain useful information from a questionnaire, I would recommend the following guidelines:

1. Create your own questionnaire rather than trying to use some other institution's. When a questionnaire has been written to suit the idiosyncrasies of an institution, the faculty receiving the questionnaire will be more likely to complete and return it.

2. Allow a sufficient amount of time to create, distribute, analyze, and share the results of the questionnaire with colleagues. Our committee took 2 years in the process.

3. Involve a variety of professors across the campus in determining the questions that need to be answered. On our committee were

history professors as well as faculty and support staff involved with helping learning disabled students.

4. Seek external support for the questionnaire from an administrator or from a committee of respected faculty members.

5. Make sure to pilot questions with faculty from all content areas. When our committee did this, we discovered from the science professors that our questions had omitted the role of labs for courses such as biology and chemistry.

Sample syllabi and faculty questionnaires both focus on academic literacy demands from the perspective of the professors teaching the courses. The next two ways of conducting reality checks rely on students and their perceptions of what it takes to succeed in a course.

Requiring Students to Interview Their Professors

The students in my elective Learning to Learn course are usually very motivated to improve their grade point averages so they can be admitted to a certain program of studies, be removed from academic probation, or qualify for a certain scholarship. Ironically, many of these students have never considered the most obvious way to improve their understanding of what is necessary for success in a particular course — see the professor. Every quarter I would urge these students to visit their professors during office hours in order to find out how to read and study for the particular courses, but only a few would do this.

Therefore, last year I instituted the Faculty Interview Assignment, which the students had to complete for one of their core content area courses within the first 2 weeks of class. I recommend to the students that they select the course they are most worried about, not the course they like the most. As illustrated in Figure 2, the students are required to ask their chosen faculty member a set of certain questions, but they are welcome to supplement their interviews with additional questions. I also encourage the students to take their lecture notes, study strategies, or paper ideas for the professor's reactions. Some students have used the time to go over a test or paper, thus receiving their professors' feedback on what they needed to do to perform better for the next test or paper.

To make sure that all students complete this assignment, I award a large number of points for it. I also share with them samples of completed assignments from past quarters so they can see what other students have learned from the experience. In addition, on the day the students hand in their assignment, I devote the class period to their discussions of the experience. Students then hear what 20 different professors expect of their students in the way of reading, listening, studying, writing, and thinking.

Figure 2. Faculty Interview Assignment

Professor's name: _____

Course taught: _____

1. *Test format and type of questions.* If you have not taken a test yet, ask about the format of the test. Make sure this is not already spelled out for you on the syllabus. Then ask the professor to describe the type of questions asked on the test. Are there questions about key terms and people or theories and generalizations? Are the questions memory-level questions or thinking-level questions that require synthesis and application? Could he/she give you a sample question to guide your study?

2. *Lecture notes:* Ask the professor for suggestions on how to make sure you have quality notes from class. Does she/he recommend that you read before attending class? After class? Both? If you have a set of lecture notes with you, ask the professor to critique them. Ask about problems you hare having such as keeping up with the pacing of the lecture.

3. *Method of test preparation:* If you have already taken a test or written paper, you may wish to go over it with the profressor. In this way, you can determine what questions you missed and why. Explain how you studied or show the professor your strategies. If you have not taken a test or written a paper, ask the professor for suggestions.

Professor's signature:_____ Date:_____

The assignment has been extremely well received by my students. In their weekly journals I ask them to comment on assignments done in this course and their concerns with their core content area courses. The following comments typify what students think of this assignment (all names are pseudonyms):

> I really hated going to see my English instructor because she seemed so unapproachable and cold during class. However, in her office she opened up to me and told me exactly what I needed to do to write "A" papers for her. It was the best 30 minutes I ever spent! I plan on going back to see her. (Tabitha)

> I found my economics professor to be really helpful during my visit. In fact, he told me that he rarely sees any of his students, but would like to. Now the professor calls on me during class and I feel I must keep up with the work not to disappoint him. (Corey)

> I showed my anthropology professor my chapter annotations just like you said. He was impressed with the idea and said I should continue annotating and putting ideas into my own words. This strategy really helped me on the first quiz. (Shawn)

This assignment has informed my students and me about the reading, writing, and thinking demands in the core courses. Serendipitously, it has also informed many professors about the Learning to

Learn course and learning strategies such as textbook annotation. The students have told me that most of their professors did not even know such a course existed. The public relations gained from such an assignment have probably been more potent than those from any newspaper article.

Conducting Student Interviews

Once students have exited a required reading course or have completed an elective course such as Learning to Learn, it is important to keep in touch with them. Most academic assistance programs designate someone to collect quantitative data such as former students' grade point averages and graduation rates as a part of their summative program evaluations. However, it is also important to collect qualitative data from the students. More specifically, it is useful to define the strategies and ideas students have used in their courses and to trace how they have modified these strategies to fit their academic and personal needs. This information, which can be collected from student interviews or questionnaires, can be useful in curricular planning as well as in defining academic demands on the campus.

To determine what strategies former students were using and modifying for their various courses, I have conducted two types of interviews. The first type was a telephone interview of students formerly enrolled in the elective Learning to Learn course. I chose the telephone interview over sending a questionnaire because I wanted to interact with the students and to ask them questions that would provoke them into describing, rather than simply checking off, strategies that they use or do not use. Telephone interviews are also a quick way to find out about students' successes and failures and the reasons behind them.

Using a set of common questions, another academic assistance instructor and I made the telephone calls over 2 weeks. Some of those questions included the following:

1. What has been your most difficult course this term? How did you study for that course? Why did you study in that manner? Did that strategy/approach work? Why do you think so?

2. If you were to recommend some new units for Learning to Learn, what would they be? Why would you like to learn them?

3. If someone asked you what you learned from Learning to Learn that made a difference for you, what would you say?

4. Have you modified any of the strategies you learned in the course? Which ones?

5. Which strategy from the course have you used most often? In which courses? Why? Which strategies have you never used? Why?

To obtain a representative sample and cross section of former students, we selected 10 students who had a cumulative grade point average of 3.00 (out of 4.00) or above and 10 students with a cumulative grade point average of 2.40 and below. All were students who had taken the course at least two quarters ago.

From these interviews I have collected a considerable amount of information. For example, I discovered that the students with the higher grades were using different strategies than the students who had the lower grades. The students with the higher grade point averages remembered the strategies by name and talked about how they used and modified them. In contrast, most of the students with the lower grade point averages could not remember the names of the strategies, nor could they talk about their use or modification. They did, however, offer suggestions on what they needed to learn — they wanted the course to teach them how to be motivated and less bored with their studies.

The second type of student interview is different in that fewer students are contacted, but the contact or interviews are more in depth. A doctoral student and I have been conducting such a longitudinal case study with a former academic assistance student whom we have interviewed and videotaped for 3 consecutive years. This student, Janie, was purposely chosen because she had maintained a 4.00 cumulative average in her core content area courses and her preveterinarian curriculum. By following Janie for such a long time we have been able to watch her modify and invent new strategies for her courses. For example, Janie told us that she studies for chemistry tests by pretending to teach someone the key concepts of the unit and by writing these concepts or formulas on a small dry erase board to support and illustrate what she is saying. I have borrowed this strategy from Janie and have taught it to my students in the elective learning strategy course.

I would recommend that both types of student interviews be employed because they provide different types of information. Interviewing requires patience, persistence, and flexibility because students are difficult to contact. In addition, interviewing requires that you ask questions that are open ended and thought provoking and that you listen carefully to what the students tell you and do not tell you. A good interviewer will then capitalize on those moments with additional probes.

Sensing the Big Picture

Learning strategy instructors should consider using a variety of reality checks because multiple methods of collecting data or information constitute what many researchers call triangulation (Merriam, 1991). The rationale of data triangulation is that a flaw in one method will be compensated for by the strength of another method. Thus, the researcher or instructor has a better opportunity for understanding the phenomenon being studied and sensing the big picture.

The big picture for learning strategy instructors is obviously an accurate appraisal of the reading, writing, and thinking demands their students encounter in academia. Once learning strategy instructors understand these academic demands, they will be better able to build curricula that facilitate their students' strategic learning.

References

Anderson, W., Best, W., Black, A., Hurst, I., Miller, B., & Miller, S. (1990). Cross-curricular underlife: A collaborative report on ways with academic words. *College Composition and Communication, 41*, 11–36.

Carson, G. C., Chase, N. D., Gibson, S. U., & Hargrove, M. F. (1992). Literacy demands of the undergraduate curriculum. *Reading Research and Instruction, 31*, 25–50.

Christison, M. A., & Krahnke, K. J. (1986). Student perceptions of academic language study. TESOL *Quarterly, 20*, 61–81.

Merriam, S. B. (1991). *Case study research in education: A qualitative approach.* San Francisco: Jossey-Bass.

Nist, S. L. (1993). What the literature says about academic literacy. *Georgia Journal of Reading, 19*, 11–18.

Pintrich, P. R., & Garcia, T. (1994). Self-regulated learning in college students: Knowledge, strategies, and motivation. In P. R., Pintrich, D. R. Brown, & C. E. Weinstein (Eds.), *Student motivation, cognition, and learning* (pp. 113–130). Hillsdale, NJ: Erlbaum.

Pressley, M. (1995). More about the development of self-regulation: Complex, long-term, and thoroughly social. *Educational Psychologist, 30*, 207–212.

Schallert, D. L., Alexander, P. A., & Goetz, E. T. (1988). Implicit instruction of strategies for learning from text. In C. E. Weinstein, E. T. Goetz, & P. A. Alexander (Eds.), *Learning and study strategies* (pp. 193–214). San Diego, CA: Academic Press.

Simpson, M. L. (1986). PORPE: A writing strategy for studying and learning in the content areas. *Journal of Reading, 29*, 407–414.

Simpson, M. L., & Nist, S. L. (1992). A case study of academic literacy tasks and their negotiation in a university history class. In C. K. Kinzer & D. J. Leu (Eds.), *Literacy research, theory, and practice: Views from many perspectives. 41st yearbook of the National Reading Conference* (pp. 253–260). Chicago: National Reading Conference.

Stahl, N. A., Simpson, M. L., & Hayes, C. G. (1992). Ten recommendations from research for teaching high-risk college students. *Journal of Developmental Education, 19*, 2–11.

Reluctant Readers: Case Studies of Reading and Study Strategies in Introduction to Psychology

Julia Beyeler

In "Reluctant Readers," Julia Beyeler provides case studies of four college students who underwent training to improve reading and learning strategies with particular emphasis placed upon the deep level strategy of reciprocal teaching. The author found that for the target course in introductory psychology, students believed that surface-level strategies — such as memorizing, acquiring facts, and learning terms — were sufficient to pass the course, and hence, those were the types of strategies employed during the semester. Strategies that seemed too difficult were not used at all.

Objective

The purpose of this study was to assist under prepared college students for college study at a small two year branch campus of a four year university in the rural Midwest where about 70 percent of the students plan to achieve a four year degree. The research guiding this study sought to determine the participants': (a) strengths and weaknesses of student study strategies in a conceptually difficult course, (b) ability to apply reciprocal teaching strategies to an Introduction to Psychology textbook with instruction, demonstration, and practice, (c) transfer of reading and learning strategies to other classes, and (d) changes in study strategies with instruction and demonstration. This study documents the participants' rationale and choices of study strategies in the above four areas.

Perspective and Theoretical Framework

Retention of college students is a high priority at many colleges and universities. Some college students drop out because they are under prepared for college study and need assistance with reading and study strategies in order to pass their classes (Weinstein & Mayer, 1985). In addition, many students need strategies for time management, metacognition, and self-regulation (Dansereau, et al. 1979). Students attending colleges and universities can benefit from strategy training (Dansereau, 1985; Grant, 1994). This study provided marginal students some strategies to deal with psychology concepts and the textbook.

The case study was based on the cognitive view of learning and followed the reciprocal teaching model pioneered by Annemarie Sullivan Palincsar and Ann Brown (1984). The process in reciprocal teaching involves students and teacher in dialogue about the meaning of a segment in a textbook. The dialog was structured to incorporate four components; *generating questions* about the content, *summarizing* the content, *clarifying* points, and *predicting* upcoming content from cues in the text from prior knowledge of the topic (Palincsar, 1987).

In addition to comprehension strategies, students need to become self-regulated learners (Zimmerman, 1990) and follow through with their learning plan. Self-regulation can develop through experience and example (Brown, 1978). When students learn how to learn, and how to manage and control their concentration, they discover that learning becomes easier and tend to improve in self-regulation (Como & Rohrkemper, 1985). This study provided marginal students with study strategies and charted the participants' use of strategies.

Methods

This was a qualitative, action research study based on case studies of four students. This method was chosen to analyze how the students changed their study strategies during a regular semester when they were taught strategies. The number of participants was limited because the researcher needed to collect an enormous amount of data to document how the participants studied and changed their strategies during the semester. The researcher chose the participants and led the research study. The basis for choosing the four participants was their score on the reading placement test taken when entering the university. The score was immediately above the cut off for developmental reading. Previous studies of students with these scores indicate that many of them dropped out or had low grades. However, the school did not require them to take a remedial reading class. The participants included both sexes and traditional, ages 18 to 24, and nontraditional, ages over 25, students. Introduction to Psychology was chosen because it was conceptually difficult and reading the textbook was important in passing the course. In addition, the professor of the psychology class was interested in student study strategies and the relationship of the strategies to the final grade.

The participants agreed to meet one hour twice a week for one semester where learning strategies for the psychology class were demonstrated and discussed. The incentive for the participants to attend sessions was to improve their study strategies. They did not receive credit or grades for their attendance.

The four students began their study strategies class with a demonstration of reciprocal teaching using the psychology textbook. After the first session when the researcher demonstrated the four steps in reciprocal teaching, participants were assigned sections in the next chapter to demonstrate reciprocal teaching to the other participants with the exception of the prediction step. That step was done when the chapter was introduced and the sections assigned.

To aid the students with self-regulation, a Proximal Goal Questionnaire was given to them to complete each week. The Proximal Goal Questionnaire included a question asking for their learning goals for the week. The next question asked for specific actions or steps to accomplish these goals. The researcher looked for specific actions, for example, "I will organize the ideas of this chapter into a semantic map" as opposed to "I will read the chapter." The information from the Proximal Goal Questionnaire provided the researcher with study goals and strategies each week. Participants were given weekly feedback concerning the goals and the strategies they planned to use. Early in the semester the Operationalize Effort Questionnaire was given to each participant to provide the researcher with information of the participants' belief of effort versus ability. Questions on this questionnaire asked the participant to compare the importance of ability with effort, list behaviors that they thought described effort, and asked them to list how they put forth effort in the psychology class.

The Learning and Study Strategies Inventory (LASSI) was administered to the students as a pre- and post-test to document changes in study strategies (Weinstein, Schulte, & Palmer, 1987) and to compare with their written and oral statements describing their application of study strategies to their studying. The LASSI is a self-report that measures ten areas found to be significant for effective study. The areas include attitude, motivation, time management, anxiety, concentration, acquiring knowledge, reading strategies including locating main ideas and supporting details, self-testing, and preparing for tests.

In helping the participants prepare for tests they were asked to write five multiple-choice questions from the unit chapters because the professor utilized multiple choice questions on the class unit tests. These questions were compiled and were part of a practice test that was typed and given to the participants during the study strategies class prior to the psychology class where the unit test was administered.

Triangulation was used when comparing final grade and class test results with study strategies identified on the Proximal Goal Questionnaire, (LASSI), evaluation of dialog in study strategy class, and formal and informal interviews.

Data Source and Analysis

A portfolio (Valeri-Gold, Olson, & Deming, 1991–92) was established for each participant. Information on learning activities was gleaned from questionnaires, interviews, self-reports, observations, summaries, adjunct study aides, and scripts from the learning strategy class. The class discussions were scripted and dialog was coded for each participant using King's (1994) classroom discussion evaluation: knowledge restating, knowledge assimilation, and knowledge integration. The test questions the students generated were coded with Pearson and Johnson's (1972) taxonomy of questions. The three taxonomies were text explicit, text implicit, and script implicit. Each participant's portfolio was checked weekly for patterns, feedback on the study strategies, and analysis of study strategies. The reasons the participants gave for not choosing a study strategy were analyzed using Convington's (1992) description of "self-handicapping strategies."

Case Studies

The following are the case studies of the four participants. The first three case studies are traditional students and the last case study is a non-traditional student. The names have been changed to protect the identity of the students.

Molly

Molly is a traditional first year, second semester female student. She works part-time at Wendy's. She also works at a public library in a small town stamping and organizing books. She rarely reads anything that is not required. When she does choose her reading, she likes to read biographies.

Molly reported at the beginning of the semester that her basic study strategy is outlining. On her first Proximal Goal Questionnaire she stated that she had trouble concentrating, thought the textbook was boring, did not think the terminology was difficult, but did learn some words. Later she stated that psychology is very complicated. As the semester progressed she read about some practical applications concerning stress, frustration, conflict, and health. She wrote, "I always thought that stress was a bad thing, but it isn't, it is perfectly normal. These chapters are getting more interesting."

Molly's ranking of satisfaction on her Proximal Goal Questionnaire for reaching previous goals on a scale of 0 to 25 went from an 18 at the beginning of the semester to a 6 at the end of the semester. Her confidence level for obtaining the goals she set for herself was low, 10 or below all semester. Molly believes that the responsibility for her grades is divided equally between her and the professor. The professor should explain what kind of test will be given, objective or essay, and then give study strategies for that type of test. The student is responsible for asking questions on the content of the course.

When Molly evaluated her performance on her first unit test she said that she followed her plan to study for nine hours. She couldn't see any pattern to her errors and felt she had selected the appropriate study strategies. She said, "I may have studied a bit too hard. I did a lot more work that I needed to do. Next time I won't do my chapter objectives in one day. I will do bits and pieces of it during the week." She wrote that for the second test she would study her notes and class handouts and do the chapter objectives. After her second unit test she stated that she studied with friends for the test. She also stated that her friends study differently than she does and believed that if she had studied by herself, she would have done better on the second test. For the third and last unit test she reported that she studied with three friends for seven hours the Saturday before the test.

When Molly reflected on her study strategies during the semester, she indicated that the changes she made in her studying included studying more with other students in the class, using the chapter objectives from the psychology instructor, reading the summaries at the end of each chapter, using flashcards for terms, and trying to answer the questions within the chapters and at the end of each chapter.

She defined effort as, "doing everything you can." She stated that effort makes "all the difference." She wrote that for Introduction to

Psychology effort meant, "read, study the notes, and reread." This information indicates that Molly was not specific in her study strategies and that she had general and global goals that were difficult to monitor.

In her interview at the end of the semester, Molly reported that she did not read the chapters in the psychology textbook, but did read the summaries at the end of each assigned chapter. She stated that she thought she gained a better understanding of psychology throughout the semester. When asked what determined her attendance in study strategies class she said it was time. If she got to her library job late, she had to make up the time. She described herself as a flighty person, who would go to study strategies class only if she felt like it.

On the LASSI (Figure 1 at the end of this article) she reported improved study strategies in all ten areas. Her unit test scores were, 81 percent, 84 percent, and 87 percent. Her average GPA at the beginning of the semester was 2.9 and her grade in Introduction to Psychology was B+. Her grade indicates that her Introduction to Psychology grade is above her previous semester average. Her GPA at the end of the semester of this study was 3.5 which would indicate that she transferred her study strategies to other classes.

Nevin

Nevin is a second semester, first year traditional student. He plans on a nursing career. He is taking biology, chemistry, and computer and software fundamentals in addition to Introduction to Psychology. He stated that the newspaper is the only reading he does that is not assigned. He usually spends one and one-half to two hours per week on the newspaper.

During Nevin's first interview he stated that in high school he had a teacher who was a big influence in his study methods. This teacher told him to read and review his class material the same day the class met. He still follows this advice.

When Nevin was asked what determined his attendance in study strategies class, he said that if he thought he understood the class lecture and the textbook he would not go to study strategies class. He stated that he did not think study strategies class would make a difference in his grade.

Nevin indicated on one of his Proximal Goal Questionnaires that he was highly satisfied with reaching his previous goals and felt very confident that he would reach the goals he set for himself in Introduction to Psychology. He had taken Introduction to Psychology the previous semester and received an F. He is taking the course for a change of grade.

During Nevin's end of the semester interview, he stated that reviewing the tests in study strategies class was helpful. He could see where he misread questions. When he studied for tests he used the study guide for a previous edition of the psychology textbook. He stated that he usually answered the multiple choice questions. He said that the application section of the multiple choice questions in the study guide were too hard, so he did not do those.

When comparing Nevin's LASSI scores (Figure 2 at the end of this article) from the beginning of the semester with those at the end of the semester, he reported lower scores in seven areas at the end of the semester. The three areas where he reported gains were information processing, use of support techniques and materials, and test strategies and preparing for tests. Nevin's unit test scores in Introduction to Psychology were 60 percent, 76 percent, and 48 percent. Nevin had a GPA of 3.4 at the beginning of the semester. He received a D+ in Introduction to Psychology. His GPA at the end of the semester of this study was 1.8. During his conference with his advisor in May he changed his major from nursing to education. His GPA indicates he did not utilize study strategies discussed or transfer them to other classes.

Bob

Bob is a first year, second semester traditional male. Bob reads every day, even when he is not in school. He enjoys murder mysteries and the newspapers. He reported that during the previous semester he studied about six hours a day. He did not study in high school. Bob likes to listen to soft music while studying. When he reads a textbook he takes notes and fills in a study guide that follows the textbook if one is available. He finds the study guide for Introduction to Psychology confusing and overwhelming.

When Bob evaluated his test strategies, he stated in his journals that his problem was not enough time. He felt that he used the most appropriate study strategies, but for the second test he planned to study longer.

During the semester he discovered that he studied best early in the morning. He was a security guard and he began taking his book with him on his rounds. He believed he was learning more since he was spending more time studying. He thought the early morning was a good time for him to learn.

Bob believes he alone is responsible for his learning. He stated that it was up to him to adjust to the different teaching styles of professors. He also stated that he earns the grades he receives. During Bob's end of the semester interview, he stated that the study strategies he found most helpful were highlighting and looking for bold type and words in italics. He used to read every word in the chapter, but now he thinks looking for bold type and italics is more helpful. He also stated that reading the summaries at the end of the chapters was important.

On one Proximal Goal Questionnaire Bob reported on a scale of 0–25 that his satisfaction of meeting his previous goals was 12 and on another questionnaire his satisfaction was 25, or he was very satisfied. He stated that he is somewhat satisfied with meeting previous goals. His goal is to "learn all he can." He states several times in the action section of his Proximal Goal Questionnaire, that he will study in all his spare time. He believes that the only person who can help him with his studying is himself. He will not ask anyone else for assistance nor will he study in a group.

Bob suggested that the study strategies class would be improved if time was spent going over the notes rather than the textbook. He stated that he learned to organize his time better this semester. He reported that the study strategies explained in the study strategies class were helpful to him. He did not explain which ones he used or how he applied them to his studying. On the LASSI (Figure 3 at the end of this article), Bob reported gains in five of the 10 study categories. He reported less use of strategies in motivation, anxiety, concentration, use of support techniques, and self-testing at the end of the semester. Bob's grades on his unit tests were 55 percent, 65 percent, and 64 percent. His GPA at the beginning of the semester was 3.0. His final grade in Introduction to Psychology was C–.

Roy

Roy, a nontraditional, second semester sophomore, stated in his introductory interview that he usually reads about six hours a week. He especially enjoys reading historical fiction. He did not study in high school. He reported that he learns best outlining his textbook as he reads. First he highlights, then he makes his outline from the words he highlighted. In preparing for a test he writes questions from his outline. He writes the questions on one page and the answers on another page. He plans to study Introduction to Psychology about one and one half to two hours per day. Roy reported that for his algebra class last semester he sometimes did his homework twice to be sure he understood the problems. He stated that he prefers learning to memorizing.

Roy reported on his Proximal Goal Questionnaires that he was highly satisfied with the achievement on his previous goals and confident he would meet his current goals. He is in college because he became disabled in his previous job. The disability caused him to seek another type of work. He believes college is his last chance to be productive. Experience has taught him that nothing comes easy. He reported that he was overwhelmed with the volume of assignments. One weekend he procrastinated because of the amount of work and then proceeded to rush through the assignments Sunday evening to get them done. The next weekend he planned shorter intervals of study and use of the whole weekend. In Roy's journal entries he describes his reading rate. He believes he is a slow reader because he tries to comprehend when he reads. This causes him to frequently go back over the material he has read for clarification. He also tries to highlight the items he deems important. Sometimes he loses his concentration and stops reading for a time.

The week before the first unit test, Roy reported that he had completed the assigned reading so he could concentrate on learning the material. He felt frustrated with all the material. His study strategy was to understand all the handout material, go over highlights in the text and learn the meaning of the major terms. After the exam he reported that he did not follow his study plan. The reason he gave for not following his plan was that he had three major examinations the same day. The amount of material he had to learn was overwhelming. He thought he missed some questions that were based on the lectures. He did not think there was a pattern to his errors. He reported that he had selected the most appropriate study strategies, but for the next test he would employ distributed practice rather than do all his reviewing at one session. He also planned to pay closer attention to class notes.

During his interview at the end of the semester, Roy stated that not until April was he able to make the connection between what he learned in the study strategies class and Introduction to Psychology. At the end of the semester he thought study strategies class would have been more helpful if the class had used the study guide more. He also wished that each person in the group would have come to class prepared to explain certain questions. He wished that the students would have been aware of the value of the study guide.

For the final unit test Roy planned to study independently. His plan included answering questions in the study guide and skipping the chapter objectives from the professor. He planned to do the multiple-choice questions in the study guide. This was a new plan for him. He changed methods because he decided that his previous strategies were not effective in helping him reach his grade goal.

Roy stated on the Operationalize Effort Questionnaire that effort is the absolute key to learning a subject. Talent and ability go to waste without effort. He stated that effort means reading to learn, striving to retain, applying material to life situations, and redoing, reading, and studying as often as necessary. When Roy operationalizes effort, he looks over the chapter to discover the main ideas, then he reads and highlights, reads the review points at the end of the chapter and checks to see if the answers are highlighted, and answers the self-test questions. On the LASSI (Figure 4 at the end of this article), Roy was above the 75th percentile in all ten categories in January, but in May he was below the 75th percentile in anxiety. His LASSI scores indicate that he used effective strategies in the other categories.

Roy's unit test scores were 83 percent on all three unit tests. Roy had a GPA of 3.8 at the beginning of the semester he received a B+ in Introduction to Psychology.

Results

*Strengths and Weaknesses of Four Students in a
Conceptually Difficult Course*

Memorization was the main study strategy utilized by the four students in this study. The textbook, *Introduction to Psychology* by D. Coon, was difficult for the participants to read so they did not read the assigned chapters. They only read the summaries at the end of the chapters, certain sections within the chapters to answer the chapter objectives, and bold face print. The students were like the surface learners described in Entwistle and Ramsden (1983) who were "game players" trying to guess the questions on the unit tests. If they viewed the assignment as too difficult, they would skip the assignment. For an example, one participant did not understand the textbook and therefore did not read it or write the summaries. Another participant could not understand the application questions in the workbook and did not complete that section. Since reciprocal teaching involved reading the textbook, reciprocal teaching was not utilized as taught after the first unit text. The participants chose another method of study.

The change participants made in study strategies during the semester when they were presented and demonstrated were from one surface strategy to another. Surface strategies as defined by Saljo, and reported in Gibbs, Morgan, and Taylor (1982) include memorizing, acquiring facts, and learning terms. Examples of surface learning that the participants utilized were memorizing the responses to the objectives from the chapters that the professor gave them to guide their studying, selective reading of the textbook, looking up answers to questions, learning terms with bold face print, and memorizing their notes.

The participants were looking for the necessary facts and principles they needed to learn in order to pass the unit tests. There was very little application of psychological theory in their lives. One example was when they read the chapter on memory. Study strategies were in the chapter and they were taught, but the participants did not want to apply new strategies while studying. This is similar to a description of a student Rose (1989) described who was failing chemistry. The student Rose described could "memorize facts and formulas but not use them to solve problems" (p. 190).

One thing that seems important is that the surface strategies participants used may have contributed to their own "deskilling." Bintz (1993) refers to students who use surface level strategies rather than deep level strategies as contributing to their own deskilling. When students try to pass a course by memorizing facts and terms rather than understanding and applying concepts they are depriving themselves of a learning opportunity. Their method of memorization will more likely be repeated in the future because of their past utilization and familiarity with the memorization skill. Students learned to utilize better techniques, but since these took more effort they chose not to use them as their primary motivation appeared to be merely passing the course with as little effort as necessary to get an acceptable grade.

The participants' use of surface learning is further exemplified by their misuse of chapter objectives as study guides. The participants used the answers for material to be memorized rather than looking up related concepts in the textbook. This focused memorization strategy was also evident in a study by Marton and reported in Gibbs, Morgan, and Taylor (1982) that described the student's use of in-text questions. Marton noted that when students utilized in-text questions they used surface level processing. When students need to incorporate deep level strategies to aid better understanding of a textbook the questions need to come from the reader's background of knowledge and experience. Marton sees his research as helping teachers understand that it is important for students to ask their own questions and for teachers to be aware of how students conceptualize the subject matter.

In summary, the study strategies of the participants in the current study were surface level learning strategies. When they changed their strategies they tended to change to another surface strategy. When they viewed studying as difficult, they tended to skip that assignment. The participants thought that if they memorized the terms, chapter objectives, and notes they would do well on the test. They were not aware that they should be rehearsing, organizing, and elaborating their understanding of concepts in the chapters.

Four Students' Application of Reciprocal Teaching Strategies to an Introduction to Psychology Textbook with Instruction, Demonstration, and Practice

During the first unit the participants were beginning to utilize reciprocal teaching in their study group. However, after the first unit test they did not perceive that reciprocal teaching was helpful so they chose other study strategies. This decision by the participants is consistent with Saljo's description of students' concepts of learning as reported in Gibbs, Morgan and Taylor (1982). The participants' decision not to read the textbook made sense to them because they believed that learning was memorizing and acquiring facts. They also believed that the facts they needed to memorize were in their notes and the answers to the chapter objectives. They did, however, look in the textbooks for information on their chapter objectives. So they did selective textbook reading to look for answers to the objectives. This is also consistent with Bintz (1993) who noted that teachers operate on the assumption that reading is an integral part of content area courses, but students report that assigned reading is not meaningful or relevant to their personal lives. And, in addition, students believe that classes require "little more than routinized identification and memorization of isolated facts from texts" (p. 613).

The summaries, questions, and class discussion early in the semester as participants were learning reciprocal teaching showed progress. After the participants chose not to utilize reciprocal teaching, the responses indicate an increase in factual questions, lack of summaries, and the class discussion included fewer integration statements at the end of the semester than at the beginning.

Four Students' Transfer of Reading and Learning Strategies to Other Classes

With the exception of Roy and Molly who utilized the application questions for the last test and spaced their study time, the participants appeared to use the strategy of memorization and cramming on all their subjects. These were the same strategies they said they used at the beginning of the semester. It was difficult for them to change to more effective strategies.

Participants stated that choosing isolated facts and memorizing them is a strategy they utilize in all their classes. They were comfortable with this strategy and the strategy had been effective in their previous classes. When their test scores were not as high as they had hoped for, they looked for different material to memorize for the next test. When different, effective strategies were demonstrated, they tried them if they were not too difficult and if they thought they were effective, used them. This is consistent with Palmer and Goetz (1988) who noted that when students feel a strategy is too difficult they refuse to utilize that strategy. However, when they did not think they were helpful or too difficult, they chose not to use them. The participants' choices of study strategies confirm the results in Entwistle and Ramsden (1983) who described students' choices of strategies as a relationship between context of learning and the approaches students use.

Some small changes did surface. For example, one participant stated that he planned to use a study guide that goes with a textbook when one is provided in the future. He also believed that the application questions were better preparation for the unit tests than memorizing the chapter objectives. In addition, he plans to think of life examples whenever he can in all future classes. Another participant plans to read summaries at the end of the chapters when they are available.

The participants did utilize reading and learning strategies that they thought effective in obtaining their desired grade. Basically, they looked for information they thought was going to appear on tests in all subjects rather then organizing and understanding the information. This confirms the research done by Nist, Sharman, and Holschub (1996) to determine students' transfer of strategy instruction to other courses. The Nist study found that students seemed to prefer rereading a text to applying or modifying the more effective strategies they were taught.

Changes in Study Strategies Four Students Made
with Instruction and Demonstration

Although there were a variety of changes, the dominant one was using the chapter objectives as the basis of selecting material to memorize. They used these as a guide to their studying. The chapter objectives guided them in which sections of the textbook to read and what material to memorize for tests.

As the semester progressed, the participants became more selective in choosing sections of the textbook to read. One participant said that he now focuses on bold face print and italics. He also spends more time with the study guide.

All of the participants became more aware of time management. They tried to space out their study. However, they still crammed for tests. Some of the participants became aware of certain times of the day when they were more alert and concentrated their study during that time.

The significant factor in participants choosing or not choosing a strategy was how they thought it would help them achieve their desired grade. One participant noted that he had not achieved his desired grade on the first two unit tests and decided to change his strategy when studying for the third test. This information indicates that students are persistent in using surface level strategies and hope that changing from one surface level strategy to another surface level strategy will help them improve their grade. Also, if the strategy seemed too difficult, they did not use the strategy. This is consistent with Palmer and Goetz (1988) who noted that when students feel a strategy is too difficult they refuse to utilize the strategy.

Importance of the Study

This study gathered qualitative information, which focused on the utilization of students' study strategies. The results can potentially help instructors in their awareness of how students learn and comprehend the content of their courses. The findings in this study can help college instructors in their understanding of how difficult it is to get some students to change their study strategies and to engage in deep-level processing of course material. In a study by Sherman (1991) describing a two-year project to improve learning strategies of college freshmen, he noted that when content instructors did not provide extensive support of the strategies taught in study strategies classes, the students did not utilize the new strategies. In the psychology class these students were taking, the instructor gave the students chapter objectives for review. The students perceived that defining the objectives was all that was necessary to pass the course. In effect, this meant that they did not need to read the entire chapter or utilize reciprocal teaching, but only needed to learn the material on the course objective sheet. This study

Figure 1. Molly's LASSI Pre- and Post-Test Percentiles

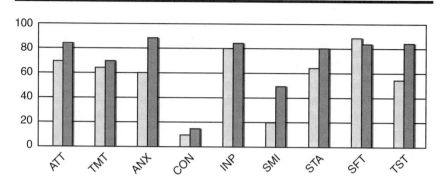

Figure 2. Nevin's LASSI Pre- and Post-Test Percentiles

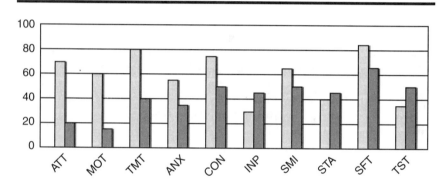

Figure 3. Bob's LASSI Pre- and Post-Test Percentiles

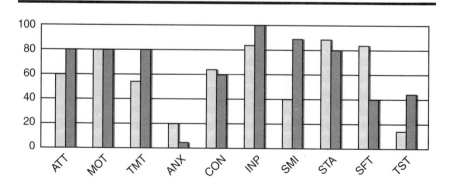

Figure 4. Roy's LASSI Pre- and Post-Test Percentiles

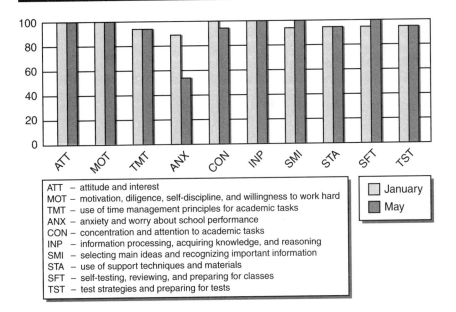

ATT – attitude and interest
MOT – motivation, diligence, self-discipline, and willingness to work hard
TMT – use of time management principles for academic tasks
ANX – anxiety and worry about school performance
CON – concentration and attention to academic tasks
INP – information processing, acquiring knowledge, and reasoning
SMI – selecting main ideas and recognizing important information
STA – use of support techniques and materials
SFT – self-testing, reviewing, and preparing for classes
TST – test strategies and preparing for tests

☐ January
■ May

indicates that students need to see a correlation between a study strategy and their final grade before they will utilize the strategy. The study also implies that the way an instructor organizes a class determines to some extent how the students will study for the class. This information is helpful to college faculty working with reluctant readers.

References

Bintz, W. P. (1993). Resistant readers in secondary education: Some insights and implications. *Journal of Reading, 36*, 604–615.

Brown, A. L. (1978). Knowing when, where, and how to remember: A problem of metacognition. In R. Glasser (Ed.), *Advances in Instructional Psychology, 1*, 77–165. Hillsdale, NJ: Erlbaum.

Brown, A. L., & Palinscar, A. S. (1985). *Reciprocal teaching of comprehension strategies: A natural history of one program for enhancing learning* (Tech. Rep. # 334). Urbana, IL: University of Illinois, Center for the Study of Reading.

Corno, L. & Rohrkemper, M. M. (1985). The intrinsic motivation to learn in classrooms. In C. Ames & R. Ames (Eds.), *Research on Motivation in Education: The Classroom Milieu, 2*, 53–90. Orlando, FL: Academic.

Covington, M. (1992). *Making the grade: A self-worth perspective on motivation and school reform.* New York: Cambridge University Press.

Dansereau, D. F. (1985). Learning strategy research. In J. Segal, S. Chipman, & R. Glaser (Eds.), *Thinking and Learning Skills: Relating Instruction to Research, 1*, 209–240. Hillsdale, NJ: Erlbaum.

Dansereau, D. F. McDonald, B. A. Collins, K. W., Garland, J., Holley, C. P., Dickhoff, G., & Evans, S. H. (1979). Evaluation of a learning strategy training program.

In H. F. O'Neil & C. D. Speelberger (Eds.). *Cognitive and Affective Learning Strategies,* 3–43. New York: Academic Press.

Entwistle, N. J., & Ramsden, P. (1983). *Understanding student learning.* New York: Nichols Publishing Co.

Gibbs, G., Morgan, A., & Taylor, E. (1982). A review of the research of Ference Marton, the Gateborg group: A phenomenological research perspective on learning. *Higher Education,* 11, 123–145.

Grant, R. (1994). Comprehension strategy instructions: Basic considerations for instructing at-risk college students. *Journal of Reading,* 38, 42–48.

King, A. (1994). Guiding knowledge construction in the classroom. Effects of teaching children how to question and how to explain. *American Education Research Journal,* 31, 338–369.

Nist, S. L., Sharman, S. J., & Holschuh, J. L. (1996). The effects of rereading, self-selected strategy use, and rehearsal on the immediate and delayed understanding of text. *Reading Psychology: An International Quarterly,* 17, 137–157.

Palincsar, A. S. (1987). Reciprocal teaching and reading comprehension: a review. *Journal of Research in Reading,* 11(1), 3–14.

Palincsar, A. S., & Brown, A. (1984). Reciprocal teaching of comprehension fostering and comprehension-monitoring activities. *Cognition and Instruction,* 1, 117–175.

Palmer, D. J., & Goetz, E. T. (1988). Selection and use of study strategies: The role of the student's beliefs about self and strategies. In C. E. Weinstein, E. T. Goetz, & P. A. Alexander (Eds.), *Learning and Study Strategies: Issues in Assessment, Instruction, and Evaluation,* 41–62. New York: Academic Press.

Pearson, P. D., & Johnson, D. D. (1972). *Teaching reading comprehension.* Chicago: Hold, Rinehart & Winston.

Rose, M. (1989). *Lives on the Boundary.* New York: The Free Press.

Sherman, T. M. (1991). Creating a disposition to learn: Promoting enduring effects from learning improvement programs. *Research and Teaching in Developmental Education,* 8(1), 37–47.

Valeri-Gold, M., Olson, J. R., & Deming, M. P. (1991–1992). Portfolios: Collaborative authentic assessment opportunities for college developmental learners. *Journal of Reading,* 35, 298–305.

Weinstein, C. E., & Mayer, R. E. (1985). The teaching of learning strategies. In M. C. Wittrock (Ed.), *Handbook of Research on Teaching* (3rd ed.), 315–327. New York: Macmillan.

Weinstein, C. E., Schulte, A. C., & Palmer, D. P. (1987). *The learning and study strategies inventory (LASSI).* Clearwater, FL: H & H.

Zimmerman, B. J. (1990). Self-regulated learning and academic achievement: An overview. *Educational Psychologist,* 25(1), 3–17.

Do as I Say, Not as I Do: High, Average, and Low-Performing Students' Strategy Use in Biology

Jodi Patrick Holschuh

This study investigated the differences in the ways that high, average, and low-performing students made use of deep-level as opposed to surface-level learning strategies in a large general education, lecture-style, introductory biology course. In addition, the study asked whether there "are differences

*in students' self-reported study strategies and their studying advice for
other students."*

*The analysis of study strategy checklists completed by 518 students
and the content analysis of student responses to an open-ended questionnaire led to the following findings: High-performing students use more
deep-level and domain-specific learning strategies than low-performing
students, and they possess good conditional knowledge about strategy use.
Low-performing students, on the other hand, generally report using
different strategies than the approaches they would suggest to a peer.*

The purpose of this study was to investigate the differences in deep
and surface strategy use of high, average, and low performing students in an introductory biology class. In addition, this study examined
differences between the strategies students reported using for test
preparation and those they would suggest a friend to use. This study
was undertaken because I see the struggles my students face in learning science in my own college reading courses. By understanding the
differences between students who are successful science learners and
those who are not, I hoped to discover ways to help students become
better equipped for the task.

Because research has indicated that strategy use is domain and
content dependent (Garner, 1988), it was important to examine the role
of deep and surface strategy use within a single domain. An introductory biology course was chosen as a research cite for several reasons.
Science is a domain where many students experience difficulty learning because they are introduced to many complex topics that may contradict their real-world experiences and because the tasks often
involve both integrating concepts and problem solving (Alexander &
Kulikowich, 1994; Nolen & Haladyna, 1990). In addition, biology is an
especially appropriate domain for this research, because the texts are
often dense and filled with difficult concepts and vocabulary, which has
been found to cause students with little science background to use
inappropriate learning strategies and to experience comprehension
problems (Glynn, 1991; Lee, Fradd, & Sutman, 1995). In fact, many science texts are written in ways that lead students to believe that learning science is merely a memorization task because of the numerous
bold-faced terms on each page. In a study of high school physics Coleman and Shore (1991) found that average performers in a course for
gifted students were not able to monitor their text comprehension
accurately, because of their strategy selection. The students never
moved beyond learning new vocabulary terms to learning the concepts
in the text. Thus, it would appear that students could experience difficulty if they approach a complex task of science learning using only
inappropriate surface approaches.

Deep and surface approaches to learning may tie into students' college performance because they are a result of students' perceptions of

academic tasks (Biggs, 1988). Students who adopt deep approaches to learning tend to personalize the task and integrate information so that they can see relationships among ideas (Entwistle, 1988; Marton & Saljo, 1997). Deep approaches to learning allow the learner to build on previous knowledge in a meaningful way which eliminates compartmentalized knowledge and facilitates long-term learning (DeJong & Ferguson-Hessler, 1996; Edmondson, 1995). Students who use deep approaches for science learning have been shown to be more successful at both selecting strategies and monitoring when comprehension breaks down (Nist, Holschuh, & Sharman, 1995). For example, Spiegel and Barufaldi (1994) found that college students who used deep strategies, such as constructing their own graphic organizers for their science course, retained more information than students who used more surface strategies such as underlining, rereading, or highlighting.

On the other hand, students who adopt surface approaches begin a task with the sole purpose of task completion rather than learning, which leads to verbatim recall or the use of rote memorization strategies (Biggs, 1988; Entwistle, 1988; Marton & Saljo, 1997). Students who adopt surface approaches view each piece of information as discrete and unrelated. Research has indicated that an overemphasis on rote learning of isolated facts and concepts can impair students' ability to interrelate scientific concepts (Anderson, 1990; Hammer, 1994a, 1994b). Surface approaches can hinder science learning because when students do not use strategies that facilitate integration of information, they may reach a point where they are unable to grasp new material (Qian, 1995; Trowbridge & Wandersee, 1994).

Learning science at the college level may primarily require deep approaches (Padilla, 1991), but Marton and Saljo (1997) pointed out that the level of processing used should be determined by the task in which students are asked to engage. If the task was merely to memorize a list of scientific terms, then surface approaches would be warranted. If, however, the task required synthesis and interpretation of information, as is most common in college science courses (Cavallo & Schafer, 1994; Larkin & Reif, 1979; Lord, 1994; Norris & Phillips, 1994; Padilla, 1991), deep approaches would be more appropriate. Padilla (1991) found that most college science courses require skills such as formulating, interpreting, analyzing, and experimenting, which would necessitate deep approaches to learning. Because science learning often requires deep approaches, students often experience difficulty in science classes. Thus, to be successful learners, students need to able to identify the level of processing required in their science classes.

Although the research on deep and surface strategy use seems to indicate that deep strategies are more effective, the studies have been limited in several ways. First, self-selection of strategies was not a factor. Many studies examined specific strategies, such as concept mapping, rather than investigating the strategies students were selecting on their own (e.g., Briscoe & LeMaster, 1991). Second, studies occurred in a laboratory, not natural setting (e.g., Blanchard & Mikkelson, 1987). Thus, the tasks were not always representative of college classrooms. Third, many of the studies did not occur within a specific domain. Students were asked about their studying in general rather than tied to a content course or specific domain. These limitations were addressed in the present study. The overall purpose of this study was to investigate the differences in self-selected deep and surface strategy use of high, average, and low performing students in an introductory biology class. By understanding the factors that differentiate high, average, and low performing students, college reading and study strategy instructors can gain insight into ways to address the difficult task of science learning.

The following questions guided this study: (a) Are there differences in study strategies of high, average, and low performing students, and (b) Are there differences in students' self-reported study strategies and their studying advice for other students? It was expected that the differences would be demonstrated by high performing students using deep strategies for learning, average students using a combination of deep and surface strategies, and low performing students using surface strategies.

Method

Participants

Participants were recruited from two large lecture sections of an introductory biology course for non-science majors. A total of 518 (349 female, 169 male) participants completed both phases of data collection; their responses were used for the data analysis. The majority of participants were female (66 percent) and European American (69 percent). The class was made up of mostly freshmen (28 percent) and sophomores (49 percent), which is typical in an introductory-level course. Eighty-seven percent of the participants were of traditional college age, between 18 and 21 years of age. The majority of participants (89 percent) reported that introductory biology was their first college-level science course.

Description of the Course

Data were gathered for this study in two sections of biology that were taught using large-lecture format with each section having an enrollment of approximately 330 students. The class met five days a week for the lecture, and students were also enrolled in a lab course, which met once each week. The professor lectured from the same set of notes for each class, used the same textbook, and gave equivalent exams in both sections. Thus, course content and exams were virtually identical for the two sections.

The professor used a visualizer (a modern overhead projector) during his lectures, which allowed him to include actual diagrams from the text as well as newspaper articles and other relevant information in his lectures. Topics included those traditionally covered in an introductory biology course (e.g., cellular reproduction, human genetics, evolution) as well as some that may not traditionally be included (e.g., sexually transmitted diseases, birth control methods). Exams consisted of multiple-choice questions in which most items required synthesis and application of multiple concepts. Thus, students perceived these tests as difficult, because the majority of the items required more than mere memorization of terms.

Several support services were offered to students in this class. The professor videotaped each lecture and made those tapes available in the Biology Learning Center. Students could view a missed lecture or fill in the gaps in their notes by listening to the lecture another time. The professor hired a student to take notes in the class, which were then put on the Internet. These notes included actual diagrams from the text, and they were added to the biology web page within a day or two after each lecture. The professor also posted several exam modules, organized by subject area, on the biology web page, which students could use for exam practice. Each module consisted of a series of 20 multiple-choice items drawn from the test bank, similar to those that students would encounter on the actual exam. On the nights before exams 2 and 4, the professor offered review sessions, which served to answer students' content-related questions. None of these supports were mandatory, but students were encouraged by the professor to take advantage of them.

Materials and Data Collection

Data collection occurred twice over a 10 week quarter. During the first data collection, which occurred after the second of four exams, students completed an open-ended questionnaire. In this questionnaire, students read the following brief scenario about a student taking introductory biology:

> Your friend Pat thinks you are an expert on study methods. Pat has a multiple-choice exam in introductory biology on Monday and comes to you for advice regarding how to study for the exam. What method(s) would you suggest to Pat and why? Please write about how you would tell your friend to study and what you believe is the key to doing well in introductory biology.

Thus, the task was to give their friend studying advice addressing both how their friend should study and what they believe the key is to doing well in their introductory biology course. The scenario was constructed based on information from the Metacognitive Awareness

Questionnaire (Corkhill, 1996), the Measure of Epistemological Reflection (Baxter Magolda, 1992), and from student responses from previous research in introductory biology (Holschuh, 1995; Nist & Holschuh, 2000).

During the second data collection, which occurred before the fourth exam, students completed a strategy checklist about how they actually studied for the course as a measure of deep and surface strategy use. The checklist contained 29 deep-strategy items and 17 surface-strategy items about the role of the texts, the notes, and the classroom supports in introductory biology (see Appendix). All items on the checklists reflected either deep strategies (e.g., "When I read my biology text, I looked for connections between ideas") or surface strategies (e.g., "I read an entire biology chapter before I stopped to think about it") for learning. Items were constructed based on information from *Developing Textbook Thinking* (3rd edition, Nist & Diehl, 1994), a textbook designed to teach effective strategies for college learning, and from students' responses from previous research in introductory biology (Holschuh, 1995; Nist & Holschuh, 2000). Thus, the checklist was constructed to reflect both general study strategies and domain-specific strategies for science learning.

Data Analysis

Data were analyzed in two ways. First, responses to the strategy checklist for all 518 participants were aggregated and coded. Means for student responses to checklist items for each group were generated and an Analysis of Variance was conducted. Second, a content analysis (Bernard, 1994; Patton, 1990) of student responses to the open-ended questionnaire was conducted on 50 randomly selected questionnaires to determine categories of response. Student responses were typed into a computer to help organize and identify patterns in the data (Patton, 1990). Similar responses were categorized together. For example, "I read the textbook" and "I do the reading" would be categorized together. Responses from the 50 questionnaires were compared with an additional 50 randomly selected questionnaires, which were also coded on computer, to be sure that all patterns in the data were expressed. Inter-rater coding indicated that an analysis of a third set of 50 questionnaires was needed. Thus, the content analysis reported in this paper reflects 150 questionnaire responses. After the data were coded, participant responses were grouped and sorted by course performance for analysis. Students who made an A or a B in the course were grouped as high performing (n = 47). Students who made a C in the course were grouped as average performing (n = 56). Students who made a D or an F in the course were grouped as low performing (n = 47). Then the responses to the questionnaire were compared with mean group responses on the strategy checklist.

Results and Conclusions

Several differences emerged when the data of study strategies of high, average, and low performers were analyzed. Findings for each question are presented below and relevant student quotations are included to explicate the conclusions.

Are There Differences in Study Strategies of High, Average, and Low Performing Students?

Results indicated that there were differences in the study strategies of high, average, and low performers in several ways. High performing students used more deep level strategies, more domain-specific strategies, and had good conditional knowledge about strategy use.

HIGH PERFORMING STUDENTS USED MORE DEEP LEVEL STRATEGIES   As shown in Tables 1 and 2, there were statistically significant differences in the strategy use of high, average, and low performing students. Although most students reported using both deep and surface strategies on the strategy checklist, high performing students reported using the greatest number of deep level strategies and the least number of surface level strategies. Conversely, low performing students reported using the least number of deep level strategies and the greatest number of surface level strategies. Average performing students fell in the middle of these two groups on the use of both deep and surface level strategies. It was expected that high performing students would use deep strategies for learning, but this finding is interesting because it appears that the ratio between deep and surface strategies used in learning makes a difference in overall course performance.

HIGH PERFORMING STUDENTS WERE MORE LIKELY TO REPORT USING DOMAIN-SPECIFIC STRATEGIES   Through further investigation of student responses to checklist items and the open-ended questionnaire it appears that the differences between high, average, and low performers goes beyond mere ratios of deep and surface strategy use. Course performance also depended on the type of deep strategies used.

High performing students were more likely to report using domain-specific strategies. In this science course it was important for students to be able to learn content-specific terms for science processes and be able to apply such information to a variety of situations. They also needed to be able to read and understand diagrams explaining complex processes. To accomplish these tasks, high-performing students reported reading for understanding, studying diagrams, comparing their text to their lecture notes, and using computerized test bank as a final review for exams. For example, one student said, "I try to get down the concepts. Memorization doesn't work unless it is a vocabulary

Table 1. Mean Scores for Student Responses to Strategy Checklist

Grouping	N	Deep Strategies	Surface Strategies
High-performing	518		
M		13.61	3.75
SD		4.26	2.33
Average-performing	518		
M		12.77	4.53
SD		4.70	2.40
Low-performing	518		
M		12.16	5.15
SD		4.64	2.57

Table 2. Analysis of Variance for High, Average, and Low Performing Students' Deep and Surface Strategy Use

Source	Df	F	p
Deep Strategies	2	10.659	.000**
Surface Strategies	2	30.898	.000**

** $p < .01$

test. That is great that the terms have been memorized, but can you apply them to scientific processes? I try to understand the in-depth reasoning." Some low and average performing students also discussed reading diagrams and understanding science processes, but most students focused on the importance of learning key terms. For example, one low performing student gave the following advice "Learn the vocabulary terms for each chapter. Multiple choice tests generally have a fair amount of vocabulary words." This is consistent with Ryan (1989) who found that often at-risk students never moved beyond memorizing terms to actual science learning. This view of learning is troublesome because an overemphasis on rote vocabulary learning can impair students' ability to interrelate concepts (Anderson, 1990).

HIGH PERFORMING STUDENTS HAD CONDITIONAL KNOWLEDGE OF STRAT-
EGY USE   Not only were high performing students better able to identify domain-specific, deep strategies for learning, but they were also able to articulate on their open-ended questionnaire responses why each strategy was appropriate for their friends to use. Thus, high performing students had good conditional knowledge. That is, they were able to discuss why the strategies they suggest are appropriate for the

task of learning science. For example one high performing student said "I believe that incorporating lecture notes into the information in the text helps [you] understand the lesson better because if one is unclear the other can clarify what was said. You should go over the notes and text together, paying attention to diagrams to help you understand the processes. Reading chapter summaries are sometimes helpful but can sometimes be extremely vague; therefore, it should not be done instead of, but in addition to other studying. After going over the text and notes it is helpful to go over practice quizzes to help you see what you still need to study." High performing students understood the value of self-testing or quizzing a friend to be sure that the information was understood. One student gave the following advice, "Get together with a study partner and go over the notes — explaining trouble spots to each other. Quiz each other about information then review [on your own] any troubles you had in the 'quiz'. This can help you know if you are ready or need more studying."

However, low and average performing students were not able to articulate the "whys." Average performing students were very procedural in their suggestions for studying. They focused on the order of how to study (first you read your book, then study the notes, etc.) but did not talk about why these procedures were appropriate. In addition, they focused on repetition of tasks (e.g. if you don't understand something you should read it over and over until you do). For example, one average-performing student said, "First, read through you[r] notes so that you know them thoroughly. Second, read through the chapter and pick out anything that is relevant and associated to what has been discussed in the book. Thirdly, take notes out of your book. Study both sets of notes — lecture and book — until you know them confidently. Fourth, when taking the exam, always cross out answers you know are not right, so that you can make an effective educated guess." This student's advice does not suggest why these activities would help their friend learn biology.

These results indicate both qualitative and quantitative differences in the deep and surface strategy use of high, average, and low performing students. That is, although all students seemed to understand that reading the text, reviewing notes, and using course supports such as computerized practice exams was important to doing well in the course, high performing students used a greater proportion of deep strategies to learn and they knew why those strategies were appropriate for learning in this science course.

Are There Differences in Students' Self-Reported Study Strategies and Their Studying Advice for Other Students?

Results indicated differences by performance group in the self-reported study strategies and studying advice for a friend.

LOW PERFORMING STUDENTS TENDED TO REPORT USING DIFFERENT STRATEGIES THAN THOSE THEY RECOMMENDED TO A FRIEND   One of the most interesting differences found in this study is that low performing students suggested that their friends use different strategies than those they reported on the checklists. Thus, even though they reported cramming for exams they suggested that their friends should start studying in advance. One student suggested, "Do as I say, not as I do . . . study class notes every night — DO NOT CRAM." They also would suggest using several different strategies in sequence, but reported using fewer strategies than they suggest to a friend. One student said, "Although this is not what I would do, I would hypothesize that Pat first go and read the chapters. I would tell Pat to divide the chapter into portions so that the reading won't become too much — and then take personal notes from the chapter. Then read over class notes and compare with the text. Then I'd suggest going to do [computer] modules and the self-tests after they have learned the material." Although it is not surprising that students who were not doing well would suggest different strategies to a friend, it is interesting that those same students did not attempt to use those strategies themselves.

However, even if low performing students did follow the advice they gave to their friend they may have continued to experience failure because they were more likely to suggest strategies that were not appropriate for the task of learning in this biology course. For example, one student said that it was important to "Rewrite all your notes neatly. Emphasizing the most imp[ortant] topics. Then reread text and notes until you understand." In addition, they suggested that their friends look for commonalties between the text and their notes ("Read the chapters paying especially close attention to the main concepts and when it is covered in both the text and notes"). One student said "I would tell Pat to review the notes and to then go over what is in the book as it pertains to the notes. Whatever is in the book and the notes is definitely worth going over more than once." Although this may be an appropriate strategy in some classes, in this biology course it would have been more important to note the differences because the professor often selected topics not covered during lecture for exam questions.

In contrast, high performing students reported using deep level strategies, and they also suggested these kinds of strategies to their friend. Their responses often started with "this is what works for me . . . " For example one student said, "what has worked for me so far is to get together *at least* once with a study partner . . . quiz each other about the information and go back over the information one last time." This result is not surprising given their success in the course.

HIGH PERFORMING STUDENTS KNEW THE KEY TO DOING WELL IN INTRO-DUCTORY BIOLOGY   On the open-ended questionnaire students were asked to tell their friend what they thought was the key to doing well in introductory biology. Most average and low performing students did not respond to this part of the open-ended question. Thus, we do not know if these students do not know the key to success in biology or if they did not see that part of the question. However, some average and low performing students responded that they simply did not know themselves the key to doing well. One student said, "I don't know the key to studying [introductory biology] because I haven't mastered it quite yet, either." Many high-performing students did respond to this question and suggested that the key to doing well is to understand the science process and to be able to apply the concepts to new situations. One student said, " . . . they need to study more than just definitions for this course. They need to understand key concepts and be able to apply them to different situations." Thus, high performing students knew the key to doing well in biology, but out of the 150 responses represented in this study, no average or low performing student was able to articulate this point.

Discussion

What do the results of this study mean for instruction? First, the result of this study indicates the need to incorporate a science-learning component into college reading and study strategy courses. Because science is a domain where students experience difficulty and because the results of this study indicate that low performing students experience difficulty due to surface strategy use, it is important for students to have the opportunity to apply strategies for science learning while they are enrolled in a college reading or study strategies course. By reading text from a difficult content area such as science, or better yet from several different content areas, students will be able to reflect on the differences in task requirements between domains when selecting strategies for learning.

Second, the results indicated that average and low performing students did not seem to understand the conditional nature of strategy use in the content-areas. High performing students were better able to select effective strategies and apply them appropriately. One way college reading and study strategies programs can help at-risk learners understand the conditional nature of strategy use is to go beyond the "whats and hows" of strategy use to discussing the reasons why one would select a particular strategy.

High-performing students were also able to articulate the reasons why each strategy was important and appropriate for the course and the tasks involved. A good way to help students in college reading or study strategy course begin to verbalize their strategy selection is through guided class discussion. Scenarios such as the one in the questionnaire allow students to reflect and make the necessary connections to add the "whys" to the "whats and hows." Thus, instruction that allow students to discuss the reasons why strategies are appropriate in certain situations should help them make effective decisions when selecting strategies for a particular task.

Third, many average and low-performing students tried to memorize terms as their main studying strategy. It is important that students realize why this is a surface strategy, and the drawbacks that memorizing terms has when compared to deep strategy use. Therefore, instruction in college reading and study strategy courses should also emphasize deep level strategies over surface strategies. We need to not only teach students deep level strategies, but also to help students understand the reasons why these strategies lead to success in learning. Thus, college reading and study strategy instruction must extend beyond modeling and direct instruction of strategies to teaching the processes underlying strategy use such as isolating, organizing, and elaborating on information.

References

Alexander, P. A., & Kulikowich, J. (1994). Learning from physics text: A synthesis of recent research. *Journal of Research in Science Teaching, 31*, 895–911.

Anderson, O. R. (1990). *The teaching and learning of biology in the United States.* New York: Columbia University.

Baxter Magolda, M. B. (1992). *Knowing and reasoning in college: Gender-related patterns in students' intellectual development.* San Francisco: Jossey-Bass.

Bernard, H. R. (1994). *Research methods in anthropology.* Thousand Oaks, CA: Sage.

Biggs, J. B. (1988). Approaches to learning and to essay writing. In R. R. Schmeck (Ed.), *Learning strategies and learning styles* (pp. 181–228). New York: Plenum.

Blanchard, J. & Mikkleson, V. (1987). Underlining performance outcomes in expository text. *Journal of Educational Research, 80*, 197–201.

Briscoe, C., & LeMaster, S. U. (1991). Meaningful learning in college biology through concept mapping. *The American Biology Teacher, 53*, 214–219.

Cavallo, A. M. L., & Schafer, L. E. (1994). Relationships between students' meaningful learning orientation and their understanding of genetics topics. *Journal of Research in Science Teaching, 31*, 393–418.

Coleman, E. B., & Shore, B. (1991). Problem-solving processes of high and average performers in physics. *Journal for the Education of the Gifted, 14*, 366–379.

Corkhill, A. J. (1996). *Metacognitive awareness questionnaire scoring guidelines with person, task, and strategy components.* Unpublished measure.

DeJong, T., & Ferguson-Hessler, M. G. M. (1996). Types and qualities of knowledge. *Educational Psychologist, 31*, 105–114.

Edmondson, K. M. (1995, April). *Promoting self-directed learning in developing or poorly defined subject areas: A problem-based course in molecular biology, genetics, and cancer.* Paper presented at the meeting of the American Educational Research Association, San Francisco. (ERIC Document Reproduction Service No. ED 387 027).

Entwistle, N. (1988). Motivational factors in students' approaches to learning. In R. R. Schmeck (Ed.), *Learning strategies and learning styles* (pp. 21–52). New York: Plenum.

Garner, R. (1988). Verbal-report data on cognitive and metacognitive strategies. In C. E. Weinstein, E. T. Goetz, & P. A. Alexander (Eds.), *Learning and study strategies: Issues in assessment, instruction, and evaluation* (pp. 63–76). San Diego, CA: Academic Press.

Glynn, S. W. (1991). Expanding science concepts: A teaching-with-analogies model. In S. W. Glynn, R. H. Yeany, & B. K. Britton (Eds.), *The psychology of learning science* (pp. 219–240). Hillsdale, NJ: Erlbaum.

Hammer, D. (1994a). Epistemological beliefs in introductory physics. *Cognition and Instruction, 12*, 151–183.

Hammer, D. (1994b). Students' beliefs about conceptual knowledge in introductory physics. *International Journal of Science Education, 16*, 385–403.

Holschuh, J. L. (1995, November). *"It all sort or gets cloudy": Voices of high and low performers in college biology courses.* Paper presented at the annual meeting of the National Reading Conference, New Orleans, LA.

Larkin, J. H., & Reif, F. (1979). Understanding and teaching problem solving in physics. *European Journal of Science Education, 1*, 191–293.

Lee, O., Fradd, S. H., & Sutman, F. X. (1995). Science knowledge and cognitive strategy use among culturally and linguistically diverse students. *Journal of Research in Science Teaching, 32*, 797–816.

Lord, T. R. (1994). Using constructivism to enhance student learning in college biology. *Journal of College Science Teaching, 23*, 346–348.

Marton, F., & Saljo, R. (1997). Approaches to learning. In F. Marton, D. Hounsell, & N. Entwistle (Eds.), *The experience of learning* (2nd ed., pp. 39–58). Edinburgh, Scotland: Scottish Academic Press.

Nist, S. L., & Diehl, W. (1994). *Developing textbook thinking* (3rd ed.). Lexington, MA: Heath.

Nist, S. L., & Holschuh, J. P. (April, 2000). *Exploring the factors that influence performance in introductory biology: A multi-layered approach.* Paper presented at the annual meeting of the American Educational Research Association, New Orleans, LA.

Nist, S. L., Holschuh, J. L., & Sharman, S. J. (1995, November). *Making the grade in undergraduate biology courses: Factors that distinguish high from low performers.* Paper presented at the meeting of the National Reading Conference, New Orleans, LA.

Nolen, S. B., & Haladyna, T. M. (1990). Personal and environmental influences on students' beliefs about effective study strategies. *Contemporary Educational Psychology, 15*, 116–130.

Norris, S. P., & Phillips, L. M. (1994). Interpreting pragmatic meaning when reading popular reports of science. *Journal of Research in Science Teaching, 31*, 934–947.

Padilla, M. J. (1991). Science activities, process skills, and thinking. In S. W. Glynn, R. H. Yeany, & B. K. Britton (Eds.), *The psychology of learning science* (pp. 205–217). Hillsdale, NJ: Erlbaum.

Patton, M. Q. (1990). *Qualitative evaluation and research methods.* Newbury Park, CA: Sage.

Qian, G. (1995, November). *The role of epistemological beliefs and motivational goals in ethnically diverse high school students' learning from science text.* Paper presented at the meeting of the National Reading Conference, New Orleans, LA.

Ryan, J. (1989). Study skills for the sciences: A bridge over troubled waters. *Journal of College Science Teaching, 18*, 373–377.

Spiegel, G. F., Jr., Barufaldi, J. P. (1994). The effects of a combination of text structure awareness and graphic postorganizers on recall and retention of science knowledge. *Journal of Research in Science Teaching, 31*, 913–932.

Trowbridge, J. E., & Wandersee, J. H. (1994). Identifying critical junctures in learning in a college course on evolution. *Journal of Research in Science Teaching, 31*, 459–473.

Additional Readings

Brothen, T., & Wambach, C. (2000). "Using factual study questions to guide reading and promote mastery learning by developmental students in an introductory psychology course." *Journal of College Reading and Learning,* 30 (2), 158–66.

Brozo, W. G., & Simpson, M. L. (2000). *Readers, teachers, learners: Expanding literacy across the content areas,* 3rd ed. Upper Saddle River, NJ: Merrill.

Carson, J. G., Chase, N. D., Gibson, S. U., & Hargrove, M. F. (1992). "Literacy demands of the undergraduate curriculum." *Reading, Research and Instruction,* 31 (4), 25–50.

Chase, N., Gibson, S. U., & Carson, J. G. (1994). An examination of reading demands across four college courses. *Journal of Developmental Education,* 18 (1), 10–16.

Chiersi-Strater, E. (1991). *Academic literacies: The public and private discourse of university students.* Portsmouth, NH: Boynton-Cook.

Congos, F. H., Langsam, D., & Schoeps, N. (1997). "Supplemental Instruction: A successful approach to learning how to learn college introductory biology." *The Journal of Teaching and Learning,* 2 (1), 2–17.

Draper, R. J. (2002). "School mathematics reform, constructivism, and literacy: A case for literacy instruction in the reform-oriented math classroom." *Journal of Adolescent & Adult Literacy,* 45 (6), 520–29.

Readence, J. E., Bean, T. W., & Baldwin, R. S. (2001). *Content area literacy,* 7th ed. Dubuque: Kendall Hunt.

Simpson, M. L. (1995). "Talk throughs: A strategy for encouraging active learning across the content areas." *Journal of Reading,* 38 (4), 296–304.

Simpson, M. L., & Nist, S. L. (1997). "Perspectives on learning history: A case study." *Journal of Literacy Research,* 29 (3), 363–95.

8

The Reading/ Writing Connection

I n the not so distant past, literacy educators viewed reading and writing as fundamentally different activities. They thought of reading as receptive in nature and of writing as expressive. However, in the past two decades a growing body of theory and research has examined the relationships between reading and writing as they influence the processes of thinking and learning. Such theory views both activities as composing processes that lead to meaning-making through interaction with text. In their now classic "Toward a Composing Model of Reading," researchers Robert J. Tierney and P. David Pearson argue convincingly that in both reading and writing the learner undertakes the cognitive activities of planning, drafting, aligning, revising, and monitoring of meaning. And in developmental education in particular, the integrated basic reading and basic writing instructional model began to gain national attention with the release of *Facts, Artifacts, and Counterfacts: Theory and Method for a Reading and Writing Course* by David Bartholomae and Anthony Petrosky in 1986.

The authors in this chapter share with us a range of ideas about the reading and writing connection in the developmental education program. Karen Quinn's article provides both a historical perspective as well as a view of the future of reading and writing instruction. Amelia El-Hindi discusses how metacognitive awareness is fostered through integrated instruction with reading and writing. Mary Deming and Maria Valeri-Gold share the reading and writing strategies they have integrated in their own classes through the teaching of Shay Youngblood's *Big Mama Stories*. Cynthia Chamblee covers how she has used reader-response theories and the process approach to writing instruction across a decade of teaching college reading at a historically black liberal arts college. Finally, the article by Maryann Feola shows how both critical and analytical comprehension skills as well as associated competencies in the language arts are promoted through the use of dramatic texts in developmental education literacy classes.

Teaching Reading and Writing as Modes of Learning in College: A Glance at the Past; a View to the Future

Karen B. Quinn

This article examines the integration of postsecondary reading and writing instruction from the late 1800s to the latter days of the twentieth century. Specific attention is given to theories, research, and practices associated with reading in the content areas, writing across the curriculum, reading and writing pedagogy, college reading programs, and reading as a discipline. Thoughts for the future are provided as well.

We hear a great deal these days about reading and writing as modes of learning (McGinley, 1992; McGinley & Tierney, 1988; Ackerman, 1993). It is often couched within teachers' or researchers' discussions of WAC, writing across the curriculum, LAC, learning across the curriculum, WID, writing in the disciplines, or CAR, content area reading. Members of each of these camps would probably acknowledge that descriptions of reading and writing as modes of learning should include the idea that both share similar purposes and processes. That is, reading and writing are not ends in themselves, but "tools," "lenses," or ways of thinking and knowing (McGinley & Tierney, 1988) which serve to help students construct knowledge or make meaning (Spivey, 1990) through dynamic interaction among a learner's existing knowledge, text, and context. Likewise, members would agree that reading and writing should be viewed as a single act of literacy (Straw, 1990) with shared cognitive processes and, as such, should be taught together for the purpose of extending thinking, expanding learning, and transforming knowledge.

Discussions about reading and writing as modes of learning in college among teachers and researchers also hinge on the idea of the acquisition of "critical literacy." Again, most would agree that successful acquisition of critical literacy in the context of higher learning means using reading and writing in ways that go beyond minimal competency and in ways which allow readers writers to carry out a complex set of demanding goals for analysis, synthesis, and original expression (Flower, 1989). Similarly, discussions of critical literacy invoke the idea that reading and writing are conceptual tools (McGinley, 1992) consisting of a learner's "literacy repertoire" made up of knowledge of different academic discourse forms and conventions which allow readers/writers to examine and explore topics.

Those of us who teach academic reading and writing at the college level or, in current parlance, who attempt to help students achieve critical literacy, follow current trends in theory, research, and practice without giving much thought to the historical circumstances which have led up to the changes in the way reading and writing are conceived, researched, taught, and even talked about today. Yet there are important landmarks in education and research that propelled the ebb and flow of the phenomenon of reading and writing as modes of learning over the years. These historical moments provide a rich understanding of the evolution of reading and writing and place our roles as practitioners of college reading and writing in the context of intellectual and pedagogical traditions spanning 150 years.

In this article, I present a brief overview of the history of reading and writing as modes of learning in college. Throughout, I attempt to shed some light on reasons why college reading and writing as practice and profession "continue to operate on the fringes of respectability" (Kerstiens, cited in Cranney, 1983), as well as separate from each other and often apart from learning. I conclude with a discussion of what we can learn from the history of reading and writing that will help practitioners (whether they espouse WAC, LAC, WID, or CAR) plan for their future roles in teaching reading and writing as modes of learning in college.

History

The good news about the history of teaching and research in reading and writing as modes of learning is that it spans a short time frame, from about the early 80's to the present. The bad news, however, is that we cannot really understand this history without reference to many other histories, to wit, the history of educational practice in reading education, in English education, in college composition, and in rhetoric. Furthermore, the history of reading and writing to learn cuts across the history of research traditions from behavioralism (1915–1970), to the cognitive revolution in the late 70's, to the current emphasis on the socially constructed nature of learning. Thus, in attempting to reflect the complex history and multidisciplinary nature of teaching and research in reading and writing as modes of learning, I draw selectively from several recent articles concerning the history of the writing across the curriculum movement (Ackerman, 1993; Russell 1987; 1989; 1990), the history of reading and writing instruction in schools (Clifford, 1987; Robinson, 1977), the history of college reading courses (Wyatt, 1992), the history of content area reading (Moore, Readence, & Rickelman, 1983), and the history of reading research (Bogdan & Straw, 1990).

The Early Years: Institutional Attempts at Integrating College Reading and Writing

While reading and writing as modes of learning is a recent phenomenon in teaching practice and research, discussions about the importance of integrating reading and writing have occurred throughout the decades beginning in the late 1800's. As early as 1894, the National Education Association's Committee of Ten (made up of presidents from ten colleges), chaired by Harvard University President, Charles Eliot, declared in a final report that reading and writing were of equal value (Applebee, 1974). And, in practice, institutions represented on the Committee of Ten did try to integrate reading and writing in ways that spanned the spectrum: At one end, at Harvard, students were required to write an essay based on reading a short passage for admission. At the other end of the spectrum, at Ohio State, a real attempt at integrating reading and writing for specific learning purposes was implemented in 1897, in the design of discipline-specific writing courses for students in agriculture, pre-med, journalism, and engineering.

The next twenty years held interesting promise for the integration of reading and writing with learning. From 1900 to about 1920, often referred to as the progressive era in education, new trends and movements at all levels of schooling were initiated. One of these, the Cooperation movement, was built on the premise that cooperation among teachers, departments, and institutions, would lead to greater student learning. At the college level, the cooperation movement in language instruction meant broadening the responsibility for language instruction by involving faculty across the curriculum. Cooperation was realized in different ways, some more successful than others.

As early as 1907, at M.I.T., students' English composition and foreign language courses included reading materials from technical courses for writing and translation exercises. As students progressed through their major course of study, their science and technical courses incorporated writing. In addition, English department faculty lectured on writing in technical courses and helped teachers from other departments design assignments. The emphasis at M.I.T. seemed to be squarely on the uses of reading and writing for communicating and learning in different contexts. This "uses" approach would be much more in line with the approach embraced by the National Council of Teachers of English (formed in 1911 by James Hosic) and by the Commission on Reorganization of Secondary Education of the National Education

Association. Both emphasized, in a report in 1917, language as communication (Hosic, 1917).

However, other models of cooperation in language instruction were not based on shared goals for integrating reading and writing with learning. Many had as their primary objective, standard, correct usage in writing. One such model at Harvard resulted in English faculty becoming what Russell (1989) has called "writing police": All instructors were required to submit really bad examples of student writing, including essays, exams, theses, to the English department where appropriate action would be taken.

The potential which the cooperation movement in higher education promised in models such as those at M.I.T. was never fully realized. Turf wars, funding battles, departmental insularity and hegemony worked against the interdisciplinary cooperation so critical to the success of this movement. In fact, many colleges and universities followed the Harvard model of cooperation in language education resulting in increased referrals to English department faculty and the burgeoning of remediation. Students were sorted, separated, and taught reading and writing as discrete skills in isolation. At Harvard, in 1915, there was a freshman composition course taught separately from a reading and study course. By 1920, both the University of Chicago and the University of Illinois had a formal college reading and study program (Stahl, Simpson & Hayes, 1992), but no formal writing course. Furthermore, there is no evidence that the reading, writing, and study skills courses at these institutions were integrated with content for learning. Ironically, a movement designed to promote integration in language and learning may have actually encouraged the instructional separation of reading from writing, isolating both from the context of subject area learning.

The Middle Years: The Impact of Professional Advocacy and Affiliation on College Reading and Writing

The 1930's, 40's, and 50's were important decades marked by the advocacy work of several professional organizations in attempting to reverse the unfortunate trend of teaching reading and writing in isolation and apart from learning. In 1936, in the book *A Correlated Curriculum* (D. Appleton-Century), members of the National Council of Teachers of English (NCTE) urged the importance of integrating reading, writing, speaking, and listening activities in schools and offered practical suggestions for ways to do so. Three years later, in 1939, a federal Blue Ribbon Commission, chaired by I. A. Richards, picked up the integrationist gauntlet and drove it into the realms of other subject areas. The Commission insisted upon the interdependence of English and other subjects and recommended the universal application of language skills as tools of critical thought across subjects. In 1947, NCTE and the Speech Association of America sponsored a conference on freshman college courses which emphasized language instruction across the curriculum. (This collaboration would lead to the founding of the Conference on College Composition and Communication). Throughout the fifties, NCTE reiterated its commitment to an integrated language arts approach.

During these same years, William S. Gray, a leading reading educator and early promoter of content area reading, would call for reading to be taught across the curriculum to all students, regardless of ability, and/or major, initiating the slogan "Every teacher a teacher of reading." Another prominent figure in the content area reading movement, Ernest Horn, advocated wide reading in the subject areas to enhance meaningful learning. Unfortunately, discussions of content area reading throughout the years rarely included writing and may be an important factor in CAR's isolation from WAC programs at the secondary and post secondary levels.

The rhetoric of combining reading and writing with learning paid off in the 40's and the 50's with the emergence of the first formal college WAC programs designed to integrate reading, writing, and learning across academic departments. The Functional Writing Program at Colgate and the Prose Improvement Committee at Berkeley were model programs which emphasized the importance of reading and writing in improving learning. The Colgate program involved helping faculty include writing assignments in their course instruction. The assignments used the reading materials of the course and promoted its educational goals in order to improve the "day-to-day learning process" of students (Russell, 1987). The Berkeley model also viewed writing as closely linked to learning and had as its goal a deeper integration of writing and learning. While faculty were not involved directly, teaching assistants from different departments taught lectures and small groups focusing on writing in their disciplines. The success of the Colgate and Berkeley models relied on their ability to deal with the highly differentiated curricula in academia. Unfortunately, the additive or "banking" (Freire, 1970) view of learning (knowledge is memorized and reproduced in tests) held fast by most practitioners in the disciplines did not quite square with the more synthetic view of learning (knowledge and personal experience are integrated and connected across courses) inherent in WAC programs such as those at Colgate and Berkeley. These two models challenged the traditional departmental divisions exalting experts and specialized knowledge, which would become so important to the expansion of universities during the 1960's. The two model programs at Berkeley and Colgate, unable to withstand the increased compartmentalization of academic work within departments, lasted only into the early 60's.

As programs were being developed to integrate reading and writing for learning across disciplines in the 40's and 50's, and as professional organizations were proclaiming the merits of integrating language arts as well as the necessity of viewing learning as the goal of language instruction, dissension among the ranks of one group, NCTE, resulted in a split among members which to this day has had serious ramifications for research and teaching practice in reading and writing as modes of learning.

From its inception in 1911 until 1947, NCTE was the professional association to which teachers of reading, English, and writing at all levels belonged. Teachers of these subjects all read the same journals, *Language Arts, English Journal,* and *Research in the Teaching of English.* They shared the same language, intellectual tradition, and research models. However, for much the same reason that NCTE was formed, in reaction to college domination of high school English curriculum and pedagogy, reading researchers and educators reacted to the domination of NCTE by teachers of college English. In response to issues of concern among elementary school reading teachers, reading specialists, clinicians, and supervisors, Constance McCullough formed the National Association of Remedial Teachers in 1947. At about the same time, another group at Temple University formed the International Council for the Improvement of Reading Instruction. By 1955, these two groups had merged to form the International Reading Association.

The break with NCTE and the formation of IRA resulted in further isolating reading from writing: discussions about integrating reading and writing no longer had a forum; reading, writing, and English teachers at the elementary, high school, and college levels had few professional opportunities to interact; and because of the elementary school focus of IRA, the teaching of reading in high school remained removed from content area learning. Even today, in most cases, English education scholars, reading researchers, and writing specialists read different scholarly journals, follow parallel but uncoordinated research agendas, and are not familiar with research and pedagogy from each other's fields.

The unfortunate legacy of this split has been particularly telling for college reading teaching as practice and profession. College reading teaching is increasingly the concern of specialists in reading, a specialty removed from English and writing (Dias, 1990). The teaching of college reading remains largely outside of the practice, and college reading teachers outside of the dialog, of WAC or WID, largely English department enterprises where discussions of research and practice in reading and writing as modes of learning most often take place. The split has made it difficult for college reading teachers to maneuver from the periphery to a more central place in making contributions to teaching and researching reading and writing as modes of learning.

*The Sixties: Influence of Curricular Reform and Open Access
on College Reading and Writing*

The 60's were an era in education unlike any other before or since. Federal monies such as those from the National Defense Education Act and the Office of Education for curricular and pedagogical reform were readily available. The impact of projects and institute programs begun during this time would resonate even up to the present. One project, in 1961, Project English was designed to reeducate English and reading teachers in ways to interrelate literature, composition, and language in the classroom. By 1966, there were 20 Curriculum Studies and Demonstration Centers around the country. However, teacher participation was so low, and the goals espoused by the programs and institutes so "out of sync" with the realities of public school classrooms, that the curricular and pedagogical experiments which were predicted to be many were, in fact, very few.

At about the same time, in 1965, the College Entrance Examination Board (CEEB), in *Freedom and Discipline in English,* proposed a three part division of high school English into language, literature, and composition. Reading was completely ignored. The net effect of this division would further isolate reading from the mainstream of content learning, in this case literature. Worse, this division tainted reading with the stigma of remediation: Literature study was for the college bound student; reading materials were for the vocationally bound.

The tripartite division of English into composition, language, and literature was attacked by participants at a historic meeting of English educators from Britain and the United States in 1966, the Anglo-American Dartmouth Conference, chaired by John Dixon. The Dartmouth Conference was a bright light on the horizon for teaching reading and writing as modes of learning. It advocated a unitary rather then a fragmentary approach to English (Dixon, 1967). One of its most important recommendations, using language to learn, was a move away from the preoccupation with literature, in the belle lettristic tradition, which was continually stressed by high school and college English teachers and organizations such as CEEB during the 60's. Unfortunately, this recommendation and others of the Dartmouth Conference were a few years too late in coming and never implemented because by the end of the 60's federal funds for education were beginning to dry up.

The 60's were a period of egalitarianism (Cross, 1971) opening the doors of education to promote equality and equal access to all Americans. Open admissions and National Defense loan monies allowed many nontraditional and minority students to attend college. Remedial programs and courses burgeoned during this time. By the end of the decade in 1969, the federal Right to Read program would be instituted as a national strategy for attacking functional illiteracy. Its singular focus on corrective attention to basic discrete reading skills, (apart from writing and learning), for nontraditional students resulted in further removing reading from writing and from content learning, supporting the "fragmentation and specialization that have moved through society . . . " (Clifford, 1987, p. 20), and marginalizing reading teaching even more as a remedial occupation.

*The Seventies: Effect of Research Trends on Teaching
College Reading and Writing.*

While the sixties did not turn out to be a particularly great era for realizing the teaching of reading and writing as modes of learning, on the research front, some interesting trends were beginning to emerge which would join the issue of reading and writing as complementary ways of making meaning and learning. Reading research would play the dominant role.

In 1963, the *Handbook of Research on Teaching* included in its list of research, a small corpus of investigations and theory supporting the integration of reading and writing for learning (Gage, 1963). English teachers learned that bringing reading into the English classroom lead to greater learning. Reading teachers learned that writing activities improved reading comprehension and that good readers were more likely to do more creative writing. Up to this point, the focus of the yearly publication of the *Handbook* had been on reading research, of which there was much more than writing, not yet a field of research and scholarship. With the exception of Bartlett's work on comprehension and memory in his 1932 book, *Remembering: A Study in Experimental and Social Psychology,* the dominant strands of reading research were readability, cloze procedure, psycholinguistics, and factor analytic studies. Even though researchers followed the behaviorist credo, studying observable behaviors, such as oral reading, word recognition, eye movements, and text features such as sentence length, number of words, and ratio of incomplete to complete sentences, here were the first attempts to link reading and writing in studies which demonstrated the impact they had on each other and on learning.

The psychometric/skills based models of reading, dominant during the 40's, 50's, and early 60's, were also being challenged by new theories of learning and language which were being used to develop new models of reading. Psychometric/skills based models of reading such as Davis' (1944/1983) and Holmes' (1953) were based on the assumption that reading is a behavior comprised of a cluster of independent skills (and sub skills) which, when measured by a test, could account for reading comprehension performance in subjects. In skills-based models, "meaning resides in the text and it is the role of the reader to translate that text into its intended meaning" (Straw & Sadowy, 1990, p. 33). Competing text-based, information-processing models of reading were advocated by researchers such as Gough (1972) and La Berge & Samuels

(1974). These models were comprised of a string of operations informed by reader knowledge (such as lexical and syntactic knowledge), as well as memory and attention. While these models placed primary emphasis on the text where meaning was assumed to reside, they acknowledged, for the first time, reader factors and how they might interact with text to influence meaning.

The interactive aspects of the text-based model of La Berge and Samuels would be expanded upon in several important models of reading developed during the 70's and 80's. These models were based on cognitive psychology, transformational-generative linguistics (first introduced in Chomsky's 1957 book *Syntactic Structures* and made more comprehensive in his 1965 book *Aspects of a Theory of Syntax*) as well as schema theory (Shank & Abelson, 1977). Psycholinguistic models such as Goodman's (1967) and Smith's (1971) viewed reading as a holistic activity, not a discrete set of skills or operations. They emphasized knowledge of the reader in making sense out of print and deemphasized the role of the text, itself. Thus, Goodman and Burke's miscue analysis (1972) attempted to understand the quality of the errors or miscues in oral reading and how they represent readers' attempts at making meaning and predictions based on their knowledge of content, discourse features, and linguistic patterns. Later interactive models such as Rumelhart's (1977) and Lesgold and Perfetti's (1978) expanded on the idea of the match between reader knowledge and text structure by hypothesizing the recursive and interactive nature of components of the reading process, including reader environment, reader knowledge of text structure and content, reader use and control of knowledge, and reader product.

Process-product debates in teaching were taking shape during the 70's also. According to Ackerman (1993), the teaching of reading and writing were openly being reconsidered, with student-centered and process models of reading and writing gaining momentum through the work of Shaughnessy (1977) on individual composing processes, Bruner (1966) on the social-psychology of learning processes, and Macrorie (1976) and Elbow (1973) on innovative classroom practices. Proponents of the whole language approach to teaching reading and writing turned attention away from the mastery of specific skills to language instruction which emphasized the acquisition of meaning through active involvement in reading and writing (Goodman & Goodman, 1977; Smith, 1982). Indeed, with the whole language emphasis on coordinating speaking, reading, writing, and listening, a move to integrate elements of language at the secondary level encouraged the reemergence of CAR or "content communication" (Dishner & Readence, 1981).

The Eighties: Cognitive Process Research and Instruction in College Reading and Writing

The 80's were a watershed decade for research in reading and writing as it moved from a long standing behavioral preoccupation with the products of reading and writing to a cognitive interest in the processes of these two language skills and their impact on learning. Schema theoretic notions of the reading process were being advanced based on Bartlett's early work on recall of North American Indian folk tales. His work showed that a person will recall certain aspects of text based on a preconceived schema or "script" which readers have stored in memory. Some sixty years later, Bartlett's important work would be invoked in a 1980 article, "Constructive Processes in Prose Comprehension and Recall," written by Rand Spiro and often credited with heralding in the cognitive revolution in reading and writing. Calling upon schema theory to explain recall results of readers, Spiro concluded that reading comprehension was as much a constructive activity as a receptive activity, with readers engaging in meaning making processes thought to be solely the domain of writers. For the first time, meaning was conceived of as residing outside of the sanctity of the text. Following on the heels of this work, other reading researchers such as Anderson and Pearson (1984), Adams and Collins (1985), and Anderson (1985) posited models built upon the assumption that a text provided direction for the reader to help him or her retrieve or construct meaning based on prior experience or schemas.

A parallel line of inquiry in writing research was also emerging in the late 70's and early 80's. Studies of writing were just beginning to be undertaken by researchers such as Emig (who actually titled a 1977 article, "Writing as a Mode of Learning"), Perl (1979), Sommers (1980), and Flower and Hayes (1981). Borrowing methods from the case study and problem-solving research of cognitive psychologists (think-aloud protocols), they studied the revisions and plans writers made in their writing with a view, like reading researchers, to understanding the decisions writers make in their writing by examining the interactions at play among text, context, and writer in the written production of language.

The new attention to the interactive, constructive nature of reading and writing and the meaning making processes involved in language production and comprehension moved a young cadre of literacy researchers in the 80's to examine the interrelationships between reading and writing and to build theories which emphasized process models of reading and writing. Pearson and Tierney would develop a composing model of reading (1984). Shanahan and Lomax (1986) would investigate comparisons among different theoretical models of reading and writing relationships. Work in the area of discourse synthesis (Spivey, 1984) and writing from sources (Kennedy, 1985; Nelson & Hayes, 1988) would begin to direct attention toward patterns of learning and reasoning which emerged when students read and wrote different kinds of texts. In the late 80's, the reading-to-write series of reports from the Center for the Study of Writing and Literacy would examine alternative perspectives on the processes and strategies which college students bring to bear on tasks requiring writing based on reading. The 80's also saw a return to classroom and teacher-based research, away from the controlled experiments of the educational and cognitive psychologists in the 70's (Vacca & Vacca, 1983).

Research begun in the mid 80's which relates directly to teaching reading and writing as modes of learning is work in the area of writing and its impact on learning. Researchers such as Newell (1984), Langer (1986), Langer and Applebee (1987), Marshall, (1987), Durst (1989), McGinley & Tierney (1989), Schumacher & Gradwohl-Nash (1991), and Penrose, (1992) found that reading with writing promotes knowledge transformation, extends and enriches students' engagement in learning, and encourages more thoughtful exploration and elaboration of ideas. Reading and writing were found to generate different patterns of cognitive behavior (Langer & Applebee, 1986) and to serve complementary and unique ways to think about a topic or a task (McGinley, 1992).

In addition to research, during the 80's three important books would appear which focused scholarly as well as public attention on reading and writing abilities of students and how they affected learning. In 1983 and 1985 respectively, *A Nation At Risk* and *Becoming a Nation of Readers* were published. Both were important clarion calls for teachers and researchers as they chronicled the abysmal failure of schools to teach students to read beyond the most basic level. Their recommendations included increased emphasis on teaching students to use reading and writing as an effective way to learn content in all subjects at all levels. Two years later in 1986, Langer and Applebee published *Writing and Learning in the Secondary Schools* in reaction to NAEP findings which indicated that high school students were unable to respond critically to reading or to write analytical responses to reading. Their recommendations included content-specific reading and writing assignments which would require students to apply, analyze, and interpret new learning. Reinforcing these recommendations, participants at the English Coalition Conference in 1989 would define reading and writing as means of discussion and learning (Lloyd-Jones & Lunsford, 1989). The move, begun in the 80's, from teaching reading and writing as ends in themselves to teaching them as modes of learning seems to be on a slow, but steady track as we head through the 90's.

The Current Scene: Encouraging Signs for Teaching
Reading and Writing as Modes of Learning

The 90's have witnessed an increased awareness on the part of teachers and researchers about teaching reading and writing as ways to learn content and academic discourse. We already see encouraging signs of this awareness in the proliferation of WAC programs currently in colleges and universities around the country. A major goal of instruction for such programs is reading and writing for learning specific subject matter. In addition, the current content orientation of composition and reading courses focuses the teaching of reading and writing less on skills and more on learning and applying new content and discourse knowledge within specific disciplines. We see this orientation evidenced in recent textbooks such as *Academic Reading* (McWhorter, 1994) and *Critical Strategies for Academic Thinking and Writing* (Kiniry & Rose, 1992) which devote half of their 500 pages to assignments requiring students to apply reading/writing strategies to learn about subject areas typically encountered in freshmen year college studies. Current interest in teaching critical thinking skills (Brookfield, 1987; Chaffee, 1993) places major emphasis on reading and writing as ways to reason, analyze, and apply one's knowledge in one subject to problem solve in another. The important new interest in examining cultural and social context in diverse discourse communities urges teachers and researchers to envision learning through reading and writing in unique and powerful ways. Moreover, teaching reading and writing as modes of learning is fortified by the current social-constructivist theory of learning (Bruner, 1986; Vygotsky, 1986) which views reading and writing as social and cultural tools for acquiring and practicing learning. Research on situated cognition (how different reading and writing contexts impact learning) and on intentional, self-directed strategic learning (McGinley, 1992) bodes well for "the possibility that students can be taught to use reading and writing together . . . based upon the thinking operations required by learners' goals." (Tierney & Shanahan, 1991)

Finally, as this brief history has shown, over the decades school reform movements have had some negative, even though unintentional, implications for the teaching of reading and writing as modes of learning. Today, the 90's school reform efforts at setting national standards for teaching and assessment in school subjects from grades K-12 may have serious ramifications for teaching reading and writing as modes of learning in schools and colleges. The Standards Project for English Language Arts, a three year collaborative effort involving IRA, NCTE, and CSR (Center for the Study of Reading), is developing national standards for classroom instruction and student learning in English. The fact that the three organizations are working together for the first time since 1947 is a recognition of the importance of teaching and assessing reading and writing together. On the other hand, concerns have been raised that the isolated treatment of subjects such as English will discourage interdisciplinary approaches to learning (Hanford, 1994). It would be an irony (but not all together surprising given the enigmatic history of teaching reading and writing as modes of learning) if the standards reform movement signaled a return to teaching and assessing reading and writing as discrete, acontextualized skills separate from the goals of student learning across the curriculum. But as Lawrence Cremin has ruefully remarked, (cited in Russell, 1987), "Reform movements are notoriously ahistorical in their outlook."

Future Directions for Teaching Reading and Writing as Modes of Learning in College

As this glance at the past shows, there were moments throughout the decades when discussions about reading and writing as modes of learning surfaced. Reform initiatives such as the cooperation movement, the establishment of early discipline-specific writing courses and writing across the curriculum programs, as well as historic meetings among professional organizations and among prominent educators promoted reading and writing to learn. Unfortunately, these discussions submerged under the weight of their advocacy, unsupported by research and theory. Today, however, discussions about reading and writing as modes of learning are emerging, buoyed by research findings that demonstrate reading and writing are powerful tools for enhancing thinking and learning and for engaging learners in a greater variety of reasoning operations (Tierney & Shanahan, 1991). Researchers studying writing in the context of reading have found that students' knowledge acquisition, skill development, thinking ability, and knowledge transformation are enhanced because students' levels of cognitive engagement both during and after reading are extended and enriched (Langer, 1986; Newell, 1984; Newell & Winograd, 1989). Other studies have shown that reading and writing encourage greater learner involvement and influence different, complementary, and unique ways to think about a topic (Kennedy, 1985; Langer & Applebee, 1986; McGinley, 1992).

While these research findings are a most hopeful sign for the vibrancy of discussions about reading and writing as modes of learning in college, an attendant instructional agenda has yet to be fully realized (Tierney & Shanahan, 1991). It is in this arena that college reading and writing teachers can contribute most to future directions for teaching reading and writing as modes of learning. However, the historical conceptions of college reading and writing, the traditional institutionalized and marginalized roles of college reading and writing teachers, and Newell and Winograd's (1989) observation that reading and writing are rarely used together to help students learn content-area information may make for interesting challenges in setting instructional agendas in reading and writing as modes of learning. And yet as Tierney has noted, " . . . a great many of the major shifts in literacy education related to reading/writing relationships were sponsored by teachers . . . " (Tierney, 1992, p. 249). There are other encouraging signs as well.

Models from WAC and CAR Programs

Curricular and instructional models for programs in Writing Across the Curriculum or Content Area Reading show promise for curriculum and instruction in reading and writing as modes of learning, as do writing to learn strategies practiced within college reading and writing courses which emphasize discipline specific literacy strategies for learning content. Curricular approaches that stress a simulations model (Stahl, Simpson, & Hayes, 1992) which "replicate the tasks and texts of a typical required, lower division course . . . " (p. 3), or which pair content courses across the curriculum with adjunct or "shadow" courses that provide practice in reading and writing for learning course topics treat students to real literacy experiences situated in the context of their own learning, thus promoting reading and writing as modes of learning. Writing to learn practices that encourage idea discussion and exchange or those that encourage students to question and explore new learning among peers and with content experts, such as learning logs or dialog journals, bring together reading, writing, and learning in a dynamic dialectic.

Implications from Current Research

Current research agendas in reading and writing point to promising new directions for instruction in reading and writing as modes of learning. Drawing on research examining the impact that different types of reading and writing activities have on comprehension and learning (Ackerman, 1991; Brown & Day, 1983; Brown, Day, & Jones, 1983; Durst, 1987; Flower, 1987; Greene, 1993; Hidi & Anderson, 1986; Kennedy, 1985; Marshall, 1987; McGinley, 1992; Newell, 1984; Quinn, 1987), researchers have found that notetaking during reading as well as summary writing and extended analytical writing based on reading impact students' planning, organizing, manipulation, and evaluation of ideas and increase their range of reasoning operations, resulting in more elaboration, integration, and extensions of ideas.

Work which explores the relationships between reading/writing multiple texts and learning as well as the relationships between situational context and learning may inform curriculum and instruction in reading and writing as modes of learning. Research studies in areas such as reading from sources (Ackerman, 1991; Durst, 1989; Flower, 1987; Greene 1993; Kennedy, 1985; Nelson & Hayes, 1988), discourse synthesis (Spivey, 1984; Spivey & King, 1989), and intertextuality (Bloome & Egan-Robertson, 1993; McGinley & Tierney, 1988; Tierney, Soter, O'Flavahan, & McGinley, 1989;) have shown how learners negotiate meaning and "crisscross" interrelationships among texts by examining factors such as students' expertise, knowledge, and ability. They have also demonstrated how learning associated with reading and writing is situationally-based, tied to specific contexts, content, and learners' purposes.

As compelling as these findings are, recent research (Langer & Applebee, 1987; Penrose, 1992) indicates that different reading/writing tasks may interfere with learning because they engage learners' thinking and reasoning processes in different ways leading to different learning outcomes. Moreover, learners' prior knowledge about content and experience with the institutional, cultural, and disciplinary practices of the academy may have a profound impact on their ability to use reading and writing as effective modes for learning (Ackerman, 1993; Tierney, 1992).

Given these research findings, future directions for teaching reading and writing as modes of learning must take into account the social and cultural worlds of college students while engaging them in a variety of learning situations representing different content areas, requiring different reading and writing tasks. Tasks that require students to read, take notes, summarize, discuss, revise, analyze, separately, together, and in different combinations are critical if students are to use reading and writing as modes of learning. Tasks that promote a metacognitive awareness of the different reading and writing roles students adopt while reading and writing in different contexts need to be encouraged as well. Activities which challenge students to understand how their uses of reading and writing are a function of topic, task, and context, how particular reading and writing activities have multiple functions, and under what conditions reading and writing enhance or interfere with learning are important for teaching reading and writing as modes of learning. Students' diverse language, literacy, and learning experiences must be drawn upon in teaching practice to ease their entry into academic discourse and to help them define their roles as literate members of a community of learners.

Additionally, the implications for instruction clearly point to the importance of teaching students how to learn from multiple text sources. Tasks that stress reading and writing interactions with many texts and with many learners, in different contexts using different content, those that require students to "traverse the topical landscape" as McGinley & Tierney (1989) describe, move students toward a view of reading and writing as nonlinear, multilayered, dynamic processes, integral to learning. Activities that encourage students to see texts as socially constructed, as conversations (re)constructed between author and readers, not as autonomous units, need to be developed. In addition, new technologies that integrate multiple sources of information — sound, images, words — into multimedia texts present exciting possibilities for teaching how learning is affected when the nature of reading and writing change.

College Teachers' Role

The long term goal of teaching reading and writing as modes of learning should be the acquisition of content, discourse knowledge, and academic literacy practices. To achieve this goal teachers must provide students with many opportunities to understand the functions that different forms of reading and writing serve for learning and how to make timely, strategic decisions about the usefulness of a specific reading/writing engagement across a task. The role of college reading and writing teachers then is to facilitate and formulate dialogs with and among students about reading and writing as modes of learning in college.

By committing to a content-based literacy program which actively engages students in learning how to use purposeful, self-directed reading and writing strategies for learning across disciplines, I believe college reading and writing teachers are well placed to lead in current and future efforts to promote reading and writing as modes of learning.

References

Ackerman, J. (1991). Reading, writing, and knowing: The role of disciplinary knowledge in comprehension and composing. *Research in the Teaching of English, 25,* 133–178.

Ackerman, J. (1993). The promise of writing to learn. *Written Communication, 10,* 334–370.

Adams, M. J., & Collins, A. (1985). A schema-theoretic view of reading. In H. Singer & R. B. Ruddell (Eds.), *Theoretical models and processes of reading* (pp. 404–425). Newark, DE: International Reading Association.

A nation at risk: The full account (1983). The U.S. National Commission on Excellence in Education. Cambridge, MA: USA Research.

Anderson, R. C., Heibert, E. H., Scott, J., & Wilkinson, I. A. G. (1985). *Becoming a nation of readers.* Washington, D. C.: National Institute of Education, National Academy of Education, Commission on Reading.

Anderson, R. C. (1985). Role of readers' schema in comprehension, learning, and memory. In H. Singer & R. B. Ruddell (Eds.), *Theoretical models and processes of reading* (pp. 372–384). Newark, DE: International Reading Association.

Anderson, R. C., & Pearson, P. D. (1984). *A schema-theoretic view of the basic processes in reading comprehension.* (Tech. Rep. No. 306). Champaign: University of Illinois, Center for the Study of Reading.

Applebee, A. N. (1974). *Tradition and reform in the teaching of English: A history.* Urbana, IL: National Council of Teachers of English.

Bartlett, F. (1932). *Remembering: A study in experimental and social psychology.* Cambridge, MA: Harvard University Press.

Bloome, D., & Egan-Robertson, A. (1993). The social construction of intertextuality in classroom reading and writing lessons. *Reading Research Quarterly, 4,* 305–333.

Bogdan, D., & Straw, S. B. (Eds.). (1990). *Beyond communication.* Portsmouth, NH: Boynton/Cook.

Brookfield, S. D. (1987). *Developing critical thinkers.* San Francisco, CA: Jossey-Bass.

Brown, A. L., & Day, J. D. (1983). Macrorules for summarizing texts: The development of expertise. *Journal of Verbal Learning and Verbal Behavior, 22,* 1–14.

Brown, A. L., Day, J. D., & Jones, R. S. (1983). The development of plans for summarizing texts. *Child Development, 54,* 968–979.

Bruner, J. (1966). *Toward a theory of instruction.* Cambridge: Belknap-Harvard University Press.

Bruner, J. (1986). *Actual minds, possible worlds.* Cambridge: Harvard University Press.

Chaffee, J. (1993). *Thinking critically* (4th ed.). Boston, MA: Houghton Mifflin.

Chomsky, N. A. (1957). *Syntactic structures.* The Hague: Mouton.

Chomsky, N. A. (1965). *Aspects of a theory of syntax.* Cambridge, MA: MIT Press.

Clifford, G. J. (1987). *A sisyphean task: Historical perspectives on the relationship between writing and reading instruction* (Tech. Rep. No. 7). Berkeley: Center for the Study of Writing and Literacy at the University of California at Berkeley and at Carnegie Mellon.

Cranney, A. G. (1983). Two decades of adult reading programs: Growth, problems and prospects. *Journal of Reading, 26,* 416–421.

Cross, K. P. (1971). *Beyond the pen door: New students in higher education.* San Francisco: Jossey-Bass.

A Correlated Curriculum: National Council of Teachers of English Committee on Correlation (1936). New York: D. Appleton-Century.

Davis, F. R. (1983). Fundamental factors of comprehension in reading. In L. M. Gentile, M. L. Kamil, & J. S. Blanchard (Eds.) *Reading research revisited* (pp. 235–245). Columbus, OH: Charles E. Merrill. (Reprinted from *Psychometrica,* 1944, 9(3), 185–197)

Dias, P. (1990). A literary-response perspective on teaching reading comprehension. In D. Bogdan & S. B. Straw (Eds.), *Beyond communication* (pp. 283–299). Portsmouth, NH.: Boynton/Cook.

Dishner, E. K., & Readence, J. E. (1981). Content reading: Past. Present! Future? In E. K. Dishner, F. W. Bean, & J. E. Readence (Eds.), *Reading in the content areas* (pp. 1–8). Dubuque, IA.: Kendall/Hunt.

Dixon, J. (1967). *Growth through English.* Reading, England: National Association for the Teaching of English.

Durst, R. K. (1987). Cognitive and linguistic demands of analytical writing. *Research in the Teaching of English, 21,* 347–376.

Durst, R. K. (1989). Monitoring processes in analytical and summary writing. *Written Communication, 6,* 340–363.

Elbow, P. (1973). *Writing without teachers.* New York: Oxford University Press.

Emig, J. (1977). Writing as a mode of learning. *College Composition and Communication, 28,* 122–128.

Flower, L. S. (1987). *The role of task representation in reading to write* (Tech. Rep. No. 6). Berkeley: Center for the Study of Writing and Literacy at the University of California, Berkeley, and at Carnegie Mellon.

Flower, L. S. (1989). Cognition, context, and theory building. *College Composition and Communication, 40,* 282–311.

Flower, L. S., & Hayes, J. R. (1981). Problem-solving and the cognitive process of writing. In C. H. Frederiksen & J. F. Dominic (Eds.), *Writing: The nature, development and teaching of written communication* (pp. 39–58). Hillsdale, NJ: Erlbaum.

Freedom and discipline in English (1965). New York: College Entrance Examination Board.

Freire, P. (1970). *Pedagogy of the oppressed.* New York: Continuum.

Gage, N. L. (Ed.). (1963). *Handbook of research on teaching.* Chicago: Rand McNally.

Goodman, K. S. (1967). Reading: A psycholinguistic guessing game. *Journal of the Reading Specialist, 4,* 126–135.

Goodman, K., & Goodman, Y. (1977). Learning about psycholinguistic processes by analyzing oral reading. *Harvard Educational Review, 47* 317–333.

Goodman, Y. M., & Burke, C. L. (1972). *Reading miscue inventory: Procedures for diagnosis and remediation.* New York: Macmillan.

Gough, P. B. (1972). One second of reading. In J. F. Kavanagh & I. G. Mattingly (Eds.), *Language by eye and by ear* (pp. 331–358). Cambridge, MA: MIT Press.

Greene, S. (1993). The role of task inlihe development of academic thinking through reading and writing in a college history course. *Research in the Teaching of English, 27,* 46–75.

Hanford, G. (1994). Educational standards and reform: The danger of fragmentation. *Educational Vision, 2*(1), 6–7.

Hidi, S., & Anderson V. (1986). Producing written summaries: Task demands, cognitive operations, and implications for instruction. *Review of Educational Research,* 56, 473–493.

Holmes, J. A. (1953). *The sub-strata factor theory of reading.* Berkeley: California Book.

Hosic, J. R. (1917). *Reorganization of English in secondary schools.* (Bureau of Education Bulletin 1917, No. 2). Washington, D.C.: U.S. Government Printing Office.

Kennedy, M. L. (1985). The composing processes of college students writing from sources. *Written Communication, 2,* 434–456.

Kiniry, M. L., & Rose, M. (1992). *Critical strategies for academic thinking and writing* (2nd ed.). Boston: St. Martin's.

La Berge, D., & Samuels, S. J. (1974). Toward a theory of automatic information processing in reading. *Cognitive Psychology, 6,* 293–323.

Langer, J. A. (1986). Reading, writing, and understanding: An analysis of the construction of meaning. *Written Communication, 3,* 219–267.

Langer, J. A., & Applebee, A. N. (1986). *Writing and learning in the secondary school.* (National Institute of Education Grant No. NIE-G-82-0027). Palo Alto, CA: Stanford University, School of Education.

Langer, J. A., & Applebee, A. N. (1987). *How writing shapes thinking.* Urbana, IL: National Council of Teachers of English.

Lesgold, A. M., & Perfetti, C. A. (1978). Interactive processes in reading comprehension. *Discourse Processes, 1,* 323–336.

Lloyd-Jones, R., & Lunsford, A. (1989). *English coalition conference: Democracy through language.* Urbana, IL: National Council of Teachers of English. New York: Modern Language Association.

Macrorie, K. (1976). *Telling writing.* Rochelle Park, NJ: Hayden.

Marshall, J. (1987). The effects of writing by students' understanding of literary texts. *Research in the Teaching of English, 21,* 30–63.

McGinley, W. (1992). The role of reading and writing while composing from sources. *Reading Research Quarterly, 27,* 227–248.

McGinley, W., & Tierney, R. J. (1988). *Reading and writing as ways of knowing and learning.* (Tech. Rep. No. 423). Champaign, IL: University of Illinois, Center for the Study of Reading.

McGinley, W., & Tierney, R. J. (1989). Traversing the topical landscape: Reading and writing as ways of knowing. *Written Communication, 6,* 243–269.

McWhorter, K. T. (1994). *Academic reading* (2nd ed.). New York: HarperCollins.

Moore, D. W., Readence, J. E., & Rickelman, R. J. (1983). An historical exploration of content area reading instruction. *Reading Research Quarterly, 18,* 419–438.

Nelson, J., & Hayes, J. R. (1988). *How the writing context shapes college students' strategies for writing from sources.* (Tech. Rep. No. 16). Berkeley: Center for the Study of Writing and Literacy at the University of California at Berkeley and at Carnegie Mellon.

Newell, G. (1984). Learning from writing in two content areas: A case study/protocol analysis. *Research in the Teaching of English, 18,* 205–287.

Newell, G., & Winograd, P. (1989). The effect of writing on learning from expository text. *Written Communication, 6,* 196–217.

Pearson, P. D., & Tierney, R. J. (1984). *On becoming a thoughtful reader: Learning to read like a writer.* (Rdg. Educ. Rep. No. 50). Champaign, IL: University of Illinois, Center for the Study of Reading.

Penrose, A. (1992). To write or not to write: Effects of task and task interaction on learning through writing. *Written Communication, 9,* 465–500.

Perl, S. (1979). The composing processes of unskiffed college writers. *Research in the Teaching of English, 13,* 317–336.

Quinn, K. B. (1987). Researching the relationships between reading and writing: The generation and elaboration of ideas from reading informational prose to writing arguments. *Dissertation Abstracts International,* 48, 09A. (University Microfilms No. 87-26,099)

Robinson, H. A. (1977). *Reading and writing instruction in the United States: Historical trends.* Newark, DE: International Reading Association.

Rumelhart, D. E. (1977). Toward an interactive model of reading. In S. Dornic (Ed.)., *Attention and performance,* (Vol. 6, pp. 573–608). London: Academic.

Russell, D. R. (1987). Writing across the curriculum and the communications movement: Some lessons from the past. *College Composition and Communication,* 38, 184–194.

Russell, D. R. (1989). The cooperation movement: Language across the curriculum and mass education, 1900–1930. *Research in the Teaching of English,* 23, 399–423.

Russell, D. R. (1990). Writing across the curriculum in historical perspective: Toward a social interpretation. *College English,* 52, 52–73.

Shank, R. C., & Abelson, R. P. (1977). *Scripts, plans, goals and understanding: An inquiry into human knowledge structures.* Hillsdale, NJ: Erlbaum.

Schumacher, G., & Gradwohl Nash, J. (1991). Conceptualizing and measuring knowledge change due to writing. *Research in the Teaching of English,* 25, 67–96.

Shanahan, T., & Lomax, R. (1986). An analysis and comparison of three theoretical models of the reading-writing relationship. *Research in the Teaching of English,* 22, 196–212.

Shaughnessy, M. (1977). *Errors and expectations: A guide for the teacher of basic writing.* New York: Oxford University Press.

Smith, F. (1971). *Understanding reading.* New York: Holt, Rinehart & Winston.

Smith, F. (1982). *Understanding reading* (3rd ed.). Orlando, FL: Holt, Rinehart & Winston.

Sommers, N. (1980). Revision strategies of student writers and experienced adult writers. *College Composition and Communication,* 31, 378–388.

Spiro, R. J. (1980). Constructive processes in prose comprehension and recall. In R. J. Spiro, B. C. Bruce, & W. F. Brewer (Eds.), *Theoretical issues in reading comprehension* (pp. 245–278). Hillsdale, NJ: Erlbaum.

Spivey, N. N. (1984). *Discourse synthesis: Constructing texts in reading and writing.* Newark, DE.: International Reading Association.

Spivey, N. (1990). Transforming texts: Constructive processes in reading and writing. *Written Communication,* 7, 256–287.

Spivey, N., & King, J. R. (1989). Readers as writers composing from sources. *Reading Research Quarterly,* 24, 7–26.

Stahl, N. A., Simpson, M. L., & Hayes, C. G. (1992). Ten recommendations from research for teaching high-risk college students. *Journal of Developmental Education,* 16, 2–10.

Straw, S. B. (1990). Conceptualizations of communication in the history of literary theory. In D. Bogdan & S. B. Straw (Eds.), *Beyond communication* (pp. 49–66). Portsmouth, NH: Boynton/Cook.

Straw, S. B., & Sadowy, P. Dynamics of communication. In D. Bogdan & S. B. Straw (Eds.), *Beyond communication* (pp. 21–47). Portsmouth, NH: Boynton/Cook.

Tierney, R. J. (1992). Ongoing research and new directions. In J. W. Irwin & M. A. Doyle (Eds.), *Reading/writing connections: Learning from research* (pp. 262–269). Newark, DE.: International Reading Association.

Tierney, R. J., & Pearson, P. D. (1983). "Toward a composing model of reading." *Language Arts,* 60, 568–80.

Tierney, R. J., & Shanahan, T. (1991). Research on the reading/writing relationship: Interactions, transactions, and outcomes. In Barr, R., M. Kamil, P. Mosenthal,

& P. D. Pearson (Eds.), *Handbook of reading research: Vol II* (pp. 246–280). New York: Longman.

Tierney, R. J., Soter, A., O'Flahavan, J. F., & McGinley, W. (1989). The effects of reading and writing upon thinking critically. *Reading Research Quarterly,* 24, 134–173.

Vacca, R. T., & Vacca, J. L. (1983). Two less than fortunate consequences of reading research in the 1970's. *Reading Research Quarterly,* 18, 382–383.

Vygotsy, L. (1986). *Thought and language.* Cambridge, MA: MIT Press.

Wyatt, M. (1992). The past, present, and future need for college reading courses in the U.S. *Journal of Developmental Education,* 36, 10–20.

Connecting Reading and Writing: College Learners' Metacognitive Awareness

Amelia E. El-Hindi

Noting that skilled learners tend to be active learners who are aware of their learning processes, El-Hindi describes a summer program focusing on reading, writing, and study strategies for incoming first-year students from underrepresented populations considered to be at-risk for college success. During the course, metacognitive instruction was promoted through the use of reading logs and of questionnaires in which students documented their thought processes as they read texts and wrote papers. Analysis of the students' logs demonstrated that they had engaged in highly strategic behaviors as they interacted with text. In addition, their awareness of the connection between reading and writing increased.

First-year college students are faced with many pressures. College life is a difficult adjustment at best and the transition from high school is overwhelming. Of the many pressures faced by this special population is the demand to integrate information from vast amounts of text. For perhaps the first time in their lives, these students must complete large amounts of reading and rapidly synthesize and communicate ideas from text. However, between 30 percent and 40 percent of first-year college students have deficiencies in the reading and writing skills necessary for college performance (Moore & Carpenter, 1985). This trend coincides with disturbing evidence cited by Brozo and Simpson (1995) which indicates that, although junior and senior high students can handle basic literacy skills, very few junior high and senior high students are gaining advanced literacy skills. Such trends pose disturbing implications for the future of first-year college students. Students who lack the sophistication to rapidly digest text could be set up for failure in reading-intensive courses. First-year students need to develop these skills early in their college careers and can do so with the help of developmental educators. This is particularly important for college students from underrepresented populations who may be considered at risk for completing their programs. Such a population is the focus of this study.

Purpose

This paper reports on a study of first-year college students who received instruction in metacognitive awareness for reading and writing. Metacognition or "thinking about thinking" involves the awareness and regulation of thinking processes. Metacognitive strategies are those strategies that require students to think about their own thinking as they engage in academic tasks. Within this study, students were taught specific metacognitive strategies for both reading and writing as part of a 6-week residential summer program. Students' use of a reflective reading journal or "reading log" was integral to the strategy instruction. The students used the reading logs to reflect on their own thinking processes as they engaged in reading and writing tasks. The focus of this article is on the students' increase in metacognitive awareness revealed by analyses of their metacognitive awareness questionnaires and their reading log entries.

Related Literature

Skilled learners tend to be active learners who are aware of their own learning processes. The use of metacognitive strategies, the awareness and regulation of cognitive activity (Baker & Brown, 1984; Flavell, 1976, 1978, 1993; Flavell & Wellman, 1977), characterizes an active learner who exercises control over the learning process (Mayo, 1993). Empirical studies show that metacognition is linked to both reading ability (Balajthy, 1986; Brown & Day, 1983; Brozo, Stahl, & Gordon, 1985; Gambrell & Heathington, 1981; Hare & Pulliam, 1980; Paris, Cross, & Lipson, 1984; Paris & Jacobs, 1984) and writing ability (Englert, Raphael, Fear, & Anderson, 1988; Raphael, Englert, & Kirscher, 1989). Empirical research also suggests that, for college learners, metacognitive awareness for both reading and writing can be enhanced by providing direct instruction (El-Hindi, 1996).

The increased attention on metacognition coincides with current definitions of literacy which suggest that reading and writing are interconnected. Brozo and Simpson (1995) indicate that reading and writing are "parallel processes" students use to gain meaning from text. Mulcahy-Ernt and Stewart (1994) appeal to a constructivist view of literacy, indicating that "writing and reading processes provide a student with the communicative tools for independent learning, the mark of a mature student" (p. 107). Today's vision of reading and writing processes suggests that they are interconnected, recursive processes used by metacognitively aware learners to actively create meaning through text. Shanahan (1990) recommends teaching reading and writing in conjunction with each other because exposing learners to both sides of the literacy process provides an understanding of the social and communicative nature of literacy. These theoretical perspectives about reading and writing form the foundation for the study reported here in which students are exposed to the interconnections between reading and writing processes through metacognitive instruction.

Methodology

Participants

Participants were volunteers from a 6-week residential academic program in Summer of 1993 for prefreshmen from a major Northern university. The program targeted incoming first-year students from underrepresented populations who were considered at risk for completing their programs. The residential program also solicited students with learning disabilities and students interested in math, science, or technology. The majority of the students were either required or encouraged to participate in the program by their academic departments. All students who enrolled in the program completed an intensive reading-writing class. Four sections of the reading-writing class were designated to receive the instruction in metacognitive awareness. Students in these sections completed reading logs as an integral part of the metacognitive instruction. The mean age of the 34 participants (13 male, 21 female) was 17.53 with a standard deviation of .56. The majority of the student participants were African American (73.53 percent), whereas a minority were either Hispanic (11.76 percent), Caucasian (11.76 percent), or Asian (2.94 percent).

Metacognitive Strategy Instruction

Metacognitive instruction for reading and writing processes was provided during the 6-week course by the researcher who worked in conjunction with two instructors. A model for the instruction (see El-Hindi, 1996) was developed based on scholarship on metacognitive processes for reading (Baker & Brown, 1984; Paris, Wasik, & Turner, 1991) and on metacognitive processes for writing (Englert et al., 1988; Raphael et al., 1989).

One important assumption of this model is that reading and writing are interactive processes linked to one another. Reading lends itself to writing and writing lends itself to reading. Another assumption of the model is that reading and writing involve three recursive phases: planning (before the process), drafting (during the process), and responding (after the process) (see Figure 1).

The metacognitive instruction involved teaching students specific strategies which corresponded to each of the three phases. As seen in Figure 1, metacognitive strategies corresponding to the planning stage

Figure 1. The interaction of various phases of the reading and writing processes.

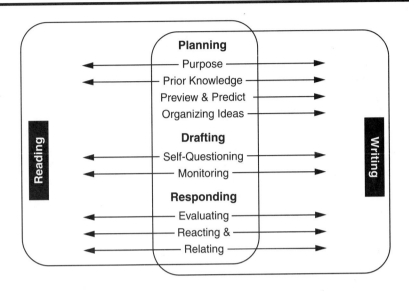

for reading included identifying a purpose for reading, activating prior knowledge, previewing text, and making predictions about text. Planning strategies for writing included identifying a purpose for writing, activating prior knowledge of a writing topic, and organizing ideas. Drafting strategies for reading included comprehension monitoring and self-questioning, strategies cited by Baker and Brown (1984) as important to effective reading. Self-questioning and monitoring were also taught as strategies which facilitated the drafting stage of writing. Learners were taught to self-question as they produced their own texts and to monitor their progress at completing a writing task.

Figure 1 also illustrates the responding phase of both reading and writing as involving evaluating, reacting, and relating. In the context of reading, students were taught to evaluate their understanding, react to the text they were reading, and relate the text to their prior experience. Within the context of writing, students were taught to evaluate their success as writers, react to their written texts as readers, and examine their texts holistically to see connections among different parts of their texts. Englert et al. (1988) identified self-evaluation of a paper's completeness as an important metacognitive activity for writing.

The model was developed and used to organize specific lessons in metacognitive awareness for reading and writing. Each metacognitive strategy was explained and demonstrated, and students practiced use of the strategies in conjunction with course reading and writing assignments.

Students completed weekly reading assignments which included chapters from the course text, *Writing with Power* (Elbow, 1981), and articles written by contemporary professional writers. Students were instructed to use their reading logs to comment on their thoughts and actions as they completed their readings for the course. For example, students would write down thoughts that came to mind when they first read the title or would use the reading log to comment on actions, such as referencing a dictionary, they would take when they encountered a word or phrase that was confusing. Students were asked to write in their reading logs each week.

Reading logs were collected and reviewed each week by the instructors. At the end of the course, reading logs were collected and photocopied for analysis. The instructors provided feedback on the reading logs by writing comments and questions in the margins. Students were given feedback and prompted to write critical commentaries on what they read, synthesize the ideas presented by the authors, and indicate how the text related to their own experience.

Assessment of Metacognitive Awareness

Metacognitive awareness was assessed by examining two sources of data: results from questionnaires designed to assess metacognitive awareness for both reading and writing, and the reading log entries generated by each student. A discussion of each data source follows.

Questionnaires for metacognitive awareness included two 36-item instruments developed as part of a larger study (El-Hindi, 1996) and used to assess students' metacognitive awareness both prior to and after the metacognitive strategy instruction. One questionnaire assessed metacognitive knowledge for reading, and the other assessed metacognitive knowledge for writing.

Each questionnaire was composed of four sets of questions. For each set of questions students responded to a specific reading or writing scenario. For example, the first scenario described a hypothetical student who was about to read an assignment for a class. After reading the scenario, students responded to the prompt, "if you were in this situation would you . . ." for nine specific activities by checking "yes" or "no" for each activity. Each activity was classified as either an activity which involved metacognition (i.e., writing down a reason for doing the reading) or an activity which did not (i.e., just starting to read without doing anything). Each response received a specific score. A yes response to a metacognitive activity was scored as a 1 and a yes response to a nonmetacognitive activity was scored as a 0. A no response to a non-metacognitive activity was scored as a 1 and a no response to a metacognitive activity was scored as a 0. For each questionnaire, the scores on all the items were added to provide an overall score of metacognitive knowledge for reading and an overall score of metacognitive knowledge for writing.

Reading log entries were requested from students as they completed their reading assignments for each week. Entries ranged in length from two to five pages. Each student generated six reading log entries which were photocopied for analysis. The "constant comparative method of analysis" was used for analysis of the reading log entries (Glaser & Strauss, 1967). The researcher completed an initial reading of all the reading log entries. Then the entries were broken down into paragraphs and each paragraph was transcribed onto an index card. The paragraphs were then sorted by the researcher according to categories which emerged from the initial reading of the full entries and were refined during the sorting process (Strauss & Corbin, 1990). According to Bogdan and Biklen (1992) data analyzed in this way provides a descriptive theory around which to organize phenomena.

The constant comparative analysis for the study's reading logs identified three major categories: (a) excerpts which showed a student's use of a particular metacognitive strategy; (b) excerpts which showed a change in the student's metacognitive awareness; and, (c) excerpts which showed the students' awareness of the connection between reading and writing. Often an excerpt would fall into more than one category and this was noted by the researcher. Still, the major categories which emerged from the data provided the means for organizing the excerpts from the reading log entries. This method of analysis allowed specific themes to emerge which captured the students' developing sophistication as readers and writers. Representative samples of entries are presented in the "Results" section. The students' identities are protected with the use of pseudonyms.

Results: Use of Metacognitive Strategies

Questionnaire Results

Results from the responses on the questionnaires indicated a significant increase in students' metacognitive awareness of reading. Prior to instruction students' mean score for metacognitive awareness of reading was 36.79 with a standard deviation of 11.11. By the end of instruction, the comparable mean score was 44.85 with a standard deviation of 9.29. A paired t-test indicated a significant gain in metacognitive awareness for reading ($t(32) = 4.66, p = .00005$).

Although scores on metacognitive awareness for reading increased significantly, scores for metacognitive awareness of writing increased but not at a statistically significant level. The mean score for metacognitive awareness of writing prior to instruction was 44.84 with a standard deviation of 8.85, and the corresponding mean score after instruction was 48.18 with a standard deviation of 6.84.

Reading Log Results

As evidenced by the entries, the students engaged in highly strategic activity as they interacted with their texts. Often the reading log entry would reveal the student's use of a particular metacognitive strategy.

Strategies most frequently illustrated by the entries included: (a) relating the text to previous experience, (b) visualizing oneself in the text, (c) talking with classmates about the reading, and (d) examining the title to make predictions about the text.

The following example from a second reading log entry shows how one student, Cathy, engages in metacognitive processes. In writing this entry, Cathy activated her own previous experience and used visualization to make sense of the text as she reacted to an author's description of a Kentucky Fried Chicken restaurant in an inner city neighborhood:

> As I read this passage I was shocked. I, too, had walked down the same street, lined with foreigners peddling their wares. I visualized myself standing at the corner near KFC staring straight towards the Apollo. Orlean encourages me to read on in this way.

Cathy's reading log entry shows her active engagement with the text. She can relate to the experience discussed by the author and actually comments on how the author would want her to read the text while visualizing herself in that neighborhood.

Another student, Marsha, demonstrated similar engagement as evidenced by the following entry from her fourth reading log in which she responded to an article about children growing up in ghetto neighborhoods:

> When I spoke to a classmate about the article he understood Freddie Brown's situation "for Freddie, poverty was not only a dearth of material comforts and opportunities; even more crippling, he wrestled with a poverty of hope." My classmate told me that he was luck [sic] to go home from school without getting harassed by a drug dealer for money, or the police thinking he's a dealer.

The excerpt shows the overall trend on the part of the students to share insights about the text with other classmates. It also shows the sense of active engagement of relating the text to previous experience and making connections between the text and their personal lives.

Another student, Nimi, articulated a detailed process for analyzing the title of one of her readings:

> I spent a lot of time analyzing this article and I began with the title. I had no idea what, "In these girls, hope is a muscle meant." First I decided to break down the title so I can decipher it. I knew what "In these girls," meant but I had a harder time with "hope is a muscle."
>
> A muscle is a part of your body that helps you move so I wrote out the sentence, Hope is a part of you that helps you move. I had an idea about the title but it was too general. So the next thing I did was look up the word muscle in my dictionary. I came up with the meanings "Power or influence especially when based on force or threats" and "To make one's

way or take control by sheer strength or force or threats or force or
control."

Now I made up a new sentence. Hope is to make one's way to take
control by sheer strength or force or threats of force or control. This
sentence made a lot more sense to me than the first one and made me
understand the title.

This critical examination of the title demonstrates Nimi's increased
metacognitive awareness for reading and her heightened engagement
with text. By the end of writing her entry, Nimi had increased her
understanding of the hidden meaning of the title and how the title fit
with the remainder of the article.

Changes in metacognitive awareness were evidenced by analysis of
the reading log entries. As students progressed through the 6-week
class, they became more critical in examining text. Early reading log
entries tended to show more summarizing of text, whereas later reading log entries tended to show more critical reflection and commentary.
Use of metacognitive strategies became more apparent as the students
wrote in their logs over time.

Sample entries from one student, Robert, illustrated this increased
metacognitive sophistication. The following series of entries, which
focus on Robert's making sense of the titles of the various articles he
read, were representative of the type of metacognitive growth revealed
by the reading log entries of the students overall.

In his first reading log entry Robert wrote: "The title, 'Making yourself at home: The baby boom generation years to settle down,' threw me
off a bit. I knew he was going to talk about staying home but the baby
boom part, I didn't understand it until I read the whole article." This
excerpt showed Robert's use of examining the title in order to make
some predictions about the text he was about to read. Robert continued
in this vein in his third entry which showed a greater sophistication in
use of this metacognitive strategy:

The first time I read the title "In these girls hope is a muscle" I was
looking for the reading assignment on the sheet. I read the title and didn't
know what to think. I thought that these girls were using hope to get
them moving. Like a muscle is able to make you move, hope gets you
motivated. I had a feeling that the article was going to be about a sport
but I didn't think it would be about basketball.

In Robert's final reading log entry, he again commented on a title
and showed a greater understanding of how a title can communicate:

When I first read the title "A Crowded Writer on the Lonely Prairie," I was
stumped. I didn't know what to think, but while reading the passage, it
came to me. The title is really sarcastic. If someone read the title alone
that person may think that the writer is crowded but it's lonely on a

prairie. That's not what it means at all. The writer is really alone because there aren't many writers that tell the story of small rural towns in the Dakotas.

This series of excerpts shows Robert's developing sophistication as a reader. He is metacognitively aware in using the title to gain insights and make predictions about the text. The excerpts also show how he refined his use of the strategy of examining the title to make predictions about the text.

Reading and writing connections were strengthened through the reading logs in addition to their allowing students to articulate metacognitive processes while reading. The logs also served as a vehicle for many participants to realize the connection between their metacognitive processes as readers and their metacognitive processes as writers.

Students' developing awareness of the reading and writing connection was a compelling insight revealed by the entries. Later reading log entries illustrated that the students reacted to the text by referring to their own experiences as writers. Jamal, wrote the following in response to an essay by Robert Hass:

> While reading this essay . . . it reminded me of the last paper I wrote on a meaningful place. The way Hass described the house where one of his babysitters lived was very similar to the way I described my grandmother's house in my paper where I wrote about the face of the house being filled with lilacs and a big tree in the front.

Consider how Jamal reflected on his own writing as he tried to make sense of the essay. This showed growing metacognitive awareness of Jamal's stance as a writer. Like Jamal, Cathy too, reflected on her role as a writer in the following excerpt from her fifth reading log entry in response to an article by Kathleen Norris:

> As I read on, I noticed that Kathleen Norris spoke of many of the same problems I had encountered in writing my paper. One of the obvious parallels was when she quoted a North Dakota Ranch woman saying, "I'd like to write about my relatives, but I'm no good at disgusting things." In writing my memoir, there were many places where I avoided telling the truth about my family.

This excerpt showed Cathy's comparison of the author she was reading with herself as an emerging writer. Another student, Robert, also demonstrated metacognitive awareness for reading-writing connections in the following excerpt in which he wrestled with his struggle to write about himself:

> The article by Jill Johnston, "Fictions of the Self" helped me to understand that anyone can write an autobiography. I'm the type of person that

hates writing about myself but from this text Johnston explains that it isn't really that hard to do. Jill Johnston used a lot of sources and I think that was a good move. She would start by saying, "I've read somewhere that . . . " and then write about the way she feels about certain statements from the sources she picked. She also describes the way she has changed after writing an article or a book. In a way I think she is trying to find herself through her writing. She wants to know who she is and what she's about. Through her writing she's finding a way to identify herself.

In writing this entry, Robert looked to the author he was reading for insights on his own writing. In later reading log entries, Robert came to grips with writing about himself and looked to the authors he read for additional clues. He demonstrated his developing awareness of himself as a reader and as a writer.

This connection between reading and writing was also expressed by Nancy who wrote the following in her fifth reading log in responding to an article by a memoirist:

I was surprised that the opening anecdote was not altogether true. To me, as a reader, it seemed very believable. He stated "but no memoirist writes for long without experiencing an unsettling disbelief about the reliability of memory, a hunch that memory is not, after all, just memory." I find this to be the case in my own writing. Because I had not been to Jamaica in so long, my memory of the place may not be completely accurate. I was not sure about the name of the housekeeper and at first I attempted to put it in, but after realizing that the name was not real I left it out.

In reading the opening anecdote, Nancy struggled with the underlying issue of the author's stretching the truth to make a point about writing from memory. She not only reflected this struggle in her analysis of the text, but she also reflected on this struggle as she thought about her own experience as a writer in the class. This reflective analysis showed metacognition of both reading and writing processes. Moreover, it demonstrated Nancy's developing awareness of the connections between reading and writing.

Nancy's example serves to illustrate how participants realized the connection between their roles as readers and their roles as writers. As they critically reflect on the processes used to understand reading text, they also reflect on their own experiences as developing writers: both examples of self-regulation of thinking processes or strategic metacognitive activity.

Reading log entries provided students with a vehicle for articulating their metacognitive processes. As analysis of the entries showed, students gained metacognitive awareness for reading and writing and also demonstrated understanding of the connections between being good readers and being good writers.

Discussion

Journals have been shown to be effective for documenting and observing metacognitive development (Newton, 1991). Analyses of the reading log entries written by the participants for this study as well as results of the questionnaire to assess metacognitive growth have indicated that such journals can assist students in articulating their metacognitive processes. In teaching college students about metacognitive processes for reading, part of the challenge is in the very articulation of processes. Students tend to read on "automatic pilot," and not realize when they have trouble comprehending or truly digesting text. Within this class, the use of the reading log caused students to actively engage in thought processes as they were completing reading for the course. By completing the reading log entries, students were required to stop, slow down, and actively think about what they were reading as opposed to simply reading text from start to finish. This slowing down proved to be beneficial to their developing awareness of reading and writing processes.

Excerpts from the reading logs also provide evidence of students' critical engagement with text. Sample excerpts illustrate students' reflections on past experience and prior knowledge to make sense of their reading. This notion is supported by the transactional view of reading which posits that meaning resides within the transaction between reader and text instead of within the text alone (Rosenblatt, 1978). This view of reading promotes the idea that students move beyond literal recall of text and into the realm of higher order thinking as they react to what they read (Kelly & Farnan, 1991).

The reading logs provided a forum for students to articulate their metacognitive processes while engaging in both reading and writing tasks. Journals, therefore, can be justified as a tool to promote metacognitive awareness on the part of college learners. Use of such journals can also assist students with realizing the connection between their roles as critical readers and their roles as critical writers.

The very words expressed by the students themselves as they struggled with their emerging voices as writers provides testimony of the power in using reading logs as a tool for teaching reading and writing skills to college learners. Consider Maurice's words in his fifth reading log entry as he reflects on how he has changed as a reader:

> When I first began to read essays, I never focused on anything that could warm me up for the reading. In other words, I would go right into the reading without thinking about the essay I was going to read. I didn't set a purpose for myself. As I began to read my final essay in this course, Memory and Imagination, I realized that I was doing things that I didn't do before.

Maurice's words give testimony to the growth he experienced as a learner throughout the course. Such awareness is, in itself, a powerful key to obtaining success in college environments. Developmental educators set out to equip their students with the tools necessary to become proficient in college. Metacognitive awareness is one such tool. Skilled learners who are metacognitively aware tend to succeed at academic tasks. This study demonstrates the effectiveness of using journals to enhance metacognitive instruction. Use of such journals also can help students realize the connection between reading and writing.

At the very least, college learning demands sophistication in gaining information from text and being able to communicate through writing. Metacognitive awareness is a key ingredient to such sophisticated literacy processes. However, too often metacognitive instruction is sacrificed to isolated skill instruction within academic support classes. Attending to metacognitive awareness within academic support classes can benefit college learners seeking to improve their reading and writing skills. Use of a reflective journal, such as a reading log, can allow students the vehicle for becoming more metacognitively aware as they approach the reading and writing demands of college courses. Furthermore, as evidenced by this study, use of reading logs can help college students understand the process of reading and the process of writing as a single act of literacy. Such an integrative view of literacy will help at-risk learners cope with the demands of college learning.

References

Baker, L., & Brown, A. (1984). Metacognitive skills and reading. In D. Pearson, R. Barr, M. Kamil, & P. Mosenthal (Eds.), *Handbook of reading research* (pp. 353–394). New York: Longman.

Balajthy, E. (1986). The relation of training self-generated questioning with passage difficulty and immediate and delayed retention. In J. Niles & R. Lalik (Eds.), *Solving problems in literacy: Learner teachers, and researcher* (pp. 41–46). Rochester, NY: National Reading Conference.

Bogdan, R. C., & Biklen, S. K. (1992). *Qualitative research for education: An introduction to theory and methods.* Boston: Allyn and Bacon.

Brozo, W. G., & Simpson, M. L. (1995). *Readers, teachers, learners: Expanding literacy in secondary schools* (2nd ed.). Englewood Cliffs, NJ: Prentice-Hall.

Brozo, W. G., Stahl, N. A., & Gordon, B. (1985). Training effects of summarizing, item writing, and knowledge of information sources on reading test performance. In J. Niles & R. Lalik (Eds.), *Issues in literacy: A research perspective* (pp. 48–54). Rochester, NY: National Reading Conference.

Brown, A. L., & Day, J. D. (1983). Macrorules for summarizing tests: The development of expertise. *Journal of Verbal Learning and Verbal Behavior* 22(1), 1–14.

Elbow, P. (1981). *Writing with power.* New York: Oxford University Press.

El-Hindi, A. (1996). Enhancing metacognitive awareness of college learners. *Reading Horizons,* 36(3), 214–230.

Englert, C. S., Raphael, T. E., Fear, K. L., & Anderson, L. M. (1988). Students' metacognitive knowledge about how to write informational texts. *Learning Disability Quarterly,* 11(1), 18–46.

Flavell, J. H. (1976). Metacognitive aspects of problem solving. In L. Resnick (Ed.), *The nature of intelligence* (pp. 231–235). Hillsdale, NJ: Lawrence Erlbaum Associates.

Flavell, J. H. (1978). Metacognitive development. In J. M. Scandura & C. J. Brainerd (Eds.), *Structural/process models of complex human behavior* (pp. 213–245). Alphen aan den Rijn, The Netherlands: Sijthoff & Noordhoff.

Flavell, J. H. (1993). *Cognitive development* (3rd ed.). Englewood Cliffs, NJ: Simon & Schuster Company.

Flavell, J. H., & Wellman, H. M. (1977). Metamemory. In R. V. Kail, Jr. & W. Hagen (Eds.), *Perspectives on the development of memory and cognition* (pp. 3–33). Hillsdale, NJ: Erlbaum.

Gambrell, L. B., & Heathington, B. S. (1981). Adult disabled readers' metacognitive awareness about reading tasks and strategies. *Journal of Reading Behavior,* 13(3), 215–222.

Glaser, B., & Strauss, A. (1967). *The discovery of grounded theory.* Chicago: Aldine.

Hare, V., & Pulliam, C. (1980). College students' metacognitive awareness of reading behaviors. In M. L. Kamil & A. J. Moe (Eds.), *Perspectives on reading research and instruction. Twenty-ninth yearbook of the National Reading Conference* (pp. 226–231). Washington, DC: The National Reading Conference, Inc.

Kelly, P. R., & Farnan, N. (1991). Promoting critical thinking through response logs: A reader-response approach with fourth graders. In P. Zutell & S. McCormick (Eds.), *Learner factors/teacher factors: Issues in literacy research and instruction. Fortieth yearbook of the National Reading Conference* (pp. 277–284). Rochester, NY: National Reading Conference.

Mayo, K. E. (1993). Learning strategy instruction: Exploring the potential of metacognition. *Reading Improvement,* 30(3), 130–133.

Moore, W., & Carpenter, L. C. (1985). Academically underprepared students. In U. Delworth & G. R. Hanson (Eds.), *Increasing student retention* (pp. 95–115). San Francisco: Jossey-Bass.

Mulcahy-Ernt, P., & Stewart, J. P. (1994). Reading and writing in the integrated language arts. In L. M. Morrow, J. K. Smith, & L. C. Wilkinson (Eds.), *Integrated language arts: Controversy to consensus* (pp. 105–132). Boston, MA: Allyn & Bacon.

Newton, E. V. (1991). Developing metacognitive awareness: The response journal in college composition. *Journal of Reading,* 34(5), 477–479.

Paris, S. G., Cross, D. R., & Lipson, M. Y. (1984). Informed strategies for learning: A program to improve children's reading awareness and comprehension. *Journal of Educational Psychology,* 76(6), 1239–1252.

Paris, S. G., Lipson, M. Y., & Wixson, K. K. (1983). Becoming a strategic reader. *Contemporary Educational Psychology,* 8(3), 293–316.

Paris, S. G., & Jacobs, J. E. (1984). The benefits of informed instruction for children's awareness and comprehension skills. *Child Development,* 55, 2083–2093.

Paris, S. G., Wasik, B. A., & Turner, J. C. (1991). The development of strategic readers. In D. Pearson, R. Barr, M. Kamil, & P. Mosenthal (Eds.), *Handbook of reading research* (pp. 609–640). New York: Longman.

Raphael, T. E., Englert, C. S., & Kirscher, B. W. (1989). Students' metacognitive knowledge about writing. *Research in the Teaching of English,* 23(4), 343–379.

Rosenblatt, L. (1978). *The reader, the text, the poem.* Carbondale: Southern Illinois University Press.

Shanahan, T. (1990). Reading and writing together: What does it really mean? In T. Shanahan (Ed.), *Reading and writing together: New perspectives for the classroom* (pp. 1–21). Norwood, MA: Christopher Gordon Publishers, Inc.

Strauss, A., & Corbin, J. (1990). *The basics of qualitative research.* Newbury Park: Sage.

Making Reading and Writing Connections with Shay Youngblood's *Big Mama Stories*

Mary Deming and Maria Valeri-Gold

Using the short story "Did My Mama Like to Dance?" as a sample reading assignment for developmental readers, Mary Deming and Maria Valeri-Gold provide examples of prereading / prewriting activities (KWL, setting the stage through the five senses, literary scavenger hunts), reading / writing activities that encourage exploration of the story at the literal, inferential, and applied levels, and postreading / postwriting activities that promote comprehension. In a very practical way, then, the authors demonstrate the potential of short fiction to engage students in the reading / writing connection.

Female characters called "big mamas" populate much of the literature about Black life in the United States. The "big mama" character is an African American woman who helps to raise and/or provide guidance to the children in a community. Youngblood (1989), an African American playwright from Georgia, portrays "big mamas" from the perspective of someone who has had first-hand experience with them in her collection of short stories, titled *The Big Mama Stories*. She affectionately defines a "big mama" as a Black woman who had a gift for seeing with her heart" (p. 12). However, when stories like those written by Youngblood (see Appendix for a list of her publications), are portrayed in commercial film, the perspective on their lives tends to be less sensitive and the characters more comic than serious. The film, *Big Momma's House* (Gosnell, 1999) is an example.

In her anthology of 12 short stories, Youngblood describes the "big mamas" and a variety of other colorful characters who inhabit Princeton, a small Georgia town located near the Georgia-Alabama border. The stories, many just short vignettes, are told through the eyes of the narrator, Rita from age six to thirteen. They can be enjoyed separately or read as a whole work. Story plots contain mature themes and are more appropriate for college students than for younger students. Themes include romantic love, courage, and initiation into adulthood, prejudice, death, friendship, abuse, injustice, religion, and sexual awakening. The language is metaphorical and moving and is used to describe many humorous situations and characters.

One short story, "Did My Mama Like to Dance?" is particularly poignant and speaks to the emotions of most readers. In this story, the main character, Rita, searches to discover more about her mother who died six years earlier. Now twelve years old, the narrator asks one of her mother's friends, Miss Corine, to tell her more about her mother's short life and premature death. Even though Fannie Mae, the child's mother, experienced a life filled with hardship, sexual abuse, and broken dreams, the child wants to hear the truth and the friend, Miss Corine, has the courage to tell it. At the end of the story, the child sorrowfully states, "I cried until my eyes hurt, till my heart was empty and my soul full. I whispered thanks into the front of Miss Corine's pink uniform, for the pain she had to bear to tell me the truth" (pp. 42–43).

The short story, "Did My Mama Like to Dance," has been very successful with college students. Students were moved by its themes. They were especially intrigued by the emphasis on family and indicated that they longed to learn more about their own families. Since this story spoke to students on such a personal level, it became an accessible arena from which to draw connections between reading and writing.

Reading and Writing Connections

The connections between reading and writing have been thoroughly examined in the past twenty to thirty years. Researchers have shown that both reading and writing are about generating meaning and that many of the reading and writing processes overlap and depend on similar cognitive elements (Shanahan, 1997). Tierney and Pearson (1983) assert that both reading and writing are comprised of similar processes and argue that both readers and writers go through the following stages to construct meaning: planning, drafting, aligning, revising, and monitoring. Furthermore, researchers conclude that instruction in one process may improve skill in the other, although not enough to eliminate instruction in either reading or writing (see for example Graves, 1978). Researchers have also demonstrated that the connections between reading and writing that are made explicit and taught in meaningful contexts are more likely to facilitate learning (Shanahan, 1988).

Rereading/Prewriting Activities

In order to activate students' prior knowledge (Anderson, 1984) and spark their interest in the short story, "Did My Mama Like to Dance," students can engage in a number of prereading and prewriting activities. A very simple, yet effective prereading/prewriting strategy is the use of a KWL chart (Ogle, 1986). Students list in three columns what they know (K) about a particular topic, what they want (W) to learn about the topic, and what they have learned (L) about the topic after they have read a story. Table 1 shows an example of a KWL chart for the short story, "Did My Mama Like to Dance?"

Another way to engage students before they read the story is to manipulate the environment to set the stage for the reading event. Our colleagues, McHaney and Schatteman (2000) suggest appealing to students' five senses — smell, touch, taste, sight, and hearing. Before students come to class, teachers can prepare the classroom with artifacts related to the story. For example, related to the story, "Did My Mama Like to Dance," the classroom might include items like jazz playing softly, mag-

Table 1. KWL Chart for "Did My Mama Like to Dance?"

Topics	K	W	L
Dumplings	A type of food	What type of food?	Little round balls of dough floating in gravy
Big Mamas	?	It is one person or a group of persons?	Women in the town who help to rear children
Blood Mama	?	Is it your real mother?	Biological mothers
Seminoles	Native Americans	Where do these Native Americans live?	In Florida long ago but were run out by white settlers
Naps	Afternoon sleep?	Are there different meanings for this word?	Naps refer to soft, fuzzy or downy surfaces; a type of hair texture.
Curling irons	Tool for hair	How do you use a curling iron?	Through the application of heat, curling irons can be used to either straighten or curl hair.
Running numbers	?	Can numbers run, like in cartoons? Does the word "numbers" stand for something else?	"Numbers" refer to a type of gambling; bettors pick numbers they hope will be drawn in a lottery.
Sulphur 8	?	Is this a type of mineral?	It is a type of hair lotion.

azines describing African American hairstyles, hair lotions and styling utensils, maps of the state of Georgia and of the city Columbia, dance magazines, and samples of southern food. Students can be encouraged to move around the room and touch different items, sample food, and enjoy the ambience of life in a small southern town in the 1950s and 60s.

Students can also participate in literary scavenger hunts before reading the short story. One of our student teachers, Amy Crisp, schedules a day in the library to conduct a computer scavenger hunt before her students start to read a novel (personal communication, April 13, 2000). Similarly, students can use the Internet to research topics related to the anthology and then share the website addresses and the results of their searches. The areas listed in Table 2 related to the story, "Did My Mama Like to Dance?" could be explored.

Other prereading/prewriting strategies that engage students include discussions, free writings, anticipation guides and previewing activities linked with teacher modeling (Deming, 2000). Because understanding vocabulary is so crucial to comprehending a text, students might be encouraged to keep a vocabulary journal that includes words suggested by the instructor and words the students themselves are interested in exploring. They may also want to collect colorful examples of dialects and special sayings.

While Reading/While Writing Activities

Students benefit from being encouraged to be active thinkers as they read and write. They can monitor whether or not they are making sense of what they are reading or writing. Again, a variety of strategies can be employed to encourage strategic, active reading that includes the use of maps, outlines, time lines, comprehension guides, and graphic organizers (Deming, 2000). Further, students can be asked to visualize a particular place or time in the short story or rewrite the story from a different character's point of view. They can also read other texts with many of the same themes. The works of Earnest Gaines, Alice Walker, Toni Morrison, and Zora Neale Hurston (among other writers), contain many of the same themes.

Specifically, students can use comprehension guides like those suggested in Herber (1978) and Alvermann and Phelps (1997) to monitor the accuracy of their reading. Table 3 provides an example. Other activities that captivate students' interest include role playing, choral readings, research and folklore projects. Students can work individually or in small groups to conduct folklore documenting projects. In particular, they might document customs, rituals or practices common to the community. They can examine the cultural and societal influence of these. Videotaped interviews and artifact collections can augment the students' work. "Big Mama" biographies could be written and illustrated. Students' work could be exhibited at state fairs and through local professional organizations.

After Reading/After Writing Activities

After completing the reading of and writing about a story or text, students can return to their KWL charts and comprehension guides to review their initial responses. They can discuss any changes they might make and write summaries individually or in small groups. In addition, they could do the following:

- Describe the importance of "big mamas" or mentors in their lives

- Describe an incident of prejudice in their lives

Table 2. Potential Research Topics Related to the Story "Did My Mama Like to Dance?"

Shay Youngblood's biography	Shay Youngblood's plays
Shay Youngblood's works of fiction	Literary criticism of Youngblood's work
Columbus, Georgia in the 1950s and 60s	African American funeral customs
African American hairstyles of the time	South Carolina Geechee/Gullah dialects
Dance and music styles of the time	Small southern town movies of the time
African American magazines of the time	Civil Right movement in the 1960s
A Shay Youngblood interview via e-mail	

Table 3. "Did My Mama Like to Dance?" Comprehension Guide

Directions: As you read this story, fill out this chart. Be sure to be able to justify your answers with examples from the text.

Literal Level: Place a check by the items that are explicitly mentioned in the story.

1. _____ Three of the characters in this story are Miss Corine, Big Mama, and Fannie Mae.
2. _____ This story is set in a beauty shop in the American South.
3. _____ Fannie Mae is dead by the time this story is told.
4. _____ Fannie Mae was raped in the white folk's park.
5. _____ A white policeman's son was accused of raping Fannie Mae and her white friend, Patty.

Inferential Level: Place a check by the items that are referred to or implied in the story.

1. _____ Miss Corine was reluctant at first to tell the narrator of the story about her mother's life and death.
2. _____ Fannie Mae's pride was her hair.
3. _____ Fannie Mae could not accept the evil treatment of black people by white people.
4. _____ Rita, the narrator of the story, has both positive and negative feelings about her blood mother, Fannie Mae.
5. _____ Many of the men in town were in love with Fannie Mae.

Applied Level: Place a check by the items that you believe are true based on your own experiences and the events in the story. Be able to provide evidence for your answers.

1. _____ In the South in the 1950s and 60s, people had to keep to their social stations and not mix races and social classes.
2. _____ Many times people in power escape punishment even when they are guilty of a crime.
3. _____ Many times the truth is very painful to hear.
4. _____ Sometimes people die because of a broken heart.
5. _____ No matter the obstacles, people should always dream and follow those dreams.

- Compare Rita, the narrator in the story with someone they have known or have read about in another story

- Describe what it is like to grow up in a one-parent household

- Describe the importance of one's family

- Define the term, "family"

- Compose a vignette about some important event or person in their lives

- Attend a Shay Youngblood play and write a critical review of it

Conclusion

Assessment of what students learn from these activities is important. Their understanding of the story can be assessed continuously as they read and write. Vocabulary exercises, journal entries, learning logs, reading guides, essays, and projects can all be used to measure students' comprehension and how well they are using reading and writing to think about these important concepts.

At the end of *The Big Mama Stories,* Youngblood acknowledges the "big mamas" in her life when she writes, "These women were my mamas. They had always been there to give me whatever I thought I needed. . . . All the stories they had told me were gifts, all the love more precious than gold" (p. 106). So now, we thank Shay Youngblood for sharing her stories and becoming a "big mama" herself to a large number of readers who are touched by her majestic language and thought-provoking vignettes.

References

Alvermann, D. E., & Phelps, S. E. (1997). *Content reading and literacy.* Boston: Allyn and Bacon.

Anderson, R. C. (1984). Role of the reader's schema in comprehension, learning, and memory. In R. C. Anderson, J. Osborn, & R. J. Tierney (Eds.), *Learning to read in American schools: Basal readers and texts* (pp. 243–257). Hillsdale, NJ: Erlbaum.

Deming, M. (2000). Reading and writing: Making the connection for basic writers. *Bwe: Basic Writing e-Journal* [On-line], *2.2.* Available: www.asu.edu/clas/english/composition/cbw/summer 2000 v2N2.

Gosnell, R. (Director). (1999). *Big momma's house.* Los Angeles: Twentieth Century Fox.

Graves, D. (1978). *Balance to basics: Let them write.* NY: Ford Foundation.

Herber, H. (1978). *Teaching reading in the content areas* (2nd ed.). NY: Prentice Hall.

Mchaney, P., & Shatteman, R. (2000). Using post-colonial literature in the classroom. Paper presented at the Georgia Read/Write Conference, Atlanta, GA.

Ogle, D. (1986). K-W-L: A teaching model that develops active reading of expository text. *The Reading Teacher,* 39, 564–570.

Shanahan, T. (1988). The reading-writing relationship: Seven instructional principles. *The Reading Teacher,* 41, 63–637.

Shanahan, T. (1997). Reading-writing relationships, thematic units, inquiry learning . . . in pursuit of effective integrated literacy instiuction. *The Reading Teacher,* 51, 12–19.

Tierney, R. J., & Pearson, P. D. (1983). Toward a model of reading. *Language Arts,* 60, 568–580.

Youngblood, S. (1989). *The big mama stories.* Ithaca, NY: Firebrand Books.

Appendix

Shay Youngblood's Publications

(1989). *The Big Mama Stories.* Ithica, NY: Firebrand. (Short stories)

(1991). *Communism Killed My Dog.* Woodstock, IL: Dramatic Publishing. (Play)

(1992). *Black Power Barbie in Hotel de Dream.* Woodstock, IL: Dramatic Publishing. (Play)

(1992). *Square Blues.* Woodstock, IL: Dramatic Publishing. (Play)

(1994). *Shakin' the Mess Outta Misery.* Woodstock, IL: Dramatic Publishing. (Play)

(1994). *Talking Bones.* Woodstock, IL: Dramatic Publishing. (Play)

(1997). *Soul Kiss.* NY: Riverhead. (Novel)

(2000). *Black Girl in Paris.* NY: Putnam Publishers. (Novel)

Bringing Life to Reading and Writing for At-Risk College Students

Cynthia M. Chamblee

Cynthia Chamblee describes a developmental reading course that has evolved across a decade of working with young men and women in a historically black liberal arts college. The course's curriculum and instruction is based on reader-response theories and the process approach to teaching writing. Chamblee also believes in the importance of integrating reading and writing processes and in the value of having students make connections to their personal experiences as they read and write. A course framework — including course readings, pre- and postreading writing activities, and autobiographical writing assignments — illustrates the recursive and continuing nature of reading and writing.

> know that whenever life throws a curve ball at me, I have to try to hit it no matter what. In other words, no matter how hard or tough the road gets, I must take a deep breath and do my best and never give up. Failure is the absence of acknowledgment. If I don't acknowledge the fact that I have the potential, I will give up to failure.

This excerpt was written by a student enrolled in a developmental reading class in a small, historically black liberal arts college in the southern U.S. Students who possess inadequate reading skills are not new to U.S. colleges and universities and are typically enrolled in developmental classes as a result of the perception that their reading skills are not adequate for learning at the college level. Many of these students, often referred to as underprepared or at risk, have experienced limited success in high school and regard reading as negative and stressful.

Other characteristics associated with them include the following: They (a) avoid reading when possible, even though they have developed sufficient cognitive skills, (b) feel that they lack control over their reading and have little metacognitive awareness of it; (c) have little sense of the reader's role and how to use reading; (d) do not consider themselves to be competent readers and do not expect to be successful in their efforts to improve their reading; and (e) lack interest in reading and see little practical value in it (Vacca & Padak, 1990).

I taught developmental reading classes for 10 years, and during those years, I was constantly searching for the means to better motivate my students to read. I was convinced that all students can improve their reading skills if they will only engage in the actual process of reading.

The purpose of this article is to describe the instructional framework that eventually evolved from the continual process of revising my course. The foundation for the framework consists of the reader response theories and the process approach to the teaching of writing, but supporting the framework are two very important, yet basic, principles — the importance of connecting the reading and writing processes and the value of helping students bring their own experiences to their reading and writing.

For the last 20 years, research has suggested that there is an intimate connection between reading and writing (Bartholomae & Petrosky, 1986; Marshall, 1987; Shaughnessy, 1977; Smith, 1983; Stotsky, 1983; Tierney & Pearson, 1983). While the research is not definitive of the exact nature of this connection or the teaching practices that best facilitate the development of the reading and writing processes, it clearly implies that reading can have positive effects on writing and vice versa.

Reading and writing are both composing processes in which the reader or writer constructs and reconstructs meaning (Tierney & Pearson, 1983); as such, they share common features. Both processes include the stages of planning, drafting, and revising (Lewin, 1992; Mulcahy-Ernt & Stewart, 1994). In the planning stage, topics to write or read about are selected, prior knowledge is activated, purposes for writing or reading are set, and predictions are made. In the drafting stage, self-monitoring of understanding and reactions take place, new information is related to what is already known, vocabulary is expanded, and important ideas are distinguished from less important ones. In the revising stage, meaning constructed through writing or reading is reconsidered, the text is improved through rewriting or rereading, and alternative interpretations are considered.

Reading and writing are also interdependent processes that are necessary and beneficial to one another (Smith, 1982). Pearson (1994) suggests the following as ways reading and writing support each other: (a) reading is an important component of the writing process, because it is through the act of reading that the writer monitors the meaning he or she has constructed; (b) the knowledge used in writing often comes from what has been read, and writing often becomes the stimulus for further reading; (c) reading provides models from which the writer can learn about genre, style, and voice; (d) reading helps the writer begin to understand the importance of structure, organization, and the conventions of language such as grammar, punctuation, and spelling; (e) reading one's own writing provides the opportunity to learn to read with a critical eye; (f) reflecting on how meaning is created during writing helps the reader better understand the role he or she must play in the construction of meaning while reading; (g) writing in response to reading allows the reader to revise the initial meaning constructed for the text; (h) writing before reading can have positive effects on comprehension as well as subsequent writing; and (i) writing provides support for comprehension skills and strategies such as determining main idea and supporting details or inferring character traits.

The evidence of the importance of the reading and writing relationship has manifested itself in integrated language arts classes and writing in the content areas. Nevertheless, courses designed for basic readers and writers often continue to separate the two processes and, therefore, fail to benefit from the important connections.

Likewise, courses designed for basic readers and writers often do not capitalize on the importance of bringing life to reading and writing. Research has suggested that when students make connections between the literature they are reading and their own lives, they are able to understand the text at a deeper level (Hynds, 1985; Nystrand & Gamoran, 1991; White, 1995). Research also suggests that when students are asked to write about their own autobiographical experiences evoked by the text, they become involved in the act of defining the point of that experience. This point, in turn, may then be used to help them better understand the point of the text (Beach, 1990).

The reading course I developed on these principles provided me with the means to better motivate my students. I began to see these reluctant readers (and writers) take an interest in what they were reading and writing and engage in lively discussions. In other words, I began to see these reluctant readers, these at-risk students, become real readers and writers — people who could engage in the processes with both authority and enthusiasm.

Course Framework

My first goal was to put my students into positions of authority; therefore, I designed the course around a topic they all knew well — life. Because the students had experienced and were continuing to experience life, they could respond with authority to what they read about others' lives. I encouraged them to make connections between what they were reading and their own lives and to agree, disagree, question, or speculate. Likewise, the students were placed in positions of authority as writers because they wrote stories about their own lives — a topic about which they were true authorities.

The reading and writing assignments for the course were divided into five sections with each section pertaining to a particular time in life — childhood, early adolescence, later adolescence, adulthood, and the senior years. For each section, the students engaged in a series of reading and writing activities related to that particular time in life. At the end of each section, they wrote a "chapter" to their autobiographies.

Course Readings

The texts chosen for each section were primarily short stories that varied in terms of content and level of difficulty, but in each section, the readings centered around a particular time in life (see Figure 1). The students were encouraged to make connections between the various stories read as well as to make connections between the stories and their own lives. They were also encouraged to note the common themes that emerged in the readings and in their own writings.

Figure 1. Examples of Course Readings

Childhood
"Discovery of a Father" (Sherwood Anderson)
"My Papa's Waltz" (Theodore Roethke)

Early adolescence
"Finishing School" (Maya Angelou)
"Bad Characters" (Jean Stafford)

Later adolescence
"Paul's Case" (Willa Cather)
"The Library Card" (Richard Wright)

Adulthood
"When the Other Dancer Is the Self" (Alice Walker)
"The Story of an Hour" (Kate Chopin)

Pre- and Postreading Writing Activities

Prior to reading the text, the students responded in writing to a prompt designed to activate the students' prior experiences and to help focus the students on the content or theme of the text. Examples of the prompts are in Figure 2.

After reading the text, the students responded to an open-ended prompt that asked them to write about their opinions of the text, their personal life experiences evoked by reading the text, the relationship of the text to other texts they had read, and the message of the text and how it could be generalized to life. This open-ended prompt gave some direction to the students in the various ways they could respond to their reading, but it also allowed the students to form their initial interpretations of the text (see Figure 3). These responses served as the starting points in the process of meaning construction.

The group discussions were a very important component of the course framework. Vygotsky's (1978) social constructivist theory of learning and development, which has contributed significantly to our understanding of the importance of the group discussion and the community of

Figure 2. Examples of Prompts for the Prereading Writing

Childhood
Describe an event from your childhood that reminds you of the expression, "You can't judge a book by its cover." How was this event significant in your life?
"After You My Dear Alphonse" (Shirley Jackson)

Early adolescence
Describe the person who influenced you to do something you knew you should not do. Who was this person, and why was he/she able to lead you astray? What significance did the event have on your life?
"Bad Characters" (Jean Stafford)

Later adolescence
Describe your dream life. What can you do to make this dream a reality? What impact will the dream have on your life if it comes true? What impact will the dream have if it does not come true?
"Paul's Case" (Willa Cather)

Adulthood
Describe your perfect mate. What attributes will you look for in a mate (personality, values, ambition, physical appearance, etc.)?
"The Guilded Six-Bits" (Zora Neal Hurston)

Senior years
Do you think you will live to be 120 years old? Discuss the reasons why you think you will or will not.
"How to Live to Be 120" (*Newsweek*)

Figure 3. The Postreading Writing Prompt

Write a very short summary of the text, then consider the following:

Did you like the story? Why or why not?

Did the story remind you of a person, an experience, or another text? Discuss.

What is the lesson of the story? How can the text be generalized to everyday life?

learners, proposed that higher psychological function appears first on the intrapsychological plane as social interactions between people and then later on the interpsychological plane as the social interactions are internalized (Wertsch, 1985). In this way, new ideas, skills, and strategies are acquired through social interactions and become the "inner speech" that later directs the individual in his or her own activities.

This scaffolding (Bruner, 1961) occurs in the literacy classroom when peers have the opportunity to discuss varying text interpretations, thereby being encouraged to consider other perspectives and to rethink their own prior knowledge and process, which may lead to the creation of a new interpretation.

Rosenblatt (1978) recommends that students be given opportunities to express their reactions to the text in writing and group discussion. She asserts that during the group discussion the students will return to the text to explain or justify their derived meanings, and they will often find that their interpretations are not the only ones justified by the text. As they hear the beliefs, opinions, and knowledge of others, they may also see that other interpretations are more meaningful, and may, therefore, revise or reject their own interpretations.

The group discussions in my classes produced the same positive results described by Rosenblatt. Initially, I had to prompt the students to return to the text to justify an idea or response, but during the discussions, I often saw the students' initial interpretations become further developed or altered in some ways. During the discussions, I would also prompt and push the students to go beyond the literal interpretations of the text, to think deeper about the text, and to consider the theme or point of the text.

Autobiographical Chapters

At the end of each of the five sections of the course, approximately every 2 weeks, the students wrote a chapter to their autobiographies (see Figure 4). The first three chapters focused on significant life experiences. The students were encouraged to elaborate an experience and then to reflect on the point or significance of the experience and how it had influenced them and helped them become the person they are today. In the fourth chapter, the students were asked to reflect on what they had previously written about their lives and then to describe their

Figure 4.

Chapters 1–3
Think about yourself as a small child (early adolescent, older adolescent). Recall an incident from this period of your life that was particularly significant. How did this incident influence the person you are today?

Chapter 4
Begin by looking back on what you have written and discovered about yourself. Describe the character that emerged. Now, think about your goals and aspirations. Describe the route you want your life to take. Where do you want to go? How will you get there? Who will be with you?

Chapter 5
Your life has come to an end. Look back on your life — your experiences, your character, your values, your beliefs. Think about who you were and what you stood for. Write your obituary.

futures, where they wanted to go and how they would be able to get there. In the fifth chapter, the students were asked to think about their past, present, and future lives and then to write their obituaries.

A Recursive and Continuing Process

As the students engaged in the reading, writing, and discussion activities, I began to see a process taking place — a process that expressed clearly that reading and writing are composing processes that are interdependent and beneficial to one another. Writing before reading was promoting a more active and enthusiastic response to the reading, and the postreading responses and discussions were providing the students with opportunities to further reflect on what they had previously read and thereby continue the meaning making process.

This process was also observed when the students engaged in writing their autobiographical chapters. The previous reading and writing activities became the seeds from which most of their stories grew, and the follow-up discussions of the autobiographical chapters indicated that writing their own stories had given the students additional opportunities to reflect back on past readings. In many cases, the students' personal stories enabled them to better understand the point or significance of stories previously read.

This process of preparation and reflection gave the students insight into how to effectively engage in the reading and writing processes. As a result, they were better prepared for their future reading and writing activities. The students were learning that reading and writing are recursive and continuing activities that do not stop after the first interpretation or draft. They were also learning the value of making personal and intertextual connections as they engaged in the reading and writing processes (see Figure 5).

Figure 5. Recursive Reading and Writing Process

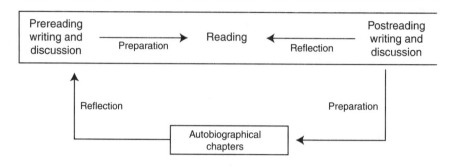

Relating Text to Life

While I do not have statistical data to prove the success of the course, each semester I sensed a greater willingness and motivation on the part of the students to engage in the reading and writing activities. I also saw their written and oral responses to the reading grow from a focus on the literal aspects of the text to the ability to think more deeply about the text — to relate the text to their own lives and to begin to consider the theme or point of the text. Likewise, their autobiographical stories improved in both quality and content as well as in their ability to elaborate on the point or significance of their own experiences.

Beach (1990) suggests that "readers move recursively back and forth between the text and their own experience, using one to reflect on the other" (p. 222). Giving students the opportunities to connect their reading and writing activities and prompting them to examine the experiences evoked by the texts may have facilitated the recursive process of preparation and reflection and may account for some of the successes observed. Encouraging the students to examine their own experiences may have helped them interpret the texts, which in turn may have helped them understand and write about their own lives, which in turn may have helped them better interpret the texts.

In writing this article, I do not suggest that this is an exact framework to be followed. In fact, the number of effective instructional frameworks is only limited by the resources available and the teacher's imagination. What I do want this article to suggest is that our basic readers and writers, our at-risk students, have potential. It is our responsibility as teachers to find ways to capitalize on that potential. Connecting the reading and writing processes and encouraging the students to bring their lives to their reading and writing appear to be two ways to accomplish this.

References

Bartholomae, D., & Petrosky, A. R. (1986). *Facts, artifacts and counterfacts: Theory and method for a reading and writing course.* Portsmouth, NH: Boynton/Cook.

Beach, R. (1990). The creative development of meaning: Using autobiographical experiences to interpret literature. In D. Bogdan & S. Straw (Eds.), *Beyond communication: Reading comprehension and criticism* (pp. 211–235). Portsmouth, NH: Boynton/Cook.

Bruner, J. (1961). *The process of education.* Cambridge, MA: Harvard University Press.

Hynds, S. (1985). Interpersonal cognitive complexity and the literary response processes of adolescent readers. *Research in the Teaching of English, 19,* 386–402.

Lewin, L. (1992). Integrating reading and writing strategies using an alternating teacher-led/student-selected instructional pattern. *The Reading Teacher, 45,* 586–591.

Marshall, J. D. (1987). The effects of writing on students' understanding of literary texts. *Research in the Teaching of English, 21,* 30–63.

Mulcahy-Ernt, P. I., & Stewart, J. P. (1994). Writing and reading in the integrated language arts. In L. M. Morrow, J. K. Smith, & L. C. Wilkinson (Eds.), *Integrated language arts: Controversy to consensus* (pp. 105–132). Boston: Allyn & Bacon.

Nystrand, M., & Gamoran, A. (1991). Instructional discourse, student engagement, and literature achievement. *Research in the Teaching of English, 25,* 261–290.

Pearson, P. D. (1994). Integrated language arts: Sources of controversy and seeds of controversy. In L. M. Morrow, J. K. Smith, & L. C. Wilkinson (Eds.), *Integrated language arts: Controversy to consensus* (pp. 11–31). Boston: Allyn & Bacon.

Rosenblatt, L. (1978). *The reader, the text, the poem: The transactional theory of the literary work.* Carbondale, IL: Southern Illinois University Press.

Shaughnessy, M. P. (1977). *Errors and expectations: A guide for the teacher of basic writing.* New York: Oxford University Press.

Smith, F. (1982). *Understanding reading.* New York: Holt, Rinehart & Winston.

Smith, F. (1983). Reading like a writer. *Language Arts, 60,* 558–567.

Stotsky, S. (1983). Research on reading/writing relationships: A synthesis and suggested directions. *Language Arts, 60,* 627–642.

Tierney, R. J., & Pearson, P. D. (1983). Toward a composing model of reading. *Language Arts, 60,* 568–580.

Vacca, R., & Padak, N. (1990). Who's at risk in reading. *Journal of Reading, 33,* 486–488.

Vygotsky, L. (1978). *Mind in society.* Cambridge, MA: Harvard University Press.

Wertsch, J. V. (1985). *Vygotsky and the social formation of mind.* Cambridge, MA: Harvard University Press.

White, B. (1995). Effects of autobiographical writing before reading on students' responses to short stories. *Journal of Educational Research, 88,* 173–184.

Using Drama to Develop College Students' Transaction with Text

Maryann S. Feola

As Maryann Feola notes, many new college students do not understand how their ideas, memories, emotions, and assumptions inform their responses to texts. When these learners discuss a text, this lack of awareness often leads to misconnections that obscure the meaning-making process.

Feola believes that dramatic literature has a great potential to lead college developmental readers to become more responsive readers. Drawing upon the ideas of Holland, Bleich, and Fish — transactive theorists who believe that meaning is formed in a reader's mind and not simply by the words on the page — Feola demonstrates how higher level critical and analytical comprehension along with competencies in the other language arts are promoted through her students' reading of dramatic texts. Excerpts from students' written work shows their improved ability to communicate their experiences, situate themselves within their work, and then describe both the commonalties and the differences between the events and characters from the play and the experiences and knowledge within their own lives.

Developmental readers often hold two misconceptions when they enter college. The first concerns their own levels of comprehension as conveyed by the number of lines they highlight in their texts with colorful marking pens. The second concerns their belief that the meaning in these lines was shaped without the influence of their personal experiences. Most incoming college students are unfamiliar with how ideas, memories, emotions, and assumptions inform their responses. Consequently, when they discuss a story, their lack of awareness often results in their making connections that obscure rather than enhance meaning.

If putting students in touch with what they bring to a text promises reading improvement, what type of literature would best facilitate the process? Dramatic literature, filled with personal conflict, emotion, and moving language, has the potential to transform students in developmental reading courses into more responsive readers. While reading drama, students become intimately involved with a character's life. This journey into someone else's beliefs, frustrations, and responses provides students with an opportunity to explore their own. In addition to serving as a window to the human condition, drama is fun and allows students to work with the kind of interest and energy that enhances their comprehension. For students likely to make egocentric assumptions, the structure of dramatic dialogue — with its distinctive oral and visual cues — enables them to define the boundaries between the text and themselves.

My use of drama in the developmental reading class is influenced by the ideas of subjective or transactive theorists, who believe meaning is formed by the reader's mind, not solely by the words on the page. Like others who enter college developmental reading courses with poor assessment scores and histories of disappointment with text, my students often have little awareness of how their attitudes and experiences affect their interaction with what they read and the world of ideas. This article discusses some components of transactive teaching that have value for developmental students reading dramatic literature.

Why Transactive Theory?

Transactive theorists contend that when we learn about ourselves — including ourselves as readers — we gain greater insight into the experiences and ideas of others. Holland (1975) believes an individual's success with a text is influenced by an "identity theme," an accumulation of the reader's needs and frustrations. This identity theme brings a "network of defenses" which must be recognized and managed during the reading process. According to Holland, a work's content must "come through the gates of [a reader's] personality" before meaning is constructed.

For a transactive classroom, Holland (1977) has offered a three-step process in which the instructor asks students to talk about their transaction with a literary text and then has each student answer the following questions: What am I bringing to this transaction? What that is especially and characteristically me am I mingling into this literary text? How does the text respond to the experiences I bring to my reading?

Bleich (1995) too has discussed how the exploration of a reader's feelings and beliefs results in increased subjective and objective awarenesses and has benefits that extend to enhanced cultural understanding. To facilitate this process, Bleich (1978) recommends a group setting, since he believes that students gain access to knowledge as a result of sharing their experiences and "re-creating" meaning. His focus on the social construction of knowledge recalls Fish's (1980) contentions regarding the authority of "interpretative communities" and Bruffee's collaborative approach for teaching communication skills (1985, 1993).

Bleich's emphasis on the importance of student collaboration and Holland's transactive approach in teaching English and literary criticism courses are useful in teaching developmental readers whose prior difficulties with text too often result in passivity and dependence on their instructors' interpretations. In contrast, working in student groups, like working in the theatre, results in effective communication among active participants.

Yet, in applying the transactive approach with college developmental readers, it must be kept in mind there are marked differences between these readers and the theorists' advanced composition and graduate students, who had more sophisticated language and critical thinking skills. Moreover, Fish, Bleich, and Holland assume that readers can consistently distinguish between what they bring to a text and what the author included. Developmental college readers, however, frequently confuse those boundaries. Consequently, for developmental readers to reap the benefits from subjective engagement, often class time must be devoted to learning how to explore and communicate carefully and accurately.

Initial Encounter with Drama

When we work with drama, my developmental reading students' difficulties with constructing meaning usually surface when they are introduced to a new idea or literary character. For example, during one semester when we began work with Arthur Miller's *A View From the Bridge* (1955), I observed that several students made little of protagonist Eddie Carbone's obsessive control of his wife and his flirtations with her niece. Their written responses to an assignment asking them to examine Eddie's treatment of Beatrice and Catherine yielded uncritical answers that did not take into account significant textual content. Their answers were based largely on memories of strong personal experiences that had been triggered by the text but not recognized by the readers. Here are three typical excerpts (all students' names are pseudonyms):

> *Matt:* Eddie is taking care of these women because they live in a dangerous neighborhood. If he's acting nervous towards them at times, it is better than taking a chance with what might happen on the street. His yelling shows he cares.

> *Tom:* It's Eddie who brings money into the house and is responsible for the family. Without Eddie, Catherine and Beatrice would be doing little better than their illegal alien cousins who move in with them. Eddie takes care of them all and puts himself out a lot.

> *Beth Ann* Beatrice needs to stop the abuse and leave Eddie. He is a bully who has no respect for her. He likes to throw his weight around and get his way. He can be generous, but it is on his terms all the time. He does care about Catherine, and she is the only person who understands him.

Initially, these students, like most of the class, were unable to discuss how they formulated their answers. Their comments suggested that their difficulty combining personal experience with significant information in the text resulted in something that was closer to rewriting the story than constructing a meaning for it. When I asked them what influenced their answers, they insisted they found them "right there in the book." It was evident they were unaware of the role experience plays in shaping a reader's response and, therefore, blamed any noticeable difference between another student's response and their own on a misreading of the text.

Employing the Transactive Approach

How can an adaptation of transactive theory be used with developing college readers so they can communicate their experiences, put themselves in the text, and articulate the links and differences between its story and their own? Because this was the beginning of the semester, my students were still learning how to listen openly to group members, how to examine alternate views, and how to rethink or rephrase an initial idea. To facilitate their efforts, I asked them to look again at Eddie's lines and answer the following questions collaboratively: What are a few major observations your group made (things you know for sure) concerning Eddie Carbone? Locate the evidence (pages and line numbers) that supports your observations. Describe any differences among group members in explaining these major observations. What suspicions does your group have regarding Eddie? What in the text shaped those suspicions? How did group members' personal ideas shape those suspicions? Explain any disagreement you had in answering these questions and how you worked to present, resolve, modify, or accept your differences.

This modification of Holland's queries into reading activities enables students to think more critically about how the characters responded to Eddie's authority. My class discussed how their initial appraisals of Eddie had been based too much on their personal responses to this character and not enough on the gestures, pauses, intonation, and other cues in the text they now spoke of as "evidence."

In the case of one student, Tom, the differences among the personal experiences of his group's members enabled him to see that a reader must be aware of the subjectivity he or she brings to a text along with what is printed on the page. He told the class how his interaction with male authority figures had shaped his first mental picture of Eddie. He discussed the changes he added because of the specifics he and his group came to regard as significant markers in the text.

The comments Matt, Tom, Beth Ann, and the other students wrote after several transactive group tasks reflected greater awareness of how they were, as Holland (1975) would say, receiving the text through the "gates of their personalities" and finding meaning in Miller's story. They became aware that this negotiation validated their own individual ideas, and they were more careful narrating, interpreting, and evaluating what was printed on the page. Their writing demonstrated that they recognized their relationship with the play, as well as that of the author and other readers. Their responses were now more thoughtful, probing, and developed.

The following are brief excerpts from Matt's, Tom's, and Beth Ann's written assessments of Catherine's behavior in the Carbone household:

> *Matt:* Catherine is suddenly growing up and it's hard for Eddie to let go. She goes from being like a child to Eddie and Bea to getting a job, falling in love, and breaking away from the family. Eddie is scared for her and, given the dangers she might face, he needs to be. On the other hand, I suppose each person in that house has the right to a life lived without interference from the others. I've heard this before from my sisters at home and the others in my group here. Now I'm wondering more about responsibility. How does it work, and what are the limits?

> *Tom:* It is hard for me to look at Catherine as a grown-up, since she sometimes acts like a kid. Does she act like this because Eddie continues to treat her like a little girl? Their conversations remind me of my own house where my parents take care of us and want our respect in return. Tempers flare and boundaries get pushed in both houses, mine and Eddie's. I think controlling one's own space is a touchy issue. . . . Yet the way Catherine and Eddie act around each other is something else, something that is frankly a little sickening. Who's his wife anyway? Why doesn't he put his eyes where they belong? Why doesn't Beatrice speak up and let out her emotions?

> *Beth Ann:* Catherine has mixed feelings about growing up. She wants to work and go out into the world, but she still wants to be Eddie's little girl. She likes to please him, maybe too much. When Catherine talks she sounds unsure about her maturity and spends a lot of time convincing everyone, especially herself, that she can be independent. It is difficult to separate from your parents, or in this case, from your guardians. Eddie's feelings towards Catherine are only adding stress. Beatrice is caught in the middle and when she tries to talk sense into Eddie and Catherine, she reminds me of my mom who hates it when my sisters and I argue with my father. But my mother, unlike Beatrice, is a strong woman who would have put a stop to the sexy way they talk and carry on with each other a long time ago.

Another group exercise followed our reading of Act I, which ends with Eddie baiting Rodolpho, the illegal alien with whom Catherine has fallen in love, into boxing with him. This arouses the anger of Marco, Rodolpho's brother, who resents Eddie's controlling, self-centered behavior. The groups itemized the textual cues they regarded as meaningful. For each character, they located lines earlier in the act that contributed to their reaction to the tension. Each student assessed one character's reaction and discussed why he or she chose this character and the personal experiences that influenced the assessment. Using the itemized list of contextual cues, each group coached one group of fellow students who reenacted the scene for the class.

While we read the second act, a point where each of the major characters is undergoing a crisis, each student wrote a one- to two-page dialogue between a character from the play and himself/herself. This miniplay included body language, intonation, pauses, and other specifics. The miniplay involved an experience, attitude, conflict, or need the student shared with the character. Before writing, each student referred to one of the collaboratively written class newsletters in which we periodically explored concerns, ideas, needs, and questions that resulted from our reading. After drafting and revising their dialogues, the students read them to group members who offered insights, support, and suggestions.

At the end of the semester, after we read Grace Paley's short story, "Wants" (1983), the class continued to identify and communicate the links between the subjective and objective. The students reread both the class newsletters and their miniplays, and each wrote a story called "Wants," centered around their personal growth.

Subsequent writing assignments and class discussions yielded increasingly critical insights and questions. Students had learned to work through the text without distorting it and use their own experiences productively in the process of creating meaning.

Construction and Communication of Meaning

Several students discussed how their groups' assessment of the actions and emphases in the play enabled them to discern more accurately how they were responding to the characters and creating meaning for what they read. Working in groups, they said, forced them to use language more selectively and purposefully. Their interaction also helped them flesh out and examine the nuances that sharpened their understanding of the characters' predicament. "Seeing" Catherine in her slip, sitting in the bathroom while Eddie shaved, raised questions that allowed the students to distinguish between their specific encounters with male role models and the character of Eddie Carbone.

I noticed that their oral and written responses were more critical and analytical. The combination of reading the play aloud and working collaboratively had necessitated listening, examining, speculating, generalizing, and reconsidering what many of them admitted they otherwise would have "just read through without giving a second thought." In this setting I saw close reading replace hit-or-miss. While they worked, the groups' disagreements and need for clarification resulted in their searching for and presenting evidence. When one group raised a question regarding the marital discord in the Carbone home, the group members supported their responses by pointing to lines where they found Eddie losing his temper, complaining, or trying to control and where they found Beatrice acting nervous while trying to defuse the tension.

Activities based on the transactive theory afforded my students the opportunity to make better use of their experiences and ideas during the reading process. I noticed they had greater facility articulating what they brought to a text and how it shaped the meaning they derived. For students who had felt like outsiders when it came to understanding literature, recognizing and utilizing their subjective experiences gave them a noticeable sense of empowerment. Developing this awareness in a group setting forced them to pay closer attention to the author's use of language and the ways different readers respond to it.

Reading together, like actors performing in a play, they became involved in a relationship where each member affected what was happening, as well as the outcome, which in this case was more skillful construction and communication of meaning. Their work had enhanced their ability to navigate between the subjective and the objective and to read between the lines, skills they need for later college work.

References

Bleich, D. (1978). *Subjective criticism.* Baltimore, MD: Johns Hopkins University Press.

Bleich, D. (1995). Collaboration and the pedagogy of disclosure. *College English, 57,* 43–61.

Bruffee, K. (1985). *A short course in writing: Practical rhetoric for teaching composition through collaborative learning.* Boston, MA: Little, Brown.

Bruffee, K. (1993). *Collaborative learning: Higher education, interdependence, and the authority of knowledge.* Baltimore, MD: Johns Hopkins University Press.

Fish, S. E. (1980). *Is there a text in this class?: The authority of interpretive communities.* Cambridge, MA: Harvard University Press.

Holland, N. (1975). *5 readers reading.* New Haven, CT: Yale University Press.

Holland, N. (1977). Transactive teaching: Cordelia's death. *College English, 36,* 276–285.

Miller, A. (1955). *A view from the bridge.* New York: Viking.

Paley, G. (1983). Wants. In I. Howe & I. W. Howe (Eds.), *Short shorts: An anthology of the shortest stories* (pp. 171–173). New York: Bantam.

Additional Readings

Bartholomae, D., & Petrosky, A. (1986). *Facts, artifacts, and counterfacts: Theory and method for a reading and writing course.* Upper Montclair, NJ: Boynton Cook.

Bernstein, S. N. (2001). *Teaching developmental writing.* Boston: Bedford/St. Martin's.

Clery, C., & Smith, A. (1993). "Evaluating reader response journals: A coding system." In T. V. Rasinski & N. D. Padak (Eds.), *Inquiries in literacy learning and instruction: 15th yearbook of the College Reading Association* (pp. 57–64). Pittsburg, KS: College Reading Association.

Daane, M. C. (1991). "Good readers make good writers: A description of four college students." *Journal of Reading, 35* (3), 184–88.

Friend, R. (2000). "Teaching summarization as a content area reading strategy." *Journal of Adolescent & Adult Literacy, 44* (4), 320–29.

Hayes, C. G., Simpson, M. L., & Stahl, N. A. (1994). "The effect of extended writing on students' understanding of content-area concepts." *Research & Teaching in Developmental Education,* 10 (2), 13–34.

Shaughnessy, M. P. (1977). *Errors and expectations.* New York: Oxford University Press.

Tierney, R. J., & Pearson, P. D. (1983). "Toward a composing model of reading." *Language Arts,* 60, 568–80.

Tierney, R. J., & Shanahan, T. (1991). "Research on the reading-writing relationship: Interactions, transactions, and outcomes." In R. Barr, M. L. Kamil, P. Mosenthal, & P. D. Pearson (Eds.), *Handbook of reading research* (vol. 2, pp. 246–80). Hillsdale, NJ: Lawrence Erlbaum Associates.

Valeri-Gold, M., & Deming, M. P. (2000). "Reading, writing, and the college developmental student." In R. F. Flippo & D. C. Caverly (Eds.), *The handbook of college reading and study strategy research* (pp.149–73). Mahwah, NJ: Erlbaum.

Wambach, C. (1998). "Reading and writing expectations at a research university." *Journal of Developmental Education,* 22 (2), 22–26.

9

Beyond the Reading/
Writing Connection

The previous chapter argued that reading and writing are similar composing activities that, when integrated in a sound pedagogical program, promote mutually beneficial competencies. This chapter expands that argument by encouraging the use of other communicative arts in college reading courses as well. In the first article, Nannette Evans Commander and Sandra Gibson describe how formal debate can be used to promote a range of literacy skills. In the second, Carolyn Beardsley Meigs and Ruth Abernethy McCreary provide the rationale and then detail the procedures for using subtitled foreign films in an integrated language approach to developmental reading.

Ideas in Practice: Debate as an Active Learning Strategy

Nannette Evans Commander and Sandra U. Gibson

For over one hundred years, we have known that integrating language arts instruction promotes literacy skills. In this article, Nannette Commander and Sandra Gibson show how debate leads students to develop and apply reading comprehension competencies through activities such as outlining, summarizing, integrating information, and thinking critically. In order to assist teachers in using debate in their instruction, a five-step instructional procedure is provided, along with a description of the benefits of this learning strategy for both students and teachers.

The purpose of a developmental reading is to teach a repertoire of skills that will enable students to succeed in their college courses. Thus, students need to learn not only discrete reading skills but, more importantly, how to transfer specific strategies to the particular tasks required of each course they may encounter. Although educational researchers have concluded it is difficult to teach transferable study skills in isolation (Dimon, 1988; Keimig, 1983), students in most developmental reading courses are not enrolled concurrently in "real" (content-area) courses. Developmental reading instructors, therefore, need to use instructional techniques that allow students to transfer reading skills to other kinds of tasks that the students perceive to be real.

With acquiring transferable skills as the goal, the question becomes one of how best to facilitate the acquisition of those skills. To that end, researchers and writers (e.g., Cross, 1987; Study Group . . . , 1984) have urged college and university faculty to involve and immerse students in the process of learning. Bonwell and Eison (1991) have described involving students in *doing* things and *thinking* about what they are doing as "active learning." Active learning strategies have proved effective for mastery of content as well as the development of thinking skills.

One active learning technique that involves students in doing things and thinking about what they are doing is formal debate (Bonwell & Eison, 1991). The process of debating may be designed to engage students in developing and applying reading comprehension skills. Additionally, students may transfer these reading comprehension skills to the very "real" task of participating in a debate. Thus, debate fosters both active learning and transferability. The following is a description of procedures for one variation of formal debate adapted for reading instruction.

Procedure

In the classroom the instructor introduces students to debate with a general discussion of the value of the debate process along with some information on the history of debate. The discussion includes illustrations of debate in everyday life, in government, and in the larger context of a democratic society. Using a handout that lists the virtues of an ideal debater, the instructor relates these virtues to characteristics of a successful reader. For example, both the ideal debater and the proficient reader are able to collect, organize, and subordinate ideas. Overall, the instructor emphasizes how debate will help students practice and apply reading skills.

Once the value of debate is established, the instructor introduces rules and general principles of the debate process. The instructor models each step of selecting a topic, forming teams, and researching the issues using example articles, summaries, and outlines. Teaching the process of debating may culminate in a mock debate before the actual debates take place. Such modeling of each step of the debate process is very effective in allaying students' anxieties about public speaking and in clarifying expectations.

Step One: Selection of Topics

Topics for school debates typically are propositions of value (a statement asserting the value or worth of something) or propositions of policy (a statement asserting that some course of action should be followed). A list of past natural debate topics illustrates for students how value and policy issues differ. For instance, whereas the resolution "Education has failed its mission in the United States" is a value issue, "All U.S. military intervention into the internal affairs of any foreign nation should be prohibited," is a policy issue. Offering examples of propositions that relate to the students' academic experience such as, "The place for Developmental Studies Programs is at the Junior College level," or "The federal government should significantly cut funds for financial aid to students," never fails to generate lively discussions. With an understanding of value and policy propositions, students have no trouble generating their own resolutions.

Step Two: Formation of Teams

Four students may volunteer or be assigned to a debate team which will argue a resolution previously agreed upon by the class. Assignments are made with the understanding that at a later time two people on the debate team will serve on the affirmative side, which supports the proposition, and two will serve on the negative side, which counters that effort. The instructor presents information about public speaking and the duties of each speaker. Students receive handouts based on a debate handbook by Ericson, Murphy, and Zeuschner (1987) which provide structure and clarify what the debates should accomplish as speakers present their arguments. A meeting of the instructor with each debate team is often effective in addressing concerns and answering questions.

Step Three: Researching the Topic

The instructor encourages students to obtain as much information on their debate topic as possible through books, magazines, interviews, or discussions. The specific assignment is for each speaker to obtain three substantive articles that will serve as the main resource for the arguments presented in the debate. Students must write a complete summary of each article isolating the main points and details. Additionally, each student must prepare two outlines presenting arguments and evidence, one for the affirmative side and one for the negative side of the debate topic. Students are most successful when each facet of this assignment is broken down into small steps. The selection of three articles on their topic may be the first experience with research for many students. Summary writing and outlining prove extremely challenging as well. Specific due dates for each task are helpful.

Step Four: Presenting the Debate

At least a week before the debates the instructor assigns students the specific roles of First Affirmative, Second Affirmative, First Negative, and Second Negative. The debate begins with the First Affirmative presenting the opening (or constructive) speech, then the First Negative, followed by the Second Affirmative and the Second Negative. The opening speeches are about 5 minutes each. After all the constructive speeches, there is a short period of cross-examination. This permits students in the audience to become involved and to clarify any points made by the speakers. It also allows a few minutes for the debaters to prepare their thoughts for the rebuttal speeches. The rebuttal speech offers each speaker an opportunity to attack the opponents' arguments in addition to the defense already presented. The sequence of the rebuttal speeches (limited to 3 minutes) is First Negative, First Affirmative, Second Negative, and Second Affirmative. The negative side has the last speech in the constructive series and the affirmative side has the last speech in the rebuttal series, which balances each side's opportunity of reply. Typically, presentation of each debate requires about 45 minutes of class time. Of course, time limits may be tailored to meet specific situations.

Step Five: Evaluating the Debate

An evaluation form completed by members of the audience and by the instructor provides feedback to the students regarding their debate. A self-evaluation form completed by the debaters as they watch a video recording of their performance provides feedback to the instructor on students' evaluation of their own performance and on the debate process in general.

FEEDBACK TO THE STUDENTS   Each person in the class completes a separate evaluation form on the affirmative team and on the negative team (see Appendix A for complete instrument). This procedure results in each team receiving a point value from each member of the audience for their debate performance. The instructor strongly urges students to assign points based on their evaluation of which team presented the most powerful argument, not on which point of view they personally agree with, and to provide written comments to each debater. The instructor collects and tallies all forms and then returns them to the debaters at the next class meeting when the class learns which team, according to the audience, has "won" the debate. The completion and collection of the evaluation forms is included in the 45 minutes previously mentioned as class time consumed by a debate. This has proved an efficient system for involving the audience, providing feedback to debaters, alleviating some of the pressure on individual performance, and encouraging collaboration of teammates.

The instructor also evaluates each individual debater with a point system utilizing the same form used by members of the audience. This provides an objective system for assigning individual grades, and, although grades of teammates seldom vary a great deal, it enables the instructor to reward individual effort.

FEEDBACK TO THE INSTRUCTOR   Finally, using a similar evaluation form (see Appendix B for complete instrument), debaters communicate to the instructor their opinion of their own debate by viewing a video recording of their performance. Students are keenly aware of being filmed and debate with a great deal of energy in front of the camera. The video recordings are also available for modeling debate procedure to students in subsequent courses. The self-evaluation form also asks for written comments regarding strengths and weaknesses of their presentation and what they learned from the debate process.

A sample of students' comments collected during Fall quarter, 1992 and Winter and Spring quarters, 1993, indicated that they found debates to be a worthwhile experience. Some comments focused on reading and writing skills, such as "I learned how to get information and facts. Also I learned how to build an outline and talk from it." Another comment was, "I learned that having a good outline to follow is important for any paper or project that I will do in the future." Another student said, "I learned to summarize information from articles, to outline it, and to present this information to a group."

Other comments addressed students' fears of public speaking. One student wrote, "I have learned to 'get over' my fear of being in front of a group of people my own age. In the past, I would not have got [sic] in front of my class to talk, but now I feel better about myself and my speaking abilities. I enjoyed doing the debate even though I was scared to death of doing it!" Another said, I have overcome my fear of speaking out in class."

Comments also reflect students' positive response to the debate experience, "I think everyone should have learned a lot about the topics and about everyone as a whole. The class really got into the debates. I feel you should keep debates in your classroom because it is a wonderful learning experience." Another student said, "I learned that I want to be a lawyer!"

Additional evaluation of the debate experience by students during Spring quarter, 1993 was accomplished using a procedure developed by Moeller (1985). Each student (N = 16) was asked to rate on a scale from 1 to 10 how valuable the learning experience of using debates was as a participant. Data indicated a mean rating of 8.6 with a standard deviation of 1.9, suggesting that students viewed the exercise positively. Each student was also asked to rate on a scale from 1 to 10 how valuable the learning experience of using debates was as an observer. The mean rating was 8.8 with a standard deviation of 2.23, supporting previous findings (Moeller, 1985) that debates are as worthwhile for listeners as they are for participants.

These data include the response of one student who said he "burned [us] on the evaluation" because he was angry that his side had lost the debate when he felt they had presented the strongest argument. While at first glance this may be considered a negative reaction, it certainly indicates how engaged the student was in the process.

Related Benefits

There are numerous benefits of incorporating formal debate into the developmental classroom. Debate actively involves students in learning comprehension strategies by requiring practice and application of skills. For instructors, debate serves as a manageable active learning technique that adapts to students of varied skill level and learning styles.

Benefits to Students

Formal debate benefits students by providing practice in many of the essential skills involved in proficient reading comprehension. Further, presenting these skills as steps in the debate process rather than as isolated tasks motivates students to become actively involved in their learning. Thus, debate has a positive impact on reading because it motivates students to engage in the following important skill activities which enhance comprehension: writing summaries, preparing outlines, integrating information, and thinking critically.

SUMMARY WRITING   There are many studies that document the positive effect of writing summaries on reading comprehension and recall abilities (Brown, Day, & Jones, 1983; Johnson, 1982; Taylor & Berkowitz, 1980). However, practicing summary writing only for the purpose of improving reading and recall is not nearly as tangible or engaging as the practice of summary writing for the purpose of a more successful debate performance in front of peers. Often students will need several attempts in order to write a summary which recognizes main points and details and is written in their own words. Debate motivates students to summarize since capturing the essence of their reading and presenting this information in a succinct manner is necessary to support their arguments.

OUTLINING   Practice with outlining assists in developing reading comprehension because outlining involves recognizing main ideas and details. Once students understand that the affirmative team's goal is to compel the audience to agree that their resolution should be adopted and that the negative team's goal is to prevent the affirmative from succeeding, they become aware how important it is to make every moment with the audience count. Debate speakers realize that they must be clear on what the main ideas are in the debate so they can communicate their ideas to the audience. Moreover, if the debaters do not know their own main ideas, they will never be able to recognize those of the opposition. When outlining serves the broader purpose of being the means by which the debater can present the most cogent argument to support the resolution, students become very motivated to think and speak in outline terms.

Reviewing the three structural elements of a debate case (issues, arguments, and evidence) not only helps students with constructing outlines but also encourages awareness of how information is typically presented in expository text. For instance, the issues, or the assertions which must be proved, may be compared to any general subject (often presented as main headings). The arguments, or the reasons for acceptance of an issue, may be compared to main ideas (often seen in the form of subheads) presented to support an issue. The evidence, or the facts and opinions that may make an assertion acceptable to the audience, may be viewed as the proof (often seen as supporting details). Sample outlines (see Figure 1) are very effective for demonstrating that all propositions are supported by major issues, and these in turn are supported by arguments which have specific evidence as their supports.

INTEGRATION OF INFORMATION   An analysis of the required tasks of a major core curriculum course indicated that a key literacy demand was integration (Carson, Chase, Gibson, & Hargrove, 1992). Students must be competent in synthesizing information from a variety of sources in order to demonstrate control of course content. For instance, in the course examined by Carson et al., students often were required to integrate material from the text with lecture notes and with supplemental texts as well. Many individuals lack experience in this type of task or lack the organizational skills necessary to accomplish this task. An example of an assignment which addresses this concern is to require that debaters note by each argument on their affirmative and negative

Figure 1. Sample Outline Presented to Students from Instructor

---

Example of Affirmative Outline

PROPOSITION: Resolved: That the Georgia legislature should vote to remove the confederate emblem from the state flag.

ISSUE: I. The flag communicates support of segregation.

ARGUMENT: A. The confederate emblem is a symbol of white supremacy.

EVIDENCE: 1. The Klansmen love the flag.

(source)   (article #3)

    2. The vote to add the confederate emblem was in 1956 to serve as a symbol of resistance to integration. (article #2)

    3. The symbol is often associated with slavery and segregation. (article #3)

ISSUE: II. It is important to preserve history.

ARGUMENT: A. There are other Confederate emblems and monuments that would honor this time period.

EVIDENCE: 1. Hundreds of statues of Confederate soldiers are in town

(source)   squares all over the state. (article #3)

    2. There are countless inscriptions, gravestones, and other public memorials to Confederates. (article #3)

    3. Jeff Davis County, Fort Benning, Toombs County, Manassas, Bartow County, Gray, Candler County, Stephens County, and scores of other Georgia places represent names which honor Confederates. (article #3)

    4. The equestrian statue of Gen. John B. Gordon outside the Capitol is a highly visible monument. (article #3)

ISSUE: III. This is an important issue facing the legislature.

ARGUMENT: A. A proposal to drop the Confederate battle emblem from the flag is Governor Miller's high-profile legislation this year.

EVIDENCE: 1. Miller said that this one vote will be the only vote for

(source)   which this General Assembly is ever remembered. (article #1)

    2. Miller gave an impassioned, high-intensity plea for new flag in four pages of his 14 page speech. (article #2)

Article #1: "Assembly Cool To Miller's Flag Plea," by Mark Sherman. *The Atlanta Journal,* January 13, 1993.

Article #2: "Governor Miller challenges lawmakers to 'do the right thing,' change flag," by Mark Sherman (Rebecca Perlman contributing). *The Atlanta Journal,* January 10, 1993.

Article #3: "A Flag That Slaps You In The Face," by Colin Campbell. *The Atlanta Journal And Constitution,* January 10, 1993.

---

outline which of the three articles supports this point of view (see Figure 1). This assignment not only provides experience with integration of information but also increases awareness of the process of synthesizing.

CRITICAL THINKING   Critical thinking has been referred to as a variety of interacting cognitive abilities which include discussing subjects in an organized way, developing evidence and arguments to support views, critically evaluating the logic and validity of information, and exploring issues from multiple perspectives (Chaffee, 1992). Formal debate involves tasks that provide experience with all of these skills. Debate particularly emphasizes presenting arguments from points of view that may be different from one's own. To present a strong case students must transcend their own bias. They must examine positions which may be totally different from their own point of view, and they may have to present a position contrary to what they really believe. Performing such a task results in an empathic understanding of opposing positions on controversial issues. Thus, debate fosters sensitivity to the author's bias as well as the debater's bias in reading materials. Because students must be prepared to debate both affirmative and negative sides of each topic, they are forced to look at the issue from both perspectives. Furthermore, students are more motivated to look at both sides of an issue in order to be prepared to counter the opposing arguments they will face during the debate.

Benefits to Instructors

Use of debate in the classroom also has benefits to reading instructors for incorporating active learning in their instructional repertoire. In spite of a number of available active learning strategies and the emphasis on the need for active learning by researchers and national reports, faculty often rely on traditional classroom presentations. Reasons cited for faculty resistance to instructional change are difficulty in covering course content, increase in preparation time, dealing with large classes, and lack of materials. Bonwell and Eison (1991) discuss the fact that perhaps the greatest obstacle to active learning strategies is the risk involved for faculty that students will not participate or that faculty will feel a loss of control. The different types of strategies promoting active learning vary in level and type of risk. The benefit of debate to the instructor is that it provides a structured, active learning strategy that involves low risk with high return. Although the faculty member must share some of the power in the classroom as he or she requires students to play major roles in their own learning, he or she does not relinquish control totally because formal debates require certain procedures be followed. Debate may provide a comfortable starting point for faculty to begin incorporating other active learning strategies.

Additionally, debate offers instructors a technique for reaching students with different learning styles. A study by Fraas (1982) empirically supports the belief that instructors should use a variety of teaching methods for reaching students with different learning styles.

Debate provides instructors with a strategy that incorporates reading, writing, speaking, and listening.

Conclusion

An important challenge of higher education today is to develop instructional techniques that help students to think creatively and critically. Developmental educators must meet this challenge while facing the special needs of high-risk college students. The motivation and excitement debate creates combined with the cognitive demands of the various subtasks in the debate process make formal debate a powerful tool for the reading instructor. For reading students, debate is an effective active learning strategy that fosters independence and competence. The numerous benefits of incorporating formal debate in the developmental reading classroom make this active learning procedure worthy of consideration.

References

Bonwell, C. C., & Eison, J. A. (1991). *Active learning: Creating excitement in the classroom* (ASHE-ERIC Higher Education Report). Washington, DC: Association for the Study of Higher Education. (ERIC Document Reproduction Service No. ED 336 049)

Brown, A. L., Day, J. D., & Jones, R. S. (1983). The development of plans for summarizing texts. *Child Development, 54,* 968–979.

Carson, J. G., Chase, N. D., Gibson, S. U., & Hargrove, M. F. (1992). Literacy demands of the undergraduate curriculum. *Reading, Research, and Instruction, 31*(4), 25–50.

Chaffee, J. (1992). Critical thinking skills: The cornerstone of developmental education. *Journal of Developmental Education, 15*(3), 2–8, 39.

Cross, K. P. (1987). Teaching for learning. *AAHE Bulletin, 39*(8), 3–7.

Dimon, M. (1988). Why adjunct courses work. *Journal of College Reading and Learning, 21,* 33–40.

Ericson, J. M., Murphy, J. J., & Zeuschner, R. B. (1987). *The Debater's Guide.* Carbondale, IL: Southern Illinois University Press.

Fraas, J. W. (1982, October). *The use of seven simulation activities in a college economics survey course.* Paper presented at the Economics in the Community College Workshop, Orlando, FL. (ERIC Document Reproduction No. ED 227 028)

Johnson, N. S. (1982). What do you do if you can't tell the whole story? The development of summarization skills. In K. E. Nelson (Ed.), *Children's Language Vol. 4.* New York: Gardner.

Keimig, R. T. (1983). *Raising academic standards: A guide to learning improvement* (ASHE-ERIC Higher Education Report No. 4). Washington, DC: Association for the Study of Higher Education.

Moeller, T. G. (1985). Using classroom debates in teaching developmental psychology. *Teaching of Psychology, 12*(4), 207–209.

Study Group on the Conditions of Excellence in American Higher Education. (1984). *Involvement in learning: Realizing the potential of American Higher Education.* Washington, DC: National Institute of Education/U.S. Dept. of Education. [ERIC Document Reproduction No. ED 246 833]

Taylor, B. M., & Berkowitz, S. (1980). Facilitating childrens comprehension of content area material. In M. Kamil & A. Moe (Eds.), *Perspectives on reading and instruction* (pp. 64–68). Washington, DC: National Reading Conference.

Appendix A

Evaluation Form*

Debate No. _____
Resolution: _____
Speakers: _____
The *affirmative/negative team* demonstrated an

Strongly Disagree		**Agree**		**Strongly Agree**
		ability to collect and organize ideas		
1	3	5	7	10
		ability to subordinate ideas		
1	3	5	7	10
		ability to evaluate evidence		
1	3	5	7	10
		ability to see logical connections		
1	3	5	7	10
		ability to think and speak in outline terms		
1	3	5	7	10
		ability to speak convincingly		
1	3	5	7	10
		ability to adapt		
1	3	5	7	10

Subtotal _____
Team Effort   +30
Total Points Earned _____

*This form may be used for evaluation of each team by the audience, the instructor, and the debater.

Appendix B

Self-Evaluation Form

Address at least two strengths of your presentation.

Discuss two areas for improvement.

What do you feel you learned from the debate process?

Please rate on a scale from 1 to 10 how valuable a learning experience you found the debates to be as a participant.

1	2	3	4	5	6	7	8	9	10

Please rate on a scale from 1 to 10 how valuable a learning experience you found the debates to be as a member of the audience.

1	2	3	4	5	6	7	8	9	10

Foreign Films: An International Approach to Enhance College Reading

Carolyn Beardsley Meigs and Ruth Abernethy McCreary

College developmental reading instructors have the opportunity to open up a world of reading experiences to their students. The article that follows describes a unique summer session program that promotes reading, writing, and viewing across extended periods of time.

In describing the program's rationale the authors draw on both theory and research regarding motivation, task engagement, prior knowledge / schema, and integration of the language arts. They also describe the instructional techniques employed with classic international films such as Diabolique, The White Rose, *and* Small Change.

wasn't even aware that I was reading," declared Lorenzo, a reluctant reader in Western Carolina University's (WCU) Summer Early Enrollment Program, after viewing the classic French film *Diabolique*. Lorenzo's reaction was similar to that of many students in the program who had had positive experiences viewing subtitled foreign-language films in their reading classes.

This was exactly the response we were seeking when we introduced the foreign film to the classroom. We wanted our students to enjoy reading while forgetting the mechanics, and to sustain the task for an extended period. This article provides the rationale and techniques for using subtitled foreign films with an integrated language approach. It also reports our students' attitudes toward viewing foreign films in reading class.

Almost 200 students enroll in WCU's developmental reading classes during the summer session. Their fall admission to the university is contingent upon success in the program. Most students in this group begin with below average Scholastic Aptitude Test (SAT) scores, reading scores on the Nelson-Denny Reading Test only at high school level, slow reading rates, and average class ranks, and are predictably likely to earn low grade point averages in college. Few are avid readers.

One of the required courses in the program is Introduction to College Reading. Its purpose is to help students improve their reading skills so that they can better cope with college study. To accomplish this goal, they are challenged to spend more time reading a variety of material, including textbooks, periodicals, reference books, microfilms, novels, short stories, and subtitles on foreign films.

Why Use Foreign Films?

The idea of using subtitled foreign films in class evolved in 1982 while we were enjoying several classic films borrowed from our university media center. We were reading continuously and were discovering films that were interesting, exciting, and sometimes of historical interest.

Before introducing the subtitled foreign film to our reading classes, we developed the following rationale: students would (1) find motivation to read, (2) experience a high level of time on task, (3) read faster to keep up with the script, (4) improve their comprehension by reading and watching, (5) learn vocabulary in context, (6) discover different cultures while building background for additional reading, (7) view classic works by famous directors, (8) build confidence by successfully reading adult material, (9) integrate language by reading, writing, speaking, and listening, and (10) actually enjoy reading.

MOTIVATION   The benefits gained from reading foreign films are based on sound educational principles. Viewing a film is motivating to students. Clary (1991) suggests that since today's young people are media oriented, films appeal to them. Keyes (1988) also encourages educators to use video to motivate unenthusiastic readers.

Adolescents experience many upheavals in their lives, forcing reading to take a back seat to other activities and concerns (Atwell, 1987). Thus, motivating adolescents is a special challenge. "Students should be surrounded by all types of print including but not limited to trade books, literature, biographies, newspapers, magazines, pamphlets, and student writing" (Irwin, 1991).

Subtitled foreign films are usually overlooked as one of the "all types of print," but they do offer another dimension.

TIME ON TASK   Reading film subtitles engages students in the process for extended periods. Chickering and Gamson (1987) substantiate that time on task is one of seven principles for helping improve undergraduate education. The amount of time students are engaged in reading "has been found to be positively and significantly related to reading achievement, regardless of the grade level" (Rosenshine & Stevens, 1984), and achievement is linked to the amount of time spent in "academic activity" (Brophy & Good, 1986).

SCHEMA THEORY   Reading foreign films exposes students to aspects of other cultures and to ideas that help them build background for future reading. Tierney and Cunningham (1984) report the value of enriching background knowledge to enhance comprehension. Poor readers tend to have little background knowledge about particular subjects, which causes them to have difficulty comprehending what they read in those areas (Anderson & Pearson, 1984). While we know the importance of activating schema (what is already known) to aid reading comprehension (Durkin, 1981), Nist and Mealey (1991) relate that college reading programs seldom consider the value of schema theory and prior knowledge. By recognizing the importance of schema in comprehension, we use and augment the backgrounds our developmental readers already possess.

INTEGRATED LANGUAGE APPROACH   Using subtitled foreign films for reading instruction affords opportunities for an integrated language approach. We avoid reading that is fragmented into subskills when "the reader is not engaged in making meaning" (Irwin, 1991) and follow such researchers as Moffett (1983), who endorses integration of learning, and Ross (1989), who recommends that students have purposes for reading, listening, writing, and speaking. "Becoming a good reader depends upon teachers who insist that students think about the interconnections among the ideas as they read" (Anderson & Pearson, 1984).

Developing the Strategy

Our first step was to preview foreign films we thought might be appropriate for our classes. This led to a list of films, all of which fulfilled the following criteria: Films should have (1) favorable reviews, (2) noteworthy directors, (3) sharp, clear English subtitles (no dubbed voices), (4) plots that are intriguing and appropriate for college students, and (5) availability on videocassette. (A list of the films we have used successfully in class appears in Table 1.)

The second step was to prepare a viewing guide to use before, during, and after each film. Each guide includes background information on the film (such as title, country and year of production, and director); a list of major characters with space to add descriptions of each; 10–12 vocabulary words to observe in context; and questions to aid in understanding the characters and plots.

Introduction of the foreign film to the class required direct instruction on viewing, since most had not watched subtitled films before and none had experienced such films as a medium for reading instruction. We informed students that since the voices would be in a foreign tongue, they would be reading English subtitles at the bottom of the screen as they watched the film. We challenged students to persist with reading subtitles even if they missed some of the words.

Students understood that each film would be paused or stopped, rewound, and rerun to keep them on target, to have them make or evaluate predictions, and to give time for writing notes on the guide.

DIABOLIQUE   Our first film, the murder mystery *Diabolique,* was adapted to Stauffer's (1969) Directed Reading-Thinking Activity (DRTA). This technique was familiar to our students, who had used the predict, read, and prove or disprove formula for short stories read in class. We felt that the best strategy would be to connect this new film medium to a proven reading method such as the DRTA; the viewer could make

Table 1. Films with English Subtitles Useful for University Developmental Reading Classes

Title, country, & director	Year	Length	Genre
The Bicycle Thief (Italy)* Vittorio De Sica, director	1948	90 min.	Social concern
The Blue Angel (Germany)* Josef von Sternberg, director	1930	103 min.	Comic tragedy
Dersu Uzala (Japan/Russia) Akira Kurosawa, director	1975	140 min.	Epic
Diabolique (France)* Henri-Georges Clouzot, director	1955	107 min.	Mystery
Diva (France)† Jean-Jacques Beineix, director	1982	123 min.	Mystery
The 400 Blows (France)* François Truffaut, director	1959	99 min.	Social concern
Jean de Florette (France) Claude Berri, director	1987	122 min.	Drama
M (Germany)* Fritz Lang, director	1931	99 min.	Crime/punishment
Manon of the Spring (France) Claude Berri, director	1987	113 min.	Drama
Orphée (France)* Jean Cocteau, director	1949	112 min.	Myth
Small Change (France) François Truffaut, director	1976	104 min.	Realism
Wild Strawberries (Sweden)* Ingmar Bergman, director	1957	90 min.	Drama
The White Rose (Germany) Michael Verhoeven, director	1983	108 min.	Historical drama

*Filmed in black and white
†Rated "R" ("restricted" — for adult viewers) by the Motion Picture Association of America (MPAA)

predictions throughout the lesson, thereby staying actively involved in the task of reading the film.

With their viewing guides in hand, students listened to the music and voices as the film began and wrote anything that came to mind. During this 2-minute introduction, students gathered impressions of the film's title (their first vocabulary word) and the type of film they would be viewing. Using music, title, and other visual clues, students made written and oral predictions about the film's genre. "The music is eerie and voices sound like children's," one student commented.

As the film resumed, students noted main characters and setting and speculated on the emerging plot. The pause mode allowed time for character description and clarification, review of predictions concerning the plot, and making brief notes on the guide.

Throughout the film, student predictions kept interest high and readers active. Occasional pausing allowed students time to check the validity of their speculations, to make new predictions, and to identify vocabulary read in the context of the film. The final scene encouraged much discussion as viewers toyed with the various diabolical plots. Students wrote epilogues for this 1955 classic and shared them in small groups.

THE WHITE ROSE   Numerous requests for additional film reading in class led to our viewing of *The White Rose,* a 1983 German film. We began with several quotations and photographs from Richard Hanser's *A Noble Treason* (1979), a written account of the same historical event, and we asked students to speculate on the who, what, when, where, and why of the story to help establish a purpose for reading.

As the film began, students quickly identified with the college campus setting and the youthful characters, a brother and sister, and participated vicariously in the college, family, and political life of these young Germans. As the story unfolded, viewers became acquainted with the period of the Holocaust and learned that some brave German citizens resisted Hitler's tyranny. This film challenged many apathetic attitudes and awakened a sense of moral responsibility for some students.

Follow-up activities included research, examination, and comparison of the White Rose resistance group to American student groups from the Sixties, and to the more recent student protestors of Beijing, China. Using large intertwining circles, students summarized their findings, which were displayed on poster boards in the room. One particularly interesting comparison was made between Munich University students of the White Rose and Kent State University students of the Vietnam era.

Students also examined their own feelings as they listed issues and causes they would champion today. Some of their concerns included the plight of Native Americans, apartheid in South Africa, world hunger, child abuse, nuclear weapons, destruction of the environment, and censorship. The class discussed personal risks they were willing to take or had taken.

Again the subtitled foreign film was a success in our reading classes. Students read eagerly and steadily and learned about an event involving college students in another time and culture.

SMALL CHANGE   François Truffaut, "the most celebrated French filmmaker of his generation" (Ophuls, 1985), had such an impact on the film industry that we wanted our students to be introduced to one of his films. To acquire a greater understanding of the 1976 *Small Change,* students used the university library to find and read film reviews and biographical information about Truffaut. They were surprised to learn that he also wrote the screenplay for and directed *Fahrenheit 451* and played a French scientist in *Close Encounters of the Third Kind.* They discovered that although most reviews praised *Small Change,* some criticized aspects of it.

After establishing background, students anticipated seeing the film. Many of the childhood episodes placed in a small French village are quite humorous and evoked rounds of laughter. (Recently a student who viewed this film with a class 3 years ago stopped on campus to reminisce about one of the incidents she vividly remembered.)

The class used viewing guides with names of major characters and key questions. After focused viewing, which involved pausing a few times to allow for questions, notetaking, and comments, students critically analyzed characters and events. They compared the teachers in *Small Change* with those in *Diabolique,* and the different ways children in *Small Change* spent their "pocket money" — the literal translation of the film's original French title.

As a follow-up activity using the writing process (Graves, 1984), each class member recorded a personal account of a childhood incident. (According to Johnson [1985], Truffaut had used newspaper accounts for most of his vignettes.) Although students wrote about something that actually happened, they freely embellished their stories. The class enthusiastically read their "published" collection, *Small Change, American Style.*

As a concluding exercise, students had the opportunity to attend a screening of Truffaut's first feature-length film, *The 400 Blows.* Aware from their earlier research that much of the film was autobiographical, they read the subtitles carefully to observe similarities and differences in the two films.

Students Respond Enthusiastically

At a campus blood drive, Chris, a student who had been in a developmental reading class 2 years earlier, chatted for a few minutes and then asked, "Do you remember that film *Diva* we saw in class? That was the best film I've ever seen." A couple of weeks later, Tim stopped in the parking lot to say that he had purchased the same foreign film! That class had been deeply engrossed in the story and characters of the film; they readily identified with the hero, who always was able to be at the right place at the right time.

Like those of Chris and Tim, other student responses to reading foreign films have been very encouraging. Using anonymous forms at the end of each term, we have assessed students' attitudes toward seeing foreign films and they have routinely evaluated the selections. Here are some of their comments:

"I had never viewed a foreign film before I came to WCU. I learned how to read the words quickly enough so when I finished reading I could look at the scenes. I liked all of the films and am glad that I was exposed to them."

"I believe that reading the films helped in my comprehension."

"I learned that you really can enjoy a movie even though you cannot speak the language. . . . "

"That's the closest I've come to reading a novel. At least it's a start!"

"These films give you insight [into[foreign countries. In *Diabolique* and others, you get to see parts of the cities and countryside."

"It was good for comprehension skills and it did make you read at a much higher speed."

"The foreign films give a brief look at the world outside the U.S. I enjoyed watching the way people live in other parts of the world. *The Bicycle Thief* was my favorite because it gave a realistic look at Italy during a time of depression"

We hope that students will continue to read from a wide variety of sources after each course is finished. Their enthusiastic response to reading films makes us believe our hope may be realized: At the end of the course, an overwhelming 88 percent of our students highly recommended foreign films for future reading classes. An additional 4 percent considered this technique a potentially useful reading method. When asked if they would like to read additional foreign films, 70 percent gave a strong affirmative response, and another 12 percent said maybe.

Reading foreign films with English subtitles has proved to be an engaging way for our college developmental readers to expand their reading interests. Students gained confidence in their ability to read adult material and developed research skills while completing written assignments related to particular films. They practiced critical reading/ thinking skills while analyzing characters and comparing facts and opinions in an integrated language setting. For our developmental students at Western Carolina University, foreign films have helped bridge the gap to college reading.

References

Anderson, R. C., & Pearson, P. D. (1984). A schema-theoretic view of basic processes in reading comprehension. In P. D. Pearson (Ed.), *Handbook of reading research* (pp. 255–291). White Plains, NY: Longman.

Atwell, N. (1987). *In the middle: Reading, writing, and learning with adolescents.* Upper Montclair, NH: Boynton/Cook.

Brophy, J., & Good, T. (1986). Teacher behavior and student achievement. In M. C. Wittrock (Ed.), *Handbook of research on teaching* (pp. 328–375). New York: Macmillan.

Chickering, A. W., & Gamson, Z. (1987). *Seven principles for good practices in undergraduate education* (Report No. HE 020318). Washington, DC: American Association of Higher Education. (ERIC Document Reproduction Service No. ED 282 491)

Clary, L. M. (1991). Getting adolescents to read. *Journal of Reading, 34,* 340–345.

Durkin, D. (1981). What is the value of the new interest in reading comprehension? *Language Arts, 58,* 23–41.

Graves, Donald H. (1984). *A researcher learns to write.* Exeter, NH: Heinemann.

Hanser, R. (1979). *A noble treason.* New York: Putman.

Irwin, J. W. (1991). *Teaching reading comprehension processes.* Englewood Cliffs, NJ: Prentice Hall.

Johnson, Julia (1985). Small change (*L'argent de poche*). In F. N. Magill (Ed.), *Magill's survey of cinema foreign language films* (vol. VI, pp. 2812–2815). Englewood Cliffs, NJ: Salem Press.

Keyes, D. (1988). Motivating unmotivated readers through media. *The ALAN Review, 15,* 20–22.

Moffett, J. (1983). *Teaching the universe of discourse.* Portsmouth, NH: Boynton/Cook.

Nist, S. L., & Mealey, D. L. (1991). Teacher-directed comprehension strategies. In R. F. Flippo & D. C. Caverly (Eds.), *Teaching reading & study strategies at the college level* (pp. 42–85). Newark, DE: International Reading Association.

Ophuls, M. (1985). Confidentially ours: Privileged moments with François Truffaut. *American Film, 10,* 16–23.

Rosenshine, B., & Stevens, R. (1984). Classroom instruction in reading. In P. D. Pearson (Ed.), *Handbook of reading research* (pp. 745–798). White Plains, NY: Longman.

Ross, E. P. (1989). How to use the whole language approach. *Adult Learning, 1,* 23–29.

Stauffer, R. G. (1969). *Directing reading maturity as a cognitive process.* New York: Harper & Row.

Tierney, R., & Cunningham, J. W. (1984). Research on teaching reading comprehension. In P. D. Pearson (Ed.), *Handbook of reading research* (pp. 609–655). White Plains, NY: Longman.

Additional Readings

Aikman, C. C. (1995). "Ideas into practice: Picture books and developmental students." *Journal of Developmental Education,* 19 (1), 28–32.

Elder, L., & Paul, R. "Critical Thinking." *Journal of Developmental Education* (Regularly appearing column).

Feola, M. S. (1996). "Using drama to develop college students' transaction with text." *Journal of Adolescent & Adult Literacy,* 39 (8), 624–28.

James, P. (2002). "Ideas into practice: Fostering metaphoric thinking." *Journal of Developmental Education,* 25 (3), 26–33.

James, P., & Haselbeck, B. (1998). "The arts as a bridge to understanding identity and diversity." In P. L. Dwinell & J. L. Higbee (Eds.), *Developmental Education: Meeting Diverse Student Needs* (pp. 3–19). Carol Stream, IL: National Association of Developmental Education.

Miholic, V. (1999). "Photography: A writer's tool for thinking, rendering, and revising." *Journal of College Reading and Learning,* 29 (1), 21–29.

———. (1998). "Using photography to heighten critical thinking." *Journal of College Reading and Learning,* 28 (2), 111–16.

Spencer, B. H., & Angus, K. B. (1998). "Demonstrating knowledge: The use of presentations in the college classroom." *Journal of Adolescent and Adult Literacy,* 41 (8), 658–66.

———. (2000). "The presentation assignment: Creating learning opportunities for diverse student populations." *Journal of College Reading and Learning,* 30 (2), 1 82–94.

10

Technology

Whether you are a dyed-in-the-wool Luddite or a Bill Gates wannabe, there can be little argument that the modern technological revolution, with all its promises and potential pitfalls, has come to stay in the ivory tower. Terms such as distance education, online education, compressed video, streaming video, Blackboard, Whiteboard, PDAs, CD-ROMs, and DVDs, which once belonged to the register of a select group of individuals in computer science or instructional technology departments, are now used and generally understood by administrators and faculty alike. Even while campus bean counters and tertiary-level politicians see technology as the savior of the bottom line, postsecondary educators — including developmental educators and learning assistance personnel — have come to embrace the potentials of technology. We must remember, however, that pedagogy should be served by technology rather than having technology dictate pedagogy. We can't afford to fall sway to the siren call of new technology, seducing us with newer, faster computers and operating systems, new generations of interactive software, more options for Web-based instruction, and ever more intriguing multimedia applications at the expense of quality pedagogy driven by theory, research, and best practice.

The articles that follow cover applications of technology in the developmental reading class today as well as the potential for technology on campus in the very near future. Alison Kuehner reviews the research on the effectiveness of computer-based instruction for the improvement of reading competencies of postsecondary students. Marsha Sinagra, Jennifer Battle, and Sheila Nicholson describe a program in which developmental reading students from two institutions responded to literature as "booktalk" partners through the use of e-mail. Next, David Caverly and Lucy MacDonald describe how developing a generation two (G2) online college reading course led to a reconceptualization and redesign of both the curriculum and instruction of the course. Finally, David Caverly provides a most interesting analysis of the current and future possibilities of technology in postsecondary education through the eyes of a hypothetical (but typical) college student and her colleagues.

The Effects of Computer Instruction on College Students' Reading Skills

Alison V. Kuehner

In this review of the research on improvement of reading competencies through computer-based instruction at the postsecondary level, the author discusses the expectations for computer-based instruction as well as problems associated with research in the field. In addition, she looks both at the research on various computer instructional methods and at comparisons of computer instruction versus traditional instruction, paying particular attention to mode of delivery, student attitudes, learning time, and student achievement. In conclusion, she determines that computer-based instruction can be used effectively with developmental readers if emphasis is placed "on good instruction via computers, rather than on computer instruction itself."

The computer revolution has hit higher education as college students increasingly receive their instruction via computers. But along with the widespread use of computers in classrooms has come concerns about their effectiveness. As Tanner (1984) says, "When a new technology is touted as having so much potential for education, its glamour cannot be allowed to obscure the need to validate its usefulness" (p. 37).

Research on computer-based instruction at the college level has been published since the late 1960s and, in 1980, the first meta-analysis was conducted (a meta-analysis uses statistical analysis on the results of many different studies to generalize from the findings). From the perspective of Kulik, Kulik, and Cohen's 1980 meta-analysis of 59 studies, results for computer-based instruction in colleges look promising. Kulik et al. reported that "the computer has made a small but significant contribution to the effectiveness of college teaching" (p. 538) particularly in terms of student achievement and students' attitudes toward their instruction. An updated meta-analysis (Kulik & Kulik,

1986) reached similar conclusions about achievement and student attitudes. Interestingly enough, both the 1980 and 1986 meta-analyses reported almost identical effect sizes for student achievement, 0.25 and 0.26 respectively, meaning that the typical control student performed at the 50th percentile in comparison to the typical computer-using student who performed at the 60th percentile. But the most striking finding of both meta-analyses was a "substantial savings in instructional time" (Kulik et al., 1980, p. 537) suggesting that computers could cut learning time to "two thirds the time required by conventional teaching methods" (Kulik & Kulik, 1986, p. 100). Still, Kulik et al. caution that the impact of computer-based instruction on student achievement at the college level is not as dramatic as gains at the elementary and secondary levels, and that other teaching methods might be just as effective as computers. These meta-analyses provide only a broad overview of the efficacy of computer-based instruction in college classrooms across many disciplines, and, as will be discussed later, may be flawed in their conclusions.

Literature reviews focusing on computers to teach reading are more cautious in their findings. Balajthy (1987), for instance, believes that the "results of research on computer-based instruction in reading are at best equivocal" (p. 63). He explains that while using computer-based instruction to supplement traditional instruction is effective, so is almost any type of supplemental instruction, whether or not it uses computers. In a recent review examining reading achievement in adult education, Rachal (1995) found "no significant differences between computer-assisted instruction (CAI) and traditional reading instruction" (p. 249) for adults reading at the ninth grade level or above.

To date, no meta-analysis or research review has looked specifically at the research on the use of computers to teach college-level reading skills. With this in mind, the goal of this paper is to examine this body of research. First, the Educational Resources information Center (ERIC) database was searched, using various combinations of the following keywords: CIA or computer-based instruction (CBI) and reading and college or college student(s). Bibliographies of articles and reports found through the ERIC search were also used to locate other relevant studies. Studies were chosen to review on the basis that they described experimental or quasi-experimental studies involving college students, at two or four-year institutions, using computers for reading instruction — either reading instruction per se or reading for study in a content area class. Only studies published since 1980 were included since software and hardware prior to 1980 is largely outdated. Also, repeat studies using the same software and conducted by the same researchers were not included, just the most recent version of the research was examined.

Expectations for Computer-Based Instruction

Much of the excitement over computer instruction is fueled by the belief that computers can help college students, sometimes in ways human teachers or tutors cannot. One of the most powerful arguments advanced for computer-based instruction is that computers can individualize instruction (Askov & Clark, 1991; Kamil, 1987; Reinking, 1987; Seigel & Davis, 1987; Turner, 1988; Watkins, 1991). Computers should be capable of adjusting the content of lessons or the rate of instruction according to the learners' needs. For example, Watkins reports on one student who needed 8 hours to complete an assignment, a pace that would exhaust the patience of most human tutors, but not an electronic one. Moreover, Taraban (1996) describes a program that could advise students as to which reading strategies work best for them. The computer monitors the student's reading behaviors and performances on exercises or quizzes, accumulates sufficient information to make correlations between the student's reading activities and performance scores, then recommends strategies that have helped the student in the past.

Computers could place in the readers' hands more control over learning, which Askov and Clark (1991) and Turner (1988) contend is empowering for low-level readers. Now with long-distance capabilities for delivering information, computers can be flexible to meet students' needs; computer instruction could conceivably be administered at various sites at any time of the day or night (Turner). Such accessibility has been recognized as advantageous for students who must juggle multiple responsibilities (Askov & Clark; Turner).

Other hypothetical advantages to computer instruction have less to do with the nature of instruction than with students' attitudes toward their learning. Particularly for the struggling student, observers report computer instruction can provide an important degree of privacy; only the computer program knows the student's skill level (Askov & Clark, 1991; Turner, 1988; Watkins, 1991). In fact, Askov and Clark contend that computer instruction provides a certain cachet. Students who might be embarrassed to admit they are taking a remedial reading class can avoid stigma by saying they are attending a computer class. Finally, researchers expect to capitalize on the excitement surrounding new technologies to motivate students to learn. In the age of television and video games, perhaps computers can engage students with graphics, animation, and game-like features in ways that will make learning fun (Kamil, 1987).

In short, optimistic educators believe computers will be patient, responsive, personalized tutors providing extra help with assignments in ways that engage and encourage learners. However, where there is hope, there is also fear, the fear that computer-based instruction will prove to be an expensive, ineffective attempt to improve learning. Askov and Clark (1991), among others, point to the high costs of installing hardware and purchasing software, of maintaining and upgrading equipment, and of providing computer training for teachers, as well as expert, technical support in the classroom or lab. Computers can crash (Kamil, 1987) and software, once installed, can be inflexible and may not exactly suit the needs of the course or the students (Kamil; Watkins, 1991). Moreover, integrating computers into the curriculum takes teacher time and energy, extra work which might cause resistance or create resentment among faculty (Askov & Clark).

Reinking (1988–89) offers some more troubling criticisms of reading software, arguing that most are neither pedagogically sound nor based on current research about the teaching of reading. Rather, he claims, assumptions underlying reading software development are fundamentally flawed. For instance, programmers rely on the misconception that reading is best taught by focusing on isolated skills, rather than on integrating these skills into the act of reading. Often these programs ignore the *process* of good readers to emphasize *products,* such as correct responses to multiple choice questions, and therefore do not teach reading comprehension so much as measure it. In short, bad software equates with poor learning. Computers, some observers warn, may not be the panacea for education.

Research-Based Answers: Computer vs. Traditional Instruction

To test hypothetical or observed advantages and drawbacks of computer-based instruction, we can turn to research. Typical research studies pit computer-based instruction against traditional teaching methods. Students in a control group might complete assignments by filling in worksheets or reading printed texts, while students in an experimental group might complete the same assignments using a computer program or by reading texts on a computer screen. An early concern of researchers was whether reading the same text in print or on a computer has any impact on reading ability. Other important research questions consider whether computer-based instruction has any effect on attitudes, learning time, or student achievement.

Mode of Delivery

Studies that examine mode of delivery investigate whether the experience of reading material on a printed page differs from reading on a computer screen. This is important because computer-based instruction, almost by definition, requires students to read significant amounts of information on a computer screen. Despite some concerns that computers might impede reading ability because of eye strain, or slow readers down, there seems to be little difference between these two reading methods. Fish and Feldmann (1987) found no significant comprehension differences among sophisticated readers (graduate students) when reading the same text on page or screen. Similarly, Askwall (1985) reported the same text presented on a computer or on paper had no effect on undergraduates' reading speed or comprehension. Therefore no detectable differences seem to exist between reading information from print or from a computer screen.

Attitudes

Most researchers agree that students have a positive attitude toward learning on computers (Balajthy, 1988; Kulik & Kulik, 1986; Kulik, et al., 1980; Lang & Brackett, 1985; McCreary & Maginnis, 1989; Mikulecky, Clark, & Adams, 1989; Wepner, Feeley, & Wilde, 1989). Only one study (Wepner, Feeley, & Minery, 1990) reported negative student reactions toward computer-based instruction, which the researchers attributed to "poor lab conditions" (overcrowded lab with outdated, unreliable hardware and software) and an "unfortunate change in instructors midway through the course" (p. 353). More typical are Mikulecky et al.'s, findings that students' attitudes toward computer-assisted instruction were strongly positive. Students reported on questionnaires that they enjoyed using the computer lessons and learned from them. In this case, the researchers maintain that students recognized the computer taught them useful reading strategies.

This positive student attitude, however, can be problematic if students confuse interest with effectiveness, cautions Balajthy (1988). That is, students in Balajthy's (1988) study rated the 2 computer-based instructional methods as being more effective than traditional workbook exercises, when, in fact, the group using workbooks showed greater achievement gains. Balajthy conjectures that students equate their interest in computer-based instruction with learning effectiveness and therefore may not, if left to their own devices, be capable of choosing the mode of instruction that would be most helpful to them. So while computers seem to motivate learning, this same motivation may misdirect students' attention toward unproductive activities and therefore not pay off in achievement gains.

Learning Time

Computer-based instruction reduces learning time (Kulik & Kulik, 1986; Kulik et al., 1980; Wepner et al., 1990; Wepner et al., 1989). Wepner et al. (1990) found students using computers could complete an entire program in the same time it took the control group to get through two thirds of the same material. The researchers noted that this 32 percent reduction in instructional time "correspond [s] precisely" (p. 352) with

Kulik and colleagues (1986, 1991, 1980) findings in their meta-analyses. Wepner et al. (1989) report a similar result in an earlier study, noting that the computer's ability to efficiently manage instruction (in this case, to calculate words per minute read and comprehension scores, and to supply reading materials) saved time since the computer users "consistently finished before the allotted time while the control group sometimes had to do their paperwork after class" (p. 8). They hypothesized that this time-saving feature of the computer may account for students' positive reactions toward computer-based instruction.

The one study to contradict these findings is Balajthy's (1988) comparison of students who used traditional workbook exercises vs. 2 groups who used 2 different computer programs to study vocabulary. As noted previously, the workbook users outperformed the computer users on vocabulary quizzes, yet these students also spent significantly less time on the text exercises. These findings suggest the workbook exercises were the most efficient use of student time (students learned the most in the least amount of time), even though students rated this method of instruction as least interesting and least effective. The fact that students spent less time on the workbook could be explained by their low-interest ratings, yet it is not clear why these exercises also proved to be more effective learning tools.

Achievement

An important concern for researchers has been whether computer-based instruction improves student achievement, achievement most often measured in quantifiable terms such as the differences between scores on pre- and post-tests. Many individual studies focusing on reading skills have found computer-based instruction to be effective for improving reading comprehension (Dixon, 1993; Grabe, Petros, & Sawler, 1989; Kester, 1982; Lang & Brackett, 1985; Mikulecky et al., 1989; Price & Murvin, 1992; Skinner, 1990; Wepner et al., 1990). Vocabulary (Culver, 1991; Lang & Brackett, 1985) and reading rate (Culver; Wepner et al., 1990) also appear to benefit from computer-based instruction. A closer look at these studies, though, raises the question of whether the *computer* or the *instruction* via the computer made the difference in student learning.

For example, studies often compare one group that receives computer-based instruction to a control group that receives no special instruction to show that computer-based instruction is effective. Price and Murvin (1992) reported that a computer program supplementing the textbook in an accounting class boosted student success rates in the course when compared to students in previous classes who had no access to the computer-assisted instruction. Similarly, Grabe et al. (1989) found that students in an educational psychology class scored better on exams when they used computer-assisted instruction to study the assigned textbook reading as opposed to studying the textbook on their own. Moreover, Mikulecky et al. (1989) looked at undergraduates in a biology class who used a computer program to help them understand the reading material as compared to a control group who studied the textbook on their own. The computer group scored significantly higher on exams, and even on subsequent exams, suggesting the computer had modeled and taught students effective reading strategies. But while both treatment and control groups worked with the same textbook for the same amount of time, only the treatment group received instruction (through the computer program) about how to identify, compare, contrast, and connect key concepts in the reading, skills that were necessary to do well on the test.

These studies seem to indicate that computer-based instruction can provide effective supplemental instruction. Another example is Kester's (1982) study in which students in basic skills classes who used computer-assisted instruction at least 2 hours a week to supplement their regular classwork made significantly greater gains in reading skills than students who did not engage in supplemental instruction. Dixon (1993) found that students completing a required remedial reading course averaged 4 years of growth in reading comprehension in the first study and 3 years of growth in a repeat study, leading Dixon to conclude that computer-assisted instruction is effective for remediating under-prepared freshmen.

It might also be that computer-based instruction, when compared to traditional instruction, provides a different type of instructional experience. Skinner (1990) compared 2 groups of students using 2 different versions of the same computer program to a control group who used text-only materials to study for a classroom management class. The computer groups performed consistently better on quizzes than the text-only group. Skinner hypothesized that the computer programs were effective study tools because they gave the students immediate feedback and were motivating. But also, students working under computer instruction were required to complete tutorial units while the text group had no such requirement.

Like the studies that indicate computer-assisted instruction helps college students' reading comprehension, studies suggest computer-based instruction can also improve students' vocabulary. In Lang and Brackett's (1985) research, college freshmen using computers to learn vocabulary and comprehension skills showed gains of one to two years in grade level reading ability over the course of the semester. This study, however, lacked a control group. Culver (1991) reports that computer instruction can improve English as a Second Language (ESL) students' vocabulary. Over the course of a semester, the researcher noted an overall increase of 3.9 grade levels in vocabulary development for students using a computerized, levelized reading program. But, like

Lang and Brackett's study, Culver's study lacked a control group against which to compare these gains.

Computer-based instruction also seems to improve students' reading rates. Wepner et al. (1990) concluded that reading rate for developmental reading students improved using computer-assisted instruction. Growth for the computer users compared to the central group was statistically significant. In this study, however, students in the computer group were able to finish all the assigned units while the control group completed only two thirds of the similar text materials. Culver (1991), too, found reading rate improvements in ESL students using computer-based instruction in a developmental reading class. The majority of students improved their reading speed, with an average 3.4 grade level increase for the semester. But, as mentioned previously, this study lacked a control group.

In most of the above cited studies, computer-based instruction did improve students' reading skills. However, attributing achievement gains to the computer alone may be misleading, since the computer often provided additional or different instruction that the control groups did not receive.

On the other hand, some studies have found computer-based instruction has little or no effect on reading skills (Burke & others, 1992; Jobst & McNinch, 1994; Kleinmann, 1987), comprehension and vocabulary (McCreary & Maginnis, 1989; Taylor & Rosecrans, 1986), or efficiency (Wepner et al., 1989). For example, in a study much like many of those cited above, Burke and others (1992) placed students into practice labs to study, either with a computer-based approach or with a text-based approach. The researchers found no significant difference in the achievement of the 2 groups. However, when compared to a group who did not use a practice lab, the 2 groups who participated in practice labs, whether computer- or text-based, scored significantly higher on a standardized reading test. This led Burke and others to conclude that the amount of practice time, not the mode of presentation, best accounts for differences in student achievement. Conversely, Kleinmann was careful to set up a study that used identical text and computer-assisted instructional materials and equal instructional time. He found that both groups made significant gains in reading achievement, and no significant difference in gains existed between the groups. Kleinmann concluded that while supplemental instruction appears to be effective for ESL students in a developmental reading program, supplemental computer-based instruction does not seem to be any more effective than supplemental traditional instruction. In fact, Burke and others and Kleinmann's studies, which directly addressed the question of whether achievement gains are due to more practice time or to computer-based instruction, suggest the answer lies in additional instructional time.

Taking a different approach, Jobst and McNinch (1994) set up a computer-based and text-based reading assignment for students in a technical writing class. Rather than create identical study materials (a case study), they deliberately constructed materials that would take advantage of each method: The printed version was cheap and easy to use; the computer version allowed for graphics and student choice about moving around in the text. Despite the researchers' expectations of increased achievement among the computer users, no significant differences were found in retention of the material or in students' exam scores. This study raised concern that the time involved in developing computer-assisted tutorials did not pay off in student results.

Analyzing student achievement when students use computers or texts is not a simple process. Some studies of computer-based instruction reveal that student aptitude might influence achievement. Two studies (Price & Murvin, 1992; Skinner, 1990) suggest that poor readers can benefit more than capable readers from computer use. Price and Murvin, who added supplemental computer-based instruction to an accounting class, reported the results of their colleague's research that students with reading skills below college level stayed in their accounting class and succeeded at higher rates than previous students. Students with college level reading skills also benefited from the computer instruction, but not as dramatically. Similarly, Skinner concluded that computer-based instruction is effective for college students, but particularly for those with a record of poor past performance. Low-achieving students using computer-based instruction scored 15 percent higher on quizzes than low-achieving students using text-based study materials. Skinner hypothesizes this improvement is due to "the structure and frequent opportunities to respond provided by CBI" (p. 358). Indeed, as noted earlier, students working under computer instruction were required to complete tutorial units while the text group had access to a human tutor with no required tutorials. In these two studies, the use of computer-based instruction to require supplemental work may be one reason less able students improved under the computer treatment when compared to students who studied on their own.

In contrast, the study by Grabe et al. (1989) illustrates a more problematic interchange between student aptitude and instructional effectiveness. In their experiment, when students were given free access to computer-assisted tutorials for study, the better students tended to use the computers. These computer users outperformed their classmates on most exams (even taking into account the fact they were better readers). Despite these advantages to computer users, the number of students using computer-assisted instruction over the course of the semester declined drastically. Researchers were not sure why this was so or why less capable students made less use of computer-assisted tutorials even though such instruction might benefit them.

Based on the above cited studies of college students, it appears that computer-based instruction can improve students' reading abilities. The majority of studies indicate that computer-assisted instruction increases student achievement. This finding, though, might be because computer-based instruction supplements or adds new instruction not provided to those students using "traditional methods." In these cases, more instruction, different instruction, or more time on task may account for the gains by computer users. Other factors, such as student ability, may further influence achievement gains of computer users. The structured approach of some computer-based instruction may help less able students who are unable to study effectively on their own.

Research-Based Answers: Computer vs. Computer Studies

Although most studies compare computer-based to text-based instruction, a few researchers (Balajthy, 1988; Blohm, 1987; Gay, 1986; Kulik & Kulik, 1986; Skinner, 1990; Taylor & Rosencrans, 1986) have examined differences among various computerized instructional methods. A key question is whether the method of computer instruction affects student achievement.

Unfortunately, no consistent terminology describes features of computer-based instruction. It is not clear, for instance, what makes a program "interactive." Nevertheless, Kulik and Kulik (1986) established three main categories of computer instruction: (a) *computer-assisted,* providing drill and practice or tutorial instruction; (b) *computer-managed,* providing evaluation, feedback, guidance, and record keeping for the student; and *computer-enriched,* serving as a tool to solve problems or as a model to illustrate ideas or relationships. Kulik and Kulik's (1986, 1991) meta-analyses found no difference in achievement among these instructional methods. All types of computer-based instruction had small but positive effects on student learning. They concluded that college students can readily adapt to a variety of computer-based instructional methods.

Another area of considerable interest is learner control vs. program control in computer-based instruction. In fact, learner control has become a field of study in itself and will only be touched on in this paper in the context of reading instruction. In learner control situations, subjects typically make decisions about how the computer program operates; for instance, they may decide whether or not to preview or review material, complete practice exercises, or do extra work if they receive low scores. In program control, the computer guides the learner's course through the program and usually "makes decisions" about whether to review material or to assign extra exercises for the learner.

Two studies (Balajthy, 1988; Gay, 1986) caution against giving poor readers significant control over their learning, whether using computer-assisted or traditional methods. In these studies, learner control hurt low-aptitude students who lacked effective learning and reading strategies. As both researchers explain, these students are unable to accurately monitor the success or failure of their own learning. In Gay's study, when students were given control over the computer program to study modules on DNA structure, subjects avoided difficult or unfamiliar material and tended to overstudy familiar topics. On the other hand, subjects with high prior knowledge of the topic under learner control conditions were significantly more efficient in their use of time than subjects with high prior knowledge under program control or than low prior knowledge subjects under learner control or program control. Blohm (1987) also found that providing proficient readers with learner control (in this case, computerized access to lookup aids, such as clarification of technical language) improved their reading comprehension. That is, competent readers successfully monitored their own comprehension and took advantage of computerized tools when compared to competent readers reading the same material via computer with no lookup aids. Both Gay and Blohm studies suggest that students can be given more learner control if their prior understanding of a topic is relatively high.

In one of the few studies comparing 2 different methods of computer-assisted instruction to traditional instruction, Skinner (1990) allowed students to use the same computer program under guided (GUIDED) or unguided (SOLO) conditions. Under the SOLO method, students were able to choose which computerized tutorials to complete, while under the GUIDED method students were required to complete entire units of tutorials. The control group used text-only tutorials. As mentioned earlier, Skinner found that low-achieving students benefited significantly from computer-based instruction. The study also revealed that students seemed to prefer the guided method of computer instruction. That is, even when students in the SOLO group could operate the program as they wished, most treated it like a GUIDED program. This finding might explain the higher levels of achievement for both the computer users and for the low-ability students, since other research suggests program control benefits less capable students.

Skinner's (1990) results, though, are contradicted by other studies. Taylor and Rosecrans (1986) also examined a control group (non-computer users) and 2 different computer-assisted treatments, being students receiving computer-assisted instruction in a structured manner and students using computer-assisted instruction during their free time (unstructured). In this study, the control group outperformed the 2 experimental groups. In another three-way study, Balajthy (1988) compared students using traditional workbook exercises to students using 2 different computer programs; a fast-paced video game and a slow-moving text exercise. In this case, the workbook users outscored the 2 groups of computer users. As in Skinner's study, students seemed motivated by the computer-based instruction (rating it as highly effective) and spent more time using the computers. But, unlike Skinner's subjects, the students in Balajthy's (1988) study did not benefit as much from the computer-based instruction as did their counterparts who studied with text workbooks.

A tentative conclusion might be that interactive yet guided practice (as advocated by Burke and others, 1992) is a beneficial approach for computerized remedial reading instruction, and, for these students, better than unaided homework. Students with more prior knowledge about a topic (Gay, 1986), or with good reading skills (Blohm, 1987) may benefit from more control over their own learning (Grabe et al., 1989). Still more research is needed to sort out the various influences of the type of computer program or instructional method and of the characteristics of the learner on achievement.

Criticisms of the Research

Although research studies should provide a more reliable, objective assessment of computer-based instruction than anecdotal or hypothetical observations, research has its limits and problems.

As noted earlier, the type and quality of computer programs vary greatly. Balajthy (1987) contends that "a variety of observers have indicated that the computer is not being well-used in the field of education" (p. 56). He also suggests there is a "lack of quality software" (p. 57), a point Reinking (1988–89) supports when he argues that most reading software is neither pedagogically sound nor based on current research about the teaching of reading. Balajthy (1987) points out that "almost all computer-based research is based on the programmed instruction model, which . . . is presently out of favor among reading researchers and teachers" (p. 56). In these situations, the software or hardware limitations may also limit the research findings. If computers are not being effectively used to teach, then researchers will not see the results of good computer-based instruction.

More troublesome, though, are claims of flawed research studies and meta-analyses. In an examination of the meta-analyses done on computer-based instruction by Kulik and colleagues, Clark (1986) claims 75 percent of the studies used were poorly designed (based on a random sampling of 30 percent of the studies included in the meta-analyses). He also notes that over 50 percent of the studies he examined failed to control the amount of instruction each group received, so that more instructional time might account for the increased learning of the computer users. Moreover, Clark points to studies in which the method of instruction differed between experimental and control groups. In these studies, the type of instruction, rather than the computer, may account for any measured effect. Reinking and Bridwell-Bowles (1991) also contend that many computer-based studies fail to properly control variables, such as time on task. Again, if the computer group is spending more time studying than the control group, this extra time, rather than the computer, might account for differences between the 2 groups.

A recurring criticism of research design is failure to control for the Hawthorne effect that tends to operate on the experimental group (Balajthy, 1987; Clark, 1986; Reinking et al., 1991). The novelty of using computers, explains Balajthy (1987), might result in increased student effort to learn. Evidence for this effect is bolstered by the finding in the most recent meta-analysis (Kulik & Kulik, 1986) that computer-based instruction is more effective over short periods of time (less than 4 weeks) and effectiveness decreases over longer periods. Perhaps, after 3 or 4 weeks, the novelty of using a computer wears off. On the other hand, shorter studies might be more tightly controlled and therefore better able to measure significant differences between the 2 groups (Kulik & Kulik, 1986). Another concern is lack of control over the "same teacher" effect. That is, if different instructors design the curriculum and/or teach the control group and the experimental group, differences in achievement might be attributed to the instructor rather than to the method of instruction. As evidence of this problem, Clark notes that when the same teacher designs both the computer and traditional instruction, computer-based effect sizes for college students reduce to insignificant levels.

In fact, when Clark (1986) re-analyzed the studies, controlling for such variables as the "same teacher" effect or instructional methods, his revised effect sizes were much lower. He concludes that meta-analyses overestimate the effect of computer-based instruction on achievement. It would appear that many of Clark's criticisms of the meta-analyses apply to the studies examined in this paper. Differences in instructional methods or time on task between control and experimental groups may account for the differences between groups.

The Correct Question?

In light of the criticisms over the research and meta-analyses, Clark (1986) contends that it is basically misleading or unproductive to pit computer-based instruction against traditional teaching methods. When studies are correctly designed, Clark asserts, no discernible differences in student achievement exist that can be attributed to computers, and there is no reason to believe that there should be. The computer, he argues, is just a delivery system for instruction. The type of instruction, rather than the means by which it is sent to the student, is paramount. Therefore, the correct question researchers could investigate productively would be how computers might deliver good instruction most effectively and cost-efficiently.

Balajthy (1987) also believes research into computer-based instruction could be more productive by focusing on the question, "In what ways can the computer improve on conventional classroom effectiveness and efficiency?" (p. 55). Unlike Clark (1986) though, Balajthy (1987) insists that research and research reviews show "there is no doubt that computer instruction is effective" (p. 55). Like Clark, Balajthy (1987) emphasizes identifying effective teaching methods, then considering how computers can effectively deliver that instruction. In this process, Balajthy (1987) advocates examining the various student-based, computer-based, or instructional factors that influence computer effectiveness.

Conclusions

As Tanner (1984) urges, we as educators should not allow the excitement of computers arriving in our classrooms and labs to blind us to the need to examine carefully how we use computers with our students. It would seem, based on the examination of research included in this review, that both Clark's (1986) and Balajthy's (1987) emphasis on good instruction via computers, rather than on computer instruction itself is important. As educational researchers, we might do well to heed Rachel's (1995) criticisms of computer-based research, noting how frequently studies lacked control over treatment time, did not randomly assign subjects to groups, or used a small number of subjects for study. His suggestions to future researchers are excellent: pre-testing and randomly assigning an adequate number of students to control and experimental groups taught by equally competent instructors; carefully documenting time on task and post-testing students after equal number of hours for each treatment; using appropriate software; and reporting methodology and findings as clearly as possible.

Despite problems with the research, in light of the studies cited here, there are some good reasons to use computers for reading instruction with college students. Computer-based instruction can provide motivating and efficient learning since two of the most significant advantages to using computers are that students have positive attitudes toward learning with computers and that computers, in most situations, can reduce instructional time.

Moreover, computer-based instruction as a supplement to traditional teaching methods appears to increase student achievement, though it is not clear whether computer-based instruction itself or the instruction given students via the computer best accounts for student gains. This uncertainty suggests that teachers need to consider carefully the computer program itself. Instruction should be based on sound pedagogy. In fact, supplemental materials or additional instruction may be provided to students to improve reading skills without computer aid. Here, some evidence indicates that remedial students can benefit more from computer instruction, but only if they are not given a significant degree of control over their own learning. For these students, program control or explicitly taught learning strategies might be more advantageous. Certainly there is promise that computers can help teach large numbers of college students, including remedial readers, but only if they are used wisely.

References

Askov, E. N., & Clark, C. J. (1991). Using computers in adult literacy instruction. *Journal of Reading, 34,* 434–437.

Askwall, S. (1985). Computer supported reading vs. reading text on paper: A comparison of two reading situations. *International Journal of Man-Machine Studies,* 425–439.

Balajthy, E. (1987). What does research on computer-based instruction have to say to the reading teacher? *Reading Research and Instruction, 27* (1) 55–65.

Balajthy, E. (1988). An investigation of learner-control variables in vocabulary learning using traditional instruction and two forms of computer-based instruction. *Reading Research and Instruction, 27* (4), 15–24.

Blohm, P. J. (1987). Effect of lookup aids on mature readers' recall of technical text. *Reading Research and Instruction, 26* (2), 77–88.

Burke, M., & others. (1992, March). *Computer-assisted vs. text-based practice: Which method is more effective?* A version of this paper was presented at the Annual Midwest Reading and Study Skills Conference, Kansas City, MO. (ERIC Document Reproduction Service No. Ed 350 046)

Clark, R. E. (1986). Instruction studies: Analyzing the meta-analyses. *Educational Communication and Technology, 33,* 249–262.

Culver, L. (1991). *Improving reading speed and comprehension for ESL students with the computer* (Practicum Report No. FLO19486). Florida, Nova University. (ERIC Document Reproduction Service No. Ed 335 960).

Dixon, R. A. (1993, March). *Improved reading comprehension: A key to university retention?* Paper presented at the Annual Midwest Regional Reading and Study Skills Conference, Kansas City, MO.

Fish, M. C., & Feldmann, S. C. (1987). A comparison of reading comprehension using print and microcomputer presentation. *Journal of Computer-Based Instruction, 14* (2), 57–61.

Gay, G. (1986). Interaction of learner control and prior understanding in computer-assisted video instruction. *Journal of Educational Psychology, 78,* 225–227.

Grabe, M., Petros, T., & Sawler, B. (1989). An evaluation of computer assisted study in controlled and free access settings. *Journal of Computer-Based Instruction, 16* (3), 110–116.

Jobst, J. W., & McNinch, T. L. (1994). The effectiveness of two case study versions: Printed versus computer-assisted instruction. *Journal of Technical Writing and Communication, 24,* 421–433.

Kamil, M. L. (1987). Computers and reading research. In D. Reinking (Ed.), *Reading and computers: Issues for theory and practice* (pp. 57–75). New York: Teachers College Press.

Kester, D. L. (1982, August). *Is micro-computer assisted basic skills instruction good for black, disadvantaged community college students from Watts and similar communities?* Paper presented at the International School Psychology Colloquium, Stockholm, Sweden.

Kleinmann, H. H. (1987). The effect of computer-assisted instruction on ESL reading achievement. *The Modern Language Journal, 71,* 267–273.

Kulik, C. C., & Kulik, J. A. (1986). Effectiveness of computer-based education in colleges. *AEDS Journal, 19* (2–3), 81–108.

Kulik, C. C., & Kulik, J. A. (1991). Effectiveness of computer-based instruction: An updated analysis. *Computers in Human Behavior, 7,* 75–94.

Kulik, J. A., Kulik, C. C., & Cohen, P. A. (1980). Effectiveness of computer-based college teaching: A meta-analysis of findings. *Review of Educational Research, 50,* 525–544.

Lang, W. S., & Brackett, E. J. (1985, February). *Effects on reading achievement in developmental education: Computer-assisted instruction and the college student.* Paper presented at the Annual Meeting of the South Carolina Reading Association, Columbia, SC.

McCreary, R., & Maginnis, G. (1989, May). *The effects of computer-assisted instruction on reading achievement for college freshman.* Paper presented at the Annual Meeting of the International Reading Association, New Orleans, LA.

Mikulecky, L., Clark, E. S., & Adams, S. M. (1989). Teaching concept mapping and university level study strategies using computers. *Journal of Reading, 32,* 694–702.

Price, R. L., & Murvin, H. J. (1992). Computers can help student retention in introductory college accounting. *Business Education Forum, 47,* 25–27.

Rachal, J. R. (1995). Adult reading achievement comparing computer-assisted and traditional approaches: A comprehensive review of the experimental literature. *Reading Research and Instruction, 34* (3), 239–258.

Reinking, D. (1987). Computers, reading, and a new technology of print. In D. Reinking (Ed.), *Reading and computers: Issues for theory and practice* (pp. 3–23). New York: Teachers College Press.

Reinking, D. (1988–89). Misconceptions about reading and software development. *Computing Teacher, 16* (4) 27–29.

Reinking, D., & Bridwell-Bowles, L. (1991). Computers in reading and writing. In Barr, R., Kamil, M. L., Mosenthal, P. B., & Pearson, P. D. (Eds.), *Handbook of reading research* (pp. 310–340). New York: Longman.

Seigel, M. A., & Davis, D. M. (1987). Redefining a basic CAI technique to teach reading comprehension. In D. Reinking (Ed.), *Reading and computers: Issues for theory and practice* (pp. 111–126). New York: Teachers College Press.

Skinner, M. E. (1990). The effects of computer-based instruction on the achievement of college students as a function of achievement status and mode of presentation. *Computers in Human Behavior, 6,* 351–60.

Tanner, D. E. (1984). Horses, carts, and computers in reading: A review of research. *Computers, Reading, and Language Arts, 2,* 35–38.

Taraban, R. (1996). A computer-based paradigm for developmental research and instruction. *Journal of Developmental Education, 20* (11), 12–14, 16, 18, 20.

Taylor, V. B., & Rosecrans, D. (1986). *An investigation of vocabulary development via computer-assisted instruction (CAI).* (ERIC Document Reproduction Service No. ED 281 168).

Turner, T. C. (1988). Using the computer for adult literacy instruction. *Journal of Reading, 31,* 643–647.

Watkins, B. T. (1991). Using computers to teach basic skills. *Chronicle of Higher Education, 38* (6) A23–26.

Wepner, S. B., Feeley, J. T., & Minery, B. (1990). Do computers have a place in college reading courses? *Journal of Reading, 33,* 348–354.

Wepner, S. B., Feeley, J. T., & Wilde, S. (1989). Using computers in college reading courses? *Journal of Developmental Education, 13,* 6–8, 24.

E-mail "Booktalking": Engaging Developmental Readers with Authors and Others in the Academic Community

Marsha D. Sinagra, Jennifer Battle, and Sheila A. Nicholson

When educators first choose to introduce technology into their classes, they often begin with e-mail. In " 'Booktalking,' " we learn how developmental reading students from two universities communicated about literature via e-mail. Qualitative analysis undertaken by the authors shows the nature of the readers' engagement with text. The authors also share some of the ways they have refined their use of e-mail as an instructional technique over the years.

There is a common perception among developmental reading teachers that their students are generally unengaged, passive readers. Recognizing that success in college demands active engagement with print, with authors, and with others in the academic community, many instructors use sustained silent reading of literature and group discussion to promote engagement. However, recent interest in fostering computer literacy, and continued efforts to enhance readers' literacy skills, awakened our interest in studying the computer as a tool to promote reader engagement with literature in our developmental reading classes. As instructors and faculty at two distant universities, Southwest Texas State University and Nova Southeastern University, we wondered how having our students use interactive E-mail exchanges to respond to well-written literature with substantive themes would affect their engagement with the assigned readings. We believed that this opportunity, based on a constructivist view of learning that affirms the learner's active role in the social construction of knowledge (Vygotsky, 1978), might build motivation for engagement with literature (Guthrie, 1996).

Little research has been done that specifically investigates the use of the computer as a medium for response to literature at the university level. However, since engaging often-unengaged students with literature was an important goal of instruction and the focus of this investigation, we looked at what researchers have said about the nature of engagement. Gambrell (1996), for example, describes the engaged reader as strategic, motivated, knowledgeable, and socially interactive. We have found in working with developmental readers that they often do not exhibit these qualities. In their review, Almasi, McKeown, and Beck (1996) define engagement during reading as "sustained personal commitment to creating understanding while one reads" (p. 108). According to these researchers, engaged readers' perceptions of themselves and their literacy tasks show (a) readers believe they are capable, (b) the task has intrinsic value for them, (c) they believe their work is interesting and important, (d) they believe their behavior influences their academic performance, and (e) they have positive affective responses. Almasi et al. (1996) found that engagement with literature is evident in students' use of "interpretive tools" while responding to literature. These tools consisted of relating text to personal experiences, using texts to support their ideas, pondering or questioning the text's meaning, and exchanging ideas and opinions with their peers.

Method

We began this study wondering what the nature of engagement with multiethnic literature would be for developmental readers when given the opportunity to respond via E-mail exchanges with counterparts at another university. We initiated a semester-long qualitative research study.

Participants

Participants included 95 developmental reading students at the two universities. They ranged in age from 17 to 27 and were ethnically diverse, including 24 Latinos, 45 European Americans, 11 African Americans, seven Asian Americans, as well as eight international students.

Procedure

Students enrolled at Southwest Texas State University were placed in their remedial reading course based on a state-mandated skills test, while Nova Southeastern University students were placed in a developmental course based on their in-house reading placement score.

We selected two multiethnic nonfiction books, Maya Angelou's *I Know Why the Caged Bird Sings* (1971) and Gary Soto's *Living Up the Street* (1985), because their substantive thematic content and well-written text might open up possibilities for grappling with issues. We divided each book into four sections for independent reading purposes. Students were assigned one or two booktalk partners from each university. Before the first booktalk correspondence, students were instructed to introduce themselves to their partners. Subsequently, they were to write to their virtual partners once a week for eight weeks. Consistent with Rosenblatt's (1978) reader response theory, students were encouraged to take an aesthetic stance by sharing their reactions, feelings, thoughts, opinions, and ideas with their booktalk partners, who were to respond in kind. Students were also asked to pose any questions they might have about the reading. Additionally, students were to respond to their partner's comments and try to answer questions raised.

The E-mail correspondence served as the primary source of data for the study. Throughout the semester, we collected hard copies of all the booktalk correspondence. Based on the frequency, length, and quality of students' correspondence, as well as classroom observations, we identified 6 students from each university whose correspondence demonstrated either high engagement, moderate engagement, or minimal engagement. At the end of the semester, these 12 key informants participated in audiotaped personal interviews intended to gather their perceptions of this computer-based response format. The transcriptions of the audiotapes served as a secondary source of data (see Appendix A for interview questions).

Analysis

Analysis of the E-mail correspondence was performed in the following manner. By reading and rereading the E-mail exchanges, we searched for patterns that would organize the data into representational categories (Bogden & Biklen, 1982). Guided by Almasi et al.'s (1996) definition, we systematically coded the E-mail exchanges by locating and marking demonstrations of engagement and labeling each with the "perceived rationale for engagement" (p. 116). For example, this response to Angelou's book — "The same situation that uncle Willy had with his problem, that a baby sitter drop him when he was small. I can relate with it because my next door neighbor had the same thing happen to him and even worst would be that the same person would take care of both of us!" — was coded as "responding to multiethnic literature/ personal Connection." We then grouped the engagement rationales that emerged from the data into four broad categories that described the types of engagement that appeared in the E-mail correspondence. These four categories, accompanied by illustrative student dialogue, were as follows:

(a) Interacting socially with virtual peers (e.g., maintaining conversation and establishing a relationship)
   "Hi Tynisha, how are you doing? Everything here is going well."
   "How was your Halloween? Are you going anywhere for Thanksgiving?"

(b) Discussing readings with virtual peers (e.g., initiating a topic, inviting opinions, confirming or clarifying ideas, processes of discussion)
   "Is there any part of the book that really grabs your attention?"
   "I relly [really] agree with what you said about the boxers. Joe Louis was fighting for his race, and the white man was fight for his."

(c) Responding to multiethnic literature (e.g., seeing personal connections, making inferences about characters, expressing empathy, exploring themes)

"We should not have racial prejudice in America because we have so many cultures in our country."

"The reason I am against Gary in that chapter is because I got rubes [robbed] three times in a year."

(d) Responding to technological aspects of the task (e.g., complaining about technology problems, being excited about the novelty of the computer and E-mail)

"I am very sorry about having your address typed wrong on the nicknames. If you want, I can forward all the ones from before to you."

"I am very excited because of this project and being able to meet new friends from an internet. This is a very fresh way of communication."

The personal interviews were also coded into participant-reported engagement rationales. Categories of rationales, with accompanying representative responses, are as follows:

(a) Intrinsic value (e.g., statements of the personal value of computers for the future)

"We were getting to know how to use the computer more for all our classes, not just computer class. In a few years when we all graduate, that's all that's going to be out there."

(b) Metacognitive awareness (e.g., reported positive affective responses about support for their learning and understanding)

"It's easy to talk about something that's in the book on E-mail. You can actually talk to other people and learn more about the book when you are talking to someone else. Like things you might have missed, or you don't understand something."

(c) Social interaction with virtual peers (e.g., pleasure in making new friends, reading different perspectives, and receiving positive feedback)

"We were talking back and forth. I talked to her about personal things. Like I shared with her when our cheerleader died."

(d) Personal connections (e.g., similarities in experiences and feelings between themselves and characters)

"I wrestled for 5 years. I went through sweat, losing weight. It took dedication and hard work. I was surprised how alike our experiences were. I was thinking this is my life."

(e) Novelty (e.g., positive affective feelings about communication via E-mail)

"It was weird being able to communicate with someone in another state without having to mail it or put a stamp on it. That was something I was never used to. Just writing someone right there and then and be replied to ten minutes later!"

Results

The analysis of the E-mail correspondence and transcripts of the audio-taped interviews provided descriptive information about the nature and categories of engagement with literature of these developmental readers at our universities. The analysis revealed that a range of engagement, from highly engaged to moderately engaged to minimally engaged, existed among the participants (see Appendix B).

Students whose correspondence demonstrated high levels of engagement contained very social and interpersonal conversations. Student inquiries about each other's academic and social activities routinely followed a warm, friendly greeting. Students often commented on weekend and holiday activities, expressing their excitement about them. As these social interactions became more comfortable, students took more risks in their book discussions. They took positions about issues raised by the authors and placed themselves in the characters' situations, while trying to explain how they would react. Partners responded in similar ways. Students used formal or academic language, with little slang. Invitations for continued correspondence beyond the end of the semester were common among the most active partners. The few references to using E-mail occurred when the system failed them and a message was returned due to an addressing problem.

The dialogue that developed among the highly engaged students relied on continued partner inquiries and subsequent responses. Students often asked each other questions about incidents in the book. Partners readily replied with additional questions of their own. Students showed strong reactions to each book's events, particularly when they could relate these events to experiences with which they were familiar. In fact, most students related their childhood experiences to those of the authors. Several pairs discussed themes and issues raised by the authors. Students talked about cultural and racial issues. They compared their feelings and experiences with the authors', but most frequently they discussed their own racial and cultural beliefs. Several students acknowledged that they learned something about a different culture, while commenting on the societal issues each author raised. In correspondence demonstrating a high level of engagement, partners continued with discussions about these issues throughout several exchanges, often responding the same day or the next.

Students identified as moderately engaged tended to write less about themselves. Usually one partner was active and tried to establish a personal relationship, but the other student did not return correspondence weekly. Most often the entries began with, "how are you?" and then launched into a discussion of the book. As a student realized that a partner was not responding on a regular basis, correspondence became brief summaries of sections read, with some comments about the issues. Partners extended invitations to discuss the book, but with the lack of full partner participation, the results turned into a "tell me what you think" query.

Both highly and moderately engaged students related the books to self and family, drawing parallels to their own experiences. However, while conversations among those identified as moderately engaged touched on similar issues as those raised by highly engaged correspondents, they lacked the in-depth exploration of concerns and issues, and there was little follow-up discussion.

In contrast, the correspondence from students identified as minimally engaged was often one-way with sporadic responses from partners. Some students encouraged personal social talk while avoiding book discussions altogether. Often students would state that they did not receive a partner's message and would ask why the partner was not writing. Frustration with non-responsive partners was evident. In several instances, students stated that they could not communicate due to trouble with the E-mail system. This was the only time students referred to the use of E-mail for this activity.

Minimally engaged students generally did not respond to themes and issues raised by the authors, and merely summarized chapters. The few exceptions were found in students' comments about racial differences. Students reacted to racial awareness and injustice; however, comments were limited to one-time statements with little elaboration. Furthermore, the use of slang expressions and non-academic language was more prevalent in the correspondence of minimally engaged students.

The personal interviews served to corroborate the findings of the analysis of the E-mail correspondence since two similar categories (Social Interaction and Personal Connections) emerged from the analysis of the transcriptions of the interviews. Two new categories emerged that related to students' perceptions of the task and of themselves as readers (Intrinsic Value and Metacognitive Awareness). Comments in these categories provided further evidence of our students' engagement. All but two of the students interviewed expressed personal difficulties with reading and writing (e.g., trouble staying focused, lack of a large vocabulary, difficulty thinking up topics to write about, difficulty elaborating on writing, necessity of rereading to comprehend, difficulties with organizing papers). Yet, they reported that booktalking helped them perceive themselves as better readers, learn about another historical period, appreciate another culture, and become competent E-mail users. The interviews revealed the perspectives of those students who demonstrated minimal engagement during the E-mail exchanges. For example, the lack of responses from the E-mail partner was a source of frustration, and dampened the spirit of engagement. One student reported that he preferred oral discussions and presentations to communication through writing. Another student expressed the desire to read self-selected books.

Discussion

This project provided us with a snapshot of students' engagement with text, with others, and with the writing task. It granted a better understanding of the nature of engagement and an opportunity to see the ways that developmental readers engaged, or failed to engage, with literature. We learned that, contrary to the common perception of these readers as passive and unengaged, many of our students did exhibit the characteristics of engaged readers reported by Almasi et al. (1996). Our students related personally to the characters' experiences, and used the text to support their ideas. They thought about and questioned the text's meaning, and exchanged their ideas with their peers. In addition, in their interviews, most students reported positive affective feelings toward the E-mail task. For the highly and moderately engaged readers, having quality literature with substantive personal and social issues was motivating. The novelty of E-mail and the competence the students gained in using this technology was also rewarding. We have learned that providing developmental students with quality literature, the novelty of E-mail, and authentic audiences can engage them in the type of academic discourse they must develop to be successful in college.

Based on these observations, we have continued to use E-mail booktalking but have refined our instruction to better support those students who remained minimally engaged. One refinement was additional modeling during class meetings with "think alouds" (Davey, 1983). We now demonstrate the process of how an active reader engages with literature. Another refinement we have used is to have our students respond to their reading in double-entry journals (Noden & Vacca, 1994) prior to writing to their E-mail partners. Having them reflect about their readings before writing has improved the quality and focus of their E-mail conversations. As we have continued to use E-mail booktalking we have chosen different multiethnic books for our students to read. We have found that quality literature that addresses both personal and social issues in nonfiction or realistic fiction selections engages our students. Finally, this study of our students' E-mail correspondence has motivated us to continue with our analysis of their correspondence by focusing next on their perceptions about gender and ethnicity.

References

Almasi, J. F., McKeown, M. G., & Beck, I. L. (1996). The nature of engaged reading in classroom discussions of literature. *Journal of Reading Behavior, 28,* 107–146.

Angelou, M. (1971). *I know why the caged bird sings.* New York: Bantam Books.

Bogden, R. C., & Biklen, S. K. (1982). *Qualitative research for education: An introduction to theory and methods.* Boston, MA: Allyn and Bacon.

Davey, B. (1983). Think aloud: Modeling the cognitive processes of reading comprehension. *Journal of Reading, 27,* 44–47.

Gambrell, L. B. (1996). Creating classroom cultures that foster reading motivation. *The Reading Teacher, 50,* 14–25.

Guthrie, J. T. (1996). Educational contexts for engagement in literacy. *The Reading Teacher, 49,* 432–445.

Noden, H., & Vacca, R. T. (1994). *Whole language in middle and secondary classrooms.* New York: Harper Collins.

Rosenblatt, L. (1978). *The reader, the text, the poem: The transactional theory of the literary work.* Carbondale, IL: Southern Illinois University Press.

Soto, G. (1985). *Living up the street: Narrative recollections.* New York: Dell.

Vygotsky, L. (1978). *Mind in society: The development of higher psychological processes.* Cambridge, MA: Harvard University Press.

Appendix A

E-mail booktalking interview questions

Using E-mail to talk about books

1. Tell me about your experience with **E-mail** booktalking.

2. What was it like using the computer to discuss books?

Interacting with others (students and authors)

3. Tell me what it was like for you to have conversations with students at another university about the books you were reading.

4. Tell me how writing your responses was different from how talking about the books in class would have been.

5. In what ways did reading about Maya Angelou's life affect you?

6. In what ways did reading about Gary Soto's life affect you?

7. Which book did you prefer? Why do you think so?

8. Tell me something you found in each book that would cause you to recommend it to a friend.

Reading and writing

9. Tell me about yourself as a reader (i.e., your interests, habits, strengths and weaknesses).

10. Tell me about yourself as a writer (i.e., your interests, habits, strengths and weaknesses).

Other

11. What do you think you learned from this experience?

Appendix B

Levels of Engagement by Presence of Subcategories

Minimally engaged

- 3–4 booktalks
- 1/4–1/2 pages
- interacting socially
  - greetings and closure
  - apologies
  - introducing
  - sharing
- responding to literature
  - connecting personally
  - expressing empathy
- responding to technology
  - having problems

Moderately engaged

- 6–7 booktalks
- 1/2–1 page
- interacting socially
  - greetings and closures
  - apologies
  - introducing
  - sharing
  - responding
- discussing reading
  - inviting
  - initiating

- – confirming
- – clarifying
- responding to literature
  - – connecting personally
  - – expressing empathy
  - – interpreting
  - – criticizing
  - – making value judgment
- responding to technology
  - – expressing interest
  - – having problems

Highly engaged

- 7–8 booktalks
- 1/2–1 1/2 pages
- interacting socially
  - – greetings and closures
  - – apologies
  - – introducing
  - – sharing
  - – responding
- discussing readings
  - – inviting
  - – initiating
  - – confirming
  - – clarifying
  - – posing alternative view
  - – elaborating
  - – dialoguing
- responding to literature
  - – connecting personally
  - – expressing empathy

- interpreting

- criticizing

- wondering

- making value judgment

- responding to technology

- expressing interest

- having problems

Techtalk: Developing Online Reading Courses

David C. Caverly and Lucy MacDonald

Institutions of higher education are rushing to put courses online to better serve the student population and to maximize the institutional reach. In their installment from the Tech Talk column of the Journal of Developmental Education, *David C. Caverly and Lucy MacDonald describe how the development of a generation two (G2) online college reading course promoted a reconceptualization of the reading program's curriculum.*

Starting with the fundamental but often overlooked principle that pedagogy must precede technology, the authors used the following three-step process to adapt an on-campus reading course to a G2 level online course: (1) basing the curriculum on research about effective college developmental reading instruction, (2) matching instructional methods to fit the semester's curriculum and selecting appropriate technological resources to deliver the instruction, and (3) piloting the online course on campus before offering it to an off-campus population. As designed, the course employs a synchronous interaction between students and instructor using e-mail, World Wide Web discussion boards, and interactive Web pages, which permit each student to complete the course at his or her own pace. Procedures for allowing you to explore the course online are provided at the end of the article.

E lsewhere we have] discussed developing an online writing course following a generation one (G1) level of distance education. Here we will share how we developed a generation two (G2) online developmental reading course, delivering a class online but adding asynchronous interaction among the students and instructor. Using technology such as e-mail, web-based discussion boards, and interactive web pages, students are able to complete a G2 course at their own time and place.

Developing a G2 course served as an opportunity for us to reconsider our existing curriculum. We realized pedagogy must precede technology (F. Christ, personal communication, July 24, 1999); that is, teaching and learning must take precedence over technological delivery systems. Following this advice, we used three steps to adapt an on-campus reading course into a G2 course: (a) adjust the curriculum around research on effective college-level readers and effective reading instruction; (b) match instructional activities to fit this curriculum, selecting technology resources to deliver that instruction and sequencing the instruction to fit a semester scenario; and (c) pilot the course as an on-campus/online course through an online course development package before delivering it off-campus through that same package.

Research Guides Instruction

We began by examining the research literature for effective reading strategies and for effective instruction to teach these strategies. We organized the reading strategies around four factors: motivation, decoding, comprehension, and transaction with text. Inquiry and explicit teaching emerged as effective instructional strategies.

Effective Reading

Effective readers are intrinsically motivated, receiving pleasure and satisfaction from an affective engagement with reading self-selected, authentic, culturally relevant texts and with the opportunity to share their emotions, feelings, and sentiments. They use the sound/symbol system effectively to fluently process text. This is developed through explicit instruction with sufficient reading practice to develop fluency. They have a substantial reading vocabulary developed through extensive reading that exposes them to words in a variety of settings, allows them to self-select which words to learn, and permits them to explore the semantic connections between these words. From wide reading, they build strong declarative and procedural background knowledge as they read to satisfy internal and external task demands. Connecting new knowledge to old they reflect on and test out what they have learned by presenting their understanding to others. They construct meaning within and across sentences as they infer what is known and what is new. Using background knowledge activation, meaning predictions, reflections upon the satisfaction of task demands, and self-corrections, they self-regulate their comprehending. They transact with the text by assuming an efferent stance when they add and change their background knowledge and an aesthetic stance when they respond emotionally (Caverly & Peterson, 2000; Nist & Holschuh, 2000)

Instructional Strategies

Additionally, specific principles of instruction to develop effective readers were found in the research literature. Inquiry lessons are best to teach concepts, whereas direct, explicit instruction is best to teach strategies. Respecting and honoring cultural and linguistic diversity connects students' out-of-school knowledge with their developing academic knowledge. Assessment informs instruction before, during, and after reading. "Considerate" material fosters instruction: "inconsiderate" material fosters transfer. Instructional scaffolds such as these help support students while they are learning.

Using these research conclusions, we revised the curriculum of our on-campus developmental reading course for a G2 course. Next, we developed instructional activities.

Match Instructional Activities to Technology

For our students who have mastered decoding and fluency, we adapted an on-campus course designed to develop comprehension, transaction with text, and motivation for reading. Inquiry lessons were developed to teach effective reading concepts such as how ordination (superordination, coordination, and subordination) and relationship text structures (categorical, causal, sequential, and comparative) are used by authors; how engagement of background knowledge, inference development, and self-regulated comprehension are required to transact with text; and how reading and discussing well-written, relevant literature can be motivating to read more. Then, we developed explicit instructional lessons to teach the processes of strategic reading following a strategy called PLAN (Preview, Locate, Add, Note; Caverly, Mandeville, & Nicholson, 1995).

Inquiry Lesson for Concepts

One example inquiry lesson we developed is how to teach the concept of text structure. That is, how authors use macrostructures to lead students to learn about the connections between ideas.

We created a web-based inquiry lesson by first engaging the students' declarative knowledge about text structure through a prelearning journal prompt and asking them to share that knowledge on a web-based discussion board (i.e., webboard). Text representing various text structures and with explicit signal words was presented via webpages followed by a peri-learning prompt on the webboard asking them to collaboratively construct the concept: "different signal words represent different text structures." Then, a postlearning journal prompt asked them to generate a list of which signal words represented which structure. If they struggled, we provided a link to resources both on- and offline where they could find other signal words.

Strategy Lesson for Processes

To teach the reading strategy of using signal words to identify text structure, we developed another series of webpages and webboard prompts that led students through modeling, guided practice, and independent practice as well as pre-, peri-, and postjournaling of what they were learning. A prejournal prompt engaged their background knowledge of how effective readers might use signal words to recognize text structure. Next, we read a considerate passage with explicit signal words to model how we use signal words to determine which text structure is present and inserted "think alouds" to verbalize our thinking processes.

To provide this classroom modeling through a G2 course, we found three technology-based solutions. A low-tech solution for modeling presents the strategy through the use of an animation program like *PowerPoint* (Microsoft, 2000) or *Flash* (Macromedia, 2000). A medium-tech solution lets students download a digital movie, using *Quicktime* (Apple, 2000) or *RealPlayer* (RealNetworks, 2000), in which they see one of us model the strategy. Students can download these movies from our webpage or from a CD-ROM that is sent to the student with the course materials. A high-tech solution delivers the digital movie through streaming video (Sinclair, 2000), which is faster than downloading and allows the originator to maintain ownership of the video. Which solution you choose depends on whether you want to provide the simplest technology to address the widest audience or to provide all three solutions, permitting students to choose a medium depending on the sophistication of their computer.

After we modeled the strategy, we provided considerate and less than considerate text examples for students to apply the strategy as well as a peri-journal to construct which techniques could be used to recognize text structure and to discuss what they are coming to understand about the strategy. Then, they were assigned to find examples of rhetorical structures in college textbooks to shut and defend to their peers on the webboard followed by a postjournal of how they adapted what they knew about text structure as they explored various textbooks. Following similar procedures, we developed other web-based inquiry and explicit lessons for the other reading concepts and processes.

After our instruction was developed, we sequenced our course: introducing the concepts of effective reading first, then teaching the processing of these concepts through PLAN, adapting PLAN to fit narrative and critical reading, and encouraging adaptation from following the steps of PLAN to constructing a plan for reading. We then arranged the course to fit a semester scenario with specific assignments due each week.

Online Course Development Package

Selecting an online course development package, *Blackboard* (Blackboard, 2000), we converted these webpages and prompts to an on-campus/online course to pilot their effectiveness. You can explore our

Reading Improvement G2 course at our site (http://courseinfo. mediasrv.swcedu/), logging in as "guest" and using "guest" as the password and then entering "RDG1300T" under the Search window. During the piloting we still met students face-to-face each week to reduce anxieties, correct misconceptions, adjust instructional webpages and prompts, replace inconsiderate text, and evaluate what parts were effective. This feedback was invaluable in the migration of this course to an off-campus/online course.

Conclusion

In developing G2 online courses we emphasize that pedagogy precedes technology. Using research of effective readers and effective reading instruction to dictate course curriculum and course instruction, using online course packages to deliver the course, and piloting the course on-campus prior to delivering it off-campus will lead to more successful experiences for you and your students.

References

Apple. (2000). *Quicktime* (Version 4.1.2) [Computer software]. Cupertino, CA: Apple Corporation.

Blackboard. (2000). *Blackboard* (Version 4.0) [Computer software]. Washington, DC: Blackboard, Inc.

Caverly, D. C., Mandeville, T. P., & Nicholson, S. A. (1995). PLAN: A study-reading strategy for informational text. *Journal of Adolescent & Adult Literacy, 39*(8), 190–199.

Caverly, D. C., & Peterson, C. L. (2000, November). *A framework for evaluating the resources for struggling college readers.* Paper presented at the annual meeting of the College Reading and Learning Association, Reno, NV.

Macromedia. (2000). *Flash* (Version 5.0) [Computer software]. San Francisco, CA. Macromedia, Inc.

Microsoft. (2000). *PowerPoint* (Version 2000) [Computer software]. Redmond, WA: Microsoft Corp.

Nist, S. L., & Holschuh, J. L. (2000). Comprehension strategies at the college level. In R. F. Flippo & D. C. Caverly (Eds.), *Handbook of college reading and study strategy research* (pp. 75–104). Mahwah, NJ: Lawrence Erlbaum, Inc.

RealNetworks. (2000). *RealPlayer* (Version 8) [Computer software]. Seattle, WA: RealNetworks, Inc.

Sinclair, J. T. (2000). *Streaming media 101.* Retrieved September 16, 2000 from the World Wide Web: http://www.builder.com/Graphics/StreamingMedia/ptag=st.b1.3883.dir2.bl_StreamingMedia.

Back to the Future: Preparing Students to Use Technology in Higher Education

David C. Caverly

Technology has been part of the developmental reading and learning strategies program for the past seventy-five years. It should not be a surprise that the nature of technology has changed in the course of those years. What is daunting, however, is the exponential nature of technological innovations in the past decade. During that decade, David C. Caverly has been the primary figure writing not only about the place of technology in developmental education programs, but also about the products available for use in such programs.

In "Back to the Future: Preparing Students to Use Technology in Higher Education," Caverly walks us through a day in the life of a technology-savvy student in a state of the art postsecondary education setting. He follows this scenario with a description of the technological developments we might observe on college campuses in just a few years. Next, Caverly draws upon his experience as a developmental educator to discuss the role of technology in developmental education and learning assistance. Finally, he offers sage advice when he notes that technology in developmental education must be used as a tool to support what research tells us about good instruction, not as a replacement for that instruction.

A graduate student e-mailed me the other day asking an interesting question. He had read an article I wrote six years ago proposing a scenario of what college would be like for students in the twenty-first century (Caverly, 1995). Now that we are in that new century, he wondered which predictions were coming true and whether we are preparing students for this new environment. Here, I'd like to respond. Let me document whether technology in post-secondary education actually has met these predictions, consider how it will change in the future, and determine our role as developmental educators to prepare students for these task demands.

"Toto, I Don't Think We Are in Kansas Anymore"

I proposed a day in the life of Cori, a college freshman in the year 2000 who responds much like Dorothy did in the *Wizard of Oz*. Here is the story that has become reality in 2001 with citations for those of you who want to read more. She awakes and unplugs her "tablet" (e.g., a laptop from Obe; Manning, 2001) which had been recharging all night. On the screen is her daytimer reminding her that she has a paper due in English Literature in two days. Reading an e-mail from her parents to write home, she responds by requesting money. An hour later, she arrives at her Chemistry class and opens her tablet to connect to all the other students in class and the professor via a wireless network (Apple

Computer, 2001; Bluetooth, 2001). As the professor balances a chemical equation on his white board, it is downloaded into her tablet, and she proceeds to collaborate electronically with Jake on the other side of the room about how the equation was balanced (Cornell Chronicles, 2000). She takes notes using a metal stylus writing directly onto her tablet's screen (Manning, 2001). When she saves her notes, her handwriting is automatically converted to Helvetica font, dated, and a reminder added to her daytimer to review the notes.

Since it is a beautiful day, she sits under an oak tree and logs into the virtual chemistry lab to complete an experiment (Model Science Software, 2001). Manipulating the chemicals using her stylus, she is disappointed as the experiment fails. Wondering why, she logs into the Learning Resources Center and searches the Chemistry class's lecture as it was automatically videotaped, converted into streaming video, and archived as a searchable database (Virage, 2001). She repeats the experiment successfully, realizing that she should have used an acid rather than a base, writes out her lab notes, and e-mails them to her professor.

Because she spent extra time on the lab experiment, she is late for her Conversational Japanese class. So, instead of being embarrassed by walking in late, she logs into the class as a virtual student. She reviews the time she missed in only ten minutes by viewing the streaming video in fast forward compressed to remove the spaces in the conversation (Simpson, 2001). Once she catches up to real time she sees four video windows on her tablet: in one corner, the professor; in a second, his overheads, whiteboard, or slide show; in a third, whichever student is speaking; and in a fourth, a student in Japan who is taking the course via distance education. The other students can see her on their tablets through a miniature video camera discreetly placed at the top of her tablet. Now that she is in real-time, she contributes to the discussion asking the Japanese student about certain idioms.

After lunch, she returns to her room to begin her paper on southern gentlemen in literature and movies. Searching the electronic database at the library, she downloads passages from electronic versions of a Faulkner novel and several video clips of Rhett Butler from the movie *Gone with the Wind*. Logging out of the library, her tablet automatically adds these references to her bibliographic database in MLA style (ISI Research Software, 2001). Satisfied with her progress, she e-mails an outline to her collaborative writing group for her part in producing their joint paper (Miller, 2000).

Her friend Jake appears at her door complaining about his paper. Networking their tablets, she sees that he has a reasonable draft although it contains several grammar and spelling errors and only print references. She makes an appointment for him with the learning center on campus to learn about using the proofing tools (Microsoft Corporation, 2001) and electronic databases. He says he doesn't know where on campus it's located. She quickly shows him the Geographical Positioning System built into his tablet which maps out the way (Travroute, 2001). She invites Jake to join her in an aerobic exercise class and leaves her tablet in her locker. She doesn't worry as she knows it can only be activated via her thumbprint (Ott, March 17, 2001). When she returns to her dorm, she is exhausted after a strenuous day of studying and falls asleep wondering what college was like for her father.

Many college students are learning with these technological opportunities as well as others that were unpredictable six years ago. The most obvious is the prevalence of Personal Digital Assistants, PDAs (CyberAtlas, 2000), small hand-held computers for keeping schedules and information. Students like Cori and Jake turn in their hypermedia papers on a CD-ROM that they "burned" (Fass, 2001) or post it on their personal webpages assigned to them by the college. They have a choice to enroll in courses at their college or through a myriad of distance education courses provided by other colleges. More and more textbooks are being produced by their professors as multimedia CD-ROMs and DVDs with connections to webpages rather than generic textbooks primarily because of the ease of updating (Rosenzweig, 1995). How do we prepare students for these learning opportunities?

We Ain't Seen Nothing Yet!

As the Bachman-Turner Overdrive sang (Bachman-Turner Overdrive, 1985), the learning opportunities of tomorrow will grow even more when Cori's little brother Mike attends college four years from now. PDAs will become more prevalent and faster using broader bandwidths (i.e., the "pipeline" allowing the speed of internet access) to deliver e-mail and internet access (Gowan, 2001). As the pipeline becomes larger and faster, more and more information access will be required by his professors. This will require a greater need for Mike to be able to synthesize information from multiple sources. Easier access to virtual reality will allow Mike to explore electrical fields (Dede, 1999) or travel through his own digestive system with a miniature camera embedded in a digestible pill (Given Imaging, 2001). Hypertext, i.e., a piece of electronic text with links, will allow Mike to read any textbook through links to any given word's pronunciation, meaning, and syntactic function (Blumberg, 2001). Biometrics like retinal scans, handprints, and voice prints will provide security for his computer and classroom attendance for his teachers (Ott, March 17, 2001).

Technology will do what it has always done; it will make Mike's life easier in some ways and more challenging in others. For example, Mike likely will enroll in a World History class where he will be required to complete inquiry-based tasks such as a Webquest (Peterson & Caverly, 2001). Here, he will be placed into a collaborative learning group to discover the skills of a historian as they conclude how and why Stonehenge was built in England.

What learning strategies will he need to have in order to succeed at this task? He and his group will have to know how to *gather* up information from a variety of primary and secondary sources including text, video, audio, graphics, and data; they will have to evaluate these sources for information relevant to their task, for what information is accurate and complete, as well as what is fact and what is opinion, all to provide evidence to support their conclusions. After gathering the information, he and his group will *arrange* it into a possible solution. This arrangement will emerge through analysis, synthesis, and compromising toward a tentative solution. Finally, Mike and his group will have to determine the best delivery system to *present* this solution. Should they use a term paper, newsletter, multimedia slide show, webpage, or video; what should be presented first, next, last; what sounds or visual images will add or distract from their presentation?

Many colleges have deemed these technological skills so important that they have implemented technology competency tests (St. Edward's University, 1999). Almost 60 percent of college professors today require e-mail of students, and 43 percent require students to access internet resources to learn from outside their textbooks and lectures (Green, 2001). This has tripled since 1995 and will continue to grow as professors take advantage of learning opportunities outside their classrooms.

Resistance Is Futile

As the Borg of Star Trek fame would say (Great Star Trek Quotes, 2001), Mike and his peers need to be prepared to succeed in these learning opportunities. First, they will need technology access. While many of Mike's peers will have technology access, increasing from an average of 32.7 percent in 1998 to 44.4 percent in 2000, the digital divide still exists for African-American (where they average only 29.3 percent access) and Hispanic students (23.7 percent), and for low income (25.1 percent for <$15–24K), single-parent (33 percent), disabled (21.6 percent), or urban (11.8 percent) and rural (7.3 percent) students (U.S. Department of Commerce, 2000).

Next, learning centers and developmental courses will have to teach new learning strategies built on old learning strategies. In the foreseeable future, students will still arrive at college needing to become more effective and efficient in the basic skills of reading, writing, and mathematics. National statistics suggest there are as many as 34 percent of students today who still need development in reading, 38 percent in writing, and 44 percent in math (National Association for Developmental Education, 1998). While these numbers will be reduced somewhat through national and local initiatives for the primary school population (Paige, 2001), there will be many more first generation students attending college, other older students retooling for a career change, still others updating their technical knowledge, and still others taking advantage of personal development opportunities (National Center for Educational Statistics, 2001).

These new "traditional" students will not only need their old basic skills developed, but they will need the new technical skills of a Knowledge Age worker (Drucker, 1994). These new learning strategies can be described by a heuristic: G.A.P. (Gather, Arrange, and Present; Caverly, Collins, DeMarais, Otte, & Thomas, 2000). Building on the basic skills of reading, writing, and math, G.A.P. teaches students how to convert data (facts and figures) into information (data that has been collected and organized) and then into knowledge (information that has been understood by placing it into a context) as they bridge the gap between information and knowledge. In the learning centers and developmental courses of tomorrow, we will have to teach the Mikes and Jakes of this world to learn how to *gather* data from a variety of sources like textbooks, laboratories, the internet, and their own research through reading and listening strategies as well as search engines and Boolean logic. They will need to learn how to *arrange* number-based data into information using spreadsheets (Dede, 1989); *arrange* word-based data into information using databases or mapping programs (Turner & Dipinto, 1992); and *arrange* visual-based data into what the author intended as meaningful information (Pinkel, 1998).

When converting this data into information, they are bridging the gap and beginning to build knowledge. However, to truly understand, they will need to extend and confirm their new found knowledge by *presenting* it to others to test out what they know, much like experiencing what we learn when we teach (Riskin, 1990). They will have to learn how to use technology such as word processing or desktop publishing to produce single media documents or other more sophisticated technology to produce multimedia documents in the form of slide shows and webpages combining text, video, audio, and graphic media.

There's No Place Like Home

As other prognosticators suggest (Damashek, 1999), the future of developmental education in the form of learning centers or developmental courses connected to discipline-based courses will have to change. Some will provide "Just in Time" instruction (Hall, 2001) where both faculty and students can learn on a needs basis how to teach with or learn through what research has found to be sound instruction (Chickering & Gamison, 1987; Peterson & Caverly, March 15, 2001) and what research has found to be effective learning strategies (Flippo & Caverly, 2000). For teaching developmental students, these effective strategies include providing collaborative learning, teaching for transfer, ongoing informal assessment, scaffolded instruction, an honoring of cultural and linguistic diversity, explicit strategy instruction, building of strategy repertoires, as well as extensive and authentic practice with student choice. For teaching learning strategies, we need to teach students to be active, constructive, strategic learners.

Notice I am proposing that technology in developmental education should be used as a tool to support what we know about good instruction and what we know about effective learning. For example, you can use e-mail to encourage collaborative discussion outside of class and to help students transfer newly learned strategies to a variety of college learning tasks; use computer-based adaptive tests to continually update student progress; and use the internet to provide a wide range of culturally and linguistically diverse learning materials. You can use better designed computer tutorials with hypermedia to provide other explicit instructional input beyond what you teach; to demonstrate the effectiveness and efficiency of various strategies designed for various tasks; and to provide a variety of authentic college level tasks for the students to choose in order to practice these strategies. You can use technology such as mapping programs, e.g., Inspiration™, 2001, to understand before, during, and after reading strategies like PLAN (Caverly, Mandeville, & Nicholson, 1995); process writing programs like *Writer's Helper* (Wresch, 1998) or bibliographic programs like *EndNote* (ISI Research Soft, 2001) to help students develop research papers, or slideshow programs (e.g., Microsoft, 2001b) to produce multimedia, or web production programs, e.g., Dreamweaver, 2001, to produce hypermedia; and spreadsheet programs (e.g., Excel, Microsoft, 2001a) and graphing calculators (Texas Instruments, 2001) to help students learn math concepts. Notice in both situations that technology is being used not to replace instruction, but rather as a scaffold to support instruction and learning as students develop.

Learning centers and developmental education courses are well placed to help develop the students of today grow to meet these demands of tomorrow. To succeed, we as developmental educators will also have to develop along with these students. This can take place through professional development activities like learning at national conferences such as those held by the National College Learning Center Association, the College Reading and Learning Association, and the National Association for Developmental Education, as well as professional institutes like the National College Learning Center Association's Summer Institute, Southwest Texas State University's Technology Institute for Developmental Educators, Learning Support Centers in Higher Education's Winter Institute, and the National Center for Developmental Education's Kellogg Institute.

Whether we like it or not, the future will come. We need to be prepared to meet it head on and grow along with our students. Isn't that why we like developmental education?

References

Apple Computer. (2001). *Airport* (v. 1.3). Cupertino, CA: Apple Computing.

Bachman-Turner Overdrive. (1985). *You ain't seen nothing yet.* Retrieved April 13, 2001 from the World Wide Web: http://www.clinton.net/~sammy/bot.htm.

Bluetooth. (2001). *Bluetooth wireless software,* http://www.bluetooth.com/.

Blumberg, R. B. (2001). *MendleWeb.* Retrieved April 14, 2001 from the World Wide Web: http://www.netscape.org:80/MendelWeb/Mendel.html.

Caverly, D. C. (1995). *Technology and the learning assistance center: Past, Present, and future.* Retrieved January 8, 1995 from the World Wide Web: http://www.schooledu.swt.edu/Dev.ed/Technology/PastPresFuture.html.

Caverly, D. C., Collins, T., DeMarais, L., Otte, G., & Thomas, P. (2000). Bridging the G.A.P. between information and knowledge: Integrating technology into developmental education. In D. B. Lundell & J. L. Higbee (Eds.), *http://www.ci.swt.edu/Faculty/Caverly/Publications/BridgingtheGap.html* (pp. 34–36). Minneapolis, MN: Center for Research on Developmental Education and Urban Literacy, University of Minnesota.

Caverly, D. C., Mandeville, T. P., & Nicholson, S. A. (1995). PLAN: A study-reading strategy for informational text. *Journal of Adolescent & Adult Literacy, 39*(3), 190–199.

Chickering, A. W., & Gamson, Z. F. (1987). *Seven principles for good practice in undergraduate education.* (ERIC Document Reproduction No. ED 282 491).

Cornell Chronicles. (2000). Look, Ma, no wires! Cornell class project tests wireless networking. Retrieved April 2, 2001 from the World Wide Web: Cornell Chronicle.

CyberAtlas. (2000). Wireless Portal users growing in numbers. Retrieved June 4, 2001 from the World Wide Web: http://cyberatlas.internet.com/big%5Fpicture/traffic%5Fpatterns/article/0%2C1323%2C5931%5F309191%2C00.html.

Damashek, R. (1999). Reflections on the future of developmental education, Part I. *Journal of Developmental Education, 23*(1), 18–22+.

Dede, C. (1999) *Maxwell movie.* Retrieved November 9, 1999 from the World Wide Web: http://virtual.gmu.edu/Maxwell.mov.

Dede, C. J. (1989). The evolution of information technology: Implications for curriculum. *Educational Leadership, 47*(91), 23–26.

Dreamweaver. (2001). *Dreamweaver* (v. 4). San Francisco: Macromedia Inc.

Drucker, P. (1994). The age of social transformation. *Atlantic Monthly, 274*(5), 53–80.

Fass, R. J. (2001). Will you really be able to play DVDs made by the Apple Super-Drive and iDVD? Retrieved April 4, 2001 from the World Wide Web: http://machardware.about.com/compute/machardware/library/weekly/aa020901b.htm.

Flippo, R. F., & Caverly, D. C. (2000). *Handbook of college reading and study strategy research.* Mahwah, NJ: Lawrence Erlbaum & Associates.

Given Imaging. (2001). *Given Diagnostic Imaging System.* Retrieved April 11, 2001 from the World Wide Web: http://www.givenimaging.com/non_usa/default.asp.

Gowan, M. (2001). Future web. *PC World, 19*(4), 105–116.

Great Star Trek Quotes. (2001). *Great Star Trek Quotes.* Retrieved April 14, 2001 from the World Wide Web: http://home.golden.net/~jip/trek/startrek/stquotes/stquotes.html.

Green, K. C. (2000). The campus computing project. Retrieved March 11, 2000 from the World Wide Web: http://www.campuscomputing.net.

Hall, P. (2001). *Teachable Moments Project.* Retrieved April 14, 2001 from the World Wide Web: http://www.ed.gov/offices/OPE/disabilities/uw-stout.html.

Inspiration™. (2001). *Inspiration™* (v. 6.0). Portland, OR: Inspiration Software, Inc.

ISI Research Soft. (2001). *EndNote* (v. 4.0). Berkeley, CA: ISI Research Soft.

Manning, R. (2001). *TabletPC.* Retrieved April 4, 2001 from the World Wide Web: http://portables.about.com/gadgets/portables/library/weekly/aa111800.htm.

Microsoft Corporation. (2001a). *Excel* (v. 2000). Redmond, WA: Microsoft Corporation.

Microsoft Corporation. (2001b). *Powerpoint* (v. 2000). Redmond, WA: Microsoft Corporation.

Microsoft Corporation. (2001). *What's new in proofing tools?* Retrieved April 13, 2001 from the World Wide Web: http://www.microsoft.com/MAC/products/office/2001/word/prooftools.asp.

Miller, S. L. (2000). Use of technology with developmental students. *The Learning Assistance Review, 5*(2), 35–39.

Model Science Software. (2001). *Model ChemLab* (v. 2.0). Waterloo, Ontario: Model Science Software.

National Association for Developmental Education. (1998). *Need for developmental education at 4-year institutions.* Retrieved April 5, 2001 from the World Wide Web: http://www.umkc.edu/cad/nade/nadedocs/psde4y98.htm.

National Center for Educational Statistics. (2001). *Digest of Education Statistics, 2000.* Washington, DC: Department of Education. Retrieved April 8, 2001 from the World Wide Web: http://nces.ed.gov/pubs2001/digest/ch3.html.

Ott, D. (March 17, 2001). *Setting the pace for instructional technology in developmental education.* Paper presented at the annual meeting of the National Association for Developmental Education, Louisville, Kentucky.

Paige, R. (2001). *Release of the Nation's report card: Fourth-grade reading 2000.* Retrieved April 14, 2001 from the World Wide Web: http://www.ed.gov/Speeches/04-2001/010406.html.

Peterson, C. L., & Caverly, D. C. (March 15, 2001). *A framework for selecting technology-supported, developmental reading programs and strategies.* Paper presented at the annual meeting of the National Association for Developmental Education, Louisville, Kentucky.

Pinkel, S. (1998). *The on-line visual literacy project.* Retrieved April 14, 2001 from the World Wide Web: http://www.pomona.edu/Academics/courserelated/class-projects/Visual-lit/intro/intro.html.

Riskin, S. R. (1990). *Teaching through interactive multi-media programming: A new philosophy of the social sciences and a new epistemology of creativity.* (ERIC Document Reproduction No. ED 327 133).

Rosenzweig, R. (1995). *So, what's next for Clio? CD-ROM and Historians.* Retrieved April 13, 2001 from the World Wide Web: http://chnm.gmu.edu/chnm/clio.html.

Simpson, D. (2001). *Streaming your video on the internet (Part 4: Compressing).* Retrieved April 4, 2001 from the World Wide Web: http://desktopvideo.about.com/compute/desktopvideo/library/weekly/aa092900a.htm.

St. Edward's University. (1999). *St. Edward's University computer competency reguirements.* Retrieved April 14, 2001 from the World Wide Web: http://itec.stedwards.edu/.

Texas Instruments. (2001). *TI-92 Plus.* Retrieved April 15, 2001 from the World Wide Web: http://education.ti.com/product/tech/92p/features/features.html.

Travroute. (2001). *Pocket CoPilot* (v. 1). Princeton, NJ: Travroute.

Turner, S. V., & Dipinto, V. M. (1992). Students as hypermedia authors: Themes emerging from a qualitative study. *Journal of Research on Computing in Education, 25*(2), 187–199.

U.S. Department of Commerce. (2000). *Falling through the net: Toward digital inclusion.* Washington, DC: U.S. Department of Commerce. Retrieved April 13, 2001 from the World Wide Web: http://www.ntia.doc.gov/ntiahome/fttn00/contents00.html.

Virage. (2001). *Virage platform enhances the educational experience at the University of Arizona.* Retrieved April 2, 2001 from the World Wide Web: http://www.virage.com/news/march_2001_arizona.html.

Wresch, W. (1998). *Writers' helper for windows* (v. 4.0). Scarborough, Ontario: Prentice-Hall Canada.

Additional Readings

Bohr, L., & Grant, J. M. (1997). "The net as literacy tool? Educators respond." *The Learning Assistance Review,* 2 (2), 5–19.

Caverly, D. C., & MacDonald, L. "Tech Talk." *Journal of Developmental Education.* (Regularly appearing column.)

Caverly, D. C., & Peterson, C. L. (2000). "Technology and college reading." In R. F. Flippo & D. C. Caverly (Eds.), *The handbook of college reading and study strategy research* (pp. 291–320). Mahwah, NJ: Erlbaum.

Knox, D. F., Higbee, J. L., Kalivoda, K. S., & Totty, M. C. (2000). "Serving the diverse needs of students with disabilities through technology." *Journal of College Reading and Learning,* 30 (2), 144–57.

Kuehner, A. V. (1999). "The effect of computer-based vs. text-based instruction on remedial college readers." *Journal of Adolescent & Adult Literacy,* 43 (2), 160–70.

MacDonald, L., & Caverly, D. C. (1997). "Distance education and the developmental educator." *Journal of Developmental Education,* 21 (2), 37–38.

Miller, S. L. (2000). "Use of technology with developmental students." *The Learning Assistance Review,* 5 (2), 35–39.

Wepner, S. B. (1990). "Do computers have a place in college reading courses?" *Journal of Reading,* 33 (5), 348–54.

Yaworski, J. A. (2001). "How to create and use PowerPoint presentations to teach reading skills." *Journal of College Reading and Learning,* 32 (1), 14–21.

Yaworski, J. A., & Ibrahim, N. (2001). "How to teach 1000 vocabulary words using the internet." *Journal of College Reading and Learning,* 31 (2), 133–42.

About the Contributors

Jennifer Battle is an Associate Professor of Curriculum and Instruction at Southwest Texas State University, where she teaches both undergraduate and graduate courses. She also serves as the Director of the Tomás Rivera Mexican American Children's Book Award, a post which grows out of her deep interest in Mexican American literature for all ages. She recently published "A Conversation with Rudolfo Anaya" in *The New Advocate.*

Laura Bauer is the Director of the Undergraduate Developmental Studies Program at National-Louis University in Chicago. She enjoys using popular culture in the developmental classroom to facilitate reading, writing, and acculturation. Recently, Dr. Bauer was a panelist for the Dallas Community College and PBS/Starlink Teleconference entitled "Developmental Education: Policy and Pedagogy." There, she demonstrated the use of an outsider art gallery exhibit to foster written communication, reading, and collaborative learning among post-ESL learners.

Julie Beyeler is Director of Learning Support Services at the University of Akron-Wayne College, where she teaches College Reading and University Orientation, along with courses in the College of Education. She researches how students study and what prompts improved learning strategies in their lives.

Dr. Louise Bohr is Associate Professor for the Reading Program at Northeastern Illinois University and has taught developmental reading at several colleges in Illinois. Her publications include articles in *The Learning Assistance Review, The Illinois Reading Council Journal, The Journal of Higher Education, Educational Evaluation and Policy Analysis, The Journal of College Student Development, The Journal of College Reading and Learning, Community College Review, Community College Journal of Research and Practice,* and *The Journal of the Freshman Year Experience.* She is also an associate editor for the *Illinois Reading Council Journal.* Her areas of interest are adolescent and adult literacy development and the application of technology for literacy development and basic writing pedagogy.

Hunter Boylan is the Director of the National Center for Developmental Education and a Professor of Higher Education at Appalachian State University in Boone, NC. He is the editor of *Research in Developmental Education,* a member of the Editorial Boards of the *Journal of Developmental Education,* the *Journal of Teaching & Learning,* and the Principle Investigator for the ongoing National Study of Developmental Education. Hunter is also the current Chairperson of the American Council of Developmental Education Associations and the former President of the National Association for Developmental Education (NADE). He has received NADE awards for "Outstanding Leadership" and "Outstanding Research," and has authored 3 books and over 70 articles, book chapters, and monographs.

Debra C. Brenner, Assistant Director of the University of Georgia's Disability Services, is active in professional organizations at the local, state, and national level and has served as Secretary of the Georgia Association of Disability Providers in Higher Education. She has published a number of articles on the deaf and hard of hearing and is particularly interested in the discrepancy in these students' SAT scores as they relate to admissions requirements.

Martha E. Casazza is a Professor at National-Louis University in Chicago, where she is also Chair of the Developmental Studies Department. She has published on a range of topics in developmental education and is a member of the editorial board for the monograph series of The Center for Research on Developmental Education and Urban Literacy. Her most recent book is *Learning and Development,* which she coauthored. In 1999 Dr. Casazza was a Fulbright Senior Scholar to South Africa.

David C. Caverly is a Professor in the Department of Curriculum and Instruction at Southwest Texas State University, where he also serves as Director of the Reading Lab. He is the Chair and Founder of the Technology Special Interest Group of the National Association for Developmental Educators. Along with publishing numerous articles in scholarly journals, he has coauthored several books, most recently the *Handbook of College Reading and Study Strategy Research* and *Building Reading Proficiency at the Secondary Level: A Guide to Resources and Collaborative Reflection.*

Dr. Cynthia M. Chamblee taught in public schools for 9 years. In 1985 she joined the faculty of Saint Augustine's College in Raleigh, North Carolina, where she taught Developmental Reading for eleven years. After receiving an Ed.D. degree, Dr. Chamblee joined the Division of Education at Saint Augustine's College as an Assistant Professor of Education and the Director of Field Experiences. Currently, Dr. Chamblee works with the Wake County Public School System where she develops and manages after-school and summer programs for low-performing elementary students.

Nannette Evans Commander is an Associate Professor at Georgia State University, where she teaches orientation and learning strategies courses. She is also the Coordinator of the Academic Excellence Unit of the Counseling Center. Her research interests include learning, cognition, and retention.

Mary P. Deming is an Associate Professor in the Department of Middle, Secondary, and Instructional Technology at Georgia State University in Atlanta, where she teaches English education and graduate reading courses. She also coordinates the Language and Literacy unit there. Dr. Deming's research interests include academic literacy and nontraditional students' preparation in teacher education.

Douglas Dierking is a professor at the University of Texas–Austin. He received his Ph.D. in Educational Psychology from the University of Texas and has a private counseling practice in Austin. He has been a consultant for many companies, helping improve employee productivity, performance, and organizational structure, and implementing change management. He also performs studies on the culture of business and nonprofit organizations.

Shevawn Eaton directs ACCESS, a comprehensive academic support program for Northern Illinois University. She has also served as president of the National College Learning Center Association. Dr. Eaton has a strong interest in assessment and program evaluation for both learning assistance and special admission programs and their contributions toward retention. Her recent publications address the psychological contributors to student retention.

Ulinda Eilers teaches first grade in the Greeley-Evans school district in Colorado, where she focuses on curriculum integration and a standards-based curriculum. In addition, she has researched the use of multicultural books written in dialect in middle and secondary public schools. Dr. Eilers also teaches in the reading department at the University of Northern Colorado.

Amelia E. El-Hindi has a Ph.D. from Syracuse University and is currently an Assistant Professor at Translyvania University in Lexington, Kentucky. She teaches in several areas including literacy, math and science, pedagogy, multiculturalism, and the psychology of learning. Her current research interests are in the area of integrating literacy with math and science instruction within elementary classrooms.

Francine C. Falk-Ross teaches undergraduate and graduate courses in literacy education at Northern Illinois University in De Kalb. Over the years, she has worked in both special and regular education programs. Her research focuses on language and literacy routines in classroom discourse and on accommodations for difficulties in literacy development within a diverse student population. Dr. Falk-Ross's articles have appeared in a number of professional journals, and she is the author of *Classroom-Based Language and Literacy Intervention: A Programs and Case Studies Approach.*

Maryann S. Feola is Professor and Assistant Chair of the Department of English, Speech, and World Literature at The College of Staten Island. She has also coordinated the Program in Science, Letters, and Society, which is the liberal arts major for students seeking certification in early childhood and elementary education. Dr. Feola publishes on pedagogy, ethnography, and English Renaissance poets and politicians, and has served as coeditor of the *Journal of College Reading.* She is the author of *George Bishop: Seventeenth-Century Soldier Turned Quaker* and is currently researching Christopher Marlowe's plays.

Sandra U. Gibson is the author of *Making As in College: Everything You Need to Know to Make Good Grades in College,* a handbook with videos.

Annette F. Gourgey, an educational psychologist and learning consultant, teaches at Baruch College and at the Borough of Manhattan Community College of The City University of New York. Along with a team from Baruch, she is developing educational software for visually impaired students. Dr. Gourgey researches cognitive, metacognitive, and affective components of the learning process. She has published widely in these areas and has served on the editorial board of Research and Teaching in Developmental Education. She also wrote high school instructional materials for the PBS-Online Democracy Project 2000.

Jeanne L. Higbee has worked in the field of developmental education since 1974, when she coordinated the Learning Skills Program as a graduate assistant at the University of Wisconsin-Madison Counseling Center. Prior to joining the faculty in the General College at the University of Minnesota, Dr. Higbee taught developmental courses at the University of Georgia. She is the 1999 recipient of NADE's Hunter R. Boylan Research and Publication Award, and she serves as editor of the NADE monograph series.

Vicki L. Holmes is an Associate Professor at the University of Nevada, Las Vegas, where she also serves as Director of the English Language Center. Her research focuses on all forms of second language writing and on vocabulary acquisition. She has served on the editorial board of the *Journal of Adolescent and Adult Literacy* and is currently active on the board of CATESOL. Dr. Holmes has published numerous articles and coauthored *Writing Simple Poems: Pattern Poetry for Language Acquisition.*

Jodi Patrick Holschuh is an Assistant Professor in the Division of Academic Enhancement at the University of Georgia, where she is an award-winning teacher. In addition to publishing articles in scholarly journals, Dr. Holschuh has coauthored several texts, including *Active Learning: Strategies for College Success* and *College Rules! How to Study, Survive, and Succeed in College.* Her wide-ranging scholarly interests include self-regulated learning, college reading and study strategies, the transition from high school to college learning, and science learning and literacy.

Jenefer Husman received her MA and Ph.D. degrees from the University of Texas, Austin, where she participated in the development and teaching of the undergraduate Learning to Learn course. As a junior faculty member at the University of Alabama, she established a developmental learning strategies course. Dr. Husman has written articles and book chapters on learning strategies course work and on student Future Time Perspectives. She is currently an Assistant Professor at Arizona State University.

Dr. Denise Johnson teaches developmental reading, literacy, and literature in the School of Education at the College of William and Mary.

Karen S. Kalivoda is Director of Disability Services at the University of Georgia, where she also serves as adjunct faculty in the Department of Counseling and Human Development Services in the College of Education. She has published widely in scholarly journals and is currently coauthoring three chapters for a book on Universal Instructional Design, which is being developed for the American College Personnel Association Media Board. Universal Instructional Design uses multimodal teaching and assessment methods to enhance learning for all students. Dr. Kalivoda is also participating in a two-year study investigating factors associated with degree completion and postschool success of college students with disabilities.

Lía D. Kamhi-Stein is an associate professor at California State University, Los Angeles, where she teaches in the Teaching English to Speakers of Other Languages program. Her publications include contributions to the journals *TESOL Quarterly, TESOL Journal, The Journal of Adolescent and Adult Literacy,* and *Lectura y Vida,* and to several books. She is the editor of *Learning and Teaching from Experience: Perspectives on Nonnative English-Speaking Professionals* (University of Michigan Press, forthcoming). Her scholarly interests are second language academic literacy, the integration of computer-mediated communication in TESOL teacher preparation, and nonnative English-speaking professionals in the TESOL field. She is the current President of California TESOL and Past Chair of the Normative English Speakers Caucus in the TESOL organization.

James R. King is professor of Childhood/Language Arts/Reading Education at the University of South Florida in Tampa. His experience includes teaching from first grade to graduate school. His articles have appeared in *Reading Research Quarterly, Journal of Adolescent and Adult Literacy,* and *Qualitative Studies in Education* among other journals. He is currently researching the construction of error and accuracy in reading and writing.

Alison Kuehner teaches composition, literature, and reading at Ohlone College in Fremont, California, both traditional and online classes. She has a BA in English from UC Berkeley, an MA in English from the University of Chicago, a single subject teaching credential from the Bay Area Writing Project at UC Berkeley, and an MA in Reading from Cal State Hayward.

Mellinee Lesley was, until recently, an Assistant Professor of Reading/ Literacy Education at Eastern New Mexico University, where she also served as the Coordinator for Developmental Reading. She has just begun, however, as an Assistant Professor of Secondary Reading Education at Texas Tech University. Dr. Lesley conducts research and publishes articles on critical literacy, developmental reading, and the literacy acquisition of special needs students.

Lucy Tribble MacDonald has a Masters Degree in English from the University of Kansas and another in Reading from the University of Oregon. She has taught Developmental Reading since 1976 and is Emeritus faculty at Chemeketa Community College in Salem, Oregon. She designed and maintains a study skills web site, *http://www.howtostudy.org* and has developed the video *How to Read a Textbook.* For the past five years, she has coauthored "Tech Talk," a column in the *Journal of Developmental Education.* She is a frequent presenter at CRLA, a mentor at the Winter Institute, and a charter member of the training team at Technology in Developmental Education Institute (TIDE).

Ruth Abernethy McCreary is the Director of the School University Teacher Education Partnership at Western Carolina University. Currently, her scholarship focuses on the use of subtitled foreign films to support reading instruction and to integrate the curriculum. She also studies ways that partnerships with schools and teachers promote learning for both public school and university students.

Donna L. Mealey received her doctorate in Reading Education from the University of Georgia and was an Assistant Professor in the Department of Curriculum and Instruction at Louisiana State University until 1994. She now lives with her family in Seattle, Washington, where she is Executive Director of Westside Baby, a nonprofit organization that provides clothing, food, books, and other essentials to needy infants and young children in the Seattle area.

Carolyn Beardsley Meigs teaches developmental reading courses in the Academic Success Program at Western Carolina University, where she also supervises interns for the Department of Elementary and Middle Grades Education. Her scholarly interests include reading strategies that support college students and experiential education.

Margaret R. Moulton, now retired, was affiliated for many years with the College of Education at the University of Nevada, Las Vegas. Most of her published work centers on language acquisition and teacher education. She is the coauthor of *Writing Simple Poems: Pattern Poetry for Language Acquisition* and has published numerous articles in scholarly journals. Dr. Moulton served on the Governors' Advisory Council on Literacy in Nevada and was also awarded the American Library Trustees Association Literacy Award and the National Award for Excellence, Laubach Literacy Action.

Sheila A. Nicholson is a lecturer in developmental and secondary content area reading at Southwestern Texas State University, where she uses electronic discussion forums in online book clubs among developmental readers at her institution and several distant ones. In addition to these forums, her research interests include strategies for struggling readers and collaborative learning strategies in online classes. Dr. Nicholson coauthored *Building Reading Proficiency at the Secondary Level: A Guide to Resources and Collaborative Reflection.*

Sherrie L. Nist is a Professor in, and currently the Director of, the Division of Academic Enhancement at the University of Georgia. She publishes regularly in professional journals and has served on the editorial boards of *Reading Research Quarterly,* the *Journal of Literacy Research,* and the *Journal of Contemporary Educational Psychology.* Professor Nist's research interests include how college students study in different disciplines, how they learn from text, and how they transition from learning in high school to learning in college. She has coauthored several books, including the recent *College Rules! How to Study, Survive, and Succeed in College.*

Lorrie Powdrill is currently completing her doctorate in Educational Psychology at the University of Texas at Austin. Her focus is on self-perceptions of socially rejected and neglected children, and she has an interest in strategic learning and child development. Her essays have been published by the National Association of Developmental Education, among others.

Karen B. Quinn was very involved in the inception of *The Learning Assistance Review* and served as its first coeditor. She also served as the Assistant Director of the Academic Center for Excellence at the University of Illinois at Chicago, where she worked for over two decades, focusing in particular on improving retention. Dr. Quinn was a personal mentor to many in the field of learning assistance, always encouraging colleagues in their professional growth and development. She is missed by many since her death early in 2002.

Jim Reynolds is a counselor at Northern Virginia Community College, where he works with students on academic and career issues and study strategies. His primary research interest is learning-centered learning, about which he has published a number of articles in *Inquiry: The Journal of the Virginia Community Colleges.*

Linda Roska received her Ph.D. in Educational Psychology from the University of Texas, Austin. She manages the Performance Measures and Progress Unit of the Division of Research and Evaluation at the Texas Education Agency. Her areas of interest are grade-level retention and high school completion.

Michele L. Simpson is a Professor of Reading in the Division of Academic Enhancement at the University of Georgia. Her research interests include the efficacy of certain learning strategies, students' beliefs about learning, and the characteristics of successful college students. Dr. Simpson's qualitative and quantitative studies have appeared in a variety of professional journals. In addition, she has published numerous articles on pedagogy and has coauthored three textbooks, along with a chapter on studying in the *Handbook of Reading Research*.

Marsha D. Sinagra is the Curriculum/Database Specialist for SIRS Publishing, Inc., where she develops online curriculum for high school students. During her tenure in higher education, she participated in numerous state and national developmental education organizations. She also coauthored "ARC: An Alternative Teaching Strategy for Developmental Reading," which was published in *Research and Teaching in Developmental Education*.

Yvonne Siu-Runyan is Professor Emerita at the University of Northern Colorado's School for the Study of Teaching and Teacher Education. She has also taught K-12 classes throughout the United States. Her professional interests center on the use of talk and language to empower and support students as they read and write and on writing across the curriculum as a means of integrative learning. She has served on the editorial boards of *The Reading Teacher* and *Language Arts*, and she is the author of *Beyond Separate Subjects: Integrative Learning at the Middle Level*. Currently, Dr. Siu-Runyan edits *The Colorado Communicator* and volunteers at the public library in Boulder, Colorado. She also tutors students and mentors parents.

Brenda D. Smith is a Professor Emerita of Georgia State University. She is the author of several books, including *Bridging the Gap, Breaking Through,* and *The Reader's Handbook*. She also coauthored *The Lifelong Reader*.

Norman A. Stahl is a Professor in, and currently the Chair of, the Department of Literacy Education at Northern Illinois University. He has also been President of the College Reading Association and Chair of the American Reading Forum. Right now he is the Historian for the National Reading Conference. His works on the history of developmental education and related topics have appeared in the field's journals on a regular basis for many years.

Linda Sweeney is an Assistant Professor at National-Louis University in Chicago, where she also serves as Program Director of Graduate Developmental Studies. Her research interests include technology and literacy as well as online learning communities. She also studies the "reading" of film and other popular media such as the Internet, and the connections between those kinds of texts and more traditional ones. Her scholarly interests and some of her publications grow out of her background as a commercial writer and romance novelist.

Maria Valeri-Gold is a Professor of Reading and Learning Strategies in the Counseling Center at Georgia State University in Atlanta. She researches retention, assessment, and the reading/writing connection. Dr. Gold has coauthored several textbooks for college developmental readers and writers, most recently *Taking Charge of Your Reading*. She has also served as President of the College Reading Association, and she is actively involved in the College Literacy and Learning Special Interest Group of the International Reading Association.

Dr. Claire E. Weinstein is Professor and Chair of the College of Education at the University of Texas, Austin. She have over 100 publications, including an assessment instrument called the Learning and Study Strategies Inventory (LASSI), which is used in more than 65 percent of the colleges and universities in the United States and has been translated into more than thirty languages. She received a Teaching Excellence Award at the University of Texas, the Developmental Educator of the Year for the State of Texas, and the Outstanding Contributions Award from the International Association of Applied Psychology, Division of Educational, Instructional, and School Psychology. She is also a member of the Board of the Center for Psychology in Schools and Education and Past-President of the Division of Educational Psychology of the American Psychological Association.

Weinstein was inducted as a Fellow of the American Council of Developmental Education Associations.

Stuart C. Werner coordinates workforce development initiatives at Northern Virginia Community College. He also serves on the executive committee of the Workplace Learning Conference and is associated with the Southern Literacy Information Communication System's Workforce Education Web site. Committed to lifelong learning, Dr. Werner's primary focus is creating learner-centered training programs for business and governmental clients.

Kenneth Wolf is an Associate Professor of Education at the University of Colorado at Denver. He has also taught school children with the Peace Corps and in American schools abroad. His research interests focus on educational assessment and teacher portfolios. Dr. Wolf has written numerous articles growing out of his research as well as the book *Leading the Professional Portfolio Process for Change.*

Nancy V. Wood is a Professor in the Rhetoric and Composition program in the English Department at the University of Texas at Arlington, where she teaches undergraduate and graduate courses in argumentation, composition theory and pedagogy, reading theory and pedagogy, nineteenth-century American literature, and Milton. She was a member of the first Texas Academic Skills Program reading committee in 1989 and is the author of a number of college textbooks, including reading textbooks.

Monica Wyatt received her Ph.D. in Reading Education at the University of Georgia. She has taught at Northern Illinois University and Fitchburg State College and currently works at the Oceanside Public Library in California. Her essays have been published in *The Journal of Reading* and *The Reading Teacher*.

Sharon Wyland holds a Master of Science degree in special education from Northern Illinois University, with Illinois teacher certification in Learning Disabilities, Behavior Disorders, Mental Retardation, and Elementary Education. She currently teaches and serves as the academic advisor for the NIU Department of Teaching and Learning in the College of Education. Prior to her current position, she coordinated support services for students with learning disabilities and attention deficit disorder for the NIU Center for Access-Ability Resources. Before coming to NIU, Sharon implemented and developed the learning disability support services program at Waubonsee Community College in Illinois. She has ten years of teaching experience in public high school special education programs.

Acknowledgments *(continued from page iv)*

Martha E. Casazza. "Using a Model of Direct Instruction to Teach Summary Writing in a College Reading Class." From the *Journal of Reading 37,* (3), November 1993, pp. 202–08. Copyright © 1993 by the International Reading Association. Reprinted with permission. All rights reserved.

Martha E. Casazza. "Strengthening Practice with Theory." From the *Journal of Developmental Reading, Volume 22* (Issue #2), Winter 1998. Published by the National Center for Developmental Education, Appalachian State University, Boone, NC 28608. Reprinted with permission of the author.

David C. Caverly. "Back to the Future: Preparing Students to Use Technology in Higher Education." From *The Learning Assistance Review,* Volume 6, Number 1, Spring 2001, pp. 51–59. Reprinted by permission of the Midwest College Learning Center Association.

David C. Caverly and Lucy MacDonald. "Tech Talk: Developing Online Reading Courses." From the *Journal of Developmental Education, Volume 24* (Issue #2), Winter 2000. Published by the National Center for Developmental Education, Appalachian State University, Boone, NC 28608. Reprinted with permission of the author.

Cynthia M. Chamblee. "Bringing Life to Reading and Writing for At-Risk College Students." From the *Journal of Adolescent & Adult Literacy 41* (7), April 1998, pp. 532–37. Copyright © 1998 by the International Reading Association. Reprinted with permission. All rights reserved.

Nannette Evans Commander and Brenda D. Smith. "Developing Adjunct Reading and Learning Courses That Work." From the *Journal of Reading 38* (5), February 1995, pp. 352–60. Copyright © 1995 by the International Reading Association. Reprinted with permission. All rights reserved.

Nannette Evans Commander and Sandra U. Gibson. "Ideas into Practice: Debate as an Active Learning Strategy." From the *Journal of Developmental Education, Volume 18* (Issue #2), Winter 1994. Published by the National Center for Developmental Education, Appalachian State University, Boone, NC 28608. Reprinted with permission by the author.

Mary P. Deming and Maria Valeri-Gold. "Making Reading and Writing Connections with Shay Youngblood's *Big Mama Stories.*" From the *Journal of College Literacy and Learning 30,* 2000–2001. Reprinted by permission of the International Reading Association, University of Pittsburgh, School, PA. All rights reserved.

Shevawn Eaton and Sharon Wyland. "College Students with Attention Deficit Disorder (ADD): Implications for Learning Assistance Professionals." From *The Learning Assistance Review,* Volume 1, Number 2, Fall 1996, pp. 5–18. Reprinted by permission of the Midwest College Learning Center Association.

Amelia E. El-Hindi. "Connecting Reading and Writing: College Learners' Metacognitive Awareness." From the *Journal of Developmental Education, Volume 21* (Issue #2), Winter 1997. Published by the National Center for Developmental Education, Appalachian State University, Boone, NC 28608. Reprinted by permission.

Francine C. Falk-Ross. "Toward the New Literacy: Changes in College Students' Reading Comprehension Strategies Following Reading/Writing Projects." From the *Journal of Adolescent & Adult Literacy 45* (4), December 2001–2002, pp. 278–88. Copyright © 2002 by the International Reading Association. Reprinted with permission. All rights reserved.

Maryann S. Feola. "Using Drama to Develop College Students' Transaction with Text." From the *Journal of Adolescent & Adult Literacy, 39* (8), May 1996, pp. 624–28. Copyright © 1996 by the International Reading Association. Reprinted with permission. All rights reserved.

Annette F. Gourgey. "Teaching Reading from a Metacognitive Perspective: Theory and Classroom Experiences." From the *Journal of Reading and Learning,* Volume 30, No. 1, Fall 1999, pp. 85–93. Reprinted by permission of the College Reading and Learning Association.

Vicki L. Holmes and Margaret R. Moulton. "Dialogue Journals as an ESL Learning Strategy." From the *Journal of Adolescent & Adult Literacy 40* (8), May 1997, pp. 616–21. Copyright ©1997 by the International Reading Association. Reprinted with permission. All rights reserved.

Jodi P. Holschuh. "Do as I Say, Not as I Do: High, Average, and Low-Performing Students' Strategy Use in Biology." From *Journal of College Reading and Learning,* Volume 31, No. 1, Fall 2000, pp. 94–107. Reprinted by permission of the author and the College Reading and Learning Association.

Denise Johnson and Virginia Steele. "So Many Words, So Little Time: Helping College ESL Learners Acquire Vocabulary-Building Strategies." From *Journal of Adolescent & Adult Literacy 39,* (5), February 1996, pp. 348–57. Copyright © 1996 by the International Reading Association. Reprinted with permission. All rights reserved.

Karen S. Kalivoda, Jeanne L. Higbee, and Debra C. Brenner. "Teaching Students with Hearing Impairments." From the *Journal of Developmental Education, Volume 20* (Issue #3), Spring 1997. Published by the National Center for Developmental Education, Appalachian State University, Boone, NC 28608. Reprinted by permission of the author.

Lía D. Kamhi-Stein. "Profiles of Underprepared Second-Language Readers." From the *Journal of Adolescent & Adult Literacy, 41* (8), May 1998, pp. 610–19. Copyright © 1998 by the International Reading Association. Reprinted with permission. All rights reserved.

Alison V. Kuchner. "The Effects of Computer Instruction on College Students' Reading Skills." From the *Journal of College Reading and Learning,* Volume 29, No. 2, Spring 1999, pp. 149–65. Reprinted by permission of the College Reading and Learning Association.

Mellinee Lesley. "Exploring the Links between Critical Literacy and Developmental Reading." From the *Journal of Reading 33* (8), May 1990, pp. 598–601. Copyright © 1990 by the International Reading Association. Reprinted with permission. All rights reserved.

Donna L. Mealey. "Understanding the Motivation Problems of At-Risk College Students." From the *Journal of Reading 33* (8), May 1990, pp. 598–601. Copyright © 1990 by the International Reading Association. Reprinted with permission. All rights reserved.

Carolyn Beardsley Meigs and Ruth Abernethy McCreary. "Foreign Films: An International Approach to Enhance College Reading." From the *Journal of Reading 35* (4), December 1991, pp. 306–10. Copyright © 1991 by the International Reading Association. Reprinted by permission. All rights reserved.

Karen B. Quinn. "Teaching Reading and Writing as Modes of Learning in College: A Glance at the Past; a View to the Future." From *Reading Research and Instruction 34* (4), Summer 1995, pp. 295–314. Published by the College Reading Association. Reprinted by permission.

Jim Reynolds and Stuart C. Werner. "An Alternative Paradigm for College Reading and Study Skills Courses." From the *Journal of Reading 37* (4), December 1993/January 1994, pp. 272–78. Copyright © 1994 by the International Reading Association. Reprinted with permission. All rights reserved.

Michele L. Simpson. "Conducting Reality Checks to Improve Students' Strategic Learning." From the *Journal of Adolescent & Adult Literacy 41* (2), October 1996, pp. 102–09. Copyright © 1996 by the International Reading Association. Reprinted with permission. All rights reserved.

Michele L. Simpson and Sherrie L. Nist. "An Update on Strategic Learning: It's More than Textbook Reading Strategies." From the *Journal of Adolescent & Adult Literacy, 43* (6), March 2000, pp. 528–41. Copyright © 2000 by the International Reading Association. Reprinted by permission. All rights reserved.

Marsha D. Sinagra, Jennifer Battle, and Shelia A. Nicholson. "E-mail: 'Booktalking': Engaging Developmental Readers with Authors and Others in the Academic Community." From the *Journal of College Reading and Learning,* Volume 29, No. 1, Fall 1998, pp. 30–40. Copyright © 1998 by the International Reading Association. Reprinted with permission. All rights reserved.

Norman A. Stahl, James R. King, and Ulinda Eilers. "Postsecondary Reading Strategies Rediscovered." From the *Journal of Adolescent & Adult Literacy, 39* (5), February 1996, pp. 368–79. Copyright © 1996 by The International Reading Association. Reprinted with permission. All rights reserved.

Claire E. Weinstein, Douglas Dierking, Jenefer Husman, Linda Roska, and Lorrie Powdrill. "The Impact of a Course in Strategic Learning on the Long-Term Retention of College Students." From *Developmental Education: Preparing Successful College Students* edited by J. Higbee & P. Dwinnel. Lawrence Erlbaum Associates, 1998. Reprinted by permission.

Kenneth Wolf and Yvonne Siu-Runyan. "Portfolio Purposes and Possibilities." From the *Journal of Adolescent & Adult Literacy, 40* (1), September 1996, pp. 30–37. Copyright © 1996 by the International Reading Association. Reprinted with permission. All rights reserved.

Nancy V. Wood. "College Reading Instruction as Reflected by Current Reading Textbooks." From *Journal of College Reading and Learning,* Volume 27, No. 3, Spring 1997, pp. 79–95. Reprinted by permission of the College Reading and Learning Association.

Monica Wyatt. "The Past, Present, and Future Need for College Reading Courses in the U.S." From the *Journal of Reading 36* (1), September 1992, pp. 10–20. Copyright © 1992 by the International Reading Association. Reprinted by permission. All rights reserved.